MARCUS SCHMÜCKER (ed.)
VIṢṆU-NĀRĀYAṆA

ÖSTERREICHISCHE AKADEMIE DER WISSENSCHAFTEN

PHILOSOPHISCH-HISTORISCHE KLASSE
SITZUNGSBERICHTE, 934. BAND

VERÖFFENTLICHUNGEN ZU DEN SPRACHEN
UND KULTUREN SÜDASIENS, NR. 40

HERAUSGEGEBEN VOM INSTITUT
FÜR KULTUR- UND GEISTESGESCHICHTE ASIENS
UNTER DER LEITUNG VON BIRGIT KELLNER

Marcus Schmücker (ed.)

Viṣṇu-Nārāyaṇa

Changing Forms and the Becoming of a Deity in Indian Religious Traditions

AUSTRIAN
ACADEMY
OF SCIENCES
PRESS

Published with the support of the Austrian Science Fund (FWF): PUB 923-Z

FWF Österreichischer Wissenschaftsfonds

Cover: Viṣṇu-Nārāyaṇa seated in the crowning of the Brahmapurīśvara temple of Puḷḷamaṅkai (Tamil Nadu), 10th c. (Photo: Charlotte Schmid)

ISBN 978-3-7001-8865-0
Printed: Prime Rate, Budapest
https://epub.oeaw.ac.at/8865-0
https://verlag.oeaw.ac.at
Made in Europe.

Accepted by the publication committee of the Division of Humanities
and Social Sciences of the Austrian Academy of Sciences by:

This publication was subject to international and anonymous peer review.
Peer review is an essential part of the Austrian Academy of Sciences Press evaluation process. Before any book can be accepted for publication, it is assessed by international specialists and ultimately must be approved by the Austrian Academy of Sciences Publication Committee.

The paper used in this publication is DIN EN ISO 9706 certified
and meets the requirements for permanent archiving of written cultural property.

Table of contents

Marcus Schmücker

Introductory remarks

The present volume (still) aims to make contributions to the study of the complex history of the deity Nārāyaṇa (later Viṣṇu-Nārāyaṇa).

The existence of many deities in Indian religious traditions should not hide the fact that, from the earliest sources up to the religious worship and practices of the present day, individual deities may have long-lasting traditions. Over time, some essential features of these deities may be seen to persist, while others may fade into the background. But the changes that arise—for example, through shifting identifications with other deities—do not contradict the continuity of certain basic structures that emerge repeatedly, albeit in ever new forms.

A few of these structures, both textual and conceptual, concern the deity Nārāyaṇa. Starting from the mention of Nārāyaṇa in Vedic texts, we can follow this deity not only to the later *Mahābhārata* and *Harivaṃśa*, but also to Nārāyaṇa's identification with Kṛṣṇa Vāsudeva, the most important deity of the Bhāgavatas. At the same time, the worship of Nārāyaṇa arose as a pillar of the Pāñcarātra tradition, and gradually came to be associated with the emerging Viṣṇuism—in the course of which Nārāyaṇa evolved into a form (and one of the names) of Viṣṇu. But the history of the development of this deity does not come to an end here, however, and leads *via* various important strands to the traditions of theistic Vedānta, in which the *one* God Viṣṇu-Nārāyaṇa becomes the centre of theological and philosophical reflection.

A few remarks on some important points of this development: It is striking when a deity comes to be identified not only with other divine figures, but also with distinctive equations such as that of sacrifice. Thus, the earliest Vedic evidence in the context of cosmological treatises not only attests to Prajāpati's identification with Nārāyaṇa as Puruṣa-Nārāyaṇa, but also indicates that the deity can be equated with the figure of the so-called Ṛgvedic Puruṣa itself—a primordial being whose slaying and subsequent dissection brought the world into existence.

This important motif persists up to epic literature. The Nārāyaṇīya, the section of the *Mahābhārata* (Mbh) that features Nārāyaṇa, still calls him the "Lord of Sacrifice," identifying him in terms of the sacrifice by which the world was created from his body parts; the Vedic Puruṣa is described here as having a hundred heads, a thousand eyes, and a thousand legs, abdomens and arms (cf. Mbh 12.326, 6–7).

In later times we may find an interesting contrast in the fact that, for Rāmānuja as well as his successors in the Vedānta tradition he pioneered—and who also equate Nārāyaṇa with the Vedic Puruṣa—the world eternally represents the body of God, but is expressly *not* sacrificed any longer. Rather, the body that encompasses the whole world, which even modifying is imperishable in its nature, belongs eternally to the God Viṣṇu-Nārāyaṇa Himself. This leads us to another peculiarity besides this connection between God and his sacrifice, and may in fact explain something about the way in which Nārāyaṇa was conceptualized—something that, for all its importance, needed full explanation: the God's relationship with water, as already attested in ancient texts. We get a sense of this relationship, by Nārāyaṇa's resting on the waters on the back of the serpent Śeṣa, which allows Nārāyaṇa to survive the period of dissolution before the world comes into existence.

The important significance of the serpent as protection against the flood of water is just as striking as God's divine manifestations (*avatāra*) that enable the God to survive in the water. We therefore also understand the function of the "oceanic" nature of Viṣṇu's manifestations like the fish, the tortoise, or the swimming boar, all of which originally belonged to Nārāyaṇa, and which are still represented in the *Mahābhārata* as his forms.

Nevertheless, as we are now aware, to reconstruct an illuminating timeline of Viṣṇu-Nārāyaṇa's development, it is necessary to examine a wide range of sources: not only textual traditions, comprising mythological, ritual, theological, and philosophical works, but also material representations, such as sculptures, inscriptions, and archaeological finds. Each contribution to this volume is rooted in a particular methodological and historical approach, be it philological, conceptual, or religious.

In their discussions, the contributors to this volume focus on many aspects of how Viṣṇu-Nārāyaṇa is connected with the origin and development of various traditions. To do this, they examine a wide range of textual material in Sanskrit, Tamil, and Maṇipravāḷa: the early Caṅkam literature of the 3rd to 6th century CE; the Vaiṣṇava text corpus, particularly the *Tivyappirabandham* (6th–9th cent. CE); Purāṇic literature, above all the *Viṣṇupurāṇa* (5th–6th cent. CE); Pāñcarātra literature; and the later (10th–14th cent. CE) literature of the philosophical and theological tradition of theistic Viśiṣṭādvaita Vedānta, in which Viṣṇu-Nārāyaṇa plays a central role. The volume places a strong emphasis on reconstructing the developmental and historical elements that shaped the "divine composition" (*Tivyappirabandham*) of Nārāyaṇa. Also examined is how Viṣṇu-Nārāyaṇa came to be seen as a single and immutable supreme God; a reconstruction of the theological arguments supporting this monotheism reveals his special nature.

In the following, a brief overview of the volume's chapters introduces the methodological and thematic approach of each author in their studies on the divine figure of Viṣṇu-Nārāyaṇa.

Eva Wilden examines some of the earliest texts that mention features of Viṣṇu-Nārāyaṇa, namely texts from the Caṅkam literary corpus and the *Kīḻkkaṇakku*, in particular analyzing statements about deities in the invocation stanzas of selected works. These invocations allow a glimpse of various non-sectarian views of religion and thus of the earliest stages of Śaivism and Viṣṇuism, before they became established traditions. These invocations, which mirror the form and meter of the poems in their respective texts, have the function of identifying religious affiliation. Moreover, Wilden points out that the poems of these texts, integrating various narrative elements, prefigure the iconic worship of Viṣṇu-Nārāyaṇa. By way of example, she presents several poems addressing particular gods that became a fixed part of their respective transmitted traditions. Moreover, based on her examination of the invocation stanzas of these poems as well as their metrical features, Wilden suggests an internal chronology of the Caṅkam corpus. Considering the invocation stanzas in combination with the colophons, she demonstrates that while the latter refer to the deity, together they have the function of anchoring these texts in their respective traditions.

The focus of the next chapter, by **Peter Schreiner**, is the *Viṣṇupurāṇa*, which, with its central statements about the God Viṣṇu, is one of the most important texts of the Vaiṣṇava tradition. For his contribution, one might apply the dictum that no theological statement about the God Viṣṇu can be made without inspecting the wording of the *Viṣṇupurāṇa*: no theology without philology. Schreiner thus presents not only the central theological views of this text, but also suggests a methodological approach based on what he calls the text's "theology": its talk of God. If examined philologically, what type of language is used to refer to the divine figure of Viṣṇu? Schreiner has determined that the *Viṣṇupurāṇa*'s theological statements focus on "praise" (*stotra*). Like Wilden, he takes up the issue of how Viṣṇu is addressed, examining descriptions of the God in expressions of praise. To develop an objective text-based criterion, he first analyses and compares the terminology of all the *stotra*s in the *Viṣṇupurāṇa*, subsuming their variations in vocabulary and expression under what he calls "paradigms" summarizing a particular aspect of the God Viṣṇu-Nārāyaṇa. These paradigms are then structured into groups by still other paradigms. This collection of paradigm structures and contents allows Schreiner to speak about the *Viṣṇupurāṇa*'s concept of Viṣṇu. The synchronic structure of the *stotra*s, which he has characterized and collected into a total of 31 paradigms, contains important information about God, the universe, and the relation between the two. He is thereby able to demonstrate that the *Viṣṇupurāṇa*'s cosmo-theology is not only divided into the realities of the world and the elements of the divine, but also includes their relationship to each other.

The next part of Schreiner's chapter examines the question of terminological layers and the use of particular key terms. When investigating a particular term, Schreiner does not isolate it from other terms, but attempts to reveal their complex links and interrelationships. In particular, he analyses statements equating Viṣṇu with the concept of cognition (*jñāna/vijñāna*). In contrast to the view of Paul Hacker, who has concluded that this concept was influenced by the Buddhist idea of *vijñānavāda*, Schreiner concludes by suggesting that since the *Viṣṇupurāṇa* considers divine cognition to permeate everything, cognition (*jñāna/vijñāna*) is seen as something that purifies the mind.

The next chapter, by **Charlotte Schmid**, draws another picture of the divine figure of Viṣṇu-Nārāyaṇa, demonstrating how different elements have combined to shape his image, not only within the Sanskrit and Tamil textual traditions, but also in the way the God is portrayed in sculpture. To begin with, she examines references to Nārāyaṇa in the works of the eleven Āḻvārs, the authors of the *Tivyappirabandham*. While Nārāyaṇa's name is mentioned in these works, she questions whether the deity on the snake might be considered a separate figure. She proceeds by asking whether certain elements associated with the name "Nārāyaṇa" might rather be connected with reclining snake deity images from Tamil Nadu that were created before the *Tivyappirabandham*'s composition. In her search for predecessors or early forms of this deity, she follows the description of snake gods in the early Tamil epic *Cilapattikāram* (6th–7th cent. CE), pointing out that gods related to snakes were quite prevalent in early South Indian history, for example Balarāma, one of the oldest snake deities of the Vaiṣṇava world. To see how snake gods and Nārāyaṇa are connected, Schmid then follows traces from North and Central India, analyzing passages from the *Harivaṃśa*. Her investigation leads to the important conclusion that the form of the reclining Viṣṇu-Nārāyaṇa did not originate in Śrīraṅga, or "Araṅkam," but rather came from North India. The process of adaptation to the local religious landscape can be delineated quite precisely. The earliest Vaiṣṇava cult image in the Tamil world is plausibly the reclining God of the Shore Temple in Mahābalipuram. Finally, a reference to a hymn in the *Paripāṭal*, one of the main Caṅkam anthologies (3rd–6th cent. CE)—which constitutes the literary background of the *Tivyappirabandham*—concludes the article with a possible clue to ancient Vaiṣṇava sources.

Katherine Young challenges the assumptions that the Āḻvārs' supreme God is Viṣṇu, Kṛṣṇa, or Nārāyaṇa. For a case study, she focuses on the four *Antāti*s of Poykai-, Pūta-, Pēy-, and Tirumaḻicai-Āḻvār (the first three dated to ca. 7th cent. CE and the fourth possibly later), more specifically on proper names, "epithetonyms," color, cosmogony, and salvific roles. She finds that there is no mention of the name Viṣṇu whatsoever in the *Antāti*s (and only four in the entire four thousand verses of the Āḻvārs, which can be justified by special circumstances). The homology is held together by several linking concepts that bridge these three components. One is the ocean, which is usually black but sometimes white, due to Nārāyaṇaṉ's association with a milk ocean. Another is the act of chanting the God's name, which usually refers to Nārāyaṇaṉ, but sometimes to Tirumāl or Kaṇṇaṉ. The third such concept is the name Tirumāl (or a variant), which is used for any of the three components of the homology and is mentioned in many contexts, but especially in oceanic, cosmogonic ones. Signifiers such as the God's feet, discus, and presence in the heart of the devotee also function as linking concepts because they appear routinely in all three components of the homology. Finally, the fact that many verses do not use proper names helps to merge these components. Through its bridging mechanisms, this homology informs each one of the *Antāti*s, though the poets differ on which of the three components they emphasize.

With this pattern in mind, Young then searches for antecedents to the three components of the homology in Sanskrit and Tamil texts. After finding many versions of myths about the ocean and a cosmogonic God in late Vedic and post-Vedic Sanskrit works, she speculates that the aniconic ocean/ocean deity might have once been important in the ancient Indus Valley Civilization, at least near the ocean, and lived on through multiple myths. To explain how the ocean comes to be a reason for Kṛṣṇa's transcendence, she suggests that this development might have occurred at Dvāraka, which had once been an Indus site and was also, according to legends, the capital of Kṛṣṇa's kingdom. Even if it was only Kṛṣṇa-worshippers who lived in the region and developed his transcendent dimension by drawing on the ocean imagery and myths, it helps us understand the homology. The addition of Nārāyaṇa to this homology probably happened a bit later, and was followed in some circles by the addition of Balarāma, who had amalgamated agricultural and serpent (*nāga*) deities.

An Ocean-Kṛṣṇa-Nārāyaṇa-Balarāma homology is also what we find when we turn to late Caṅkam works (in Tamil), composed just before the first Āḻvārs or perhaps contemporaneously with them. However, while the *Antāti* poets maintain the early Ocean-Kṛṣṇa-Nārāyaṇa homology, they have eliminated Balarāma. Young suspects that this happened because the Āḻvārs emphasized an *ekānta* tradition (worship of one God, which can be traced back to the *Nārāyaṇa Upaniṣad*, connected with the Atharvaveda) and probably did not like the Balarāma addition to the Ocean-Kṛṣṇa-Nārāyaṇa homology, because Balarāma was sometimes viewed as an independent or semi-independent deity. Young surmises that because a popular form of the Atharvaveda tradition had integrated many non-Vedic local traditions by the 5th century CE, it was trying to maintain its "Vedic" status in the face of criticism from orthodox Brahmins that it did not belong to the Vedic tradition. The Āḻvārs likely inherited this mindset and were ignoring, if not purging, some aspects that had accrued to its tradition, such as Balarāma.

Kṛṣṇa *or* Nārāyaṇa cannot be the Āḻvārs' supreme God, Young thinks, because that would be reductive of the Ocean-Kṛṣṇa-Nārāyaṇa homology, which is central to all the *Antāti*s. As for Viṣṇu, how could he be the supreme God if the poems never mention his name? To explain his absence, Young proposes that those who followed the Atharvaveda in a general or popular sense might have long viewed the followers of Viṣṇu as competitors or representatives of an exclusive (or orthodox) Brahmanism. Given the tensions between Atharvavedins and orthodox Brahmins, especially as the latter began to move into the temple milieu, the *Antāti* poets probably inherited this refusal to acknowledge Viṣṇu. Young concludes that the name Viṣṇu should not be applied anachronistically to the God of the *Antāti* poets. Rather, we need to look to subsequent developments in Śrīvaiṣṇavism: to the late 9th century, when inscriptions in the Tamil world begin to mention the word *vaiṣṇava*; followed in the second half of the 10th century by the term *śrīvaiṣṇava*, perhaps designating Brahmin Vaiṣṇavas; and then to the 12th century, when a text first uses the term *śrīvaiṣṇava* to characterize a *sampradāya* that names Viṣṇu (identified with Nārāyaṇa and Vāsudeva) as the supreme deity, but has also integrated the poetic legacy of the Āḻvārs and (mono)theistic Vedānta.

Marion Rastelli investigates concepts connected with the deities Vāsudeva, Viṣṇu, and Nārāyaṇa as found in several *Saṃhitā*s of the Pāñcarātra tradition. She pursues the question of whether, according to the *Pāñcarātra Saṃhitā*s, the gods Viṣṇu, Vāsudeva, and Nārāyaṇa are the same deity. She arrives at the conclusion that while descriptions of the pure creation do differentiate between Vāsudeva, Viṣṇu, and Nārāyaṇa, in the *śāstrāvatāra* stories and in ritual descriptions, no distinction between the three gods can be found. Nonetheless, different *man-*

tras are used for their manifestations: the twelve-syllable *mantra* (*dvādaśākṣaramantra*) brings forth Vāsudeva; the eight-syllable *mantra* (*aṣṭākṣaramantra*), Nārāyaṇa; and the six-syllable *mantra* (*ṣaḍakṣaramantra*), Viṣṇu. Examining the use of these three *mantras* in earlier and later Pāñcarātra texts, Rastelli is able to demonstrate different levels of influence from both Vedic and non-Vedic traditions.

The contribution of **Gerhard Oberhammer** examines the development of Pāñcarātra and the God Viṣṇu as seen in Vāmanadatta's *Saṃvitprakāśa* (9th cent. CE), including, like Rastelli, the relationship between God and his manifestation in *mantras*. The three chapters of the *Saṃvitprakāśa* represent a monistic doctrine of the Pāñcarātra tradition. In contrast to the anonymous literature of early India, here we encounter an author who can, to some extent, be apprehended historically. In his *Saṃvitprakāśa*, Vāmanadatta reflects on the type of language needed to express the supreme being. Focusing on this problem of the relationship between language and transcendence, Oberhammer demonstrates that it is not possible to conceive of a supreme God if descriptions of that God are in conventional language. Such language does not understand God as God, but distorts him. Again, we see here the importance of the language of praise: Oberhammer presents several verses from the "praise" (*stuti*) chapter on Viṣṇu.

As described by Oberhammer, from the perspective of the individual soul, the God Viṣṇu can be experienced upon final release, even though he is said to be beyond human cognition. An important means for reaching the presence of Viṣṇu is applying the two functions of language: while it communicates a linguistic meaning, it is also able to point to a transcendent reality. Thus, in this context, language has a double function, although these two functions seem contradictory. Language represents the objectifiable phenomenal reality of *what* there is, but at the same time conveys the transcendent religious experience of God. Oberhammer describes how Vāmanadatta reflects on this double character of language and pursues the question of how God can be directly experienced in meditation. Starting from the idea that reality is composed linguistically, a special distinction in Vāmanadatta's concept of language is elaborated: in relation to God, language does not say *what* he is, but rather *whereof* God is, without objectifying him.

Oberhammer's distinction between God's manifestation in the world and his transcendence beyond the world is also at the heart of **Gérard Colas**'s contribution. Colas discerns between two concepts: a concrete world in which God manifests himself, and a transcendent God who surpasses the world as the single highest principle.

Colas does not pursue this distinction philosophically, but historically. He presents a conceptual-historical overview of two different concepts of God as they developed until the 12th century: God "as a generic or paradigmatic model for the various sectarian creator-gods and that of a metaphysical creator God beyond sectarian gods." The concept of a metaphysical God is found in the earliest Indian sources. Colas pays particular attention to the criticism—beginning in the 2nd century CE and increasing until the 6th century—of the existence of a creator God and the assumption that this God is the ultimate cause of the world.

In his contribution, Colas uses the terms "deism" and "theism" to differentiate between two approaches toward conceiving of a supreme being—one based on human reasoning, the other on belief. Colas elaborates the historical development of deistic arguments used to defend the idea of a creator God against mainly Buddhist criticism. He also demonstrates that this criticism did not eliminate rational concepts of a creator God, but reinforced them and gave them intellectual weight, especially in the Nyāya-Vaiśeṣika tradition. Colas also shows that the separation between deist and theist ideas did not last, but that they eventually merged in the theistic Vedānta tradition.

For the later post-Rāmānuja tradition, **Erin McCann** focuses on the theology of Piḷḷai Lokācārya (13th–14th cent.) and his discussions about the correct means for attaining the Lord. By teaching an extreme dependency on the Lord, who manifests as everything, Piḷḷai Lokācārya articulated a means to salvation (*upāya*) that stood in stark contrast to the prevailing soteriological paradigm of *bhaktiyoga* set forth by Rāmānuja, the progenitor of Śrīvaiṣṇavism. Though Piḷḷai Lokācārya accepted the meditative and ritual practices of *bhakti* as a means to salvation, he emphasized the indivisibility of God from these means. While the seeds of such an idea are evident in the works of Rāmānuja, Piḷḷai Lokācārya insists that attaining liberation can only be brought to fruition through surrender (*prapatti*) and love of the teacher (*ācāryābhimāna*). These concepts rest soundly on what he understands as the essential nature of God's relationship to humanity. Since humans are utterly dependent upon God, who is the goal of any practice, God must also be the means. Thus, we find salvation redefined as God himself, whereby all the various modes by which one reaches God—such as the *arcāvatāra* (an image form usually found in temples), the *ācārya* (teacher), the individual Śrīvaiṣṇava, and the entire community of believers—are manifestations of God's accessibility and compassion on earth.

Marcus Schmücker also explores the post-Rāmānuja development of a personal God, with his focus on the ideas of the 13th-century theologian and philosopher Veṅkaṭanātha. As shown by Schreiner, the early *Viṣṇupurāṇa* already displays aspects of theology inasmuch as it not only deals with God and the world, but also with God's relationship to that world; by the time of Veṅkaṭanātha, one major consideration, based on deeper philosophical reflection, had become how an eternal being can be related to changing, non-eternal beings. What transformation (*pariṇāma*) is necessary for there to be a relationship between God, souls, and the world? To answer this question, Veṅkaṭanātha develops and applies a concept of relational unity. In several of his works, Veṅkaṭanātha cites a central sentence from the *Bṛhadāraṇyaka Upaniṣad* (1.4.7) to corroborate this idea of transformation. Schmücker elaborates the relevance of this in Veṅkaṭanātha's theology, namely, that the concept of God's eternity depends on how transformation is defined. Indeed, the universe remains the same despite its being transformed. While an object (*rūpa*) can vanish, its name (*nāma*) remains. In his theology, Veṅkaṭanātha deals with the linguistic paradigm of denotation and denotated object. He develops a concept of irreducible language, using this to show that the central concept of substance and state, representing God and his body, also follows the concept of eternal language, that is, the language of the Veda. Veṅkaṭanātha's concepts of "state" (*avasthā*) and eternal "substance" (*dravya*) are based on the central idea that a designation always exists to unite name and form: a designation continues to exist even if the designated thing is absent. In the same way, a substance continues to exist even if its states are absent (because they, too, still exist). Schmücker examines the extent to which this concept, based on an Upaniṣadic idea, is implemented in Veṅkaṭanātha's theology, including other theological concepts like the will of God, which Veṅkaṭanātha also interprets as based on the scheme of substance and state.

In summary, the long history of Viṣṇu-Nārāyaṇa is ultimately a history of how his image was defined. This changed many times depending on the genre of text in which the deity was featured. There are various approaches to such a history: describing the deity's special characteristics, uncovering elements of earlier deities that were later identified with the more powerful and supreme deity, analyzing the intentions of the deity's followers, or determining what abstract (universal) concepts of God were used by those striving for salvation.

What might be deduced from the contributions to this volume is that, with regard to Viṣṇu-Nārāyaṇa, thinkers in India endeavored to bring together different traditions or conceptual strands in order to preserve them as a unity. This, however, was not unification: contradictory elements were also included in the concept of this God. The tendency to unify differences may be a special feature in the development of this monotheism. It goes hand in hand with an image of a personal God accessible to all social groups, not a God who represents a distant goal or is accessible only to privileged believers.

Some early versions of the articles collected in this volume were presented at the workshop with the former title "Forms and the Becoming of a Deity in Religious Traditions: The God Viṣṇu-Nārāyaṇa," held at the Institute for the Cultural and Intellectual History of Asia of the Austrian Academy of Sciences in May 2011.

The editor offers his sincere apologies to all of the participants for the publication's delay, which was due to several unavoidable circumstances, and wishes to thank all of the contributors to this volume for their constant encouragement to complete it, as well as for having so patiently awaited its publication.

Eva Wilden

The plurality of god(s) as a poetic concept in the early Tamil invocation stanzas

Tamil devotional literature is generally believed to have started around the 6th century, with the three times hundred *Antāti* stanzas of Poykai-, Pēy- and Pūtattāḻvār on the Vaiṣṇava side, and with diverse poems or songs from Kāraikkālammaiyār on the Śaiva side. All these works have found entry in the respective canons of their traditions, that is, around the 10th century, in the Vaiṣṇava *Nālāyirat Tivyappirapantam* and somewhat later in the Śaivite twelve *Tirumuṟai*. A number of poems from the earlier *Caṅkam* corpus are accepted as predecessors, along with the three theistic cantos from the poetic epic *Cilappatikāram* (XII, XVII, XXIV). Yet another source is not generally taken into consideration, namely the invocation stanzas (*kaṭavuḷ vāḻttu*, literally "praise of the deity") which exist for the greater part of the so-called secular literature of the first millennium, most notably for the works of the *Caṅkam* and the *Kīḻkkaṇakku*. These two corpora are today counted, well in accordance with a good thousand years of poetological history, as the major and minor classics of Tamil. One of the difficulties that arise when dealing with such material is the notorious dating problem. While we already have rather vague notions of when most of the poetry was composed, the additional material, especially if we view the matter at a manuscript level, is even more dubious, because of its fluid nature and *a priori* may have been added at any time between the 6th century (the date of the first Veṇpā poems) and the time the manuscript in question was copied, say between the early 18th and the 20th centuries.

With respect to this problem I would argue that it is possible to suggest an internal chronology for many of these poems, not only on the basis of metrical considerations, but also by the position they take in the textual tradition, for example by being included in commentaries, and by the theistic conceptions that can be gleaned from them. As far as the *Caṅkam* invocations are concerned, I have argued elsewhere in detail that, by comparison with a number of poems from the theistic cantos of the *Cilappatikāram*, the poem today counted as *Kuṟuntokai* 1 can best be explained as an invocation by origin.[1] It is part of a layer of poetic vision that does not focus on the deity directly, but on his or her space or constitutive attributes, such as the hill or the spear for Murukaṉ, or the flute for Kṛṣṇa. In this context it has to be remembered that the older type of worship shining through in the earlier parts of the *Caṅkam* corpus is characterised by the link between a deity (mostly non-personal and as yet without "story") and a location such as a mountain or a tree. The attributes, then, are the part that is capable of representing or manifesting the deity on earth, that is, the poems in question show a pre-form of iconic worship with a first integration of narrative elements. This stage precedes that of the series of five invocations by Pāratampāṭiya Peruntēvaṉār, which in turn point to a composition after the late-comers in the classical corpus (*Paripāṭal* and *Tirumurukāṟṟuppaṭai*), but before the establishment of Śaivism as a major force, because it is in this series that Śiva begins to play a predominant role, while Viṣṇu takes a form (reminding one of the cosmic man myth known from the *puruṣa* hymn *Ṛgveda* X.90) that is prominent neither in the *bhakti* corpus nor in the Tirumāl hymns of the *Paripāṭal*.[2]

---

1 The relevance of the invocation stanzas for the genesis and relative chronology of the *Caṅkam* corpus is discussed in chapter III.1 of Wilden 2014. *Kuṟuntokai* 1 runs thus:

cem kaḷam paṭa koṉṟ' avuṇar tēytta	"Red the ground from killing, the demon reduced
cem kōl ampiṉ cem kōṭṭ(u) yāṉai	by red-stemmed arrows, red-tusked [his] elephant,
kaḻal toṭi cēey kuṉṟam	anklets, bracelets—the Red one's hill
kuruti pūviṉ kulai kāntaṭṭē.	full of Malabar lilies, bunches of blood-flowers."

2 One issue to be mentioned is the poem found among the anonymous quotations in Nacciṉārkkiṉiyar's commentary on *Tolkāppiyam Po-*

Apart from the six hymns already mentioned, the *Caṅkam* corpus encloses two further candidates for invocation stanzas, namely that of the *Kalittokai* and the *Tirumurukāṟṟuppaṭai*, the first of the Ten Songs, *Pattuppāṭṭu*. It has been argued before (for example by Vaiyāpurip Piḷḷai 1956: 24) that the *Tirumuruku* might be viewed as the *kaṭavuḷ vāḻttu* of the *Pattuppāṭṭu*, and indeed there are a number of arguments to support such a hypothesis. To begin with, it has to be kept in mind that an invocation is supposed to mirror in poetic form and metre the type of poems found in the text it precedes. This means that, although it is not customary to have an invocation of 317 lines (as has the *Tirumuruku*), one might argue that this is simply because we do not have other long poems[3] in any of the comparable anthologies, and that, just like the other *Caṅkam* invocations, it represents the average length of a poem in the collection.

Secondly, the general expectation is to find an invocation stanza as a prelude to the text in question, not as a part of the text itself, as is definitely the case with the *Tirumuruku,* which is needed to fill the

---

ruḷḷatikāram 91 that has been brought forward by the editor of that text, Kaṇēcaiyar 1948, as a possible candidate for the lost invocation of the *Patiṟṟuppattu*. This poem betrays it late origin not only by content, but even more so by metre, clearly being a revival type of Āciriyappā with no less than six metrical feet in twelve lines that would not have been acceptable to the old standard.

3 Here a table for the relation between invocation and anthology. The only poem not perfectly following suit is that of the *Naṟṟiṇai*, which with seven lines is slightly short.

Text	Number of lines per poem	Number of lines for Invocation
Naṟṟiṇai	9–12	7
Akanāṉūṟu	13–31	16
Puṟanāṉūṟu	variable	13
Aiṅkuṟunūṟu	3–5	3
Kalittokai	variable + stanzaic	17 + ib.
Pattupāṭṭu	103–782	317
Kuṟuntokai	4–8	4 and 6

number of ten songs. Interestingly, in that respect parallels can be found in a number of other cases. Controversial, as a matter of fact, is the *Puṟanāṉūṟu*, where the song by Peruntēvaṉar is, in all editions, counted as No 1. However, since the end of the anthology is lost, it stands to reason that this is a recent development and an attempt to cut losses: according to this count, what would have vanished at the end would be just the last part of poem 400 plus the final colophon. But, as otherwise the *Puṟanāṉūru* resembles in every respect the other old anthologies, it looks far more likely that what is printed as number 400 is in fact the remainder of No 399, that the whole sequence has to be counted one downwards and that accordingly the alleged No 1 is the usual pre-positioned *kaṭavuḷ vāḻttu.*

A clearer case in point is the *Kalittokai,* where the invocation is unequivocally and officially counted as poem No 1, and referred to as *kaṭavuḷ vāḻttu,* and in its place commented on by the commentator Nacciṉārkkiṉiyar. To this poem we will have to come back when we have dealt with the *Kīḻkkaṇakku.* Among those eighteen there are after all four that officially and with commentarial record have their invocations integrated into the main text, namely *Tirukkuṟaḷ*, *Nāṉmaṇikkaṭikai*, *Ciṟupañcamūlam* and *Paḻamoḻi.*[4] Thus we could easily argue that the *Pattuppāṭṭu* compiler was but following one of the trends current in his period by putting the *Tirumuruku* in the first position of the Ten.

The strongest argument against such a hypothesis is that Nacciṉārkkiṉiyar, the *Pattuppāṭṭu* commentator, should not have mentioned the fact and should not have called the *Tirumuruku* a *kaṭavuḷ vāḻttu.* I would counter that by the time of Nacciṉārkkiṉiyar, in about the 14th century, the *Tirumuruku* had long outgrown its original role as a praise poem in the beginning of the *Pattuppāṭṭu.* Not only had it been integrated into the Śaiva canon itself, but it also was a popular devotional hymn in its own right. It was not in need of classification.

---

4 We might consider this phenomenon as a reinterpretation of convention that has a parallel in the Sanskrit tradition, where there is the famous example of Pāṇini's beginning the treatise with an auspicious word, *vṛddhi*, as is explained by Patañjali.

Moreover, if we see matters from a poetic point of view, the *Tirumuruku*, just as the other invocations, is alien in spirit and content to the anthology it precedes, while at the same time emulating the form, and in this case in an even more sophisticated way than can be said of the others. The *Tirumuruku* has to be seen as a creative adaptation of the traditional genre Āṟṟuppaṭai (sending a bard on the way to a wealthy patron) of which there are four specimens found among the *Pattuppāṭṭu*. As such it is famously structured by the six places of worship it describes, but in addition it can be said to subsume six types of poetic approach to the deity, the first of which, under the heading Tiruparaṅkuṉṟam, delivers a vignette of Ceyyōṉ in an Akam setting of Kuṟiñci, as the lord of a hill (not a temple) where various types of devotees dance, headed by the familiar types of *pēy makaḷ* and *cūrara makaḷir*.

Coming back finally to the *Kalittokai* invocation, it underlines the status of the whole anthology as a late production. As the Kali itself, its sophisticated metre and stanzaic form presuppose significant further development. Metrically speaking, it is unreasonable to suppose that Veṇpā, which is one of the elements constitutive of Kali metre, has developed later than the Kali that is based on it. This means that the Kali could not have been composed before the whole set of the *Kīḻkkaṇakku,* whose predominant metre is Veṇpā, but has to be placed somewhere in the middle of them. Needless to say, that it also presents us with a far more developed view of lord Śiva and his consort. Important is this poem nevertheless, because it is the only one that accords a role of significance to any of the female deities.

The advantage of invocations as a poetic type is that they allow, in contradistinction to the material from the *bhakti* corpora, a glimpse at a non-sectarian view on religion. They preserve a far greater variety and also a number of mixed forms, presumably in accord with the personal preferences of their authors, who might be anything from the author of the respective anthology, its compiler or, simply, its copyist. The poems to be taken up in this context are those that I judge to be a fixed part of the transmission, namely in addition to the eight from the *Caṅkam* corpus eleven plus one decade for the *Kīḻkkaṇakku*.[5] Among these nineteen plus ten poems, six are unequivocally Vaiṣṇava (in one sense or another), four are Śaiva, three Kaumāra, and one is for Śiva's son, Gaṇeśa. Four poems praise several gods, and they employ at least three different types of poetic technique to that effect, beginning with simple enumeration up to *double entendre* and mere allusion. Another subset remains in the abstract, not identifying any personal deity, namely one single stanza plus the decade. It might not be by chance that these verses belong to the two most well-known and important didactic texts in the collection, namely the *Tirukkuṟaḷ* and the *Nālaṭiyār*.

Another type of stanza, which for the time being is cautiously called "colophon stanza", should be considered here, firstly in order to begin to understand better how the transmission of text-additional material worked. It usually is found at the end of the text, while the invocation is found at the beginning, so that the pair of them could be seen as a sort of bracket around the text. It usually contains information on content, structure and authorship of a text. Secondly, in some of those verses again recourse to a deity is taken, in one case we might even have a *double entendre* with a poetic and a theistic reading.

The following tables list the stanzas that have to be considered and suggest their religious affiliation which cannot be termed obvious in all cases:

5 Those are normally counted as eighteen (as in *Patiṉeṇkīḻkkaṇakku*), but there is some amount of fluctuation as to which are the eighteen texts concerned, so that here we shall deal with a list of nineteen texts.

Table 1: Stanzas connected with the *Caṅkam* corpus

text = 7(8?) + 6	invocation	colophon stanza
Kuṟuntokai	2 (Murukaṉ)	1 (*Eṭṭuttokai*)‖ /
Naṟṟiṇai	1 (Nārāyaṇa)	/
Akanāṉūṟu	1 (Śiva)	1 (arrangement)
Puṟanāṉūṟu	1 (Śiva)	/
Aiṅkuṟunūṟu	1 (Śiva or Nārāyaṇa)	1 (authors)
Patiṟṟuppattu	[1 suggested; Śiva]	/
Kalittokai	1 (Śiva)	1 (authors)
Paripāṭal	/	1 (number + topics)
Pattupāṭṭu	1? (Murukaṉ)	1 (*Pattuppāṭṭu*)

Table 2: Stanzas connected with the *Kīḻkkaṇakku*

Kīḻkkaṇakku **= 11 (+10) + 10**	**invocation**	**colophon stanza**
Aintiṇai Aimpatu	/	1 (Māṟaṉ Poṟaiyaṉ)
Aintiṇai Eḻupatu	1 (Gaṇeśa)	/
Tiṇaimoḻi Aimpatu	/	/
Tiṇaimālai Nūṟṟaimpatu	/	1 (author unnamed)
Kainnilai	/	/
Kār Nāṟpatu	/	1 (Kūttar; Kṛṣṇa?)
Kaḷavaḻi Nāṟpatu	/	/

Nāṉmaṇikkaṭikai	2 (Nārāyaṇa/Trivikrama/ Kṛṣṇa)	/
Tirikaṭukam	1 (Trivikrama + Kṛṣṇa)	2 (both Nallātaṉ)
Ciṟupañcamūlam	1 (Trivikrama)	2 (Kāriyācāṉ)
Ācārakkōvai	/	1 (Peruvāyiṉ Mu i)
Ēlāti	1 (the four and twenty-four)	1 (Kaṇimētai)
Iṉṉā Nāṟpatu	1 (Śiva, Balarāma, Kṛṣṇa, Kumāra)	/
Iṉiyavai Nāṟpatu	1 (Śiva, Kṛṣṇa, Brahmā)	/
Mutumoḻikkāñci	/	/
Paḻamoḻi	1 (Trivikrama)	1 (Muṉṟuṟaiyaraiyar; lord in the shade of the Aśoka tree)
Iṉṉilai	1 (Śiva)	/
Nālaṭiyār	1 (*kaṭavuḷ*)	
Tirukkuṟaḷ	1st decade (*iṟaivaṉ*)	‖ 1 (*Kīḻkkaṇakku* stanza)

What is it that the invocation stanza and colophon stanza have in common, except for the fact that they both appear to be an important additional element in the transmission of a text? The most immediate answer to this question is perhaps that both have the function of anchoring the text in a tradition, the colophon stanza in a literary tradition that preserves an ordered collection of human artefacts and the invocation stanza in a cult tradition that views the recitation of poetry as one possible communal activity in a group whose identity is intimately linked with their religious affiliations. Interesting and perhaps telling is the distribution of metres. While, as already mentioned, invocation stanzas mirror the text they belong to, at least for the period under consideration, the colophon stanzas are usually in Veṇpā, the very metre developed with the *Kīḻkkaṇakku*. We might thus draw conclusions as to the genesis of the tradition of stanzas; they cannot have developed with the earlier *Caṅkam* texts that do not yet employ Veṇpā. They might plausibly go back to the period of arranging the anthologies, which fits in with the religious picture to be gleaned from the invocations, that is, somewhere around the 6th century.

As interesting as the stanzas to be found are those that are missing. For the *Caṅkam* corpus invocations are only lacking for the incomplete texts, that is, *Patiṟṟuppaṭṭu* and *Paripāṭal*, both cases where the beginning has been lost. This seems to show that the convention was already firmly established, but this picture is not altogether confirmed by the *Kiḻkkaṇakku*. Out of nineteen candidates eight come without invocation, namely *Aintiṇai Aimpatu*, *Tiṇaimoḻi Aimpatu*, *Tiṇaimālai Nūṟṟaimpatu*, *Kainnilai* and *Kārnāṟpatu*—in other words, all the Akam anthologies except for one, the *Aintiṇai Eḻupatu*—as well as *Kaḷavaḻināṟpatu*, *Ācārakkōvai* and *Mutumoḻikkāñci*. The only one among them that is fragmentary and thus might be suspected to have lost its invocation is the *Kainnilai*. As far as the colophon stanzas are concerned, they never seem to have been covering the whole ground. The rationale for them possibly is that they were made when there was information to be preserved. Each of the hyper-anthologies has one (with deviations in various manuscripts) that enumerates the texts assembled in the collection. The additional ones contain information as to arrangement and authorship within the anthology. For the *Caṅkam* corpus they are absent in the cases of the older anthologies with no principle of arrangement (*Kuṟuntokai*, *Naṟṟiṇai* and *Puṟanāṉūṟu*), while for the *Patiṟṟuppattu* one could ask the question whether the verse was lost. However, one might argue that the information given in the verse is always of the kind not preserved by the text itself or by its colophon. In the *Patiṟṟuppattu* the Paṭikams could be thought sufficient in that respect. For the *Kīḻkkaṇakku* for the time being ten verses of this type are known, all of them naming the author or the compiler, a tradition that is continued for example in the *Tivyappirapantam*. However, the situation of transmission is somewhat precarious and not very well studied. It is likely that a fresh investigation of manuscripts will bring to light further material.

In accordance with the endeavour of the current collective volume that aims at throwing more light on the development of Vaiṣṇavism, the invocations which betray some sort of Vaiṣṇava affiliation shall make the beginning. Since the *Caṅkam* verses are relatively well known they can be passed over here quickly. The one for the *Naṟṟiṇai* is remarkable in that it stands in relative isolation.

mā nilam cēv aṭi āka tū nīr
vaḷai naral pauvam uṭukkai āka
vicumpu mey āka ticai kai āka
pacum katir matiyamoṭu cuṭar kaṇ āka
iyaṉṟa ellām payiṉṟ' akatt'
aṭakkiyavētam mutalvaṉ eṉpa
tīt' aṟa viḷaṅkiya tikiriyōṉē.

That [his] red feet be the great land, that [his] garment
be the curved, roaring ocean with pure water,
that [his] body be the sky, that [his] hands be the [four] directions,
that [his] eyes be the sun with the fresh-rayed moon,
that he, who has concealed inside [himself and] who resides in all that is,
is the first in the Vedas, they say,
he with the shining discus to cut off evil.

The cosmic deity along with the Vedic associations it presents is a type neither found in the *Paripāṭal* nor prominently featured in the *Tivyappirapantam* (I have so far not located any direct parallels). The three-liner from the *Aiṅkuṟunūṟu* is amusing because it forms a text book illustration for a *śleṣa*:

nīla mēṉi vāl iḻai pākatt'
oruvaṉ iru tāḷ niḻal-kīḻ
mū vakai ulaku mukiḻttaṉa muṟaiyē.

Viṣṇu:
Under the shade of the two feet of the One
with blue body [and] a place [taken by her] with pure jewels
the world unfolded one by one in three parts.

Śiva:
Under the shade of the two feet of the One
with a blue throat [and her with] pure jewels as one part
the world unfolded one by one in three parts.

In fact, the larger body of the poem is unequivocal, but there are a few words that are awkward in either of the two possible readings. In the case of Nārāyaṇa, here amalgamated with Kṛṣṇa, with his blue body, *pākattu* has to be taken as a reference to the chest where the goddess Śrī is found, while so often the word is used in the description of Ardhanārīśvara, Śiva depicted with one masculine and one feminine side. In the case of Śiva, who has the goddess Umā as one part of him, it is *nīla mēṉi* that obstructs a smooth reading, for *mēṉi* has to be understood as "throat" (blue by the cosmic poison he has swallowed), while its usual meaning is "body".

The five further unequivocally Vaiṣṇava stanzas belong to four of the *Kīḻkkaṇakku* didactic anthologies, namely *Nāṉmaṇikkaṭikai* with two verses, *Tirikaṭukam*, *Ciṟupañcamūlam* and *Paḻamoḻi*. None of these texts is popular today and so far, none of them have been translated into English, although they are part of the Cemmoḻi programme for the translation of Classical Tamil texts.

The first verse from the *Nāṉmaṇikkaṭikai* slightly transgresses the norm with five lines instead of the usual four (which is not exactly irregular, but far less frequent). In style it brings to mind the later of the two *Kuṟuntokai* invocations, which give a similar description of Murukaṉ, totally based on colour.[6] This might signal the wish to es-

---

tāmarai puraiyum kāmar cēv aṭi	Red the foot, in beauty similar to lotuses,
pavaḻatt' aṉṉa mēṉi tikaḻ oḷi	glittering brightness the body, like corals,
kuṉṟi ēykkum uṭukkai kuṉṟiṉ	[his] dress [red] like Kuṉṟi seeds, long the spear

tablish an intertextual relationship with the probably not much earlier tradition and the series of Peruntēvaṉār.

mati maṉṉum māyavaṉ vāḷ mukam okkum.
katir cērnta ñāyiṟu cakkaram okkum.
mutu nīrp paḻaṉattut tāmarait tāḷiṉ
etir malar maṟṟu avaṉ kaṇ okkum. pūvaip
putu malar okkum niṟam.

The moon resembles the bright face of the permanent tricky/dark one.
The sun joined with rays resembles [his] discus.
The blossoms again flowering on the stalks of the day lotus
in tanks with old water resemble his eyes. The new blossoms
of bilberry resemble [his] colour.

The second is very different and could easily come, for example, from one of the early *Antāti*s:

paṭiyai maṭi akatt' iṭṭāṉ aṭiyiṉāṉ
muk kāl kaṭantāṉ muḻu nilam akkālattu
āṉ nirai tāṅkiya kuṉṟu eṭuttāṉ kōviṉ
arumai aḻitta makaṉ.

He who put the earth inside [his] belly, he who with [his] feet
in three times traversed the whole ground at that time,
he who in order to protect the cow herd lifted the mountain,
is the boy who took care of the king's difficulty.

Both the construction and the technique of allusion are familiar, as well as the cosmic deeds of the deity, which are related probably to three incarnations, namely Nārāyaṇa (who takes the world into himself), Trivikrama and Kṛṣṇa, first as a young cowherd and then as the helpmate of Arjuna.

Of the same mould is the poem from the *Tirukaṭukam*, here restricted to allusions to the act of Vāmana and from the life of Kṛṣṇa:

---

neñcu paka eṟinta am cuṭar neṭu vēl	of beautiful glow, thrown to split the heart of the hill
cēval-am koṭiyōṉ kāppa	–since the one with the cock on [his] banner stood guard
ēmam vaikal eytiṉṟāl ulakē.	the world attained a day of joy.

kaṇ akal ñālam aḷantatūum kāmaru cīrt
taṇ naṟum pūm kuruntam cāyttatūum naṇṇiya
māyac cakaṭam utaittatūum im mūṉṟum
pūvaip pū vaṇṇaṉ aṭi.

Measuring the world vast in area and bending
the wild lime tree with cool fragrant blossoms of desirable excellence
and kicking the deceptive cart that approached—all these three
[is] the foot of him with the colour of bilberry flowers.

A priori I do not see any decisive difference between such poems and those integrated into the Vaiṣṇava canon, and it is likely too that they go back to about the same period. In a slightly different league is the following verse from the *Paḻamoḻi*, in that its syntax is considerably more complex, as literary Veṇpā likes to have it.

arit' avitt' āc' il uṇarntavaṉ pātam
viri kaṭal cūḻnta viyaṉ kaṇ mā ñālatt'
uriyataṉiṉ kaṇṭ' uṇarntār ōkkamē pōlap
periya taṉ āvi peritu.

The feet of him who removed what is difficult [and] understood faultlessly,
are great like the height of those who have understood, seeing it as the one possessing
the huge world vast in area surrounded by the expansive sea,
great is his strength.

Here we somehow have a play on the double meaning of the verb *uṇartal*, used at the same time to describe the cognitive faculty of god for perceiving and understanding the world and that of the devotee for perceiving god. But the exact point of the simile eludes me. Out of key is only the verse counted as the first in the *Ciṟupañcamūlam*:

muḻut' uṇarntu mūṉṟ' oḻittu mūvātāṉ pātam
paḻut' iṉṟi āṟṟap paṇintu muḻut' ētti
maṇ pāya ñālattu māntarkk' uṟuti ā
veṇpā uraippaṉ cila.

> Humbling himself masterly without fault before the feet of the one who does not age,
> having understood the whole, having accomplished the three [steps], praising the whole,
> as strength for the people of the extensive earth world,
> he speaks a few Veṇpās.

Here we find an element of praise for Trivikrama, but otherwise it looks much more like a reference to the author or compiler of that text, only that the name is missing. In tone and form it is very similar to the author stanzas prefixed to the *Antāti*s, and here we see the first occasion where a verse of that type is found at the beginning, not as part of the final colophon as in the other cases.[7]

A beautiful example of such a stanza with the poet's name and at least the possibility of religious affiliation is the one that belongs to the *Kārnāṟpatu*:

mullaik koṭi makiḻa moy kuḻalār uḷ makiḻa
mellap puṉal poḻiyum miṉṉ' eḻil kār tollai nūl
vallār uḷam makiḻat tīn tamiḻai vāḻkkumē
col āynta kūttar kār cūḻntu.

> For the mind of him with the flute to rejoice, delightfully decked with jasmine creepers,
> For the minds of those with curls delightfully decked with jasmine creepers to rejoice
> the ancient book on the flashing graceful clouds, from which soft floods flow,
> for the minds of those who master [it] to rejoice he has blessed sweet Tamil,
> Kūttar who chose words encompassing the rainy season.

Here the first line is ambiguous, and, since Tirumāl-Kṛṣṇa is the god of Mullai and the rainy season, the topic of the *Kārnāṟpatu* series of

---

[7] Today's editors generally print these stanzas at the beginning of the text, seeing them as a sort of *ciṟappup pāyiram* (a laudatory preface, as a rule made by somebody else, in contradistinction to the author's preface, *pāyiram*), but this is not conform to the manuscript tradition.

poems, it is highly likely that it was deliberately shaped so. If this is the case, we would have here a second early instance of associating Kṛṣṇa with the flute, besides the verses *Cilappatikkāram* 17.19-21.

If we now turn our attention to the non-Vaiṣṇava material, as far as the *Kīḻkkaṇakku* are concerned, Śaivism is far less widely spread. The *Caṅkam* corpus comes with three poems unequivocally devoted to Śiva, the two well-known ones from the series of Peruntēvaṉār for the *Akanāṉūṟu* and the *Puṟanāṉūṟu* plus the later one from the *Kalittokai* (counted as *Kalittokai* 1) that is less well known and the only one giving a prominent place to the *devī,* two good enough reasons to quote the full poem here:[8]

āṟu aṟi antaṇarkku aru maṟai pala pakarntu
tēṟu nīr caṭai karantu tiripuram tī maṭuttu
kūṟāmal kuṟittataṉ mēl cellum kaṭum kūḷi
māṟā pōr maṇi miṭaṟṟu eṇ kaiyāy kēḷ iṉi.

paṭu paṟai pala iyampa pal uruvam peyarttu nī
koṭukoṭṭi āṭum-kāl kōṭu uyar akal alkul
koṭi purai nucuppiṉāḷ koṇṭa cīr taruvāḷō?

maṇṭu amar pala kaṭantu matukaiyāl nīṟu aṇintu
paṇṭaraṅkam āṭum-kāl paṇai eḻil aṇai mel tōḷ
vaṇṭu araṟṟum kūntalāḷ vaḷar tūkku taruvāḷō

kolai uḻuvai tōl acaii koṉṟai tār cuval puraḷa
talai aṅkai koṇṭu nī kāpālam āṭum-kāl
mulai aṇinta muṟuvalāḷ muṉ pāṇi taruvāḷō
eṉa āṅku
pāṇiyum tūkkum cīrum eṉṟu ivai
māṇ iḻai arivai kāppa
āṇam il poruḷ emakku amarntaṉai āṭi.

---

8 While traditionally *Kalittokai* 1 has never been counted as one of the Peruntēvaṉār series, in recent years a manuscript has been found that claims him to be the author [Rajeswari 2009]. For reasons of metre, morphology and contents, however, this seems unlikely.

Announcing many rare secrets (Veda words) to brahmins who know the path,
hiding clear water in [your] matted hair, goring the three cities with a fiery [arrow],
listen now, you with eight arms [and] sapphire throat of unrelenting battle
with [your] fierce demon [troops], who go according to [your] intention, without being told:
While many beaten drums sound, you dispelling many forms:
At the time [you] dance the Koṭukoṭṭi, will she with high-curved broad hips
[and] a waist resembling a creeper give the melody taken?
At the time [you] dance the Paṇṭaraṅkam, winning many vehement battles
by [your] strength, adorned with ashes, will she with soft shoulders touched by grace [and] tresses in which bees sound give the ascending rhythm?
At the time you dance the skull dance, taking a skull in [your] palm,
tying the hide of the murderous tiger, while the Laburnum garland is rolling on [his] neck,
will she with a smile that adorns [her] breast give the beat in front [of you][9]?
That is to say,
while the young woman with glorious jewels
guards these: melody and rhythm and beat,
you keep dancing, not a small wealth for us.

In accordance with the custom of using for the invocation the metre of the text it precedes, the poem is composed in the stanzaic Kali form. The image of Śiva projected here is not the one familiar from the Peruntēvaṉār invocations—that of bull rider, Ardhanarīśvara and Gaṅgādhara—but that of a dancer, a figure otherwise especially evoked in the Tiruvalaṅkāṭṭu decades of Kāraikkālammaiyār (6th c.). Moreover, he is supported, if not downright supervised, by the god-

9 Or: "will she give the first beat?"

dess. If so, I do not see any direct contemporary parallel. Morphology and semantics likewise speak for a later origin; the Middle Tamil negative absolutive *kūṟāmal* occurs along with a series of Sanskrit loan words (*caṭai*, *tiripuram*, *paṇṭaraṅkam*, *kāpālam*), except for the first unprecedented in classical poetry.

Far more conservative in several ways is the only purely Śaivite invocation attested for the *Kīḻkkaṇakku*, that of the *Iṉṉilai*, if ever the *Iṉṉilai* has to be counted among the *Kīḻkkaṇakku* at all, which is disputed.[10] From the perspective of primary sources, i.e., manuscripts, we find contradictory evidence. While not a single surviving serial *Kīḻkkaṇakku* manuscript seems to contain the text of the *Iṉṉilai*, the anonymous mnemonic stanza that enumerates the texts included in the anthology makes mention of it.[11] However, since neither the search and analysis of manuscripts nor the wording and interpretation of the stanza can be regarded as done,[12] the verse shall be quoted nevertheless:

---

10 For a discussion, see Vaiyāpurip Piḷḷai 1954: 80f.; for an English summary, see Zvelebil 1994: 251f.

11 *nālaṭi nāṉmaṇi nāṉāṟpat' aintiṇai-mup-*
pāl kaṭukam kōvai paḻamoḻi—māmūlam
iṉṉilai col-kāñci-uṭaṉ ēlāti eṉpavē
kainnilai avām kīḻkkaṇakku.

1. *Nālaṭi[yār]*, 2. *Nāṉmaṇi[kaṭikai]*, the four *Nāṟpatu* (3. *Kaḷavaḻi Nāṟpatu*, 4. *Kārnāṟpatu*, 5. *Iṉṉānāṟpatu*, 6. *Iṉiyavai Nāṟpatu*), the *Aintiṇais* (7. *Aintiṇai Aimpatu*, 8. *Aintiṇai Eḻupatu*, 9. *Tiṇaimālai Nūṟṟaimpatu*, 10. *Tiṇaimoḻi Aimpatu*), the one in three parts (=11. *Tirukkuṟaḷ*), 12. *[Tiri]kaṭukam*, 13. *[Ācārak]kōvai*, 14. *Paḻamoḻi*, *Māmūlam* (=15. *Ciṟupañcamūlam*), 16. *Iṉṉilai*, with *Colkāñci* (=17. *Mutumoḻikkāñci*), 18. *Ēlāti*, they say, 19. *Kainnilai*—those are the *Kīḻkkaṇakku* (the minor classics).

12 As it is given here, the enumeration seems to be of nineteen texts, while eighteen (*patiṉeṇ*) unequivocally is the traditional figure, incorporated into the full title *Patiṉeṇkīḻkkaṇakku*. One possible way out of the dilemma might be to understand *iṉṉilai* ("of pleasing condition") as an attribute to *col-kāñci* instead of reading it as a separate title.

vēla<u>n</u> tarīiya viri caṭaip pemmā<u>n</u>
vāl i<u>l</u>ai pākattu amariya ko<u>l</u>u vēl
kū<u>r</u><u>r</u>am kata<u>l</u>nt' e<u>r</u>i ko<u>n</u><u>r</u>aiya<u>n</u>
kūṭṭā ulakam ke<u>l</u>īiya malintē.

The lord with expansive matted hair brought by the spear-carrying [priest],
the Laburnum wearer inhabited half by [her with] pure jewels
who angrily throws [his] rich spear at Kū<u>r</u><u>r</u>am (Death),
let the united world joyfully join [him].

Unlike the majority of *Kī<u>l</u>kkaṇakku,* the *I<u>n</u><u>n</u>ilai* is not composed in Veṇpā metre, but in the older Āciriyappā, and the same is true for its invocation. It has been attributed to Peruntēva<u>n</u>ār, and indeed it has similarities with the *Caṅkam* invocations, which might be deliberate if indeed the text has to be seen as a forgery. From the point of view of the contents, what is significant is a certain amount of oscillation between Śiva and Muruka<u>n</u>. While the attributes (matted hair, Laburnum, female half) and the divine deed (killing of Death) belong to Śiva, the spear-carrying priest (*vēla<u>n</u>*) is connected with Muruka<u>n</u>.

As far as Muruka<u>n</u> is concerned, the *Kī<u>l</u>kkaṇakku* do not have a single invocation exclusively dedicated to him, while for the *Caṅkam* corpus he shared the first place with Śiva. Not only can he claim the two *Ku<u>r</u>untokai* invocations already referred to, but, if the *Tirumurukā<u>r</u><u>r</u>uppaṭai* can indeed be counted as a *kaṭavuḷ vā<u>l</u>ttu* as argued above, with 317 lines he commands more material than all the other verses to all other deities put together.

Gaṇeśa, however, the stepchild of first-millennium devotional literature, gets one stanza with the *Aintiṇai E<u>l</u>upatu,* the only among the small Akam anthologies to be endowed with an invocation at all.

eṇṇum poruḷ iṉitē ellām muṭitt' emakku
naṇṇum kalai a<u>n</u>aittum nalkumāl, kaṇ nutali<u>n</u>
muṇṭattā<u>n</u> aṇṭattā<u>n</u> mūlattā<u>n</u> nalam cēr
kaṇṭattā<u>n</u> ī<u>n</u><u>r</u>a kaḷi<u>r</u>u.

Having sweetly accomplished all poetic elements that count he grants us all the joined arts, the elephant bull brought forth at an auspicious moment by the bald one with an eye on [his] forehead, who is the cosmic egg [and] the root.

So here the elephant god is praised for his relation to the arts (part of which, we presume, is the *Aintiṇai Eḻupatu*),[13] but as much space, namely half the stanza, is given to the description of his father Śiva.

Coming to the poems that praise more than one deity, all four praise some form of Viṣṇu and Śiva as a minimal pair. The *Aiṅkuṟu-nūṟu* that has already been quoted evokes Nārāyaṇa-Kṛṣṇa and Ardhanarīśvara, the other three refer to further partly named, partly unnamed deities. One stanza precedes the text that is variously called, in the literary tradition, *Iṉiya Nāṟpatu*, *Iṉiyavai Nāṟpatu* or *Iṉiyatu Nāṟpatu*.

kaṇ mūṉṟ' uṭaiyāṉ tāḷ cērtal kaṭitu iṉitē,
tol māṇ tuḻāy mālaiyāṉait toḻal iṉitē,
munturap pēṇi mukam nāṉk' uṭaiyāṉaic
ceṉṟ' amarnt' ēttal iṉitu.

---

13 In this respect similar, although more concrete, is the second early invocation stanza to Gaṇeśa known to me, probably somewhat later but still from the 1st millennium, that is, the first of three coming with the *Pārata Veṇpā*, the oldest Tamil version of the *Mahābhārata* surviving in more than a handful quotations. There the god's relation to the text is spelt out: he has written or copied it. The verse is remarkable too for its genre mix, for though it is positioned like a *kaṭavuḷ vāḻttu*, it actually enumerates the benefits to be derived from reciting the text, as is the purpose of the *phalaśruti*, normally positioned at the end of a text:

ōta, viṉai akalum ōṅku pukaḻ perukum
kātal poruḷ aṉaittum kaikūṭum – cītap
paṉi kōṭṭu māl varaimēl pāratap pōr tīṭṭum
taṉik kōṭṭu vāraṇattiṉ tāḷ.

When one recites [the praise of]
the foot of the elephant with the single tusk
that inscribes the Bhārata war on the huge mountains with cold dewy peaks, [past] deeds will depart, high fame will increase,
all the desired objects will draw near.

> Fast joining the feet of him who possesses three eyes is sweet,
> worshipping him who has a garland of old glorious Tulsi is sweet,
> going to, staying with [and] praising him who possesses four faces,
> judging [him] to have priority, is sweet.

Here the wording employed to express veneration for the familiar triad of gods, Śiva, Viṣṇu and Brahmā, is playfully individual, no doubt because it has to be read as an allusion to the anthology title; *Iṉiya Nāṟpatu* means "The Forty on What Is Pleasing". The epithets chosen to refer to the gods are among the basic stock items in devotional poetry, i.e., the three eyes for Śiva, the Tulsi garland for Viṣṇu or Kṛṣṇa and the four faces for Brahmā.

More interesting is the poem of the *Iṉṉā Nāṟpatu* ("The Forty on What Is Unpleasant"), attributed to the famous classical poet Kapilar, who after all he had composed for the old anthologies, also took the trouble to produce the Kuṟiñci Hundred of the *Aiṅkuṟunūṟu*, the *Kuṟuñcippāṭṭu* among the Ten Songs and, last but not least, the Kuṟiñci portion of the *Kalittokai*, so that by now he should have indeed reached the ripe age of about 600 years.

> *muk kaṇ pakavaṉ aṭi toḻātārkk' iṉṉā,*
> *poṟpaṉai veḷḷaiyai uḷḷāt' oluk' iṉṉā,*
> *cakkarattāṉai maṟapp' iṉṉā, āṅk' iṉṉā*
> *cattiyāṉ tāḷ toḻātārkku.*

> Misery to those who do not worship the feet of the Venerable one with three eyes,
> misery acting without thinking of the White one with the golden Palmyra palm,
> misery forgetting him with the discus, as much misery
> to those who don't worship the feet of the Spear-bearer.

The technique is the same as for the sister anthology, with a play here on the idea of being conducive to misery. The group of deities addressed here consists of four members, evoked in a similar manner by their attributes, only two of which are identical with the group of three. Here we have three-eyed Śiva, Balarāma with the Palmyra banner, Kṛṣṇa with the discus and Murukaṉ under the name Cattiyāṉ (< Skt. *śakti-dhara-* "spear bearer"). That this group is not the product of chance is shown by at least one parallel from the *Puṟanāṉūṟu*, the famous 56 (PN 56.1-14). The first eight lines in that poem enumerate with some more detail the same sequence of four gods as models of behaviour for the Pāṇṭiya king.

ēṟṟu valaṉ uyariya eri maruḷ avir caṭai
māṟṟ' arum kaṇicci maṇi miṭaṟṟōṉum
kaṭal vaḷar puri vaḷai puraiyum mēṉi
aṭal vem nāñcil paṉai koṭiyōṉum
maṇṇuṟu tiru maṇi puraiyum mēṉi
viṇ uyar puḷ koṭi viṟal veyyōṉum
maṇi mayil uyariya māṟā veṉṟi
piṇimuka ūrti oḷ ceyyōṉum.

The one with a sapphire throat, with a battle-axe difficult to avert,
with shining matted locks resembling a flame, become high in victory on a bull,
and the one with a Palmyra banner, with a ploughshare desirous of killing,
with a body resembling a spiralled conch grown in the sea,
and the one desirous of victory, with a bird banner high to the sky,
with a body resembling a polished brilliant sapphire,
and the bright ruddy one, whose vehicle is Piṇimukam,
of unaltered victory that is elevated on a sapphire peacock.

This song has a number of peculiarities that make it look like a late intrusion in the *Puṟanāṉūṟu*. It describes a series of personalised gods in a way that is absolutely typical of the period under consideration here, that is, not before the 6th century and possibly in the early 7th. It is put into the mouth of yet another of the fluid reappearing poets, namely Nakkīraṉ, the son of Kaṇakkāyaṉār from Maturai (Maturaik Kaṇakkāyaṉār makaṉār Nakkīraṉār),[14] who is not only supposed to have left behind several poems in the early anthologies, but also the *Neṭunalvāṭai*, and, more to the point here, the *Tirumuru-kāṟṟuppaṭai*, besides being famous as the first commentator on Akam

---

14 On the various possible identities of Nakkīraṉ, see Gros 1983: 90f., and Zvelebil 1986: 65f.

poetics, writer of the commentary on the *Iṟaiyaṉār Akapporuḷ*. It has two late and rare Sanskrit loans, one of them being Piṇimukam, the name of Murukaṉ's elephant, likewise referred to in the *Tirumuruku*, and *yavaṉar*, referring to Greek traders. Last but not least it shows a number of smaller metrical irregularities which are symptomatic of the later revival Āciriyappā.

I would draw the conclusion that, firstly, here we are touching on a certain milieu of literates involved, in one way or another, in giving the corpus the structure we know today. Secondly, I would conclude that in that milieu there was a group where indeed the above series of four gods was worshipped. If that is accepted, it would yield us the key to one more of the verses which address a plurality, but which so far seem cryptic, namely the one of the *Ēlāti*:

aṟu nālvar āy pukaḻc cēv' aṭi āṟṟap
peṟu nālvar pēṇi vaḻaṅkip peṟu nāṉ-
maṟai purintu vāḻumēl maṇ oḻintu viṇṇōrkku
iṟai purintu vāḻtal iyalpu.

While seeking the red feet of choice fame of the six [times] four,
if, habitually esteeming the worthy four, one lives
performing the four Vedas, when leaving behind the earth,
living as lord of the celestials [comes] naturally.

Here we see as an invocation a verse of one kind typical for the signature verse of the *bhakti* corpus, the one that would be termed, in Sanskrit, the *phalaśruti*, the fruit to be gained from listening to or reciting the text thus graced. Gaining heaven is one of the elementary achievements aspired to by a devout human. Only here the implication of listening or reciting is left inexplicit; the *Ēlāti* itself is not referred to, and indeed here we are only at the beginning of the text, while the signature verse naturally belongs to the end. We might see this as a phase of experiment with form. As far as the deities evoked are concerned, the twenty-four remain mysterious, while the four I suggest reading as Śiva, Balarāma, Kṛṣṇa and Murukaṉ.[15] As an ex-

[15] An alternative reading, however, might be a Śaivite one, taking the twenty-four as to refer to the gods, while the four could also be the

ample for the praise of deity in the abstract, the invocation of the Nālaṭiyār may be quoted. The first decade of the Kuṟaḷ would be the second case in point, but that has already been translated a sufficient number of times.

vāṉ iṭu villiṉ varav' aṟiyā vāymaiyāl
kāl nilam tōyāk kaṭavuḷai yām nilam
ceṉṉi uṟa vaṇaṅkic cērtum, 'em uḷḷattu
muṉṉiyavai muṭika' eṉṟu.

Because truth is unpredictable, like the [rain]bow put in the sky,[16]
the god whose feet do not touch the ground let us join,
bowing so that [our] heads touch the ground, saying
"Let the thoughts contemplated in our minds be perfected".

Here the attitude of human to god certainly falls into the pattern of *bhakti*, that is, of personal devotion to the deity with the hope of

---

traditional group of the four Śaivite saints, Campantar, Appar, Cuntarar and Māṇikkavācakar. What speaks against such an interpretation in my view is time: Māṇikkavācakar is a comparatively late one the spot, in about the 9th century. Still, it has to be admitted that we have no means of proving that all the *Kīḻkkaṇakku* invocations go back to the early period of compilation and a later date for basically any stanza currently cannot be excluded. Moreover, tradition holds that Kaṇimētaiyār was a Jain, and accordingly there are commentaries attempting to give a Jain interpretation to the invocation stanza. But the same claim is made for the author of the *Ciṟupañcamūlam*, whose invocation stanza refers to Trivikrama. And if we look at the wording of the *Ēlāti* stanza, there is more than one element that connects it to the familiar cosmos of "Hindu" deities. To begin with, the reference to paying homage to the "red feet" of someone is very clearly a *bhakti* topos. Secondly, Jains are not really expected to do service to the four Vedas, by far the most obvious interpretation of *nāṉmaṟai*.

16 The first line poses difficulties of understanding, but I suggest to read a pre-positioned explanation of why it is necessary to turn to god: because truth (here presumably of the spiritual, liberating kind) literally "does not know of coming", i.e. is elusive unless given by god, just as the rainbow whose appearance is unforeseen and not under the control of humans.

spiritual improvement and finally, one presumes, heaven or liberation.

This brings us to the end of the theistic share in the satellite stanzas insofar as they are usually printed.[17] We have seen, though in uneven distribution, veneration of a number of, from the point of view of *bhakti* literature, major and minor deities of the Hindu pantheon—Murukaṉ, Śiva with most of his celebrated aspects and accompanied by the goddess, Gaṇeśa, Viṣṇu in most of his incarnations, his brother Balarāma, Brahmā—as well as references to more abstract forms of "god". It is easy to perceive that with the invocation stanzas to the two major classical hyper-anthologies of Tamil literature we are not dealing with a chance collection of stray verses unevenly distributed over an indefinite number of centuries, but with a group of verses that stand in close intertextual relationship with each other and with the texts they are attached to. Even apart from aspects of literary form, content and metre, the various conceptions of divinity seem far more fluid and individual than would easily be explicable if we were to accept the late dates currently assigned to these stanzas.[18] If indeed the 7th century has seen the advent of "Śaivism" and "Vaiṣṇavism" as it transpires from the great *bhakti* works assigned to that period, greater liberty must have either still been possible at that time, even for persons acting within the sphere of royal courts such as that of the Pāṇṭiyas, or these stanzas must predate those oeuvres. In short, these neglected verses on the margin of classical literature allow us rare glimpses into the crystallisation of poetic forms, the formation of the corpus and the religious sentiments of a literary milieu before the pervasive sectarian splits.

---

[17] That is, except for those associated with the *Tirumurukāṟṟuppaṭai*, which have been collected and edited by Emmanuel Francis (cf. Francis 2017: 319–351).

[18] Given dates vary between the 8th century (Champakalakshmi 2011: 166) and the 9th century (Marr 1985[1958]: 70ff.), although Zvelebil 1994: 555 seems to advocate the 7th century, at least for the stanzas of Peruntēvaṉār.

Bibliography

Primary Literature

Ācārakkōvai

Ācārakkōvai, Pu. Ci. Puṉṉaivaṉanāta Mutaliyār (ed. + comm.), Caivacittānta Nūṟpatippuk Kaḻakam. Tirunelvēli 1939.

Aiṅkuṟunūṟu

Aiṅkuṟunūṟu mūlamum paḻaiyavuraiyum. U. Vē. Cāminātaiyar (ed. + comm.), Vaijayanti Accukkūṭam. Ceṉṉapaṭṭaṇam 1903 (2nd ed. Kaṇeṣa Accukkūṭam, Ceṉṉapaṭṭaṇam 1920; various repr. by UVSL).

Aintiṇaiyaimpatu

Aintiṇaiyaimpatu mūlamum uraiyum. Rā. Rākavaiyaṅkār (ed.), Tamiḻccaṅkamuttiracālai. Maturai 1912.

Aintiṇaiyeḻupatu

Aintiṇaiyeḻupatu paḻaiya uraiyōṭum. Āṉanta Rāmaiyar (ed.), Nōpil Accukkūṭam. Ceṉṉai 1931.

Akanāṉūṟū

Neṭuntokai ākum Akanāṉūṟu mūlamum paḻaiya uraiyum [old comm. for KV-90, new comm. for 91-160]. Vē. Rā. Rākavaiyaṅkār/Rājakōpālāryaṉ (eds.), Kampar Pustakālayam, Kamparvilāsam. Mayilāppūram, Śrīmuka v° = 1933/34.

Cilappatikāram

Cilappatikāram mūlamum arumpatavuraiyum aṭiyārkkulallār uraiyum. U. Vē. Cāminātaiyar (ed.), Madras 1892 (rep. of the 5th edition 1955).

Ēlāti

Ēlāti viruttiyuraiyuṭaṉ. Ti. Cu. Pālacuntaram Piḷḷai (ed.), Caivacittānta Nūṟpatippuk Kaḻakam. Tirunelvēli 1939.

Iṉiyavai Nāṟpatu

Iṉiyavai Nāṟpatu paḻaiya uraiyum viḷakka uraiyum. Es. Vaiyāpurip Piḷḷai (ed.), Āciriyar Nūṟpatippuk Kaḻakam. Ceṉṉai 1949.

Iṉṉānāṟpatu

Iṉṉānāṟpatu paḻaiya uraiyuṭaṉ. Ca. Vaiyāpurip Piḷḷai (ed.), Cakti Kāriyālayam. Ceṉṉai, Maturai 1944.

Kaḷavaḻi Nāṟpatu

Kaḷavaḻi Nāṟpatu mūlamum uraiyum. Na. Mu. Vēṅkaṭacāmi Nāṭṭār, Vā. Makātēva Mutaliyār (eds.), Caivacittānta Nūṟpatippuk Kaḻakam. Tirunelvēli [no date].

Kalittokai

Kalittokai mūlamum nacciṉārkkiṉiyār uraiyōṭum. I. Vai. Aṉantarāmaiyar (ed.), Tamiḻp Palkalaik Kaḻakam, Tañcāvūr 1984 (rep. in one vol. of two books from 1925, 1931).

Kārnāṟpatu

Kārnāṟpatu. Na. Mu. Vēṅkaṭacāmi Nāṭṭār (ed. + comm.), Caivacittānta Nūṟpatippuk Kaḻakam. Tirunelvēli 1925.

Māmūlam

Kaṭukaṅ Kaṭikai Māmūlam patavurai viḷakkavuraiyuṭaṉ. Pu. Ci. Puṉṉaivaṉāta Mutaliyār (ed.), Caivacittānta Nūṟpatippuk Kaḻakam. Tirunelvēli 1966.

Kuṟuntokai

Kuṟuntokai, Critical Edition and Annotated Translation + Glossary and Statistics. Eva Wilden (ed.), 3 volumes, EFEO + Tamilmann Patippakam. (Critical Texts of Caṅkam Literature 2.1-2.3). Ceṉṉai 2010.

Mutumoḻikkāñci

Mutumoḻikkāñci. Cē. Kiruṣṇamācār (ed.), Mu. Caṭakōparāmānujācāryar (comm.), Ār. Jī. Accukkūṭam. Ceṉṉai 1939.

Nālaintiṇai

Nālaintiṇai patavurai viḷakkavuraikaḷum. A. Naṭarācapiḷḷai (ed.), Caivacittānta Nūṟpatippuk Kaḻakam. Tirunelvēli, Ceṉṉai 1935.

Nāṉmaṇik Kaṭikai

Nāṉmaṇik Kaṭikai mūlamum uraiyum. Ca. Vaiyāpurip Piḷḷai (ed.), Cakti Kāriyālayam. Ceṉṉai, Maturai 1944.

Naṟṟiṇai

Naṟṟiṇai, Critical Edition and Annotated Translation + Glossary. Eva Wilden (ed.), 3 volumes, EFEO + Tamilmann Patippakam. (Critical Texts of Caṅkam Literature 1.1-1.3). Ceṉṉai 2008.

Paḻamoḻi

Paḻamoḻi mūlamum paḻaiya uraiyum. Nārāyaṇa Aiyaṅkār (ed.), Maturait Tamiḻc Caṅkam. Maturai 1922.

Paripāṭal

Paripāṭal mūlamum āciriyar parimēlaḻakariyaṟṟiya uraiyum. U. Vē. Cāminātaiyar (ed.), Kamarṣiyal Accukkūṭam. Ceṉṉai 1918 (2nd ed. 1935; various reprints of the UVSL).

Tirumuṟai 11

Patiṉōrān Tirumuṟai. Āṟumukanāvalar (ed.), Vittiyānupālaṉayantiracālai. Ceṉṉapaṭṭaṇam, paritāpi v° = 1852/53.

Patiṟṟuppattu

Patiṟṟuppattu paḻaiyavuraiyum. U. V. Cāminātaiyar (ed.), Vaijayanti Accukkūṭam. Ceṉṉapaṭṭaṇam 1904 (2nd ed. Kamarṣiyal Accukkūṭam, Ceṉṉapaṭṭaṇam 1920, Lipaṛṭi Accukkūṭam, Ceṉṉapaṭṭaṇam 1941, various rep. by UVSL).

Pattuppāṭṭu

Pattuppāṭṭu mūlamum Nacciṉārkkiṉiyar uraiyum. U. V. Cāminātaiyar (ed.), Tirāviṭātnākara Accukkūṭam. Ceṉṉai 1889 (2nd ed. Kamarṣiyal Accukkūṭam, Ceṉṉai 1918, 3rd ed. Kēcari Accukkūṭam, Ceṉṉai 1931; various rep. by UVSL).

Puṟanāṉūṟu

Puṟanāṉūṟu mūlamum uraiyum. U. V. Cāminātaiyar (ed.), Vē.Tā. Jūbili Accukkūṭam. Ceṉṉai 1894 (2nd ed. 1923, 3rd ed. 1935, various rep. by UVSL).

Pāratavēṇpa

Peruntēvaṉār Pāratam eṉṉum Pāratavēṇpa. A. Kōpālaiyaṉ (ed.), Centamiḻ Mantiram Puttakacālai. Mayilāppūr, Ceṉṉai 1925.

Patiṉeṇkīḻkkaṇakku

Patiṉeṇkīḻkkaṇakku. Es. Rājam (eds.), Ceṉṉai 1959.

Patiṉeṇkīḻkkaṇakku

Patiṉeṇkīḻkkaṇakku. Mu. Caṇmukam Piḷḷai (ed.), 3 vol. Mullai Nilaiyam. Ceṉṉai 1996, 2009 (repr.).

Tiṇaimālainūṟṟaimpatu

Tiṇaimālainūṟṟaimpatu mūlamum uraiyum. Rā. Rākavaiyaṅkār (ed.), Tamiḻccaṅkamuttiracālai. Maturai 1927.

Tirukkuṟaḷ

Tirukkuṟaḷ mūlamum Parimēlaḻakar uraiyum. Vaṭivēlu Ceṭṭiyār (ed.), 3 vol., Maturaip Palkalaikkaḻakam, 1904, 1972–1976 (repr.).

Tolkāppiyam Poruḷatikāram

Tolkāppiyam Poruḷatikāram 1-5, Nacciṉārkkiṉiyam. Ci. Kaṇēcaiyar (ed.), Tirumakaḷ Aḻuttakam, Cuṉṉākam 1948.

Secondary Literature

Champakalakshmi 2011

R. Champakalakshmi, Vaiṣṇava Concepts in Early Tamil Nadu. In: *Religion, Tradition, and Ideology. Precolonial South-India*. New Delhi: Oxford University Press 2011, pp.165–196 [rep. from *Journal of Indian History*, vol. I, No. 150, part III, 1972]

Gros 1983

François Gros, La littérature du Sangam et son public. In: *Purṣārtha* 7 (1983) 77–107.

Francis 2017

Emmanuel Francis, The Other Way Round: From Print to Manuscript. In: Vincenzo Vergiani, Daniele Cuneo, Camillo Alessio Formigatti (eds.), *Indic Manuscript Cultures through the Ages: Material, Textual, and Historical Investigations*. Berlin: deGruyter, pp. 319–351.

Marr 1985

John Ralston Marr, *The Eight Anthologies. A Study in Early Tamil Literature*. Madras 1985 (print version of a PhD dissertation of 1958).

Nandakumar 2007
P. Nandakumar, *Eladi, Tamil Classic by Ganimedhaiar*. Translated into English. Dravidian University, Srinivasavanam, Kuppam 2007.

Pope 1893
George Uglow Pope, *The Nālatiyār or Four Hundred Quatrains in Tamil*. Introduction, translation and notes. Oxford: Clarendon Press 1893.

Rajeswari 2009
T. Rajeswari, Pālaikkali Verses and Their Authors. In: *Between Preservation and Recreation: Tamil Traditions of Commentary*. Proceedings of a Workshop in Honour of T.V. Gopal Iyer. Ed. by Eva Wilden [Collection Indologie 109]. Pondichéry: IFP-EFEO, pp. 255–268.

Ramachandra Dikshitar 2000
V.R. Ramachandra Dikshitar, *Tirukkuṟaḷ in Roman Transliteration with English Translation and Tamil Text*. Chennai: The Adyar Library and Research Centre, 1949, 2nd ed. 1994, 2000 (repr.).

Vaiyāpurip Piḷḷai 1954
S. Vaiyāpurip Piḷḷai, *Ilakkiya Maṇimālai*. Ceṉṉai 1954, 2nd ed. 1957.

Vaiyāpurip Piḷḷai 1956
S. Vaiyāpurip Piḷḷai, *History of Tamil Language and Literature* (Beginning to 1000 A.D.). Madras: New Century Book House 1956, 1988 (repr.).

Wilden 2014
Eva Wilden, *Manuscript, Print and Memory: Relics of the Caṅkam in Tamilnadu*. [Studies in Manuscript Cultures 3]. Berlin: de Gruyter 2014.

Zvelebil 1986
Kamil Veith Zvelebil, Brief Prolegomena to Early Tamil Literary History: Iṟaiyaṉār, Tarumi, Nakkīrar. *Journal of the Royal Asiatic Society of Great Britain and Ireland* 1 (1986) 59–67.

Zvelebil 1994
Kamil Veith Zvelebil, *Lexicon of Tamil Literature*. [Handbuch der Orientalistik Bd. 9]. Leiden, New York, Köln: E.J. Brill 1994.

Peter Schreiner

Theology of Viṣṇu in the *Viṣṇupurāṇa*

Introduction

In order to extract or distil something like "theology" from the *Viṣṇupurāṇa* (ViP) two analytical procedures have been applied which will be briefly described and the result of which form the core of this presentation.

In the first part, the literary genre of *stotra* (hymns of praise) is chosen as an important locus of talking about God (Viṣṇu).[1] The vocabulary[2] of all *stotra*s in the ViP is analysed and classified into semantic fields[3] according to what is mentioned, described or talked about addressing God in praise. The variations of vocabulary and expression constitute the "paradigm" for talking about a particular aspect of the concept of God. The totality of paradigms thus established includes paradigms which structure this totality. Structure and content together constitute the concept of Viṣṇu that characterizes the ViP.

---

1 This paper is based on my unpublished Habilitationsschrift, "Die Hymnen des Viṣṇupurāṇa: Materialien zur Textanalyse des Viṣṇupurāṇa". Tübingen 1980.

2 Other elements and perspectives by which *stotra*s or (any other puraṇic sub-genre) could be described and analysed are, e.g., literary style (including metre, refrain, formulaic expressions, compounds, particles, etc.) and intertextual comparison (e.g., Viṣṇu-*stotras* vs. Śiva- or Devī-*stotra*s, *stotra*s in the ViP vs. *stotra*s in the *Liṅgapurāṇa*, etc.; cf. Schreiner 1990: 426–441). Other literary genres that have been or could be analysed are episodes, mythological narratives, dialogues, (philosophical, theological, cosmological) tracts, attributions of merit (*śravaṇa-phala*).

3 This term, though part of the technical terminology of semantics, linguistics, lexicography, history of concepts, etc., is used here without reference to any specific authority in these disciplines.

The second part consists of the analysis of conceptual keywords of philosophical or theological import based on "cross sections", i.e., the examination of all occurrences of a word in the whole text (a procedure which obviously presupposes the availability of a digitized version of the examined text). Theoretically, one might postulate that such a cross section should be carried out for every vocabulary item in all the paradigms; but the effort would be forbidding, the results are not likely to modify substantially what can be derived from exemplary cross sections. I restrict myself to summarizing the results of examining *jñāna/vijñāna*.[4]

If these procedures are taken as programmatic methodological tools in Purāṇa research, they obviously need to be supplemented by intertextual comparison as the tool and method that introduces a historical perspective into this type of textual analysis. This dimension has been deliberately excluded from this presentation. Its importance, however, cannot be overemphasized.

The two procedures document that the ViP, while praising the deity,[5] also say much about the world. Its theology is a cosmo-theology. The world in its relation to God is a layered universe with beginning and end, and a period of subsistence in between. God in relation to this world assumes all three of the "*trimūrti*-functions". The sequence of creation, maintenance and retraction of the world demands that time is part of reality, as divine, and of divinity as ultimate reality.

The world, as produced from God, participates in his ultimate reality; the term for this dimension is *vijñāna* or *jñāna*. In it, epistemology and metaphysics seem to meet and to mingle. Viewed from the worldly perspective, it means that God can be cognized because everything participates in the cognitive dimension of reality—a dimension which characterizes, singularly and absolutely, only God.

Thus, reality is layered and God is the highest reality (*paramārtha*) and therefore is more real than the world. But the world and its

4 *Paramārtha*, and *parama-pada*, *yoga*, *bhakti*, *māyā* and *pūjā/ārādhana* are further keywords that have been analysed.

5 I choose this word deliberately in order to avoid the gender problem; Viṣṇu is masculine; as God he is more properly considered neuter.

parts are not ultimately unreal. The parts cannot be separated from the whole. The recognition of what the parts and the whole share and have in common, viz. cognition, identifies with this common dimension and liberates from the provisionality of identifying only with the parts.

Though these traits of the concept of God in the ViP are (taken individually) not new in the Indian history of ideas, at least their combination characterizes the ViP as a whole and thus can be attributed to what can be called the "milieu" which produced the final redaction of this Purāṇa.

1.1 *Stotras* in the *Viṣṇupurāṇa*

The title of this paper consists of several irritating singulars which require some clarification. "The *Viṣṇupurāṇa*" is a parlance which in western Purāṇa research must be considered provocative if not meaningless after Willibald Kirfel. Purāṇas are *a priori* considered texts belonging to the genre of anonymous literature, which do not have an author and thus do not have a singular origin—in time and in space. In the process of transmission and migration such texts have been modified, enlarged, abbreviated. The changes can affect the literary form as well as the content. Thus, to want to say anything about "the" ViP without asking about the specific layer in its development runs the danger of being considered unscientific and naive.

The comparative method has been considered the most promising tool for discovering chronological layers. By comparing wording (as is practiced for the preparation of critical editions) Kirfel's *Purāṇapañcalakṣaṇa*[6] aims at a kind of critical edition of those passages in (theoretically) all Purāṇas which talk about *sarga*, *pratisarga*, *manvantara*, *vaṃśa*, *vaṃśānucarita*. Taking the next step, Hacker applied comparison to a myth (its plot, descriptions, religious milieu and theological terminology). Next to Narasiṃha in the Prahlāda-episode, other *avatāra* myths have been handled in a similar manner (Kūrma, Varāha, Paraśurāma, Vāmana, Buddha—Kṛṣṇa already and with

---

[6] Kirfel 1927.

different guiding questions by Ruben[7]). None of these studies considered any of the studied Purāṇas as unified texts about which one could confidently speak in the singular.

By choosing to study the *stotras* in *the* ViP I did not originally intend to question or denounce this presupposition; rather, I wanted to expand the repertoire of what can be compared in Purāṇas (and between the different layers of one Purāṇa) by the category "literary genre". Were those hymns (in historical perspective) an integral part of the episode or context in which they occurred? To answer this question one needs to compare the *stotras* amongst themselves, the *stotras* and their content with the content of the episode, the occurrence of the *stotras* in other versions of the same episode in other Purāṇas, the occurring *stotras* with the *stotras* in the parallel episodes.

The content of *stotras* evokes the second singular, "theology". *Stotras*, i.e., hymns of praise, are (in the ViP) generally addressed to a deity. In praising the deity, they state affirmatively what or how the deity is, what he (or she or it) did and how he (or she or it) acted. Hymns of praise thus speak *to* a deity and *about* the deity, whom they address. This is "theo-logy", "god-talk", not in the sense of a scientific discipline or an ideological system, but in a general sense of "speaking about god/God". And, if *stotras* are addressed to different deities, they should also document different theologies.

Can at least the singular of Viṣṇu survive the irritation of a critical reading of the title? Yes and no. No, because Viṣṇu is not just called Viṣṇu. For the purpose of this study I speak of Viṣṇu where the text may speak of Viṣṇu (292 times), Hari (187), Keśava (65), Kṛṣṇa (312), Hṛṣīkeśa (7), Janārdana (67), Bhagavat (237), Govinda (61), Nārāyaṇa (30).[8] No again, because the name Viṣṇu is used for different aspects and functions of this deity.[9] Yes, if what the ViP

---

[7] Rüping 1970; Gail 1977a: 127–168; Gail 1977b. Tripathi 1968. Ruben 1943. The method has been also applied to other myths, cf. Bock 1984 and Mertens 1998.

[8] The numbers are meant only to indicate roughly the proportions of frequency; the title *bhagavat*, e.g., is not only to Viṣṇu.

[9] As an example, for the simultaneous multiformity of Viṣṇu on an episodic level, see 1,9.86-89 (the quoted text and references are that of the

says about Viṣṇu (its theology) adds up to a consistent system and view of "god and the world", a cosmo-theology with traits (on the level of terminology, of conceptualization, of order and values) that make it distinctive—as a theology of Viṣṇu and as the theology of the *Viṣṇupurāṇa*.

As already mentioned, the most explicit way of speaking about God (and thus of practicing "theo-logy") in the ViP are the *stotra*s (hymns of praise) addressed to the deity. The following observations are primarily based on the analysis of the *Viṣṇustotra*s in the ViP.

1.2 Establishing a corpus of hymns of praise

In order to establish the corpus of hymns of praise by a text-immanent and formal, objectifiable criterion, I examined the use of the word "praise" (*stu-* and derivates).[10] It allows identifying hymns of praise as those sections which are called *stuti*, *stotra* or *stava*, or are introduced and/or concluded in the ViP by explicitly mentioning that somebody *praised* or was praised by these passages.

1,2.1–1,2.7*	Parāśara praises Viṣṇu
1,4.12–24	Earth praises Varāha
1,4.31–44	Sanandana, etc. praise Varāha
1,9.39–56	Brahmā praises Viṣṇu
1,9.60–64	Devarṣayaḥ praise Viṣṇu
1,9.68–73	Deities praise Viṣṇu
1,9.115–130	Indra praises Śrī
1,12.53–75	Dhruva praises Viṣṇu
1,14.23–43	Pracetasas praise Viṣṇu

critical edition: *The Critical Edition of the Viṣṇupurāṇam*, ed. by M.M. Pathak, 2 vols., Vadodara 1997–1999). In the *Amṛtamanthana*-episode Kṛṣṇa-Hari-Keśava is actively involved under at least four forms. He is present as the tortoise at the base of the mountain, he participates among the gods as well as among the Daityas in the churning, he stands invisibly on the mountain.

10 This is in effect the methodological procedure of a terminological "cross section" as exemplified for other terms in part 2 of this paper.

1,15.55–58	Kaṇḍu praises Viṣṇu
1,19.64–86	Prahlāda praises Viṣṇu
1,20.9–13	Prahlāda praises Viṣṇu
3,5.16–25	Yājñavalkya praises the sun
3,17.11–34	Deities praise Viṣṇu
5,1.35–51	Brahmā praises Viṣṇu
5,1.55–59	Brahmā praises Viṣṇu
5,2.7–20	Deities praise Devakī
5,7.48–57	Kāliya's wives praise Kṛṣṇa
5,7.59–74	Kāliya praises Kṛṣṇa
5,18.48–58	Akrūra praises Kṛṣṇa
5,20.82–92*	Vasudeva praises Kṛṣṇa
5,23.27–46	Mucukunda praises Kṛṣṇa
5,29.23–29	Earth praises Kṛṣṇa
5,30.6–23	Aditi praises Kṛṣṇa
5,30.76–78	Indra praises Satyabhāma
6,8.59–63*	Parāśara praises Viṣṇu

The chosen criterion leads to the inclusion of 5,30.76–78 (Indra addressing Satyabhāma). Mucukunda's hymn (5,23.27–46) does not begin at the beginning of a verse. Indra's statement (5,30.76–78) does not contain any formulas of veneration, but it does contain theological assertions (*trimūrti*-functions, identity with the world). The hymns of the Kāliya episode are not called "praise" by the narrator but rather in the hymns themselves (by reflecting about the impossibility to praise adequately). Applying this element of content leads to the inclusion 5,29.23–29. The earth praises by reflecting about praising and uses the word *stuti* (v. 28).

The other hymnic passages (marked by asterisks) can be included only by extending the formal criterion of selection. They are Vasudeva's hymnic prayer (5,20.82–92, where theological description of Kṛṣṇa as deity is combined with formulas of submission and requests for mercy), as well as the introductory and concluding prayers by the narrator; they qualify by style and content as hymns.

Other hymnic descriptions by Parāśara should perhaps be classified among the theological tracts (e.g., 3,3.22–31; 2,8.98–107; 2,12.37–47). These passages raise the problem that the hymns of praise are indeed not the only passages in the ViP that are theological. But for a first attempt to identify this theology a formal textual criterion seems preferable.[11]

The Indian attitude towards purāṇic *stotras* (or more generally to any praise of any deity) tends to take their statements less than seriously due to the presupposition that praise implies that one is prepared to say anything and everything about the praised deity. This is based on the conviction that praising means to state the greatness, the exceptional qualities and admirable deeds of the praised person. In doing so the same thing can be said about different deities. Thus, what is said in a *stotra* is not specific and should not be taken to be specific. The literary genre ("praise") would determine the content of the text or of this particular text genre to a degree that the interpretation of the content is deemed meaningless. God is great, greater, the greatest—and anything within the greatness becomes accidental, arbitrary, fortuitous.

I beg to disagree. Viṣṇu and Śiva are iconographically different; their deeds and the episodes in which they are involved are different. Why should their theology be the same? As a comparativist I must concentrate on the differences, and the working hypothesis states that similarities are originally the result of contact, imitation, competition, rivalry, complementariness, inclusivism, substitution, and whatever other strategies and mechanisms one might discover.

---

[11] There are other passages in the ViP which stand out by their theological or perhaps more specifically theographical content: they describe Viṣṇu. The literary form may be that of a "tract" or that of a dialogue of instructions; the stylistic diction is often hymnic. Examples are 2,8.98-2,8.107: hymnic description; 2,12.37-47: Viṣṇu as the All and as cognition; 3,3.22-31: Parāśara's hymnic description of *brahman*, where *brahman* is a form of Viṣṇu; 5,3.10-11 and 5,3.12-13: Vasudeva and Devakī address the new-born Kṛṣṇa; 5,7.35-42: Baladeva's acclamation reminding Kṛṣṇa of his divinity; 5,9.23-33: Kṛṣṇa's acclamation reminding Bala of his divinity; 5,7.2-17 and 5,7.26-33: Akrūra's joy and apprehension about meeting Kṛṣṇa; 5,31.41-43: Śiva addressing Kṛṣṇa; the instructions given by Prahlāda, Bharata or Ṛbhu. A comparison—using the same criteria and parameters—of the corpus of theographic passages with the hymns is likely to confirm that the Viṣṇu theology of the ViP is indeed comprehensive and characteristic of the whole text.

That God Viṣṇu is everything, is the All and is all, that he is even more than all, stands above all and above the All, transcends all, is however specifically true for the theology of the ViP.[12] In order to grasp and describe this specificity it is essential *how* Viṣṇu's allness is expressed. After all, we can know about and understand the thinking of the authors of the ViP only by analysing their ways of expressing themselves and of using words.[13]

Among the first observations will probably be that themes and formulations repeat themselves. This invites and allows one to abstract from the variations, themes and formulations in order to establish the categories and the structure that underlie the repetitions. What is said about Viṣṇu's allness and transcendence apparently was not formulated arbitrarily, could not be formulated arbitrarily.

1.3 Paradigms of praise

In order to illustrate the kind of text from which my procedure abstracts, let me include the translation of the first few verses of the hymns by the gods to Viṣṇu from the Māyāmoha-episode (3,17.11–18).

> The deities said:
> Through this acclamation that we shall utter
> for the homage of Viṣṇu, the lord over the worlds,
> may He be favourable,
> the gracious, the one of the beginnings.

---

12 In historical perspective it appears that the ViP is probably the first Purāṇa that uses *stotras* to such an extent and uses them to express mainly Viṣṇu's allness. It may well be that the mentioned Indian attitude belongs to the *Wirkungsgeschichte* of the ViP; other theologians imitated or competed with the avowed greatness of Viṣṇu in the name of their god(s) and thus by generalizing and universalizing the structure of theological statements about Viṣṇu made the theological assertion of god's greatness and allness a cliché devoid of specificity.

13 I must presuppose that their way of expressing themselves was intentional and meaningful. However, the risk of over-interpretation is real.

Who can praise Him, the Great Self,
from whom all beings are born
and in whom they will be absorbed?

Yet, destroyed is our bravery
by the destruction wrought by our enemies
and we strive for a new existence –
we shall praise you
though your true being
does not fall within the domain of words.

You are earth, water, fire,
and wind and space,
the whole inner sense,
primordial matter and the spiritual person
that transcends the former.

Your body is just one
consisting of anything formed and unformed
beginning with Brahmā and down to the plants
with differences due to time and place.
Lord, one of your forms is standing before you
which formerly arose from the lotus of your navel;
to it, helping with creation
and one with Brahmā, homage!

We also are a form of yours
distinguished as Śakra, Sun, Rudra, Vasus,
as Aśvins, wind, moon and the others,
to it that is one with the demons, homage!

To your form, Govinda, that is characterized by pretentiousness
and that lacks insight, forbearance and discipline
to it that is one with the demons, homage![14]

---

14 *devāḥ ūcuḥ*
ārādhanāya lokānāṃ viṣṇor īśasya yāṃ giram
vakṣyāmo bhagavān ādyas tayā viṣṇuḥ prasīdatu ‖ 3,17.11 |
yato bhūtāny aśeṣāṇi prasūtāni mahātmanaḥ |
yasmiṃś ca layam eṣyanti kas taṃ saṃstotum īśvaraḥ ‖ 3,17.12 |

If the statements of the *stotras* are considered as variants of expressions of a central structure, the collections of variants of the different statements will show what they have in common. One obtains the *paradigm* of theological statements in the ViP, i.e., the words and/or concepts which can be substituted for each other, because they are attested as variants of (or in) the same theologoumenon, i.e., an item, point, or teaching of theological relevance.

The words or ideas subsumed under a paradigm are not synonyms in a narrow sense, but they function as equivalents within a structure. The way in which paradigms are related to each other, or subsumed one under the other, is essential. The fact that the words or ideas which function as equivalents are often diachronically distinguishable, i.e., the fact that they stem from different schools or contexts or can be attributed to different modes of thinking (e.g., Sāṃkhya cosmogony and mythological cosmology) conditions the breadth and depth of the theology that made use of them.

Applied to the interpretation of the hymns in the ViP, and of their theology, this means: It is less important *that* everything can be said about Viṣṇu, while the constellation and elements which constitute Viṣṇu's universality and uniqueness, and how they interrelate, are important. The milieu from which this theology might stem, the redactors' intentions and the message of the text are likely to be found more reliably in the structure than in the occurrence or omission of a single element, stylistic peculiarity or any other building block of the whole. The constellation or structure of (praising) statements about

---

tathāpy arātividhvaṃsadhvastavīryā bhavārthinaḥ |
tvāṃ stoṣyāmas tavoktīnāṃ yāthārthyaṃ naiva gocare ‖ 3,17.13 |
tvam urvī salilaṃ vahnir vāyur ākāśam eva ca |
samastam antaḥkaraṇaṃ pradhānaṃ tatparaḥ pumān ‖ 3,17.14 |
ekaṃ tavaitad bhūtātman mūrtāmūrtamayaṃ vapuḥ |
ābrahmastambaparyantaṃ sthānakālavibhedavat ‖ 3,17.15 |
tatreśa tava yat pūrvaṃ tv annābhikamalodbhavam |
rūpaṃ sargopakārāya tasmai brahmātmane namaḥ ‖ 3,17.16 |
śakrārkarudravasvaśvimarutsomādibhedavat |
vayam evaṃ svarūpaṃ te tasmai devātmane namaḥ ‖ 3,17.17 |
dambhaprāyam asaṃbodhi titikṣādamavarjitam |
yadrūpaṃ tava govinda tasmai daityātmane namaḥ ‖ 3,17.18 |.

Viṣṇu is composed by the paradigms of these statements grouped according to topic. The following sketch[15] of this structure deliberately does not take the diachronic perspective into consideration. The classification according to topics and the nomenclature for the subject matter of each topic attempt to find labels or umbrella concepts that should serve as a descriptive tool and as a starting point for their critical discussion. The scheme and its nomenclature are a heuristic device. If it describes adequately the conceptual framework and profile of this text, it could serve as reference for the comparison with other texts with different profiles.

Survey of *stotra* paradigms on "Viṣṇu and the world"

[1]	spirit, *Geistprinzip*
[2]	world
[2.1]	metaphysics, levels of material evolution
[2.1.1]	matter
[2.1.2]	psyche, consciousness and cognition
[2.1.3]	senses and elements
[2.2]	beings and things
[2.2.1]	cosmography and geography
[2.2.2]	time and its divisions
[2.2.3]	classes of (living) beings
[2.2.3.1]	gods
[2.2.3.2]	living beings
[2.2.3.3]	humans
[2.2.3.4]	non-human, semi-divine, demonic beings
[2.2.3.5]	animals
[2.2.3.6]	plants
[2.3]	mythological paradigm
[2.3.1]	iconography
[2.3.2]	*viśvarūpa*
[2.3.3]	divine actions on earth

[15] For an explication of each paradigm, see below.

[2.4]	human life
[2.4.1]	suffering
[2.4.2]	salvation
[2.4.2.1]	salvific activities/behaviour
[2.4.2.1.2]	sacrifice
[3]	modalities of relation between Viṣṇu and the world
[3.1]	degrees of reality
[3.2]	cause and effect
[3.3]	whole and parts, one and many
[3.4]	thing and name
[3.5]	*trimūrti*-functions

That these topical groups and concepts *are* indeed something in the text is confirmed by the fact that the complete vocabulary of the *stotra*s can indeed be classified with their help.[16] I construe and present the paradigms by briefly summarizing the meaning and content of a classifying concept in the light of the corresponding Sanskrit vocabulary listed in the footnotes (occasionally with additions like compounds that characterize the context, a disambiguating typical verbal root, etc. in parentheses).[17]

---

[16] This claim ought to lead to a discussion about the details of the operationalisation of its verification: lemmatisation, disambiguation, polysemy, contextualisation (e.g., if *agre* is used to describe how the earth is placed on the top of the boar's tooth, the word does not have theological relevance), syntax (more than a hundred occurrences of *ca*, other particles, pronouns, nominal composition, negations [an analysis of positive vs. negative terminology and its potential structural relevance, e.g., concerning the correlation of specific negative statements remains a desideratum]), style (refrains, formulaic expressions of veneration, e.g., 38 times *namas*, 5 times *śaraṇam* – elements which very likely do have theological and systematic relevance).

[17] Basis is the digital version of the text in which word boundaries are marked (i.e., Sandhi is resolved) and from which an index (most comfortably a KWIC Index) of the *stotra* passages has been established. The references in the text can be found in the electronic text that is being made available on the internet.

As a conceptual system the polar duality of a cosmo-theology comprises *a priori* the realities of a world ("cosmo"-) [2] and a divinity ("theology") [1] but must also include the conceptualization of how the two are related [3]. That the God is said to be one and all-inclusive gives a monistic dimension to the system; that the worldly material realities are many gives a pluralistic hue to the other pole. The metaphysical aspect of speaking about the world is indebted to Sāṃkhya; the concrete worldly realities are spoken of in a predominantly mythic manner (heavens, underworlds, classes of beings, etc.). None of the three constituents (i.e., conceptual fields) can make sense without the two others [3]. They constitute a triangle, but the fact that "spirit" [1] stands at the top is justified not by a logical priority but by the temporal aspect included in the system. The cosmos ([2] with all subsections, including its metaphysical realms) stems from the spiritual, the Viṣṇu-aspect of reality and is periodically absorbed in it. There is nothing outside of or independent of Viṣṇu. But the worldly dimension of reality exists within a system of becoming and dissolving. And since the worldly dimension of reality is an aspect of divinity, God is not conceivable without the rhythm of becoming and dissolving. The *trimūrti*-functions conceptualize the temporal aspect of this cosmo-theology quite clearly; it must be considered a central, innovative element of the Viṣṇu-theology of the ViP.

The universe, the constituents of which provide the material for describing Viṣṇu, is an ordered universe and in that sense a cosmos. For its metaphysical and cosmological section, it is the Sāṃkhya philosophy which provides the frame. This world view accepts two separate, independent realms of reality, one matter, the other spirit. These realms of reality are ontologically independent; they are functionally related as subject and object or as "enjoyer" and "enjoyed".[18]

[1] spirit, "*Geistprinzip*"

Theologically speaking, Viṣṇu comprises everything, spirit and matter, divinity and world, and would therefore form a category outside of this scheme. Sāṃkhya philosophy offers to the Viṣṇu theologians

---

18 *bhuj-*, *bhoga(-pradāna)*, *sākṣin*.

a concept or category which allows cosmology and theology to form a continuum. The hierarchical scheme of steps of evolution and levels of reality was/is continued "on top" by a concept of God who does not exist side by side (next to) the world but simultaneously *in* the world and *beyond* the (material) world. This category functions as focus or meeting point for concepts of spirit, transcendence, purity, infinity, of being beyond words, non-worldliness (expressed *via negativa*), etc. The terms in this paradigm may not all stem from Sāṃkhya philosophy (or did not enter into the classical system). That is why this paradigm is not primarily a Sāṃkhya paradigm but one of Viṣṇu theology that utilizes Sāṃkhya and thereby modifies it.[19]

[2] world

There are two aspects to material reality. There is matter as a principle of the same standing as spirit, a "metaphysical" realm of reality (though this term is evidently a misnomer, since the principle of matter cannot be beyond matter) [2.1 metaphysics, levels of material evolution]. And there is, secondly, matter in its concrete forms [2.2 beings and things] which are connected with the material principle by a process of evolution or transformation.[20]

The first sub-paradigm concerns matter as a principle which is the origin of all evolved realms of reality and of all things; it can therefore be called the "unevolved" or the "unmanifest". It is the matrix and cause of all products of evolution (which is evoked by transla-

---

19 **[1] spirit, *Geistprinzip***
puruṣa, pumān, puruṣottama, brahman, ātman, paramātman, paramabrahman, parabrahman, paramārtha, para, paramapada, paramarūpa,
eka, na anya, svarūpa,
guhyam, jyoti, pāra,
jñāna, vijñāna, parā vidyā, bodha
(positive:) *śuddha, viśuddha, śāśvata, sanātana, nitya*
(negative:) *aja, akṣara, akṣaya, avyaya, acintya, anirdeśya, aprameya, ameya, acyuta, nirguṇa, nirañjana, amala, nirmala, niradhiṣṭha, niravadya, nirdvandva, niṣprapañca, ananta, anādi, amūrta*

20 *pariṇāma, pravṛtti, vyākṛ-, vikāra, vṛddhi*

tions like "primordial nature", "*Urnatur*") and the ground in which everything is absorbed.

[2.1.1] matter

The material principle is and has three "traits" (*guṇa*, "*Grund-züge*"), qualities which are constituents. Their imbalance starts the process of evolution and the differences and variations in their proportions are responsible for the differences between different conditions and concrete things. These processes of evolution and differentiation are connected to the divine principle by the concept of energy (*śakti*). I suspect that the triad of the concepts *virāṭ*, *saṃrāṭ*, *svarāṭ* belong to the same conceptual field.[21]

[2.1.2] consciousness and cognition

The first phase of evolution produces a level of reality which may be subsumed under consciousness and cognition. It is material and in its cosmological dimension and potentiality comprises everything. It permeates the levels subordinated to and originated from it (I-consciousness and the faculties of the senses of cognition and action). This level of "psychic" realities appears as little differentiated in the vocabulary of the *stotras*.[22] The five vital breaths (*prāṇa*) appear as further principles and have perhaps been integrated into the Sāṃkhya scheme from upaniṣadic sources.[23]

---

21 **[2.1.1] matter**
prakṛti, *pradhāna*, *avyakta*, *avyākṛta*, (*tri-*)*guṇa*, *sattvādi*,
kāraṇa, *layasthāna*
śakti
virāṭ, *saṃrāṭ*, *svarāṭ* (?)

22 **[2.1.2] cosciousness and cognition**
buddhi, *mahān*, *antaḥkaraṇa*, *guhā* (?), *manas*, *cetas*, *prāṇa*

23 I use "Sāṃkhya" and "upaniṣadic" as convenient labels to characterize "milieus" that can be distinguished historically and according to the sources that fall under each term. This is only a heuristic device to conceptualize that the tradition presupposed by the ViP consists of different strands; these strands may touch and intertwine and are not meant to suggest consecutive stages of development.

[2.1.3] senses and elements

The next level of evolution (it is a top-down process) remains in the realm of principles and does not yet produce concrete separate things. First appear the five senses, then five realms of objectivity ("that-ness", the word *tanmātra* itself does not appear in the *stotras*) which correspond to what each sense can perceive (in principle) and then the five elements[24] which are characterized by five principal attributes ("that-ness"), each correlated with one sense function.[25] The five senses of action do not play a role in the scheme of principles according to the ViP.

Everything else in the world is composed of these elements. The philosophical texts of Sāṃkhya do not (to my knowledge) contain schematic lists of [2.2] beings and things (with perhaps one exception from the MBh 12,290). The vocabulary of the *stotras* allows one to recognize a number of categories from the realm of manifest, cosmic, material reality which supplement the paradigm of Sāṃkhya cosmology. I repeat only the headings; each category is represented by a number of synonyms and/or different beings:

---

[24] *bhūta* is of course multivalent: "thing" as in *bhūtabhedāḥ*; "past" as in *bhūtabhaviṣyatī*; "identical with" as in *sarvabhūta*. And the word for "earth" may refer to geography or to the personification.

[25] **[2.1.3] senses, elements**
indriya, śabda-ādi, gandha, sparśa, rasa
[elements]

(earth)	(water)	(fire)	(air)	(space)
urvī	*salila*	*vahni*	*vāyu*	*ākāśa*
bhūmī	*āpaḥ*	*agni*	*anila*	*nabhaḥ*
medinī	*ambu*	*anala*	*pavana*	*kha*
bhū	*jala*		*pāvaka*	*gagana*
mahī	*toya*			*vyoman*

[2.2] beings and things[26]
[2.2.1] cosmography and geography[27]
[2.2.2] time and its divisions[28]
[2.2.3] classes of (living) beings
[2.2.3.1] gods[29]
[2.2.3.2] living beings[30]
[2.2.3.3] humans[31]

---

26 [2.2] objects (summarily)
grāhya, bhogya-viṣaya, vedya, (akhila-)jagat, prapañca, vyakta, carācara, sthāvara-cara, sthāvara-jaṅgama, bhūta, rūpāṇi, samaṣṭi-vyaṣṭi, viṣaya, gocara, sṛjya, kārya.

27 [2.2.1] cosmography and geography
loka (jana-, mahar-, brahma-, tapas-, svar-, bhuvar-, bhū-) svarga, devaloka, naraka, bhuvana(-traya), dyāvāpṛthivī, diśaḥ.

graha, ṛkṣa, tārak, tāraka, nakṣatra, vimāna, sūrya, soma, candramas, indu:

pṛthivī, mahī, śaila, sarit, nadī, payonidhi, samudra, grāma, pattana, kharvaṭa, kheṭa.

28 [2.2.2] time and its divisions
kāla(-sūtra), kalā, kāṣṭhā, nimeṣa, muhūrta, ahar, niśā, rātryahanī, rātri, saṃdhyā, gharmasīta-ambhas, kalpa.

29 [2.2.3] classes of (living) beings
[2.2.3.1] gods
amara, deva, devatā, devī, tridaśa, sura, divaukasa, divya, brahma, rudra (trilocana, pinākadhṛk, paśupati, śiva), indra (śakra, śatakratu, devarāja, vṛtraripu), agni, yama (pretarāja), samīraṇa, marut (sg., pl.), *aśvinau, vasavaḥ, rudrāḥ, ādityāḥ, sūrya, arka, savitṛ, nāsatyau, pūṣan, prajāpati, aryaman, vidhātṛ, soma (candra), varuṇa (toyeśa), dhanapati, sādhyāḥ, viśvadevāḥ.*

30 [2.2.3.2] living beings
jīva, dehin, śarīrin, (sthāvara-) jaṅgama, cara(-acara).

31 [2.2.3.3] humans
manuṣya, manuja, nara, puṃs
brāhmaṇa, kṣatra, vaiśya, śūdra.
It is revealing that the social classes derive from God, and that this order is thereby identified with God, but that woman and the whole field of

[2.2.3.4] non-human, semi-divine, demoniac beings[32]
[2.2.3.5] animals[33]
[2.2.3.6] plants[34]

[2.3] mythological paradigm for God

Besides the philosophical paradigm for "spirit" the *stotras* know a mythological paradigm for God [2.3], a term chosen for the personified divinity which has names, titles and epithets, which acts in the world that is constituted by it, and about which the purāṇic episodes narrate. The title *bhagavat* is not exclusively used for Viṣṇu (in the *stotras* also for Brahmā, Agni).[35] The philosophical [1] and the mythological paradigm [2.3] overlap, they occur only as intermingled in the hymns. Yet these observations only document that both paradigms are complementary and mutually dependent. Titles and appel-

---

family relations (wife, sons, etc.) feature only in characterizations of *saṃsāra*.

[32] [2.2.3.4] non-human, semi-divine, demoniac beings
siddha, muni, ṛṣi, sūri, pitṛ, preta, guhyaka, kuṣmāṇḍa, gandharva, kiṃnara, daitya, rākṣasa, yakṣa, piśāca, niśācara, asura, nāga, apsaras, cāraṇa.

[33] [2.2.3.5] animals
paśu, pipīlika, khaga, pakṣin, nāga, (mahā-)uraga, sarpa(-jāti), mṛga, sarīsṛpa, pannaga.

[34] [2.2.3.6] plants
gulma, tṛṇajātayaḥ, pādapa, mukhya, stamba, mahīruh, latā, vṛkṣa, sthāvara.

[35] **[2.3] God (mythological)**
Acyuta, Adhokaja, Ananta, Kṛṣṇa, Keśava, Govinda, Janārdana, Nārāyaṇa, Vāsudeva, Viṣṇu, Hari, Harimedhas
īśa (deva-, devadeva-, bhuvana-, sarva-, sarvabhūta-, bhūta-, bhūtabhavya-, parama-, viśva-, sakala-),
īśitva,
īśvara (parama-, sura-, sarva-), tridaśottama,
puruṣottama, nātha (sura-, jagan-), deva, devadeva,
pati (jagat-, prajā-, kartṛ-, tridaśa-, yajña-, ādya-),
prabhu, bhagavān, vibhu, vedhas (?), *svāmin,*
Aniruddha, Pradyumna, Saṃkarṣaṇa, Vāsudeva.

lations that indicate God's lordship and sovereignty might also be classified under the *trimūrti*-functions (*sthiti* in particular). The iconographic details [2.3.1][36] mentioned in the text may be considered part of the mythological paradigm, as are the terms that describe the *viśvarūpa* [2.3.2][37] which has clearly human and corporeal traits. The iconographic aspect of Viṣṇu's identity with all and the All reflects the parlance of the *Puruṣasūkta* and the *Bhagavadgītā*.

[2.3.3] divine actions on earth

Similar to the distinction of a paradigm for "spirit" and a paradigm of "God" one should differentiate God's being the (metaphysical) cause [3.2] from his episodic actions on earth [2.3.3][38] Here also there are connections to philosophical questions (e.g., concerning the one material cause over against the many products; paralleled by the problem of a partial presence of God, *aṃśāvatāra*). Descent, embodiment, protection of the good, showing grace, death and punishment for the wicked: these are the kind of activities mentioned in the *stotras*. The overlap with the *trimūrti*-functions is obvious.

---

36 [2.3.1] iconography
gadā, cakra, śārṅga, asi (*-dhṛk, -bhṛt*), *śaṅkha-dhara, abjalocana, puṇḍarīkākṣa,*
śeṣe śī-

37 [2.3.2] *viśvarūpa*
viśvamūrti, bahurūpa, sahasramūrti
viśvataḥ cakṣuḥ, bahuvaktrapada, sahasra-śīrṣa, -pat, bāhu.

38 **[2.3.3] divine actions**
(*aṃśa-*)*avatāra, aṃśena lokam āyā-, śarīra-grahaṇa,*
upakṛti, (*martyānām*) *upakāra*(*ka*)*, sarvalokarakṣa, dharma-trāṇa, go-brahmaṇa-hita, hitāya*
viśvasya bhū, uddhāra, uddhṛ-, tejasā āpyāyanam
damana, daṇḍamipāta, daityanirjaya, han-
śaraṇam, prapanna-ārtiharaṇa, aśubham hṛ-, darśanaṃ dā-, varaṃ dā-, vibhūtiṃ dā/kṛ-,
varcaṃ dā-, padaṃ nidhā-, kṛpā, kṣamā, aiśvarya, prasāda, abhayaṃ kṛ-, śubhāśubhaṃ paś-, sarvasākṣin, agha naś-, pavitratā (*kṛ-*).

[2.4] human life

A fourth comprehensive paradigm within the cosmic aspect of reality concerns the description and evaluation of things with regard to beings. How are things to be valued concerning human values and aims, particularly concerning the highest value and aim, i.e., salvation or liberation? I call this paradigm [2.4] human life and divide it into two subsections. The first, suffering [2.4.1],[39] serves to classify all terms and concepts which describe human life as painful and unredeemed, as well as the objects of human striving (a number of items in the list of objectives stem from the wishes addressed to Śrī-Lakṣmī in ViP 1,9) or the attitudes which cause the suffering.

The second, salvation [2.4.2],[40] includes also the terms for talking about salvific behaviour, i.e., actions that lead to salvation or contrib-

---

39 **[2.4 human life]**

[2.4.1] suffering
saṃsāra(-śrama, -cakra), mohasaṃplava, janman(-ādi), jarā, mṛtyu, jīvita
duḥkha, (a-)sukha, tāpa(-traya), svapna(-ādi), jāti(-svabhāva), viṣaya(viṣayin), māyā (saṃsāramātṛ), mohinī, māyāmoha, mohāndhatamas.

[2.4.1.1] erroneous attitudes
asaṃbodha, kāma, icchā, kopa, krodha, klama, garva, tandrī, doṣa, tāpa, dambha, dīna, dveṣa, prīti, paritāpa, bhaya, raga, bhrānti (-jñāna, -darśana), manoratha, mamatva, moha (mohita, mūḍha), viḍambanā, vrīḍā, asvarūpavid

[2.4.1.2] false objectivities
kalatra, dārāḥ, bhāryā, putra, kula, aiśvarya, rājya, bala, kośa, gṛha, goṣṭha, dhana, dhānya, vairi-pakṣa-jaya, aripakṣakṣaya, paśu, paricchada, mitrapakṣa, śarīra, suhṛdvarga, vibhūṣaṇa

40 [2.4.2] salvation
mukti, mokṣa, (ātma-vimukti), nirvāṇa, nivṛtti, pāra, paramapada, niṣṭhā, dhāman, paramārtha, paraṃ tattvam, siddhi, jñāna, ātma-vijñāna, gati.

[2.4.2.1] salvific activities/behaviour
cint-, jñā-, vid-, (pra-)paś-, dṛś-, prāp-
sāṃkhyajñāna, dhyāna
tap-, ārādh-, (sam-)arc- (gandha, puṣpa, anulepana), stu-, stuti
prāp-, praṇam-, prapad-

ute to reaching this aim. The sub-paradigms, Veda [2.4.2.1.1][41] and sacrifice [2.4.2.2],[42] are singled out simply because of the large number of terms.[43] Insofar as God's identity with the cosmos makes God also identical with the world as the condition of human suffering and lack of salvation, the polarity of spirit and matter is analogous to the polarity of salvation and suffering. God can be identified with the object or subjective of salvific actions as well as with the actions by which redemption/liberation can be achieved (sacrifice in particular), indirectly even with the conditions from which liberation is desired (*māyā*). The epistemological terms apply on the metaphysical level insofar as Viṣṇu *is* cognition; salvation consists in actively identifying with it.

[3] modalities of relation between spirit and the world

Besides the vocabulary, which describes the totality of what is there, i.e., the totality of what is comprised by God's allness, there is another group of paradigms which concern the modalities in which the spirit aspect of the deity and the world are interrelated [3]. This third group of paradigms concerns the systematic correlation of the realms and levels of reality. Evolution, creation and immanence are the pro-

---

manīṣi, yogin, bhakta, śuddha-cetas, svarūpavid, jñānavid, yajvin

41 [2.4.2.1.1] Veda
śabdabrahman, veda, dve vidye, trayī, śākhā, śākhāpraṇetṛ, ṛg, yajus, sāman, atharvan, OṂ, vedāṅga, śikṣā, kalpa, dharmaśāstra, nirukta, chandas, jyotiṣa, vyākaraṇa,
nyāya, mīmāṃsā, itihāsa-purāṇa,
anvīkṣikī, vārtā, daṇḍanīti,
pravṛtta, nivṛtta (*karman*)

42 [2.4.2.1.2] sacrifice
yajña, yajñavidyā, kartṛ, bhoktṛ, yaṣṭṛ, yajvin
karma, kriyā, upakaraṇa, karaṇa, kārya, phala
vaṣat, svāhā, svadhā
agnayaḥ, hutāśa(*na*)
yajñapumān, -puruṣa, -pati, mūrtidhara
havya, kavya, sudhā, amṛta, havis, huta

43 This indicates of course priorities characteristic of the milieu of the ViP.

cesses by which this world-view is related to God. The theological problem seems to have been how to reconcile God's being all with God's oneness.

Being *one* was apparently only thinkable as uniformity, but being *all* had to allow for the multiplicity and difference of things. One can recognize several patterns or strategies of dealing with the tension between unity and plurality by which a solution (consisting in a description of the relation of God and world, which was apparently felt to be satisfying and sufficient) was achieved. This is why the "theology" of the ViP can justly be called a cosmo-theology.[44]

The first modality of describing this relation is derived from Sāṃkhya philosophy, viz., the idea of a sequence of **degrees of realities [3.1]** or **realms of reality**,[45] classified along parameters of subtle and gross, small and large, permanent and transient. In classical Sāṃkhya the sequence of stages applies only to matter (where emanation proceeds from subtle to gross etc.). For the Viṣṇu theologians of the ViP the realms of matter and of spirit are connected by the same pattern. In this adaption intermediate levels are often omitted and only two levels, grades or aspects are mentioned (e.g., two forms of the Veda, two forms of knowledge); but they are levels or aspects of reality as one, not an expression of a dualism.

---

44 "Cosmological monotheism" is the term used by Angelika Malinar for the *Bhagavadgītā* (cf. Malinar 2007). A comparison of the theologies of ViP and BhG falls outside the scope of the synchronic approach chosen for this paper, but is an important desideratum.

45 **[3.1] Degrees or realms of reality**

aṇu, aṇīya	*guru, gaurava, garīya*
sūkṣma, sūkṣmatara	*sthūla*
avyakta	*vyakta*
alpa, hrasva	*bṛhat, dīrgha*
para	*apara*
akṣaya, nitya, akṣara	*kṣaya, kṣara*
avyaya, aja, ananta	*vyaya*
dve vidye, dve brahmaṇī	

Cf. above under [2 world] and fn. 18.

Secondly, God and the world are related to each other as **cause and effect** [3.2],[46] i.e., as the material and the things formed from the material, or as the substrate and its manifestations (which may overlap with the first pattern). I would include here all statements about God being the foundation or basis of the world.[47] But this "material" cause is spirit. This concept of spirituality is linked or mediated with its material products by concepts like *sattva* and *(vi)jñāna*. Thus, God exists in the realm of manifold of things, and the plurality of things participates in God as a dimension of unity. Inasmuch as it is material causality that characterizes God's relation to the world, causality merges into immanence and forms the logical basis of the many statements and terms that express allness.

[3.3] whole and parts, One and many

Thirdly, God and world, unity and plurality correlate as the whole to its parts or as the One to many [3.3].[48]

[3.4] thing and name

Form and name constitute the individuality of things and make them distinctive and name-able. God's forms make him describable, as the *stotras* document by their enumerations time and again. Thus, one

---

[46] **[3.2] cause and effect**
kārya, hetu
sattva, satya
jñāna, vijñāna, vidyā, vedya
mahiman
āśraya, ālambana, ādhāra,
ālaya, āspada, mūla, nābhi,
bīja, dhāman, pratiṣṭhā,
saṃśraya, sthāna

[47] This may imply a link to the function of maintenance within the *trimūrti* functions; see below.

[48] **[3.3] whole and parts, One and many**
sarva, akhila, aśeṣa,
niḥśeṣa, viśva, sakala,
samasta
bheda, avayava, aṃśa, vibhāga
viśeṣa, pariccheda
vyatirikta, pṛthakbhūta, bahurūpa

can also conceptualize the relation of God and world as that of a thing to the words that name it [3.4].[49] Especially through the concept of form, there is here a link to the first and the second mode of relation.

These observations make it clear that God and the world, as poles of a relation, are not unconnected. Rather each pole throws a particular light on what can be said about the other. Totality and the distinctive existence of things are substrates for plurality, parts, and appellations, which are thus effects in the objective and the psychical realm. The one thing can manifest and emanate in its appellations and relations just like a material cause in its transformations. Attributed to God the emanation of relations is linked to God's energy (*śakti*) and is considered as his manifest but not ultimate creation (*māyā*). Totality is not the sum of equal constituents but is constituted by the common relation to the substrate. In that sense, any statement about the world can become a statement about God. The world is a form of God, God has taken the world as his form.

The question *why* plurality exists at all, why God let plurality emanate, is not asked. However, plurality, separateness, being caused, etc. are considered as provisional, derivative; they are characteristics that derive from God ontologically, but at the same time they are conditions which soteriologically need to be overcome.

[3.5] *trimūrti*-functions

The most pervasive paradigm to describe the relation of God and world (besides the degrees of reality, cause and effect, part and whole, one and many, thing and name) are the three functions ascribed to the *trimūrti* [3.5].[50] At the beginning of the ViP (in the last

---

[49] **[3.4] thing and name**
viṣaya, vastu, artha, vedya, bhinna(-artha, -buddhi)
jihvā-dṛk-gocara, viśeṣaṇa(-gocara)
rūpa, mūrti, svarūpa, vapus, tanū, deha
śakti, māyā
vāc, ukta, udīr-, upacāra, kalpanā, vikalpa(na), jāti, nāma, saṃjñā, saṃjñita, vācaka, saṃsūcika

verse of the first chapter) the threefold relation between Viṣṇu and the world is summarized: the world originates from Viṣṇu, is sustained in Him and He is the world, and He ends its existence; this is because, it is added, He is the world.[51]

The scheme of the *trimūrti* functions is expressed by terms of different provenience and it seems to be modified and enlarged by these concepts. That the *guṇa*s are included underlines that all three functions (and the respective conditions of the world) concern the realm of matter; all three functions state the worldliness of Viṣṇu. The con-

---

50 **[3.5] *trimūrti*-functions**

Brahmā, Hiraṇyagarbha	Viṣṇu, Hari	Śiva, Rudra Śaṅkara, Pinākadhṛk
sṛṣṭi	*sthiti*	*pralaya*
sarga, (sam)-udbhava,	*saṃsthāna*	*saṃhāra, saṃyama*
utpatti, prabhava	*pālana*	*(vi-)nāśa, apyaya*
prasūti		*nidhana*
bīja, yoni		
kāraṇa	*kārya*	
bhāvana	*bhava*	
ādi	*madhya*	*anta*
kartṛ	*vikartṛ*	*saṃhartṛ*
dhātṛ	*goptṛ*	*grasiṣṇu*
praṇetṛ	*pātṛ*	
	vedhas	
	yajña	
rajas	*sattva*	*tamas*
pravṛtti	*prakāśa*	*niyam*
	jñāna	
	tejas	
	śakti	
	māyā (?)	
samudgam-		
sṛj-		
jan-		
bhūta	*bhavya*	*bhaviṣya*
yataḥ	*yaḥ*	*yasmin*
tvattaḥ	*tvam*	*tvayi*

51 *viṣṇoḥ sakāśād udbhūtaṃ jagat tatraiva ca sthitam* | *sthitisaṃyamakartāsau jagato 'sya jagac ca saḥ* ‖ 1,1.31 ‖.

cepts of Sāṃkhya are incorporated in this Viṣṇu theology (not vice versa). The predominantly static descriptions of the other paradigms gain a dynamic dimension, which is also indicated by God being identical with time.

If the scheme of the *trimūrti*-functions is understood as the matrix for the conceptualization of the relation between God and world, and thus as providing the structure that orders the paradigms of Viṣṇu theology in the ViP,[52] then it is striking that it is primarily the function of maintenance where concepts from different traditions were assimilated: Sāṃkhya terminology, vedic ritual, upaniṣadic parlance about a spiritual absolute, mythological ways of speaking. This is documented, for example, by the equivalence of *sattva* and cognition (*Erkenntnis*), by the maintaining power of sacrifice, by *OṂ* as epitome of spirit and highest reality, by *parama-pada* as a simultaneously metaphysical and mythological entity, by the equivalence of functioning as cause and as substrate.

At first sight the paradigms, salvation [2.4.2] and salvific actions [2.4.2.1], do not seem to have a place in this structure. At the same time, it is striking that the function of reabsorption, resolution and destruction is underrepresented among the three functions. This impression is corrected if salvation [2.4.2] is classified as representing the third function (rather than as an aspect of human life and activity in the context of maintaining the world). Salvation is to be taken as liberation from the world and from the cosmos. The ViP treats cosmic dissolution and the individual reabsorption as instances of the

---

52 This observation implies that Hacker's systematization and interpretation of the theological formula can be modified. Hacker ordered epithet and statements about Viṣṇu as follows:

"A. Viṣṇu an sich: als Höchstes Selbst. B. Viṣṇus Beziehung zu anderem Seienden:1. Alles ist von Viṣṇu. 2. Viṣṇu ist in allem. 3. Viṣṇu ist alles. 4. Alles ist in Viṣṇu. [...]

C. Viṣṇu als Vereinigung der Gegengesätze.

D. Viṣṇus ‚Kraft' (śakti)." (Hacker 1960: 81f.; this systematization is also used by Rüping 1970: 34f.) C can be considered an aspect of A; B2 and B3 as well as D can be subsumed under the function of maintenance.

same general concept of *pralaya* (cf. 6,3-4). And God's interference with the inner worldly order does not only uphold or reinstitute cosmic order, it may in its destructive aspect of killing the wicked lead to their salvation (e.g., Śiśupāla).

Evidently, this structure of the theology of the hymns and of the ViP is an abstraction which cannot be found as such in the text. However, as a conceptual construct, it fits the individual *stotra*s no less than the totality of *stotra*s and the philosophical or theological tracts in several of the episodes. It is also reflected in the order of topics in the ViP which begins with creation and ends with dissolution or liberation. This implies that, as a conceptual structure permeating the ViP as a sample of anonymous literature, it characterizes the thinking not only of an individual author but of the totality of authors, redactors and compilators (including copyists) whose intentions and concepts, whose religion and theology characterize the ViP. The analysis of the literary genre "hymn of praise" (*stotra*) leads to a surprisingly coherent picture of a viṣṇuitic theology which allows one to speak of a distinctive point of view of its authors/redactors, and thus of the ViP.

The fundamental doctrine of this theology concerns God's identity with all and with the All. Thereby, cosmology and theology become co-extensive, without however becoming identical. Rather, they are correlated like a lower and a higher truth. This distinction likely reflects a yogic experience of meditative withdrawal and a mode of cognition through which cosmology and theology merge into soteriology. The text says little about the concrete practices or about the state of liberation. Subject of the analysed statements is God (which is not surprising, since the *stotra*s are addressed to Him). One can infer the higher mode of cognition as goal of meditative, identifying absorption, and as directed at God's transcendent aspect. Further, there are indications that this directedness can be understood as "taking refuge", which would then make the achieved liberation a gift granted by God.

Even though the structure of the paradigms is a systematizing abstraction, it is likely that the authors/redactors of the ViP were aware of it and applied it consciously. The most convincing argument for this observation is the central position of the theological formula

(1,1.31 and parallels, cf. fn. 50) and its repetitions. The fact that the text of the ViP covers the span from creation and manifestation of the world until its dissolution suggests interpreting the sequence of the text (narrated time) as a projection of Time as metaphysical and theological principle onto the literary level.

The *trimūrti*-functions and the identification of Viṣṇu with Time form, so to speak, the horizontal axis, while the Sāṃkhya scheme of evolution, *satkāryavāda*, and a hierarchy of levels of reality, the conditions of the cosmos and of the things in it, form a vertical axis. The dynamic character of these coordinates is due to the conviction that the three functions or conditions are recurring events. Thus, the system of coordinates needs to be inscribed into a circle in which linear time can be imagined to be bent backwards towards its beginning. Or, alternatively, the processes and realities covered by this cosmo-theology would cover only one quadrant of the coordinates, while the system requires allowing for a time before time, for reality outside and above (at least in a geographic representation and its two dimensions) the manifested cosmos. The ViP would probably call these dimensions of reality "Viṣṇu".

2. Conceptual cross sections

If it is justified to study, analyse and interpret the ViP as a whole and as a unity, then the examination of individual key words or key concepts suggests itself as another procedure that can help to describe the conceptual profile that characterizes and unifies the text. We cannot know anything about Viṣṇu, or about the theology of Viṣṇu, or about the believers in this Viṣṇu, or about the authors of such a theology, if it is not expressed or at least indicated in the text. That is to say, the pathway to an understanding of intellectual, conceptual, spiritual entities (all of these adjectives could in German be conveniently covered by "*geistige Größen*") like Viṣṇu, God, theology (as the discipline of knowledge or the attitude of cognition and insight or as the consequences of presupposed dogmatic decisions) must start from the words used by the text (and, thus, from philology). The first part of this paper looked at all the words used in the *stotra*s; the following, second part will look at *all* the occurrences of one word in the text, thus making a cross section, a terminological *Querschnitt* through the ViP.

The distinction between word (term) and concept is useful and important: several different terms may be used to indicate the same concept; and, a concept may emerge only as the sum and as the result of complementarity of several terms. This would be relevant even if we were thinking and talking in Sanskrit, in the same Sanskrit as the authors of the text. It is even more relevant if understanding of the conceptual universe of the text involves translating and formulating it in a different language (German or English being the target languages of understanding in our case). The following part will document[53] only an abbreviated extract[54] and the results of one example of a terminological cross section by examining *jñāna/vijñāna* as key terms for the understanding of the metaphysics of cognition in the ViP.[55]

As a first result it may be mentioned in passing that both terms are used interchangeably. The following chapters and episodes are marked by the frequency of occurrences of the words and by the fact that *jñāna* and *vijñāna* both occur.

1,22	the four kinds of cognition
2,13-14	Bhārata-episode
2,15-16	Ṛbhu-Nidāgha-dialogue
3,18	Māyāmoha-episode
5,18	*stotra* by Akrūra to Viṣṇu

---

[53] In times of the electronic availability of texts, the presentation of the material that constitutes the foundation of an interpretation loses importance, since everybody has his or her own search algorithms and tools and formats of presentation. My own procedures date from the beginnings of the use of electronic tools in Sanskrit philology (before 1980). Further, I shall not present all of the material (the Sanskrit wording, a translation, analytical observations, comparisons, etc.).

[54] I did not consider the (ca. 230) occurrences of verbal forms of the root *(vi-)jñā*, but only the occurrences of *jñāna* and *vijñāna*.

[55] For a more extensive summery of the theological profile of the ViP, see the commentary (*Kommentar*) in *Viṣṇupurāṇa*: Schreiner 2013.

5,30	*stotra* by Aditi
6,6-7	Khāṇḍikya-Keśidhvaja-dialogue

Besides these, the following passages which have *jñāna*, but not *vijñāna* need to be considered:

1,2	*maṅgala*
1,4	*stotra* of the Earth and of the Yogis
2,6; 2,12	passages attributed to Parāśara, the narrator
6,4-5	chapters on eschatology
6,8	conclusions on the ViP

I cannot present the exegesis of all passages (which are more than 120) but hope that the selected instances exemplify the theological importance and extension of the concept. "Cognition" (German "*Erkenntnis*") may not be the most fortuitous translation, but it is consistently, concordantly with the use of *jñāna/vijñāna* in Sanskrit. Occurrences of *jñāna* and *vijñana* are treated together.

Viṣṇupurāṇa 1,4.38-41 is a passage that documents well the complexity of *vijñāna* in a systematic context; and, since the passage has been dealt with by Kirfel and by Hacker,[56] it may serve to introduce the diachronic perspective as well.

You alone are the Highest Reality,
no one else, o guardian of the world.
Yours only is the greatness
By which is permeated anything, be it endowed with life or not.
What is seen as having form
is considered by people who are not *yogins*
as your world-form,
by a cognition which is error
even though you are one with cognition.
People without understanding
Consider the whole world which is essentially cognition
as having the things as its form,
(and therefore) they err around
In a flood of bewilderment.
Those, however, who know about cognition

---

[56] Kirfel 1927; Hacker 1960: 350; 351.

and whose spirit is cleansed
consider this whole world
as a form of yours, as one with cognition, o Highest Lord![57]

These verses were included in Kirfel's *Purāṇapañcalakṣaṇa* (p.18–19) since they occur also in PdP (1,3.48-54 and 5,3.41-46, depending on the edition). Hacker extrapolated three stages:

1.) ViP 1,4.40, teaching that the world consists of cognition which reflects Buddhist *vijñāna-vāda* ("*Nur-Erkenntnis-Lehre*").
2.) ViP 1,4.41, modifying the Buddhist teaching by identifying this cognition with Viṣṇu, which must have happened before the ViP since it occurs also in PdP.
3.) 1,4.39, an addition to this, specific for the ViP, which repeats that it is Viṣṇu who is cognition and adds that only *yogins* can realize this.

The change of metre after verse 37 suggests that verse 38 be included in the passage under discussion. It belongs also to PdP which, however, reads *paramātmā* for *paramārtha*. If *paramārtha* is included in interpreting *vijñāna*, it can be seen in terminological and argumentative relation to the *arthasvarūpa* of verse 40. And it becomes less convincing to see in verse 40 "*eindeutiger Einfluß der buddhistischen Nur-Erkenntnis-Lehre*". For, the empirical reality is differentiated from a highest reality that is characterized as a subtle, all pervading substance of cognition, perhaps analogous to the *sattva*-principle. The consciousness of *yogins* is constituted by that reality; by its purification the Highest Reality can be cognized as existing in everything. Such a "*Nur-Erkenntnis-Lehre*" or *vijñānavāda* need not be directed polemically against Buddhists, nor need it be inclusivisti-

---

[57] *paramārthas tvam evaiko nānyo 'sti jagataḥ pate* |
tavaiṣa mahimā yena vyāptam etac carācaram || 1,4.38 |
yad etad dṛśyate mūrtam etaj jñānātmanas tava |
bhrāntijñānena paśyanti jagarūpam ayoginaḥ || 1,4.39 |
jñānasvarūpam akhilaṃ jagad etad abuddhayaḥ |
arthasvarūpaṃ paśyanto bhrāmyante mohasaṃplave || 1,4.40 |
ye tu jñānavidaḥ śuddhacetasas te 'khilaṃ jagat |
jñānātmakaṃ prapaśyanti tvadrūpaṃ parameśvara || 1,4.41 |.

cally appropriated from Buddhists. Rather, it can be (should be) understood as a viṣṇuitic version of Sāṃkhya-Yoga teachings. Cognition as Highest Reality pervades (*vyāpta*) all empirical things (*artha*); it can be seen and thus known. That is why those who have purified their mind can be called *jñānavidaḥ* (v. 41), knowers of cognition; that is why cognition can be called a form of God that can be seen. This reality is not the negation of the reality of the empirical world, abstracted from its being cognized; it is rather the theologically founded argument for the unity of everything (everything) with regard to divine reality which is its foundation and cause (material cause).

The logical and ontological problem does not seem to be the relation between the different levels of reality, but rather the reality of plurality and of differences in view of the uniqueness and singularity of the (material) cause (e.g., 5,33.47-49).

The fact that in the passage just discussed the cross section on *vijñāna* overlaps with the cross section on *paramārtha* is an important index for establishing the importance of both words.

The same observation holds for 1,6.13 where the cross section of *vijñāna* overlaps with the cross section on *parama-pada*.

> They enjoyed living as they wanted; having purified their inner sense, free from blemishes due to (maintaining their) observances, (these) pure beings lived free from all impediments.
> And when their mind is purified (and) Hari, the pure one, is ever present in their purified inner sense, they see pure cognition and thereby the step that is called after Viṣṇu.[58]

The context speaks about the origin of the *varṇa* system and of the institution of sacrifice. An important concept is that of purity. Observation of *dharma* makes free of blemishes (*nirmala*) and is the precondition for a higher goal. He who has made his inner sense (*antaḥkaraṇa*) and his mind (*manas*) pure and has established Hari in himself, "such a person sees Hari, the pure one, and thereby the step that

---

58 *yathecchāvāsaniratāḥ sarvabādhāvivarjitāḥ* |
śuddāntaḥkaraṇāḥ śuddhāḥ sarvānuṣṭhānanirmalāḥ || 1,6.12 |
śuddhe ca tāsāṃ manasi śuddhe 'ntaḥsaṃsthite harau |
śuddhajñānaṃ prapaśyanti viṣṇvākhyaṃ yena tat padam || 1,6.13 |

is named after Viṣṇu." The cognition and the deity, the human mind and the object of such (salvific?) vision as well are called pure. Cognition is in this context another expression for that all-pervasive reality which is simultaneously God, mind and cosmic principle.

The formulaic expression (similar to a refrain) about a place or condition "which is Viṣṇu's highest step" known from *Ṛgveda* 1,22 belongs in the ViP to the repertoire of the authors of *stotra*s. But it occurs also outside of *stotra*s in passages which stylistically resemble *stotra*s and describe Viṣṇu with hymnic diction (introduction 1,2.16 and conclusion 6,5.68; tracts like 1,6; 1,22; 2,7; 2,8). It is a dimension of content which ties together different subgenres in this Purāṇa. The episodic anchors are the Dhruva episode (who desires the highest position and becomes the highest, polar point of the cosmic egg) and the Trivikrama episode (the latter not being told extensively but mentioned in 3,1.42-43 and 3,2.18). The religious anchor is a soteriology which is linked to an ascetic-meditative-yogic way and aims (in analogy to the cosmic localisation of the highest step) at a step or level which is above worldly involvement and fetters. The milieu to which the ViP can be assigned is therefore (further) characterized by its respect for the vedic tradition and yogic practices. This amounts to a combination of a *karmamārga* and a renunciatory *jñānamārga*. If both coexist in the ViP it is tempting to postulate that ritually committed *brahmin*s and philosophically inclined *saṃnyāsin*s were coexisting and perhaps competing in this religious milieu.

Of the more than hundred relevant testimonies of *jñāna/vijñāna*, so far only two have been discussed, and only one more can be added, viz. chapters 3,17-18, the Māyāmoha-episode. The only explicit mention of Buddhism and *vijñānavāda* is found in this episode. The demons are taught as an anti-vedic doctrine that everything consists of cognition. This statement is paraphrased or explained as meaning that the world has no real foundation (*ādhāra*).[59] Therefore the world has the reality of objects of erroneous cognition (3,18.18-19).[60]

> Māyāmoha said: If your desire aims at heaven and at extinction, o counter-gods, then enough of that wicked normative regulation involving the killing of animals; you should gain awareness!
> You should recognize that all this consists of nothing but cognition. Be aware of my words! Those who have gained awareness did proclaim thus!
> This world, without foundation and completely corrupted by passion, etc., errs around in the straights of existence and aims at the objects of an erroneous cognition.[61]

This teaching that the world has no (ontological) foundation does not contradict what the ViP otherwise says about *vijñāna*, if the erroneous cognition consists in taking the objects of desire as real rather than recognizing them as one with Viṣṇu.[62] God is identified with the object of an upaniṣadic *jñānamārga*, i.e., with *brahman*, *ātman*, *paramātman* without leading to an illusionism. God is "principle", i.e., beginning and foundation of all reality, including everything in the cosmos. The cosmos and individual things are real because they are forms of God who is their basis and substratum. There are degrees of

---

59 Elsewhere in the ViP it is one of God's functions to be the basis or foundation of the world.

60 Otherwise, error is described as the restriction of perception to the differences between things and the non-perception of what they have in common as underlying reality.

61 *māyāmoha uvāca*:
svargārthaṃ yadi vo vāñchā nirvāṇārtham athāsurāḥ |
tad alaṃ paśughātādiduṣṭadharmaṃ nibodhata || 3,18.17 |
vijñānamayam evaitad aśeṣam avagacchata |
budhyadhvaṃ me vacaḥ samyag budhair evam udīritam || 3,18.18 |
jagad etad anādhāraṃ bhrāntijñānārthatatparam |
rāgādiduṣṭam atyarthaṃ bhrāmyate bhavasaṃkaṭe || 3,18.19 |.

62 The general acknowledgement of Vedic *dharma*, however, will have to be understood to imply the rejection of animal sacrifice, while for the counter-gods, it is included in the Vedic *dharma* that makes them invincible.

reality as well as degrees of cognition and the two correspond to each other because both have their base (*ādhāra*) and their material cause in the same cognitive substance (*vijñānamaya*). This is identical with God as another of his forms. God's allness or universality is the point of reference for all realities and all cognitions without the lower degrees being eliminated by the higher. Both are anchored in Viṣṇu. The condition or method for attaining the higher degrees of cognition is an assimilation of cognition and the organs of cognition to the one universal reality in and behind all differences. This is achieved by *yoga*, i.e., concretely by purification and abolition of all obstacles.

Decisive for the evaluation of such a purāṇic position is whether it is deemed a meaningless cliché, a manner of speaking that allows for the saying of everything and anything without an identifiable standpoint, or whether the allness and universality of Viṣṇu reflects a genuine theological or religious commitment which in the course of purāṇic textual history, sectarian rivalries and increasing literary shallowness has only later turned into a cliché. The evidence of what the *stotras* say about Viṣṇu and of the conceptual cross sections testifies to a genuine, multifaceted and thus lively literary and theological activity.

Thus, the Māyāmoha episode does not profoundly disturb the overall profile of the ViP. It confirms a point of reference for a relative chronology (whatever the Buddhologists may offer as the date for *vijñānavāda*) but does not make the ViP appear as a reaction to *vijñānavāda*. The passages on *jñāna*/*vijñāna* do not reveal a buddhistic character (*Prägung*) of this concept and doctrine.

Cosmological, theological and spiritual-practical teachings complement each other and combine in the passages of the ViP that deal with cognition; they form a composite yet complex picture of multiple links and interrelations. A conscious and strong wish to conform to the norms of Vedic tradition and to brahminical values and practices is an undeniable trait of this picture.

If the discussed passages made plausible that the ViP documents a specific and distinct structure of theological thinking which we could compare with other systems (from other texts), if the methods of arriving at the system of the ViP are adequate and thus applicable to other texts, if the attempt to look at a Purāṇa as a meaningful unity (represented by a conceptual structure on the literary level, e.g., by the outline of the text or by use of a literary genre like hymns) did not lead to a dead end but to a better understanding of the history of Viṣṇuism and of the place of the ViP in it, if, thus, this presentation succeeded in turning the assumptions behind any one or all three of these "ifs" into acceptable conclusions, then Purāṇa research may have made a small step forward, and our understanding of the theology of Viṣṇu may have been expanded. The latter is succinctly summarized in the following verse from a *stotra*:

> You are the only one
> considered by the Wise
> as that highest step at the top
> recognized as cognition.
> Nothing that (presently) exists with a form of its own
> is independent from you,
> neither anything past or future
> o you transcendent (highest) Self!
>
> *ekas tvam agryaṃ paramaṃ padaṃ yat* |
> *paśyanti tvāṃ sūrayo jñānadṛśyam* |
> *tvatto nānyat kiṃcid asti svarūpaṃ* |
> *yad vā bhūtaṃ yac ca bhavyaṃ parātman* || 5,11.46 |.

Bibliography

Primary Literature

ViP
Viṣṇupurāṇa. The Critical Edition of the Viṣṇupurāṇam, ed. by M.M. Pathak, 2 Vols., Vadodara 1997–1999.

Secondary Literature

Bock 1984
Andreas Bock, *Der Sāgara-Gaṅgāvataraṇa-Mythus in der episch-purāṇischen Literatur*. [*Alt- und Neu-Indische Studien* 27]. Stuttgart: Franz Steiner Verlag 1984.

Hacker 1960a
Paul Hacker, Purāṇen und Geschichte des Hinduismus. Methodologische, programmatische und geistesgeschichtliche Bemerkungen. In: *Orientalische Literaturzeitschrift* 55 (1960) 341–354.

Hacker 1960b
Ibid., *Prahlāda. Werden und Wandlungen einer Idealgestalt.* Beiträge zur geschichte des Hinduismus. Teil I; Teil II. [Akademie der Wissenschaften, Abh. Geistes- u. Sozialwiss. Kl. Jg. 1959, Nr. 9; 13, pp. 517–663; pp. 889–993]. Wiesbaden: Steiner 1960.

Gail 1977a
Adabert Gail, Viṣṇu als Eber in Mythos und Bild. In: *Beiträge zur Indienforschung*. Ernst Waldschmidt zum 80. Geburtstag gewidmet. Berlin: Veröffentlichungen des Museums für Indische Kunst 1977, 127–168.

Gail 1977b
Ibid., *Paraśurāma, Brahmane und Krieger. Untersuchungen über Ursprung und Entwicklung eines Avatāra Viṣṇus und Bhakta Śivas in der indischen Literatur.* Wiesbaden: Otto Harrassowitz 1977.

Kirfel 1927
Willibald Kirfel, *Das Purāṇa Pañcalakṣana. Versuch einer Textgeschichte.* Leiden: Brill 1927.

Malinar 2007
Angelika Malinar, *The Bhagavdgītā. Doctrines and contexts*. Cambridge: Cambridge University Press 2007.

Mertens 1998
Annemarie Mertens, *Der Dakṣamythus in der episch-purāṇischen Literatur. Beobachtungen zur religionsgeschichtlichen Entwicklung des Gottes Rudra-Śiva im Hinduismus*. Wiesbaden: Otto Harrassowitz 1998.

Ruben 1943
Walter Ruben, *Krishna*. Konkordanz und Kommentar der Motive seines Heldenlebens. Istanbul 1943.

Rüping 1970
Klaus Rüping, *Amṛtamanthana und Kūrma-Avatāra. Ein Beitrag zur puranischen Mythen- und Religionsgeschichte*. Wiesbaden: Otto Harrassowitz 1970.

Schreiner 1990
Peter Schreiner, Purāṇische Stotras im Vergleich. In: *XXIV. Deutscher Orientalistentag vom 26. Bis 30. September1988 in Köln*. Ausgewählte Vorträge, Werner Diem, Abdoljavad Falaturi (eds). Stuttgart 1990, 426–441.

Schreiner 2013
Id., *Viṣṇupurāṇa. Althergebrachte Kunde über Viṣṇu.* Aus dem Sanskrit übersetzt und herausgegeben von Peter Schreiner. Berlin: Verlag der Weltreligionen 2013.

Tripathi 1968
Gaya Charan Tripathi, *Der Ursprung und die Entwicklung der Vāmana-Legende in der indischen Literatur*. Wiesbaden: Otto Harrassowitz 1968.

Charlotte Schmid

Elements for an iconography of Nārāyaṇa in the Tamil land: Balarāma and a lost Vaiṣṇava world

Introduction

> [His] reclining on the milk, [His] dwelling in Araṅkam [Śrīraṅgam] of old, [His] sleeping on the banyan[-leaf]: Who would know the earth's unique essential Principle, the celestials' true God, the rare Entity [lying on] water the way I have known [Him]?[1]

This stanza[2] by Tirumaḻicaiyāḻvār is part of a hymn to a deity called Nārāyaṇa by this author. This saint poet is one of the 12 Āḻvārs, who composed the *Nālāyirat Tivyappirapantam* (or *Tivyappirapantam*, Tiv.), "The Sacred Collection of Four Thousand Verses" (6th–9th c.), an early anthology of poems from Tamil Vaiṣṇava Bhakti [Tiv.].[3] Three

---

1 Tirumaḻicaiyāḻvār, *Nāṉmukaṉ Tiruvantāti* 3 (Tiv. 2384):

pāliṟ kiṭantatuvum paṇṭu araṅkam mēyatuvum,
ālil tuyiṉṟatuvum ār aṟivār, – ñālattu
oru poruḷai vāṉavar tam meyp poruḷai, appil
aru poruḷai yāṉ aṟinta āṟu.

There is no critical edition of the *Tivyappirapantam*. I use the edition of Jagathratchagan 2002, where the *sandhi* is deleted, the final short *u* sometimes marked and other choices (like punctuation marks) are made – some might certainly be criticized but this is beyond my competence. The numbering of the stanzas given in brackets refers to this edition. If no reference is given, translations of cited texts are mine.

2 Translation by Suganya Anandakichenin, to whom heartfelt thanks are due for that; for the translation of this stanza, see also, *infra*, fns 4, 5 and 6.

3 Tirumaḻicaiyāḻvār is considered one of the first Āḻvārs by many authors, see Hardy 1983: 265–269, who postulates the 6th or early 7th c. for the first *Antāti*s.

different manifestations of the god are referred to here:[4] the deity lying on the ocean or creator god, the deity residing in Śrīraṅgam, and the god child (Kṛṣṇa) sleeping on a fig-leaf floating on the primordial ocean. This is Nārāyaṇa's "way", *āṟu*. This Tamil word also means river and, to my opinion, affords a play on words equating the course of a river (*aṟu*)[5] and the way (*āṟu*) the god who is "*aru poruḷ*", "rare Entity", Supreme Being) manifests himself.[6] Water defined here as the substance of the god thus allows three images of reclining deities to merge into one single idol, that of the Śrīraṅgam island in the Kāvēri River [fig. 1 and 2].

The icon of Śrīraṅgam here praised is an anthropomorphic deity lying on a multi-headed snake. The stucco image that is today worshiped in this prominent Vaiṣṇava site of South India is popular and well-known [fig. 2].[7] Long before the contemporary representations, the antiquity of this image is attested through numerous mentions in the *Tivyappirapantam*.[8] The familiar iconography of "the Great one [*peru-*

---

4 The term *paṇṭu*, meaning "antique", may be applied either to the ocean on which the god reclines in ancient times or to the site where he manifests, Araṅkam. The latter option was chosen in this translation but the ambiguity may also be intentional in order to stress the fact that the river is an embodiment of the antique milk-ocean.

5 Another term may echo this play of words: *ñālam* means "world, earth" but also "magic". In this last sense, it comes from the Sanskrit *jāla*, which has two different meanings: "illusion, artifice" as a noun but "watery, aquatic" as an adjective.

6 One can understand the two *poruḷai* of this stanza as direct invocations to the god. In the translation by Sri Rama Bharati (in the edition of Jagathrachagan 2002: 681) the celestials appear as the first ones to know the ways the deity manifests itself.

7 The idol itself may not be viewed by non-Hindus. Not all the details of the literary descriptions of the Āḻvārs match the present icon, see Champakalakshmi 1981: 70 (see *infra*, fn. 56 for comments on the usage of stucco for cult-images of Viṣṇu before the 6th–7th c. CE). But the main scheme is this one, as well as peculiar details of the representation to which I will return below.

8 In the *Tivyappirapantam*, the deity enshrined in Śrīraṅgam is the most often mentioned of all the deities linked to a site. The eleven stanzas the

mā<u>n</u>aṭikaḷ] of Śrīraṅgam", or "Ananta-nārāyaṇa of Śrīraṅgam", as the deity is called in early inscriptions of the site (10th and 11th c.), is commonly considered a representation of the Nārāyaṇa aspect of Viṣṇu. It is acknowledged that the sculpture had a specific importance in the Tamil country where reclining deities were the earliest depicted of the Vaiṣṇava tradition. The stanza of Tirumaḻicai underlines the complexity of this multi-layered image. Indeed, this image already had a long history when it made its appearance at the tip of the Indian peninsula, but the specific transformations that it underwent there added to its complexity.

This paper examines the iconography used to represent Nārāyaṇa in Śrīraṅgam and elsewhere in the Tamil land. The focus will be on one aspect in particular, namely, how the elder brother of Kṛṣṇa, Balarāma, or Saṃkarṣaṇa,[9] was connected to the elaboration of the image and concept of Nārāyaṇa. Balarāma does not feature prominently in the *Tivyappirapantam* where Nārāyaṇa and Kṛṣṇa are prominent. Thus, to begin, the data of the *Tivyappirapantam* anthology will be investigated from

---

poet Madhura Kavi devotes to another Āḻvār constitute the only work of the *Tivyappirapantam* where Śrīraṅgam does not appear and some works of the anthology are devoted entirely to this site/deity. It is particularly prominent in the 55 strophes of Toṇṭaraṭippoti to the Lord of Śrīraṅgam and in the 10 strophes of Tiruppā<u>n</u> Āḻvār, who, both, consecrated their whole works to the deity of Śrīraṅgam. It is very important in Kulacēkarar Āḻvār (31 stanzas of 105). It takes an important place in Periyāḻvār (35 stanzas of 473) and Āṇṭāḷ (10 stanzas of 173), less important but still considerable given the number of stanzas in Tirumaṅkaiyāḻvār (73 stanzas of 1134), comparable thus to the works of Tirumaḻicai (14 stanzas of 216). Śrīraṅgam is a minor theme in Poykai (1 stanza of 100), Pūtattāḻvār (4 stanzas of 100), Peyāḻvār (2 stanzas of 100) and Nammāḻvār (12 stanzas of 1296). Given that Poykai, Pūtattāḻvār and Peyāḻvār are considered among the earliest authors of the *Tivyappirapantam*, the fact that the site is less important in these three works shows how necessary research led on geographical and chronological basis is; for steps towards such a survey, see Hardy 1983: 256–269.

9 The elder brother of Kṛṣṇa is known under various names. Balarāma is quite common in the *Mahābhārata* while Saṃkarṣaṇa is used in the *Harivaṃśa*.

two perspectives, that are Nārāyaṇa as a name and the deity lying on a snake as a form. A connection between the two is well established in the *Tivyappirapantam*. Still, the scrutiny of the *Tivyappirapantam* anthology reveals a number of opaque aspects in the development of the Nārāyaṇa cult in the Tamil land. Are specific qualities of the name "Nārāyaṇa" associated with a lying snake-deity in Tamil dating before the *Tivyappirapantam*? Is it possible to discern specificities of their association in the Tamil country? In fact, in the multi-faceted text of the *Tivyappirapantam*, the forms in which Nārāyaṇa and Kṛṣṇa are visualised can be linked to the original appearance of Balarāma, one of the oldest snake deities of the Vaiṣṇava world. To demonstrate this point, an exploration of the *Tivyappirapantam* will be complemented with earlier data from the Tamil region: on the one hand, the *Cilappatikāram* (Cil.), a long poem usually designated as a Tamil epic (6th–7th c.), and, on the other, various early sculpted images found in the Tamil lands. Balarāma is clearly perceptible in these two bodies of work.

However, the characteristics of many of the reclining Vaiṣṇava deities alluded to in the *Cilappatikāram* or sculpted in the Tamil country do not fully correspond with the *Tivyappirapantam*. They do not always correspond either with the model of reclining deities elaborated earlier and further north on the Gupta territory (4th–6th c.). Their features lead us down the path of ancient Vaiṣṇava trends in the Tamil land and to carefully consider the contribution of Saṃkarṣaṇa-Balarāma to the Nārāyaṇa thread. To conclude, as a possible clue to ancient Vaiṣṇava models that have largely been erased by the passage of time, examined will be a hymn from the *Paripāṭal*, one of the main anthologies of Caṅkam (3rd–6th), a corpus that appears today as one of the literary background elements of the *Tivyappirapantam*.

This survey will be based on texts in both Tamil and Sanskrit, together with the sculptural tradition of the Tamil region. The overview it provides will perforce be brief, since under consideration is a span of time covering more than a millennium and an area corresponding to the entire Indian Peninsula. It is thus intended as general presentation only; each point certainly deserves a much more detailed study. Among the numerous Sanskrit texts, in addition to the *Mahābhārata* (Mbh; 4th c. BCE–4th c. CE) and Purāṇic texts (a genre thought to have appeared in the 4th or 5th c. CE), I have made extensively use of the *Harivaṃśa*.

This *khila*, (necessary) "complement" of the *Mahābhārata* usually thought to have largely been composed between the *Mahābhārata* and the Purāṇic literature in terms of genre, mythology—and date as it is usually thought to have been composed between the 2nd and 4th c. AD. As a third basis of the analysis, investigated will be a number of relevant inscriptions ranging chronologically from a Prākṛt epigraph of the 1st BCE from North India to inscriptions of the 10th century found in South India. Identifying some sculptures being a central aim of the survey, sculptures form a third basis of the analysis. Even if this proved quite elusive, a not unusual outcome, by drawing a link between South and North, it highlights the fruitfulness of the confrontation between archaeological data and texts, asserting the existence of forms of Hinduism beyond authoritative, often text-based ones.

Nārāyaṇa in the *Tivyappirapantam*: a name to be chanted, a form to be seen

The stanza of Tirumaḻicai cited first is exemplary of the complexity of an anthology that, enriched as it was by a number of earlier sources, often contains varying associated levels of realities or forms. In this case, posture and water weave traditions of distinct origins together. Nārāyaṇa, the Śrīraṅgam icon and Kṛṣṇa are linked one to the other by the water on which they lie and by their reclining posture.

On the one hand, a Sanskritic background is prominent. First, the name "Nārāyaṇa", which appears in the first stanza of the hymn (*nāṉ mukaṉai nārāyaṇaṉ paṭaittāṉ*, "Nārāyaṇa created the Four-faced one [Brahmā]") keeps Sanskrit characteristics in the whole *Tivyappirapantam* in contradistinction to many other names given to the deity of the *Tivyappirapantam*.[10] The commonality of the use of the name Nārāyaṇa in the *Tivyappirapantam*, under different spellings, more or less

[10] Some names are properly Tamil, like "Māl", "Mālōṉ", and "Māyōṉ"; others are equivalents of Sanskrit names, like "Araṅkaṉ" and "Nārāṇaṉ", Tamil transpositions for "Raṅga" (here transformed into an anthroponym) and Nārāyaṇa. The later appears also as Nārāyaṇar or Nārāyaṇaṉ and in the form of the eight syllabled *mantra*, *tiruveṭṭu eḻuttu*.

tamilised, is a token paid to the Sanskrit tradition.[11] Secondly, the link established between Nārāyaṇa, the water and the child floating on a fig-leaf corresponds to an explanation of the nature of Nārāyaṇa given in several Sanskrit texts.[12] It appears in the *Mahābhārata*[13] where the sage, Mārkaṇḍeya, who is the unique being to survive the final dissolution of the universe, wanders in the primeval ocean. [14] One day, Mārkaṇḍeya sees a child in a cradle on the branch of a banyan tree, who invites him to enter inside his body. The sage sees all the worlds inside what is then called Supreme Being (*mahātman*). When he is expelled, he sees the god again but this time as a child seated on the banyan tree, who explains that he is Nārāyaṇa, "for the waters (*nara*) are my course (*ayanaṃ*)" in a verse found in several texts, including the *Manusmṛti*. If details differ then from one version of the episode to the other, such as the one found in one appendix (1.41) of the *Harivaṃśa* and several *Purāṇas*, the main scheme remains. While roaming in the primeval ocean Mārkaṇḍeya meets a sleeping *ādi-puruṣa*, a primeval being, who swallows him; when the sage emerges out of this deity, a child, who was sleeping on the branch of a banyan tree explains he is Nārāyaṇa. Our attention should be drawn here to its similarity with the stanza of the Āḻ-

---

11 For references see Narayanan 1987: 168; for a discussion about the importance of this name in the *Tivyappirapantam*, see Young 2007: 181–183; for the importance it gained in the Śrīvaiṣṇava tradition, see Carman/Narayanan 1989: 159–175.

12 On the Tamil side, *Cilappatikāram* 17.33.1 *aṟu poruḷ ivaṉ eṉṟē amarar kaṇam toḻutu ētta* ("Saying 'he is the supreme being (*poruḷ*) to determine (*aṟu*)', the group of the celestials prayed with joined hands") may be the first reference to the mythology of Sanskrit origin transformed into Tamil texts to give birth to a new motif. The same formula *aṟu poruḷ* is used in *Cilappatikāram* and in Tirumaḻicai's stanza.

13 See Mbh 3.180–221.

14 This episode in Sanskrit texts has been the focus of a few recent studies; see Brinkhaus 2000, Couture 2007: 73–97. In her PhD dissertation, Lynn Marie Ate 1978: 379–385 proposes a survey of the motif in the *Tivyappirapantam*.

vār.[15] The brief and lyric stanza of the *Tivyappirapantam* echoes the story found in Sanskrit literature; the definition of the deity of Śrīraṅgam as "the substance of water" adapts a traditional Sanskrit etymology of the name of Nārāyaṇa to a Tamil context.

On another hand, the stanza of Tirumaḻicai is deeply rooted in the Tamil soil. It links the mythology of Nārāyaṇa with the physical characteristics of the site of Śrīraṅgam. The posture of the reclining deity mirrors the position of the island in the Kāvēri River, which provides a tangible representation of the milk-ocean or primeval sea [fig. 1]. Moreover, the vision of the child sleeping on a banyan leaf is one of these typical Tamil motifs that developed from Sanskrit texts to give birth to devotional patterns distinct from their original sources. While it did originally develop from Sanskrit texts, it became distinct from them. In the early Sanskrit texts, the child does not sleep on a leaf, whereas in South India this element becomes part of a grander mythical whole, in which the god not only swallows the worlds but spits them out.[16]

Such equivalence of deities and places can be considered typical of Tamil Bhakti. While praising a deity of such or such place is less common in the Vaiṣṇava corpus than in the Śaiva Tamil corpus, the *Tēvāram*, in the *Tivyappirapantam* the iconography of a deity reclining on a snake does play an important role in what I would call the *bhakti* (devotion) of the place. Allusions to the reclining form are quite prominent in

---

15 Mbh 3.187.3: *āpo nārā iti proktāḥ saṁjñānāma kṛtaṁ mayā | tena nārāyaṇo 'smy ukto mama tad dhy ayanaṃ ||*.

16 In my opinion, this mythological event not found in Sanskrit texts is clearly inspired by the episode of Mārkaṇḍeya. *Contra* Ate (1978: 382) who feels uncertain about the parallel between the Tamil motif and early Sanskrit texts narrating the vision of Mārkaṇḍeya. L. Ate proposes that the Aurva-myth, built around the figure of a destructive fire incarnated in a child, is to be associated with the mythological event alluded to in the Tiv. See also Carman/Narayanan (1989: 163, fn. 7), who pointed out that the myth of Mārkaṇḍeya's vision is not mentioned in itself by the Āḻvārs. However, I would underline that Mārkaṇḍeya appears in the characters identified in an inscription engraved in the cave of the reclining deity of Nāmakkal (8th c.? see *infra*, p. 118).

the anthology. On the archaeological side, the fact that the earliest reclining Vaiṣṇava deities were cut directly in bedrock was a clear means for uniting them with the place at they are worshipped.

Thus, this single stanza of Tirumaḻicai appears to set an ancient and vast Sanskrit tradition into the Tamil landscape. The same type of adaptation to Tamil literature and/or territory is encountered in many other stanzas of the *Tivyappirapantam.* The name Nārāyaṇa and the appearance of the deity lying on a snake are two of the primary elements then used. The association between these two features is not always this close as it is in Tirumaḻicai's stanza. The name and the form present sometimes characteristics of their own quite separately from each other; indeed, the variations in the way these two representations of Nārāyaṇa appear in the anthology underlines the uncertainty in their association.

Since there is not enough space here to cover all their aspects, I will just summarize their main characteristics through specific examples. For the sake of clarity, I will consider each work of the *Tivyappirapantam* in the order they appear in the anthology, taking the vaṭakalai order of it as it is the one of the editions I have used. Such order is not chronological and the first two authors we encounter, Periyāḻvār and Āṇṭāḷ, are certainly not to be considered as the earliest Āḻvārs. Even if there is a general consensus on the *Antāti*s as being the earliest works, the chronology of the *Tivyappirapantam* is still much debated and also outside my competence.[17] The approach adopted here keeps in mind that each author may also be considered independently. Moreover, the *Tivyappirapantam* is a corpus that is not easily cut from a long tradition of devotion that did not necessarily focus on "Nārāyaṇa" as a name or in the forms of reclining deities. I will conclude this part of the survey with a brief synthesis to compare the relevant data with the position of the *Antāti*s, widely acknowledged as the earliest strata of the anthology.

The *Tivyappirapantam* opens with a hymn of the *Tirumoḻi* by Periyāḻvār. This *pallāṇṭu*, a hymn to invite the deity to wake up, has the devotee sing as follows:

---

17 The main study remains Hardy 1983 (see pp. 261–269 for a summary of the issue of chronology); some of his proposals about internal and external chronology can be challenged as recently demonstrated in the case of Nammāḻvār case by Wilden 2014: 317–333.

> You from countryside and city[18] who, having the intention to sing 'homage to Nārāyaṇa', giving access to the good (*naṉku aṟiya*), ...[19].

The awakening of the deity is paralleled to the process of the deity's manifestation. The poem is addressed to "the Lord having for bed a hooded snake" (*pain nākaṇaip paḷḷkoṇṭāṉukku*). These verses have been chanted in Śrīraṅgam from at least the 10th century in the presence of the deity enshrined there; they are considered to address him explicitly.[20]

In the entire *Tirumoḻi* of Periyāḻvār, chanting "Nārāyaṇa" maintains specific virtues. The formula "*namō nāraṇā*" ("homage, o Nārāyaṇa", with a vocative corresponding to a Tamilised form of *nārāṇaṉ*) is associated with the Vedic tradition (Tiv. 438), to which a kind of magic is attached. If one chants it at the hour of death, he will not come again on this earth (Tiv. 372). But Periyāḻvār's work is largely devoted to the childhood of Kṛṣṇa. While it includes poems dedicated to sites, including Śrīraṅgam (Tiruvaraṅkam), where the Lord has a serpent for a bed (*araṅkatt(u) aravaṇaip paḷḷiyāṉē*), the name Nārāyaṇa often designates Kṛṣṇa as a child[21]—and thus the form lying on a snake engages in unexpected activities, stopping to cry or sucking Yaśodā's breast (Tiv. 51). When it is said that the deity sleeping on the ocean has come to live in the ocean of the poet's heart, it seems clear that this is the merging of distinct deities from other contexts (Tiv. 471). The name Nārāyaṇa is used as a designation for the supreme deity. This supreme deity takes various shapes but the foremost of all and the source of all others, including Kṛṣṇa himself, is that of a deity reclining on a snake.

---

[18] The term *nakaram* translated here by "city" might also be understood as "temple". In that case, the poet would be inviting the people in the temples (devotees or Brahmins and/or other people specialized in such or such service to the god, etc.) like those often mentioned in inscriptions engraved in Tamil from the 9th c. onwards. The ambiguity might also be intentional.

[19] *nāṭum nakaramum naṉkaṟiya namō nārāyaṇāya veṉṟu, pāṭumaṉamuṭaip pattaruḷḷīr* (Tiv. 4).

[20] It must be stressed however that while the name Araṅkam often appears in the whole corpus of Periyāḻvār, it is not mentioned in this very first hymn.

[21] See, for example, "Nārāyaṇa" being called to bathe (Tiv. 159) or becoming the talk of the town when he seduces a young girl (Tiv. 290), etc.

In the two works by Āṇṭāḷ that follow that of Periyāḻvār, Nārāyaṇa is again a designation for Kṛṣṇa, with whom the poetess celebrates her own wedding (see Tiv. 556, 563 for instance). While she sings in honour of Keśava, this one is a form (*mūrti*) of Nārāyaṇa (*nārāyaṇaṉ mūrtti, kēcavaṉaip pāṭavum*, Tiv. 480), the god praised with a thousand names (Tiv. 514). Those who sing the hymns of Āṇṭāḷ are in fact repeating the formula "*namō nārāyaṇāya*" ("Homage to Nārāyaṇa", Tiv. 555). The poetess may have wanted to attract the power attached to a formula where Sanskrit dative has been kept to the Tamil hymns she authors. She often calls her Lord the one who sleeps on the ocean of milk (see Tiv. 475, 551) or the one who takes his place on a serpent-bed (Tiv. 524). In the decade to the Lord of Śrīraṅgam this form is duly acknowledged (see Tiv. 608). He is described as the "One of Tiruvaraṅkam who lies upon a snake whose mouths [spit] fire" (*tīmukattu nākaṇai mēl cērum tiruvaraṅkar*, Tiv. 607–616). As in Periyāḻvār's hymns, the name Nārāyaṇa and the form of a deity lying on a snake function as a reference name and a reference shape. They are not always explicitly associated with one another but in the two worlds of sound and sight they seem to play an equivalent role.

The next Āḻvār of the anthology, Kulacēkarar, sings the deity of Śrīraṅgam quite extensively, calling his Lord "Nārāyaṇa". This deity is said to lie on a snake-bed:

> In the middle of the Poṉṉi river (Kāvēri), provided with firm banks,
> The Lord whose body is dark as the sea has taken his bed in lying down on the snake of Tiruvaraṅkam.
> With the desire to be satisfied in seeing him to the fill of his eyes,
> The one provided with a parasol and a heroic army, whose victories brighten the sword,
> The king of Kūṭal, the generous Kulacēkarar,
> composed this hymn, as a garland of rhythmic Tamil.
> Those who master it shall attain the feet of Nārāyaṇa [Nāraṇaṉ] of auspicious shining.[22]

---

22 Kulacēkarar 1.11 (Tiv. 657):
tiṭarviḷaṅku karaip poṉṉi naṭuvu pāṭṭut tiruvaraṅkattu aravu aṇaiyil paḷḷi koḷḷum

In Kulacēkarar's work, "for their tongue to be bruised, saying 'Nārāyaṇa'" (*nāttaḻumpu eḻa nāraṇā eṉṟu*, Tiv. 661), the devotees of the Lord of Śrīraṅgam (Araṅkaṉ) invoke Nārāyaṇa in a kind of ecstasy. The poet repeatedly describes the Lord of Tiruvaraṅkam (*tiruvaraṅkap perunakaruḷ*)[23] as a god lying

> on the resplendent king of serpents called Aṉantaṉ, a bed of effulgent whiteness shining with ornaments on which he resides (*aravaracap periñcōti aṉantaṉ eṉṉum aṇiviḷaṅkum uyar veḷḷai yaṇaiyai mēvi*, Tiv. 647).

The connection between the deity and the land where the temple stands is established by the Kāvēri River whose waters lap the feet of a snake-reclining Lord. The brilliance of the deity, and more specifically of his snake counterpart who sometimes spits fire, is often stressed.

In the five works that follow, namely, the *Tirucantaviruttam,* which is the first composition of Tirumaḻicai to appear in the *Tivyappirapantam,* the two works of Toṇṭaraṭippoṭi, the poem by Tiruppāṇ, and the one by Maturakavi, the name Nārāyaṇa is not met. This is surprising as the deity of "Araṅkam surrounded by the Golden River" (*poṉṉicūḻ araṅka(m)*, Tiv. 870) and the form of the deity lying on the snake are often encountered—with the exception of the poem by Maturakavi, a hymn in honour of another Āḻvār (Nammāḻvār). Toṇṭaraṭippoṭi gives the exact unusual position of a representation facing south:

> Having seen the blackness (*mā*) sleeping on a snake, our father, the deity (*kaṭavuḷ*) of the ocean-hue, looking towards Laṅkā in the Southern direction, showing his back in the Northern direction, having placed his foot in

---

kaṭalviḷaṅku karumēṉi yammāṉraṉṉaik kaṇṇārak kaṇṭu ukakkum kātal taṉṉāl
kuṭaiviḷaṅku viṟal tāṉaik koṟṟa oṉ vāḷ kūṭalar kōṉ koṭai kulacēkaraṉ coṟ ceyta
naṭaiviḷ aṅku tamiḻ mālai pattum vallār nalantikaḻ nāraṇaṉ aṭikkīḻ naṇṇuvārē.

[23] The word *nakar* used here can be understood as meaning a town, or city, or an abode, or a mansion, (see *supra*, fn. 18 on *nakaram*). It could thus allude either to the city of Śrīraṅgam or more precisely to the temple where the deity is enshrined.

> the Western direction, having put his head in the Eastern direction, alas my body melts, what can I do, people of the world![24]

"Nārāyaṇa" reappears in the three works by the most prolific of the Āḻvārs, Tirumaṅkaiyāḻvār, which are next in the *Tivyappirapantam* (according to the *vaṭakalai* order here followed). According to the motto of the first hymn in this series, Nārāyaṇa is the main name of the deity: "I have discovered the name 'Nārāyaṇa'" (*nāṉ kaṇṭukoṇṭēṉ nārāyaṇā eṉṉum nāmam*, Tiv. 948–957).[25] Still, the name "Nārāyaṇa" is not so frequent in these three compositions. Although the god is said to be lying on a snake and surrounded by the swift waters of the Kāvēri, in the five hymns to the deity of the site of Śrīraṅgam (Tiv. 1378–1427), the name Nārāyaṇa is not mentioned.[26] On the contrary, the name applies to deities associated with sites like Naṅkūr and Tirumāliruñcōlai, where a reclining form is not the main idol, and while a deity reclining on a snake is nonetheless very present from the beginning of the *Periyatirumoḻi* to the end, with similar formulas.[27] Finally, Tirumaṅkaiyāḻvār associates Nārāyaṇa with "Nara", repeating the famous pair Nara-Nārāyaṇa of the *Nārāyaṇīya* of the *Mahābhārata* (see *nara-nāraṇaṉ-ē*, Tiv. 1218,

---

[24] Tiv. 890: *kuṭaticai muṭiyai vaittuk kuṇaticai pātam nīṭṭi,*
vaṭaticai piṉpu kāṭṭit teṉticai yilaṅkai nōkki,
kaṭalniṟak kaṭavuḷ entai aravaṇait tuyilumā kaṇṭu,
uṭal eṉakk(u) urukumālō eñ ceykēṉ ulakattīrē.

[25] The word *nāmam* has several meanings other than "name", such as the name of the mark worn by the Vaiṣṇava devotees or "reputation, fame". The Tamil vocative of Nārāyaṇa denotes the usage of a formula of homage. One should say "O Nārāyāṇa".

[26] The site of Śrīraṅgam is also mentioned in individual stanzas of many other hymns by Tirumaṅkaiyāḻvār.

[27] See "saying 'O you the supreme one (*paramā*)' lying on the bed that is an auspicious (*nal*) snake having one thousand hoods", *paṇaṅkaḷ āyiram uṭaiya nal aravu aṇaip paḷḷikoḷ paramā eṉṟu* (Tiv. 963), or "supreme light lying on the bed that is a snake…", *pāmpiṉ aṇaip paḷḷi koṇṭāy parañcōtī* (Tiv. 2028).

1552; *naraṉ-ē nāraṇaṉ-ē*, Tiv. 1611; *nara-nāraṇaṉ āy*, "having become Nara-Nārāyaṇa", Tiv. 1898).[28]

Therefore, in the works by Tirumaṅkaiyāḻvār, although equivalence seems clear between Nārāyaṇa as a name and the deity lying on a snake as a form, these two ways of referring to the god are also used quite independently from each other.

Nārāyaṇa appears in the formula "homage to Nārāyaṇa" (*namō nāraṇā eṉṉum*, Tiv. 2138; *namō nāraṇā eṉṟu*, Tiv. 2176) in the following work, by Poykaiyāḻvār, whereby the poet's tongue praises the one having a serpent for a bed (Tiv. 2144). The equivalence between Nārāyaṇa (name) and the lying deity (form) is clear-cut in this piece. Still the reclining form is encountered more frequently than the name Nārāyaṇa.

The next Āḻvār, Pūttatāḻvār, uses Nārāyaṇa (*nāraṇaṉ*), as the name of the deity from the very beginning of his work diversely called, of course, in the various places he manifests (see Tiv. 2183). The name saves from hell (Tiv. 2247) and Pūttatāḻvār is enlightened by his vision of the deity, saying:

> I have seen the [light of the] day (*pakal*), I have seen Nārāyaṇa, first I saw him in my dreams, then in reality... (Tiv. 2262).[29]

The form of the god lying on a snake is also found, as for instance in Tiv. 2277:

> The Lord of Aṭṭiyūr rides a bird, sleeps on a snake provided with spots of bright gems [...].[30]

Yet, such references are infrequent in this work, whereas many sacred sites are cited, including Śrīraṅgam. Thus, the form lying on a snake

---

28 On this pair in the Tamil country, see Champakalakshmi 1981:165–167. However, I do not think that the mentions of those two in the *Tivyappirapantam* correspond to the two *vibhava*s (manifestations) of this name in Pāñcarātra texts, because they appear with none of the other *vibhava*s.

29 Tiv. 2262: *pakal kaṇṭēṉ nāraṇaṉaik kaṇṭēṉ kaṉavil mikak kaṇṭēṉ mīṇṭu avaṉai meyyē.*

30 Tiv. 2277: *attiyūrāṉ puḷḷaiyūrvāṉ, aṇimaṇiyiṉ tutti cēr nākattiṉ mēl tuyilvāṉ* [...].

does not appear here as an equivalent of the name Nārāyaṇa but as one of the many shapes the supreme deity may assume.

The Āḻvār that follows, Pēyāḻvār, uses the name Nārāyaṇa to pay homage to the one who has many names (Tiv. 2289). References to the deity lying on a snake are quite often found. As in Periyāḻvār's *Tirumoḻi*, the deity came to abide in the heart of the poet (Tiv. 2296) and accomplishes the feats of the Kṛṣṇa biography (see, for instance, Tiv. 2311).

The stanza presented at the opening of this paper has already demonstrated how much Nārāyaṇa imbued with his presence the *Antāti* of Tirumaḻicai, which comes next in the anthology. The name Nārāyaṇa appears throughout the work, from the first stanza (Tiv. 2382) to the last where the conclusion states that Nārāyaṇa (*nāraṇaṉ*) is the cause (*kāraṇaṉ*), what has been learnt (*kaṟṟavai*) and what must to be studied (*kaṟpavai*), (Tiv. 2477).[31] "Nārāyaṇa" appears regularly (Tiv. 2388, 2394, 2395, 2412, 2453, etc.) and is to be recited (Tiv. 2445). Here too, as we have already seen with Āṇṭāḷ and Kulacēkarar, the Lord reclines in the ocean on a fire-spitting serpent (Tiv. 2391). The equivalence between the deity lying on a snake and the name of Nārāyaṇa is delineated precisely.

In the three short works by Nammāḻvār that follow, Nārāyaṇa as a deity seems to fade away. The name appears as one of the names of Kṛṣṇa but among many others (Tiv. 2649). It is used more often in the longer *Tiruvāymōḻi*. As in several other works of the Āḻvārs "Nārāyaṇa" is prominent here; the specificity is attached to the chanting of the name, which is infused with special powers, like in the decade 10.5 (Tiv. 3935–3945) where "Nāraṇaṉ" the designation of the Lord reclining on the serpent, is said to be *tirunāmam* (an auspicious name, title, etc.). On the other hand, the deity of Nammāḻvār is rarely said to recline on a serpent, even if the decade 2.8 of the *Tiruvāymoḻi* is addressed to a deity sleeping on a snake (a hymn considered to be sung in honour of the sleeping deity of Trivandrum). Nonetheless, this form is occasionally mentioned (see, for instance, Tiv. 3818).

---

31 Tiv. 2477: *kāraṇaṉ nī kaṟṟavai nī kaṟpavai nī, nal kiricai, nāraṇaṉ nī naṉku aṟintēṉ nāṉ.*

It also appears when the deity is said to be the one having a lotus in his navel, like in other works of the *Tivyappirapantam* but more prominently here (*paṟpa-nāpaṉ*, see Tiv. 3084–3085). This is the form of the creator god sleeping on a snake, a lotus appearing in his navel. It is difficult, however, to perceive in Nammāḻvār's works a clear equivalence between Nārāyaṇa as a name and the deity lying on a snake as his primary form.

Such—too brief—survey is to be complemented by other texts, by archaeology and by elements for a chronology of the Āḻvārs as follows.

First, regarding the Sanskrit background of the name, some scholars have already pointed out the usage of Nārāyaṇa as a *mantra* in the *Tivyappirapantam* (see Narayanan 1987: 11, 49, 117, 165; Young 2007: 182–183). It must be stressed that this is the only Vaiṣṇava god name that comes directly from the Sanskrit tradition. While it is tamilised in some stanzas,[32] usage of a Sanskrit dative is noticeable in others. Secondly, this name is very present in the earliest works of the corpus, the *Antāti*s. Thirdly, the importance of the name Nārāyaṇa can be compared with the prominence of the site of Śrīraṅgam in the *Tivyappirapantam*, but the positions of this name and this site are not linked to one another and the references to the name and the site are of a different nature. Śrīraṅgam is thus less mentioned in the *Antāti*s than in most of the other works, while the name Nārāyaṇa is often encountered there. In contradistinction, the name "Nārāyaṇa" is absent from some of the works of the anthology, while Śrīraṅgam is present in all of them, as is the deity lying on a snake.[33] Fourthly, regarding the link between Nārā-

[32] On the power attached to the name of Nārāyaṇa as the *tirumantra*, referring to the sacred eight syllables in the Śrivaiṣṇava community (including in its Tamilised form "Nārāṇaṉ"), see Narayanan 1987: 117.

[33] See, *supra*, fn. 8. The name of the deity as Raṅganātha is a related thread. The "scene" (*raṅga* in Sanskrit, *araṅkam* in Tamil) alluded to in this name is the universe itself where the deity takes several forms. The locus of his incarnation is "the scene", Araṅkam or Śrīraṅgam, a name the place already had in Caṅkam literature (see *infra*, fn. 54). If this name may correspond, as it does in the Tamil tradition, to the stage where the god listens to the hymns of the *Tivyappirapantam*, the Sanskrit strand cannot be ignored. The form the god takes at this place or on that stage "Araṅkam",

yaṇa as a name and the reclining deity of Śrīraṅgam, it is important to point out that this deity is mainly known in the *Tivyappirapantam* as the one of Araṅkam that is the deity of a place. In some poems, this god is clearly referred to as the deity of the temple (*nakar*, *kōyil*) of Tiruvaraṅkam, i.e., Śrīraṅgam. The earliest known inscriptions of the site present a similar picture. First these call the deity the god of Tiruvaraṅkam. Then, in some inscriptions from the 11th century, the presence of the snake part of the god is signaled by a designation of the god that was not encountered before: Ananta-Nārāyaṇa. The case of Śrīraṅgam, which is the most prominent site of the *Tivyappirapantam*, appears to be exemplary: the physical form of the deity reclining on a snake constitutes the main link between the name Nārāyaṇa and the site.

Thus, while chanting of the name Nārāyaṇa appears a prominent feature of the textual universe of the *Tivyappirapantam*, the physical characteristics of the sites reveal themselves to be an important element in allowing this name to be pronounced, while the form, i.e., lying on a snake, has autonomy of its own. The latter may be the link between a name of which the Sanskrit origin was acknowledged and the sites of the Tamil land where Vaiṣṇavism is accommodated. But the *Tivyappirapantam* is a vast body of poems by several authors. If the case of Śrīraṅgam is definitely archetypal, the variety of the treatments in the anthology of the name Nārāyaṇa as well as of the form of a deity reclining on a serpent is no small matter. In other words, is it always relevant to try to untangle one from the other in the *Tivyappirapantam*? The snake form is firmly associated with the mythology of Nārāyaṇa as a supreme deity, even if the name "Nārāyaṇa" is not always used to designate it. Thus, allusions to this form function as a reminder of a supreme being

---

i.e., a materialization of a mythical element, is to be conceived like a first manifestation of the deity or a pre-manifestation of the deity, or as the source of all of them and the universe itself. It is a link between the non-manifest and the manifested world. Each and every temple/site attached to the *Tivyappirapantam* may be considered from this perspective; the concept gains a specific importance in Śrīraṅgam, "The Sacred stage", because—I think—the physical characteristics of the site allow for a materialization of a deity lying on waters and/or this stage where the Lord manifests.

having several names. One of these is "Nārāyaṇa". Its specificities are not apparent enough to assert that its link with the reclining form has its source in Sanskrit texts.

The specific characteristics of Nārāyaṇa as a name and of its figures reclining on a snake as a form, together with special features of the Śrī-raṅgam site, are found more manifest in the *Cilappatikāram*, a text corresponding to an earlier stage of the Vaiṣṇava movement in the Tamil land. Some passages in the thirty cantos of this Jain long poem are pre-bhaktic in a number of ways, since they present praises in honour of precise, personalized deities. In doing so, the text speaks of specific places and forms—while also introducing Nārāyaṇa.

Vaiṣṇava deities in the *Cilappatikāram*

The *Cilappatikāram* tells the story of a faithful wife, Kaṇṇaki, who is married to Kōvalaṉ. Kaṇṇaki's husband is killed in the city of Maturai to which the second book of the epic is devoted. Canto 17 evokes the celebration of rituals to conjure the absence of Kōvalaṉ, gone for Maturai. These rituals are celebrated in a cowherd camp in honour of this aspect of the Vaiṣṇava deity brought up in a cowherd settlement, that is Māyavaṉ, one of the Tamil names of Kṛṣṇa. The canto ends with a vision of the god being praised, saying:

> Eyes are not eyes that haven't seen the dark Lord
> With red feet, eyes and lips;
> The great Lord, Māyavaṉ, who appeared as a god
> And clasped the entire world in his navel
> Of the flowering lotus. Eyes are not eyes
> That blink on seeing the Lord.[34]

---

[34] Cil. 17.36. 1–5; trans. by Parthasarathy 2004: 178:
Periyavaṉai māyavaṉai pēr ulakam ellām
viri kamala unti uṭai viṇṇavaṉai kaṇṇum
tiruvaṭiyum kaiyum tiruvāyum ceyya
kariyavaṉai kāṇāta kaṇ eṉṉa kaṇṇē
kaṇ imaittuk kāṇpār tam kaṇ eṉṉa kaṇṇē.

The text is from the U.Vē. Cāminātaiyar edition. I have split the *sandhi*.

The stanza that follows gives the name of this deity. It appears in the last line, like a revelation:

> Tongues are not tongues that haven't praised the Lord
> Who frustrated the wiles of foolish Kaṃsa;
> Who went as an envoy of the Pāṇḍavas to the sound
> Of Vedic chants, and was praised in all four directions
> By a hundred people. Tongues are not tongues
> That haven't uttered the name "Nārāyaṇa".[35]

As in the *Tivyappirapantam*, Nārāyaṇa appears here as a name to be sung. Also found here is a specific play on words, the Tamil term for tongue, *nā*, and the initial syllable of "Nārāyaṇa". The devotee sees his deity as the one having a lotus in his navel. This is the *paṟpa-nāpaṉ*, the one having a navel of lotus, mentioned in the *Tivyappirapantam* like the one lying on the snake. From the Sanskrit tradition (and the earliest known sculptures located in North India) the navel from which the lotus grows belongs to a reclining anthropomorphic figure. Thus, in this Tamil praise, the devotee chants the god under his name of Nārāyaṇa while visualising him under the form of a reclining figure with a lotus issuing from its navel. This association is similar to evocations met in many poems of the *Tivyappirapantam.*

Considered in the light of the entire *Cilappatikāram*, these stanzas do not match the *Tivyappirapantam* very closely however. To provide a complete overview of non-buddhist, non-jain deities in the *Cilappatikāram* is beyond the reach of this paper. But certain elements on the Vaiṣṇava side of the picture can be investigated. In the clusters of temples mentioned as located in such or such city, Vaiṣṇava gods appear; also Vaiṣṇava deities of specific places and forms are integral parts of the scenery. Within these two categories, snake-deities are prominently mentioned—and they do not always correspond with the reclining Nārāyaṇa of the *Tivyappirapantam.*

---

[35] Cil. 17.37, 2–5; trans. by Parthasarathy 2004: 178:
kaṭantāṉai nūṟṟuvarpāl nāl ticaiyum pōṟṟa
paṭarnt' āraṇam muḻaṅka pañcavarkkut tutu
naṭantāṉai ēttāta nā eṉṉa nave nārāyaṇā eṉṉā nā eṉṉa nave.

Canto 5 of the *Cilappatikāram* describes a festival dedicated to Indra in the city of Pukār. The "temple of the White one who has a bright coiled body" (*vāl vaḷai mēṉi vāliyōṉ kōyilum*, Cil.5.171), thus having a snake as body appears here together with the temple of Indra and the temples of the great Lord (*periyōṉ*, i.e., Śiva), of the six-faced one (Murukaṉ) and of the blue deity (*nīla mēṉi neṭiyōṉ*, Kṛṣṇa). The temple of the white, bright, coiled body can safely be said to be a temple dedicated to Balarāma. The traditional iconography of Balarāma, the elder brother of Kṛṣṇa to which we will return, is one of a *nāga*, i.e., a multiheaded snake doubling a human figure by running along his back.

Such form presents many common traits with the one used to represent Nārāyaṇa in the Tamil land. The association between Balarāma with Nārāyaṇa himself is remarkably close and early: as we will see in more detail later, Balarāma is an embodiment of Nārāyaṇa according to textual sources; he was one of the first known representations in the sculpted tradition. Their association necessitates the mediation of Kṛṣṇa, and this deity is also duly mentioned in Canto 5, as the blue deity of the Pukār temples. How to distinguish Balarāma and Nārāyaṇa in this case? The white color that is typical of Balarāma is put forwards as distinctive and the reclining posture associated with the iconography of Nārāyaṇa is not mentioned. Their association necessitates the mediation of Kṛṣṇa, who is also duly mentioned in Canto 5, as the blue deity of the Pukār temples.

In canto 9, the temple of the "white snake-deity of Pukār" is again mentioned (*pukār veḷḷainākar tam kōṭṭam*, 9. 10). It appears in a list composed otherwise of deities typical of the Tamil land, namely the deity of the city of Pukār, Murukaṉ and Mācattaṉ, elements linked to a Vedic background, like the thunderbolt of Indra (to whom a temple is dedicated), and gods that can be considered pan-Indian, such as the sun and the moon.[36] Neither Śiva nor Viṣṇu appears in one of their usual forms in this passage and a Vaiṣṇava devotional strand is represented by Balarāma only.

---

36 The temple of the tree of the immortals and the temple of the Nirgrantha (the Jain deity) are also included in the list.

In canto 10, when Kaṇṇaki and Kōvalaṉ leave their native town of Pukār, they first circumscribe "the temple of the One having the color of sapphire (*maṇṇivaṇṇaṉ*) who rests in yogic sleep on the snake of beautiful lustre."[37] This Pukār temple is of a deity of contrasted colors, of a dark Lord sleeping on a luminous snake. In such a deity one can recognize the figure of Nārāyaṇa as praised in the *Tivyappirapantam.* The brilliance of the snake-part, however, points towards one specificity of Balarāma, to whom a temple was dedicated in Pukār.

In canto 11, when leaving "Araṅkam" (Śrīraṅgam), Kaṇṇaki and Kōvalaṉ met a Brahman who declares that he wants "to see with his own eyes" (l. 52–53):

> [The one who] like a blue cloud on a vast and golden Mountain,
> having expanded on milk, is stretched lying,
> the rare splendor possessing a head which has the capacity of being expanded into one thousand so it is praised and worshipped by many as the bed of sleep [or "as his half", *pāyal*],
> in the Kāviri of expanded waves, the vast, big, island,
> the reclining beauty of the Tiru-chested One.[38]

The precise object of the vision is not so clear. Two main elements seem equated with each other: a reclining deity whose head expands into a thousand and an island (*turutti*). But the island may as well be part of a comparison concerning only the bed or half of the deity as given in the last line of the passage. What is clear is that a deity lying on a snake provided with many (a thousand) heads is described and that this deity has two colors: a dark, cloud-colored part, and a golden, lus-

---

37 Cil. 10.9–10: *aṇi kiḻar araviṉ aṟituyil amarnta*
maṇivaṇṇaṉ kōṭṭam valam ceyāk kaḻintu.

38 Cil. 1.35–40: [...] *nīla mēkam neṭumpoṟ kuṉṟattup*
pālvirint(u) akal(am)ātu paṭintatu pōla
āyiram viritteḻu talaiyuṭai aruntiṟaṟ
pāyaṟ paḷḷip palartoḻu tētta
viritiraik kāviri viyaṉperu turuttit
tiruvamar mārpaṉ kiṭanta vaṇṇamum.

The Tamil word *pāyal* (*pāyar*) means "bedding, sleep" or "half". This may be an intended pun.

trous one, like the pattern already depicted in canto 10. This pattern is well attested in ancient Sanskrit texts where the "dark" Kṛṣṇa finds an ideal complement in the whiteness of his brother Balarāma. I assume Śrīraṅgam is being used to stress the complementarity of those two gods, united in the island's silhouette.

The deity lying on a snake of Śrīraṅgam is thus clearly acknowledged in the *Cilappatikāram*, where it is described along patterns of comparison encountered in earlier Sanskrit texts. Two deities are intrinsically linked to each other, in the double body of a reclining snake-deity, where the dark, human body of Kṛṣṇa is contrasted with the bright, multi-hooded *nāga,* who is Balarāma.

In canto 14, a temple of Balarāma in Maturai is mentioned. It is described as "the temple of the white one brandishing a plough" (*mēḻiv alaṉ uyartta veḷḷai nakaramum*, 14.9).[39] The plough is a characteristic attribute of this deity as much as the white is his color.

In additions to the mentions of the god having the world in his navel and the chanting of Nārāyaṇa already referred to, canto 17 contains several references to Balarāma as the elder, "Muṉṉai", who, white "as the moon" (*mati puraiyum*, 17.26), dances with Kṛṣṇa and the young female one "Piṉṉai" (see 17.14, 17, 26–28). But a snake form is not stated, while another snake deity of the Vaiṣṇava domain appears with the serpent Vāsuki used as a rope in the myth of the churning of the ocean (17.32).

In canto 26, in the book of Vañci, the Cēra capital, "the snake deity who bears the firm earth bows his head".[40] A little later in the same canto some pray to the deity "who resides in a yogic sleep at Ātakamāṭam".[41] In canto 30, the same temple is mentioned (l. 51, *āṭaka māṭat taravaṇaik kiṭantōṉ*). Today the deity of Ātakamāṭam is considered to be one of Trivandrum, a seashore deity sleeping on a snake-god.

---

[39] The plough is the characteristic attribute of Balarāma in texts; it is attested in archaeology as early as the Aï Khanoum coins dated to the 2[d] c. BCE (see *infra*, p. 119).

[40] Cil. 26.34: *uravu maṇ cumanta aravut talai paṇippa.*

[41] Cil. 26.62: *āṭakamāṭatt(u) aṟituyal amarntōṉ.*

Vaiṣṇava deities having snake-forms are thus rather common in the *Cilappatikāram*. They must be understood against the general background of other references in this text to Vaiṣṇava gods. In canto 6, three forms of Viṣṇu (Kṛṣṇa, "the deity who measured the earth", and the deity who fights Baṇa) are listed as dancers, together with Śiva, Kāmā, Durgā and some goddesses including Tiru (Lakṣmī), a warrior-like goddess, and Indra's wife. In canto 11, after a description of the snake-deity of "Turutti" (Śrīraṅgam), Neṭiyōṉ (a Tamil name for Viṣṇu as "the tall one") of Vēṅkaṭam is described, as holding a discus and a conch, having the color of clouds, and appearing on the peak of the hill (Cil. 11.41–42). In the same canto, a hill is described, that is said to be devoted to Tirumāl (l. 91). The description that follows mentions three holy ponds inside a cavern and the Cilampāru, a river that flows at the foot of the hill. This is identified as the Vaiṣṇava site of Tirumāliruñcōlai. There the devotee is to recite the *mantra*s of five and eight syllables (l. 128–129). The deity praised here has a decorated bird for a banner (l. 136). Later, in the same canto, the Lord of the high crown, who measured the whole earth, is mentioned (*nīḷ nilaṅ kaṭanta neṭumuṭi aṇṇal*). Canto12 is dedicated to the goddess. She is said to be Māl's (Viṣṇu's) sister (l. 68). In addition to the passages already cited, Kṛṣṇa and his younger consort Piṉṉai are consistently present in canto 17, where various feats of Kṛṣṇa are given (lifting the Govardhana mount, stealing butter, etc.) but also the churning of the ocean. At the beginning of canto 18 the leading devotee of the rituals celebrated in canto 17 goes to adore the feet of Neṭumāl, on the banks of the Vaiyai (the river that flows in Maturai). In canto 22 (l. 60), Neṭiyōṉ is used as a term of comparison for one of the four guardian-deities of Maturai. Several characteristics of another guardian-deity are the same as those of Balarāma's (plough, color of pure gold). The plough is among the characteristic attributes of still a third deity.[42] In canto 25, a river is compared to the garland on the chest of Neṭiyōṉ (l. 21).

---

42 Many lines of this canto do not appear in all manuscripts. They may therefore be considered as interpolated and I cite here only the lines appearing in all manuscripts (translated by Parthasarathy 2004: 196). Still, the lines that were probably interpolated may be relevant from a historical point of view. In these, the four guardian deities of Kūṭal (*kāval teyvam*) correspond to

In the Vaiṣṇava domain as portrayed in the *Cilappatikāram*, it is conspicuous that a great number of snake-deities appear. Moreover, in each city—after which are named the three books of the Epic, Pukār, Maturai and Vañci—there is a Vaiṣṇava snake form. The deity of Śrīraṅgam adds an important site to these three. The description of the god sleeping in the middle of the Kāvēri River is the longest of any Vaiṣṇava deity met in the text, save the one devoted to the deity of Vēṅkaṭam. At first glance, the significance of snake forms in the *Cilappatikāram* corresponds to that found in the *Tivyappirapantam*, where there are also numerous deities said to be reclining on a multi-hooded snake. Similarly, the prominence of the deities of Śrīraṅgam and Vēṅkaṭam in the *Cilappatikāram* is similar to what is found in the devotional anthology of which these two are the most important deities. Still, even if the correspondence between the name and the form of the reclining deity in canto 17 corresponds to what can be considered an important tendency of the *Tivyappirapantam*, this is the only passage in the whole epic where the name Nārāyaṇa is encountered. The names given to Vaiṣṇava deities are diverse (Tirumāl, Neṭiyōṉ, Neṭumāl, Māyavaṉ, and also formulas like *uvaṇac cēval uyarttōṉ*, the one having a *garuḍa* for mount, etc.) but Nārāyaṇa is not common. This name to be chanted is not attached to any of the Vaiṣṇava deities associated with precise sites, nor does it appear in precise circumstances, with the exception, perhaps, of the hill near Maturai where a *mantra* of eight syllables must be recited. How the link between these two (name and form) was established, and whether such a link was important in the period of the composition of

---

four different modes of life: Brahmins, warriors (the one compared to Neṭiyōṉ), merchant-class and t farmers. The last two deities are much less clear than the first two. The third one holds the plough and is clearly stated being the deity of the farmlands. Still, this god also holds a scale, is said to be the god of the merchants and is compared to the god having the moon in his coiffure (Śiva). The fourth deity is of the farmers, also holds a plough and is connected to agricultural work. The third and the fourth deities of this group are redundant in numerous ways and both can be associated with Balarāma, but Balarāma's characteristic being white is attributed only to the third god. The group does not correspond to the one given elsewhere (and later) as an explanation of the ancient name of *nāṉmaṭakūṭal* for the city, see Gros 1968: xxvii–xxix, Hardy 1983: 236–237, see also *infra*, fn. 112.

the *Cilappatikāram* is unclear. On another hand, Balarāma the plough bearer is one of the prominent snake deities of the *Cilappatikāram*. Indeed, he is much more present than would be expected after reviewing the *Tivyappirapantam*.

The archaeology of the Vaiṣṇava sites in the Tamil country helps clarifying the matter. It confirms the antiquity of specific snake deities in the Tamil land suggested by the *Cilappatikāram* and the *Tivyappirapantam*. It may allow one to outline how these were linked with Nārāyaṇa, as a name and concept.

Archaeology of reclining deities in the Tamil Country

The literary descriptions of the deity of Śrīraṅgam presented in the *Cilappatikāram* and the *Tivyappirapantam* often emphasize natural settings which imbue the image with a sort of self-manifested (*svayambhu*) character. A similar physical correspondence is also noticeable in the earliest known South Indian shrines of Vaiṣṇava deities. A vast majority of them is consecrated to reclining deities [fig. 3 and 4].[43] The rock-cut Vaiṣṇava deity in the Shore Temple of Mahābalipuram was originally surrounded by the waving sea,[44] as is clearly indicated by its

---

43 For surveys of these images see Soundara Rajan 1967, Champakalakshmi 1981: 66–79, and Parimoo 1983. The gigantic reclining god of the site of Uṇḍavaḷḷi in Andhra Pradesh (close to Vijayawada) was probably carved before the sculptures found in Tamil Nadu but its date is debated (6 th–7th c.). This much damaged sculpture has been reworked in stucco and it is today difficult to be sure of the original iconography. Still, this rock-cut piece is situated in a cave and seems to share many of the characteristics with images of the Tamil land produced from the 8th or 9th century, like the two arms of the main deity and the many secondary characters waging war against Madhu and Kaiṭabha.

44 Another deity lying on a snake has also been carved in the 7th century at the same site, Mahābalipuram, but, considering its present position, on a side wall of a cave, it was probably not a cult-image, or not the main cult-image of the so-called Mahiṣamardinī cave where it is located.

location as well as by texts, both in Sanskrit and Tamil.[45] The deity of the temple of Veḵka in Kāñcīpuram lies in the water of a river, already referred to in a Caṅkam work, the *Perumpāṇāṟṟupaṭai* as well as in the *Tivyappirapantam*.[46] The deity of Trivandrum worshipped today along the sea might be the one of the Cēra country mentioned in the *Cilappatikāram*.[47] At these four sites, I think that real water was part of the representation: the cyclic floods of the rivers in Śrīraṅgam and Veḵka, the tides of the sea in Mahābalipuram and Trivandrum were used to enact the phenomenon of destruction and creation that shapes the mythology of the deity reclining on a snake [fig. scenery 2].

The reclining deity of Pukār mentioned in the *Cilappatikāram* may have been similar since the city stood on the mouth of a river. Archaeologically, the original site of Pukār has not been located precisely enough to say more about this deity however. The situation is quite the

---

45 See the poem of Tirumaṅkaiyāḻvār (Tiv. 1088–1107) on the deity reclining on earth (*talacayaṉaṉ*), in Kaṭalmallai, the "sea-richness" that is Mahābalipuram. I consider this hymn (end of the 8th c.–beginning of the 9th?) as a testimony to the specificity of the iconography of the image when calling the deity "the one reclining on the earth". The snake part does not appear here. This unusual characteristic would have been acknowledged by the poet, who reminds the devotee of the presence of the sea with the formula *kaṭalmallai talacayaṉaṉ*, the one reclining on the earth in the sea-richness. In a Sanskrit work attributed to Daṇḍin (8th–9th c.?), the Avantisundarīkathā, a carving of Viṣṇu reclining on a snake (*bhujaga-vara-śayanam-anugṛhṇataḥ*, l. 13 on p. 13 in the edition of K.S. Mahādeva Śāstrī) situated in Mahāmallapuram is said to have its lotus-feet brushed by the sea (*uru-taraṅga-hasta-saṃvāhyamāna-pāda-paṅkajasyormi-mālino*; see also l. 19 on p. 14 where the body of the god is beaten by the waves). This text may be much later than often accounted for and this testimony may have nothing to do with the image of the Shore Temple—where no snake is represented contrary, to what is said in the description in this text. Still, the mention of the waves of the sea attests to the ocean being known in medieval times in the representation of a reclining Viṣṇu in Mahābalipuram, be it that of the Shore Temple or another one at the same site; on the later possibility, see Francis 2009: 356–359, fn. 200; for the use of the waters of the sea in the scenery, see Smith 1996.

46 See Champakalakshmi 1981: 38.

47 See Champakalakshmi 1981: 37–39.

same for Maturai. The references in the *Cilappatikāram* to a temple dedicated to a snake-deity are rather vague, while the archaeology of what is today a bustling city—one that has for long been an epicenter of Tamil literature—is difficult to handle. I will take a closer look at this in the last part of this paper.

Still, archaeology has uncovered information at several other sites where, carved directly in bedrock, Vaiṣṇava icons attest to an early arrangement with nearby surroundings which may have been sought out specifically.[48] In the Vaiṣṇava rock-cut shrines of Malayatipaṭṭi [fig. 4] and Tirumayam, located south of the delta of the Kāvēri, of Ciṅkavaram some one hundred kilometres south of Kāñcīpuram, on a boulder in Toṇṭūr in the same area [fig. 3], and in one of the caves of Nāmakkal, in the heart of contemporary Tamil Nadu, huge cult-images of deities reclining on a multi-hooded snake were carved during the 7th–9th century.

Together with the deity of the Shore Temple, from an archaeological point of view these sites constitute the core of the most ancient known Vaiṣṇava cult-sites in the Tamil land.[49]

48 There is an element of chance in the fact that today we know many ancient rock-cut images of Vaiṣṇava deities. Once carved out of a rock, such idols lasted many more centuries than other types of representations. Still, a comparison with contemporary and geographical close-by Śaiva sites reveals the importance of the link with the soil. The first *liṅga*s in the Tamil country were not rock-cut, even inside caves of the same age than the Vaiṣṇava deities under examination. In contradistinction, the early Vaiṣṇava cult-images of reclining forms can be rock-cut even outside caves. Most of them are huge works with dimensions larger than any other carving known from the same period of time. Moreover, as already mentioned, at several sites water is part of the representation. In Mahābalipuram other natural elements were used for at least one other representation, the one of Kṛṣṇa lifting the Govardhana mount.

49 Temples housing other types of cult-images of Viṣṇu dated to the same period are scarce. Most are situated in sites where a contemporaneous reclining form was located. Examples are the built temple of the Vaikuṇṭhaperumāḷ of Kāñcīpuram, several cave temples and one built temple in or near the site of Mahābalipuram. A standing Viṣṇu from the Pallava period was discovered close to Mahābalipuram at Ciṟutavūr; see Francis/Gillet/Schmid 2003: 438–441.

With the exception of the icon in the Viṣṇu shrine of the Shore Temple, to which I will return below, the iconography of these early representations of the Tamil land is quite homogeneous. Like the present-day icon of Śrīraṅgam, these images consist of a human body with two arms lying on a snake that has five or seven heads. The proper right arm of the human part of the deity is stretched to the head. The deity does not hold attributes. In the caves, the deity is surrounded by several other figures carved in relief on the back and side walls around the main icon. Those sculpted at Nāmakkal are identified in a Sanskrit inscription engraved on a beam above the image.[50] Such figures provide a narrative background, developed in Epic and Purāṇic texts, and alluded to in the devotional *Tivyappirapantam* or the Jain *Cilappatikāram*.[51] The two demons, Madhu and Kaiṭabha, are the major opponents of the reclining form of the god in the texts and are the most common figures in the sculptures.[52] A fierce combat is depicted. Still, the sculptural tradition presents the main deity as quietly sleeping on a snake-bed, leaving the other characters to enliven the stage.

Thus, according to both texts and material testimony, the deity reclining on a snake was the main early Vaiṣṇava form in the Tamil land, often involving the use of natural settings. The Lord of Śrīraṅgam was also of this type, situated opposite the ancient Cōḻa capital of Uṟaiyūr.[53]

---

50 See Srinivasan/Srinivasan 1965; Champakalakshmi 1981: 72.

51 Kālidāsa also mentions some of them when evoking Viṣṇu about to incarnate as Rāma in the tenth canto of the *Raghuvaṃśa*.

52 These secondary characters are also found with the reclining deity of the so-called Mahiṣamardinī cave relief in Mahābalipuram (see *supra*, fn. 44) as well as, it seems, the deity carved in the Andhra cave of Uṇḍavaḷḷi (see *supra*, fn. 43) also presents. The latter may be more ancient than the other carvings under consideration here.

53 Kōvalaṉ and Kaṇṇaki go to the temple of the Jain ascetics close to Śrīraṅgam before leaving Uṟaiyūr (Cil. 11.5–9). Maybe the Sanskrit name Uragapura, the "City of the Snake" given to a city situated in the southern bank of the Kāvēri in the Cāḷukya tablets of Gadval, dated 674 (see Hultzsch 1910, *Epigraphia Indica* 10.22) refers to Uṟaiyūr; see also Hari Rao 1976: 15. If this is the case, this name echoes the importance of snake deities in

The name "Araṅkam" given to this place in the *Cilappatikāram* also appears in a poem of the *Akanāṉūṟu*, one of the earliest anthologies of Caṅkam literature.[54] This is the "scene", from Sanskrit *raṅga*, where a flood-festival takes place. In the Vaiṣṇava tradition, the scene is this world, where Viṣṇu-Nārāyaṇa manifests himself whereas the deity is the scene's master, *nātha*. These two functions are both apparent in the common designation of the deity of Śrīraṅgam in the *Tivyappirapantam* and in inscriptions as "Raṅga-nātha."[55] This name is also used for other reclining Vaiṣṇava deities in Tamil country, but perhaps as an echo of the Śrīraṅgam deity. The site of Śrīraṅgam weaves a specific form, a sacred stage and a specific landscape together with several texts. In my view, it is the form embedded in a site that constitutes the earliest and the main element of the devotion here, to be connected with the importance of what can be defined as the *bhakti* of the place in the *Tivyappirapantam.*

The form of the reclining Viṣṇu-Nārāyaṇa did not originate in "Araṅkam" but came from North India. Thus, the process of adaptation to the local religious landscape can be delineated quite precisely. The earliest known Vaiṣṇava cult-image in the Tamil land is plausibly the reclining god of the Shore Temple [fig. 5]. This form seems exceptional: the deity is provided with four arms, no snake is represented, and the sea-water was the couch of the deity.[56]

Although the absence of the snake and the addition of arms are puzzling in the south of the Peninsula, they match with North Indian traditions available to us through Sanskrit texts on the one hand, and with North Indian carvings on the other.

---

the area. However, there are other cities identified with Uragapura, such as Maturai and Nāgappaṭṭanam.

[54] *Akanāṉūṟu* 137, see Hari Rao 1976: 24.

[55] This name of the deity of Śrīraṅgam appears in the Sanskrit portion of the bilingual (Sanskrit and Tamil) plates of Aṉpil, dated 959–960.

[56] It can also be supposed that elements made of perishable material originally augmented the image. In the caves south of the Kāvēri, many elements are depicted in stucco on the interior back walls of the cult-cells. The image of Śrīraṅgam is also made of stucco.

Earliest images of deities reclining on snakes: North and Central India

The earliest sculptures of a deity reclining on a snake belong to sites of North and Central India. Those provide a range of representations being the first known of their kind. Examples are found at Bhītargāon, Udayagiri, Deogaḍh and Sultānganj, where a deity reclines on a multi-headed snake. A blooming lotus opens above him. The Brahmā seated on this flower and the reclining posture allow for these sculptures to be safely identified as the one called Nārāyaṇa, the creator aspect of Viṣṇu.

In the brick temple of Bhītargāon (Uttar Pradesh; Kanpur district), the god was depicted on a terracotta panel, half-seated without any supplementary arm.[57] A stem comes out of his navel. On its blooming flower, a one-headed Brahmā is represented. To his side the two demons Madhu and Kaiṭabha, each holding a mace, have been modeled.

Some two hundred kilometres further south, at the site of Udayagiri (Madhya Pradesh, some sixty kilometres north-east of Bhopal), the Vaiṣṇava deity reclining on a snake has been cut directly into the rock and is adapted to the physical characteristics of the site. The stretched-out deity fits the narrow corridor where it is sculpted.[58] Although it is damaged, we can safely assume that the reclining god had four arms, and that the supplementary right arm was stretched to be placed very close to the head of the anthropomorphic body. The image is too worn to be certain the god hold attributes, but it is probable that he did not, since weapons are represented as independent figures (*āyudhapuruṣa*)

---

57 On this temple, see Zaheer 1981. The panel is now in the Indian Museum of Calcutta; the description given in Zaheer (1981: 93–94) is quite accurate. It is difficult to be precise about its date. It may be contemporary to the other sculptures mentioned here but it could also be slightly earlier or later (on the date of the temple itself, see Zaheer 1981: 160–163). The fact that Brahmā has only one head here speaks in favour of an early date and Williams 1982: 82–84 also inclines towards an early date for this temple.

58 According to Willis (2009: 30–37), rain was also part of the rituals celebrated in connection with the reclining Viṣṇu. This is another element linking this sculpture with the early South Indian Vaiṣṇava sites.

above the lying deity. This image is dated to the beginning of the 5th century.[59]

More than a hundred kilometres to the north of Udayagiri, the deity carved on an exterior wall of the Vaiṣṇava structural temple of Deogaḍh is in better condition. It is dated to the first half of the 6th century,[60] rather close in time to the Mahābalipuram site in South India. In this case it is certain that the four-armed human body reclining on a seven-headed snake does not hold attributes (that are represented as *āyudhapuruṣa* below him). The god is relaxed, his half-closed eyes turned towards the viewer.

This is a well-known image, considered as one of the first representations of Nārāyaṇa. However, the originality of the carved panel of Deogaḍh is far from being acknowledged; the lotus where Brahmā is seated does not come from the navel of the human figure as in the other known examples but from the coils of the serpent. This makes the snake-part of the deity the main actor in the process of creation.

The last sculpture to be mentioned here is found much further east, at the site of Sultānganj located in the present-day Bihar (Bhāgalpur district).[61] Sculpted directly into a rock along a river whose water laps the deity's feet as in some of the South Indian sites; this Viṣṇu reclining on Śeṣa has four arms and holds a rosary and a conch. A one-faced Brahmā is seated on the lotus issuing from the navel of the human part of the deity. The carving is dated between the end of the 5th and the end of the 6th century. With a one-faced Brahmā and a rosary held by the main deity, it illustrates the variety of the iconography of the reclining form when it was first conceived.

While the god may be two- or four-armed, hold this or that attribute or hold none, the figure of Brahmā have one or four faces, and the secondary characters vary, a multi-headed snake is present in all four works, always depicted as the form on which the human body lies. This is testimony to the importance of this element in the sculptural tradition.

---

[59] See Williams 1982: 42–47.

[60] See Williams 1982: 131–137.

[61] See Sachchidanand 1967 and Asher 1980: 30–31.

These four sculptures were carved in a territory where inscriptions dated in Gupta era are found to praise a deity lying on the ocean. But these epigraphs never refer to the snake part of the Lord. For instance, the second verse of the Valkhā copper-plates discovered near Bagh more than a hundred kilometers to the south-west of Indore in Madhya Pradesh (4th c.?) reads as follows:

> [To Viṣṇu] who reclines upon the wide and spotless couch that is the unique ocean (*ekārṇava*), whose sleep (*nidrā*) is praised in song by the bees of the lotus born of his navel.[62]

The first verse of a stone inscription at Maṇḍasor (two hundred kilometers to the north of Bagh), dated to 404-405 CE, gives a similar picture:

> Obeisance to that Thousand-Headed Puruṣa whose soul is boundless and who sleeps on the waters of the bed-like four oceans [...].[63]

Likewise, there is no mention of a snake in any Gupta-period epigraphs evoking a reclining Viṣṇu. However, if one keeps these inscriptions in mind while "reading" the carvings, it is possible to understand the snake as a representation of waters. An alternative exercise would be to visualize the deities in the epigraphs with the sculptures in mind. When doing so, the snake body of the depicted god becomes apparent. Such exercises may sound theoretical, but they could account for the differences in documents produced contemporaneously in a culturally consistent area. Texts and sculpted tradition would define their own sphere separately but would be related to the same concept.

When one turns towards South India, the situation is more confusing however. If the snake represents waters, what are the real waters of many of the South Indian sites—starting with the Shore Temple of Ma-

---

62 See Ramesh/Tewari 1990: 1–3. These plates were discovered near Bagh; they may be dated to the 4th century CE. In one of the plates a temple to Nārāyaṇadeva is mentioned. These copper-plates are discussed in Willis 2009: 70–73.

63 Transl. by Bhandarkar 1981: 265. See Bhandarkar 1981: 261–266 for a presentation, the text and a translation of this inscription. R.G. Bhandarkar also commented on it in the introduction (pp. 125–127) where this author cites a verse giving the etymology of Nārāyaṇa (Mbh 3.187.3, see *supra*, fn. 14) to prove the identification of Viṣṇu with Nārāyaṇa.

hābalipuram—intended to be? A closer look at the encounters between texts and sculpted tradition allows the deity of the Shore Temple to be placed into a continuum, while pointing towards distinct strands within the process of transmission from North to South India.

Texts and the sculptural tradition

It must first be kept in mind that the archaeological testimonies of the Gupta territory attest the establishment of a religious tradition in which a Vaishnava deity emerged as a supreme Lord, regardless of which deities preceded this major figure and be incorporated into him. In this tradition, the creator god is represented under the form of a lying snake-deity.

Secondly, the inscriptions of the Gupta period are not the only texts that do not mention a snake when praising a reclining deity. In the epic and Purāṇic literature, the creator god of the Vaiṣṇava tradition is said to be lying on the waters of the ocean but mention of a snake seldom occurs. As mentioned at the beginning of this paper, the traditional etymology of "Nārāyaṇa" emphasizes the connection of the deity with the waters:

> The waters are called *nāras*: I gave them the name; therefore, I am called Nārāyaṇa, for the waters are my course.[64]

If depictions of this verse in stone resulted into a reclining snake-deity from the 5th century, texts seem to have followed their own tradition, a tradition in which a snake does not fit. One of the very few times the snake is mentioned is in the same book 3 of the *Mahābhārata*:

---

64 Mbh 3.187.3; transl. by van Buitenen 1981: 591. See *supra*, fn. 15 for the text; see also the explanation given in the *Nārāyaṇīya-parvan*: "Eternal as I am, I am the one sole Refuge of all men. The waters have been called by the name of 'Nārā', for they originated from Him called 'Nara'. And since the waters, in former times, were my refuge, I am, therefore, called by the name Nārāyaṇa" (*narāṇām ayanaṃ khyātam aham ekaḥ sanātanaḥ* | *āpo nārā iti proktā āpo vai narasūnavaḥ* | *ayanaṃ mama tat pūrvam ato nārāyaṇo hy aham* || Mbh 12.328.35).

> The blessed Viṣṇu, the everlasting source of all creatures, the eternal Person, slept solitarily on his ocean bed in the vast coil of the boundlessly puissant snake Śeṣa.[65]

The deity sleeps *in* the coils of the snake and *on* the ocean. The intricacy of the three combined elements of ocean, snake, and deity, is quite peculiar. Similarly, in the *Nārāyaṇīya-parvan* of the *Mahābhārata* in which Nārāyaṇa is the supreme deity, associated in many ways with the ocean of milk, there is only one mention of the snake on which the deity reclines (12.335.58).[66] The astonishment of Madhu and Kaiṭabha seems appropriate, leading them to then ask: "Why is he sleeping provided with coils?" (*eṣa kiṃ ca svapiti bhogavān* Mbh 12.358.61d). Indeed, what is the link between the coils of a snake and the supreme deity? The *Nārāyaṇīya-parvan* presents many forms of Nārāyaṇa. Several mentions of a horse-headed figure as well as the boar form—both of which belonging to the sculptural tradition—are encountered a number of times.[67] But the snake-part of the reclining deity does not appear to be entirely comprehensible.

In the slightly later *Harivaṃśa*, the association of Nārāyaṇa with a figure reclining on a snake is a complex issue. In canto 31, which presents the different manifestations of Viṣṇu, the fight against Madhu and Kaiṭabha is part to a mysterious manifestation of the lotus; no deity lying on a snake appears.[68] Similarly, in canto 42, where the fight be-

---

[65] Mbh 3.194.9; trans. by van Buitenen 1981: 611. *prabhavaḥ sarvabhūtānāṁ śāśvataḥ puruṣo 'vyayaḥ | suṣvāpa bhagavān viṣṇur apśayyām eka eva ha | nāgasya bhoge mahati śeṣasyāmitatejasaḥ.*

[66] Mbh 12.335.58: "Highly effulgent and imbued with the pure quality of Goodness, the body of the Supreme Lord lies on the excellent hood of a snake that seemed to throw out flames of fire for the resplendence attached to it." *ātmapramāṇaracite apām upari kalpite | śayane nāgabhogāḍhye jvālāmālāsamāvṛte.*

[67] In the Tamil region, a horse-headed form of Nārāyāṇa has been carved on the 8th c. Pallava temple of the Vaikuṇṭha Perumāḷ in Kāñcīpuram.

[68] This manifestation appears in two other passages of the *Harivaṃśa*. It is expanded in one of the appendices of the critical edition (as are also other manifestations of Viṣṇu) and has been examined extensively in Couture 2007.

tween Nārāyaṇa and the two demons is narrated, no snake-bed is mentioned. While this does not prevent snake-forms to appear elsewhere in the text, usually their association with the supreme deity (called Nārāyaṇa) necessitates the mediation of the elder brother of Kṛṣṇa, to whom I will return in a moment. Finally, the *Viṣṇupurāṇa* quotes the famous verse giving the etymology of the name of Nārāyaṇa (*Viṣṇupurāṇa* 1.4.6), but there are no more snake bodies in this text than in the Gupta-period inscriptions.

Nor is the snake form recorded in the most ancient southern epigraphy. The name "Nārāyaṇa" is met in one of the first inscriptions of the Pallavas, found in Andhra Pradesh, where donations are made to Nārāyaṇa.[69] Then, the royal eulogies, the Sanskrit Pallava corpus located in the northern part of the Tamil Nadu (6th–9th) knows the supreme creator god as a deity sleeping on the ocean of milk.[70] The inscriptions found in the Pāṇḍya territory (7th–9th) present a similar picture. To Nārāyaṇa a grant is made in a stone inscription,[71] while in the metal tablets, Nārāyaṇa is a creator god.[72]

In none of these epigraphs is the snake-part of the deity being alluded to. However, in the same period of time, the inscription of Nāmakkal lists a good number of characters associated with the myth of the reclining deity.[73] And the image of the Shore Temple of Mahābalipuram turns out to be an integral, matching part of these Sanskrit texts in the

---

[69] See the 4th century *prākṛt* tablets of Carudevī, Mahalingam 1988, No. 4. Nārāyaṇa is also the name given to a god in a Tamil inscription in the North Arcot district, dated using a Pallava regnal year (of about the end of the 9th c.), see Mahalingam 1988, No. 228.

[70] See, e.g., the tablets of Rāyakōṭa, st. 1. Viṣṇu is the mythical ancestor of the Pallavas and as such appears in many inscriptions recording the mythical genealogy of the dynasty. The deity is then the one from which a lotus springs (plates of Paḷḷāṅkōyil [6th c.] and of Kasakkudi [mid-8th c.]). In the first two stanzas of the Paṭṭattālmaṅgalam plates (end of the 8th century) the deity lying on the ocean is beautifully described.

[71] See, e.g., Krishnan 2002, No. 75.

[72] See the tablets of Śrīvaramaṅgalam, Krishnan 2002, No 11.

[73] See *supra*, fn. 50.

Tamil land. Since the god lies on the ocean itself, a snake bed needs not to be represented. From the 9th century the picture becomes clearer with various bilingual inscriptions. In the two languages then used, Sanskrit and Tamil, the contrast is similar to the one encountered between texts and carvings in North India.

In the Taḷavāypuram plates (dated 910 CE),[74] we find two mythological accounts of the Pāṇḍya dynasty. The first is in Sanskrit. The creator god from whom everything came, including the line of the Pāṇḍyas, is called "Nārāyaṇa". Brahmā appears on the lotus of Nārāyaṇa, engaged in reciting the Vedas. No snake is mentioned. But in the Tamil eulogy that follows, the deity is described, with Sanskrit terms, as the one lying on "the high bed" called "serpent who is the Lord of other serpents".[75]

With these two preambles, the equivalence is clearly stated. Nārāyaṇa is the creator god of Sanskrit texts. In Tamil, he is represented as a deity lying on a snake, as in contemporary sculptures from the Tamil area. The Tamil part of the epigraph is rather close to some poems of the devotional *Tivyappirapantam* in asserting these points. Carvings appear to reference this case. From a visual point of view, the creator god carved in North and Central India is indeed a reclining *nāga*. The ancient iconography of the latter category of deities, where a multi or single hooded snake is superimposed on a human body, has been used in the creation of an image of the deity lying on an ocean. The early *nāgas* are standing deities. The first known representations of Viṣṇu as a creator are reclining *nāgas*.

However, because they are four-handed, the latter *nāgas* are peculiar. In their representations, the traditional iconography of a *nāga* with two arms is associated with the shape of a four-armed deity. As I have shown elsewhere, such a figure combines the earlier representations of Balarāma and Kṛṣṇa.[76] The iconography of Balarāma was the main mold in this case and if the importance of Kṛṣṇa in the formation of

---

74 Found in the Tirunelvēli district; see Krishnan 2002, No 61.

75 l. 68–69, *bhujamgama purassarabhogi eṉṉum poṅk' aṇai*, text: Krishnan 2002: 74.

76 See Schmid 2010: 255–313.

Viṣṇuism becomes more and more acknowledged, the importance of Balarāma will be less studied.

Balarāma and Nārāyaṇa

My contention is that the material of the Tamil country provides another clue regarding the significant position once held by the deity Balarāma (Saṃkarṣaṇa) in Vaiṣṇava traditions, a significance visible in earlier data, of North Indian origin.

The elder brother of Kṛṣṇa proved to be an important deity from the 2nd BC until at least the 4th CE in a vast area covering the Gangetic plain but also expanding farther. Kṛṣṇa and Balarāma are found as a pair in various records, including archaeological finds like the famous coins from Aï Khanoum, and texts like *sūtra*s of Patañjali, the *Mahābhārata* and the *Harivaṃśa*.[77] In the Ghosūṇḍi and Hāthibāḍā epigraphs, found close to each other in the present-day Rājasthan and dated to the 1st BC, this pair is associated with Nārāyaṇa.[78] In the sculptural tradition of the first three centuries of the Common Era, Kṛṣṇa and Balarāma are the most visible forms of those deities appearing in the *Mahābhāra-*

---

[77] See the commentary of Patañjali *ad sūtra* 2.2.24 of Pāṇini, where the desire is expressed that the power of Saṃkarṣaṇa the second part of Kṛṣṇa or his double increase with that of Kṛṣṇa (*saṃkarṣaṇadvitīyasya balaṃ kṛṣṇasya vardhatām*). *Harivaṃśa* 51.2–5 is emblematic; here it reads that the two boys moved together as one (*anyonyagatau*); that from their childhood, they had only one body (*bālyād evaikatāṃ gatau*) and one mind (*ekamantradharau*); that the two were from a unique model (*eka-nirmāṇa-niryuktāu*), shared the same bed, seat and food; that both did the same thing (*ekakāryāntaragatāu*). Finally, they appeared as if one body was divided into two parts (*ekadehau dvidhā kṛtau*) and for people these two were living the childhood of a unique being.

[78] These inscriptions are two different copies of a same text. They have been published and commented on often (see Schmid 2010: 84–87). The text speaks of an "enclosing wall [round] the stone object of worship" (*pūjāśilāprākāro*), called "Nārāyaṇavāṭakā", for the two divinities Saṃkarṣaṇa-Vāsudeva (*bhagavadbhyāṃ saṃkarṣaṇavāsudevābhyāṃ*), built by a king who is referred to as *bhāgavata* and who was celebrating an *aśvamedha*.

ta. Few others were represented in sculptural form. I would claim that carved representations of Kṛṣṇa and Balarāma were the icons corresponding to what is called early Bhāgavatism since they figure prominently in these rare materials that are the earliest testimonies to this movement.[79]

During this early period, Balarāma underwent a considerable iconographic evolution becoming represented mainly as a *nāga*, stretching his right arm with an open palm above his head (see figs 6 and 7).[80] When different forms of Viṣṇu appeared in inscriptions, from the 4th century CE, and the theory of the various manifestations of this deity was developed in texts and sculpture, the iconography of Viṣṇu was inspired by the earlier iconography of both Kṛṣṇa and Balarāma. That Balarāma was the model of the deity reclining on a snake is enlightened by the three following passages of the *Harivaṃśa*.[81]

The description in canto 40 of Brahmā's abode or the "divine sanctuary of Nārāyaṇa" (*divyaṃ nārāyaṇāśramam*, *Harivaṃśa* 40.1d), "famous because of his name" (*svena nāmnā parijñātaṃ*, *Harivaṃśa* 40.3) is the first relevant passage. This is the deity's "own abode, similar to the ocean" (*sa tatrāmbupatiprakhyaṃ dadarśālayam ātmanaḥ* *Harivaṃśa* 40.4ab), where "he took his thousand-headed form, binding his chignon of matted hair, and walked towards his couch" (*Harivaṃśa* 40.7):[82]

---

[79] On early Bhagavatism, see Colas 2003, who, however, states that he uses mainly texts and, thus, does not cover the sculptural tradition.

[80] See Schmid 2010: 268–284.

[81] The manifestation of the lotus that is mentioned before all the other manifestations in the canto 31 of the critical edition and developed in its appendix I.41, should also be noted. There Nārāyaṇa sleeping on the ocean is also prominently mentioned, see Couture 2007.

[82] *Harivaṃśa* 40.7:
sa tatra praviśann eva jaṭābhāraṃ samudvahan |
sa sahasraśirā bhūtvā śayanāyopacakrame ||.

> Hari, the foremost of those observants of vows, was lying on a divine couch, cooled by the clouds and by the ocean, engaged in the *ekārṇava* (unique-ocean) vow.[83]

This text corresponds to the inscriptions of the Gupta period. The deity lies on a couch, in a unique ocean, *ekārṇava*, which is also mentioned in the Maṇḍasor inscription. He has one thousand heads. As in the Purāṇas and the sculpturl tradition the gods turn to this Lord for assistance; he is the source of the manifestations of the deity.

Canto 58 links this deity to Balarāma. Kṛṣṇa raises the spirits of Balarāma (who shall fight against a demon), saying:

> Remember that you are the body itself of the worlds at the time of dissolution; know what you become when the oceans become one.
> Remember that your original form is the cause of ancient gods, Brahmā and water; [remember] also your own features and splendour.[84]

This discourse echoes the traditional definition of Nārāyaṇa as the embodiment of waters and thus matches the *Tivyappirapantam* vision of a deity who is "the substance of water". One variant recorded in numerous manuscripts confirms the bond between Balarāma and Nārāyaṇa, since the expression "the body itself of the worlds" is replaced by the name Nārāyaṇa: "Remember that you are Nārāyaṇa Himself [his body] (*nārāyaṇātmāṇam)* at the time of dissolution...".[85] One is the substitute for the other.

---

83 *Harivaṃśa* 40.9:
sa śiśye śayane divye samudrāmbhodaśītale |
harir ekārṇavoktena vratena vratināṃ varaḥ ||.
The translations here given are based on the French translation of A. Couture (1991).

84 *Harivaṃśa* 58.36–37:
smarārya tanum ātmānam lokānāṃ tvaṃ viparyaye |
avagacchātmanātmānam samudrāṇāṃ samāgame ||
purātanānāṃ devanāṃ brahmaṇaḥ salilasya ca |
ātmavṛttapravṛttāni saṃsmarādyaṃ ca vai vapuḥ ||.

85 *Harivaṃśa* 58.36ab: *smara nārāyaṇātmāṇam lokānāṃ tvaṃ viparyaye* | [...].

Canto 70 gives a clear picture of the relation between the reclining deity and Balarāma. When on his way to Mathurā, Akrūra, a devotee of Kṛṣṇa, plunges into the waters of the Yamunā River, saying:

> I will worship the Lord of serpents, the Lord of all worlds, in this lake of Yamunā, with the chanting of the divine *bhāgavata mantra*s.
> I bow in front of this snake whose heads are adorned with auspicious *svastika* marks, having a thousand heads, the god Ananta, dressed in black.
> [...]
> In the middle [of the *sarpaloka*], with a thousand heads, with a banner of a golden palm leaf, carrying a plough in one hand and a pestle (*musala*) near his belly,
> dressed in black, of white complexion, with a white face, wearing one earring, intoxicated (*matta*), sleeping (*supta*), seated on the white seat of his own serpentine body.[86]

Then Akrūra

> saw the killer of enemies with his long arms smeared with paste of red sandal, the one with a lotus flower from his navel, with white complexion, attractive with his effulgence,
> the king of serpents, the Lord of the Ekārṇava, the powerful one worshipped by great snakes such as Vāsuki.[87]

These verses mention all the iconographic markers of Balarāma, palm tree, plough, pestle, the unique earring, the white complexion, as well as his appearance as a snake as indicated by the mention of a thousand

---

[86] *Harivaṃśa* 70.17–18: *yamunāyā hrade hy asmin* | *toṣyāmi bhujageśvaram* | *divyair bhāgavatair mantraiḥ* | *sarvalokaprabhuṃ yataḥ* || *śrīmatsvastikamūrdhānaṃ* | *praṇamiṣyāmi bhoginam* | *sahasraśirasaṃ devam* | *anantaṃ nīlavāsasam* || *Harivaṃśa* 70.10–11. [...] *tasya madhye sahasrāsyam* | *hematālocchritadhvajam* | *lāṅgalāsaktahastāgram musalāpāśritodaram* || *asitāmbarasaṃvītam* | *pāṇḍuraṃ pāṇḍurānanam* | *kuṇḍalaikadharaṃ mattam* | *suptam amburuhekṣaṇam* ||. On this passage, see Couture 1986.

[87] *Harivaṃśa* 70.21–22: *raktacandanadigdhāṅgam* | *dīrghabāhum ariṃdamam* | *padmanābhaṃ sitābhrābham* | *bhābhir jvalitatejasam* || *dadarśa bhogināṃ nātham* | *sthitam ekārṇaveśvaram* | *pūjyamānaṃ dvijihvendrair* | *vāsukipramukhaiḥ prabhum* ||. It is also worth looking at the whole canto 70 in which other verses would be relevant; see more specifically 70.19–20 in between the two citations given here.

heads, the serpentine body, etc. Balarāma is the sleeping one who has a lotus flower issuing from his navel; he is the Lord of the *ekārṇava*, the unique ocean.

Such visualizations seem to me to record cult tendencies similar to the one that has inspired the representation of the Deogaḍh temple, where the lotus springs directly from the coils of the snake. Balarāma as a snake-deity was himself considered—at least by some devotees, and in a few different contexts—as the form of the divine creator or Nārāyaṇa. In *Harivaṃśa* 38, the *asura* Kālanemi plans to kill Nārāyaṇa. For him this deity is "Viṣṇu for the gods; Vaikuṇṭha for the celestials; Ananta for the snakes who live in water." In other words, the same deity can be seen from one's own devotional perspective. But indicating a specific devotional perspective is not easily done in carvings. Having made the lotus of the creation rise out the snake coils is, I think, the way chosen in Deogaḍh to denote a specific perspective, one in which the snake part of the deity is given special importance.

These materials place the focus on Balarāma. In North India he was the first Vaiṣṇava snake deity represented in the early period before the 5th century, a time when the emergence of the classical Hindu Viṣṇu is documented.[88] The importance of this specific snake-deity has been erased over time. It has also probably suffered from the *ex post facto* look at the earliest known clues; that what is related to later dominant devotional streams is more easily perceptible.

It seems little more of the original contribution of Balarāma can be detected. The data from North India might be considered testimony of an ancient trend that disappeared over the course of time, starting in the 5th or the 6th century. Nonetheless analyzing of texts and archaeology of the Tamil land up to the 10th century throws unexpected light on the importance of this deity in ancient times.

---

88 During the Gupta period, several types of sculptures may be considered as being representations of Nārāyaṇa. As a continuation of the Kuṣāṇa-period depictions, Nārāyaṇa is represented as a boar, identified as such in an inscription, in Eran (Madhya Pradesh).

Balarāma in the Tamil land: Caṅkam literature

From its careful recording in the *Cilappatikāram*, in Tamil inscriptions, and in the sculptural tradition prior or concurrent to the *Tivyappirapantam*, the importance of the form of the deity lying on a snake as well as of the name and concept of Nārāyaṇa in the Tamil land is clear. The figure lying on a snake is a major iconographic form for Vaiṣṇava deities, and is the form given, in particular, to Nārāyaṇa, the one having a lotus coming out of his navel, like in Śrīraṅgam. The name of Nārāyaṇa should be sung along with what appears to be formulas in the *Tivyappirapantam* that were already relayed in the *Cilappatikāram*, not to mention the Vedic *mantra*s, explicitly cited in this Jain text (Cil. 11.128). Moreover, in the *Cilappatikāram*, Balarāma is depicted as a prominent deity. He appears either in a cluster with other gods, or as the elder of Kṛṣṇa. In the latter case, which corresponds to the canto 17 of the text, the bodies of contrasted colors of Kṛṣṇa and Balarāma echo one another, evoking the two bodies constituting a snake-deity. Worshiped in temples and being the other half of Kṛṣṇa, Balarāma appears as one of the main deities of Hinduism in the *Cilappatikāram*.

There is material in the Caṅkam corpus that corresponds to these elements. Mentions of deities are quite rare in this body of texts since it is primarily secular—with the exception of the *Tirumurukāṟṟupaṭai* (dedicated to Murukaṉ) and the *Paripāṭal* (which presents hymns dedicated to Murukaṉ and Tirumāḷ). Mentions of Balarāma thus signal the importance of the deity. They also allow enable a better understanding of the *Cilappatikāram* passages.

Balarāma appears in two poems of the *Puṟanāṉūṟu*, one of the earliest Caṅkam anthologies. In *Puṟanāṉūṟu* 56 he is invoked as:

> the god having as emblems a palm tree [and] a plough hot because of killing, whose body resembles a twisted circle sleeping on the ocean (l. 3).[89]

---

[89] *kaṭal vaḷar puri vaḷai puraiyum mēṉi* is a reference to the whiteness of the god, whose body (*mēṉi*) is compared to a conch (*vaḷai*) twisting (*puri*) while growsing in the ocean (*kaṭal*): "[his] body comparable to the conch twisting while growing in the ocean". Since *vaḷar* has several meanings, including to lengthen, to sleep, to grow, and to extend, I wonder whether this line might not be understood also as hinting that the deity extends and

This reference is found after an invocation to Śiva and before one to the deity of the color of the sapphire having a bird on his banner (Kṛṣṇa-Viṣṇu) and one to Murukaṉ. These are the "four whose power shields the world" (*ñālam kākum kāla muṉpiṉ*, 1.9, trans. by Hart-Heitzfeld 2002: 43). The whiteness of the deity is referred to in the same poem, on 1.12 where he is "Vāliyōṉ" (the White one). The same group of deities is praised in the invocatory stanza of the *Iṉṉa Nāṟpatu* ; the group is exactly the same as that appearing in the 5th canto of the *Cilappatikāram*.[90]

In *Puṟanāṉūṟu* 58, Balarāma is paired with Kṛṣṇa. The two kings of Maturai and Uṟantai (Uṟaiyūr) are described as follows:

> As if the god who carries a palmyra palm on his banner and whose skin is as white as milk and the one who wields the discus, the dark-colored god, those two great beings were to stand together [...]. (trans. by Hart-Heifetz 2002: 45).

Maturai is the city of Kṛṣṇa in the *Cilappatikāram* Balarāma may be more particularly associated with Uṟaiyūr—which is in the vicinity of Śrīraṅgam.

The North Indian influence as indicated by the presence of deities such as Śiva, Kṛṣṇa, and Balarāma in these two poems allows us to hypothesize these two poems belong to a later layer of the anthology (3rd–5th c.?). But the same pair Kṛṣṇa-Balarāma appears in *Naṟṟiṇai*, another one of the early anthologies, whose most poems are even less likely to be later works:

---

sleeps on the ocean, with his body twisted into a circle (*puri vaḷai* [circle is the first meaning of *vaḷai*]). Thus "[his] body comparable to a twisted circle expanding in the ocean" could be an allusion to the coiled body of a snake: "[his] body comparable to a twisted circle expanding in the ocean".

90 For the *Iṉṉa Nāṟpatu* invocatory stanza, see the chapter of Wilden in this volume pp. 21–49. There Balarāma is found as "the White one with the golden Palmyra Palm" (trans. E. Wilden).

With waterfalls, glowing white like the white one (*vāliyōṉ*),
On the mountain side, black like the black one (*māyōṉ*).[91]

The contrasting colors of Māyōṉ (the Black one, i.e., Kṛṣṇa), and Vāliyōṉ (the White one, i.e., Balarāma) are found here, just as they are in the description of the Śrīraṅgam image in the *Tivyappirapantam*. In my view, this contrast appears again in the invocatory stanza of the *Aiṅkuṟunūṟu*, another of the earliest anthologies wherein the praise is addressed to the deity regularly unfolds the world as "the unique one of two united halves, with whiteness in a dark body."[92] The periods of destruction and creation of the universe which compose the mythological background of Nārāyaṇa—can be understood in various ways. This is possibly what we are encountering in this stanza also.

In the *Kalittokai*, one anthology in which some of the last Caṅkam (6-7th c.?) compositions were collected, various names and attributes of Balarāma also are found. He is the one with a plough (*Kalittokai* 36.1), has a palm-tree as his emblem (*Kalittokai* 104.7), wears unique earring (*Kalittokai* 105.11), and is the white one (*Kalittokai* 104.8; 105.11). These references appear at the beginning of the poems that is in this part of the hymn containing elements of a visual mythological background in the *Kalittokai*. Balarāma appears either alone (*Kalittokai* 36) or as one of the group already encountered several times: Kṛṣṇa, Balarāma, Śiva, Murukaṉ in *Kalittokai* 104; Kṛṣṇa, Balarāma, Śiva, Murukaṉ, Indra as well as Yama in *Kalittokai* 105. Balarāma is linked closely to Kṛṣṇa since, in hymns 104 and 105, Kṛṣṇa is mentioned just before or after Balarāma.

---

91 *Naṟṟiṇai* 32.1–2; text and translation by Wilden 2007 (1), p. 122: *māyōṉ aṉṉa māl varai kavāaṉ, vāliyōṉ aṉṉa vayaṅku veḷ aruvi.*

92 *nīla mēṉi vāl iḻai pākatt' oruvaṉ iru tāl niḻal-kīḻ, mū vakai ulaku mukiḻttaṉa muṟaiyē.* This stanza implies several plays of word. The formula *vāl iḻai* (translated here considering *iḻai* as a verbal root meaning associated very closely) can be understood as "of pure jewels" (with *iḻai* as a substantive, ornament) and is commonly attributed to women. Such play of words allows the stanza to allude to both Viṣṇu and Śiva, see Wilden in this volume, pp. 21–49. I thank Eva Wilden for having explained this stanza to me and discussed about it at length.

The *Paripāṭal* belongs approximately to the same chronological stage of Caṅkam literature than *Kalittokai*, but it is a devotional anthology and thus falls under another category. The pair here formed by Balarāma with Kṛṣṇa is of considerable importance.[93] Balarāma is praised in the very first stanza in explicit terms:

> One thousand, spread, full of divine power, [your] great heads,
> Having the power of spitting fire, are rising above your crown,
> Having Mā (Lakṣmī) on the large chest of [your] circular body of immaculate whiteness,
> Red and rising are the tusks of the high and beautiful bamboo above which is brandished
> [Your] circular plough of bending mouth, oh you of the unique earring, you the unique one![94]

This first stanza of the anthology as known today can be considered a tribute to Balarāma as an elder. The stanza that follows is devoted to Kṛṣṇa. The two deities are associated so closely in this praise that it be-

---

[93] The following presentation of the *Paripāṭal* is based on the unrivalled publication of François Gros 1968.

[94] *Paripāṭal* 1.1–5:
āyiram viritta aṇaṅku uṭai aru talai
tī umiḻ tiṟaloṭu muṭi micai aṇavara
mā uṭai malar mārpiṉ mai il vāl vaḷai mēṉi
cēy uyar paṇai micai eḻil vēḻam ēntiya
vāy vāṅkum vaḷai nāñcil oru kuḻai oruvaṉai.

This stanza has been understood in various ways. The French translation of F. Gros is worth quoting here, as it is the basis of the translation above given (1968: 2): “Mille, déployées, redoutables, les têtes insignes / Au pouvoir de cracher le feu se dressant par-dessus ta couronne, Mā sur ta large poitrine, un teint de conque blanche immaculée, Un bel éléphant brandi qui mange un bambou haut dressé, Une charrue courbe au soc tranchant : Tu es l’Unique à l’unique anneau”, see also the comments of Gros on p. 167: variants comprise *paṉai*, the palm-tree for *paṇai*, bamboo, and *mēḻi*, the plough for *y-eḻi* (in *micai eḻil*), which are two of the attributes of Balarāma. Whether one follows the text here chosen or not, the praise is addressed to Balarāma, holding a plough, having a unique earring, being white and provided with the thousand heads of a snake-deity.

comes difficult to distinguish between them.[95] For instance, Lakṣmī is first said to be on the large chest of Balarāma, then five lines later she spreads out on the chest of the god of the color of the *pūvai* flower, the dark Kṛṣṇa (l. 8). This seems to illustrate the unity of the two bodies, the white snake-deity on the one hand, the dark human figure on the other.[96]

Hymn 2 is in honour of Tirumāl. It starts with a description of the dissolution of the worlds, then continues with images of creation. The deity being praised presents several characteristics that establish a link to the most ancient information we have about Nārāyaṇa, Kṛṣṇa, and Balarāma. Three forms of the deity, indeed, are mentioned here: the boar, Balarāma, and Kṛṣṇa that are the earliest concrete forms of Nārāyaṇa in North India.[97] Throughout the hymn Balarāma is mentioned abundantly as a comparing object for Tirumāl. This deity of the dissolution *par excellence* is the elder, white like a conch, with a gold palm-tree as his emblem (l. 21-22). Two myths are alluded to in the course of the poem: the story of the boar who marries the earth, and a fight in which palm-trees are destroyed (l. 41-47). The latter is one of two deeds attributed to Balarāma in the *Harivaṃśa* and becomes a siege led by Kṛṣṇa in the *Tivyappirapantam.* In the *Paripāṭal* passage, it is impossible to say which of the two brothers leads the siege.[98] Thus, it is

---

[95] Lines 14–25 are not understandable (see Gros 1968: 2–3, 168–170). Still, it is clear they develop the theme of a deity formed of two contrasted parts, one dark, the other bright, which are united in a unique god.

[96] Line 31 reads, "The father of the two (*iruvar*), o Māl of glowing jewels" (*iruvar tātai ilaṅku pūṇ māl.* Here I follow the understanding of Gros). This image is perhaps similar to the one of the invocatory stanza of the *Aiṅkuṟunūṟu*: the bright half of the deity being designated by a formula alluding to the jewels of the deity (see *supra*, fn. 92).

[97] The boar is one of the earliest forms of Nārāyaṇa, appearing as such in the sculptural tradition since the 3rd CE and named as such in Gupta-period inscriptions (see also, *supra*, fn. 88).

[98] This combat is included in a long comparison for the fights waged by the Lord. Since it is a comparison for the main deity of the hymn, it is plausible the figure who is fighting is somebody else; on this fight as a shadow motif in the *Tivyappirapantam*, see Schmid 2013.

perhaps reflecting the progressive fading of Balarāma from devotional works. While the deed is not clearly attributed to Kṛṣṇa, it is no longer said to be achieved by Balarāma.

Paripāṭal 3 focused clearly on the Dark one, Kṛṣṇa, who fights various demons. Yet, the end of the hymn again combines Kṛṣṇa and Balarāma in one and the same form. The deity is the Black and the White, the cowherd and the guardian, etc. and the poem ends with an evocation of the deity who has a lotus issuing from his navel.

In the fourth hymn to Tirumāl (*Paripāṭal* 4), Balarāma is described in lines 36-48. He is a snake-deity, with a palm-tree and plough as emblems. But the poem concentrates on Viṣṇu-Kṛṣṇa, of whom it mentions several manifestations: Balarāma is one of them, mentioned after the lion and the boar manifestations and followed by a vigorous attack against snakes through a description of their enemy, Garuḍa, adorned with snakes as his captured prey.

The fifth Vaiṣṇava hymn of the anthology, *Paripāṭal* 13, devotes several verses to a deity of one thousand heads lying in yogic sleep in the milk-ocean (*aṟituyil*, the same expression used in the *Cilappatikāram* to describe the snake-deities). The description is followed by an evocation of the one having a plough for a weapon, on the one hand, and of the boar form of the deity, on the other. This passage concludes as follows: the God is "the unique one having divided himself into three forms" (*mū uru ākiya talaipiri oruvaṉai*, l. 38). Here, a specific relation is established between the snake deity, Balarāma, and the boar manifestation, which appears quite close to the situation encountered in North India during the four first centuries CE regarding the representations of Nārāyaṇa.[99]

Hymn 15, which is devoted to the deity of Iruṅkuṉṟam or Māliruṅkuṉṟam, seems closer to the inspiration of the two first hymns. It stresses the proximity of two deities, who are Kṛṣṇa and Balarāma.[100] The poem praises the site of "two having a single action", who are said to be indivisible and one, "like a word and [its] meaning, though they

---

[99] See, *supra*, note 97.

[100] See Gros 1968: 264.

differ in their divine forms in each aspect!"[101] The two gods are also compared to the shore and the water of the sea dashing on the rocks (l. 12), calling to mind the Shore Temple of Mahābalipuram. Iruṅkuṉṟam is the place of a god "close to" and "combined with" the "one wearing a gold cloth", "like a lengthening darkness mixed with the whiteness of water", a description of contrasting colors with which we are now familiar.[102] The water, this element snake-deities are linked with, is often mentioned. The description of the place seems to develop the fundamental landscape as already encountered in a comparison in *Naṟṟiṇai* 32: here is a dark mountain provided with glowing white waterfalls; it embodies the complementarity of the two deities.

Balarāma is the older of the two deities. He is provided with numerous snake-heads (l. 21). The description in l. 54-62, evokes his iconographic markers (brightness, single earring, a plough and a pestle [a stick full of anger]), as well as those of one who is like a dark mountain, having a bird on his banner, provided with discus and conch (Kṛṣ). The hymn concludes with a prayer to the Two of great fame (or, as we will see, literally, to the "two-mountain", which is of great fame) *peru peyar iruvarai*.

This poem is in honour of a particular place, mentioned several times as "Iruṅkuṉṟam" (see l. 14, 24, 53, 65) or "Iruṅkuṉṟu" (l. 35 and 45), the dark mountain. It is also called Māliruṅkuṉṟam (l. 17 and 23), the dark mountain of Māl. The same place is often praised in the *Tivyappirapantam* under the name Māliruñcōlai, and it also appears in the *Cilappatikāram* (see *supra*, p. 95, 105). This place is today the important Vaiṣṇava site called Tirumāliruñcōlai, 19 kilometres north of Maturai the name "The dark mountain (*kuṉṟam*)" has changed into "the dark grove (*cōlai*)", then following indications given in *Paripāṭal* 15, a transformation to which we will return with the hymn of the appendix on which this paper will conclude. The name of the site, Iruṅkuṉṟam, "the dark mountain" (l. 14, *iruṅ kuṉṟam*), in which *iruṅ* is from *irumai*,

---

[101] *Paripāṭal* 13, l. 12–13: *pulliya col um poruḷ um pōla um, ellām vēṟu vēṟu uruviṉ oru toḻil iruvar.*

[102] *Paripāṭal* 13, l. 27–28: *maṉ puṉal iḷa veyil vaḷāva iruḷ vaḷarvu eṉa, poṉ puṇai* uṭukkaiyōṉ *puṇarntu amar nilai.*

darkness, seems to be used in this case as a play on words, according to which the site is presented as the "mountain of the two"; i.e., *iru kuṉṟam*. Indeed, the last line of the poem praises *iru-varai*, which draws the attention to *iru* as the abbreviated form of *iraṇṭu*, the second. *Iru-varai* itself may correspond either to *iru* and *varai* that is "the mountain of the two" or to an accusative ending *–ai* added to *iruvar*, the two. The two options point towards the dual of the deity embodied in the mountain.

This all too brief presentation of the Vaiṣṇava hymns in the *Paripāṭal* highlights the ambiguity of the snake-deity. To separate the two bodies, one several-headed snake and one human, is probably often irrelevant. Is the snake deity represented only under the animal form, or as a combination with the human form also? I propose that these poems are playing with this ambiguity in order to express what was conceived, at the time of the composition of some of them at least, as one fundamental complementarity between Balarāma and Kṛṣṇa. In doing so they indicate the important role played by the "Elder", the Lord of snakes, or Balarāma.

Thus, the two schemes encountered in the *Cilappatikāram* are already met in Caṅkam literature. In the *Puṟanāṉūṟu*, Balarāma appears in a cluster of deities. And in the *Naṟṟiṇai*, Kṛṣṇa and Balarāma constitute a specific pair according to a model already encountered in the most ancient material, found in North India. If this second scheme is more operative in the devotional hymns of the *Paripāṭal*, from one text to the other, a line of transmission can be drawn between all this early material. This line seems to disappear in the *Tivyappirapantam*., where Balarāma is seldom encountered. The important topic of Kṛṣṇa's infancy in the *Tivyappirapantam* would have provided opportunities for Balarāma to appear as he did in the *Harivaṃśa.* But deeds known to be of Balarāma in the *Harivaṃśa* are commonly credited to Kṛṣṇa in the *Tivyappirapantam* (Schmid 2013). The sculptural tradition seems to follow a similar pattern, gradually absorbed into the Nārāyaṇa visual model he has inspired, Balarāma would have paled in significance.

In fact, the carvings of deities lying on snakes of the Tamil land do not correspond to the model developed in the Gupta territory and also favored in the Cāḷukya sites of South India from the 6th century onwards. The four arms given to the god of the Shore Temple are unique in the Tamil country. The stretching of one arm close to the ear with an open palm, the other arm slightly bent above the snake coils, are found in images scattered throughout the Tamil country from the 6th or 7th century. These are much closer to the iconography of Balarāma promoted first during the Kuṣāṇa period in North India. The deity of the Shore Temple appears to illustrate a text-oriented strand; the other reclining deities of the Tamil country seem to have belonged originally to other patterns closer closer to the sculpted tradition. The latter is known through the examples of Central India where a serpent is represented as a necessary complement of the human deity; these are in line with farther north and earlier sculptures in which a two-handed snake deity is depicted as a man with a massive snake running along his back, its coils visible on each side of the human figure, its multi-headed hood blooming above the humane head of the fantastic being.

How the two-handed iconographic scheme became prevalent in the Tamil land is far from clear, but the persistence of one ancient iconography linked to Balarāma to here represent the creator god as a snake-deity with two hands can only make one wonder. These images stand as testimonies to ancient streams of devotion, different than those we know as they became the dominant ones.

There is, in fact, one more poem to be assessed in the *Paripāṭal*. It belongs to the section of the "fragments" (*tiraṭṭu*) of the anthology. It testifies to the difficulty of defining Vaiṣṇava deities in Caṅkam literature in ways accustomed to when studying the Sankrit corpus.

A Fragment from the *Paripāṭal*

The first text included in the *tiraṭṭu* section in the 1918 *editio princeps* of the *Paripāṭal* by U.Vē. Cāminātaiyār is a poem of 82 lines. This poem, variously called "Fragment I" or "Annexure I",[103] is cited in commentaries but not found in any of the known manuscripts of the *Paripāṭal*. Perhaps it was difficult to accommodate this poem in an anthology that is traditionally considered as having comprised hymns to

[103] See Gros 1968: 144, Seshadri 1996: 235.

Tirumāl (8 poems), Murukaṉ (31 poems), the Vaiyai (26 poems), Maturai (4 poems), and Koṟṟavai (1).[104] Overall, indeed, these 82 lines are considered to be devoted to Tirumāl and thus, seven out of the eight hymns mentioned in the tradition as devoted to Tirumāl would have been transmitted.[105] But the case may be more complex than this as the modern authors consider that the hymn praises Ādiśeṣa (Āticēṭaṉ) or the Primeval snake on whom Tirumāl reclines.[106] The snake and Tirumāl are one and the same deity; still a specific focus is put on the snake-part of the deity in this hymn. Let us examine it. "Fragment I" praises a site called Iruntaiyūr,[107] or the deity in Iruntaiyūr:

> O you, the deity (*celvaṉ*) settled in Iruntaiyūr, [that place] associated with many ghats of sweet water! (*tīm nīr mali tuṟai mēya, iruntaiyūr amarnta celva niṉ*, l. 4-5).

This genre, the praise of a place, is illustrated in the anthology by the hymn 15, the praise of Iruṅkuṉṟam, or Māliruñcōlai. Dedicated to deities of sites, *Paripāṭal* 15 and Fragment I stand as literary ancestors to some poems of the *Tivyappirapantam.*

The deity of Iruntaiyūr is a snake-deity. Listed are "the temple of the *nāga* whose head [bears] the earth" (*pū muṭi nākar nakar*, 1. 59), "the temple of the Lord (*celvaṉ*) inhabiting (*keḻu*) the mountain, whose neck is adorned by two bright dots" (*iru kēḻ utti aṇinta eruttiṉ, varai keḻu celvaṉ nakar*, l. 48-49). Cobra hoods are decorated with two dots and this physical characteristic that is rarely mentioned in texts, leaves no doubt as to the nature of the Lord of Iruntaiyūr. As could be expected for a snake-deity, water floods the scenery. The rain comes from the mountain up to the bank where the temple is located (l. 1-5; see also the bank of the pond where the god resides, l. 63). In this territory the pools grow larger, like big stars expanding in the sky (*viṇ vīṟṟirukkum kaya*

[104] See Gros 1968: xiii. Only poems in honour of Tirumāl, Murukaṉ and the Vaiyai have survived in the manuscripts of the text, to which the *tiraṭṭu* section is added in the editions.

[105] See Gros 1968 lvi, 144 for comments.

[106] See Cāminātaiyār 1995: 227; Seshadri 1996: xxx–xxxi, 235.

[107] See Gros 1968: xxviii, 144, 297.

mīn̲ viri takaiyin̲, kaṇ vīr̲r̲irukkum kayam, l. 12-13)[108] and one sees "the paddy-fields cherished by Tiru" (*tiru naya takka vayal* l. 17), "while swollen waterfalls resound with large drums" (*taṇṭā aruviyoṭu iru mu-l̲avu ārppa*, l. 52).

The mythological events here narrated to illustrate the power of the deity correspond to the nature of the Lord of a site of such nature. A specific version of story of the churning of the ocean is given (l. 64-79). The deity of Iruntaiyūr takes on the form of the rope needed to do the churning whereby the one who holds the discus (*āl̲iyān̲*) pulls this rope by its two ends. In this way, the deity of Iruntaiyūr protects Mount Meru and holds the earth. If the churning of the ocean is one of the famous deeds of Viṣṇu, here the hero is "Āl̲iyān̲", the discus bearer, or the one who has the form of the snake, used as a rope. This is followed by a praise of the deity who became the snake-rope of Śiva's bow when the latter god destroyed the three cities (l. 76-78). With these accounts of two divine deeds of Viṣṇu and Śiva, the *nāga* appears as the necessary instrument of divine victory over the *asura*s.

The fragment concludes with a praise addressed to the god "who has a thousand fearful (*aṇaṅku*) rare heads spread out" (*aṇaṅku uṭai aru talai āyiram viritta*, l. 79) and who is surrounded by a group of his attendants (l. 80), a typical trait of *nāga* deities.

Hymns 1, 2 and 15 of the *Paripāṭal* can be considered in honour of Tirumāl, united with the snake-deity Balarāma, while "Fragment I" honours the snake part of the supreme deity whose "human" figure appears only along the mention of the one who holds a discus in the episode of the churning. While the two parts of the supreme deity, the snake and the "human" one, are so close that they may fuse, the object of the praise in "Fragment I" is a multi-headed snake. The evocation of one of Śiva's exploits enhances the importance of a snake deity who is not actingt only in the sphere of Tirumāl. In *Cilappatikāram* (17.32.1) the deity used as a rope in the churning is Vāsuki as it is in the *Mahābhārata*, in which Vāsuki is also the snake taking the shape of the

---

[108] The understanding of this poem and the translations here given follow the translation into French by Gros (1968: 144–147). Many lines are debatable and as Eva Wilden pointed out to me this text might not be always understandable in its present state.

string-bow of Śiva during the fight against the three cities. As this exploit of Śiva is alluded to elsewhere in the *Paripāṭal* but in hymns devoted to Cevvēl (Murukaṉ), the snake-deity of "Fragment I" seems less closely associated with Tirumāl than with the proper *nāga*'s part of the deity.

The god of Iruntaiyūr is presented as the object of devotion for a large range of people. Vedas prominent in the Nārāyaṇa mythology are mentioned together with the Brahmins in this poem (l. 18) but merchants and cultivators also inhabit the site. The crowd of worshippers is impressive. In lines 33-45 listed are women, important people mounted on elephants, elders, and beautiful, knowledgeable individuals who "incessantly gathering, grow at the feet [of the Lord]" (*iṭai oḻivu iṉṟi aṭiyuṟaiyār īṇṭi*, l. 55).

Where was Iruntaiyūr? Kūṭal of the four quarters (*nāṉmāṭakkūṭal*) that is the ancient name of Maturai appears in the third line of the poem and the site praised in this poem is today thought to be Kūṭalaḻakar, the Viṣṇu temple situated in the present-day Maturai.[109] Two of the Āḻvārs, Periyāḻvār and Tirumaṅkaiyāḻvār are said to have sung Kūṭalaḻakar and that would make it an early site dedicated to Kṛṣṇa-Viṣṇu-Nārāyaṇa or the deity of the *Tivyappirapantam*. However, one searches in vain for anything in the said poems of the *Tivyappirapantam* referring to Kūṭal-

[109] After having reviewed the relevant bibliography, Gros 1968: 297 considers this identification doubtful but nevertheless situates the site in a suburb of Maturai, following an identification proposed in 1906 by T. A. Gopinatha Rao, whose papers were unavailable to me, and M. Raghava Iyangar (see 1938 [collected papers]: 241–244). These scholars were in fact trying to locate the temple of Neṭumāl, mentioned at the beginning of *Cilappatikāram* 18 (l. 4, see *supra*, p. 10538) and in the ancient commentary of the text called "*Irunta-vaḷam-uṭaiyār*". I thank Jean-Luc Chevillard for having read this passage with me. This site is today considered being the temple of Kūṭalaḻakar, that is the Vaiṣṇava temple dedicated to Kṛṣṇa located in Maturai itself. It houses a seated form of the deity as a main idol. This form matches with the word *irunta*, "seated", appearing in "Irunta-vaḷam-uṭaiyār" and Iruntaiyūr (on this correspondence, see the commentary of Cāminātaiyār, 1995: 231). This hypothesis seems widely accepted, as, for example, Champakalakshmi (1990: 51–52).

a<u>l</u>akar or to any precise deity.[110] Periyā<u>l</u>vār would have sung his *Tirup-pallāṇṭu*, already referred to in the first part of this paper, in Kūṭala<u>l</u>a-kar. The form lying on a snake is mentioned in one stanza of the concerned hymn (see Tiv. 9), but is not a prominent figure in the poem. Nothing else calls for an association with a site called Iruntaiyūr. As for the sole stanza by Tirumaṅkaiyā<u>l</u>vār considered in praise of Kūṭala<u>l</u>a-kar, it does not refer to a snake-form. The deity has four arms, holds a discus and conch, and resides in Kō<u>l</u>i and Kūṭal.[111] The mention of Kū-ṭal is the only element shared with "Fragment I" of the *Paripāṭal*—but since Kō<u>l</u>i and Kūṭal were the two capitals of the Cō<u>l</u>as and the Pāṇḍ-yas, the presence of Viṣṇu in those two places is nothing unusual. Moreover, even if the location of the present-day temple of Kūṭala<u>l</u>akar might constitute a link with stanzas mentioning Kūṭal in the *Tivyappi-rapantam*, establishing these as praises to the Lord of Iruntaiyūr raises more difficulties than it solves. The place-name Iruntaiyūr is found nowhere in the *Tivyappirapantam*. That absence is surprising, given, firstly, the antiquity of the site of Iruntaiyūr indicated by its connection with the *Paripāṭal* and, secondly, the number of place-names mentioned in the *Tivyappirapantam*.

But there is another trail that can be followed. The name itself of "Iruntaiyūr" may imply a play of sound to echo the Iruṅku<u>n</u><u>r</u>am/Mā-liruṅku<u>n</u><u>r</u>am of *Paripāṭal* 15, a site that is praised in the *Tivyappirapan-tam* under the name Tirumāliruñcōlai. Maturai is indeed mentioned in *Tivyappirapantam* stanzas devoted to this important Vaiṣṇava temple located, as mentioned above, on the banks of a river only 19 kilometres

[110] In a note available on the website Tamil Arts Academy (http://www.tamilartsacademy.com), entitled "Balarāma in Tamil Nadu", R. Nagaswamy also seems to favour "Fragment I" as a praise to Balarāma.

[111] *Paripāṭal* 9.2.5 (1762):
kō<u>l</u>iyum kūṭalum kōyil koṇṭa
kōvalarē oppar ku<u>n</u><u>r</u>am a<u>n</u><u>n</u>a
pā<u>l</u>iyum tōḷum ōr nā<u>n</u>ku uṭaiyar
paṇṭu ivar tammaiyum kaṇṭa<u>r</u>iyōm
vā<u>l</u>iyarō ivar vaṇṇam meṇṇil
mā kaṭal pō<u>n</u><u>r</u>u uḷar kaiyil veyya,
ā<u>l</u>i o<u>n</u><u>r</u>u ēnti ōr caṅku pa<u>r</u><u>r</u>i
accō oruvar a<u>l</u>akiyavā.

from Maturai (Kūṭal. see Tiv. 545, for instance). The complementarity of the two deities, theme of *Paripāṭal* 15, may be echoed in "Fragment I". *Paripāṭal* 15 (the earliest known text in honour of Iruṅkuṉṟam/Māliruṅkuṉṟam) specifically praises the mountain, the *kuṉṟam*, *kuṉṟu* of the place-name. "Fragment I" is honouring a river, a ghat. Its waters come from the mountain in an evocation of the ancient images of the mountain and its waterfalls used to suggest the fusion of Kṛṣṇa and Balarāma in Caṅkam literature. Iruṅkuṉṟam is given as the site of a pair, *iruvarai* (*supra*, p. 131). This play on words could find an echo in a play on sound with "Iruntaiyūr."

Could it be possible that a mountain and a ghat of the same site were the object of two separate hymns? If one accepts this hypothesis, *Paripāṭal* 15 and "Fragment I" would be consecrated to two complementary, yet distinct deities of the same area. These would have been located either at the same site or close by, if one considers the present-day position of Kūṭalaḻakar and Tirumāliruñcōlai to reflect the ancient situation. At both sites, a mountain and water are the two main elements of the sacred place, but the emphasis is laid either on the mountain (Iruṅkuṉṟam) or the place of water (Iruntaiyūr). This harkens back to the comparisons of other Caṅkam pieces, where a mountain and its waterfalls illustrate the complementarity of Kṛṣṇa and Balarāma.

According to this suggestion, *Paripāṭal* 15 would be more specifically devoted to the Kṛṣṇa part of Tirumāl and "Fragment I" to the snake half of the deity, Balarāma. The fact that the two mythical deeds in the narration can be attributed to the snake deity Vāsuki, and are not characteristic of Balarāma (who is the other half of Māl in *Paripāṭal* 15) might be another indication of the gradually withdrawal of Balarāma's who has nearly disappeared in the *Tivyappirapantam.*

Regarding the connection between Iruntaiyūr and the Maturai of the four temples mentioned in "Fragment I", another link can be established.[112] As we have seen above, in the *Cilappatikāram* one temple of

[112] Maturai is called *nāṉmāṭakkūṭal* in "Fragment I" of the *Paripāṭal*; for a discussion of this epithet, see Gros 1968: xxvii–xxix. The epithet *nāṉmāṭam* given here to Kūṭal is understood as a reference to four (*nāl*) quarters or temples (*māṭam*). The formula reminds is clearly reminiscent of the description of Maturai that opens canto 14 of the *Cilappatikāram* where four

Balarāma in Maturai (Kūṭal) is mentioned at the beginning of the 14th canto, when Kōvalaṉ reaches Maturai, and the description of one of the four guardian-deities of the city in canto 22 applies to Balarāma in a number of ways.[113] These two passages in the epic allow to propose that one of the four temples of Kūṭal, whether or not located in the Kūṭalaḻakar of today, was originally consecrated to Balarāma. This is a viable hypothesis given the present state of research. But there are enough elements to argue that "Fragment I" of the *Paripāṭal* was originally dedicated to a site where a snake-deity, maybe Balarāma, was worshipped as one half of Tirumāl. It seems that this place deity was later included in—or excluded from—a devotional movement that transformed the conception of the site, as well as the ancient poem associated with it. Either the poem was no longer considered a part of the whole to which it originally belonged, or, perhaps, it was produced from the very beginning by a different devotional stream.

This hypothesis is consistent with sectarian trends noticeable in the *Tivyappirapantam.* The later anthology may only attest that Balarāma worship became so completely absorbed in the Nārāyaṇa-Viṣṇu-Kṛṣṇa cult that it was no longer relevant to distinguish Balarāma from an increasingly complex deity. However, the fact that "Fragment I" does not appear in the known manuscripts of the *Paripāṭal,* where Tirumāl is prominent, gives weight to the idea that sectarian attitudes gradually promoted certain deities at the expense of the cult and literature devoted to others.

---

temples are distributed in the city: "a temple of the one having an eye opening in his forehead (Śiva)", "a temple of the one having a *suparṇa* kite for mount" (*uvaṇac cēval*, a *garuḍa*; Viṣṇu), "a temple of the White one brandishing a plough" (our Balarāma), and "a temple of the one having a cock as an emblem (Skanda-Murukaṉ): *nutalviḻi nāṭṭat tiṟaiyōṉ kōyilum, uvaṇac cēval uyarttōṉ niyamamum, mēḻivala ṉuyartta veḷḷai nakaramum, kōḻic cēvaṟ koṭiyōṉ kōṭṭamum.*

[113] On this description in canto 22, see *supra*, fn. 42. The lack of clarity in the latter passage may point towards a period of transition between different worlds dominated by distinct deities.

Conclusion

In the *Tivyappirapantam*, one of the main names of the deity being praised is Nārāyaṇa. It encompasses many others and is to be chanted at the hour of death. It corresponds with the vision of a deity reclining on a snake, which proves to be a central image that even encompasses the others. This name and this form are the ones of a supreme god characterized by his creative power, towards whom the other names and forms go, or from whom they proceed. This name and this form were used for localizing a pan-Indian deity through the two domains of sound and vision. But the link between the name, the concept, and the form exhibits differences from one author or text to another, and from one site to the other. Śrīraṅgam is an archetypal case in the *Tivyappirapantam*. The above analysis was aimed to demonstrate the multi-layered character of its reclining deity and the importance of the physical characteristics of the site in the development of the worship of Nārāyaṇa in this place.

Similarly, the association of Nārāyaṇa with the reclining form of the Vaiṣṇava domain is less than clear in earlier documents than it is in the *Tivyappirapantam*. The numerous Vaiṣṇava snake-deities of the *Cilappatikāram* do not always correspond to one representation of Nārāyaṇa, while some signal the presence of Balarāma, the "elder" (*muṉṉai*) represented as a *nāga* from the very beginning of the Common era. The survey of the available archaeological data from North India—where deities portrayed lying on a snake were first carved—has led to make several working hypotheses. It is here proposed that the snake imagery has been used to represent the creative powers of a deity who is able to split and manifest himself in several different forms, as well as the waters to which the snake is linked. The eventual prominence of the snake-form in the Tamil land may record similar ways of conceiving the process of the supreme deity's manifestation in the material world. And the hypothesis of a dissemination of the early Bhāgavata movement in which Balarāma played an important part, seems tenable.

It also been shown that Balarāma—portrayed as a *nāga*—was important in early texts in the Tamil country. The erosion of his importance seems to have taken place between the end of the Caṅkam period and the beginning of the composition of the Bhakti hymns (6th–9th c.). It is possible that Balarāma tended to vanish while the theory of the *avatāras* of Viṣṇu gained in importance: as a double-bodied snake who is one with Kṛṣṇa, Balarāma does not fit into the *avatāra* scheme, which presupposes forms referring to a single supreme being, not to two supreme bodies.

With this tentative analysis of the iconographical process, based on the most frequently encountered representations of Nārāyaṇa in Tamil country, three points shall be highlighted.

First, in numerous documents, the relation between Kṛṣṇa and Nārāyaṇa was initially conceived as a relation between three distinct, yet close deities, a group that includes Balarāma. The family bond linking Kṛṣṇa and Balarāma in the mythological discourse, the name and the order of the *vyūha*s, and the iconographic tradition uniting two different bodies in a single one, all attest to this close association and to the importance of Balarāma/Saṃkarṣaṇa in an early stage of Nārāyaṇa worship.

Secondly, the importance of Balarāma and of the snake-imagery points towards contacts between North and South India at an early stage. Cult tendencies attested in North and Central India during the first four centuries of the Common era seem also to appear in the Caṅkam corpus. This was a time when the elder brother of Kṛṣṇa was a quite important deity, perhaps in another strand of Vaiṣṇavism than those which later became dominant. Both the Balarāma of the Tamil texts and the rock-carved figures of Nārāyaṇa attest to the diversity of transmission processes from North India to the southern part of the peninsula. If the deity praised in a poem presently called a "Fragment" of the *Paripāṭal* has to be recognized as a snake-deity, its precise identity remains difficult to establish. This ambiguity equally speaks of antique, devotional streams that have been lost and eventually absorbed into others. In fact—and this will be the third and last point of our conclusion—the snake imagery found in carved representations is a witness of a fruitful dialogue between the worlds of images and that of texts. In the earliest Sanskrit texts, one rarely finds mention of a snake morphology for deities. However, in the Tamil land, once reclining *nāga*s were carved, they were echoed in texts, thereupon giving rise to further images in both texts and sculptures. It thus appears that the visual tradition was as important as the textual one in the process of disseminating a culture usually considered grounded in Sanskrit literature. Giving snake-deities an importance that was subsumed in the texts, sculptures establish quite distinct links between several areas of the Indian peninsula. Their contribution to the building of Hinduism from North to South appears to have been fundamental.

Acknowledgements

Heartfelt thanks are due to Marcus Schmücker who organized a workshop where many issues touched in this paper were raised, and to my dear colleagues Suganya Anandakichenin, Jean-Luc Chevillard, Dominic Goodall, and Eva Wilden who discussed several points with me at length (including translations).

Bibliography

Primary Literature

Aiṅkuṟunūṟu
Aiṅkuṟunūṟu, Mūlamum Uraiyum, Catāciva Aiyar ed., Ceṉṉai: Institute of International Institute of Tamil Studies, 1999.

Avantisundarīkathā, K.S. Mahādeva Śāstrī, TSS n° 172, Trivandrum: University of Travancore, 1954.

Cilappatikāram
Cilappatikāram Iḷaṅkōvaṭikaḷaruḷiceyta cilappatikāramūlamum arumpatavuraiyum aṭiyārkku-nallāruraiyum, Cāminātaiyar, U. Vē. ed., Ceṉṉai: U. Vē. Cāminātaiyar nūl nilaiyam, 2001 [1892].

Harivaṃśa
Harivaṃśa, critical edition by Vishnu Sitaram Sukthankar, S. K. Belvakar & Parashuram Lakshman Vaidya: vol. I, *Introduction, critical text and notes*. Poona: Bhandarkar Oriental Institute, 1969; vol. II, *Appendices*, Bhandarkar Oriental Institute, Poona 1971.

Kalittokai
Kalittokai Maturaiyāciriyar Pārattuvāsi Nacciṉārkkiṉiyar Uraiyuṭaṉ, Ceṉṉai: South Indian Saiva Siddhanta Works Publishing Society, 1999 [1943].

Mahābhārata
Mahābhārata, critical edition by Vishnu Sitaram Sukthankar *et alii,* Poona: Bhandarkar Oriental Institute, 1933-1963.

(Nālāt) Tivyappirapantam
Nālāyirativiyappirapantam. Four Thousand Hymns of Twelve Alwars and Commentary by Dr. S. Jagathratchagan. English rendered from the Sacred book by Sri. Rama Bharati, Chennai: Āḻvārkaḷāyvumaiyam, 2002.

Naṟṟiṇai
Naṟṟiṇai, A Critical Edition and an Annotated Translation of the Naṟṟiṇai, Eva Wilden. [*Critical Texts of Cankam Literature* 1]. Chennai: École française d'Extrême-Orient/Tamilmann Patippakam.

Paripāṭal[1]
Le Paripāṭal. Texte tamouḷ. Introduction, traduction et notes par François Gros. [*Publications de l'Institut Français d'Indologie* 35]. Pondichéry: Institut Français d'Indologie 1968.

Paripāṭal[2]
Paripāṭal, Parimēlaḻakaruraiyum, U. Vē. Cāminātaiyar ed., Ceṉṉai : U. Vē. Cāminātaiyar nūl nilaiyam 1995 [1918].

Puṟanāṉūṟu
Puṟanāṉūṟu, Cu. Turaicāmi Pillai ed., 2 vols, Ceṉṉai: Tirunelvēli Teṉṉintiya Caivacittānta Nūṟ Patippukkaḻakam 2002 [1958].

Viṣṇupurāṇa
Viṣṇupurāṇa and Śrīdhara's commentary. Bombay: Veṅkateśvara Press 1967.

Secondary Literature

Ate 1978
Lynn Marie Ate, *Periyāḻvār's Tirumoḻi.* A Bāla Kṛṣṇa Text from the Devotional Period in Tamil Literature. PhD dissertation, University of Wisconsin. Madison 1978.

Asher 1980

Frederick M. Asher, *The Art of the Eastern India, 300-800*. Minnesota: University of Minnesota Press 1980.

Brinkhaus 2000

Horst Brinkhaus, The Mārkaṇḍeya-Episode in the Sanskrit Epics and Purāṇas. In: *On the Understanding of Other Cultures*. Proceedings of the International on Sanskrit and Related Studies to commemorate the Centenary of the Birth of Stanislaw Schayer (1899–1941), Piotr Balcerowitz, Marek Mejor (eds.), Warsaw: Oriental Institute, Warsaw University 2000, pp. 59–70.

van Buitenen 1981

Johannes Adrianus Bernardus van Buitenen, *The Mahābhārata, 2. The Book of the Assembly hall. 3. The Book of the Forest*. Chicago/London: The University of Chicago Press 1981.

Champakalakshmi 1981

R. Champakalakshmi, *Vaiṣṇava Iconography in the Tamil Country*. New Delhi: Orient Longman 1981.

Champakalakshmi 1990

Id., The sovereignty of the Divine: The Vaiṣṇava Pantheon and Temporal Power in South India. In: *Essays in Indian History and Culture, Felicitation Volume in Honour of Professor B. Sheik Ali*, H.V. Sreenivasa Murthy, B. Surendra Rao, Kesavan Veluthat, S. A. Bari (eds.), Delhi: Mittal Publications 1990, pp. 49–66.

Carman/Narayanan 1989

John Braisted Carman, Vasudha Narayanan, *The Tamil Veda, Piḷḷāṉ's Interpretation of the Tiruvāymoḻi*. Chicago: University of Chicago Press 1989.

Colas 2003

Gérard Colas, History of Vaiṣṇava Traditions: An esquisse. In: *The Blackwell Companion to Hinduism*. Oxford: Blackwell Publishing. 2003, pp. 229–270.

Couture 1986

André Couture, Akrūra et la tradition Bhāgavata selon le Harivaṃśa. In: *Sciences Religieuses/Studies in Religion* 15/2 (1986), pp. 221–232.

Couture 1991
Id., *L'enfance de Krishna*. Paris: Les éditions du Cerf/Presses de l'Université Laval, Québec. 1991.

Couture 2007
Id., *La Vision de Mārkaṇḍeya et la manifestation du lotus. Histoires anciennes tirées du Harivaṃśa (éd. cr., Appendice I, n° 41)*. [Hautes Études Orientales 43, Extrême-Orient 7]. Paris: École Pratique des Hautes Études, Sciences historiques et philologiques 2007.

Francis 2009
Emmanuel Francis, *Le discours royal. Inscriptions et monuments pallava (IVème-IXème siècles)*, PhD dissertation, Institut Orientaliste, Louvain-La-Neuve 2009.

Francis 2013
Id., *Le discours royal dans l'Inde du Sud ancienne. Inscriptions et monuments pallava (IVème-IXème siècles). Tome I, Introduction et sources.* [*Publications de l'Institut Orientaliste de Louvain* 64]. Louvain-La-Neuve: Université Catholique de Louvain Institut Orientaliste 2013.

Francis/Gillet/Schmid 2006
Emmanuel Francis, Valérie Gillet, Charlotte Schmid, Trésors inédits du Pays tamoul. Chronique des études pallava II. Dans: *Bulletin de l'École française d'Extrême-Orient* 93 (2006 [2008]), pp. 431–484.

Hari Rao 1976
V.N Hari Rao, *History of the Śrīrangam Temple*. [Sri Venkateswara University Historical Series]. Tirupati: Sri Venkateswara University 1976.

Hart/Heifetz 2002
George Luzerne Hart & Hank, Heifetz, *The Puṟanāṉūṟu, Four Hundred Songs of War and Wisdom, An Anthology of Poems from Classical Tamil*, New Delhi: Penguin Books India 2002,

Hardy 1983
Friedhelm Hardy, *Viraha-Bhakti. The Early History of Kṛṣṇa Devotion in South India.* Delhi: Oxford University Press 1983.

Hultzsch 1910
Eugen Hultzsch, Gadval Plates of Vikramaditya I., A.D. 674. In: *Epigraphia Indica* 10 (1909-10), pp. 100–106.

Nanditha 1980
Krishna Nanditha, *The Art and Iconography of Vishnu-Narayana*, Taraporevala/Bombay: Taraporevala Sons & Co. 1980.

Narayanan 1987
Vasudha Narayanan, *The way and the goal: Expressions of devotion in the early Śrī Vaiṣṇava Tradition*. Washington D.C.: Institute for Vaishnava Studies 1987.

Parthasarathy 2004
R. Parthasarathy, *The Cilappatikāram of Iḷaṅkō Aṭikaḷ. An Epic of South India, Translated, with an Introduction and Postscript*. [Translations from the Asian Classics]. New York: Columbia University Press, Penguin Books India 2004.

Ramesh/Tewari 1990
K. V. Ramesh, and S. P. Tewari. *A Copper-Plate Hoard of the Gupta Period from Bagh, Madhya Pradesh*. New Delhi: Archaeological Survey of India, 1990.

Ratan 1983
Parimoo Ratan, *Sculptures of Śeṣaśāyī Viṣṇu. Survey, Iconological Interpretation, Formal Analysis*. Baroda: Maharaja Sayajirao University of Baroda 1983.

Raghava Iyangar 1938
M. Raghava Iyangar, *Collected Essays. A Selection from the Writings of Sri. M. Raghava Iyangar*, published by his sons, R. Seshadri Iyangar, R. Narayana Iyangar, On the occasion of his Sixty-first Birthday Celebration 24th July. Madras: R. G. Press 1938.

Sahai 1967
Sachchidanand Sahai, Note sur une nouvelle sculpture indienne de Viṣṇu couché. In: *Arts asiatiques* 16 (1967), pp. 53–57.

Schmid 2010
Charlotte Schmid, *Le Don de voir, premières représentations krishnaïtes de la région de Mathurâ*. [PEFEO, monographien 193]. Paris: Publications de l'École française d'Extrême-Orient 2010.

Schmid 2013
Id., The contribution of Tamil literature to the Kṛṣṇa figure of the Sanskrit texts: The case of the *kaṉṟu* in *Cilappatikāram* 17. In: *Bilingualism and Cross-cultural Fertilisation: Sanskrit and Tamil in Mediaeval India*, Whitney Cox, Vincenzo Vergiani (eds.) [Collection Indologie 120]. Pondichéry: École française d'Extrême-Orient/Institut Français de Pondichéry, 2013, pp. 15–52.

Smith1996
Walter Smith, The Viṣṇu Image in the Shore Temple at Māmallapura. In: *Artibus Asiae* 56 1/2 (1996), pp. 19–32.

Soundara 1967
Rajan, K. V. Soundara, The Typology of the Anantaśayī Icon. In: *Artibus Asiae* 29/1 (1967), pp. 67–84.

Srinivasan/Srinivasan 1965
K.R. Srinivasan, P.R. Srinivasan, Atiya Inscriptions from Nāmakkal. In: *Epigraphia Indica* 36.4 (October 1965), pp. 131–138.

Young 2007
Katherine K. Young 2007, Brāhmaṇas, Pāñcarātrins, and the Formation of Śrīvaiṣṇavism. In: *Studies in Hinduism* IV. On the Mutual Influences and Relationship of Viśiṣṭādvaita Vedānta and Pāñcarātra. [ÖAW Sph 756 = BKGA 54]. Gerhard Oberhammer, Marion Rastelli (eds). Vienna: Austrian Academy of Sciences Press 2007, pp. 179–261.

Wilden 2014
Eva Wilden, Nammāḻvār as a Master of *tiṇaimayakkam* – Transposition Techniques in the Akam Songs of the *Tiruvāymoḻi*. In: Valérie Gillet (ed.), *Mapping the Chronology of Bhakti, Milestones, Stepping Stones, and Stumbling Stones.* [Collection Indologie 124]. Pondichéry: Institut français de Pondichéry, École française d'Extrême-Orient. 2014, pp. 317–333.

Willis 2009
Michael Willis, *The Archaeology of Hindu Ritual*: *Temples and the Establishment of the Gods*. Cambridge: Cambridge University Press 2009.

Zaheer 1981
Mohammad Zaheer, *The Temple of Bhītargāon*. Delhi: Agam Kala Prakashan 1981.

Fig. 1. Śrīraṅgam Island, seen from the Trichy fort (Photo by Emmanuel Francis).

Fig. 2. Popular picture (collected in July 2006, Śrīraṅgam. Photo by Charlotte Schmid).

Fig. 3. The reclining figure of Toṇṭūr, 8th–9th c.
(Photo by Emmanuel Francis).

Fig. 4. The reclining deity of the Malayatipaṭṭi cave, 8th–9th c.
(Photo by Dominic Goodall).

Fig. 5. The deity of the Shore Temple of Mahābalipuram, 6th–7th c. (Photo by Emmanuel Francis).

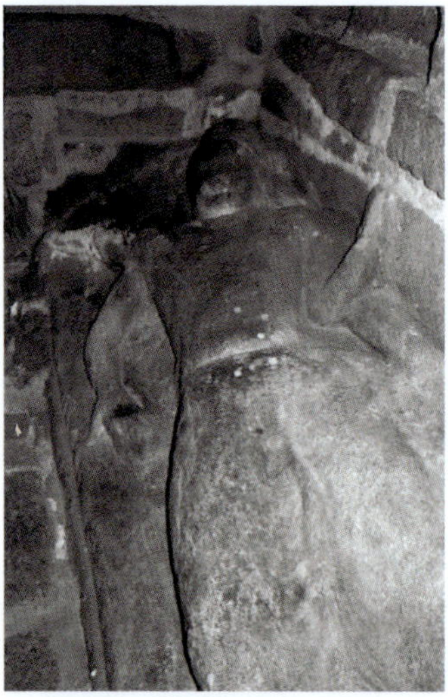

Fig. 6. Balarāma, Mathurā, 2nd–3rd c.
(Mathurā Museum. Photo by Charlotte Schmid).

Fig. 7. The representation of the four *vyūhas*, 3rd–4th c. CE (Mathurā Museum. Photo by Charlotte Schmid).

Katherine K. Young

Who is the Āḻvārs' supreme God?

The conventional understanding of the name Śrīvaiṣṇavism is that it is a Hindu sect located in South India which worships the god Viṣṇu and the goddess Śrī.[1] Its scripture includes the Tamil poems of the Āḻvārs composed between the seventh and ninth centuries C.E. and eventually canonized and called the Tamil Veda or the Sacred Collection of the Four Thousand (Verses) (*Nālāyirat Tivyappirapantam*).[2] Most people today assume that the Āḻvārs' supreme god is Viṣṇu. This idea is rein-

---

1 The word *vaiṣṇava* in the *Mahābhārata* has no sectarian definition but simply means relating to or belonging to Viṣṇu (Dasgupta [1931] 1985: 98). The word appears in inscriptions in Tamil country by the late 9th century and the 10th century—SII 24.1 (AR 69 of 1892), 24.2 (AR 70 of 1892), 24.4 (AR 72 of 1892)—and by the second half of that century *śrīvaiṣṇava* (a *karmadhārya* compound, that is, adjective plus noun), probably means the auspicious (*śrī*) *vaiṣṇava*s. (SII 24.11, 12). This might signify just the auspicious (*śrī*) devotees of Viṣṇu in a general sense, or the addition of *śrī* might indicate a specific type of *vaiṣṇava* such as Brahmin *vaiṣṇava*s. The compound *śrīvaiṣṇava* can also be taken as a *bahuvrīhi* compound containing a *dvandva*, that is, those belonging to, in the sense of devotees, of Śrī and Viṣṇu. I think this meaning developed only with the formation of the Śrīvaiṣṇava *sampradāya*, drawing on the importance of Śrī and Viṣṇu in the writings of Yāmuna and Rāmānuja.

2 There are twenty-four works in this corpus. The title of the collection is a *maṇipravāḷa* term (a mix of the Tamil word *nālāyira* and the Sanskrit words *divya* and *prabanda* in Tamil orthography). I have found no evidence of this term up to the 19th century, although the term *divya-prabandham*(s) is found long before that, initially referring to Nammāḻvār's *Tiruvāymoḻi* or his four works. Four thousand refers to the approximate number of verses in the corpus; the number has been rounded off and understood as the total of four groups of a thousand verses each, which symbolize the four Vedas. Śrīvaiṣṇava scripture also includes the Sanskrit Vedas (*śruti*) and by extension *smṛti* works.

forced by the prevalence of the Gupta understanding of Viṣṇu with his *avatāras* of varying number, which spread throughout the subcontinent from the fourth century C.E. But it is odd that the name Viṣṇu (Tamil Viṭṭu) is used *only four* times[3] in the four thousand Āḻvār verses. This suggests to me that the Āḻvārs do not consider Viṣṇu or a homologized Viṣṇu-Nārāyaṇa-Kṛṣṇa as their supreme god, and so they must belong to a distinct tradition that only later was integrated into Śrīvaiṣṇavism.

The matter of the Āḻvārs' supreme god is even more complicated. Determination of supremacy is problematic because in general the Āḻvārs do not use proper names but rely on cryptic mythic or poetic imagery that alludes to identification. Moreover, they have a theological assumption of one supreme god with many names, epithetonyms,[4] forms, and functions[5] albeit with some restrictions. When the Āḻvārs do mention a specific name, they refer usually to Māl/Tirumāl (the dark one), Kaṇṇaṉ (Sanskrit Kṛṣṇa) but also Nāraṇaṉ/Nārāyaṇaṉ (Sanskrit Nārāyaṇa). This brings me to my question: Just who is the Āḻvārs' supreme god?

My research suggests that ocean imagery abounds in the four thousand Āḻvār verses and is central to a cosmogony, which I take here as a synonym of cosmology in the religious sense of the nature of the universe that makes human life possible. The cosmogony has a common structure—a cycle of virtual destruction of the earth/universe, preservation of it in the sense that something remains, and rescue/re-manifestation/re-creation of it (henceforth, abbreviated as virtual destruction, preservation, and re-creation). The Āḻvār verses allude to different myths or variants of the same myth that belong to each phase in this tripartite

---

3 *Periyāḻvārtirumoḻi* 2.3.5; *Periyatirumoḻi* 11.5.9; and *Tiruvāymoḻi* 2.7.4 and 2.7.5. Viṇṇu, which could be derived from Viṣṇu, generally means sky or heaven in their verses and never the supreme god.

4 Examining proper names by no means solves the issue of which god is supreme. Many references to the deity are by epithet (the one who is X, has X or does X) or by location (the one who resides in X). I call these names based on epithets "epithetonyms." Many proper names were probably once epithetonyms such as Kṛṣṇa, the one who is black/dark.

5 Cf. Poykai 44.

cycle: virtual destruction (by floods, eating, or swallowing), preservation (as earth, child, germ of all things, soul of the universe, serpent, island), and rescue/re-creation (by a boar,[6] a god who takes three great steps,[7] a dwarf who grows to the size of the universe,[8] or a figure who emerges from the deity's navel and then re-creates the world[9]). Some Āḻvār verses allude to just one phase of the tripartite cycle such as destruction through a flood or extension/re-creation through three steps. Other verses reduce a phase of the cycle to just a synecdoche such as the final step (the supreme heaven) or the feet of the god.[10]

---

6 The boar (*ēṉam*, *kēḻal*, and *varākam* from Sanskrit *varāha*) is mentioned in *Śatapatha Brāhmaṇa* I.8.1-6. Prajāpati assumes the form of a boar and lifts the earth out of the primeval waters by raising it on its tusks. The boar is also mentioned in *Śatapatha Brāhmaṇa* XIV.1.2, which describes how after a fight with a demon, he raised the earth out of the ocean with his tusks.

7 The epithet of the one who takes three great steps (*trivikrama*) later becomes a proper noun.

8 The dwarf (*vāmaṉ/vāmaṉaṉ* from *vāmana*) is the one who grows tall through three great steps. In the *Rāmāyaṇa*, we encounter a more developed version of this myth. Here the supreme god becomes a dwarf to subdue the *asura* King Bali's pride. "He asks for a gift of land measuring the size of his three steps. When granted the boon, he enlarges himself into a wonderfully giant form, and measures the entire earth with his three steps. King Bali is finally sent to rule the nether world" (Desai 1973: 98-99).

9 This figure becomes known as Brahmā.

10 The question is whether these are just independent creation myths or whether they are related through homologies (assimilation through analogy or equation) and other types of transformations, including additions and subtractions of key elements. My hypothesis is that a cosmogonic myth related to the ocean (also minimally anthropomorphized as a deity residing on the ocean) once existed in the Indus Valley Civilization, which likely developed its own mythic transformations leading to variants over time. After this civilization weakened or collapsed, its myths or mythic fragments were absorbed into the worldviews of groups on its borders, one of which (the Vedic) moved over time to the Gangetic heartland, generating more variants in the process, and another moved inland from Indus settlements on what is now the Gujarat coast. South of the Vindhya mountains, the ocean god and tripartite cosmogony were more prominent, despite the pos-

With this background in mind, I search for information related to the deity such as proper names, epithetonyms, and concepts of supremacy and soteriology in the four *Antātis*[11]—*Mutal Tiruvantāti, Iraṇṭām Tiruvantāti, Mūṉṟām Tiruvantāti,* and *Nāṉmukaṉ*[12] *Tiruvantāti*—written supposedly by the four earliest Āḻvārs (Poykai, Pūtam, Pēy, and Tirumaḻicai) respectively.[13] These works have approximately the same length, about one hundred verses each, and are written in *veṉpā* meter. I then compare the results of my translations[14] to what is found about Viṣṇu, Kṛṣṇa, and Nārāyaṇa in northern Sanskrit works and the late Tamil *Caṅkam* works, which likely preceded or overlapped with those of the early Āḻvārs. I conclude by offering a new view of the *Antāti* poets' view of the supreme god and his history, which I think applies to the other Āḻvārs as well.

---

sible development of variants there too, which eventually travelled further south and into Tamil country.

11 *Antāti* refers to the stylistic feature of having the final (*anta*) letter, syllable or foot of the last line the same as the beginning (*āti;* Sanskrit *ādi*). By extension, the end of the work is the same as its beginning (*Tamil Lexicon* vol. 1, 1982, 82).

12 The title of this work *Nāṉmukaṉ Antāti* is intriguing. It literally means the one-with-four-faces (= Brahmā) *antāti*. Although there are some references to him, he is by no means the focus of the *Antāti*. If one were to follow the pattern of the titles—first (*mutal*), second (*iraṇṭām*), and third (*mūṉṟām*) *Antāti*s—then the next one should just have the word fourth.

13 Hardy 1983: 266. Scholars have assumed that the order of these *Antāti*s is also the chronological order of the Āḻvārs themselves. But Tirumaḻicai seems to me to be a later poet with his focus on Araṅkam and his putdowns of other deities, which are akin to the putdowns of Tirumaṅkai Āḻvār. If Tirumaḻicai were a later poet, it is possible that a redactor wanted to group all the *Antāti*s of the same length together and therefore chose a title that had at least the word four in it. That said, I include Tirumaḻicai here so that I can compare four works of about equal length.

14 The translations here are my own unless otherwise noted. After this article was submitted, a book including translations of the first three *Antāti*s, an extensive introductory essay with philological explanations, an epilogue and appendices on the names and epithets of deities, incarnations, mythic episodes, temples, and toponyms was published (Wilden 2020).

Setting the stage

As mentioned, it is commonly accepted that the deity of the Āḻvārs is Viṣṇu who is also known by the names of his incarnations (*avatāra*s).[15] Friedhelm Hardy has a somewhat different identification. In his *Viraha-Bhakti: The Early History of Kṛṣṇa Devotion in South India*, a book that focuses on emotional devotion (*bhakti*) to Kṛṣṇa, Hardy takes up the question of the relation of Kṛṣṇa, Viṣṇu, and Nārāyaṇa in the Āḻvārs' works. He argues that "The religious awareness of Kṛṣṇa as a historical person on the one hand, and the tendencies to deify him, in fact to see in him the Vedic god Viṣṇu or the absolute Bhagavān on the other, created a contrast and a theological tension. How can one and the same 'person' be 'historical' and eternal-absolute?"[16]

Hardy thinks that the deification of Kṛṣṇa occurred by association with Viṣṇu or the more general epithet 'Bhagavān.' He suggests that the *avatāra* concept developed specifically in the context of Kṛṣṇa—the need to hold together the transcendent and human aspects of the god—and only then was extended to include the "incarnations" of other figures. However, Hardy says that he wants to keep Kṛṣṇa and Viṣṇu conceptually distinct to acknowledge those who see Kṛṣṇa as both the supreme god and a human form on earth, and those who view Viṣṇu as supreme and Kṛṣṇa as but one of many incarnations.[17] This distinction, he says, is important for the Tamil *Caṅkam* references. He assumes that Kṛṣṇa is the key figure in these works because "*the only real name ren-*

---

[15] For instance, "They held that Visnu or one of his avatars (incarnations) confers upon devotees the grace that is necessary for total surrender (*prapatti*) to him" (Britannica, The Editors of Encyclopaedia. "Alvar." Encyclopedia Britannica, 15 Nov. 2018. https.//www.britannica.com/topic/ Alvar. Accessed 3 March 2022). See also Wikipedia. "Alvars": "The Alvars or Azhwar ... were Tamil poet-saints of South India who espoused *bhakti* (devotion) to the Hindu god Vishnu..." (en.wikipedia.org. Accessed 3 March 2022). The same identification is made by most scholars. For example, Vasudha Narayanan comments: "The Tamil devotees who sang in praise of Viṣṇu were called Āḻvārs ...." (Narayanan 1987: 1).

[16] Hardy 1983: 23.

[17] Hardy 1983: 24.

dered into Tamil is Kṛṣṇa. 'Viṣṇu,' 'Vāsudeva,' 'Nārāyaṇa,' and so on have no direct Tamil replicas ... Kṛṣṇa is synonymous with Vāsudeva, Viṣṇu, Nārāyaṇa, Bhagavān, all names which denote the 'personal absolute.'"[18] So now Hardy wants to have the analysis both ways: a distinction should be maintained between Kṛṣṇa and Viṣṇu, but also no such distinction need be maintained.

Just how messy this issue of identity can become is evident in Hardy's analysis of the name Māyōṉ.[19] He presents eight textual "fragments" from the Tamil *Caṅkam* corpus prior to the time of the Āḻvārs that mention this name Māyōṉ. He identifies #1[20] as definitely the Kṛṣṇa of Mathura/Vraja tradition because it refers to a festival on the *tiruvoṇa* (Śravaṇa) star. I agree; this identification is possible because Śravaṇa is Kṛṣṇa's birthday in other texts. Hardy's fragment #7,[21] which pairs Vāliyōṉ and Māyōṉ is obviously a specific reference to Balarāma (*vāl* is derived from Sanskrit *bāla*) and Kṛṣṇa, because the two have been closely connected if not identified in Sanskrit works such as the *Harivaṁśa*.

Regarding fragment #2,[22] Hardy attributes the one who is the color of the ocean (*mun-nīr Vaṇṇaṉ piṟaṅ*)[23] as of a "more general Vaiṣṇava nature." But what does that mean, especially in light of his analysis of the next two fragments: #3 (lines 371-3) and #4 (lines 402-4) of the *Perumpāṇāṟṟupaṭai?* He says that these are "perhaps ... more typical of Nārāyaṇa."[24] The former refers to the one who reclines on the serpent

---

18 Hardy 1983: 23.

19 Hardy 1983:150 ff. and Appendix V: 606 ff.

20 *Maturaikkāñci* lines 590-599.

21 *Naṟṟiṇai* 32, lines1-4.

22 *Perumpāṇāṟṟupaṭai* line 30.

23 I translate this as the lord who is the one with the color of the three-fold sea, which seems to be an allusion to the three-fold cosmogony. According to the *Tamil Lexicon* (vol. 6, 1982, 3268), *mu-n-nīr* can mean the "sea as having the three qualities of forming, protecting, and destroying the earth," taking *mu-n* as *muṉṟu* or three.

24 Hardy 1983: 153.

couch and the latter to the one who gives birth to the one with four faces, that is Brahmā, in the navel of Neṭiyōṉ.[25] It is intriguing that here Hardy assumes that Nārāyaṇa and not Viṣṇu is associated with sleeping on the serpent couch, creation, and dark blue color, despite an earlier statement that Kṛṣṇa's supremacy comes from his identification with the god Viṣṇu and that the one who is the color of the ocean belongs to a more general Vaiṣṇava nature![26]

Despite making some distinctions, Hardy concludes that because the color of this god is dark—he is the color of the ocean, a sparkling polished sapphire, an elephant, and a mountain, or more generally because he is said to have a body of dark color—this god must be Kṛṣṇa because Kṛṣṇa means black, and the name Māyōṉ is a literal translation into Tamil: the one who is black.[27] But perhaps in times past, Kṛṣṇa, who needed a transcendent aspect, was simply merged with a supreme deity who was independently described as dark or black such as a god of the dark ocean.

Hardy has little to say about a Nārāyaṇa strand except for a brief historical note on the process of Kṛṣṇa's apotheosis via linkage in the *Mahābhārata* with Nara-Nārāyaṇa or Nārāyaṇa's link with Indra, Viṣṇu or Arjuna/Kṛṣṇa. He also mentions cryptically another transmission of a "Nārāyaṇa of some obscure independent origin ... [who later] entered the Pāñcarātra and other branches of Vaiṣṇavism as the personal absolute."[28] This is not very helpful. According to Narayanan's catalog (1987, Appendix1), there are only 6 references to Nara-Nārāyaṇa in the entire four thousand verses and 5 of these are found in just one late

---

25 Hardy translates this as the Exalted One, but it really means the one who grows tall, from *neṭu* meaning to grow tall (*Tamil Lexicon* vol. 4, 1982, 2336).

26 Of Hardy's eight fragments, two are specifically about Kṛṣṇa; three are about an oceanic, cosmogonic god; and three, which I have not mentioned here, are too general to determine whether they are Viṣṇu, Kṛṣṇa, or Nārāyaṇa. This hardly makes a case that the *Caṅkam* antecedents identify Kṛṣṇa as the key god.

27 Hardy 1983: 220.

28 Hardy 1983: 23-24.

work, the *Periyatirumoli̲*, and none in the four *Antāti*s being discussed here.[29]

My own concern is that the names, epithets, and descriptions of the deity whom the Āl̲vārs' considered supreme have not been examined thoroughly in their poems, and that a textual study combined with a search for antecedents might provide clues to his identity and history, even the Āl̲vārs' identity and history. I turn now to my case study: the supreme deity in the four *Antāti*s.

The four *Antāti*s: an introduction

In this section, I will give an overview of descriptions of color, references to sleeping on the ocean or on a serpent couch on the ocean, the tripartite cosmogony (virtual destruction, preservation, and re-creation), proper names, and salvific motifs in the four *Antāti*s, based in large part on Narayanan's "Catalog of Myths and Names in Āl̲vār Poetry"[30].

---

[29] I have argued elsewhere that there is no specific Pāñcarātra Āgamic content in the four thousand verses because there are other viable interpretations for any evidence produced such as numbers, patterns of worship, branding, mantras, and details of temple architecture (Young 2006: 203-210). Now, after doing the present study, I think another explanation is also possible. There were proto-Pāñcarātra traditions in the temples, possibly including priests, but the Āl̲vārs likely avoided mention of them because they were trying to distance themselves from aspects of this tradition for reasons that will become clear later in my discussion.

[30] Narayanan 1987, Appendix 1. Because this catalog was not computer-generated, I found some additional references. More recently, Wilden (2020) have created a study of names, descriptors, and myths for the first three *Antāti*s, which are based on a digitalized text. However, it is difficult to compare my results with the verse counts that can be generated from their glossary and appendices, because I have aggregated some names into one category when I consider them variants, and I have included Tirumal̲icai in my counts, whereas their study is based on just the first three Āl̲vārs. That said, I find that my general conclusions regarding verse counts are supported by this more recent study.

Narayanan has detected 41 references in these works to the one of the color of the dark ocean (Kaṭalvaṇṇaṉ, Nīrvaṇṇaṉ) and by extension other epithetonyms based on darkness: Māṇikkam (the one who has the color of a garnet[31]); Maṇivaṇṇaṉ (the one who is the color of a jewel or blackness); Mukilvaṇṇaṉ (the one who is the color of a [dark] cloud); Kārvaṇṇaṉ (the one of black or *kāl* color); Kāyāpūvaṇṇaṉ (the one of the color of the [dark] Kāyā flower), and Koṇṭavaṇṇaṉ (the one of cloud color). She finds 27 references to swallowing/eating the world. In addition, she is has detected 46 references to the one sleeping on the ocean or on a serpent on the ocean. The following chart shows the number of occurrences of these epithets that I have detected in the four *Antātis*.

Chart 1: The Ocean God

	dark color	swallows the worlds	sleeps on the serpent or the ocean of milk
Poykai	11	6	15
Pūtam	10	5	8
Pēy	11	9	13
Tirumaḻicai	9	7	10
total	41	27	46

If I consider just proper names in Narayanan's catalog, I find that in the *Antātis*, there are 10 references to the proper name Kaṇṇaṉ, 20 to Nāraṇaṉ/ Nārāyaṇaṉ,[32] and 63 to Tirumāl/Māl. Because the latter name includes what I consider variants — Neṭumāl/Neṭiyāṉ/Neṭiyōṉ referring to the one who grows tall), Ceṅkaṇmāl (the Māl with red eyes), and Māyaṉ/Māyavaṉ (the one who is dark, illusive, or wondrous)[33]—the

[31] The word "gem" (*maṇi*) is some contexts means specifically sapphire, garnet, or ruby.

[32] Narayanan's catalog mentions only 15 references; it has left out those to Nāraṇaṉ in Poykai. When these are added plus a few others I have found, my total is 20.

[33] *Māl* means the one who is black. I consider Neṭumāl (the one who grows tall), a variant because it contains *māl* but also Neṭiyāṉ/ Neṭiyōṉ because it

name Tirumāl/Māl and its variants considered collectively is far more common than the other proper names.

Chart 2: Key Names of God

	Māl etc.	Nāraṇan̲/Nārāyaṇan̲	Kaṇṇan̲
Poykai	19	3[34]	2
Pūtam	20	5	3[35]
Pēy	16	1	2
Tirumal̲icai	16	10	4
total	71	19	10

Regarding what I consider figures associated with the cosmogony, Narayanan has 13 references to the boar, 42 to the wide-stepping one, 14 to the dwarf, and 25 to Ayan̲/Nān̲mukan̲ (Brahmā).[36] With this background in mind, I now examine the first *Antāti*.

---

means the one who grows tall, elsewhere identified as Māl. Similarly, Ceṅkaṇmāl (the Māl with red eyes) is a variant because it contains *māl.* Māyan̲/Māyavan̲ are variants, because *mā* can mean black and by extension black person (see *Tamil Lexicon* vol. 5, 1982, pp. 3142, 3165, 3174, 3175 and *A Dravidian Etymological Dictionary* (DED) 1984, #4781. The fact that *mā* can also mean great, beauty, illusion, desire, or love (DED #4786, 4814) or can be derived from Sanskrit *māyā* (illusion; magic) was creatively exploited by the poets.

34 There is no separate category in Narayanan's catalog for Nāraṇan̲/ Nārāyaṇan̲. Two of these three references to him are found in Poykai 57 and 59 under the category "Sacred Names." I have found one other reference in Poykai 5.

35 Narayanan lists two. I have located three.

36 Although there are quite a few references to Ayan̲/Nān̲mukan̲ (Brahmā), I summarize the references to him only in this note because he is always secondary and is not in contention for being supreme.

Poykai mentions Nān̲mukan̲ (Brahmā) 6 times in several contexts: one is his abode on the Lord's navel (vs. 28, 33, 56, 59); another is his worship by Irāvaṇan̲ (45), and yet another is how his skull became a begging bowl (v. 46).

Mutal Tiruvantāti by Poykai

In this section, I search for references to ocean imagery, proper names, and supremacy and soteriology in Poykai's *Antāti.*

Ocean imagery: According to Narayanan's catalog, Poykai mentions the one of a dark color 11 times, the one who sleeps on the serpent in the ocean of milk[37] 15 times, and the one who swallows the worlds 6 times. She does not catalog other figures associated with the ocean and cosmogony, perhaps because she views Viṣṇu as containing all these or because she is looking only for what she considers *avatāras*.

A very common epithetonym refers to the god who is the color of the (dark) ocean.

> The foremost [of the gods] are the three. Among these three, the ocean-hued one (*nīr vaṇṇaṉ*) is the foremost. Without the grace of the one who is

---

Pūtam mentions him 5 times; I have removed one verse from Narayanan's count (v. 69) because I do not consider it a reference to Nāṉmukaṉ but to the supreme god who is described as having a lotus navel. Pūtam says that Nāṉmukaṉ worships the serpent-reclining Lord's feet (v. 12) or Māl (v. 17); that he sits on the Lord's navel (v. 37); and that he poured water that became the Kaṅkai (Gaṅgā) (v. 78).

Pēy mentions him 2 times and refers to the Lord as a child lying in Nāṉmukaṉ's lap when Irāvaṇaṉ came (v. 77), and how Nāṉmukaṉ cannot completely understand the Lord's glories (v. 97).

Tirumaḻicai mentions him 12 times and often expresses the Lord's supremacy by saying how the Lord creates Nāṉmukaṉ (v. 1), how he has Nāṉmukaṉ as part of his body (v. 4), how he is the Lord of Nāṉmukaṉ and Civaṉ (v. 96) and how people will never worship these two (v. 66). With even greater hyperbole, Tirumaḻicai proclaims how worshippers of the Lord become gods even to Nāṉmukaṉ and Civaṉ (v. 91). In addition, Tirumaḻicai mentions how Nāṉmukaṉ washed the Lord's feet with water that fell on Civaṉ's hair, and how that water then became the Kaṅkai (Gaṅgā) (v. 9). We are also told that the results of penance are received from Nāṉmukaṉ (v. 19).

37 Her references in this category are often not "sleeping on serpent in ocean of *milk*" but rather "being on the ocean" or "sleeping on the ocean," which is usually described as dark.

> beneficent and the cause of everything in this world [surrounded by] the great ocean, the grace of many [other gods] is lacking.[38]

Here the ocean-hued one is described as supreme over the three, that is, the *trimūrti*, which usually refers in Sanskrit texts to Brahmā, Viṣṇu, and Śiva. If we were to consider Viṣṇu as the supreme god, this verse would contain a redundancy (Viṣṇu is both beyond the *trimūrti* and is one of the gods of the *trimūrti*).

The ocean is so important to this poet that he personifies it as in the apostrophe "O Great Dark Ocean." The personified dark ocean is named Māl, which literally means "the dark one" in Tamil, and we are told that he has a beautiful dark body. Poykai describes the ocean in various ways. He sometimes makes a connection between the ocean and anything of dark color such as a cloud, a gem, or a mountain. He describes the ocean as deep (vs. 39, 83) or mighty (v. 68). The poet refers elsewhere to the god being so great and omnipresent that he contains the ocean and all else within himself (v. 73).

This dark ocean deity is often described as reclining or sleeping on the ocean or on a serpent bed on the ocean or on a leaf there. With reference to reclining on a serpent bed on the ocean, we find this verse.[39]

> Afraid, saying "I have wasted many days," I cried. Now, after seeing the one on the serpent bed (*aravaṇai mēl*), I worshipped the feet of the one who has the color of the ocean, has captivating red eyes and who rests [there] while the ocean caresses [his] feet with waves.[40]

---

mutal āvāṉ mūri nīr vaṇṇaṉ—mutal āya
nallāṉ aruḷ allāl nāma nīr vaiyakattu,
pallār aruḷum paḻutu (Poykai 15).

39 See also vs. 55, 62, 68, 85.

40 *paḻutē pala pakalum pōyiṉa eṉṟu, añci*
aḻutēṉ. arav' aṇai-mēl kaṇṭu — toḻutēṉ
kaṭal ōtam kāl alaippa kaṇvaḷarum cem kaṇ
aṭal ōtam vaṇṇar aṭi. (Poykai 16).

Elsewhere, Poykai elaborates on the idea of the serpent as coiled (v. 62) or thousand-hooded (v. 32).[41] Sometimes he refers directly or indirectly to an actual temple where the god resides in his reclining form such as Veḫkā (v. 77). There are more general allusions to the posture of the deity as reclining, sitting, or standing. And in several verses, the poet describes the god as sleeping on a banyan leaf on the ocean after swallowing the earth.

> O great dark ocean! What effort did you make to be always touching his auspicious form when Māl sleeps, the one with beautiful dark body [and] red eyes [who reclines] on the ocean, having swallowed the earth, [and] rests on a banyan leaf?[42]

The god also assumes the form of a child sleeping on the banyan leaf.

> Having swallowed the seven worlds, you once took the form of a child and slept on a banyan leaf. This is the truth they say. Was the banyan [leaf] on that day within flood waters of the ocean, in the sky, [or] on the earth? You who lifted the mountain surrounded by rich groves, tell.[43]

There are other references to eating/swallowing the earth/universe (*ulakam*) (vs. 1; 9), which suggests its virtual destruction. The poet elaborates on this,

> Saying "are these the seven worlds destroyed by you, with eyes blazing with anger, which arose again?" My tongue will not praise, even a bit, anyone except Māyavaṉ who revealed himself completely to the Veda-knowers.[44]

---

41 The snake is such an important image that in verse 53 the poet declares: "Tirumāl has a snake (*tirumaṟku aravu*)" and then describes how it becomes a parasol (as the head of a cobra), a seat, a pedestal, and an armrest.

42 *mālum karum kaṭalē, eṉ nōṟṟāy, vaiyakam uṇṭ'*
āliṉ ilai tuyiṉṟa āḻiyāṉ, — kōla
karu mēṉi cem kaṇ māl kaṇpaṭai-uḷ, eṉṟum
tiru mēṉi nī tīṇṭa peṟṟu (Poykai 19).

43 *pālaṉ taṉat' uruv' āy ēḻ ulak' uṇṭ' āl ilaiyiṉ*
mēl aṉṟu nī vaḷarntatu mey eṉpar — āl aṉṟu
vēlai nīr uḷḷatō viṇṇatō maṇṇatō?
cōlai cūḻ kuṉṟ' eṭuttāy collu (Poykai 69).

44 *ceṟṟ' eḻuntu tī viḻittu ceṉṟa inta ēḻ ulakum*

In addition, Poykai alludes to eating/swallowing the worlds when describing how the god contains everything—the ocean, mountains and so forth—within himself (v. 73). There are also references to rescuing the earth/world by lifting it up[45] as in the following.

> When was the ocean (*kaṭal*) churned? From the ocean (*nīr*), which world was lifted? I do not know anything about these [matters]. On that day, the ocean (*āḻi*) is where you slept after you destroyed and preserved this earth that you created, lifted, swallowed, and spat out![46]

The ocean is so important for Poykai that he elaborates on it whenever he can, for instance, by describing the earth as surrounded by the ocean but also the ocean during the flood being without the earth (v. 61). On occasion, Poykai alludes to the myth found in Sanskrit sources of how the *devas* and *asuras* churned the ocean to obtain ambrosia.

The re-creation of the earth is another important theme. In one verse, it is the god's very growth or expansion that produces the world again (v. 3). Another way of expressing the extension or measuring of the earth is the idea of the three great strides. This in turn becomes connected to the myth found in Sanskrit texts of how the god deceives the *asuras* to obtain a bit of land the size of his dwarf body. Poykai alludes to this myth on three occasions. Although he does not use the word dwarf (*māṇi*)—in fact, none of the *Antāti* poets do—he does refer to Māvali (Sanskrit: Mahābali) who took the gift of land and grew (vs. 36, 50, 79).

---

maṟṟ' ivaiyā eṉṟu vāy aṅkāntu muṟṟum
maṟaiyavaṟku kāṭṭiya māyavaṉai allāl
iṟai ēṉum ēttāt' eṉ nā (Poykai 94).

45 In addition, there are direct and indirect references to the rescue of the earth by the boar (Poykai 10, 26, 84, 91), who lifts it on his tusk.

46 *eṉṟu kaṭal kaṭaintatu? ev ulakam nīr ēṟṟatu?*
oṉṟum ataṉai uṇarēṉ nāṉ. aṉṟ' at'
aṭaitt' uṭaittu kaṇpaṭutta āḻi, itu nī
paṭaitt' iṭant' uṇṭ' umiḻnta pār (Poykai 2).

Proper names: Poykai uses the name Māl and its variants 19 times; these refer mainly to the ocean (vs. 42, 53), cosmogony (vs. 7, 19, 21, 61, 69, 92, 96), and worship (vs. 52, 58, 70, 75) with one reference to Māl's supremacy (v. 52) and one to the man-lion (v. 31). In verse 64, Poykai says that he will not praise any deity except Tirumāl. As for the variant Māyavaṉ, Poykai uses it in two verses that allude to how one should worship only this god (vs. 80, 94), one about cosmogony (v. 94), and one as a vocative (v. 100).

In Poykai's *Antāti*, the name Kaṇṇaṉ occurs only twice (vs. 7; 56). In verse 7, in the context of the creation of the quarters and their respective gods, the one who is the color of the black sea, who churned the ocean, and who is Neṭumāl (the Māl who grows tall) is identified with Kaṇṇaṉ. In another verse, the name Kaṇṇaṉ appears in connection with the god's lotus navel.

> Besides prattling so his names will come, who can know our Lord?[47] So be it. Even Ayaṉ (Brahmā), although being within the fragrant lotus [Kaṇṇaṉ's navel], cannot see Kaṇṇaṉ's lotus feet.[48]

In the previous verse (55), Poykai also describes Āyaṉ—the cowherd, an allusion to Kaṇṇaṉ—as the one who reclines on the serpent bed and says that the devoted servants give praise to Āyaṉ's name.

There are several Tirumāl/Māl verses that allude to Kaṇṇaṉ.[49] One is to him as the charioteer, one to events in his early life, and one to the cosmogony, more specifically to the one who ate the worlds and then emptied out his stomach. In this context, the poet impishly makes a connection to Kaṇṇaṉ by asking whether the butter given by the cowherd dame Yacōtai (Yaśodā, his foster mother) was sufficient to fill his empty stomach. The catalog gives other references to incidents in the life of Kṛṣṇa (many known to the *Harivaṁśa*) without mentioning his name such as killing various demons (13 references) or wrestlers (1),

---

47 Pemmāṉ is an alternative form of Perumāṉ, meaning the "great one".

48 *pērē varap pitaṟṟal allāl em pemmāṉai*
ārē aṟivār. atu niṟka. nērē
kaṭi kamalatt' uḷ iruntum kāṇ-kilāṉ kaṇṇaṉ
aṭi kamalam taṉṉai ayaṉ (Poykai 56).

49 For instance, Poykai 8 and 92.

being a cowherd (1), stealing and eating butter/yoghurt (4), being tied to a mortar (2), participating in the Kurukṣetra war (1), lifting Govardhana (6), and performing the Kuravai dance (1). The catalog also refers to some items that belong only to the South Indian milieu such as Nappiṉṉai (1), the conquest of seven bulls (2), going between two *maruta* trees (6), dancing with pots (1), and breaking the Kuruṇṭu tree (3).

Narayanan's catalog has no specific category for Nāraṇaṉ/ Nārāyaṇaṉ (only a category for Nara-Nārāyaṇa) but does mention 2 references to Nāraṇaṉ by Poykai under the category of "sacred names" and the subcategory "*namō nāraṇa,* sacred 8, and *tirumantra,*" in other words, the category of *mantra.* They appear in my Chart 2 for Nāraṇaṉ/Nārāyaṇaṉ.

Namō nāraṇā literally means "salutations, O Nāraṇaṉ." This has been considered a *mantra* in the later tradition and possibly here too. The word *mantra* does not appear in this verse. But it does in the immediately following one (v. 58), which refers to worship with flowers and incense and then to *mantra*s. Because of their proximity, we can assume that the name Māl, which also appears in this verse, is equated with the Nāraṇaṉ in the previous verse and that *namō nāraṇā* is likely the *mantra.* There are several other key references to *mantra*s and reciting a sacred name in this decade, but no other proper name is mentioned.

On two other occasions, Poykai mentions the word *mantra* or *namō nāraṇā.* One verse advises one to worship Tirumāl with garlands, sacrifices, *tantra*s and *mantra*s, and names (v. 70). Another verse connects chanting "*namō nāraṇā*" with going to the great refuge (the god is not named).

> There is a tongue in every mouth; there is speech for chanting ceaselessly *namō nāraṇā*; there is a path to go to his great refuge without returning. How can someone go on the path to hell?[50]

---

[50] *nā vāyil uṇṭē namō nāraṇā eṉṟ'*
ōvāt' uraikkum urai uṇṭē mūvāta
mā kati kaṇ cellum vakai uṇṭē eṉ oruvar
tī kati kaṇ cellum tiṟam? (Poykai 95).

We may take *namō nāraṇā* here as a *mantra*. The words *namas* and *mantra* are associated *only* with the name Nāraṇaṉ in Poykai's verses (aside from one connection of the word *mantra* and Tirumāl in verse 70, which likely is equated with Nārāyaṇaṉ in the previous verse).

There is only one cryptic connection between the name Nāraṇaṉ, the ocean, and dark color. In verse 5, which is a comparison of Nāraṇaṉ and Araṉ (Śiva), Nāraṇaṉ is associated with the [*garuḍa*] bird, the four Vedas (*nāṉmaṟai*), the mountain, the ocean (*nīr*), protection, the discus, and the color of a cloud. Ocean here might refer to the white ocean, because Nāraṇaṉ is elsewhere connected to the white ocean. If so, it is odd that he is also described as the color of a cloud because the color of a cloud implies darkness and that is usually aligned with mention of the dark ocean. In Poykai's following verse (6), Nāraṇaṉ has the color of the flood waters. Usually, however, he does not have these epithets of having dark color or being on the dark sea.

Supremacy and soteriology: We have already seen that the ocean-hued one is the foremost among the three (presumably, an allusion to the *trimūrti*). And we can presume that all the cosmogonic activities already discussed indicate supremacy. Poykai has directly linked these activities with the ocean and cosmogony but also with both Māl and Kaṇṇaṉ. In addition, one verse, albeit without mentioning a proper name, refers to the deity who measured the earth as the first cause and the foremost of all (v. 14) and another refers to him as being the ruler even of the gods (v. 97). Again, it is striking that there are no connections of Nāraṇaṉ with the dark ocean or cosmogonic imagery aside from one reference to ocean (its color is not stipulated) and one to dark color in a list of epithets (v. 5) although he mentions a milk (ocean) on which the god lies once (v. 68). Rather, we find the name Nāraṇaṉ in the context of chanting names and salvation.

As for soteriology, Poykai refers to how some sages learned yoga as the gate to salvation (v. 4) but also that chanting his names (none are mentioned) is the means to avoid the path to hell (v. 81). Meditating on his name also allows one to visualize him.

> To see clearly his two feet [and] make our minds serene, meditate on[51] the sacred name (*tirunāmam*) of he who became a lion to fight the one [demon] who was full of pride.[52]

Elsewhere, he connects chanting with a specific name such as Nāraṇaṉ or Tirumāl (v. 70) and says that chanting *namō nāraṇā* enables one to avoid the path of evil (v. 95).[53]

> I feared the harsh karma standing nearby. Being afraid, to join your sacred feet to remove my fear, worshipping with this beautiful garland I have chanted the garland of words uttering *namō nāraṇā*.[54]

The beginning and end of a work often frames it and might provide clues about the author's view of supremacy. The beginning of the *Mutal Tiruvantāti* focuses on the ocean and cosmogonic activities. Whereas the first verse is general—it is about offering this garland of verses at the Lord's feet—the second identifies key activities of this deity connected with the ocean: churning it, sleeping on it, rescuing the earth but later eating it (that is destroying it) and later still remaking it again. The third verse describes more specifically how the earth was remade

---

51 The word *eṇ* at the end of the verse is problematic. It can mean mantra (*Tamil Lexicon* vol. 1, 1982, 517), or it can be an abbreviated form of *eṭṭu*, which means eight. If the latter, this would be an allusion to the mantra with eight syllables (*oṁ namo nārāyaṇāya*). Because Poykai uses the name Nāraṇaṉ and never *oṁ namo nārāyaṇāya* or even *nārāyaṇaṉ,* I am inclined to reject this meaning. *Eṇ* can also mean to count or consider. I do not think "count" makes any sense in this context, but we could translate the verb as "consider." Another possibility is to take *eṇ* as an abbreviated form of the verb *eṇṇu* (*Tamil Lexicon* vol. 1, 1982, 519), which can mean "meditate on." This, I think, best fits the context.

52 *eḷitil iraṇṭ' aṭiyum kāṇpataṟk' eṉ uḷḷam*
teḷiya teḷint' oḻiyum cevvē. kaḻiyiṉ
poruntātavaṉai poral uṟṟu, ari āy
iruntāṉ tiru nāmam eṇ (Poykai 51).

53 For soteriology, see also Poykai 6, 51, 55, 56, 57, 67, 76.

54 *ayal niṉṟa val viṉaiyai añciṉēṉ añci*
uya niṉ tiru aṭiyē cērvāṉ nayam niṉṟa
nal mālai koṇṭu 'namō nāraṇā' eṉṉum
col mālai kaṟṟēṉ toḻutu (Poykai 57).

through the god's growth by means of his three steps from the edge of the ocean through space. The fourth refers to how some sages learned yoga as the gate to salvation. The fifth compares Aṟaṉ (Śiva) and Nāraṇaṉ (who is described with several descriptors including a cryptic reference to the ocean). The sixth refers to the temple Araṅkam (which has the reclining god as its main image) and the god having the color of the flood waters (*ōtam nīr*); it links this temple hyperbolically with the poet's worship of him from birth to death. In the seventh, the poet makes his first explicit reference to Kaṇṇaṉ where, as we saw, he is identified with the color of the dark ocean, the one who churned the ocean, and Neṭumāl.

Turning now to the end of the *Antāti*, we find that verse 95 is an important Nāraṇaṉ reference, because it identifies chanting *namō nārāyaṇā* with avoiding the path of evil. After various epithetonyms, we are told in the penultimate verse (v. 99) that the lord always exists in the hearts of his devotees, in Vēṅkaṭam, and in Poykai's own heart. The poet sometimes lists various places where the Lord dwells, but it might be significant that this verse refers to Vēṅkaṭam, which is the most important sacred place for this Āḻvār (and the other early Āḻvārs). In the final line of the final verse (v. 100), the poet calls out "O Māyavaṉ (*māyavaṉē*)" and then says "meditate on the lord" who wears the *tuḻāy* (*tulasī*) garland, who is then named Kēcavaṉ (Keśava). One might wonder why Kēcavaṉ is featured in the final verse. I suspect it is because the poet wants to connect two incidents involving feet: Kēcavaṉ (Kaṇṇaṉ) who kicked the cart with his foot and the god who measured the world with his foot.

In sum, in Poykai's *Antāti*, oceanic and cosmogonic imagery are predominant and suggest supremacy. I think we can speak of a supreme ocean god who is usually identified by epithetonyms, not proper names. But when the latter do occur, they are the names Māl or its variants but occasionally Kaṇṇaṉ and in one instance Nāraṇaṉ. By contrast, the key proper name aligned with chanting is usually Nāraṇaṉ. The fact that it is connected to the word or context of *mantra* is significant. Other general references to chanting the name or names of god mention the means to salvation or the goal of salvation variously expressed as freedom from old age, avoiding the path to hell, or protecting us from hell.

The other early *Antātis*

Having looked in detail at the first *Antāti* by Poykai, I will avoid lengthy repetition of the themes of ocean, color, reclining, cosmogony, supremacy, and soteriology for the other three *Antātis—Iraṇṭām Tiruvantāti* by Pūtam, *Mūṉṟām Tiruvantāti* by Pēy, and *Nāṉmukaṉ Tiruvantāti* by Tirumaḻicai—because these are very similar, some poetic flourishes and different emphases notwithstanding. Instead, I offer a summary with illustrations and only then turn to the three *Antāti*s for some specific observations.

Overview of ocean imagery: I begin by noting some of the phrases used for the ocean god and the cosmogonic myth. These poets commonly combine words for ocean (*nīr*, *āḻi*, *appu*, *kaṭal*), flood waters/deluge (*puṉal*, *veḷḷam*, *ōtam*), sometimes with adjectives such as *kār* (dark), *mā* (dark or great), or *tiru* (auspicious). Regarding the one who is the color of the ocean, for instance, we find *nīr āḻi vaṇṇaṉ*, *āḻi vaṇṇaṉ*, *puṉal vaṇṇaṉ*, *kaṭal vaṇṇā*, *kaṭal nīr vaṇṇaṉ*, *kaṭal vaṇṇaṉē*, and *pēr ōtam vaṇṇar.*

Words for residing in, reclining/sleeping on the ocean, on a serpent on the ocean, on a serpent couch/bed, or on a leaf often just add the third person masculine ending *āṉ* to the nouns for sea (*kaṭal*), to mean "the one who [is or is on] the sea" (*kaṭalāṉ*) or combine words for sea with a verb such as *uḷ* (to be), *kiṭa* (to lie down as in sleep), and *tuyil* (to sleep) as in *kaṭal nīr uḷḷāṉ*, *kaṭal kiṭakkum*, and *āḻil tuyiṉṟatuvam.* The serpent bed (*nākattaṇi* or *aravaṇai*) is found in many phrases as is just the word serpent (*nāki*, *pāmpu*, *aravam*). The poets speak too of reclining on the banyan leaf. Some reclining references mention a specific temple, which is known to have a reclining image of the deity such as Araṅkam or Veḵkā, sometimes in the context of the god's three postures: reclining, sitting, and standing. On occasion the poets use several words for water or ocean no doubt for metrical reasons. Sometimes the Āḻvārs refer to other myths about the ocean such as how the *deva*s and *asura*s churned it to obtain ambrosia from its depths as in Pēy's "having churned the great/dark ocean" (*mā nīrkkaṭal kaṭaintu*) (v. 33).

Pēy also elaborates on this by describing the churning rope was a snake named Vācuki (Vāsuki) (Pēy 64, 82).[55]

Finally, these Āḻvārs use the basic vocabulary of destroy or eat/swallow, recline, sleep, spit out, lift/take, make, measure, pervade, and create. Pūtam, for instance, refers to Māyaṉ who seized the earth, swallowed the earth, and spat out the earth" (*maṇkoṇṭu maṇṇuṇṭu maṇ umiḻntu māyaṉ*) (v. 36).[56] In addition, these *Antāti* poets refer to the myth about the lord coming in disguise (as a dwarf) or with deceit, begging for or taking the earth from Māvali (Mahābali), and stretching out/growing to become the universe (Pūtam 23, 34, 61, 89, 99; Pēy 52, 83). Here are some examples of these common themes.

> The One who is beautiful rests on the [serpent] bed — which is without beginning or end with hoods decorated with precious gems, while the ocean's rising and falling waves are tossed in different directions — [and] came to recline on a couch in my heart itself! I am your servant![57]

> Resolutely worship, O heart, his feet. The one with the cool garland came as a wonder (*māyā*) child in the flood waters after rescuing the good earth and reclined there on a leaf of the banyan tree in the moving waters of the great ocean.[58]

It is striking how the Āḻvārs superimpose the image of the *reclining* ocean god onto the *standing* image of the god at Vēṅkaṭam, the fore-

---

55 *malai āmaimēl vaittu, vācukiyaic cuṟṟi*
talai āmai tāṉ oru kai paṟṟi, alaiyāmal,
pīṟak kaṭainta perumāṉ tiru nāmaṁ
yāvarkkum kūṟṟu (Tirumaḻicai 49).
The language is very similar to Pēy 46. See also Pūtam 68.

56 For cosmogonic references, see also Pēy 19, 43, 28, 45, 67.

57 *paṇint' uyarnta pauva paṭu tiraikaḷ mōta*
paṇinta paṇi maṇikaḷālē aṇintaṅk'
aṉantaṉ aṇai kiṭakkum ammāṉ aṭiyēṉ
maṉam taṉ aṇai kiṭakkum vantu (Pēy 15).

58 *muyaṉṟu toḻu, neñcē mūri nīr vēlai*
iyaṉṟa maratt' āl-ilaiyiṉ-mēlāl payiṉṟ' aṅk' ōr
maṇ nalam koḷ veḷḷattu māya kuḻavi āy
taṇ alaṅkal mālaiyāṉ tāḷ (Pēy 53).

most place of pilgrimage in the northeastern part of Tamil country. In one verse, Pūtam identifies the god of gods with the ocean-reclining god (*kaṭalāṉ*) and he, in turn, is said to be the one at Vēṅkaṭam (*vēṅkaṭattāṉ*) (v. 28). In another verse, the poet even equates a sacred bath at Vēṅkaṭam with one in the cosmic ocean where the god reclines (v. 69). Pūtam also makes an indirect link between the reclining god (at Araṅkam) and soteriology, for at this place he opens the gate to his city (*nakara vācal*) (v. 88).[59]

The supreme god is sometimes described[60] as he who is on the milk ocean (*pāl kaṭalāṉ*) (Pūtam 3). Pūtam playfully describes the god of the dark flood waters (*māl ōtam*) and Śrī as the goddess of the milk flood waters (*pāl ōtam*) (v. 42). Pēy mentions the one on the milk ocean (*pāl kaṭalāṉ* (vs. 11, 31, 32, 61) or the one whose body has the color of the milk ocean as in the following.

> That day the color of his feet that strode the worlds was that of the [crimson] lotus, the color of his body that of the milk ocean (*pāṟkkaṭal*), the color of his crown that of the radiance of the sun-discus. Is not that the beauty of the one who has the precious discus![61]

---

[59] Even to this day, devotees want to go through a special door within the Araṅkam (Śrīraṅgam) temple on the very auspicious day of *vaikunta ēkātaci* (Sanskrit: Vaikuṇṭha Ekādāśi), believing that it will make it possible for them to attain heaven.

[60] I find some translators read milk/white into descriptions of the ocean where the word milk/white does not exist. This creates the impression that the white ocean is the dominant imagery, which is not the case. Rather, it is the dark ocean. That said, the ocean is certainly a bridge or swing concept that functions to link the Ocean, Kṛṣṇa and Nārāyaṇa thereby facilitating homologization.

[61] *aṭi vaṇṇam tāmarai aṉṟ' ulakam tāyōṉ,*
paṭi vaṇṇam pār kaṭal nīr vaṇṇam, muṭi vaṇṇam
ōr āḻi veyyōṉ oḷiyum, akt' aṉṟē
ār āḻi koṇṭāṟk' aḻaku? (Pēy 5).

Pūtam's *Iraṇṭām Tiruvantāti*: The oceanic, cosmogonic god who has the dark color of the ocean is often not named but occasionally he is called Tirumāl. Pūtam tells us this.

> You measured the world that day, O Tirumāl, becoming tall. In the past, you lifted the earth that day, they say. That day you churned the dark ocean and then bridged that great ocean. The lord is the one who has the body of the great, dark sea.[62]

Elsewhere Pūtam calls Tirumāl as Neṭumāl, Neṭiyāṉ, or Neṭiyōṉ in the cosmogonic context because, as already mentioned, *neṭu* means to grow tall, which refers to his cosmic growth at the time of creation (vs. 5, 11, 97, 99, 100). Māl is mentioned, moreover, in the context of supremacy. Māl is the god who is worshipped by other gods, is the king of gods, or the master (vs. 17, 90, 97, 99), although sometimes this descriptor occurs with other unrelated epithets, making the verse more general in nature. Pūtam uses the name Tirumāl too in the context of worship; he calls out "O Tirumāl," says he praises his feet alone, and uses ecstatic imagery of singing and dancing around him (v. 32). His worship frees him from further rebirth (v. 42). In one verse (v. 64), the poet asks Tirumāl's permission to chant his names. As for other names in this cluster, Pūtam uses the vocative Māyāvaṉē in a list of vocatives (v. 58), Māyaṉ once in the cosmogonic context (v. 36), and once when describing the god as full of wonders (v. 83).

From all this, one might think that Pūtam views the name Māl (and its variants) as the name of supreme god. After all, Pūtam mentions Māl and its variants 22 times in his work and in many different contexts. But looking at the beginning of Pūtam's *Iraṇṭām Tiruvantāti* causes one to question this assessment. The very first verse, which draws an analogy between the emotions of the poet and lighting a lamp, mentions the proper name Nāraṇaṉ. The second verse mentions the name Nāraṇaṉ as well.

---

[62] *nī aṉṟ' ulak' aḷantāy nīṇṭa tirumālē*
nī aṉṟ' ulak' iṭantāy, eṉparāl, nī aṉṟu
kār ōtam muṉ kaṭaintu piṉ aṭaittāy mā kaṭalai
pēr ōtam mēṉi pirāṉ (Pūtam 30).

> If we know well Nāraṇaṉ's names and chant his names in his [sacred] places (*tāṉa*), we become celestials ornamenting heaven. Is not that the nature of our king of the bowing gods?[63]

We encounter this name somewhat later in verse 20 where we are told that those who know the names of Nāraṇaṉ and praise him will live. Verse 66 puts this idea even more strongly by saying that chanting the name Nāraṇaṉ (*nāraṇaṉ pēr ōti*) prevents one from going to hell (*naraka*). Elsewhere, the Āḻvār ecstatically proclaims the importance of Nāraṇaṉ for him (v. 81).

The final five verses of Pūtam's *Antāti* do not mention Nāraṇaṉ at all. Rather, verse 95 alludes to the cosmogony, and verse 96 describes the god who is reclining on the serpent as the one of the three (sacred Vedic) fires. The next verse (97) refers to being brought up as a cowherd and again refers to reclining on the serpent. Verse 98 mentions swallowing the seven worlds (along with several other epithetonyms based on various activities of Kaṇṇaṉ). The penultimate verse refers to Perumāṉ, Neṭiyāṉ, and Māl. And the final verse begins with the vocatives Mālē, Neṭiyōṉē, and Kaṇṇaṉē and concludes by referring to the poet's love (*aṉpu*) of the god. In short, the beginning of Pūtam's *Antāti* is more explicitly Nāraṇaṉ-oriented than the end, which does not mention his name at all, referring rather to the ocean, cosmogony, and the life of the cowherd.

Regarding the proper name Kaṇṇaṉ, it appears in only three of Pūtam's verses. The first (v. 49) refers to calling out the name of the lord so that it resounds throughout the universe, the second (v. 64) addresses Kaṇṇaṉ as the substance of the Epics and then asks Tirumāl's permission to let him chant his names, and the third (v. 100) is simply found in a list of vocatives.[64]

---

63 *ñāṉattāl naṉk' uṇarntu nāraṇaṉ taṉ nāmaṅkaḷ*
tāṉattāl maṟṟ' avaṉ pēr cāṟṟiṉāl vāṉatt'
aṇi amarar ākkuvikkum aḵt' aṉṟē naṅkaḷ
paṇi amarar kōmāṉ paricu? (Pūtam 2).

64 Pūtam also uses the name Māl or its variant Tirumāl in the contexts of assuming the form of a lion (v. 18) or wrecking the cart or killing a demon calf by dashing it on the wood-apple tree (which are allusions to Kaṇṇaṉ) (v. 19). The poet connects an allusion to Kaṇṇaṉ (the one who was suckled

What are we to make of all this? The ocean god and the name Māl and its variants certainly occur in the cosmogonic context, and these names are found in a variety of other contexts. Pūtam refers to Nāraṇaṉ in the context of worship (the work begins with his name and the metaphor of offering the lamp of devotion and knowledge to him), chanting, and emotional experience. Pūtam makes references to chanting the name Nāraṇaṉ; however, he never uses the word *nāmo*, which might be the indicator of a *mantra*. Nor does he speak about *mantras* in general. He does, however, make general references to chanting names to fulfill desires (v. 92).[65] Chanting is also found in the context of "wandering, reciting the names, and becoming holy men (*tīrttakār*)" (v. 14). This might be a clue that some of the early Āḻvārs were itinerant, spreading their garland of verses from temple to temple where they worshipped with proper words and flowers (v. 10).

Pēy's *Mūṉṟām Tiruvantāti*: In his first seven verses, ocean imagery predominates. The poet refers to the god's dark ocean-hue (several times), his residing on the ocean, and his cosmogonic acts of making, swallowing, and remaking the universe. His first reference to a deity's proper name is to Tirumāl in the second verse. The fact that seeing him and his consort is linked to the salvific context of destroying rebirth[66] is particularly powerful.

---

by his foster mother Yacōtai), moreover, to the measuring of the earth (v. 9).

[65] See also Pūtam 2, 6, 10, 14, 20, 33, 38, 44, 64, 73, 77, 92.

[66] "Seven births" is a euphemism for constant rebirth. Although the poets often speak of salvation as here and now, one may surmise that this is really "as if" here and now for hyperbolic effect, because of the many references to heaven (the celestial realm), which implies that only at the time of death is one freed from the cycles of rebirth and goes to heaven.

> Today I saw your anklet [feet]. I destroyed rebirth forever! I saw you, O Tirumāl, who noticed and raised Tiru[67] that day to your mountain-like, gold-ornamented chest with the *tulāy* flowers. After seeing you, I took [you] into my heart![68]

Pēy mentions Tirumāl, Māl, Māyaṉ, Māyavaṉ, and Neṭumāl/Neṭiyāṉ (altogether 20 times) in a cosmogonic context, sometimes with ocean color or imagery (vs. 4, 13, 18, 20, 33, 36, 83, 93). These names are used too in references to where the god resides (the Veda, the ocean, several specific temples) (vs. 14, 97, 30, 59, 69) and in general references to his supremacy (vs. 30, 97). They are also found in references to how the poet waits for his grace (v. 78) and experiences him in his heart (vs. 83, 94). All these names seem to be interchangeable and do not line up with a specific context, although there are several examples of names with *neṭu* in the cosmogonic context and names with *māyā* in the context of hard to see or marvel including marvel of the cosmogony (vs. 36, 83, 94). Pēy's interest in the cosmogony when connected with the names Māl and so forth seems focused more on the god's strides and feet than on the ocean or color of the ocean per se. The poet often aligns the god's feet with love, worship, and salvation (vs. 7, 14, 17, 18, 59, 69, 95).

By contrast, Pēy refers to Nārāyaṇaṉ only once, and that is in the context of chanting the god's names in the context of worship, which is followed by the name Kaṇṇaṉ in the cosmogonic context.

> Chanting his many names, saying Nārayaṇā, let us worship with folded hands, O good heart. Come together. Let our eyes see Kaṇṇaṉ who has the cool *tuḻāy* garland which attracts humming bees — the one who swallowed [and] spat out the earth-world.[69]

---

67 Tiru here is the earth who is lifted out of the sea so that the world is remanifested.

68 *iṉṟē kaḻal kaṇṭēṉ, ēḻ piṟappum yāṉ aṟuttēṉ,*
poṉ tōy varai mārvil pūm tuḻāy aṉṟu
tiru kaṇṭu koṇṭa tirumālē uṉṉai
maru kaṇṭu koṇṭēṉ maṉam (Pēy 2).

69 *nāmam pala colli nārāyaṇā eṉṟu*
nām aṅkaiyāl toḻutum, nal ṉeñcē, vā, maruvi

Pēy makes only one other reference to chanting the names, which is more general: "reciting your names" (*pēr ōta*) (v. 10) and describes the mundane benefits that will occur through such chanting. As for Kaṇṇaṉ, Pēy mentions him directly on only one other occasion (v. 87), a vocative, which is followed by a description of his dark body.

In the last decade of his *Antānti*, Pēy first describes how the supreme god crosses over from the cosmos to his own heart. He mentions Tirumāl and key features of the cosmogonic myth such as growing tall or becoming a child and sleeping on a leaf on the ocean (v. 93). This idea of crossing-over reaches a crescendo when the poet ecstatically announces that the god stood, sat, and then lay down in his heart (v. 94). Next the poet describes the god's power in his form of the man-lion (v. 95) and then in two verses (vs. 96; 97) sings of his supremacy (celestials praising his feet and how even the one who resides on the great lotus (*mā malarāṉ* or Brahmā) and the one with the matted locks (*caṭaiyāṉ* or Śiva) cannot understand his glories. The final three verses describe the god as protector of the universe and people (from going to hell) (vs. 98, 99, and 100), his weapons, and finally how his consort Tiru on his chest is our refuge. If Pēy shows any preference at all at the end of his *Antāti*, it is to the god of the cosmogonic myth, but as he personally experiences him in worship of his feet or in his heart. As for preferring any specific name, that is Māl and its variants, certainly, not Nāraṇaṉ or Kaṇṇaṉ.

Tirumaḻicai's *Nāṉmukaṉ Tiruvantāti*: The final *Antānti* for consideration is the one by Tirumaḻicai. Tirumaḻicai mentions Māl and its variants 12 times: as lord (v. 14), as cosmogonic (vs. 5, 36) as against those who do not praise him (v. 6), as linked to Rāma (v. 8), and as his feet (vs. 27, 55). In addition, he mentions exclusive devotion to Māl (v. 27), places where he reclines (v. 36), salvation (vs. 65, 69), names to hear or praise (vs. 69, 85), the lord as in his heart (v. 92), and the lord as the essence of the Vedas (v. 69).

---

maṇ ulakam uṇṭ' umiḻnta vaṇṭ' aṟaiyum taṇ tuḻāy
kaṇṇaṉaiyē kāṇka nam kaṇ (Pēy 8).

But he mentions the name Nārāyaṇaṉ or Nāraṇaṉ almost as many times (10). This is often in the context of saying how he is supreme over other gods. In the very first verse, he says, for instance, that "I make known this deep truth: Nārāyaṇaṉ is the one who created Nāṉmukaṉ (Brahmā) and Nāṉmukaṉ created Caṅkaraṉ (Śiva) from himself." At the end of the verse, he commands: "Understand this fully" (v. 1).

Because of a cryptic reference to "reclining on the milk" in verse 3, we can assume that Tirumaḻicai is alluding to Nārāyaṇaṉ because he is the one associated with the milk ocean. Reclining is the prominent motif in this verse because the reclining god at the Araṅkam temple is mentioned, the one sleeping on the banyan leaf, and once again the god [reclining] on water.

Several other verses mention the one who is Nārāyaṇa. In one verse, Tirumaḻicai (v. 7) calls out "O Nārāyaṇa" (*nārāyaṇē*) and says that his grace (*aruḷ*) will come to him sometime, because they cannot be without each other. Another verse says that Nārāyaṇaṉ is the object of truth for liberation (*vīṭu*), the first cause according to the Veda (*vēta mutaṟpporuḷ*), and the goal for the celestials (v. 13). The next verse (14) says that "those who do not cherish the name Nārāyaṇaṉ" will go to hell (v. 14). Yet another verse (31) refers to Nāraṇaṉ lifting the curse of Nāṉmukaṉ on Araṉ (Śiva) and says that those who do not praise him will suffer. In one verse (67), Tirumaḻicai identifies Nārāyaṇaṉ with the first cause, knowledge and virtue, and promotes the chanting of his name.

Turning now to the end of this *Antāti*, we see that the penultimate verse (95) describes how the Āḻvār has overcome rebirth (*piṟappiṭum-pai*), having abandoned the world. He says: "I will see now the place that is above (i.e., heaven) (*mēlai iṭa nāṭu*). The final verse (96) again belongs to the competitive motif and describes Nāraṇaṉ as the god of Īcaṉ (Iśa or Śiva) and Nāṉmukaṉ (Brahmā), the first cause, and all that is known and to be known.

Tirumaḻicai refers to the proper name Kaṇṇaṉ four times. One refers to how he contains the whole world in his stomach (v, 32). Another refers to Māyaṉ who reclines on the ocean and Kaṇṇaṉ who reclines on the riverbank, with the poet declaring "I know the way (*vakai aṟintēṉ*)" (v. 50). Still another verse (80) says that one day long ago, Kaṇṇaṉ hid the world [in his stomach] and protected [it] when the deluge spread. It then switches to the present saying that singing and dancing (*pāṭiṉa āṭiṉa*) is spreading throughout the world, and so you should quickly take refuge in the lord. Verse 93 simply contains the vocatives *kaṇṇaṉē* (O Kaṇṇaṉ), *kōṉē,* (O King) and *kuṇapparaṉē* (O supreme god with [excellent] qualities) and refers to his protection in the deluge.

In short, Tirumaḻicai uses the name Māl and its variants in many contexts, but it is very clear that he is focused most strongly on Nārāyaṇaṉ as the supreme god and ultimate cause (which is stated abstractly, however, and rarely in the context of the cosmogony). He also connects Nārāyaṇaṉ with the celestials and with chanting as the way to overcome rebirth or hell and attain heaven.

***Antāti* comparisons:** From this examination of the four *Antāti*s, I have noticed individual differences, usually a matter of emphasis within a common theology. For instance, Poykai emphasizes both the names Māl (and its variants) and Nāraṇaṉ but uses these names generally in different contexts—cosmogonic and chanting/soteriological respectively. Pūtam does the same. Pēy also mentions Māl and variants in a variety of contexts, but he ignores Nāraṇaṉ/Nārāyaṇaṉ altogether aside from one reference in the context of chanting. As for Tirumaḻicai, he too mentions Māl and variants in a variety of contexts but focuses on Nāraṇaṉ/Nārāyaṇaṉ, sometimes with reference to chanting but especially with reference to supremacy (defined abstractly not cosmogonically) over other gods.

There are also differences in the concept of supremacy in the poems. In some poems supremacy is associated with the ocean and a god reclining on the ocean or serpent couch on the ocean or leaf on the ocean. This supreme god has cosmogonic roles. As Neṭumāl/Neṭiyāṉ/Neṭiyōṉ, he is the one who grows tall in the act of extending and thereby re-creating the world. He is also the reclining god who has the four-faced god (Brahmā) located on his navel.

The aniconic ocean alludes to that which is truly transcendent and primordial, without specific name, and therefore beyond name, and minimally described as dark, with turbulent flood waters, waves and so forth. Even when the ocean is personified as the god residing on it, the aniconic symbol of water provides the basis for the concept of the god's supremacy as that which is beyond all forms, ideas, even words, and for his cosmogonic roles of virtual destruction, preservation, and re-creation. Not only do the poets posit the ocean as supreme and primary, they also emphasize it by alluding to every variant of the tripartite cosmogony that they can. They go even further, it seems, by integrating any ocean imagery even if not related per se to ideas of transcendence or cosmogony. The proper names connected to supremacy as the ocean or ocean god are generally Māl and variants but also in several cases Kaṇṇaṉ.

However, in other poems, supremacy is associated with heaven or paradise. *Antāti* poets refer to heaven as sky (Poykai 68), the protected city of the celestials (Pūtam 88), the heavenly world (Pūtam 90), Vaikuntam (Pēy 61), the heavenly city (Pēy 62) or the place that is above (Tirumaḻicai v. 95). In this context the celestials/immortals (*amar*, *amarar*, *vāṉōr*, *viṇṇor*) are often mentioned (as in Poykai 13, 45, 46 and Pūtam 2, 3, 11, 26, 41, 45, 90, 92). The proper name connected to this concept of supremacy is almost always Nāraṇaṉ/Nārāyaṇaṉ. The oceanic supremacy is far more common than the paradisial supremacy, but both are acknowledged.

Finally, it is important to note that the distinctions—Ocean, Kṛṣṇa, and Nārāyaṇa—within the concept of supreme deity are held together by several swing concepts, though the swing often favors one of these. The connection of Nārāyaṇa's white ocean with the dark ocean likely functions to connect the two, even though references to the dark ocean are more common. General references to chanting the name/names or more specific references to chanting the names of Tirumāl or Kṛṣṇa or Nārāyaṇa also likely operate as a swing concept, even though references to chanting the name (or *mantra*) of Nārāyaṇa are more common.

There are several other swing concepts, I think. These include worship of the supreme deity's feet, the idea that he is in the heart of the devotee and certain iconographic details such as the conch or discus. The name Māl/Tirumāl, even though it signifies the dark one, may function to some degree as a swing concept. Besides his oceanic, cosmogonic imagery, his name is found in other contexts such as worship, supremacy over other gods, or soteriology. Thus, this name has the broadest range of contexts. The fact that the Āḻvārs often do not use proper names but only epithets helps to sustain the idea of one supreme deity.

With this analysis in mind, I turn now to antecedents to the *Antāti*s in Sanskrit and Tamil works to see if I can find ways of explaining the similarities and differences that I have detected. Given the regional and linguistic complexity and enormous time span involved, this must be a selective, but I hope representative, overview.

Antecedents to the *Antāti*s in northern, Sanskrit works

In this section, I search for ocean imagery, especially cosmogonic allusions, as well as the early history of Viṣṇu, Nārāyaṇa, and Kṛṣṇa.

Ocean imagery: One of the main antecedents to the description of the supreme god in the *Antāti*s being discussed here would be an oceanic and cosmogonic god. We first glimpse such a deity in the late strata of the *Ṛgveda*, which refers to a god emerging from the primeval waters.[70] A more elaborate version of this is also found in this text;[71] it refers to the germ of all things (including the gods) existing in the waters on the navel of the unborn one.

The ocean or primeval waters are sometimes described as flood waters. The *Śatapatha Brāhmaṇa* refers to a flood, rescue of Manu (the original man) by a boat pulled by a fish, and the re-creation of the universe from the primeval waters by means of a sacrifice. The story goes like this. A fish warns Manu of a coming flood and tells him to build a boat. When the flood begins, Manu is told to tie the boat to a horn on the fish's head so that the fish can pull the boat with Manu safely to a northern mountain. This occurs, the boat is tied to a tree, the waters subside, and Manu offers ghee, sour milk, whey, and curds into the waters. From these offerings into the waters, a woman is born. Manu worships and "exerts" himself with her, which generates human beings and

---

70 *Ṛgveda* 10:121:7-8.

71 *Ṛgveda* 1:24.7.

everything else desired.[72] The passage then links this woman with the figure of Īḍā, the deified sacrificial food.

Jan C. Heesterman has analyzed this passage and similar ones (found in the *Kāṭhaka Saṁhitā*, *Vādūla Sūtra* and several *Śrauta* works) in "The Flood Story in Vedic Ritual."[73] He argues that they are expressions of agonistic conflict of groups *within* the Vedic tradition, if not the opposition of order and disorder within the human condition itself.[74]

Johannes Bronkhorst[75] challenges Heesterman's explanation by pointing out that these oppositions may belong to ethnically different groups of people, a division that might have once been rooted in an opposition between Aryans and non-Aryans as reflected in the *Ṛgveda* account of the fight between the *asura*s and the *deva*s. (He qualifies this by saying that conflict between groups might have been only occasional and, in any case, conflict between groups need not presuppose an Aryan invasion hypothesis). Pointing to new ideas that appear in the texts, Bronkhorst comments that internal cultural conflicts or those of the human condition need not be the reason for changes in religion up to the common era. Rather, following the lead of the archaeologist George Erdosy,[76] he suggests that it could well be that a locally emerging ethnic group of northwestern India, distinguished by a set of social and religious institutions, was interacting with a population that had been well-established for at least a millennium with its own culture. Gradually, these two cultures were assimilated in varying ways, the resulting hybrid ones proving attractive enough that they spread and integrated more cultures, often being further transformed in the process.

I think that this scenario of gradual integration of different cultural groups (perhaps, but not necessarily, ethnically different) is indeed what is suggested by Heesterman's own study of the flood story. The passages that he discusses show a development from the time of the late

---

72 Heesterman 1985: 59-60 citing *Śatapatha Brāhmaṇa* I: 8:1.1-11.

73 Heesterman 1985: 59-69.

74 Heesterman 1985: 59.

75 Bronkorst 1999: 33-57.

76 Bronkhorst 1999: 17 citing Erdosy 1993: 46-49 and 1995: 3.

Ṛgveda to the *Mahābhārata*. Heesterman himself admits that the earliest version of the flood story found in the *Śatapatha Brāhmaṇa* seems to be tacked on to the Īḍā story with its sacrificial motifs so that the result clearly falls into "two independent parts—the flood on the one hand, the goddess Īḍā on the other"[77]—with the hinge between the two not convincing. In the *Vādūla* version, there is some integration and in the *Śrauta* texts the flood story is almost swallowed up by the sacrificial orientation. However, in many related Vedic myths and rituals, there is no such triumphant absorption of water symbolism by fire symbolism. Rather, tensions and anomalies—with traces of the underlying incongruity of water and fire symbolism—remain. There are also myths that feature water as the primary substance.

The *Śatapatha Brāhmaṇa* says, for example, that Prajāpati, a creator god, took the form of a fish, tortoise, and boar.[78] The *Taittirīya Āraṇyaka*,[79] moreover, describes how the lord of creatures, Prajāpati, becomes a boar and rescues the earth from the flood; after he wipes the moisture from her, she extends. In another version in this work,[80] Prajāpati sees a lotus leaf and then dives into the waters. The seeds of the idea of the dwarf who grows and extends in different directions can also be found in the *Śatapatha Brāhmaṇa*, *Taittirīya Saṁhitā*, and *Taittirīya Brāhmaṇa*.[81]

Another possible instance of the integration of the oceanic cosmogony into Vedic mythology is the god Brahmā. The word *brahmā*, from *bṛh*, which means to grow or expand, is reminiscent of the three steps that extend to become the created world or the dwarf who grows to become the world. Brahmā's association with the navel of the god reclining on the ocean and creation suggests that the one who grows or

77 Heesterman 1985: 61.

78 *Śatapatha Brāhmaṇa* I.8:1-6.

79 *Taittirīya Āraṇyaka* 7.1.5.1.

80 *Taittirīya Āraṇyaka* 1.1.3.5 ff.

81 *Śatapatha Brāhmaṇa* I.2:5, *Taittirīya Saṁhitā* II:1:3, and *Taittirīya Brāhmaṇa* I:6:1). See Desai 1973: 98-99.

expands belonged to the oceanic mythos before being considered a Vedic creator deity.

Although we catch only glimpses of the oceanic, cosmogonic field of meaning in the late Vedic and post-Vedic texts, there is enough to suggest that it must have been archaic and common to warrant its integration into the Vedic tradition, albeit piecemeal. The oral traditions of the non-Vedic groups no doubt had other versions that favored a cosmogonic account focused on water, with the fire cult in a minor position (as it is in the Tamil *Antāti*s of a much later time). As Vedic culture integrates more influences from the hinterlands and then extends south of the Vindhyas, it seems to become more influenced by the oceanic tradition. This becomes apparent in the *Mahābhārata*, multiple homologies and new hybridities notwithstanding.[82]

Before looking at these developments, I must survey key Vedic references to Viṣṇu and Nārāyaṇa, which will figure in my later analysis.

Viṣṇu: In the late strata of the *Ṛgveda*,[83] Viṣṇu is associated with measuring or traversing the universe with three great strides. Scholars have long argued that Viṣṇu's three steps refer to the rising, mid-day, and setting sun,[84] but there is another explanation, I think, and that is the idea that the three steps originally belonged to the re-creation phase of the cosmogony, which was at first outside the Vedic tradition (as was Viṣṇu once himself given his early description as an *asura* and the fact that there are only a few hymns dedicated to him in the *Ṛgveda*[85]). The

[82] I should point out that the kind of development being discussed here could also include a parallel history of Śiva from his epithetonym (the auspicious one) to his identification with the tripartite cosmogony, especially the destruction phase.

[83] *Ṛgveda* 1:22:17; VII: 100:4; and I: 155:6. See Desai 1973: 98.

[84] Desai 1973: 97.

[85] In the Vedas Viṣṇu is a very minor deity (only five hymns are addressed to him), and even in the late Vedas and Brāhmaṇas, he is mainly connected with the sacrifice, sun, Indra, and Varuṇa. See also Das Gupta [1931] 1985: 105 ff.

three great strides became epithetonyms (Trivikrama, Vikrama, and Tripada), and they were condensed even further to the god's feet, the part (feet) representing the whole (the strides and creation). (Adoration of the god's feet became an important aspect of subsequent *bhakti* religion.)

Because the Vedic tradition was focused on the ritual fire, which could be symbolically connected to the sun as celestial fire, it emphasized Viṣṇu's three great steps or extension of the god, akin to the rising sun, and on the epithetonym "the pervader" (*viṣṇu*), which suggests that by his steps he creates the universe and becomes it by pervasion.

The *Mahābhārata* describes Viṣṇu in a very different way. His cosmogonic role is now also related to the ocean: "the blessed Viṣṇu, the everlasting source of all creatures, the eternal Person, slept solitarily on his ocean bed in the vast coil of the boundlessly puissant snake Śeṣa."[86] The ocean god as Śeṣa supports, in the sense of preserves, this treasure-filled earth. Śeṣa means remainder or residue; here it suggests that after the virtual destruction of the universe, something remains that will be the source of re-creation.

Moreover, the *Mahābhārata* has an easy acceptance of other names for Viṣṇu such as Vāsudeva, Hari, and Nārāyaṇa. In the *Viṣṇusahasranāma* (a list of the thousand names of Viṣṇu),[87] we are told that when Bhīṣma was dying, Yudhiṣṭhira asks him:

> Who is the one deity (*daivatam*) in the universe? Who is the one refuge (*parāyaṇam*)? By praising whom, by worshipping whom can people obtain auspiciousness (*śubham*)? What is the *dharma* of all *dharma's* that is supreme in your view? What repetition of names (*japa*) frees people from the cycles of birth?[88]

---

86 *Mahābhārata* 3.194.9; Van Buitenen trans. vol. 2, 611). For the significance of the serpent imagery in this verse see Schmid in this volume, p. 121ff.

87 The *Viṣṇusahasranāma* is found in *Mahābhārata* 13.135. 679-683.

88 *kim ekaṃ daivataṃ loke kiṁ vāpy ekaṃ parāyaṇam*
stuvantaḥ kaṁ kam arcantaḥ prāpnuyur mānavāḥ śubham
ko dharmaḥ sarvadharmāṇām bhavataḥ paramo mataḥ
kim japan mucyate jantur janmasaṁsārabandhanāt.

Bhīṣma replies that one should chant the thousand names of Viṣṇu who is the all-pervading Supreme Being who is Brahman. When one examines the first verse of the *Viṣṇusahasranāma*'s list of names, it begins with Viśvam (the pervader) and then Viṣṇuḥ. The following verses include some names that are also found in the Āḻvārs.[89] The epithetonyms in this list of names refer, moreover, to the god as destroyer, pervader, and creator and to other activities that suggest acquaintance with an ocean god and cosmogony,[90] although the *Viṣṇusahasranāma* prefers philosophically abstract epithetonyms (a *Gītā*-type vocabulary). In addition, the *Viṣṇusahasranāma* includes names for praise such as *stavyaḥ*, *stavapriyaḥ*, *stotram*, *stutiḥ*, and *stōtā* and the idea that praise of the deity by chanting his names produces mundane and supermundane (salvific) results.

Viṣṇu comes into prominence in the *Viṣṇu Purāṇa* (ca. 4th century C.E.). According to Peter Schreiner,[91] this text refers to Viṣṇu (292 times), Hari (187), Keśava (65), Kṛṣṇa (312), Hṛṣīkeśa (7) Janārdana (67), Bhagavat (237), Govinda (61), and Nārāyaṇa (30). It intrigues me that although the name Viṣṇu is certainly prominent, there is ostensibly even greater importance given to the name Kṛṣṇa and other names/epithetonyms especially associated with him. Schreiner characterizes the *stotras* or hymns of praise of this text as theological, metaphysical, and cosmological drawing from the *Puruṣasūkta*, the *Bhagavadgītā*, and Sāṅkhya philosophy. There is a complementary mythological paradigm (here Brahmā arises from Viṣṇu's navel) focused mainly on the creation and manifestation of the world until the time of destruction rather than the whole cycle of destruction, preservation, and re-creation. The idea of Viṣṇu's final or supreme step refers to the cosmic act but on the

---

(*Mahābhārata* 13:135.2-3). (Young trans.)

[89] For instance, Keśavaḥ (#23; 648), Kṛṣṇaḥ (#57; 550), Mādhavaḥ (#72; 167; 735), Madhusūdanaḥ (#73) Nārāyaṇaḥ (#245), Brahmā (#663).

[90] Vikramaḥ (#78), Vāmanaḥ (#152), Govindaḥ (#187; #539), 657), Kapīndraḥ (#501; boar), Trivikramaḥ (#530), Tripadaḥ (#534), Mahāvarāhaḥ (#538). Two names even suggest the ocean god: Padmanābhaḥ (#48; 196; 346) and Apām nidhiḥ (#323) (the sea as a place for storing up the waters).

[91] See Schreiner in this volume, p. 54.

individual level to the path that includes both Vedic ritual and renunciation. "A conscious and strong wish to conform to the norms of Vedic tradition and to brahminical values and practices," Schreiner says, "is an undeniable trait of this picture."[92]

Nārāyaṇa: Nārāyaṇa makes his first appearance in the *Śatapatha Brāhmaṇa* but without oceanic symbolism.[93] Here he is called Puruṣa-Nārāyaṇa. "Under the instructions of Prajāpati, the impersonal cosmic principle in Brāhmaṇa literature, [he] places in a pantheistic mood all the worlds and all the gods in his own self and his own self in all the worlds and all the gods, thus becoming, by the power of sacrifice, the Universe itself."[94] In another passage in this text, Puruṣa-Nārāyaṇa is associated with a five-day sacrifice that makes him omnipresent, supreme, and the source of creation. This alludes to the self-sacrifice of Puruṣa, the primeval man, as first described in the *Puruṣasūkta* belonging to a late stratum of the *Ṛgveda*.[95] The idea of the primeval man is reminiscent of Manu (which means man, representative man, or father of human beings) in the flood story.[96]

The *Nārāyaṇa Upaniṣad*, a late *Upaniṣad* (date?),[97] describes Nārāyaṇa as the god who creates not only the universe but also Brahmā, Rudra, Indra, and all beings, which harkens back to the Puruṣa-Nārāyaṇa of the *Śatapatha Brāhmaṇa*.[98] Nārāyaṇa is further described as the

---

92 See Schreiner in this volume, p. 85.

93 *Śatapatha Brāhmaṇa* xii.3-4 cited by Dasgupta [1931] 1985, 347.

94 Das Gupta vol. 7, [1931] 1985, 347 citing *Śatapatha Brāhmaṇa* xii.3-4.

95 *Ṛgveda* 10:90.

96 Monier-Williams 1963, 784. The *Mahābhārata* view that Nārāyaṇa was originally a man, saint, or *ṛṣi,* a view that gave rise to the pair Nara-Nārāyaṇa, need not detain us here, for there are no references in the *Antātis* and only six in the entire *Divyaprabandham* to Nara-Nārāyaṇa.

97 Sanskrit text available at https://sanskritdocuments.org under Viṣṇu: Nārāyaṇa Upaniṣad.

98 *Śatapatha Brāhmaṇa* xii. 3-4 cited by Dasgupta vol.7 [1931] 1985, 347.

eternal one, Brahmā, Śiva, Indra, time, directions, and everything that is manifest. Nārāyaṇa is the god who is one (*deva eka*). He pervades all (*sa viṣṇur eva bhavati sa viṣṇur eva bhavati*). The *Upaniṣad's* other main message is about how by chanting the eight-syllable *mantra* (*aṣṭākṣaramantra*) "*oṁ namo nārāyaṇāya*," one will attain good health, long life, prosperity, the immortal state (*amṛtatvam*), liberation from the cycle of births (*janmasaṃsāra*), and the realm of Vaikuṇṭha (*vaikuṇṭha bhuvavanalokam*). The *Upaniṣad* goes on to say that the seat of Nārāyaṇa is the lotus of the heart. After more epithets such as being causeless and the cause of everything, we are told that the *Atharvaveda* is foremost (*etad atharva śiroyo 'dhīte*) and that chanting the *mantra* three times a day will eliminate all sins. Moreover, the one who chants this will attain the merit of the study of all the Vedas (*sarvavedapārāyaṇapuṇyaṃ labhate*) and will attain oneness (*sāyujya*) with Nārāyaṇa.

What is of special interest here is that chanting the *mantra* replaces the performance of Vedic rites three times a day, chanting it substitutes for study of the Vedas, and chanting it fulfills all desires including salvation in Vaikuṇṭha. Thus, whereas the *Upaniṣad* is certainly linked to the Vedic tradition, it also undermines it by promising an easier path through chanting the *mantra*. This is an important antecedent for a Vedic religion available to everyone.

In the *Mahānārāyaṇa Upaniṣad* (ca. third century – first century B.C.E.), "Nārāyaṇa is the Supreme Reality designated as *brahman*. Nārāyaṇa is the highest (Self). Nārāyaṇa is the supreme Light (described in the *Upaniṣads*). Nārāyaṇa is the infinite Self. Nārāyaṇa is the most excellent meditator and meditation."[99] This text makes several references to water as the primary and causal element in the context of creation,[100] which suggests integration of an oceanic cosmogonic god.

---

[99] *Mahānārāyaṇa Upaniṣad* XIII-4 translated by Vimalananda [1957] 2010. I have added diacritical marks to the quotations from this translation.

[100] The following quotations are from Vimalananda trans. [1957] 2010: "The Lord of creation, who is present in the shoreless waters" (I-1); "From whom the creatrix of the world, Prakṛti, was born, who created in the world creatures out of elements such as water" (I-4-5); "Through the power of whom the great Causal Waters holding within it the power of unfoldment and the capacity to produce fire" (I-11-7); "the waters which create fire and

However, most of this text uses Vedic imagery associated with the sun and fire and connects Nārāyaṇa to other gods in the Vedic pantheon at this time such as Indra, Varuṇa, Soma, Brahmā, and Viṣṇu. One verse anticipates or parallels (depending on how we date these texts) the *Mahābhārata* in its juxtaposition of the three names Nārāyaṇa, Vāsudeva, and Viṣṇu: "May we know Nārāyaṇa. For that may we meditate upon Vāsudeva. May Viṣṇu impel us towards it."[101] It is intriguing that there is an allusion to the Lord's feet that sounds vaguely cosmogonic and salvific: "He who is rendered holy by the ancient, widespread, sanctifying feet ... crosses over evil deeds and their effect. Having been rendered holy by the naturally pure and purifying feet of the Lord ... may we overcome our enemies, the sins."[102] Despite the fact that some verses give importance to water as the primary and causal element, the actual name Nārāyaṇa is not connected to the ocean and cosmogony per se even though one verse says: "The supreme represented as the ocean has overflown to the whole creation ..." (I-70). Rather, cosmogonic functions are the prerogative of intermediary figures such as *prakṛti* or Prajāpati.

The *Mahābhārata* explicitly connects the name Nārāyaṇa with a white ocean in several places. Nārāyaṇa's abode is said to be Śvetadvīpa,[103] an island paradise where the celestials (enlightened ones) live, located on the milk ocean north of Mount Meru.[104] The sage Nārada visits

support the Vedic acts of worship (in order to endow it with such potency); who is the one God ruling over all the rest" (I-11-8); "Salutation to fire hidden in water" (I-57); "Verily all this is water. All the created beings are water. The vital breaths in the body are water ... Vedic formulas are water. Truth is water. All deities are water. The three worlds denoted by Bhuḥ, Bhavaḥ, and Suvaḥ are water. The source of all these is the Supreme denoted by the syllable 'OM'" (XXIX-1). Some of these verses are from the *Paramātmasūkta* and *Hiraṇyagarbhasūkta* of the *Yajurveda Saṁhitā*.

[101] I-29, Vimalananda trans. [1957] 2010.

[102] I-51, Vimalananda trans. [1957] 2010.

[103] Das Gupta vol. 7, 678.

[104] This image of the island in the sea might have inspired the idea of the island as the "remainder" in some versions of the second phase of the cosmogony, which in turn probably inspired shrines (as the remainder) on an

him there. This idea of Nārāyaṇa's abode or refuge can be related to an etymology of the word *nārāyaṇa* taking *nāra* as men/human beings and *ayana* as abode or place of refuge.[105] Here we find ocean symbolism, but the ocean is *white*, not dark.

Another association of Nārāyaṇa with the ocean occurs in the description of Mārkaṇḍeya during the virtual destruction of the universe (*Mahābhārata* 3.185-187).[106] The sage Mārkaṇḍeya describes how once long ago, a fish tells Manu that when the time comes for everything on the earth to be destroyed in a deluge, you must build a sturdy ark with a cable attached so that the fish can pull you and the seven seers across the ocean. This came to pass and "Then the fish pulled the ark to the highest peak of the Himālaya [where it was moored]."[107]

Mārkaṇḍeya next describes his own experience of being alone and trying to swim to a place of refuge during such a deluge. One day he saw a large banyan tree in the flood waters with a child sitting on a branch in a cradle. The child suddenly opens its mouth wide, and Mārkaṇḍeya is powered into it. There he sees the entire earth after which he is expelled from the mouth.[108] He sees the Large Spirit in the guise of a child and says to him, "God, I wish to know yourself and this supernal wizardry!"[109] In reply, the god in the form of a child, says:

---

island, Araṅkam being a case in point, especially if they were subject to flood waters.

[105] *Nāra* means relating to or proceeding from men, humans, or mortals, and so Nārāyaṇa would mean the son of the original man (Monier-Williams 1963, 536). If we take *ayana* as a place of refuge, then Nārāyaṇa would be the abode or refuge of men (p. 84). Monier-Williams notes that *nāra* can also mean water and says that *Manu* I.10 was probably invented to explain the name Nārāyaṇa. (p. 536). I will return to *Manu* I.10.

[106] Van Buitenen, trans. vol. 2, 583-593.

[107] *Mahābhārata* 3.185. 25-45. Van Buitenen, trans. vol. 2, 584.

[108] *Mahābhārata* 3.186. 80-95. Van Buitenen, trans. vol. 2, 589.

[109] *Mahābhārata* 3.186.110-125. Van Buitenen, trans. vol. 2, 589.

> [...] You have taken refuge with me ... The waters are called *nāras*: I gave them the name; therefore, I am called Nārāyaṇa, for the waters are my course. I am the creator of all creatures as well as their destroyer ... As Śeṣa I support this treasure-filled earth that is girt by the four oceans [...].[110]

The passage goes on to describe how Nārāyaṇa once became a boar and pulled the earth out from the water and comments that the *Ṛgveda*, *Sāmaveda*, *Yajurveda* and the *Atharvans* have come from him and return to him.[111] Nārāyaṇa then says:

> I am the one of three strides .... I am the one called Nārāyaṇa ... As the soul of the universe, I sleep ... not as a child though disguised as one until Brahmā wakes up ... [then] I shall as one create from this my body space, earth, light, wind, and water [...].[112]

This story is obviously a development and variant of the account in the *Śatapatha Brāhmaṇa* previously mentioned about how a fish warns Manu about a coming flood, and after Manu builds a boat, the fish pulls him in it to safety and moors it to a northern mountain and tree.[113] That text, remember, also describes how Puruṣa-Nārāyaṇa places all the worlds and all the gods in his own self and his own self in all the worlds. The image of the child might also be extrapolated from the *Śatapatha Brāhmaṇa* reference to Manu as the primeval man and the idea of a figure who begins to grow large. In addition, the reference to the banyan tree in the *Mahābhārata* could harken back to the tree to which the boat was anchored in the *Śatapatha Brāhmaṇa*. The banyan tree, after all, represents the tree of life and immortality.

The Epic story transforms the cosmogony into a marvelous hierophany—a vision of the virtual destruction, preservation, and re-creation of the universe—and more specifically, the explicit identification of Nārāyaṇa with this cosmogony and the boar. It is interesting that in the *Mahābhārata* a new etymology is given for Nārāyaṇa. Instead of the abode or refuge (*ayana*) of men (*nāra*), he is the course (*ayana*) of the

---

[110] *Mahābhārata* 3.186.110-125. Van Buitenen, trans. vol. 2, 591.

[111] *Mahābhārata* 3.187.1-15. Van Buitenen trans. vol. 2, 591.

[112] *Mahābhārata* 3.187. 30-50. Van Buitenen trans. vol. 2, 592-593.

[113] *Śatapatha Brāhmaṇa* I. 8. 1-10.

waters (*nāra*). But why is *nāra* the word for waters in a Sanskrit text when the Sanskrit word for water is *āpa*?[114] Either this link to his name simply was made to affiliate him more closely with a common myth about the waters (and the cosmogony), or it was done knowing of a Dravidian word for water (*nāra*).[115] We encounter other aspects of an oceanic cosmogony associated with Nārāyaṇa in this Epic passage. For instance, the soul of the universe disguised as a child asleep is Nārāyaṇa, the one who is described a few lines before as a child sitting on a cradle-bed in a branch of the banyan tree. This passage also mentions Śeṣa, the one remainder who supports, in the sense of preserves, the earth.

Some Epic passages focus on Nārāyaṇa as the supreme deity; in others he is equated with Viṣṇu and Vāsudeva-Kṛṣṇa-Hari. These names and equations exist within a general concept of monism described as *ekānta*,[116] which is linked in turn to moral purity and emotional devotion to the supreme and gracious personal god who has many names.

In the *Nārāyaṇīya* (pertaining to Nārāyaṇa) section of the *Mahābhārata* (i.e., the Śāntiparvan, a late addition), *ekānta* has been circumscribed to the name Nārāyaṇa, which is to be chanted. For instance, Nārada in his worship of Nārāyaṇa performed duly a great many *japa*s relating to Nārāyaṇa.[117] Similarly, King Uparicara-Vasu performed *nārāyaṇa-japa*s. "When Yudhiṣṭira and his brothers became devoted to Nārāyaṇa on hearing Bhīṣma's narrative, they were engrossed in regular *japa* (*nit-*

---

[114] *Manu Saṁhitā* 1.10 is a similar verse but equates *nāra* with the Sanskrit word for water (*āpo nāra iti*). See also *āpo nārā iti proktā āpo vai narasūnvaḥ, ayanaṁ mama tat pūrvam ato nārāyaṇo hy aham* (*Mahābhārata* 12.328.35).

[115] Although the common Tamil word for water is *nīr*, the variant *nāram* also exists. See *Tamil Lexicon* vol. 4, 1982, 2225. *Nāram* is not in the DED.

[116] Expressions of monism are found elsewhere. For example, besides the *Upaniṣads*, the *Mahābhārata* experiments with monism, some passages presenting an equivalence of names such as Viṣṇu, Vāsudeva, Nārāyaṇa, Kṛṣṇa, and Hari and some indicating one deity is supreme but has many names (such as Viṣṇu with his thousand names).

[117] *Nārāyaṇīya* 344.26. Das Gupta vol. 7, 667.

yaṃ japya-parāḥ) and uttered the name of Nārāyaṇa (*nārāyaṇa udīrayan*)."[118] In the story of Nārada's visit to Śvetadvīpa,[119] the island paradise located on the milk ocean north of Mount Meru, which is the abode of Nārāyaṇa, there is further description of these Nārāyaṇa *ekāntins* who have become celestials through moral purity, *bhakti,* and divine grace and worship the god there. Their mental *japa* is fixated completely on him as is their exclusive devotion (*ekānta-bhakti*) and with folded hands they utter *namaḥ*, which alone brings about a beatific vision, a burst of joy, and personal feeling.[120] One chapter (338) gives two hundred names for Nārāyaṇa, another chapter (341) gives various names of Kṛṣṇa, and yet another chapter (346) describes the merit one obtains when hearing about Nārāyaṇa's greatness.

According to Charlotte Schmid elsewhere in this volume,[121] the *Harivaṁśa*, which is a *khila* or complement to the *Mahābhārata* dated 2nd to 4th century C.E., identifies Nārāyaṇa with Kṛṣṇa and Balarāma to whom I now turn.

Kṛṣṇa: Hardy has discussed what he thinks is Kṛṣṇa's early history.[122] Admitting that he cannot arrive at an Ur-form, he points to some early references such Pāṇini IV.3.98 which contains the name Vāsudeva, who is associated with Arjuna and may imply Kṛṣṇa, and the Besnagar inscription of about 115 B.C.E., which speaks of a *bhāgavata* worshipper of Vāsudeva who is then identified with Kṛṣṇa. Most of Hardy's analysis draws from the *Bhagavadgītā* with brief mention of Kṛṣṇa's identification with Nara/Nārāyaṇa or correspondences with Indra/Viṣṇu or Arjuna/Kṛṣṇa. Hardy includes the development of the concepts of *avatāra* (incarnation) and *vyūha* (emanation) in his early history. Thus, his reconstruction of the early history of Kṛṣṇa avoids the

---

118 *Nārāyaṇīya* 339:134-135. Das Gupta vol. 7, 676.

119 Das Gupta vol. 7, 667, 670-672.

120 Das Gupta vol. 7, 675.

121 See Schmid in this volume, p. 92f.

122 Hardy 1983,17-25.

ocean imagery and the cosmogony in the *Mahābhārata*, even when it is linked with Kṛṣṇa in the *Nārāyaṇīya* and *Harivaṁśa.*

I turn now to the *Harivaṁśa*. In this work, Kṛṣṇa has a close relation with Balarāma, sometimes identified as his brother. Balarāma, the white god who carries a plough (which suggests he has been an agricultural deity) assimilates or is assimilated into the image of a serpent deity belonging to *nāga* traditions. Images of these *nāga*s include ones with human bodies, bodies that are half-human and half-snake, and those that are completely snakes. They often belong to bodies of water and are guardians of treasure. (The Epic's image of Viṣṇu reclining on a serpent *couch* is also an example of this assimilation with *nāga* traditions.) Schmid traces how Balarāma and Kṛṣṇa are integrated with serpent images. Balarāma's serpent body eventually becomes the serpent couch on which he or Kṛṣṇa reclines. He is identified with Kṛṣṇa in other ways. They are paired as the white and black gods or they are considered merged, as one.[123]

Having searched for antecedents to the *Antāti*s' concept of supreme deity in northern Sanskrit texts, some comparisons of the *Antāti*s and the Sanskrit texts are in order. For instance, the *Antāti* poets are much closer to versions of the cosmogony in which oceanic and cosmogonic imagery dominate than many accounts of the late Vedas where water and fire imagery are first juxtaposed with fire gradually becoming dominant.

As noted, the supreme deity in the *Antāti*s is generally described as having dark color, especially the color of the sea. He reclines on the sea or on a serpent couch on the sea and many of his epithetonyms refer to a tripartite cosmogony (virtual destruction, preservation, and re-creation). The poets mention rescue or re-creation by a boar, a dwarf who grows tall, or the four-faced one residing on the navel of the supreme deity. In the *Antāti*s, these features are generally associated with an ocean god often called Tirumāl or Kaṇṇaṉ. We have found antecedents for all of this in the northern Sanskrit works, especially the late *Mahābhārata* (*Nārāyaṇīya*) and the *Harivaṁśa.*

---

[123] See Schmid in this volume, p. 134f.

Despite some overlap of the *Antāti* content and these northern sources, there are significant differences. For instance, in the *Nārāyaṇīya*,[124] the pair Nara and Nārāyaṇa are prominent figures, the story of Nārada visiting in Śvetadvīpa is featured, and there is mention of the four *vyūhas* with Vāsudeva as supreme. In addition, this work mentions the greatness of Brahmins, various stories of sages and kings, Viṣṇu taking the form of Hayagrīva, the Sātvatadharma that had been taught by the Lord and repeatedly forgotten, stories about Vyāsa, many references to sacrifices, a cosmogony related to the *Puruṣasūkta*, and Pāñcarātra elements (this work has been described as the "earliest literary Pāñcarātra text"[125]). These features, which belong to the proto-Bhāgavata-Pāñcarātra-Sātvatadharma tradition, are not found in the *Antāti*s or are dramatically transformed.

There are also significant differences in descriptions of Nārāyaṇa in these sources and the *Antāti*s. The Mārkaṇḍeya passage has a cosmogonic image of the supreme god as if a child sleeping on the waters, which is identified with Nārāyaṇa who is then described as the creator of all creatures as well as their destroyer and the one who as Śeṣa supports the earth that is surrounded by the four oceans. But for some reason, the *Antāti* poets rarely read cosmogonic roles into the figure of Nārāyaṇa despite this precedent even though they know the story (the *Antāti* poets mention the name Mārkaṇḍeya twice[126]). Nor do they describe Nārāyaṇa per se lying on the ocean or on a couch in the ocean aside from two exceptions: one is Poykai 68 where he lies on the white ocean but does not have cosmogonic activities and does not recline on a couch. And one is Tirumaḻicai's *Tiruvantāti* 3, which has a cryptic reference to the one "reclining on the milk" that leads one to surmise that the verse is about Nārāyaṇa because he is the one connected to the milk ocean. If Tirumaḻicai was a late Āḻvār, it is possible that by his time, it was more common to read cosmogonic roles into the figure of

---

124 For the following, I draw on the summary of chapters of the *Nārāyaṇīya* by Swami Harshananda in "Nārāyaṇa" (www.hindupedia.com/en/Nārāyaṇiya).

125 See Rastelli in this volume p. 217.

126 Poykai 94 and Tirumaḻicai 15.

Nārāyaṇa. Alternatively, if Tirumaḻicai lived at Araṅkam, which is on an island, he might have known about *Cilappatikāram* 35-40, which describes the god at Araṅkam, as reclining on the milk [ocean],[127] or he might have known about the *Mahābhārata*'s description of the island Śvetadvīpa as Nārāyaṇa's paradise.

A comparison of the *Antāti*s with the descriptions of Nārāyaṇa in the northern sources must also mention Nārāyaṇa's connection with chanting. The Āḻvārs' references to chanting the *mantra namō nāraṇā* as means to fulfill all mundane desires and to be freed from *saṁsāra* and to attain heaven is obviously the *Nārāyaṇa Upaniṣad*'s *oṁ namo nārāyaṇāya.* The idea of chanting his *mantra*s developed into chanting his names by the time of the *Mahābhārata*'s promotion of *ekānta-bhakti* and *japa*. The fact that the Āḻvārs equated reciting the names of Nāraṇaṉ with recitation of the Vedas (e.g., Pūtam 38: *avaṉ pēr ōtuvatē nāviṉāl ōttu*), which can function as an "easy" substitution for arduous Vedic training, reminds one too of the *Nārāyaṇa Upaniṣad*, which suggests that everyone can attain salvation by this easy method of chanting Nārāyaṇa's *mantra.* Moreover, the word *namas* plus the name Nārāyaṇa appears in both the Epic and the *Antāti*s in the context of chanting. So does the aspect of folding the hands together while chanting. We have also encountered many references to the god being in the heart (*neñcu, maṉam, uḷḷam*) of the devotee. These echo the *Nārāyaṇa Upaniṣad*'s statement that the seat of Nārāyaṇa is the lotus of the heart.[128]

As for the case of Viṣṇu, it is striking that unlike many *Mahābhārata* passages that call the supreme deity Viṣṇu and use sacrificial imagery, the *Antāti*s do not mention Viṣṇu at all, although mention of the one taking three steps or measuring the world as in *ulaku aḷanta* or *maṇ aḷanta* are common in the cosmogonic context of the ocean deity.[129]

[127] The description of the deity is different from other texts, including the *Antāti*s, where the god who is blue/dark is reclining on the dark ocean but here the ocean is milk or white-colored.

[128] See Schmücker, "Epilogue" in Wilden 2020: 341–347, for an analysis of how the poets refer to the heart. He traces the "mystical function" of the heart to the *Atharvaveda*.

[129] Poykai 9, 14,17,76, 84; Pūtam 5, 9, 23, 30, 91

Furthermore, there is only one cryptic reference to Vedic fire ritual imagery in the *Antāti*s (Poykai 12), although homage is paid many times to the four Vedas (*nāṉ maṟai*; *nāl vēta*), which are variously described as eternal, melodious, well-recited, created through Ayaṉ (Brahmā), or being the god himself who is their inner meaning.[130] Thus, it seems that the *Antāti* poets come from a different northern stream than that of Epic passages in which the name Viṣṇu is easily linked with other names such as Nārāyaṇa, Vāsudeva, and Kṛṣṇa or that of the *Viṣṇu Purāṇa*, which emphasizes a vedicized Viṣṇu albeit one with some integration of oceanic symbolism. For example, when the *Antāti* poets allude to the *Viṣṇusahasranāma*, it is really another version in which Nārāyaṇa is the supreme god with a thousand names (*āyiram pēr*) (Poykai 65; Pūtam 73). Moreover, the early Āḻvārs rarely use the *Viṣṇusahasranāma*'s philosophically abstract epithetonyms (a *Gītā*-type vocabulary) as names.

Finally, the *Harivaṁśa* has many references to Baladeva/Balarāma, the white god with the serpent body and plough in hand, but the *Antāti* poets ignore him.

Antecedents to the *Antāti*s in Tamil works

For possible antecedents to the *Antāti*s, one must also look to Tamil poetry of the late *Caṅkam* period likely composed before the time of the early Āḻvārs even though overlap cannot be ruled out.[131] Schmid here in this volume has discussed relevant verses in the *Puṟanāṉūṟu*, *Naṟṟiṇai*, *Aiṅkuṟunūṟu*, *Kalittokai*, *Paripāṭal*, and *Cilappatikāram*,[132] and so there is no need to repeat these again. Rather, I will just make a few observations.

---

130 For examples of these epithets, see Poykai 33, 37, 60, 68, 94; Pūtam 45; Pēy 11, 14, 31, 38, 39, 84.

131 Wilden says the verdict on this matter is not yet in (Wilden, "Introduction" in Wilden 2020: 5).

132 See Schmid in this volume p. 125ff. for translation and discussion of relevant passages which can be dated between the 5th and 7th century.

First, all these Tamil works have verses with most of the names, epithetonyms and cosmogonic motifs found in the Āḻvārs. The *Cilappatikāram*, for instance, mentions the names Tirumāl, Māl, Māyavaṉ, Neṭiyōṉ, Neṭumāl, Kaṇṇaṉ, and Nārāyaṇaṉ. The *Paripāṭal* calls the supreme deity Tirumāl. The first hymn in the Tirumāl section refers to the deity's dark color, his feet, and his connection to Brahmā and creation. The next hymn begins with a description of the annihilation of creation with reference to the waters or the flood. There are many other epithets in this hymn and in the final two hymns to Tirumāl that refer to the supreme deity's feet and the boar who rescues the earth. These motifs are found in the Āḻvār verses.

Second, just as the *Cilappatikāram*, with one exception, does not use the proper name Nārāyaṇaṉ in the context of cosmogony but only in the context of chanting and soteriology, so do the *Antāti*s. This indicates that the Tamil Bhāgavata tradition and the Āḻvār *ekānta* tradition, despite some differences, had a common source. Otherwise, we would expect to see Nārāyaṇaṉ as the cosmogonic god reclining on the snake, which had already been described in the *Mahābhārata* passage about Mārkaṇḍeya (though there is one exception).

The late *Caṅkam* works differ from the *Antāti*s in several other important ways. Vāliyōṉ is an important deity in the late *Caṅkam* works (as he was in the *Harivaṁśa*) as the white god who holds a plough in his hand, has snake symbolism, and is closely associated with the black god Kaṇṇaṉ, so much so that they have one body or Kaṇṇaṉ reclines on the cobra couch, which represents Vāliyōṉ. The first hymn of the *Paripāṭal*, for instance, begins with a description of the deity reclining on his serpent bed under a [cobra] canopy and then describes his white complexion and his plough. In the second hymn, we are told that this supreme deity was manifested by the one who is white and the one who is dark (obviously, Balarāma and Kṛṣṇa). The *Antāti* poets do not mention Vāliyōṉ specifically; there are, however, several allusions to white and dark and one possible allusion to his white body (Pēy 5).

Final thoughts

Now back to Hardy's argument that the Āḻvārs' supreme god is really Kaṇṇaṉ because Māl is simply the Tamil translation of Kaṇṇaṉ, from *kaṇha*, the Prakrit of Sanskrit *kṛṣṇa*, which literally means dark or black.

It is true that Māl means literally black or dark color, and that Māl and its variants are the most common words for the supreme god in the *Antāti*s. Given the pre-eminence of ocean imagery, I think that long before this religion came to Tamil country, Kṛṣṇa had been homologized to an oceanic, cosmogonic god. I find in three of the *Antāti*s (Pēy's being the exception) that when the poet uses the name Kaṇṇaṉ, the actual name, it refers to the ocean god and cosmogony. There are also indirect references that link Kaṇṇaṉ and the ocean as in "the one reclining on a bright serpent who destroyed the 'hundred' (that is, the Kauravas) in the *Mahābhārata* war" (v. 94). When the human Kṛṣṇa needed a transcendent dimension, the idea of the transcendent dark oceanic, cosmogonic god must have been available and easily connected to the literal meaning of Kṛṣṇa as black/dark.

Because the ocean was an aniconic image and the ocean god had only slight anthropomorphism, the dark ocean or just the idea of the supreme dark deity had pride of place, as it were, which is likely why we find Māl (and variants) as the most common proper name in the *Antāti*s. Put otherwise, this name places the emphasis on transcendence and supremacy and avoids emphasis on the human, which the name Kaṇṇaṉ suggests because of the many allusions to stories about his life.[133]

Now what about Hardy's theory that Nārāyaṇa might be the transcendent aspect of Kaṇṇaṉ in the Āḻvārs' poems? Before doing this detailed study, I thought that I would find Nāraṇaṉ/Nārāyaṇaṉ as the key name for the oceanic, cosmogonic god in the *Antāti*s. Nārāyaṇa, after

---

[133] Because any cultus or priests of an ocean god had long disappeared, assuming they had once existed, the idea of the ocean as primal and cosmogonic must have continued only in myths. This means that the ocean as transcendence could easily be homologized with different deities in various places and times, which kept the imagery of the ocean alive, dynamic, and pluriform.

all, is the common name used for the god who reclines on the ocean or serpent bed on the ocean in some passages of the *Mahābhārata* and several *Purāṇa*s. It is also the name for the reclining image of the god in the temples of Tamil Nadu today.

To my surprise, whereas the poets explicitly link the names Māl/Tirumāl and occasionally Kaṇṇaṉ with the dark ocean and the oceanic cosmogonic god, they rarely link explicitly Nāraṇaṉ/Nārāyaṇaṉ with these. And they rarely connect the name Nāraṇaṉ/Nārāyaṇaṉ with the name Kaṇṇaṉ in a specific context. Rather, in the *Antāti*s, the name Nāraṇaṉ/Nārāyaṇaṉ is found mainly in the contexts of chanting and soteriology, variously described as destruction of all sins, avoiding hell or rebirth, or going to the city of the king of the good celestials.

I suspect the oceanic, cosmogonic god and Kṛṣṇa must have been the first homologization and occurred early in the history of Kṛṣṇa. I also suspect that this occurred in Dvāraka located on a river that empties into the nearby Arabian sea in what is now Gujarat (the Kathiawar peninsula). An island just off the coast called Bet Dvāraka was once an Indus Valley site, which means that aspects of its religion (the aniconic ocean and the oceanic, cosmogonic deity?) could have remained in the area long after the civilization collapsed. According to much later stories, Kṛṣṇa migrated to this area after he fought with his uncle at Mathura and ruled his Dvāraka kingdom from his residence on the island. Although, we have only archaeology and legend to go on, it is conceivable that Kṛṣṇa was there and that after his death he was apotheosized by integrating the oceanic, cosmogonic god as his transcendent dimension. Of course, it is also possible that it was followers or devotees of Kṛṣṇa living in Dvāraka who associated him with the oceanic cosmogonic deity. Aside from these two possibilities, it is hard to explain the connection of the ocean and Kṛṣṇa as king or cowherd.

The addition of Nārāyaṇa to this homology was probably a bit later and under the influence of those associated with the *Nārāyaṇa Upaniṣad*. We know that this Upaniṣad was affiliated with the *Atharvaveda*, for it proclaims: “this Atharva is known as foremost” (*etad atharva śiroyo 'dhīte*). Even though much of Atharvavedin history is obscure, there are clues that some in this tradition helped mediate the post-Vedic world as it expanded beyond its heartland, absorbing local traditions, and engaging with early temples. They were experimental in many ways.[134] It seems that in the Dvāraka region, they had promoted a homology of Nārāyaṇa (as represented by their *Nārāyaṇa Upaniṣad*) and the already homologized "Ocean-Kṛṣṇa" deity. Over time, multiple strands of this tradition likely developed, all acknowledging the homology. Some would have emphasized Kṛṣṇa and Balarāma (he was supposedly one of Kṛṣṇa's kinsman who had assimilated an agricultural deity, *nāga* or serpent cults, and the figure of Kṛṣṇa himself in various versions of his apotheosis, including the four *vyūha*s,[135] as we see in some passages of the *Mahābhārata* and the *Harivaṁśa*). Others would have emphasized Nārāyaṇa.

It has been suggested that there was a major traumatic event at Dvāraka—a massive tsunami or an earthquake (this calls to mind the stories of Dvāraka being swallowed up by the sea). If so, this likely prompted migrations inland to the central plateau and elsewhere, including toward the south.

Eventually strands of the Ocean-Kṛṣṇa-Nārāyaṇa Bhāgavata religion entered Tamil country and amalgamated with the poetic culture of the Tamil bards. Because the *Caṅkam* bards moved from ruler to ruler seeking patronage, so too they might have sought patronage from temples, whatever the deity, by singing of the god as if a generous ruler.[136] The *Perumpāṇāṟṟupaṭai*, in which a bard asks another bard for directions to the place of the reclining god, is a possible example of a late *Caṅkam* bardic connection with a Bhāgavata temple. But it is hard to tell. This work does not describe the bard actually in the temple or with

---

134 Cf. Young, 2007, 210-217.

135 At first, these had been emanations of Vāsudeva-Kṛṣṇa and his kinsmen, the deified Vṛṣṇi heroes, one being Balarāma who came to be represented in sculpted form from the second century C.E. as Schmid has traced here in this volume. And even when these figures merged with major deities such as Nārāyaṇa, becoming the four successive emanations (*vyūha*s) of the supreme deity, Balarāma continued as an independent form. Because these figures had independent cults, this might have been problematic for those who identified especially with the Nārāyaṇa component of the early homology with its *ekānta* orientation.

136 Cf. Wilden, "Introduction," in: Wilden 2020: 9.

a temple role of singing the deity's praise. It is important to note that the Āḻvār poems, not just those of the early Āḻvārs, have no direct mention of bards, only poetic allusions to their instruments such as the *yāḻ* and drum. It seems that the Āḻvārs have displaced the bards, if they indeed had had a role in Bhāgavata temples.[137]

Following Schmid, I have noted that the Āḻvārs do not mention Balarāma. Why? I suspect it had something to do with the idea of the Āḻvārs belonging to an *ekāntin* strand of Bhāgavatism. As we have seen, there had long been a Nārāyaṇa *ekānta* orientation (worshipping just one god) beginning with the *Nārāyaṇa Upaniṣad*'s reference to the one god (*eka deva*) and the emphasis on exclusive devotion, worship, and *japa* in later Nārāyaṇa passages of the *Mahābhārata* and the *Harivaṁśa*.

The Āḻvārs do not mention *mantra*s to Kṛṣṇa and his associates (which might have been common in other strands of Bhāgavata religion. Rather, the *mantra*s found in Āḻvār poems refer directly or indirectly to Nārāyaṇa. Does that mean Nārāyaṇa is really their supreme god? I once thought so, but I now think that would be reductive of the central Ocean-Kṛṣṇa-Nārāyaṇa homology that remains alive and well in the verses by Poykai, Pūtam, Pēy, and Tirumaḻicai who mention all three, though they emphasize different components of their homologized "supreme" god. From their poems, it is hard to tell more about the Āḻvārs' identity. They identify generally with the four Vedas, and they often praise Brahmins. However, they consider themselves distinct: pre-eminently poets (*kavi*).

If there was still an active Atharvavedin component to the Āḻvārs' identity that might also explain the virtual absence of the name Viṣṇu in the Āḻvārs' verses. Despite the overlap in Viṣṇu, Nārāyaṇa, and Kṛṣṇa histories I think there had long been conflict not only between the Atharvavedins and the Brahmins of the three Vedas but also between the Atharvavedins and the more Brahmanized Vaiṣṇavas such as the Vaikhānasas and those represented in the *Viṣṇu Purāṇa*, which, in

---

137 There are indications that bards continued to have connections to Murukaṉ temples even after he was considered the son of Araṉ/Īcaṉ (Śiva) and also had connections to Śaiva temples.

Schreiner's words already cited, had "A conscious and strong wish to conform to the norms of Vedic tradition and to brahminical values and practices ....".[138] And I think that this could explain why groups affiliated with the *Atharvaveda* such as the Āḻvārs shunned the name Viṣṇu, especially as orthodox Brahmins began to shift from their sacrificial and meditative practices to temple ones.[139]

After the age of the Āḻvārs, some of their poetic works continued in temple traditions of recitation, especially Nammāḻvār's *Tiruvāymoḻi*. In the late 9th century and first half of the 10th century, as mentioned at the beginning of this analysis, inscriptions began to mention Vaiṣṇavas, and in the second half of the 10th century we hear of Śrīvaiṣṇavas, the auspicious Vaiṣṇavas, who might be Brahmins. Whoever they were, they linked their traditions to those of the Āḻvārs. This orientation was further developed in the late 12th century by Rāmānuja's disciples who describe their lineage as beginning with Nāthamuni, whom they connected to Nammāḻvār, but also by the first commentary on the *Tiruvāymoḻi* by Rāmānuja's disciple Piḷḷāṉ. It is only from this time, I think, that we can speak of the sect we now call Śrīvaiṣṇavism.

I must leave further discussion of this obscure history for another time. Let me conclude by saying that this study has tried to clarify the identity of the Āḻvārs' supreme deity by pointing to the homologized Ocean-Kṛṣṇa-Nārāyaṇa. This study has also tried to clarify the identity of the Āḻvārs themselves as participating in some way in an *ekānta* tradition with roots in an Upaniṣadic tradition affiliated with the *Atharvaveda* but which over time integrated local traditions such as those at Dvāraka.

Finally, this study has recovered from the dustbin of history the importance of what was once an important aniconic or minimally iconic ocean god who destroys, preserves, and re-creates, possibly a supreme

---

138 See Schreiner in this volume, p. 81.

139 For instance, it took a long time for the phrase "four Vedas," the *Atharvaveda* being the fourth, to be commonly accepted by "orthodox" Brahmins who identified only with the three Vedas. In the Pāli Canon and the Jātakas, Brahmins are conventionally described as going to the end of the three Vedas. Up to the 7th century, inscriptions in regions such as Orissa often mention the three Vedas when describing Brahmins.

god of the Indus civilization who was absorbed in various ways into subsequent late Vedic and then Hindu myths and cosmogonies.

Bibliography

Bharati 2002
Rama Bharati, English Translation. In: *Nalayira Divya Prabandam.* Four Thousand Hymns of Twelve Alwars and Commentary by S. Jagathratchagan. Chennai 2002.

Bronkhorst/Deshpande 1999
Johannes Bronkhorst, "Is There an Inner Conflict of Tradition?" In: Johannes Bronkhorst and Madhav M. Deshpande (eds.) *Aryan and Non-Aryan in South Asia: Evidence, Interpretation and Ideology. Proceedings of the Michigan-Lausanne International Seminar on Aryan and non-Aryan in South Asia.* Ann Arbour: University of Michigan 1999, pp. 33–57.

van Buitenen 1981
Johannes Adrianus Bernardus van Buitenen, *The Mahābhārata, 2. The Book of the Assembly hall. 3. The Book of the Forest.* Chicago/London: The University of Chicago Press 1981.

Burrow/Emeneau 1984
T. Burrow, M.B. Emeneau, *A Dravidian Etymological Dictionary.* 2nd revised ed. Oxford 1984.

Colas 2003
Gérard Colas, History of Vaiṣṇava Traditions: An espuisse. In: *The Blackwell Companion to Hinduism.* Oxford: Oxford: Blackwell Publishing. 2003, 229–270.

Das Gupta 1931
Mrinal Das Gupta, Early Viṣṇuism and Nārāyaṇa Worship. In: *Indian Historical Quarterly.* Vol. VII, no.1/no.2. 1931.

Desai 1973
Kalpana Desai, *Iconography of Viṣṇu*. New Delhi 1973.

Fitzgerald 2004
James L. Fitzgerald, trans., ed., annotator, *Mahābhārata*. Vol 7. Chicago: University of Chicago Press 2004.

Gonda 1969
Jan Gonda, *Aspects of Early Viṣṇuism*. Delhi: Motilal Banarsidass 1969.

Hardy 1983
Friedhelm Hardy, *The Early History of Kṛṣṇa Devotion in South India*. Oxford 1983.

Heesterman 1985
Jan C. Heesterman, *The Inner Conflict of Tradition: Essays in Indian Ritual, Kingship, and Society*. Chicago: University of Chicago Press 1985.

Jaiswal 1967
Suvira Jaiswal, *The Origin and Development of Vaiṣṇavism* (Vaiṣṇavism from 200 B.C. to A.D. 500). Delhi 1967.

Nanditha 1980
Krishna Nanditha, *The Art and Iconography of Vishnu-Narayana*, Taraporevala/Bombay: Taraporevala Sons & Co. 1980.

Mani 1984
Vettam Mani, *Purānic Encyclopaedia*. A Comprehensive Dictionary with Special Reference to the Epic and Purāṇic Literature. Delhi: Motilal Banarsidass [1964], 1984 (reprint).

Matchett 2001
Freda Matchett, *Kṛṣṇa, Lord or Avatāra? The Relationship between Kṛṣṇa and Viṣṇu: in the context of the Avatāra Myth as Presented by the Harivaṁśa, the Viṣṇupurāṇa and the Bhāgavatapurāṇa. Curzon Studies in Asian Religion.* Richmond 2001.

Monier-Williams 1963
Monier Monier-Williams. *A Sanskrit-English Dictionary*. Etymologically and Philologically Arranged with special reference to Cognate Indo-European Languages. New Edition, Greatly Enlarged and Improved with the collaboration of E. Leumann, C. Capeller and other Scholars. Oxford 1899, 1963 (repr.).

Nālāyira Tivyaprapantam
Nālāyira Tivyaprapantam. Sri Bhagwat Ramanuja Siddantha Prachar Sabha (Regd.) Mumbai, 2005.

Narayanan 1987
Vasudha Narayanan. *The Way and the Goal.* Expressions of Devotion in the Early Śrīvaiṣṇava Tradition. Washington D.C.: Institute for Vaishnava Studies, Center for the Study of World Religions 1987.

Narayanan 1987. Appendix 1, See Narayanan 1987.

Paripāṭal
Le Paripāṭal. Texte tamouḷ. Introduction, traduction et notes par François Gros. [*Publications de l'Institut Français d'Indologie* 35]. Pondichéry: Institut Français d'Indologie 1968.

Parthasarathy 1992
R. Parthasarathy, *The Cilappatikāram of Iḷaṅkō Aṭikaḷ. An Epic of South India, Translated, with an Introduction and Postscript*. [Translations from the Asian Classics]. New York: Columbia University Press 2004.

Tamil Lexicon
Published under the authority of the University of Madras. 6 vols. Madras 1982 (repr.).

V. S. Sukthankar et. al. 1969
Harivaṃśa, critical edition by Vishnu Sitaram Sukthankar, S. K. Belvakar & Parashuram Lakshman Vaidya: vol. I, *Introduction, critical text and notes*. Poona: Bhandarkar Oriental Institute, 1969.

Vimalanandana 1957
Swami Vimalanandana, trans. *Mahanarayana Upanishad;* www.philaletheians.co.uk [uploaded 21 June 2010]; first published by Sri Ramakrishna Math, Chennai, 1957.

Wilden 2020
Eva Wilden (ed.) with the collaboration of Marcus Schmücker, *The Three Early Tiruvantātis of the Tivyappirapantam* [Collection Indologie 143; NETamil Series 7]. Pondicherry: École française d'Extrême-Orient 2020.

Young 1978
Katherine K. Young, *Beloved Places* (*ukantaruḷiṉanilaṅkaḷ*). The Correlation of Topography and Theology in the Śrīvaiṣṇava Tradition of South India. (Ph.D. dissertation, McGill University). Montreal 1978.

Young 2002
Id., Om, the Vedas, and the Status of Women with Special Reference to Śrī-vaiṣṇavism. In: *Jewels of Authority*. Women and Textual Tradition in Hindu India. Laurie L. Patton (ed.). Oxford: Oxford University Press 2002, 84-121.

Young 2007
Katherine K. Young 2007, Brāhmaṇas, Pāñcarātrins, and the Formation of Śrīvaiṣṇavism. In: *Studies in Hinduism* IV. On the Mutual Influences and Relationship of Viśiṣṭādvaita Vedānta and Pāñcarātra. [ÖAW Sph 756 = BKGA 54]. Gerhard Oberhammer, Marion Rastelli (eds). Vienna: Austrian Academy of Sciences Press 2007, pp. 179–261.

Young 2014
Id., Śrīvaiṣṇava Topoi: Constructing a South Indian Sect through Place. In: *Mapping the Chronology of Bhakti: Milestones, Stepping Stones, and Stumbling Stones.* Ed. Valérie Gillet. Pondichéry: École française d'Extrême-Orient 2014, 335-364.

Internet sources

https://sanskritdocuments.org. See Viṣṇu: *Nārāyaṇopaniṣat*. Site visited 25 November 2020.

www/hindupedia.com/en/Narayaniya. Swami Harshananda, "Nārāyaṇa." Site visited 25 November 2020.

https.//www.britannica.com/topic/Alvar. Britannica, The Editors of Encyclopaedia. "Alvar." Encyclopedia Britannica, 15 Nov. 2018. Site visited 3 March 2022.

Wikipedia. "Alvars": "(en.wikipedia.org. Accessed 3 March 2022).

Marion Rastelli

Viṣṇu, Vāsudeva, and Nārāyaṇa in the *Pāñcarātra Saṃhitā*s[1]

At the time the *Pāñcarātra Saṃhitā*s were compiled,[2] it had already long been established that Viṣṇu, Vāsudeva, and Nārāyaṇa were a single figure. However, does this mean that these names were used interchangeably for the supreme god without any differentiation? Or are distinct features of these originally different deities still preserved in the *Saṃhitā*s?

To answer these questions, I will examine the concepts related to these names in various contexts in the *Pāñcarātra Saṃhitā*s. These contexts are (1) the representation of god as creator and (2) as the promulgator of the *Saṃhitā*s, (3) the role of Viṣṇu, Vāsudeva, and Nārāyaṇa in various groups of deities, (4) the representation of god in ritual prescriptions, and (5) the meaning and ritual usage of the *mantra*s of Viṣṇu, Vāsudeva, and Nārāyaṇa.

God as creator

As monotheistic religions generally do, the Pāñcarātra considers its supreme god to be the creator of the world. The *Saṃhitā*s often describe various kinds of creations, which are sometimes related to each other and sometimes are not. These creations are "pure creation" (*śuddhasarga*), which generally includes the creation of the deities that form the pantheon of the Pāñcarātra and of individual souls,

---

1 I would like to thank Katharine Apostle for suggesting various stylistic corrections of the English manuscript.

2 The earliest extant Pāñcarātra *Saṃhitā*s were probably composed no earlier than the 9th century (Sanderson 2009: 62–70).

and the creation of the material world. In addition, the creation of the world is sometimes described in a traditional mythological manner with Brahmā as the executive creator.

Most characteristic for the Pāñcarātra is pure creation, during which the various deities, such as the Vyūhas, Vyūhāntaras, and Vibhavas, come into existence. The ultimate source of this creation is very often called Vāsudeva, who is identified with the supreme *brahman*. It is very rarely called Viṣṇu or Nārāyaṇa.

In the *Jayākhyasaṃhitā*, it is Vasudeva, identified with the *brahman*, from whom the deities Acyuta, Satya, and Puruṣa, the individual souls (*jīva*), and the *avatāras* arise.[3]

In the *Sātvatasaṃhitā*, it is Vāsudeva[4] who divides himself in order to become manifest as the three Vyūhas, Saṃkarṣaṇa, Pradyumna, and Aniruddha (SS 3.5-7, 4.8-11).

In the *Nāradīyasaṃhitā*, creation starts with Vāsudeva, who, interestingly, is identified with the supreme Śiva.[5] For the purpose of play (*krīḍā*) and enjoyment (*bhoga*)[6], a subtle, white, shining body made of glowing energy (*tejas*) arises for Vāsudeva, who is also called Viṣṇu in this state. He then becomes Vāsudeva with a white body and four arms, who subsequently generates Saṃkarṣaṇa. Saṃkarṣaṇa then creates Pradyumna, and Pradyumna creates Aniruddha, who is equated with Nārāyaṇa (NārS 1.25c-46).

According to the *Pādmasaṃhitā* and the *Viśvāmitrasaṃhitā*, the latter probably being based on the former, a two-armed Vāsudeva,

---

3 JS 4.2-14b. For a translation of this passage into German, see Rastelli 1999a: 387f. The divine beings arising during the pure creation are not called Vyūhas in the JS.

4 Who is also identified with the *brahman*; cf. SS 2.4.

5 See also NārS 9.25. In several passages of the NārS, Śaiva influences can be found (e.g., in the description of the various hells in NārS 9.56-67; cf. TAK 3 *s.v. naraka*), but they have not yet been examined in detail.

6 For this purpose of creation, cf. also NārS 1.72ab: "Creating and destroying in this way, the lord plays like a child" (*evaṃ sṛṣṭvā ca saṃhṛtya bālavat krīḍayan prabhuḥ*).

resembling a pure crystal, arises from the supreme *brahman*.[7] From him arises another Vāsudeva with four arms. This Vāsudeva divides himself into two parts from which another Vāsudeva, resembling a pure crystal, and Nārāyaṇa, resembling a dark ocean, come into existence. Out of Vāsudeva Saṃkarṣaṇa is born, out of him, Pradyumna, and out of him, Aniruddha. From these four deities a further 24 deities[8] and several other divine beings arise. Finally, from Aniruddha the world comes into existence (PādS *jp* 2, ViśS 4; cf. below, p.219).

In the examples given up to now, it is Vāsudeva, usually identified with the *brahman* and considered the supreme god, who is the starting point of pure creation. However, there are also examples in which Vāsudeva, while the origin of pure creation, is not the most supreme being. Here, in the hierarchy of creation, Viṣṇu, who is identified with Nārāyaṇa and Hari, stands above Vāsudeva.

This designation can already be found in the *Nārāyaṇīya*, the earliest literary Pāñcarātra text. In it, Nārāyaṇa is the supreme god. With a few exceptions,[9] in this text Vāsudeva, although identified with Nārāyaṇa, is either only mentioned in connection with the Vyūhas[10] or explicitly described as a manifestation of Nārāyaṇa.[11]

---

7 The PādS does not call the entity from which Vāsudeva arises *brahman*, but its description must signify the *brahman*: "[There is] a Light which is without beginning, middle and end, without growth and decay, unshakeable, eternal, incomparable, eternally satisfied, pure, having every form [and yet] having no form, beyond the darkness, imperishable" (PādS *jp* 2.6c-7: *ādimadhyāntarahitam avṛddhikṣayam acyutam* ‖ 6 *nityaṃ nirupamaṃ jyotir nityatṛptaṃ nirañjanam* | *sarvākāraṃ nirākāraṃ tamasaḥ param avyayam* ‖ 7; translation by Schwarz Linder 2012: 277). The ViśS does not describe or designate any kind of entity from which Vāsudeva arises.

8 These 24 deities are the twelve Vyūhāntaras (see below, p. 227), another Vāsudeva, another Saṃkarṣaṇa, another Pradyumna, another Aniruddha, Puruṣottama, Adhokṣaja, Nṛsiṃha, Acyuta, Janārdana, Upendra, Hari, and Kṛṣṇa (PādS *jp* 2.21-28).

9 MBh 12.325.4 (130), 326.113, 331.9.

10 MBh 12.326.24-39, 332.15-18. Cf. also Bock-Raming 2002: 174–177.

11 MBh 328.36, 335.87.

One of the examples from the *Saṃhitās* for this concept is found in the *Sanatkumārasaṃhitā*. Here, all deities are parts of Nārāyaṇa (*nārāyaṇāṃśajāḥ*).[12] The beginning of the origination of the deities is marked by Sadāviṣṇu, homologous to the non-manifest (*avyakta*) Vāsudeva. From him arises Mahāviṣṇu, equal to (the Vyūha) Vāsudeva, from Mahāviṣṇu arises the goddess Śānti, and from her arises Viṣṇu, homologous to Saṃkarṣaṇa. The deities arising next are the goddess Śrī, Pradyumna, homologous to Brahmā, Sarasvatī, Aniruddha, and Rati (SanS *ir* 6.1-10).

In the *Ahirbudhnyasaṃhitā*, it is Vāsudeva, too, who divides himself in order to be manifested in the shape of the three Vyūhas (AS 5.15c-44). However, the most supreme being is Viṣṇu, who in this context is identified with Nārāyaṇa and Hari:

> The supreme *brahman*, Nārāyaṇa, in which all effects have fallen into sleep, is uniform in every respect, the abode of everything, untouched. (2) Possessing the complete inactive six qualities, it resembles the windless sky. His *śakti*, in the form of inactivity and emptiness, (3) awakens by her free will at any time for any reason. Being the self of the supreme *brahman*, of Hari, the *śakti* (4) flashes up as a goddess at some point like lightning in the sky. This power flashing in the [windless] sky [of the *brahman*] is called *śakti*. (5) She manifests the various pure and impure things and [divine (?)] manifestations. [Her] self-created freedom of will [that arises] when she awakens (6) is the will which is characterized by watching.[13] It is called Sudarśana. It is Hari's *kriyā*[*śakti*]; it is [his] valour, glow, and strength. (7) And the things that, moving on the substrate (*bhitti*)[14] that is she herself, become manifest are Viṣṇu's *śakti* as *bhūti*[*śakti*]. It is composed of an infinitesimal part of the [great] *śakti*.[15]

---

[12] Matsubara (1994: 120) points out that this concept derives from the Nārāyaṇīya, where the Vyūhas are considered to be manifestations (*mūrti*) of Nārāyaṇa (MBh 12.326.66-70).

[13] Cf. the explanation of the word *sudarśana* in AS 2.7c-9.

[14] In this context, *bhitti* means the substrate of something such as the canvas of a painting. In this verse, the *śakti* is described as the substrate on which the world or the things that constitute the world appear. The term *bhitti* appears also in AS 3.7cd and in the LT; cf., e.g.: "Or he should

Viṣṇu, who possesses the six divine qualities of knowledge (*jñāna*), supremacy (*aiśvarya*), power (*śakti*), strength (*bala*), valour (*vīrya*), and glow (*tejas*) in an inactive mode, becomes Vāsudeva only when these qualities awaken on account of Viṣṇu's will:

> The simultaneous awakening of the qualities of knowledge, supremacy, strength, etc., which are made of *śakti*, is characterized by the absence of inactivity. (26c-27b) The Venerate Vāsudeva, who is characterized by the manifestation of the [qualities], and the supreme primary matter (*prakṛti*) are produced by Viṣṇu's will. The *śakti* of the pervading Viṣṇu is the primary matter of the world. (27c-28) On account of the differentiation between the *śakti* and the possessor of the *śakti*, [god] is called Vāsudeva. (29ab) (...) The infinite Venerate Viṣṇu, who possesses the *śakti*, the supreme person, who possesses the complete inactive six qual-

---

regard the world like a painting on myself who is the substrate" (LT 43.32ab: *mayi vā bhittibhūtāyāṃ citravat saṃsmarej jagat* |); "Through my own will I manifest the whole world on the substrate that is myself" (LT 13.22ab: *ātmabhittau jagat sarvaṃ svecchayonmīlayāmy aham* |); and LT 22.9-10b, 50.9cd, 51.25cd. The term *bhitti* is probably borrowed from the Pratyābhijñā system; see Ratié 2011: 656–668.

15 AS 5.2-8: *prasuptākhilakāryaṃ yat sarvataḥ samatāṃ gatam* | *nārāyaṇaḥ paraṃ brahma sarvāvāsam anāhatam* ‖ 2 *pūrṇastimitaṣāḍguṇyam asamīrāmbaropamam* | *tasya staimityarūpā yā śaktiḥ śūnyatvarūpiṇī* ‖ 3 *svātantryād eva kasmāc cit kvacit sonmeṣam ṛcchati* | *ātmabhūtā hi yā śaktiḥ parasya brahmaṇo hareḥ* ‖ 4 *devī vidyud iva vyomni kvacid uddyotate tu sā* | *śaktir vidyotamānā sā śaktir ity ucyate 'mbare* ‖ 5 *vyanakti vividhān bhāvān śudhāśuddhān samūrtikān* | *tasyā unmeṣam ṛcchantyāḥ svātantryaṃ yat svanirmitam* ‖ 6 *prekṣaṇātmā sa saṃkalpas tat sudarśanam ucyate* | *sā kriyā tad dharer vīrya ṃtat tejaś ca balaṃ ca tat* ‖ 7 *vyajyante ye ca te bhāvāḥ svabhittiparivartitāḥ* | *sā bhūtir viṣṇuśaktiḥ sā śakteḥ koṭyaṃśakalpitā* ‖ 8. A translation of this passage (varying in details from this one) can also be found in Matsubara 1994: 203f. and Bock-Raming 2002: 35f. Also in other passages, the AS often emphasizes that the very beginning of creation is Viṣṇu's will, which is his *śakti*. See, e.g., AS 3.30, 36, 4.20, 21, 23-24, 43, 5.60, 6.20, etc. At times it is also said that it is Nārāyaṇa's or Hari's *saṃkalpa* (e.g., AS 4.15 and 18), but Viṣṇu is mentioned much more often, perhaps due to metrical reasons.

ities [and] resembles the motionless sea, (32c-33b) [becomes] the infinite, eternal Venerate Vāsudeva on account of the simultaneous awakening of the six qualities, which was ordered by him.[16]

The *Lakṣmītantra*, which bears many similarities with the AS, resembles it also in this case. Vāsudeva is the beginning of the pure creation (LT 4.12-18, 6.15c-16, 7.5-7). But the state before the pure creation is the *brahman*, which in a next step divides itself into Nārāyaṇa, also called Viṣṇu or Hari,[17] and Lakṣmī.[18] Lakṣmī is the *śakti* that is the initial power to start creation as described in the AS.[19]

Bock-Raming, who compared the descriptions of pure creation in the SS and the AS, came to the conclusion that while the SS teaches that Vāsudeva is the supreme god, the AS, although partly based on the SS, teaches that Hari-Viṣṇu-Nārāyaṇa is the god that is identical with the *brahman*. Thus, the AS secondarily added this god in comparison to the SS (Bock-Raming 2002: 168–173). The examples from various *Saṃhitā*s described above show us that this difference

---

16 AS 5.26c-29b and 32c-34b: *guṇāḥ śaktimayā ye te jñānaiśvaryabalādayaḥ* ‖ 26 *teṣāṃ yugapadunmeṣaḥ staimityavirahātmakaḥ* | *saṃkalpakalpito viṣṇor yaḥ sa tadvyaktilakṣaṇaḥ* ‖ 27 *bhagavān vāsudevaḥ sa paramā prakṛtiś ca sā* | *śaktir yā vyāpino viṣṇoḥ sā jagatprakṛtiḥ parā* ‖ 28 *śakteḥ śaktimato bhedād vāsudeva itīryate* | (...) *ananto bhagavān viṣṇuḥ śaktimān puruṣottamaḥ* ‖ 32 *pūrṇastimitaṣāḍguṇyo nistaraṅgārṇavopamaḥ* | *ṣaṇṇāṃ yugapadunmeṣād guṇānāṃ svapracoditāt* ‖ 33 *ananta eva bhagavān vāsudevaḥ sanātanaḥ* |. For a translation of these passages, see also Matsubara 1994: 206.

17 E.g., in LT 4.1-2, 6.4.

18 LT 2.15c-16: "*Brahman* embraces both the principle of existence and its state of existence, hence It (*brahman*) is the eternal state (*padam*). (When differentiated) the existing principle is the god Nārāyaṇa and its state of existence is the supreme Lakṣmī, i.e. myself. Therefore, *brahman*, the eternal, is called Lakṣmī-Nārāyaṇa because the I-identity is always inherent in I-hood" (*bhavadbhāvātmakaṃ brahma tatas tacchāśvataṃpadam* | *bhavannārāyaṇo devo bhāvo lakṣmīr ahaṃ parā* ‖ 15 *lakṣmīnārāyaṇākhyātam ato brahma sanātanam* | *ahaṃtayā samākrānto hy ahamarthaḥ prasidhyati* ‖ 16; translation by Gupta 1972: 9).

19 See LT 2.19-36.

between teaching that either Vāsudeva or Viṣṇu-Nārāyaṇa is the most supreme source of pure creation is not only a matter of singular modification of the doctrine, but also continues on in the time of the later *Saṃhitā*s.

The creation of the material world is often explained by the concept of creation borrowed from the Sāṃkhya, in which 24 principles (*tattva*) constituting the material world emerge from primary matter (*prakṛti*).

This explanation of the creation of the material world can stand side by side with the other explanations of creation, such as pure creation, without being related to them. An example for this can be found in JS 3.2-9b.[20] Here, only the successive coming into existence of the *tattva*s out of the primary matter is described, without relation to any of the other concepts of creation or to a supreme god.

However, the creation of the material world can also be related to the supreme god, the creation of divine *śakti*s and of deities. In the ParS 2,[21] for example, creation starts on account of an order (*niyoga*) of the *parama puruṣa* (ParS 2.26). In AS 6, the "impure creation" (*śuddhetarasṛṣṭi*), as it is called here, like the "pure creation" has its starting point in Viṣṇu's will (*saṃkalpa*; e.g., AS 6.20) that urges the *bhūtiśakti* to evolve into the various constituents of the material world. In LT 5, it is a small part of the supreme *śakti* (LT 5.1-3) that stimulates the creation of the material world. Yet, the examination of this concept of creation has no relevance for the main question of this paper, namely, if Viṣṇu, Vāsudeva, and Nārāyaṇa are identified or preserve distinct features.

As I have already mentioned, in the mythological creation stories Brahmā is the executive creator of the world. Usually the supreme god, being in the state of yogic sleep (*yoganidrā*), creates a lotus, arising from his navel, and/or a golden egg. From this lotus arises Brahmā, who then creates the material world. The name given to the

---

20 For a translation into German, see Rastelli 1999a: 383f.

21 For a description of the creation according to the ParS, see Czerniak-Drożdżowicz 2003: 108–118.

supreme god in this context varies. In the JS it is Viṣṇu,[22] in the ParS it is the "supreme man" (*parama puṃs*, ParS 1.49), in the AS it is Hari (AS 41.5), in the ĪS (20.119c-121b) and the *Hayaśīrṣapañcarātra* it is Nārāyaṇa (H 1.10 and 13),[23] and in the NārS it is Vāsudeva (NārS 1.72).

However, another deity plays an eminent role in several versions of this creation story, namely, Aniruddha, the last of the four Vyūhas, who has a particular relation to Nārāyaṇa. Already in the *Nārāyaṇīya*, it is Aniruddha from whom the lotus arises in which Brahmā is born.[24] In the NārS, the god from whom the navel lotus arises is also Aniruddha (NārS 1.64). As I have mentioned above, Aniruddha is equated with Nārāyaṇa in the NārS (1.46).

In PādS *jp* 3, the starting point of the creation through Brahmā is Nārāyaṇa. Nārāyaṇa creates water;[25] in this great ocean Durgā, who is a part of Aniruddha (*aniruddhāṃśajā*), creates a *nyagrodha* tree in which Padmanābha, who is also a part of Aniruddha, arises. Padmanābha creates a golden egg from his navel. From the egg emerges a lotus, and in the lotus Padmanābha creates Brahmā, who then creates the world.[26]

According to ViśS 5, which is probably based on the PādS *jp* 3, the creation of the world stems from Aniruddha (ViśS 5.1); but, in fact, its description begins with Nārāyaṇa, who creates water. In the water, he creates a golden egg from which Brahmā appears. On

---

22 See JS 2.60, where Viṣṇu is described as the supreme cause (*parama kāraṇa*). For a translation into German of the JS's mythological creation story, see Rastelli 1999a: 378–382.

23 The mythological creation stories of these three texts are versions of the Madhu-Kaiṭabha story, of which several versions can be found also in the *Mahābhārata* and the *Viṣṇudharmottarapurāṇa*; cf. Bock 1987.

24 MBh 12.326.69, 328.14c-15, 335.19; see also 12.327.63.

25 Traditionally, Nārāyaṇa is closely related to water, cf., e.g., Matsubara 1994: 100f.

26 PādS *jp* 3.1-7b. In the story, there is still some turbulence until the creation is complete, but this is not of interest in the context of our topic.

seeing him, Nārāyaṇa, who is now called Viṣṇu, orders Brahmā to create the world.[27]

Also, in SanS *ir* 6.17-28, which actually does not describe the creation of the world, but the "gross creation" (*sthūlasṛṣṭi*), i.e., the creation of several lower deities, it is Aniruddha who creates the first water and from whose navel a lotus arises. From the lotus then an egg emerges, out of which Brahmā is born.

The *Mudgalopaniṣad*–which is "one of the minor and later upaniṣads", an explanation of the *Puruṣasūkta* and a document of a Pāñcarātric Viṣṇuism, attempting to harmonise with Vedic lore (Gonda 1968–69: 101)–teaches that Puruṣa-Nārāyaṇa is the supreme god. He divided himself into four parts. Three-fourths of him were in the highest firmament. The other fourth was Aniruddha-Nārāyaṇa, who ordered Brahmā to create the universe (MudU 351,30-352,9).

In all these texts we find the concept that it is Aniruddha who came into existence immediately before Brahmā, who then created the world. The model for this was probably the *Nārāyaṇīya*, the text in which this concept is found for the first time. There, Aniruddha as

---

[27] ViśS 5.1-5: "Kāśyapa: 'You said that the creation of the world [comes] from the Venerable Aniruddha himself. We heard repeatedly that Brahmā creates the worlds. I am very curious to know if this is true or not true. Tell me everything now, o Guru!' Viśvāmitra: 'In the beginning, the eminent god Nārāyaṇa, whose abode is the ocean of milk, the Lord, desiring to amuse himself, created the waters by his own will and put his luminous semen into them. A golden egg that shines like ten millions of suns came into existence. From the [egg], Brahmā himself arose, the grandfather of all worlds. Having seen him, the Venerable Viṣṇu ordered [him] to create the worlds.'" *kāśyapaḥ – aniruddhāj jagatsṛṣṭiḥ sākṣād bhagavatas tvayā* | *uktā yat sṛjati brahmā lokān ity anuśuśruma* ‖ 1 *tat satyaṃ kim utāsatyaṃ mahat kautūhalaṃ hi me* | *vartate jñātum adhunā kathyatām akhilaṃ guro* ‖ 2 [*viśvāmitraḥ–*] *devo nārāyaṇaḥ śrīmān kṣīrārṇavaniketanaḥ* | *ādau vinodam anvicchan svātantryeṇātmanaḥ prabhuḥ* ‖ 3 *apaḥ sṛṣṭvā svakaṃ vīryaṃ nidadhe tāsu cojjvalam* | *hairaṇyam aṇḍam abhavad ravikoṭisamaprabham* ‖ 4 *tasmād abhūt svayaṃ brahmā sarvalokapitāmahaḥ* | *taṃ dṛṣṭvā bhagavān viṣṇur lokasṛṣṭyartham ādiśat* ‖ 5.

the last of the Vyūhas serves as a link between the creation of the deities and that of the world.

But why is Aniruddha in particular related to Nārāyaṇa? Are not all Vyūhas manifestations of Nārāyaṇa?[28] An answer can perhaps be found in the iconography. Here, the reclined deity with a lotus arising from his navel is generally considered to be Nārāyaṇa.[29] From here it is only a small step to equate Aniruddha, a lotus arising from his navel, with this god.

God as promulgator

According to the Pāñcarātra tradition, its authoritative texts, the *Saṃhitā*s, were revealed by god himself. Almost every *Saṃhitā* starts with a narrative (the so-called *śāstrāvatāra* story) which relates how, where, and to whom the teachings of the Pāñcarātra were revealed.[30] These stories are closely related to the *Nārāyaṇīya* and adopt many of its motifs.[31]

According to the *Nārāyaṇīya*, the supreme god is Nārāyaṇa (identified with Viṣṇu and Hari[32]), and it is he who revealed the Pāñcarātra.[33]

---

[28] Cf. fn. 12.

[29] See, e.g., Champakalakshmi 1981: 69–76 and Schmid 103ff. in this volume.

[30] For a study of these *śāstrāvatāra* stories, see Oberhammer 1994.

[31] Cf. Grühnendahl in Schreiner 1997: 362–370, Rastelli 2006: 161–168, Rastelli 2008: 257 fn. 5.

[32] E.g., in MBh 12.324.29-30.

[33] MBh 12.326.100-101b: "Nārada again proclaimed this *Mahopaniṣad*, which was endowed with the four Vedas, which was made by means of Sāṃkhya and Yoga, which he (?) called 'Pañcarātra' [and] which was sung by Nārāyaṇa's mouth." (*idaṃ mahopaniṣadaṃ caturvedasamanvitam | sāṃkhyayogakṛtaṃ tena pañcarātrānuśabditam ‖ nārāyaṇamukhodgītaṃ nārado 'śrāvayat punaḥ* |); and 12.337.63-64b: "The knower of the entire Pañcarātra is the Venerable one himself. And in all these

In contrast, in the *śāstrāvatāra* stories of the *Pāñcarātra Saṃhitās*, not much difference is made between Viṣṇu, Vāsudeva, and Nārāyaṇa. Although certain *Saṃhitās* state that it was Viṣṇu, Vāsudeva or Nārāyaṇa who promulgated the Pāñcarātra or the respective *Saṃhitā*, the various gods are frequently identified with one another.[34]

In addition to being the promulgator of the Pāñcarātra, Nārāyaṇa also appears in some of the *śāstrāvatāra* stories in another form, namely, as the son of Dharma. In the *Nārāyaṇīya*, Nārāyaṇa, together with his brothers Nara, Hari, and Kṛṣṇa, is a manifestation of the supreme Nārāyaṇa. He and Nara practise austerity (*tapas*) and teach the sage Nārada in the Badarī hermitage.[35] Some *Saṃhitās* allude to

---

sciences, o best of kings, Nārāyaṇa, the Lord, is observed as the basis according to the tradition [and] according to knowledge." (*pañcarātrasya kṛtsnasya vettā tu bhagavān svayam* | *sarveṣu ca nṛpaśreṣtha jñāneṣv eteṣu dṛśyate* || *yathāgamaṃ yathājñānaṃ niṣṭhā nārāyaṇaḥ prabhuḥ* |). Cf. also the story of Brahmā's seven births in MBh 12.336.13-50.

[34] Viṣṇu is the promulgator of the Pāñcarātra according to JS 1.40c-48b (identified with the *brahman*, Acyuta, and Nārāyaṇa in JS 1.21c-23), AS 11.62c-65b (in the *śāstrāvatāra* story, the deity actually teaching the AS is Śaṇkara, i.e., Śiva; see, e.g., AS 1.18), NārS 1.18 (identified with Vāsudeva), MārkS 1.22c-23b (identified with Nārāyaṇa in MārkS 1.16), BharS 1.4. Vāsudeva is the promulgator according to SS 1.17c-18b (Vāsudeva is implied by *cakrapāṇi* according to Alaśiṅga Bhaṭṭa's commentary ad loc.; he is identified with Acyuta and Viṣṇu in SS 1.19), PārS 1.77 (ĪS 1.25), ĪS 1.54 (identified with Hari in ĪS 1.47), ViṣṇuS 1.22 and 31. Nārāyaṇa is the promulgator according to JS *adhika pāṭha* 1, ŚrīpṛśS 1.44 (identified with Hari in ŚrīpṛśS 1.35), ViśS 1.70c-78 (identified with Hari in ViśS 1.75), AnS 2.2. ParS 1.33c-34b calls the promulgator of the Pāñcarātra *parama puruṣa*. The promulgator of the LT is the goddess Śrī (LT 1.56-61). The PādS is revealed by Keśava (PādS *jp* 1.32). According to BhT 2.1-6, the Pāñcarātra was revealed by Hari, the BhT itself is proclaimed by Paraśurāma.

[35] MBh 12.321.8-10b: "For Nārāyaṇa, the soul of the universe, who has four manifestations, the eternal one, was born as the son of Dharma—so my father told me—in former times, in the *kṛtayuga* in the *svāyambhuva* period, o great king, [namely,] as Nara, Nārāyaṇa, Hari, and Kṛṣṇa. Among these, both Nārāyaṇa and Nara, the imperishable ones, practised

these important personages known from the *Nārāyaṇīya*. In the NārS, for example, the sage Gautama, when visited by Nārada, says that the two ascetics Nara and Nārāyaṇa had predicted that Nārada would teach him.[36]

Viṣṇu, Vāsudeva, and Nārāyaṇa in groups of deities

As already indicated, in the Pāñcarātra tradition Viṣṇu, Vāsudeva, and Nārāyaṇa do not only appear as the supreme god, but are also included in various groups of deities who, in turn, are manifestations of the supreme god.

Vāsudeva is the first of the four Vyūhas, the others being Saṃkarṣaṇa, Pradyumna, and Aniruddha.[37]

Viṣṇu and Nārāyaṇa belong to the group of the twelve Vyūhāntaras. The Vyūhāntaras arise from the Vyūhas during pure creation. Keśava, Nārāyaṇa, and Mādhava originate from Vāsudeva; Govinda, Viṣṇu, and Madhusūdana from Saṃkarṣaṇa; Trivikrama, Vāmana, and Śrīdhara from Pradyumna; and Hṛṣīkeśa, Padmanābha, and Dāmodara from Aniruddha.[38] These twelve deities are also known as

---

austerity." (*nārāyaṇo hi viśvātmā caturmūrtiḥ sanātanaḥ* | *dharmātmajaḥ sambabhūva pitaivaṃ me 'bhyabhāṣata* || *kṛte yuge mahārāja purā svāyambhuve 'ntare* | *naro nārāyaṇaś caiva hariḥ kṛṣṇas tathaiva ca* || *tebhyo nārāyaṇanarau tapas tepatur avyayau* |).

36 NārS 1.6-15b. Also, PārS 1.73c-74b ≈ ĪS 1.42 allude to Nara and Nārāyaṇa. BhT 1.10 mentions the *mahāyogin* Nārāyaṇa (for this designation of Nārāyaṇa, see also MBh 12.335.84 and 337.17).

37 For examples, see NārS 1.25c-46 or SanS *ir* 6.1-10 described above on pp. 219 ff. There are two concepts in the *Saṃhitās*: to consider Vāsudeva as one of altogether four Vyūhas, or to oppose Vāsudeva to the three Vyūhas Saṃkarṣaṇa, Pradyumna, and Aniruddha; see here Rastelli 2006: 284f., n. 875.

38 E.g., AS 5.46-49b. These twelve deities are identical with the first twelve of the 24 *mūrtis* whose origination is described in PādS *jp* 2.21-28. See also Rastelli 2006: 348–350.

the tutelary deities of the months (*māsādhipa*, *māseśa*) within the Pāñcarātra and also in other traditions, from which the Pāñcarātra probably adopted them.[39]

The twelve deities do not bear many individual features by which they can be distinguished from each other. One distinguishing feature is their difference in colour. According to most of the sources, Nārāyaṇa is visualised as being white;[40] the AS and the PādS describe him as being dark.[41] Viṣṇu is described as being yellow[42] or red[43].

Nārāyaṇa is one of the 38 or 39 Vibhavas.[44] The SS (12.136c-148 [≈ TS 24.328c-340]) describes him together with Nara, Hari, and Kṛṣṇa and thus identifies these Vibhavas as the four sons of Dharma known from the *Nārāṇīya* (see above, p. 226). According to the SS, Nara is devoted to recitation (*japa*), Nārāyaṇa to Yoga, Hari to the ritual (*kriyā*), and Kṛṣṇa to religious austerities (*tapas*). They are described as being red, white, golden, and dark.

Viṣṇu, Vāsudeva, and Nārāyaṇa belong to the nine *mūrti*s or nine Vyūhas. The nine *mūrti*s are Vāsudeva, Saṃkarṣaṇa, Pradyumna, Aniruddha, Nārāyaṇa, Brahmā or Hayagrīva, Viṣṇu, Narasiṃha, and Varāha.[45] According to AgniP 25.4c-5 (≈ GarP 1.11.37), their col-

---

39 See Rastelli 2006: 350–355.

40 PauṣS 36.150, SS 8.58, PārS 23.73, ŚrīprśS 9.68.

41 AS 26.36, PādS *kp* 14.73. According to ViṣS 11.153, Nārāyaṇa is light-coloured, dark, or red.

42 AS 26.39, PādS *kp* 14.73, ŚrīprśS 9.68.

43 PauṣS 36.156, SS 8.58, PārS 23.74. According to ViṣS 11.167c-168a, Viṣṇu is red or dark. The other distinguishing mark of the Vyūhāntaras is the different distribution of the four attributes of discus (*cakra*), mace (*gadā*), lotus (*padma*), and conch (*śaṅkha*) among their four hands (see Rastelli 2006: 355–357).

44 On the number of the Vibhavas, see Rastelli 2006: 363–365.

45 E.g., PauṣS 10.3-33, 33.4-13 (Brahmā), AgniP 25.1-5b, 49.10-19b (Brahmā), PādS *kp* 18.62d-63 (Hayagrīva), PārS 17.96c-99 (Hayagrīva). For further references, see Rastelli 2007: 200–202.

ours are like that of saffron (*javā*, AgniP) or white (*sita*, GarP) (Vāsudeva), the colour of dawn (*aruṇa*), of turmeric (*haridrā*), blue (*nīla*), dark (*śyāma*) (Nārāyaṇa), red (*lohita*), like that of a (dark?) cloud (Viṣṇu), of fire, and yellow as honey (*madhupiṅga*). According to *Hayaśīrṣapañcarātra* 24 (parts of it ≈ AgniP 49.10-19b), Vāsudeva, having two arms, carries the conch (*śaṅkha*) and shows the *varadamudrā* (24.3-4b); Nārāyaṇa has four arms and carries a lotus, conch, mace, and discus (24.11 abc and 22.5c-6); and Viṣṇu has eight or four arms and also carries various attributes (24.17-19b).

Finally, Viṣṇu is part of the group of Mahāviṣṇu, Sadāviṣṇu, and Viṣṇu as described in SanS *ir* 6 (see p. 219).

As can generally be seen from the various groups of deities taught by the Pāñcarātra, the Pāñcarātra pantheon tends to include many deities or divine manifestations that are traditionally identified with Viṣṇu, and thus the Pāñcarātra incorporates many other traditions into its own. However, the mere fact that the three deities under discussion are also part of various groups does not give us much information, especially since almost no distinctive features of them are taught, with the exception of Nārāyaṇa as one of the Vibhavas that are Dharma's sons.

However, one fact deserves closer attention, namely, the relation of the three deities to one another. When compared to Viṣṇu and Nārāyaṇa, Vāsudeva often holds a more prominent position. We find that it is Vāsudeva who is usually the starting point of pure creation. As the various divine manifestations arise during pure creation, Vāsudeva is also the origin of the deities appearing in the defined groups, and thus, if he is part of one of these groups, he takes the primary position among them.

God in rituals

The Pāñcarātra is a tradition in which the performance of rituals plays a major role. There are various kinds of rituals: among others, the daily ritual, regular or irregular temple festivals and processions (*utsava*), consecrations (*pratiṣṭhā*) of cult images and temples, initiations (*dīkṣā*), rites of reparations (*prāyaścitta*).

With regard to the question of this paper, the prescriptions of two kinds of rituals have been examined: the daily ritual and initiation rites. In the daily ritual, god is made present by means of *mantra*s and mental visualisations in a suitable place and then gratified by means of various offerings and services. At particular moments during initiation rites, the initiand comes in close contact with god. Thus, one can examine whether specific names for god are used in certain sub-rites of these rituals or whether specific manifestations of god are made present.

To answer this briefly at the beginning: In both types of ritual it appears that generally no difference is made between Viṣṇu, Vāsudeva, and Nārāyaṇa.

I will give only one detailed example for each type of ritual: During the bath (*snāna*), which is the first element of the daily ritual, the bathing place is transformed into a *viṣṇutīrtha*, a bathing place in which Viṣṇu is present. The *Jayākhyasaṃhitā* uses the word *viṣṇutīrtha* several times (JS 9.28, 29, 32) and then describes the mental ritual by which such a *viṣṇutīrtha* is made: the whole universe is mentally incinerated and rid of water. The bathing place is then imagined as having the nature of the transcendent Viṣṇu. The worshipper visualises water falling onto the bathing place. Above the water he visualises Nārāyaṇa, through which the bathing place obtains the nature of Nārāyaṇa:

> Then he should make the bathing place together with its water supreme by means of the two meditative fixations (*dhāraṇā*).[46] By means of the ritual that is determined by the prescription, (35) he should fill the entire [universe] from the *ādhāraśakti* up to the sphere of [god's] will (*saṃkalpa*) with fire that is covered in garlands of flames. (36) He should make the world without water and he should visualise the bathing place as the body of the transcendent (*śānta*) [god]. He should first make the [water], which resembles a dewdrop [in size and] which was [mentally] created

46 The phrase "two meditative fixations" indicates what is described in the following passage: the mental burning of an object and its mental recreation by showering it with water.

only in such an extent, descend again into the transcendent Viṣṇu consisting of consciousness. Then he should visualise that the torrent of the *brahman*, which has devoured streams and waves of water, has come forth by means of the *śakti* and falls impetuously, and he should fill the entire [universe] that resembles the moon up to the abode of the *brahman*. (37-39) By means of [these] steps of observation, he should first continually visualise this union of the entire [universe] with the nature [of god]. In its centre, he should offer a throne to the lord and visualise the lord Nārāyaṇa, who resembles ten million of moons, who is covered in a multitude of waves of pure nectar, who is powerful, richly endowed with a number of *śakti*s, [and] who ejects nectar juice [from his mouth] on it, o Brahmin. If one performs it like this, the bathing place will have the nature of Nārāyaṇa.[47]

Creating a *viṣṇutīrtha* by giving a bathing place the nature of Nārāyaṇa can only be understood if Viṣṇu and Nārāyaṇa are identical.[48]

---

[47] JS 9.35-42: *dhāraṇādvitayenātha tīrthasya sajalasya ca* | *paramīkaraṇaṃ kuryād vidhidṛṣṭena karmaṇā* || 35 *ādhāraśakter ārabhya saṅkalpaviṣayāvadhi* | *vahninā pūrayet sarvaṃ jvālāmālāvilena ca* || 36 *niram mayaṃ jagat kṛtvā tīrthaṃ śāntatanu smaret* | *śānte saṃvinmaye viṣṇau bhūyas tad avatārya ca* || 37 *niśāmbukaṇasaṅkāśam iyattākalpitaṃ purā* | *smṛtvā śaktiprabhāvena brahmasroto vinirgatam* || 38 *dhārākallolasaṅgīrṇaṃ patamānaṃ tu vegataḥ* | *ābrahmabhavanaṃ sarvaṃ pūrayec chaśisannibham* || 39 *vilokanapadaiś śaśvat saṅghaṭṭaṃ taṃ tu bhāvayet* | *samaste prāk svarūpeṇa tanmadhye tv āsanaṃ prabhoḥ* || 40 *datvā tadupari brahman smaren nārāyaṇaṃ prabhum* | *candrakoṭisamaṃ śuddhasudhādhārāgaṇāvṛtam* || 41 *sāhaṃ śaktisamūhāḍhyaṃ prodgirantaṃ sudhārasam* | *evaṃ kṛte sati bhavet tīrthaṃ nārāyaṇātmakam* || 42.

[48] Other examples for the general identity of the three deities in the prescriptions of the daily ritual are JS 13.87d-89 (making Nārāyaṇa/Vāsudeva present in one's eyes in order to purify the offering implements by means of gazing [*nirīkṣaṇa*]), LT 36.32c-33b (visualisation of Viṣṇu /Nārāyaṇa), NārS 2.16-17 (visualisation of Viṣṇu/Vāsudeva/Hari), PārS 6.227-229 (invitation of Vāsudeva/Hari), 6.367-368b (≈ PauṣS 37.58cd and 31.65ab; bow to Hari/Viṣṇu), BhT 17.10 (invitation and worship of Vāsudeva in the fire), 17.58 (worship of Viṣṇu in the fire).

A ritual that is very often described in the context of initiation rites is the laying on of the so-called Viṣṇu hand (*viṣṇuhasta*). The initiating *ācārya* makes Viṣṇu present on his right hand, which he then places on the initiand's head. This hand is always called *viṣṇuhasta*; it is never called *vāsudevahasta* or *nārāyaṇahasta*. The reason for this may be metrical or perhaps the term *viṣṇuhasta* became a sort of proper name for this ritual. The reason is probably not that Viṣṇu, in contrast to Vāsudeva or Nārāyaṇa, is implied. This can be seen in a verse from the *Nāradīyasaṃhitā*:

> Then, at the end of the initiation, the *guru* should lay the Viṣṇu hand on [the initiand's head], by which [the initiand's] soul becomes identical to Vāsudeva.[49]

The *mantras* of Vāsudeva, Nārāyaṇa, and Viṣṇu

I mentioned that generally no differences are made between Viṣṇu, Vāsudeva, and Nārāyaṇa in the prescriptions for the daily ritual. However, there are exceptions. The *Śrīpraśnasaṃhitā* is such an exception. In its prescriptions for the daily ritual a differentiation is made between Viṣṇu, Vāsudeva, and Nārāyaṇa. In its daily ritual three different *mantras* are used: the twelve-syllable *mantra* (*dvāda-*

---

[49] NārS 9.321: *atha dīkṣāvasāne tu viṣṇuhastaṃ dadet guruḥ* | *yena dattena bhavati vāsudevasamaḥ pumān* ||. The reason why the initiand becomes identical to Vāsudeva is because the *dvādaśākṣaramantra* is used. The whole ritual of laying on the *viṣṇuhasta* is described in NārS 9.321-344.

Other examples for the general identity of the three deities in the prescriptions of the initiation are JS 16.125cd (*puṣpāñjali* for Viṣṇu), 16.198 and 276 (visualisation of Nārāyaṇa), 16.294c-296b (the initiand, having become identical with Viṣṇu, receives a stream from "Vāsudeva's ocean"), 16.299c-300b (visualisation of Viṣṇu), NārS 9.24-26 (visualisation of Viṣṇu/Vāsudeva), ViśS 9.23 (Viṣṇu receives a part of the cooked food offering [*caru*]), 9.51 and 63 (Nārāyaṇa is visualised), BBS 1.5.67c-68b (by worshipping Nārāyaṇa one attains Hari), 1.5.90cd (the body of a Vaiṣṇava has the form of Viṣṇu himself).

śākṣaramantra): *oṃ namo bhagavate vāsudevāya*, the eight-syllable *mantra* (*aṣṭākṣaramantra*): *oṃ namo nārāyaṇāya*, and the six-syllable *mantra* (*ṣaḍakṣaramantra*): *oṃ namo viṣṇave*.

In the tantric traditions, to which the Pāñcarātra belongs, *mantras* are not mere linguistic formulas, but manifestations of god.[50] They have a linguistic form, such as the three *mantras* just mentioned, but also a visual form, which is often anthropomorphic.

Thus, the *aṣṭākṣaramantra* is not only a formula devoted to Nārāyaṇa, as its wording suggests, but it is also a manifestation of Nārāyaṇa. According to the ŚrīprśS, it is visualised in the following way:

> He should visualise the all-pervading god Nārāyaṇa with four arms, having a noble body, being served by [his] weapons, discus and others, [in colour] resembling a dark cloud, with eyes longish like a lotus leaf, wearing yellow garments, being gentle, with earrings shining with jewels, adorned with a bracelet, a bracelet on the upper arm, a necklace and the *kaustubha* [jewel on his breast], that all are glittering, sitting on a lion throne made of jewels, accompanied by Śrī and Bhūmi, bestowing liberation to the one having resorted [to him].[51]

The *dvādaśākṣaramantra* is a manifestation of Vāsudeva, and it is visualised as follows:

> He should visualise the all-pervading Vāsudeva with two arms, lotus eyes, a body like a pure crystal, wearing a diadem and earrings, illustrious by means of a garland of forest flowers, with a *śrīvatsa* on his breast, gleaming, with a neck bent by the *kaustubha* [jewel], his breast

---

[50] On the nature of *mantras* in the Pāñcarātra, see Rastelli 1999a: 119–140.

[51] ŚrīprśS 28.99c-102b: *caturbhujam udārāṅgaṃ cakrādyāyudhasevitam* ‖ 99 *kālameghapratīkāśaṃ padmapatrāyatekṣaṇam* | *pītāmbaradharaṃ saumyaṃ ratnojjvalitakuṇḍalam* ‖ 100 *sphuratkaṭakakeyūrahārakaustubhabhūṣitam* | *ratnasiṃhāsanāsīnaṃśrībhūmisahitaṃ vibhum* ‖ 101 *dhyāyen nārāyaṇaṃ devaṃ śritānāṃ muktidāyakam* |. See also the very similar description in ŚrīprśS 52.41c-44b.

occupied by Yogalakṣmī, as high as the highest, residing in supreme heaven.[52]

The *ṣaḍakṣaramantra* is a manifestation of Viṣṇu. It is visualized as follows:

> He should visualise the eternal Viṣṇu as dark like a cloud, with four arms, carrying the conch, the discus, and the mace, as the internal controller, the Lord, who glitters because of his diadem and other [ornaments], the god who is accompanied by Śrī and Bhūmi, served by great *ṛṣis* such as Sanaka and by many sages, sitting on a lotus seat.[53]

Having prescribed the preparatory purification rites that always mark the beginning of the daily ritual, the ŚrīprśS describes the ritual placing (*nyāsa*) of the *aṣṭākṣara-*, the *dvādaśākṣara-*, and the *ṣaḍakṣaramantra* on the worshipper's hands and the body, by which he is divinized (ŚrīprśS 28.74-96b). However, this does not mean that all three *mantras* are used: only one is used, depending on which *mantra* was installed in the image being used for worship.[54]

---

52 ŚrīprśS 28.108c-110: *dvibhujaṃ puṇḍarīkākṣaṃ śuddhasphaṭikavigraham* ‖ 108 *kirīṭakuṇḍaladharaṃ vanamālāvirājitam* | *śrīvatsavakṣasaṃ bhrājat kaustubhānatakaṃdharam* ‖ 109 *yogalakṣmyā samākrāntabāhumadhyaṃ parāt param* | *parame vyomni tiṣṭhantaṃ vāsudevaṃ smared vibhum* ‖ 110. See also ŚrīprśS 52.19-20b.

53 ŚrīprśS 28.113d-115: *dhyāyed viṣṇuṃ sanātanam* ‖ 113 *meghaśyāmaṃ caturbāhuṃ śaṅkhacakragadādharam* | *antaryāminam īśānaṃ kirīṭādivirājitam* ‖ 114 *śrībhūmisahitaṃ devaṃ sanakādimaharṣibhiḥ* | *sevitaṃ sūribṛndaiś ca padmaviṣṭarasaṃsthitam* ‖ 115.

54 See ŚrīprśS 28.73-74b: "O Ramā, at the *pūjā*, the *guru* should place exactly this *mantra* on his body, which has been placed on the respective image among the images that are standing, sitting or have other forms at [its] consecration by the one possessing the *mantra*." (*sthityāsanādibimbānāṃ pratiṣṭhānāṃ yathā rame* | *yena mantreṇa yad bimbaṃ yathānyastaṃ ca mantriṇā* ‖ 73 *tanmantreṇaiva pūjāyām ātmano 'pi nyased guruḥ* |). Also, according to SanS *br* 9.10-11, the *nyāsa* by means of the *dvādaśākṣara-* or the *aṣṭākṣaramantra* are alternatives.

ŚrīprśS 28.117-119b describes still another simpler alternative of placing these *mantras* on the body, namely, placing them on the six

Having performed the *mantranyāsa*, the mental worship (*mānasayāga*) begins. Here, also, alternatives are given. For worship, Vāsudeva is visualised as having four arms—thus in a lower form than the Vāsudeva with two arms described above[55]—and as accompanied by Yogalakṣmī or the god who is accompanied by Śrī and Bhūmi. This, as we have seen above, can refer to both Viṣṇu and Nārāyaṇa (ŚrīprśS 28.125-128b).

For the actual physical act of worship, which follows the mental worship, god is transferred from the main image (*mūlārcā*) to a vessel (*pātra*). The two-armed, luminous Vāsudeva present in the main image is asked to go to the vessel and thus, he changes his form. He becomes the four-armed Vāsudeva and has the colour of a dark cloud.[56]

The ŚrīprśS then describes how Viṣṇu and his consorts Śrī and Bhūmi are invited into vessels and worshipped.[57] This, again, is probably an alternative to the invitation of Vāsudeva.

The prescriptions of the daily ritual of the ŚrīprśS are an example that shows us that although Vāsudeva, Nārāyaṇa, and Viṣṇu are often considered identical, they can also be distinguished from each other. The main means for determining their difference is the linguistic and visual form of their *mantra*s. By means of the *dvādaśākṣara*-, the *aṣṭākṣara*-, and the *ṣaḍakṣaramantra* they can clearly be differentiated.

So let us now look at these *mantra*s. What is their history? How are they used? And are there distinctive groups of followers of these *mantra*s? At least the *dvādaśākṣara*- and the *aṣṭākṣaramantra* are

---

limbs (*ṣaḍaṅga*) of heart, head, tuft of hair (*śikhā*), cuirass (*kavaca*), eyes, and weapon (*astra*).

55 The ŚrīprśS follows the PādS's teachings on the various divine manifestations (see above, p.228) as it is generally based on this text; cf. the list of parallel lines of these two texts in the edition of the ŚrīprśS, pp. lxvii–lxxxix.

56 ŚrīprśS 28.182c-217.

57 ŚrīprśS 28.222-234b. See also ŚrīprśS 28.300c-301b.

not specific to the Pāñcarātra. The *dvādaśākṣaramantra* and its wording are mentioned in the *Baudhāyanagṛhyaśeṣasūtra* (3.7.8). The *aṣṭākṣaramantra* is described in *Nārāyaṇopaniṣad* 3-4, which according to Young (2002: 86) is the earliest reference to it. They are also used in the Vaikhānasa and other Vaiṣṇava traditions.[58] I could not find any early reference for the *ṣaḍakṣaramantra*, but perhaps it was also used very early and is not specific to the Pāñcarātra.

In the Pāñcarātra, the importance of these three *mantra*s varies in the *Saṃhitā*s. Let us look at the tradition's texts in a chronological order.

In the *Svāyambhuvapāñcarātra*, one of the earliest extant Pāñcarātra texts surviving in a Nepalese manuscript dated 1026 CE and presently being edited by Diwakar Acharya, the *dvādaśākṣaramantra* is the main *mantra* (*mūlamantra*).[59] The *aṣṭākṣaramantra* is also mentioned once (SvP 8.38).

In the *Jayottaratantra*, also one of the early extant Pāñcarātra texts surviving in Nepal and being edited by Diwakar Acharya, the three *mantra*s under discussion are not mentioned at all. The main *mantra* (*mūlamantra*) of this text is *oṃ kṣīṃ kṣiḥ* (*Jayottaratantra* 1.14-17). The *Jayākhyasaṃhitā*, which is based on the *Jayottaratantra*, teaches the same *mūlamantra* and expands it by a so-called *mūrtimantra* with the wording *nārāyaṇāya viśvātmane hrīṃ svāhā* (JS 6.62-69). The wording shows us that this *mantra* is a manifestation of Nārāyaṇa—although according to its visual form it is actually the four-faced Vaikuṇṭha[60]—but it is not the *aṣṭākṣaramantra*. The JS mentions the *aṣṭākṣaramantra* in two places (JS 18.80, 22.40), but it does not play an important role in the text.

---

58 Colas 1996: 228. The *aṣṭākṣaramantra* is also frequently mentioned in the Prabandham; see Hardy 1983: 471.

59 *Svāyambhuvapañcarātra* 7.4. On the *Svāyambhuvapañcarātra*, its date and its *mantra*s, see also Sanderson 2009: 62–67. A text that is closely related to the *Svāyambhuvapañcarātra* is the *Devāmṛtapañcarātra*, which survives in a Nepalese manuscript probably from the 12th century (Sanderson 2009: 63, fn. 68).

60 See *Jayottara* 1.20-22 ≈ JS 6.73-76.

The *Sātvatasaṃhitā* teaches the worship of god in three forms of manifestation: as supreme god, as Vyūha, and as Vibhava. Accordingly, it teaches several mantric systems.[61] The *mantra*s for the Vyūhas in a particular form, namely in the waking state (*jāgrat*) in the order of reabsorption,[62] are *oṃ puruṣāya namaḥ*, *oṃ satyāya namaḥ*, *oṃ acyutāya namaḥ*, and *oṃ bhagavate vāsudevāya namaḥ* (SS 5.68c-79). The last *mantra* is the *dvādaśākṣaramantra*, which is also mentioned several times in the ritual prescriptions of the SS.[63] The *aṣṭākṣara*- and the *ṣaḍakṣaramantra* are not mentioned at all.

The *Pauṣkarasaṃhitā* (the third of the three jewels [*ratnatraya*] of the Pāñcarātra)[64] does not teach a specific mantric system, or a group of deities with one deity in its centre, that is specific to this text.[65] So it is difficult to say what is considered to be the most important *mantra* of the PauṣS. However, the three *mantra*s under discussion are mentioned several times.[66]

The wording of the main *mantra* of the *Paramasaṃhitā* is also unclear. Chapter 6, which is devoted to the description of the various *mantra*s important for the ParS, does not contain it. However, it also does not describe one of the three *mantra*s under discussion, which shows that they are not the most important *mantra*s for the ParS, although they are mentioned several times.[67]

In the *Lakṣmītantra* and the *Ahirbudhnyasaṃhitā*, neither the three *mantra*s, nor any one of them, are the main *mantra*s. Nor are

---

[61] For a detailed description of these mantric systems, see Rastelli 2006: 427–429.

[62] Cf. for this form of the Vyūhas Rastelli 2006: 342–347.

[63] E.g., SS 6.4, 106, 25.65, 107, 126, 165, 179, 343.

[64] The JS, the SS, and the PauṣS are considered the three jewels (*ratnatraya*) of the tradition; see JS *adhika pāṭha* 2-3, PRR 47,7-9.

[65] Cf. Rastelli 2006: 429.

[66] E.g., PauṣS 27.135-137, 37.57, 38.203, 41.129, 42.26, 143c-144, 43.162c-163b.

[67] E.g., ParS 3.46, 54, 6.38, 16.38, 43, 50-51.

they mentioned very often. However, their importance is emphasised in a few passages of these texts.

The most important *mantra* of the LT is called *tārikā*. It is the syllable *hrīṃ* and a manifestation of the goddess Lakṣmī.[68] The *mūlamantra* of the AS is *sahasrāra huṃ phaṭ* (AS 18.34-39b), the *mantra* of Sudarśana, the personification of Viṣṇu's discus, which is the main deity of this text.[69]

In a chapter that is devoted to the *mantra oṃ*, the LT writes that according to the injunction of the Pāñcarātra, there are three *padamantras*[70] of *oṃ*, namely, the *ṣaḍakṣara-*, the *aṣṭākṣara-*, and the *dvādaśākṣaramantra*. To this, the LT adds a fourth *padamantra*, namely, the so-called *jitaṃtemantra*. These four *mantras* together with the *mantra oṃ* are called the *vyāpakamantras*, which may be understood as the *mantras* applicable everywhere (see below, p. 240).[71]

---

68 LT 25.36c-38. The *tārikā* takes the place of the *mūlamantra* of the JS, from which the LT adopts its passages on the daily ritual. Compare, e.g., JS 11.10 (placing the *mūlamantra* on the thumb and the four goddesses Lakṣmī, Kīrti, Jayā, and Māyā on the four other fingers) and LT 35.61-62b (placing the *tārikā* on the thumb and the four goddesses on the four other fingers).

69 See, for example, AS 28.27-28, which describes the invitation of Sudarśana into the worshipper's heart in order to worship him mentally.

70 A *padamantra* is a *mantra* that consists of several words (*pada*) (LT 21.14ab and commentary *ad loc*).

71 LT 24.67c-74: "In the prescription of the Pāñcarātra, there are three *padamantras* of the [*mantra oṃ*], [namely,] *viṣṇave namaḥ*, *namo nārāyaṇa* and *namo bhagavate vāsudevāya*. *jitaṃ te puṇḍarīkākṣa namas te viśvabhāvana* | *namas te 'stu hṛṣīkeśa mahāpuruṣa pūrvaja* ‖ is the fourth *padamantra* of the *praṇava*, o destroyer of strongholds. (...) Only the *tāraka* (i.e., *oṃ*) and the four [*mantras*] beginning with it are praised as the five *vyāpakamantras* in the Pāñcarātra." (*padamantrās trayo 'sya syur vidhāne pāñcarātrike* ‖ 67 *viṣṇave nama ity evaṃ namo nārāyaṇāya ca* | *namo bhagavate pūrvaṃ vāsudevāya cety api* ‖ 68 *jitaṃ te puṇḍarīkākṣa namas te viśvabhāvana* | *namas te 'stu hṛṣīkeśa mahāpuruṣa pūrvaja* ‖ 69 *padamantraś caturtho 'yaṃ praṇavasya puraṃ-*

The AS, which otherwise hardly mentions the mantras under discussion, describes *yantras* for the *ṣaḍakṣara*, the *aṣṭākṣara-*, and the *dvādaśākṣaramantra* in great detail (AS 22.14c-48 and 23.1-14b). Further, it gives a long and detailed commentary of these three *mantras* from a Viśiṣṭādvaita Vedānta point of view in chapter 52.[72]

The *Sanatkumārasaṃhitā* is difficult to date. According to Smith (1975: 494), it is also "grouped among the 'oldest' works of the *Pāñcarātrāgama*", as passages from it are quoted in Yāmuna's *Āgamaprāmāṇya* (ĀP pp. 160f.). However, some parts that describe rituals that are rather characteristic for public worship in great temples, as given in later *Saṃhitās*,[73] probably do not belong to the earliest portions of the Pāñcarātra text corpus. According to the SanS, there are two *mūlamantras*, the *aṣṭākṣara-* and the *dvādaśākṣaramantra*.[74]

Now we come to the later *Saṃhitās*, which were all composed in South India and which are definitely orientated to public temple wor-

---

dara | (...) *kevalas tārakaś caiva catvāraś ca tadādikāḥ* | *pañcaite vyāpakā mantrāḥ pāñcarātre prakīrtitāḥ* || 74).

72 By the way, chapter 53 of the AS is devoted to a commentary on the *jitantemantra*, the fourth *padamantra* of the LT. See for the *vyāpakamantras* also below, p. 236.

73 An example for this is the distinction between *ekaberavidhi* and *bahuberavidhi*. In the former kind of worship, only one (the main) image is used for worship and ablutions; in the latter, not the main image, but an image especially meant for ritual worship (*karmārcā*) is used for worship and ablutions (SanS *br* 6.46c-49). Other examples are the great numbers of ablutions (*snapana*) described in SanS *śr* 8, or the temple procession (*utsava*) in SanS *śr* 9.

74 SanS *br* 9.10c-11b: "In this Tantra, Parameṣṭhin taught that the main *mantra* is twofold, the eight-syllable [*mantra*] and then the twelve-syllable *mantra*." (*mūlamantro dvidhā proktas tantre 'smin parameṣṭhinā* || 10 *aṣṭākṣara tato mantro dvādaśākṣara eva ca* |). The wording of the two *mantras* is taught in the prose text following verse *br* 11.4cd; the wording of the *aṣṭākṣaramantra* is also described in SanS *ir* 2.56c-59. SanS *ṛr* 7.4c-7 teaches the mantric elements of *deva*, *ṛṣi*, and *chandas* for the two *mantras* (for these mantric elements, the concept of which derives from the Vedic Anukramaṇīs, cf. Rastelli 2006: 207–209).

ship in opposition to the earlier texts, which mainly describe individual worship.[75] In almost all of these texts, one or two or all three of the *mantra*s under discussion are *mūlamantra*s.

In the *Nāradīyasaṃhitā* and the *Pārameśvarasaṃhitā*, the *mūlamantra* is the *dvādaśākṣaramantra.*[76] On some occasions[77] the *aṣṭākṣaramantra* is also mentioned, but it is not as important as the *dvādaśākṣaramantra*. The *ṣaḍakṣaramantra* is not mentioned at all in the NārS and only twice in the PārS;[78] the *vyāpakamantra*s also are mentioned twice, though it is not explicitly said which *mantra*s apart from the *dvādaśākṣaramantra* belong to them.[79]

The *mūlamantra* of the *Īśvarasaṃhitā* is the *aṣṭākṣaramantra.*[80] It is in the forefront one of the three *vyāpakamantra*s:

> Among all *viṣṇumantra*s, three *mantra*s are comprehensive (*vyāpakāḥ*). The first is the eight-syllable [*mantra*] of Nārāyaṇa, the second is the twelve-syllable [*mantra*] of Vāsudeva, [and] then [comes] the six-syllable [*mantra*] of Viṣṇu, O chiefs among the *yogin*s. These three *mantra*s are applicable to all manifestations (*mūrti*) [of god]. Therefore the other *mantra*s have only the respective manifestation as their object. And all manifestations can also be worshipped by means of the three comprehensive (*vyāpakatritayena*) *mantra*s. By means of the other *mantra*s, only the respective manifestation can be worshipped. Therefore, the three comprehensive *mantra*s are the best among all *mantra*s.

---

75 For this shift from the earlier to the later *Saṃhitā*s, see Rastelli 2006: 91–96.

76 See NārS 3.3-77 for a detailed description of the *dvādaśākṣaramantra* and its ritual worship (*sādhana*) in order to gain *siddhi*s, 8.67ab, 9.259c-262; PārS 4.5cd, 24, 15.397ab; and Rastelli 2006: 425f.

77 E.g., NārS 9.260, 12.45, 14.79; PārS 14.237, 243, 19.437.

78 PārS 10.25 (= PauṣS 42.166) and 19.437.

79 PārS 9.49 and 10.97.

80 ĪS 2.51cd, 62-68. The *aṣṭākṣaramantra* also plays an important role in the *māhātmya* of Nārāyaṇādri, the place to which the ĪS is affiliated (see below, pp. 247).

Among all three comprehensive [*mantras*], the eight-syllable *mantra* is the best one.[81]

As seen by this statement, the ĪS mentions all three *mantras* quite often.[82]

The *Pādmasaṃhitā* prescribes the performance of the daily *pūjā* by means of the *aṣṭākṣara-* or the *dvādaśākṣaramantra* (PādS *cp* 3.51). It even describes two different *maṇḍalas* for the worship of the one or the other *mantra*. The *maṇḍala* for the worship of the *dvādaśākṣaramantra* or Vāsudeva consists of a lotus with twelve petals and a wheel with twelve spokes on which several groups of deities, often consisting of twelve, are placed; Vāsudeva himself or the *dvādaśākṣaramantra* is placed on the twelve points (*bindu*) of the receptacle (*karṇikā*) of the lotus. The *maṇḍala* for the worship of the *aṣṭākṣaramantra* or Nārāyaṇa consists of a lotus with eight petals and a wheel with eight spokes, on top of which groups of eight deities are placed.[83]

The PādS devotes long passages to the *dvādaśākṣara-* and the *aṣṭākṣaramantra* (PādS *cp* 24.1-148b and 25), describing their wording, their mantric elements, and prescriptions to master them and to perform rituals for the obtainment of supernatural powers (*siddhis*). Especially the rites that can be performed after having

---

81 ĪS 23.52-56b: *sarveṣu viṣṇumantreṣu mantrāḥ syur vyāpakās trayaḥ* | *ādyaṃ nārāyaṇāṣṭārṇaṃ dvitīyaṃ dvādaśākṣaram* || 52 *vāsudevasya yogīndrās tato viṣṇuṣaḍakṣaram* | *sādhāraṇās tv ime mantrās trayaḥ sarvāsu mūrtiṣu* || 53 *anye tu manavas tattanmūrtimātraparā hy ataḥ* | *vyāpakatritayenārcyāḥ sarvā api ca mūrtayaḥ* || 54 *mantrair anyais tu sampūjyās tattanmūrtaya eva hi* | *tasmāt sarveṣu mantreṣu vyāpakatritayaṃ varam* || 55 *triṣv apy eṣu vyāpakeṣu mantro hy aṣṭākṣaro 'dhikaḥ* |. See also ĪS 21.461. ĪS 19.287 speaks of five *vyāpakamantras* headed by the *aṣṭākṣaramantra*.

82 *aṣṭākṣaramantra*: e.g., ĪS 1.66, 2.51, 68, 5.105, 6.69, 10.198; *dvādaśākṣaramantra*: e.g., ĪS 15.377, 16.14, 37, 68, 103, 160; *ṣaḍakṣaramantra*: e.g., ĪS 16.69, 19.866.

83 PādS *cp* 7.65-81b. PādS *cp* 7.81c-82b mentions a further *maṇḍala* for the worship of the 24 *mūrtis* on 24 lotuses. SanS *ir* 4.33 also mentions a *vāsudeva-* and a *nārāyaṇamaṇḍala*.

mastered the *aṣṭākṣaramantra* show that this *mantra* has taken over the place of the *mūlamantra* of the JS. Many rites that the JS describes as performable after having mastered the *mūlamantra* are described as being performed with the *aṣṭākṣaramantra* in the PādS.[84] The *ṣaḍakṣaramantra* is mentioned only once in the PādS (*kp* 28.111). Thus, its role is not important in this text.

The *Viśvāmitrasaṃhitā* and the *Śrīpraśnasaṃhitā* have close relations to the *Pādmasaṃhitā*.[85] In the ViśS, using the *aṣṭākṣara-* or the *dvādaśākṣaramantra* in the daily *pūjā* are also alternatives,[86] and this text also describes a *vāsudevamaṇḍala* and a *nārāyaṇamaṇḍala* (ViśS 15.61-73b and 73c-77[87]). Here, the *ṣaḍakṣaramantra* is not mentioned even once.

The ŚrīprśS has already been discussed. In comparison to the other *Saṃhitās* it is interesting that here the role of the *ṣaḍakṣaramantra* in the daily *pūjā* is equal to that of the other two *mantras*.

Now let us summarize what we know about the various *Saṃhitās*: Among the earliest extant *Saṃhitās*, which probably have their origin in North India, only the *Svāyambhuvapañcarātra* teaches the *dvādaśākṣaramantra* as *mūlamantra*. In the *Jayottaratantra* and the "three jewels" (with the exception of the *dvādaśākṣaramantra* for a

---

84 E.g., the rites for the neutralisation of poison (JS 26.22-24b, PādS *cp* 25.254-256), subjugation (*vaśīkaraṇa*) of other beings (JS 26.24c-30, PādS *cp* 25.102-120), attainment of prosperity (*puṣṭi*) (JS 26.51-55, PādS *cp* 25.214c-218), the attainment of a magic sword (*khadga*) (JS 26.60-63, PādS *cp* 25.156c-168b) or of a magic pill (*gulikā*) (JS 26.67-72b, PādS *cp* 25.183c-187b).

85 For the ViśS see, e.g., its prescription for the initiation (*dīkṣā*) in chapter 9, which is probably based on PādS *cp* 2. For the ŚrīprśS, see fn. 55.

86 E.g., ViśS 10.69. The wording, mantric elements, etc. of the two *mantras* are described in ViśS 6.28c-69 and 7.1-23b.

87 Although this passage does not contain any lines that are literally identical with lines from the PādS passage describing these *maṇḍalas* (*cp* 7.65-81b), the two passages are quite similar. Thus it is likely that the ViśS passage is based on that of the PādS.

particular Vyūha form in the SS) none of the three *mantra*s under discussion are the *mūlamantra*. In the ParS[88], the LT and the AS they are not the *mūlamantra* either, although great importance is attached to all three *mantra*s in the latter two texts. The SanS teaches the *aṣṭākṣara-* and the *dvādaśākṣaramantra* as *mūlamantra*s, and in many of the later South Indian *Saṃhitā*s which are oriented to public temple worship, at least one of these two *mantra*s is the *mūlamantra*. Except for the ŚrīprśS, the *ṣaḍakṣaramantra* is far from having the same importance as the two other *mantra*s.

The *Svāyambhuvapañcarātra* shows us that the *dvādaśākṣara-mantra* was used in the Pāñcarātra already quite early, but on the basis of the other early *Saṃhitā*s, we see that it was not the *mūlamantra* for all Pāñcarātrins. The LT and the AS have a lot in common. Both are influenced by the Kashmirian Śaivism and the Viśiṣṭādvaita Vedānta, and some passages agree verbatim.[89] In its ritual prescriptions the LT is based on the JS,[90] while the AS shows some similarities with the SS.[91] This means that they are ritually influenced by texts that probably have their origin in North India.[92] The LT and the AS

---

88 According to Czerniak-Drożdżowicz 2003: 29, the ParS may have been composed in South India.

89 Cf. Rastelli 2006: 273–276.

90 The descriptions of the daily ritual in LT 34.92c-40.119 and JS 9-15 are quite similar; see also Gupta 1972: XVIIIf.

91 In both texts god is worshipped on various *āsana*s (SS 6.2-75, AS 28.29c-79b), which is not described in other early texts such as the JS or the PauṣS. Generally, the AS is partly based on the SS. In AS 5.59, e.g., it explicitly refers to the SS (see also Rastelli 2006: 362, fn. 1144).

92 Many scholars think that the early Pāñcarātra *Saṃhitā*s have their origin in North India (see, e.g., Gonda 1977: 54–56), but convincing proofs are still pending (cf. also Sanderson 2001: 35). For a collection of data that could point to a North Indian origin of the JS see Rastelli 1999a: 25–27. To these data one should add that manuscripts of the JS have been found in Nepal (see Sanderson 2009: 67, fn. 77).

themselves, however, were probably composed in South India.[93] Could it be that the importance of *aṣṭākṣara-* and the *ṣaḍakṣaramantra* increased in these texts under the influence of South Indian traditions? We know that the *aṣṭākṣaramantra* was used by the Āḻvārs (see fn. 58), and in the Viśiṣṭādvaita Vedānta, it became important after Rāmānuja, as can be seen, for example, in Parāśara Bhaṭṭa's commentary on it in the *Aṣṭaślokī*.[94]

The LT mentions people who are, among other things, devoted to the *aṣṭākṣara-*, *dvādaśākṣara-* and *ṣaḍakṣaramantra* (LT 17.19c-20), in a chapter that deals with *prapatti,* taking refuge in god, even if Oberhammer (2004: 137f.) is right that it does not have its origin in the Viśiṣṭādvaita Vedānta tradition. It is probably of South Indian provenance.

So, it is easily possible that the *aṣṭākṣaramantra* became more important on account of the influence of South Indian traditions worshipping Nārāyaṇa. But how can we explain the increase of importance of the *dvādaśākṣaramantra* and, to a lesser degree, of the *ṣaḍakṣaramantra* in the later texts?

Let us look at the groups that prefer to use one of these *mantras*, which may give us a hint as to how to answer this question.

Some *Saṃhitās* teach the division of the Pāñcarātra into four Siddhāntas: Āgamasiddhānta, Mantrasiddhānta, Tantrasiddhānta, and Tantrāntarasiddhānta. In this context, *siddhānta* means sub-tradition. This means that there are four sub-traditions of the Pāñcarātra.[95]

The supreme authority of the Āgamasiddhāntins, the members of the Āgamasiddhānta, is the Ekāyanaveda, most likely a merely mythical text that is described as the *dharma* of the *kṛtayuga*, the Golden

---

[93] Both texts offer interpretations of mantras from the *Yajurveda* in the *Taittirīya* recension, which was prevalent in South India (Sanderson 2001: 38).

[94] See Young 2007: 185. According to Lakshmithathachar ($\bar{I}S_{2009}$, vol. 2, p. 81, fn. 13), the *aṣṭākṣaramantra* is the only *mūlamantra* of the Rāmānuja school.

[95] For a detailed description of the four Siddhāntas, see Rastelli 2006: 185–251.

Age of Indian mythical chronology. The Ekāyanas, as they are also called, do not undergo an initiation (*dīkṣā*) but they have the authority (*adhikāra*) to perform the ritual from childhood. They worship Vāsudeva and his four Vyūhas, and their most important *mantra* is the *dvādaśākṣaramantra.*[96] One *Saṃhitā* written by an Āgamasiddhāntin is the PārS,[97] and in this case, the *mūlamantra* is indeed the *dvādaśākṣaramantra* (see above, p. 239), which supports the theoretical statements of the texts.

The Mantrasiddhānta is described in different ways in the PārS and the PādS, but the description of the PādS, which itself belongs to the Mantrasiddhānta,[98] makes clear that it is in close association with Vedic traditions. Its followers not only belong to the Pāñcarātra, but also to a Vedic school (*śākhā*).[99] According to the PādS (*cp* 21.25c-29), they worship the two-armed Vāsudeva without his Vyūhas, and using Vedic *mantras* (*trayīmantra*).

The *Bhārgavatantra*, which is partly based on the PādS,[100] describes two kinds of Pāñcarātrins, which it refers to as either "pure" (*śuddha*) or "mixed" (*miśra*) ones. The pure ones belong to the Ekāyanaveda, the mixed ones to the Vedas. The *mantra* of the first is the *dvādaśākṣaramantra*, that of the second the *aṣṭākṣaramantra* (24.17-18). Although the BhT, which belongs to the second group, i.e. the Mantrasiddhānta,[101] describes the persons affiliated with its own sub-

---

96 See Rastelli 2006: 191–209 and 2003: 4–7.

97 See Rastelli 2006: 251f.

98 See PādS *jp* 1.86cd: "Among these, the Mantrasiddhānta called *Pādma* is set forth." (*teṣv ayaṃ mantrasiddhāntaḥ pādmasaṃjño 'bhidhīyate* ‖) and the PādS's description of the Mantrasiddhānta in PādS *cp* 21.2-29 (on the latter passage, see Rastelli 2006: 229–233).

99 See Rastelli 2006: 229–233.

100 See, e.g., BhT 24.19-20 ≈ PādS *cp* 21.36-38b. Compare also BhT 24.22 and PādS *cp* 21.43.

101 According to BhT 24.22-29, only the persons affiliated with the Veda (*traividya*) have the authority (*adhikāra*) to perform ritual worship for others (*parārtha*). BhT 24.23 calls such persons *mantrasiddhāntaniṣṭha*. In its description of the Siddhāntas (22.88-93), the BhT describes the

tradition in a very idealised way, one of their characteristics is informative for us: "He considers himself a remnant (*śeṣa*) and the supreme god the owner of the remnant (*śeṣin*)."[102] This shows clearly that the *miśra* not only belongs to the tradition of the Pāñcarātra and the Vedic orthodoxy, but also to the Viśiṣṭādvaita Vedānta,[103] just as Yāmuna did, for example.[104]

We have little information about the Tantra- and the Tantrāntarasiddhānta. The followers of the Tantrasiddhānta worship the nine *mūrti*s (see above, p. 227); they have given up the Veda and follow only the Tantra. They use the *dvādaśākṣara-* and other *mantra*s. The Tantrāntarasiddhāntins worship god in one of his other manifestations, e.g., as one of the Vibhavas. They belong to both the Tantrāntarasiddhānta and the Veda.

What can we conclude from this information? The *dvādaśākṣaramantra* is related with "non-Vedic" traditions. It belongs to the Āgamasiddhānta, following the Ekāyanaveda, and to the Tantrasiddhānta, whose followers "have given up the Veda". The *aṣṭākṣaramantra*, according to the *Bhārgavatantra*, is a characteristic of the Veda-oriented group. Thus, a hasty conclusion may be that the importance of the *aṣṭākṣaramantra* was increased by the influence of Pāñcarātric groups, who also belonged to Vedic traditions, such as the representatives of the Viśiṣṭādvaita Vedānta. As a reaction to this, the groups belonging to the Ekāyanaveda, and thus being outside the Vedic orthodoxy, may have emphasised the *dvādaśākṣaramantra* devoted to Vāsudeva. The *ṣaḍakṣaramantra* then may have been formed in analogy to the two other *mantra*s in order to also have a manifestation of Viṣṇu—we do not know by which group. A

Mantrasiddhānta in the first place, which also indicates its preference for it.

102 BhT 24.11ab: *ātmānaṃ manyate śeṣaṃ śeṣiṇaṃ parameśvaram* |.

103 For the concept of *śeṣa* and *śeṣin,* describing the relationship between soul and gold, which is characteristic for the Viśiṣṭādvaita Vedānta, see, e.g., Carman 1974: 147–157.

104 See Rastelli 2006: 218f. or 2003: 9 (based on Neevel 1977: 35f.).

closer look at other texts shows us, however, that it was not as simple as that. The PādS—the author of its main part is also a representative of the Mantrasiddhānta—does not emphasise the *aṣṭākṣaramantra* in contrast to the *dvādaśākṣaramantra*. According to it, the *dvādaśākṣaramantra* is a characteristic of the Āgamasiddhānta, but the PādS itself does not show a preference for the *aṣṭākṣaramantra*. Further, according to the PādS, it is Vāsudeva and not Nārāyaṇa who is worshipped by the Mantrasiddhāntins.

Concerning the ĪS, the *Saṃhitā* whose *mūlamantra* is the *aṣṭākṣaramantra*, the situation is different again. In its description of the Siddhāntas (ĪS 21.560-581b), the Āgamasiddhānta takes the first place. In a story told in chapter 21, the five sages Śāṇḍilya, Aupagāyana, Mauñjyāyana, Kauśika, and Bharadvāja are taught the Ekāyanaveda by Viṣṇu in the *kṛtayuga*. Later the Ekāyanaveda disappeared, and the *Saṃhitā*s were revealed. After that, Śāṇḍilya and the others performed their worship according to the prescriptions of the *Sātvatasaṃhitā*, and they initiated pupils from their own families who studied the Vedic *kānvī śākhā* and were devoted to the Veda and Vedānta. After initiation they were qualified for worship for their own purposes and those of others.[105] The SS is equated with the Mantrasiddhānta.[106] That means that these pupils were followers of the Mantrasiddhānta, affiliated with the tradition of the Pāñcarātra and a Vedic school, just as described in the PādS. The relation of such a sub-tradition with the *aṣṭākṣaramantra* matches what was said above. However, the ĪS also relates the *aṣṭākṣaramantra* to the Ekāyanaveda. Chapter 20 of the ĪS contains a *māhātmya* of Nārāyaṇādri (Tirunārāyaṇapuram temple, Melkoṭe), the place to which the ĪS is affiliated, which narrates how it came about that Nārāyaṇa is present there. In this *māhātmya*, the *aṣṭākṣaramantra* plays an eminent role: it is the means by which Nārāyaṇa enables Brahmā to create the world, and by which Nārāyaṇa is subsequently worshipped by Brah-

---

[105] ĪS 21.513-557b. Cf. also Rastelli 2006: 238–240.

[106] The same passage of ĪS 20.198c-203 describing the SS (see fn. 109) is re-used in the description of the Mantrasiddhānta in ĪS 21.571-576b.

mā.[107] Later Brahmā taught the *aṣṭākṣaramantra* and also the Mūlaveda, i.e., the Ekāyanaveda,[108] to his son Sanatkumāra (ĪS 20.196-197c). From the Mūlaveda, the *Sātvatasaṃhitā* came into existence.[109]

Let us recapitulate all the relations and equations outlined thus far. Nārāyaṇādri is a place in which Nārāyaṇa is manifest and worshipped. Nārāyaṇa is manifested through the *aṣṭākṣaramantra*. The ĪS is affiliated to Nārāyaṇādri and (therefore?) teaches the *aṣṭākṣaramantra* as its *mūlamantra*. The ĪS is also affiliated to the SS, which is equated with the Mantrasiddhānta which arose from the Mūlaveda.

The author(s) of the ĪS, despite being related to the Mantrasiddhānta, held the Āgamasiddhānta or Ekāyanaveda/Mūlaveda in high esteem for reasons we do not know at present. This can be concluded from the description of the Āgamasiddhānta as the first among the Siddhāntas and by the emphasis of the origin of the Mantrasiddhānta in the Āgamasiddhānta[110] Another clue is the fact that the *Pārameśvarasaṃhitā*, a text belonging to the Āgamasiddhānta, served as a model for the ĪS.[111] By relating the *aṣṭākṣaramantra*, its own *mūlamantra*, to the Mūlaveda/Ekāyanaveda/Āgamasiddhānta, the ĪS es-

---

[107] ĪS 20.129-134b, 156, 178, 181.

[108] *mūlaveda* is another name for *ekāyanaveda*, see, e.g., ĪS 1.18c-25 (18d ≈ PārS 1.32d, 19 ≈ PārS 1.57c-58b, 20-22b ≈ PārS 1.33-35b, 22c-25 ≈ PārS 1.74c-77) and Rastelli 2006: 157f.

[109] See ĪS 20.197d-203. This passage does not explicitly say that it is the *Sātvatasaṃhitā* which arises from the Mūlaveda, but the description of the text arising from it fits very well to the *Sātvatasaṃhitā*. For an explanation of this, see Rastelli 2006: 227–229 (here PārS 19.533c-538 is dealt with, which is a parallel of ĪS 20.198c-203).

[110] By contrast, according to the PādS, the *Mantrasiddhānta* does not arise from the *Āgamasiddhānta*; see PādS *cp* 21.2-13 and Rastelli 2006: 229.

[111] Cf. Rastelli 2006: 59. The ĪS borrowed many passages from the PārS. See, e.g., ĪS 3.1 ≈ PārS 6.1; 3.2-4 ≈ PārS 6.8-10; 5c-6b ≈ PārS 6.20; 7-12b ≈ PārS 6.21c-26; 12c-19b ≈ PārS 6.28c-35b; 20-21b ≈ PārS 6.41c-42. See also the parallel passages in ĪS 1 and PārS 1 presented in Rastelli 1999b: 82f. and Matsubara 1994: 28–30.

tablishes a link in its own tradition to the Ekāyanaveda that it originally may not have had. In conclusion, we can say that there is still much to reveal about the history of the three *mantra*s expressing Vāsudeva, Nārāyaṇa, and Viṣṇu, and their way into and development within the Pāñcarātra. The examples from the various *Saṃhitā*s, however, show us that there cannot be one valid explanation for all the *Saṃhitā*s, but that complex processes dependent on the individual environment of each *Saṃhitā* must have taken place.

Let us now summarize the results of our examinations. The question of whether Viṣṇu, Vāsudeva, and Nārāyaṇa are completely identified in the Pāñcarātra Saṃhitās or whether they still preserve distinct features cannot be answered in the same way for all contexts. In the descriptions of pure creation there are two tendencies that teach either Vāsudeva or Viṣṇu-Nārāyaṇa as their most supreme source. In the *śāstrāvatāra* stories no difference is made between the three gods. Being parts of various sets of deities, they are differentiated but not with very distinct features. In rituals, the early Pāñcarātra texts do not make a difference between the three gods either, but a gradual differentiation between them by means of their *mantra*s became popular, probably under the influence of other traditions, which is in itself a subject for future research.

Bibliography and Abbreviations

Primary Literature

AgniP

Agnipurāṇa. Agnipurāṇa of Maharṣi Vedavyāsa. Ed. by Āchārya Baladeva Upādhyāya. [The Kashi Sanskrit Series 174]. Varanasi 1966.

AnS

Aniruddhasaṃhitā. Aniruddha Samhita, one of Divyasamhita in Pancharatra. Ed. by A. Sreenivasa Iyengar. Mysore 1956.

AS

Ahirbudhnyasaṃhitā. Ahirbudhnya-Saṃhitā of the Pāñcarātrāgama. 2 vols. Ed. by M.D. Ramanujacharya under the Supervision of F. Otto Schrader. Revised by V. Krishnamacharya. [The Adyar Library Series 4]. Adyar 1916, ^{2}1986 (first repr.).

ĀP

Āgamaprāmāṇya. Yāmuna. Āgamaprāmāṇya of Yāmunācārya. Ed. by M. Narasimhachary. [Geakwad's Oriental Series 160]. Baroda 1976.

ĪS

Īśvarasaṃhitā. Īśvarasaṃhitā Anantācāryais saṃśodhitā. [Śāstramuktāvaḷī 45]. Kāñcī 1923.

$\bar{I}S_{2009}$

Īśvarasaṃhitā. Crit. ed. and translated in Five Volumes. Vol. 2 By M.A. Lakshmithathachar. Revised by V. Varadachari. [Kalāmūlaśāstra Series 43]. New Delhi/Delhi 2009.

GarP

Garuḍapurāṇa. The Garuḍa Mahāpurāṇam. Ed. Khemarāja Śrīkṛṣṇadāsa. Delhi 1984 (reprint).

Jayottaratantra

Jayottaratantra. Forthcoming critical edition being prepared by Diwakar Acharya.

JS
Jayākhyasaṁhitā. Crit. Ed. with an Introduction in Sanskrit, Indices etc. by Embar Krishnamacharya. [Geakwad's Oriental Series 54]. Baroda 1931.

NārU
Nārāyaṇopaniṣad. Nārāyaṇopaniṣad. In: The Vaiṣṇava-Upaniṣads with the Commentary of Śri Upaniṣad-brahma-yogin. Ed. by A. Mahadeva Sastri. [The Adyar Library Series 8]. Adyar 1953², 167–173.

NārS
Nāradīyasaṃhitā. Nāradīya Saṁhitā. Ed. by Rāghava Prasāda Chaudhary. [Kendriya Sanskrita Vidyapeetha Series 15]. Tirupati 1971.

ParS
Paramasaṃhitā. Paramasaṁhitā [of the Pāñcharātra]. Ed. and translated into English with an introduction by S. Krishnaswami Aiyangar. [Geakwad's Oriental Series 86]. Baroda 1940.

PādS
Pādmasaṃhitā. Padma Samhita. Crit. Ed. by Seetha Padmanabhan and R.N. Sampath (part I), Seetha Padmanabhan and V. Varadachari (part II). [Pāñcarātra Parisodhanā Pariṣad Series 3, 4]. Madras 1974, 1982.

PārS
Pārameśvarasaṃhitā. Pārameśvarasaṃhitā Govindācāryaiḥ saṃskṛtā, anekavidhādarśādibhiḥ saṃyojitā ca. Śrīraṅgam 1953.

PauṣS
Pauṣkarasaṃhitā. Sree Poushkara Samhita. One of the Three Gems in Pancharatra. Ed. by Sampathkumara Ramanuja Muni. Bangalore 1934.

PRR
Pāñcarātrarakṣā, Veṅkaṭanātha. Śrī Pāñcarātra Rakṣā of Śrī Vedānta Deśika. Crit. Ed. with Notes and Variant Readings by M. Duraiswami Aiyangar and T. Venugopalacharya with an Introduction in English by G. Srinivasa Murti. [The Adyar Library Series 36]. Madras 1942.

PLSS
Pratiṣṭhālakṣaṇasārasamuccaya, Vairocana. The Hindu Deities Illustrated according to the Pratiṣṭhālakṣaṇasārasamuccaya. Compiled by Gudrun Bühnemann and Musashi Tachikawa. [Bibliotheca Codicum Asiaticorum 3]. Tokyo 1990.

BaudhGŚS

Baudhāyanagṛhyaśeṣasūtra: In: Bodhâyana Gṛiyasutra. Ed. by R. Shama Sastri. [Oriental Library Publications. Sanskrit Series 32-55]. Mysore 1920.

BBS

Bṛhadbrahmasaṃhitā. Nāradapañcarātrāntargatā Bṛhadbrahmasaṃhitā. etat pustakaṃ Ś. Veṇegāvakarabhiḥ saṃśodhitam. [*Ānandāśramasaṃskṛtagranthāvaliḥ* 68]. Poona 1912.

BharS

Bharadvājasaṃhitā. Transcript 421 of the Institut Français, Pondichéry.

BhT

Bhārgavatantra. Bhargava Tantram (A Pancaratragama Text). Ed. by Raghava Prasad Chaudhary. [Ganganath Jha Kendriya Sanskrit Vidyapeetha Text Series 8]. Allahabad 1981.

MārkS

Mārkaṇḍeyasaṃhitā. Mārkaṇḍeya Saṃhitā. Tirupati 1984.

MudU *Mudgalopaniṣad*. In: One Hundred & Eight Upanishads (Îsha & Others.) with Various Readings. Ed. by Wâsudev Laxmaṇ Shâstrî Paṇśîkar. Bombay 1932^{4}.

MBh

Mahābhārata. The Mahābhārata for the First Time Crit. Ed. by Vishnu S. Sukthankar, S. K. Belvalkar et al. 19 vols. Poona 1933–1966.

YMD

Yatīndramatadīpikā, Śrīnivāsācārya. In: Śrî Bhâshya Vârtika, A Treatise on Viśisthâdvaita Philosophy; also: Yatîndra Mat Dîpikâ, By Nivâsâ Chârya son of Govindâ Chârya, And Sakalâchâryamat Saṅgrah. Ed. by Ratna Gopâl Bhaṭṭa. [Benares Sanskrit Series 123 & 133]. Benares 1907, 1–47.

LT

Lakṣmītantra. Lakṣmī-Tantra. A Pāñcarātra Āgama. Ed. with Sanskrit Gloss and Introduction by V. Krishnamacharya. [The Adyar Library Series 87]. Madras 1959, 1975 (repr.).

ViśS

Viśvāmitrasaṃhitā. Viśvāmitra Saṁhitā. Crit. ed. by Undemane Shankara Bhatta. [Kendriya Sanskrit Vidyapeetha Series 13]. Tirupati 1970.

ViṣṇuS
Viṣṇusaṃhitā. The Viṣṇu Saṁhitā. Ed. by M.M. Gaṇapati Sāstrī. With an Elaborate Introduction by N.P. Unni. [Trivandrum Sanskrit Series 85]. Delhi 1991 (rev. ed.).

ViṣS
Viṣvaksenasaṃhitā. Viṣvaksena Saṁhitā. Crit. ed. by Lakshmi Narasimha Bhatta. [Kendriya Sanskrit Vidyapeetha Series 17]. Tirupati 1972.

ŚrīprśS
Śrīpraśnasaṃhitā. Śrīpraśna Saṃhitā. Ed. by Seetha Padmanabhan with the Foreword of V. Raghavan. [Kendriya Sanskrit Vidyapeetha Series 12]. Tirupati 1969.

SanS
Sanatkumārasaṃhitā. Sanatkumāra-Saṃhitā of the Pāñcarātrāgama. Ed. by V. Krishnamacharya. [The Adyar Library Series 95]. Adyar 1969.

SvP
Svāyambhuvapāñcarātra. Forthcoming critical edition being prepared by Diwakar Acharya.

SS
Sāttvatasaṃhitā. Sātvata-Saṁhitā. With Commentary by Alaśiṅga Bhaṭṭa. Ed. by Vraja Vallabha Dwivedi. [Library Rare Texts Publication Series 6]. Varanasi 1982.

SSBh
Sātvatasaṃhitābhāṣya, Alaśiṅga Bhaṭṭa. See SS.

H
Hayaśīrṣapañcarātra. The Hayasirsa Pancharatram. Ādikāṇḍa. Ed. Bhuban Mohan Sāṅkhyatīrtha. 2 Vols. Rajashahi 1952, 1956.

Secondary Literature

Bock 1987
Andreas Bock, Die Madhu-Kaiṭabha-Episode und ihre Bearbeitung in der Anonymliteratur des Pāñcarātra. In: *ZDMG* 137/1 (1987) 78–109.

Bock-Raming 2002
Andreas Bock-Raming, *Untersuchungen zur Gottesvorstellung in der älteren Anonymliteratur des Pāñcarātra.* [Beiträge zur Indologie 34]. Wiesbaden: Harrassowitz 2002.

Carman 1974
John Braisted Carman, *The Theology of Rāmānuja. An Essay in Interreligious Understanding.* New Haven, London: Yale University Press 1974, Bombay 1981 (repr.).

Champakalakshmi 1981
R. Champakalakshmi, *Vaiṣṇava Iconography in the Tamil Country.* New Delhi: Orient Longman 1981.

Colas 1996
Gérard Colas, *Viṣṇu, ses images et ses feux. Les métamorphoses du dieu chez les vaikhānasa.* [Monographies 182]. Paris: Presses de l'École Française d'Extrême-Orient 1996.

Czerniak-Drożdżowicz 2003
Marzenna Czerniak-Drożdżowicz, *Pāñcarātra Scripture in the Process of Change. A Study of the Paramasaṃhitā.* [Publications of the de Nobili Research Library 31]. Vienna: Sammlung De Nobili 2003.

Gonda 1968-69
Jan Gonda, The Mudgalopaniṣad. In: *WZKSO* 12-13 (1968-69) *Beiträge zur Geistesgeschichte Indiens: Festschrift für E. Frauwallner*, pp. 101–113 (= J. Gonda, Selected Studies. Presented to the author by the staff of the Oriental Institute, Utrecht University, on the occasion of his 70th birthday. Vol. 3. Leiden: Brill 1975, pp. 499–511).

Gonda 1977
Ibid., *Medieval Religious Literature in Sanskrit.* [A History of Indian Literature 2/1]. Wiesbaden: Harrassowitz 1977.

Gupta 1972
Sanjukta Gupta, *Lakṣmī Tantra. A Pāñcarātra Text. Translation and Notes.* [Orientalia Rheno-Traiectina 15]. Leiden: Brill 1972.

Hardy 1983
Friedhelm Hardy, *Viraha-Bhakti. The early history of Kṛṣṇa devotion in South India.* Oxford: Oxford University Press 1983.

Matsubara 1994
Mitsunori Matsubara, *Pāñcarātra Saṃhitās & Early Vaiṣṇava Theology. With a Translation and Critical Notes from Chapters on Theology in the Ahirbudhnya Saṃhitā*. Delhi: Motilal Banarsidass 1994.

Neevel 1977
Walter G. Neevel, *Yāmuna's Vedānta and Pāñcarātra: Integrating the Classical and the Popular*. [Harvard dissertations in religion 10]. Missoula, Montana: Scholars Press 1977.

Oberhammer 1994
Gerhard Oberhammer, *Offenbarungsgeschichte als Text. Religionshermeneutische Bemerkungen zum Phänomen in hinduistischer Tradition*. [Publications of the de Nobili Research Library 31]. Vienna: Sammlung De Nobili 1994.

Oberhammer 2004
Ibid., *Zur spirituellen Praxis des Zufluchtnehmens bei Gott (śaraṇāgatiḥ) vor Veṅkaṭanātha. Materialien zur Geschichte der Rāmānuja-Schule 7*. [Veröffentlichungen zu den Sprachen und Kulturen Südasiens Heft 36]. Vienna: Austrian Academy of Sciences Press 2004.

Rastelli 1999a
Marion Rastelli, *Philosophisch-theologische Grundanschauungen der Jayākhyasaṃhitā. Mit einer Darstellung des täglichen Rituals*. [Beiträge zur Kultur und Geistesgeschichte Asiens Nr. 33]. Vienna: Austrian Academy of Sciences Press 1999.

Rastelli 1999b
Id., Zum Verständnis des Pāñcarātra von der Herkunft seiner Saṃhitās. In: *WZKS* 43 (1999) 51–93.

Rastelli 2003
Id., The Ekāyanaveda in the Pāñcarātra Tradition. Paper read at the 12th World Sanskrit Conference in Helsinki, July 2003. http://ikga.oeaw.ac.at/Mat/rastelli_ekayanaveda.pdf (22 May, 2012)

Rastelli 2006
Id., *Die Tradition des Pāñcarātra im Spiegel der Pārameśvarasaṃhitā*. [Beiträge zur Kultur und Geistesgeschichte Asiens Nr. 51]. Vienna: Austrian Academy of Sciences Press 2006.

Rastelli 2007
Id., The "Pāñcarātra Passages" in Agnipurāṇa 21-70. In: Dominic Goodall, André Padoux (eds.), *Mélanges tantriques à la mémoire d'Hélène Brunner. Tantric Studies in Memory of Hélène Brunner.* [Collection Indologie 106]. Pondicherry: Institut Français de Pondichéry 2007, pp. 187–229.

Rastelli 2008
Id., Von der Offenbarung Gottes zur "vedisch-orthodoxen" Tradition: Zur Begründung der Autorität der Tradition des Pāñcarātra. In: *Glaubensgewissheit und Wahrheit in religiöser Tradition. Arbeitsdokumentation eines Symposiums.* Gerhard Oberhammer, Marcus Schmücker (eds.). [Beiträge zur Kultur und Geistesgeschichte Asiens Nr. 60]. Vienna: Austrian Academy of Sciences Press 2008, pp. 255–280.

Ratié 2011
Isabelle Ratié, *Le Soi et l'Autre. Identité, différence et altérité dans la philosophie de la Pratyabhijñā.* [Jerusalem Studies in Religion and Culture 13]. Leiden, Boston: Brill 2011.

Sanderson 2001
Alexis Sanderson, History through Textual Criticism in the study of Śaivism, the Pañcarātra and the Buddhist Yoginītantras. In: François Grimal (ed.), *Les sources et le temps. Sources and Time. A Colloquium, Pondicherry, 11–13 January 1997.* [Publications du Département d'Indologie 91]. Pondicherry: Institut Français de Pondichéry 2001, pp. 1–47.

Sanderson 2009
Ibid., The Śaiva Age. The Rise and Dominance of Śaivism During the Early Medieval Period. In: Shingo Einoo, Jun Takashima (eds.): *From Material to Deity. Indian Rituals of Consecration.* [Japanese Studies on South Asia 4]. Delhi: Manohar 2005, pp. 41–349.

Schreiner 1997
Reinhold Grühnendahl, Angelika Malinar, Thomas Oberlies, Peter Schreiner, *Nārāyaṇīya-Studien.* Peter Schreiner (ed.). [Purāṇa Research Publications 6]. Wiesbaden: Harrassowitz 1997.

Schwarz Linder 2014
Silvia Schwarz Linder, *The Philosophical and Theological Teachings of the Pādmasaṃhitā. Studies on the History, Self-understanding and Dogmatic*

Foundations of Late Indian Buddhist Philosophy. [Sitzungsberichte der Österreichischen Akademie der Wissenschaften, Philosophisch-Historische Klasse 853]. Vienna: Austrian Academy of Sciences Press 2014.

Smith 1975
H. Daniel Smith, *A Descriptive Bibliography of the Printed Texts of the Pāñcarātrāgama.* Vol. 1. [Geakwad's Oriental Series 158]. Baroda: Oriental Institute 1975.

TAK 3
Tāntrikābhidhānakośa III. Ṭ-PH. *Dictionnaire des termes techniques de la littérature hindoue tantrique fondé sous la direction de Hélène Brunner†, Gerhard Oberhammer et André Padoux.* Direction éditoriale du troisième volume: Dominic Goodall, Marion Rastelli. [Beiträge zur Kultur und Geistesgeschichte Asiens Nr. 76]. Vienna: Austrian Academy of Sciences Press 2013.

Young 2002
Katherine K. Young, *Om*, the Vedas, and the Status of Women with Special Reference to Śrīvaiṣṇavism. In: *Jewels of Authority. Women and Textual Tradition in Hindu India.* Laurie L. Patton (ed.). Oxford: Oxford University Press 2002, pp. 84–121.

Id., Brāhmaṇas, Pāñcarātrins, and the Formation of Śrīvaiṣṇavism. In: *Studies in Hinduism IV. On the Mutual Influences and Relationship of Viśiṣṭādvaita Vedānta and Pāñcarātra.* Gerhard Oberhammer, Marion Rastelli (eds.). [Beiträge zur Kultur und Geistesgeschichte Asiens 54]. Vienna: Austrian Academy of Sciences Press 2007, pp. 179–261.

Gerhard Oberhammer

On the dialectic of language and mysticism in Vāmanadatta's *Saṃvitprakāśa**

The name of God is a remarkable phenomenon. In it, the problem of "religion"[1] but in consequence also the difference between "religion" and theology as well as their mutual interaction are gathered as the light at the focal point of a lens. The name of God is, on the one hand, a symbol of God and a *linguistic sign of His identity*, in contradistinction to the gods of other traditions; occasionally, as for example in Hinduism, it is also historical evidence for the transformation of the manner in which God is experienced within one's own tradition. On the other hand, the name is the way of addressing God while speaking to Him and thus it is no longer a sign, but an expression of the subject's relationality towards transcendence and in this way it is a religious act as such, in which the phenomenon of "religion", together with the his-

---

* I would like to thank Professor Raffaele Torella for his kindness expressed in allowing me to use his new, unpublished critical edition of the SPra (*prakaraṇa*s I-IV, 54) so that I could use an essentially improved text of Vāmanadatta. In all original quotations from the SPra I introduce (T) in the body of the text whenever I follow the version of Raffaele Torella. Printing mistakes of Mark S.G. Dyczkowski's edition are not accounted for here.

I would like to express my deep gratitude to my colleague Halina Marlewicz, who took the effort to translate the German version into English.

The German version of this article was published under the title *Monistische Gotteslehre und Spiritualität Vāmandattas. Ein religionshermeneutischer Versuch.* [*Publications of the de Nobili Research Library, Occasional Paper 9*]. Wien 2016, pp. 9–25.

1 The term "religion" is to mean the religion in its existential dimension and not as a socio-cultural phenomenon.

toricality of human mind, becomes discernible. As such it holds within, as it were, a germ of the whole experience of the tradition and the relation to transcendence as it is realized in that very tradition. It is the "seed" because, as the actual expression, it is conditioned by the particular existential situation of the subject and his historically actualized integration in the *Memoria* of his tradition, and so the relationality of the subject through this *Memoria* can be enriched or constricted in accordance with the current circumstances.

What is notable and crucial for the religious hermeneutics is that it is only through this verbalization, held as a seed within the act of "addressing by name" and put into language as a theological articulation of faith, that transcendence acquires its "face" and can be encountered as a "mythical presence" in the religious act. That this face is not "idolatrically" alienated results from the evocative nature of addressing God, due to which transcendence, in spite of its "mythic familiarity", is encountered without being appropriated and thus taken for granted.

Formerly I have called this phenomenon of the verbalization of transcendence[2] a "mythisation", and was surprised to find a similar idea in Vāmanadatta's *Saṃvitprakāśa* with a different function and therefore with a different significance.

Vāmanadatta, probably an older contemporary of Abhinavagupta, is, much like the latter, a monist as far as his ontological standpoint is concerned. Regarding his religious affiliation, however, he is a Vaiṣṇava and a Pāñcarātrin. In fact, in many *Saṃhitā*s of the Pāñcarātra one finds a tendency towards monism, in the sense of an attempt to effectively combine the dimension of the divine and the worldly existence of the practitioner (*sādhaka*), or else the manifoldness of the world and the one transcendent God. It is this unarticulated, latent, in a manner of speaking, monism that Vāmanadatta seeks to apprehend and argue for in his philosophical-theological reflection, the *Saṃvitprakāśa* (=SPr).[3] The available text of the *Saṃvitprakāśa* begins with the fundamental observation:

---

2 Cf. Oberhammer 2005: 191–211.

3 Cf. *Saṃvitprakāśa by Vāmanadatta*. Edited with English introduction by Mark S. G. Dyczkowski. Varanasi 1990.

In the form of subject (-*vedakarūpeṇa*) and object (*vedya-*), due to [their] inner and outer state (*vyavasthā*), this conceptual representation (*saṃkalpaḥ*) the nature of which is to differentiate (*bheda-*), makes this [transcendental being] manifold (*vibhedayati*). ‖ 1 ‖

This [in itself] is neither outside nor inside, nor in the object of knowledge, nor in the subject, neither between, nor in the middle. This is [something] totally other. ‖ 2 ‖

What is inaccessible for the conceptual representations (*vikalpa-*), undistorted (*akadarthita-*) by words and unaffected by conditioning circumstances (*upādhi-*), this I praise as the highest abode of Viṣṇu [=Viṣṇu's presence] (*vaiṣṇavam padam*). ‖ 3 ‖ [4]

Despite the missing beginning,[5] in which this *tat* must have been specified, these three verses do implicitly contain some decisive ideas. The reality of Viṣṇu—which in the text is only evoked without being mentioned as such—is inaccessible to the knowledge of men (*saṃkalpa*). This knowledge is by nature representative and substantiates itself in language,[6] because the nature of language is necessarily differentiating. One cannot say that this reality is determined by external circumstances (*upādhi*) by which it can be apprehended, as other systems teach. Also one cannot equate it with the subject of cognition, and even

4 SPr I, 1-3: *vedyavedakarūpeṇa bahirantarvyavasthayā* | *bhedapradhānasaṃkalpo vibhedayati tat tathā* ‖ 1 ‖ *na tad antar na tad bāhye na vedye vedake na ca* | *nāntarā na ca madhye 'pi sarvathāpi tad anyathā* ‖ 2 ‖ *yad vikalpair anākrāntaṃ yac chabdair akadarthitam* | *yad upādhibhir amlānaṃ naumi tad vaiṣṇavaṃ padam* ‖ 3 ‖.

5 Reasons: the reference to *tat* is missing; the SPr I, 136 speaks of 160 verses (*śaṣṭyuttaraṃ ślokaśatam*). In fact, only 137 are extant and the rest are missing.

6 In the 3rd chapter, Vāmanadatta, in the context of the representations, speaks of the idea of *vikalpaśabdaḥ*. See SPr III, 3: *vikalpaśabdo lokārthaprasiddhyā na hi sārthakaḥ* | *kiṃ tu śāstraprasiddhyaiva sa cāsmin apratiṣṭhitā* ‖ 3 ‖; III, 8: *vikalpaśabdasyānye kiṃ śabdāḥ paryāyatāṃ gatāḥ* | *sā vā teṣāṃ yad etasya teṣāṃ caikarthatocyate* ‖ 8 ‖; III, 10: *vikalpaśabdatvaṃ vācyaṃ yadi kiñcit prakalpayet* | *itare 'pi tadarthaṃ na nārthavantaḥ kathaṃ kila* ‖ 10 ‖; III, 18: *yāvad vikalpaśabdasya kaś cid artho na sādhitaḥ* | *tāvad viśeṣaṇaṃ nāyaṃ śabdamātro nirarthakaḥ* ‖18 ‖.

less can it be found in any external object. It is something totally other (*sarvathāpi tad anyathā*), even if Vāmanadatta subsequently remarks the following in verse 5:

> Everyone knows [one's own] essential form (*svarūpam*). The highest (*paraḥ*) [however] is not an object of cognition of anyone (*jñeyo na kasya cid*). You are the very own essential form which is omnipresent (*sarvagam-*); by you all this [whole] world is permeated.[7]

The reality of Viṣṇu, though evoked here, just as it also was in the first extant *śloka*s of the *Saṃvitprakāśa*, remains beyond human cognition. Even if it can be thought of as pervading the whole world, it is accessible only as the awareness of psychic phenomena which in the 5th verse is understood as the form (*svaṃ rūpam*) of the Highest. Human thought can capture the reality of Viṣṇu only in the mode of a representation determined by language, "distorted" due to its distinguishing character. Therefore, Vāmanadatta's conceptuality opens itself for the spiritual dimension of an existential meditation as an approach to the experience of the transcendental absolute. This experience is not possible in the system of (conceptual) representations, but only in the immediate experience of one's own self, with the attention focused on the depths of the "self-awareness" ("*Bei-sich-sein*"), always being emptied of representations and concepts. Unfortunately, Vāmanadatta never speaks more extensively about such a meditation, yet he does mention levels of the reality that can obviously characterize the decisive moments of the meditation, and therefore offer clues for its understanding.

> With regard to you, Lord, [the following] levels of the resting stages (*viśramabhūmayaḥ*) of the meditating subject are taught: ‖ 86cd ‖
>
> First there is the real one (*vastu*), then the [phenomenal] being (*bhāvaḥ*); afterwards the object (*arthaḥ*) and then the activity (*kriyā*). In this way, that which is primarily intended by you (*īpsitatama*) is acting, ‖ 87 ‖

---

7 SPr I, 5: *sarvaḥ svarūpaṃ jānāti paro jñeyo na kasyacit* | *rūpaṃ svaṃ sarvagaṃ ca tvaṃ tvayedaṃ pūritaṃ jagat* ‖ 5 ‖. Elsewhere (SPr I, 15ab) Vāmanadatta clarifies: "By you all this is pervaded. In you everything is founded." *tvayā sarvam idaṃ vyāptaṃ tvayi sarvam idaṃ sthitam* |.

because this fourfold form (*rūpam*) ends, in the case of every [phenomenal] being, with the activity. Hence you, being one of the fourfold nature (*caturātmā*), having permeated (*āvṛtya*) everything, are present.

‖ 88 ‖[8]

Unfortunately, the text is basically just an enumeration of terms that are not further explained. Yet it is important not only because we get to know something about the way this meditation is experienced, but also because—for Vāmanadatta—it seems to have a spiritual importance. Firstly, the text shows—by the locative singular of the one addressed (*tvayi*), the object of meditation—that this is not a theoretical consideration, but should rather be seen in the perspective of religious existence and in this way, it serves as the subject's effort towards salvation. Thus, this addressing also establishes a relation between the four levels of meditation and the reality of Viṣṇu himself. The levels can be understood as monistic-idealistic interpretations of the four manifestations of Viṣṇu (*vyūha*) in the process of creation.

It is further noticeable that these four levels of meditation not only represent progressive stages of the meditating subject's consciousness, but that they are also phenomenal aspects of reality. These levels, however, can be understood in the perspective of Vāmanadatta's monism of consciousness as the phenomena of divine consciousness, and therefore they substantiate his ontological view. By enumerating these levels, the text conveys a certain insight into how the world and its beings are constituted in a transcendental-idealistic manner as the phenomena of consciousness and through a hierarchical sequence of the levels, which undoubtedly appear one after another in a temporary sequence. They allow us to understand a certain direction of the meditative effort as well as the dynamism of the meditative "deconstruction" of these phenomena in the enumerated sequence. Thus, the decisive concept is obviously *bhāva-*, appearing in the sentence between the

---

8 SPr I, 86cd-88: *tvayy etāḥ kathitā nātha dhyāyiviśrāmabhūmayaḥ* ‖ 86 ‖ *vastu pūrvaṃ tato bhāvaḥ paścād arthas tataḥ kriyā* | *tayā yad īpsitatamaṃ tava tat karmasaṃjñitam* ‖ 87 ‖ *kriyāntaṃ sarvabhāveṣu cātūrūpyam idaṃ yataḥ* | *caturātmā tvam eko 'taḥ sarvam āvṛtya tiṣṭhasi* ‖ 88 ‖. (T)

final real (*vastu*) and the *artha-*, obviously the "thing", which represents the beings of the world.

It is hardly by chance that Vāmanadatta characterizes the transition from the real being (*vastu*) to the worldly object (*artha-*) by this concept (*bhāva-*), which, as different from the concept of being, implies the aspect of becoming and—in the context of transcendental monism—is to be understood in the sense of becoming present in the consciousness. The concept of *bhāva-* implies the transcendental conditioning of the object-perception by linguistic representations, and connects this concept with the response in the consciousness of the subject, aside from its closeness to the concept of *bhāvanā* ("making present"), and its technical sense of the primary meaning of the verbal root in grammar.[9] In the context of our quotation, the concept of *bhāva-* can only mean the transcendental structure of language-determined thinking, by which the reality (*vastu*), monistically understood in the cognition, becomes the phenomenal being. In our everyday consciousness it is perceived as the object (*artha-*).

Elsewhere Vāmanadatta expresses this distinction of the subject and object of cognition in the following way, emphasizing clearly the *aprioric* function of language:

> Only the power of the language (*vākprabhāvaḥ*) as such divides that which is in itself undivided into real objects, due to the fact that it has to be used [by language]. ‖ 7 ‖
>
> Just as the [word-]division in the expression "the head of Rahu" is not real (*vastavaḥ*), in the same way the linguistic distinction as something to be known (*vedyatve bhedaśābdaḥ*) in the case of Ātman is not real. ‖ 8 ‖
>
> Just in the way one takes the external form located in the eye [i.e., perceived] as one's own form, in the same way one [also] takes the object of cognition, namely, consciousness, in the stage (*sthita*) of knowledge as one's own form. ‖ 9 ‖ [10]

---

9 See Renou 1957: 243–244.

10 SPr I, 7-9: *kevalaṃ vākprabhāvo 'yaṃ yad abhinnam api svayam* | *vibhedayati sā vastuṣv iti kartavyatāvaśāt* ‖ 7 ‖ *yathā rāhoḥ śira iti śabde bhedo na vāstavaḥ* | *tathā svātmani vedyatve bhedaḥ śābdo na vāstavaḥ* ‖

The religious-hermeneutical value of language as *a priori* conditioning of the *saṃsāric* reality, which Vāmanadatta qualifies as error (*avidyā*, *mithyājñānam*) as well,[11] becomes visible also when he (in continuing the previously quoted text[12]) says of language:

> You, being one of the fourfold nature (*caturātmā*), having pervaded (*āvṛtya*) everything, are there as latent [language] (*śānta-*), as *Paśyantī*, as a medium-sized [and] as *Vaikharī*. Because fourfold language expresses your body in a fourfold way. ‖ 88cd-89 ‖
>
> As [namely language] due to its own nature (*nijātmanā*) pervades the whole world, so language (*bhāratī*) shines forth everywhere having been penetrated (*anuviddhā*) [lit. 'pierced'] by you. ‖ 90 ‖ [13]

Here language that Vāmanadatta elsewhere characterizes traditionally as the *śakti* of God or philosophically leads it back to the consciousness as its origin,[14] is ascribed to God in the way it works to the extent that consciousness appears as being permeated by Him. Even though God is in this case only indirectly involved in the production of the world by the appearance of language, the text offers here a clue in

---

8 ‖ *yathā cakṣuḥsthitaṃ rūpaṃ bāhyaṃ svaṃ rūpam īkṣate* | *tathā jñānasthitā saṃvij jñeyaṃ svaṃ rūpam īkṣate* ‖ 9 ‖. (T)

11 SPr I, 102f.: *sā ced vilīnā tvadbhaktyā naṣṭo bhedaḥ sthitaikatā* | *avidyeyam iyaṃ māyā mithyājñānam idaṃ nu tat* ‖ 102 ‖ *yad acitraikarūpe tvayy advaye dvayadarśanam* | *māyātvam etad evāsyā yan nāśas tattvadarśanāt* ‖ 103 ‖. (T)

12 SPr I, 86ff.; cf. fn. 8.

13 SPr I, 88cd-90: *caturātmā tvam eko 'taḥ sarvam āvṛtya tiṣṭhasi* ‖ 88 ‖ *śāntarūpātha paśyantī madhyamā vaikharī tathā* | *catūrūpā catūrūpaṃ vakti vāk tāvakaṃ vapuḥ* ‖ 89 ‖ *yathānayā jagad viddhaṃ sarvam eva nijātmanā* | *tathā tvayānuviddheyaṃ sarvato bhāti bhāratī* ‖ 90 ‖. (T)

14 See SPr I, 76-80: *saṃvinmūlād varṇaparṇā jñānastambhāt sarasvatī* | *prāg aghoṣā sanādānu puṇyatīrthā pravartate* ‖76‖ *tvatpravṛttā prāṇāyati śaktiḥ sā viśvam ojasā* | *pratiyāntī punas tvāṁ sā saṁkocayati saṃbhavat* ‖77‖ *kāryānurūpaṃ sā rūpaṃ tathā nāmāpi bibhratī* | *nirvāhayati viśvasmiṃś citrāṃ yātrāṃ carācarāṃ* ‖78‖ *sā vaikharī mantravarṇā nihanti tamasaḥ sthitim* | *manaḥsamāśrayā hantī madhyamā rājasīm api* ‖79‖ *nihanty avidyāṃ paśyantī tadūrdhvaṃ prāṇagocarā* | *tvadātmabhūtā sā śāntā samaṃ sarvaprakāśikā* ‖ 80 ‖.

order not to misunderstand Vāmanadatta's monism of consciousness. The worldly phenomena are not "empty of reality". It is the divine being itself—as the sustaining principle of consciousness—that constitutes their reality. Vāmanadatta's monism does not rest on the fact that the multitude of phenomena is unreal, but on the fact that the being of all the phenomena is God Himself. If, in these verses, God is to be taken as involved in the activity of language as the principle that alienates the unity of the divine being in the form of the multitude of phenomena, then the multitude of the worldly phenomena gains a sort of validity and reality, which is willed by God. Such a point of departure allows Vāmanadatta's approach to avoid a possible irreality, the sublation of the divine revelation in the Tantra, and also the manifoldness occurring in the religious practice of *mantra* and the manifestations (*mūrti*) of God. In this manner, even they, just like the manifoldness of the world, do not become sublated as "empty of reality", in terms of illusionistic approach, but are finally theologically testified in their phenomenological manifestations. Thus, they are testified as means of salvation to be possibly taken not in an absolute sense as leading to the union with God, but as a preparation to salvific knowledge. In this way, both the manifoldness of the world and also the salvific nature of the Pāñcarātra revelation are creations of God according to the real meaning of the word, in spite of their idealistically founded phenomenality in the consciousness of man.

In order to explain how this is to be realized, Vāmanadatta mentions the example of a golden earring. It is real as such only as gold, while as an earring it appears as something particular merely because of the special design and form, which exists only as a phenomenal entity. In the perspective of Vāmanadatta's transcendental monism, the phenomenal being is precisely that coming into the appearance of the reality of divine being in the *aprioric* conditionality of human cognition determined by language. While language—which is embedded in its being in the divine creative power—becomes the co-cause of creation and not an illusion obscuring the nature of God, the manifoldness of creation is possible only due to language, even if it is ultimately false as a phenomenon of human knowledge. However, language—due to God's acting—means reality, just like the illusionary "snake" of the Advaita is still real as a rope, since otherwise the illusion of the serpent would not be possible. If this is the case, there arises a philosophical explanation of how man, the absolute transcendence of God notwithstanding, can have a pre-rational access to this transcendence. The phenomenality of worldly reality is then no longer merely the non-real content of false cognition, but ultimately the medium in which the reality of God (even if it is still alienated by the representative cognition of man) is encountered and can become the reason for the human search for salvation.

If the language of the first extant verses of the *Saṃvitprakaśa* is not the rhetoric of hymnal poetry, but rather a serious philosophical statement, then in Vāmanadatta's predicating Viṣṇu as the only, totally other reality, it must also be accounted for that it withdraws as "inaccessible through words". Thus, it would finally be only a symbol of His transcendence, predicating nothing about him, yet serving as an indicator towards the symbolized one, but not in the way of explicit knowledge. It is with this religious familiarity, which presupposes the experience of His reality, that Vāmanadatta constantly addresses God in the entire first *prakaraṇa* and continues to do so elsewhere.

Is it therefore possible to have the awareness of the transcendent God as a symbolized one? In other words: can one have—analogous to Vāmanadatta's understanding of the Advaitic concept of the illusory serpent—an experience of the manifold world without a simultaneous experience of a transcendent God who is understood as monistic-transcendental? Vāmanadatta seems to give an answer to this question in a short passage of his *Saṃvitprakāśa*:

> As the proper form of an exceptionally clear crystal is perceived [only] if it is coloured by something else, ‖ 53 ‖
>
> in the same way your "body" (*vapuḥ*), O Noble One, can be [perceived only] in relation to the [phenomenal] being. Due to its complete flawlessness it is not perceived separately by [men] (= *dvaitapaṇḍita*-?). ‖ 54 ‖
>
> But this is why the crystal, separate from the colouring, is not non-existing nor is your flawless body [non-existent], if the form of the phenomenal being is given up. ‖ 55 ‖
>
> Like the proper ontic state (*sthitiḥ*) of a universal, if particular cases are left out, cannot be demonstrated and [yet] it is there, ‖ 56 ‖

[or] in the same way the proper ontic state of gold, of the earrings, etc., if one takes away the state [of gold], is there, in the same way there is your eternal, ever proper and pure ontic state of your consciousness (*saṃvinmayī*) which, due to the negation of joys and sorrows, is apperceived [only] through your very consciousness. ‖ 57 ‖

The reality (*padam*), free from every determination (*nirviśeṣa-*) undivided (*nirvibhāga-*), free from every limitation (*saṅkaṭavarjita-*), the spirit which is its own light, which is pure, I praise as the eternally manifested *brahman.* ‖ 58 ‖ [15]

The text is not a direct predication and the terminology applied with regard to the problem it relates is not very explicit. It requires interpretation, less in the sense of the history of philosophy, but more in the philosophical and hermeneutical sense: the crucial concepts and their explanations seem to correspond to those which Vāmanadatta uses in other later places in order to characterize levels of meditation.[16] He does this in such a way that the concept of *bhāva-* in the expression *bhāvasaṃyuktam* and, respectively, the concept of *vapu* in the above passage would correspond there to the concepts of *bhāva-* and *vastu. Bhāva-* is the phenomenal, language-determined reality of worldly beings, and *tavakaṃ vapuḥ*, the proper reality of Viṣṇu, as far as man can think of it in his thought as a proper being of the world. If it is further correct that the concepts in both passages get their meanings in the context of an internal experience, they should primarily be considered in the perspective of the religious hermeneutics in connection with the experience of God. If the experience of the phenomenal being

---

[15] SPr I, 53-58: *atyantācchasvabhāvatvāt sphaṭikasya yathā svakam* | *rūpaṃ paroparaktasya nityam evopalabhyate* ‖ 53 ‖ *tathā bhāvasamāyuktaṃ bhagavaṃs tāvakaṃ vapuḥ* | *atyantanirmalatayā pṛthak tair nopalabhyate* ‖ 54 ‖ *naitāvatāsau sphaṭikaḥ pṛthaṅ nāsty eva rañjanāt* | *bhāvarūpaparityaktā tava vā nirmalā tanuḥ* ‖ 55 ‖ *yathoddhṛtaviśeṣasya sāmānyasya nijasthitiḥ* | *pṛthaṅ na śakyā nirdeṣṭuṃ na ca tan nāsti tāvatā* ‖ 56 ‖ *yathoddhṛtakuṇḍalādeḥ kanakasya svayaṃ sthitiḥ* | *evaṃ nityā nijā śuddhā sukhaduḥkhaniṣedhanāt* | *svasaṃvedanasaṃvedyā tava saṃvinmayī sthitiḥ* ‖ 57 ‖ *aviśeṣaṃ nirvibhāgam adeśam kālavarjitam* | *svajyotiś cidghanaikātaṃ naumi brahma sadoditam* ‖ 58 ‖. (T)

[16] See SPr I, 87; cf. fn. 8.

is *a priori* determined by language, then so is also the experience of Viṣṇu in the everyday consciousness at first bound to the thought which is structured in language. Therefore, there arises, on the one hand, an issue in how language can possibly condition the phenomenal reality of beings and, on the other hand, how mediating an internal experience—or at least the experience of God in faith—becomes possible: an experience, which as such has to start unavoidably with consciousness structured by concepts and language, if it should have an actual meaning for a man.

Vāmanadatta seeks the answer to this concern in the psychological processes of meditation, when he makes the transition from the experience of phenomenal subjects to that of the proper reality of Viṣṇu dependent on the "renouncement" or "giving up"[17] of the phenomenal being. Yet, this poses the question of how this giving up can be possibly assumed, if in the experience of Viṣṇu the giving up is as such not possible at all. In any case, also for Vāmanadatta meditation must start with the representation of a phenomenal being insofar as a person cannot think outside of language. So, in any case, it is language that must ensure the transition in question. If this is true, then the transition from *bhāva-* to *vastu* as stages of meditation—and therefore also the giving up (*tyāga-*) of the phenomenality (*bhāvarūpaṃ*) of Viṣṇu's body—can be situated only in the dynamics of language. Changing the content of meditation must be ingrained in the nature of the phenomena of language itself. Thus, there appears a certain dialectic in the nature of language (of which Vāmanadatta does not speak explicitly) that is to be presupposed as a *de facto* structure of meditation.

To begin with, speech, as a linguistic phenomenon, "makes present". Therefore, as Vāmanadatta would say, speech differentiates by singularizing. By means of language, the content of meditation becomes an "object" that (due to the semantic content) is differentiated from others of its class, by which the phenomenal being of the one existing, which is *bhāva-*, occurs (reaches a certain state) and becomes a self-contained structure through which the world in its multiplicity

---

[17] SPr I, 55cd; cf. fn. 15.

is present. The "world" is, so to speak, the system of word-meanings.[18] Yet this also does not seem to be the whole truth for Vāmanadatta. That which is thought of in language, that of which language speaks, is not what it conveys. It is not even a part of its sense. Language transcends its linguistic meaning (the sense of the word), breaks through the hermetism of its structure dialectically, as it were, and evokes that what was meant by language in language.

Vāmanadatta himself reflects on this phenomenon in the light of his conceptual system in connection with the question as to whether representation (*vikalpa*) is fit to grasp the *ātman* or the *paramātman*, respectively, in meditation.

> The function of the representation does not apply to one's own *ātman* nor to the Highest Self (*paraḥ*). ‖ 22cd ‖
>
> Nor is the representation apprehended while one "considers oneself as" [when in meditation]; therefore, the representation is not really there [in the meditation]. There is no contact of the Highest [Self] with it, like [in the situation when there is no intercourse]. ‖ 23 ‖
>
> [The function of the representation] does not also apply to one's own *ātman*. For what should it be in the case of one's own *ātman*? Since the function of the representation is useless in the case of evident things. ‖ 24 ‖
>
> But the whereabouts of meditation (*saṃbhāvanāspadam*)[19] can be grasped in "considering-oneself-as" owing to the representation, if the distinction of "considering-oneself-as" in thought is overcome. ‖ 25 ‖
>
> [Yet] when there is unity of the reality (*vastvaikye*) there is only the diversity of names (*nāmabhedaḥ*), not being based on both respectively. Therefore the talk of being grasped is useless. [On the contrary], one's own *ātman* should be like [he is experienced in meditation]. ‖ 26 ‖

---

[18] See SPr III,1f.: *yasya māyāparispandavihitā viśvasaṃsthitiḥ* | *asmadvikalpasaṃkalpahartāraṃ ahaṃ nataḥ* ‖ 1 ‖ *sarvo vikalpaḥ saṃsāra ity ukter ayam āśayaḥ* | *yad asattvaṃ sṛteḥ sattvaṃ śuddhāyāḥ saṃvidaḥ sthitam* ‖ 2 ‖. (T)

[19] Namely *ātman* or *paramātman*.

> therefore the representation is nothing else but cognition being purified [of representations]. Thus, the representation with regard to one's own *ātman* is without alternative. ‖ 27 ‖ [20]

In these verses Vāmanadatta does not expressly investigate the problem of how language "evokes" one's own Ātman as divine reality without being designated by words. If one considers the connection between language and representation in the context of Vāmanadatta's monism of consciousness, the representation in "considering-oneself-as" turns into a relation of language to reality insofar as the content of representation fades away when there is no longer a direct reference of language, and thus consciousness "is evoked". As Vāmanadatta formulates it,

> In the end there remains the statement that the word-reference is the object of the representation, because if words have no reference, the object of the representation is not there. ‖ 11 ‖ [21]

In this way, language, being limited in its referential function to representation, establishes the cognition of objects. However, representation has for Vāmanadatta a function that exceeds its relation to language. It is this phenomenon of human psyche that is in immediate relation to consciousness, because—in order to become a cognition—it must be made aware of in the consciousness; it must become something of which one is conscious in the consciousness. And therefore, it is the disposition of being-aware-of that supports the totality of representations due to the fact that they are realized by the subject, while the representations as such, realized in the consciousness, conceal the

---

20 SPr III,22cd-27: *vyāpāraś ca vikalpasya na svātmani pare 'pi vā* ‖ 22cd ‖ *nābhimānagṛhīto 'pi vikalpas tena naiva san* | *parasya tenāsaṃsparśo yathāvad agates tataḥ* ‖ 23 ‖ *vyāpāraḥ svātmani na ca siddheḥ svātmani tena kim* | *na hi siddheṣu bhāveṣu vyāpāraḥ phalavān bhavet* ‖ 24 ‖ *abhimānagṛhītaṃ tu bhavet saṃbhāvanāspadam* | *vikalpād abhimānasya matibhede prasādhite* ‖ 25 ‖ *vastvaikye nāmabhedo 'yam etayor na svarūpataḥ* | *gṛhītoktir ato vyārthā svātmaivāstu tathāvidhaḥ* ‖ 26 ‖ *tasmād vikalpaḥ saṃśuddhād vijñānān nātiricyate* | *tenaiva nirvikalpo 'yaṃ vikalpaḥ svātmani sthitaḥ* ‖ 27 ‖. (T)

21 SPr III,11: *vikālpārthaś ca śabdārtha ity uktiḥ paryavasyati* | *nirarthakatve śabdānāṃ vikalpārtho yato na san* ‖ 11 ‖. (T)

reality of consciousness itself. This is, in the similar way, valid also for the meditation practiced in order to cognize the reality of the Ātman. It starts with everyday consciousness, that is, with the consciousness "alienated" or "concealed" by representations and dialectically "deconstructed" with the help of the hiding aspect of the representations of this "concealment"—precisely the "I" representation, which turns the reality of consciousness into the consciousness of the individual. Due to this, consciousness alone becomes non-alienated by representations, and appears itself as such. Vāmanadatta expresses this in another passage in the following way:

> The process, O Mādhava, by which the "I"-producing is dissolved, is produced by you and is of your nature. ‖ 100cd ‖
>
> Therefore, it is you [alone] who remains. The differentiation (*bheda-*) lasts for him [i.e., a man] as long as there is the "I"-fancy (*ahaṃmānitā*) with regard to the Ātman. ‖ 101 ‖
>
> When this one is dissolved through devotion to you, differentiation is destroyed and oneness is established. ‖ 102ab ‖ [22]

Given the background of Vāmanadatta's reflection, it becomes possible to interpret the last verses of the previous quotation[23] and to integrate them into the following thread of thought. The duality arising from the representations of one's own Ātman, conditioned by the phenomenon of "taking-oneself-for" in meditation, is eliminated the moment the meditating subject realizes that both representations refer to one and the same reality and that the differences due to the representations are only nominal ones. They are not rooted in the nature of the intended reality and are therefore considered to be unreal. Thus, the insight that arises after the "deconstruction" of the two representations is in itself not at all different from the awareness belonging to a consciousness—free-from-representations—that conditions them. This insight is therefore no longer a representation, but the consciousness it-

---

22 SPr I,100cd-102ab: *karmedaṃ tvatkṛtam api tvanmayaṃ yena mādhava* ‖ 100 ‖ *vilīnāhaṃkṛti tatas tvam eva pariśiṣyate* | *etāvataiva bhedo 'sya yad ahaṃmānitātmani* ‖ 101 ‖ *sā ced vilīnā tvadbhaktyā naṣṭo bhedaḥ sthitaikatā* | 102ab. (T)

23 SPr III,25cd-27; for text and translation cf. above pp. 269.

self of the Ātman, which arises as the "awareness-of-itself" of self-consciousness.

One thinks of Ludwig Wittgenstein, who substantiates the same problem at the end of his treatise in another perspective and in a different understanding of life.

> There are, indeed, things that cannot be put into words. They make themselves *manifest.*[24] They are what is mystical. (6.522) [...]
>
> My propositions are elucidatory in this way: he who understands me finally recognizes them as senseless, when he has climbed out through them, on them, over them. (He must so to speak throw away the ladder, after he has climbed up on it.) He must transcend these propositions, and then he will see the world aright. (6.54) [25]

In both authors there is noticeable, even if not *expressis verbis*, that particular phenomenon of speech from which an understanding of "religion" arises. In experiencing language and its inherent dialectics—as intended for the *presence* of the one evoked by the language of "religion"—the "hermetism" of the meaning of that which is articulated changes into the openness towards the *presence* of the one who is evoked by the articulation. This is the one who remains transcendent to what is said; the one who, as Wittgenstein says, just *shows* itself, and of whom Vāmanadatta, from his perspective, can only say that he can appear only when the linguistically determined fact of being the phenomenon (*bhāva-*) is given up.

How is it possible, however, to eliminate the alienating phenomenal dimension of conceptual knowledge from linguistically conditioned knowing? This seems to be what is happening, if our attempt to understand Vāmanadatta is correct, in the language-dynamics of the meditative process, which occurs on the horizon of self-awareness. Starting from the phenomenal experience of faith and from what is inherent in linguistic expression, the consciousness of the subject is directed—by the "deconstruction" of what is directly expressed—towards that *of which* language speaks, no longer towards what it says. Thus, it becomes mythically present. The immediacy of transcendence

---

24 Emphasis is mine.

25 Wittgenstein, *Tractatus logico-philosophicus*, no. 6.522, 6.54.

occurs, which is no more expressible in language than it is in concepts of knowledge. Yet is there. As Wittgenstein says: it *shows* itself. What is it that shows itself? Inasmuch as consciousness no longer has not any "particularizing" content, not even in the sense of a reflective self-consciousness), the object of meditation is precisely that which is being encountered without being representational. It is the appearing one to whom the meditating subject turns in addressing it. For Vāmanadatta this is, of course, the infinity of consciousness, in its inexhaustible fullness, unlimited and differentiated from everything else, non-relativizable by anything, and metaphorically, as illumining and light-like as the Absolute. By the use of the metaphor he avoids being constrained by the limiting power of speech and concepts. But concerning this ultimately "non-expressible" in language experience, which changes into the monistically interpreted emancipation (*mukti*), Vāmanadatta, in the fourth *prakaraṇa* of his *Saṃvitprakāśa*, says the following:

> By means of your own Self, which has given up every ritual prescription (*kalpaḥ*), due to the [so-manifested] uniformity (*sāmyāt*), there occurs the cessation of the stream of psychic representations (*saṃkalpasantatiḥ*). When [this] uniformity has been fixed in the lotus of the heart by having firmly fastened [himself] in the middle of the lotus, [the meditating subject] reaches one's own, free-of-any-activity (*kalanā*) flawless nature (*tattvam*), of which consciousness is the proper form (*citsvarūpam*). ‖ 91cd-92 ‖
>
> When he does not want to gain anything [anymore] whatever is here [on earth], neither does he want to escape from it, nor does he want to do anything [and] his thinking is free from faults of hatred, then he, whose bounds have disappeared, reaches [his] proper form (*svarūpam*) due to this uniformity. ‖ 93‖
>
> When his mind is not as if obscured by a dark cloud (*meghaniṣanna-*), and wholeheartedly (*sakalātmavṛttyā*) does he no more desire to be and he, in spite of his efforts, does not attain a neutral view, then he approaches his own nature (*tattvam*), his perfect proper form. ‖ 94 ‖
>
> When he is unable to continue living (*viruddhavṛttiḥ*) and has understood his inborn nature, then having fulfilled everything in every manner and having been freed of all, [untouched] like the ether, verily with the pure

heart, similar to a flowing river [he] indeed comes to [his] proper form (*svaṃ rūpam*). ‖ 95 ‖

When he then reaches the uniformity in every respect, and does not feel any urge to go on in his body, nor in the heart, nor in the throat, nor in the head, [and] the activities of thinking outside and inside have ceased, then [his] ancient [genuine] form is attained. ‖ 96 ‖

[Then] he knows no differentiation whatsoever of sentient and non-sentient, indifferent, he feels no pulsation [of life] (*spandaḥ*) in the space of [his] heart, he, whose entire being is only light; then this ancient [genuine] form [of his] has been reached. ‖ 97 ‖ [26]

In a manner different from the one known from the excerpts discussed (in which the linguistic "alienation" of the transcendent God as the "world" was the central issue), the text conveys Vāmanadatta's ultimate, philosophically valid "mythisation" of God. Though God, as a mythical personhood, is present throughout the whole of *Saṃvitprakāśa* (in invocations of traditional piety in the religious encounter) He becomes the divine "Thou" by being addressed with the intimateness of the second person singular. He becomes radically de-mythologized (though not *expressis verbis*) in the above-quoted text, and also becomes—so to speak—"mystagogically" deepened in a new

---

[26] SPr IV,91cd-97: *svenātmanā sakalakalpanirākṛtena saṃkalpasaṃtatinivṛttir upaiti sāmyāt sāmyaṃ tathā hṛdayapadmasamāśrayeṇa | madhye nidāya kamalasya ca citsvarūpaṃ svaṇ tattvam eti vimalaṃ kalanāvimuktaḥ* ‖ 92 ‖ *nāyaṃ jighṛkṣati yadā kim apīha vastu no vā jahāti na cikīrṣati kiñcid eva | vidveṣadoṣaparivarjitacittavṛttiḥ sāmyāt svarūpam upayāti nivṛttabandhaḥ* ‖ 93 ‖ *nāyaṃ yadā bhavati meghaniṣannacitto no vā bubhūṣur api tatsakalātmavṛttyā | no madhyamām api dṛśaṃ pratiyāti yatnāt tattvaṃ tadā samupayāty akhilasvarūpam* ‖ 94 ‖ *tattvaṃ yadā nijam avaitya viruddhavṛttiḥ sarveṇa sarvaracitaṃ rahitaṃ ca sarvaiḥ | ākāśakalpam athavā calasindhutulyaḥ svaṃ rūpam eti hi tadā pariśuddhabuddhiḥ* ‖ 95 ‖ *sarvatra sāmyam upayāti yadā svadehe nādhikyam eti hṛdaye na ca kaṇṭhamū<r>dhnoḥ | saṃvidvicāraśithilā bahir antarasya prāptaṃ tadā bhavati rūpam idaṃ purāṇam* ‖ 96 ‖ *bhedaṃ na vetti jaḍacetanayor yadaiva na spandate hṛdayasadmani madhyasaṃstha[ḥ] | bhārūpamātrapariśeṣitasarvabhāvaḥ prāptaṃ tadā bhavati rūpam idaṃ purāṇam* ‖ 97 ‖. The quoted verses (91cd-97) are not part of Torella's manuscript. Therefore, I follow in this case only the printed version given by Mark S.G. Dyczkowski.

mythisation, due to ontological monism of Vāmanadatta. This mythisation is understood as the subject's own infinity, which manifests itself in the hour of the subject's death. God's reality is experienced as the "[lasting] inner nature" (*tattvam nijam*),[27] as "that, which is the very nature [of the subject]" (*tattvam ... akhilasvarūpam*)[28] and finally as "this ancient [genuine] form" (*rūpam idaṃ purāṇam*).[29]

The present textual passage apparently (though indirectly) speaks of the event of the intended ending the *saṃsāric* existence, which in that period—in Northern India, but also, though in less explicit terms, in Southern India—was known as an extraordinary power (*siddhi-*) of the tantric Sādhaka, as a ritual realization of the emancipation.[30] The content of the text's statements should not, in fact, be misunderstood as pious formulations, but must rather be taken literally. If one takes seriously the described condition of mind of the meditating subject, there can be no doubt that this makes further living impossible. And furthermore, if taken seriously at least, the ultimate remarks should be understood[31] as a phenomenological description of dying.

The existential condition of the subject in this (meditative) process is, however, not only an anticipation of emancipation in view of Vāmanadatta's monism, but also an attempt of an inexplicit new mythisation of God's transcendence. Such an attempt comes from the perspective that God remains inaccessible by both language and conceptual representation as the "totally different one". The decisive term in that attempt seems to be the one of *sāmya-*, which at first is translated here (perhaps uninformatively) as "uniformity" and eventually requires interpretation. What does *sāmya* mean in the present context?

In any case, due to the context, it is not to be assumed that the concept refers to a psychic attitude of the subject towards another (such as "equanimity", "indifference" or the like). In view of the finality of

---

27 SPr IV 95.

28 SPr IV 94.

29 SPr IV 96 and 97.

30 For the *Sāttvata-*, *Jayākhya-* and *Pādma-Saṃhitā*, cf. Schwarz Linder 2014: 281ff.

31 SPr IV 95-97.

the intended event, there is no other being. What seems to matter much more in the context, however, is the inner condition of the subject, which concerns the subject himself as such. This is especially noticeable when he gives up differentiating, particularizing language and wants to experience the unlimitedness and unity of his non-relativized reality. If this is true, then the context entails that the term does not mean a linguistically tangible factuality, but rather a meditative experience of the subject, in which he becomes conscious of the reality which reaches beyond conceptually differentiating representations, a reality which is no longer "denotable", yet one that is not nothing, and which corresponds to the experience of *vastu* as a level of meditation that is reached when one "goes beyond"[32] the phenomenal being (*bhāva-*).

This would mean that the "uniformity" (*sāmya*) in the sense of "unity" is the non-differentiation of the subject in himself as his unalterable nature, which is inalienable by language and no longer subject to the *a priori* forms of "object" and "subject".

Therefore it is the experience of the unity between the inherent consciousness of the subject and the divine being in meditation that is in no way experienced as different and thus as a limited reality, but is instead experienced as by nature *infinite* and beyond the *static* of a linguistically expressed fact. Yet this infinity of oneself is not the trivial negation of finitude, but is instead an evocation of the dynamic fullness of unlimited, infinite, ever-renewing actuality of the subject. Through the linguistic delimitation of a definite "what", this essence would be an unchangeable and static content of cognition. By *not not* being determined as such, the reality experienced by the subject appears as ever-new and therefore dynamic origin of consciousness (*saṃvit*).[33] This condition of the subject, about which it is here argued to be a final stage, is obviously to be understood as a further reflection

---

32 See above, p. 260ff.

33 See SPr I 25: "That which is free from the [*a priori*] form of object and subject and is producing reality (*bhāvakaḥ*), is you, O Vāsudeva; [and] therefore [you are] consciousness as the source [of everything]." *vedyavedakarūpābhyāṃ yac chūṇyaṃ bhāvakaṃ ca yat* | *tad eva vāsudeva tvam tataḥ saṃvitsamudbhavaḥ* ‖ 25 ‖.

on a meditative experience and not as a description of the state of emancipation. This is substantiated for the first and only time in SPr IV, 92. It means that it has a function of mythisation, which is supposed to enable an encounter with transcendence, a mythisation by which transcendence gets a "face" and thus structures the theism of the Pāñcarātra monistically. According to Vāmanadatta: the God, in His relationality, already escapes in the *saṃhitā*s due to both the concrete personal representation already in them and the relatively non-specific metaphor of light (from a concrete personalized representation). This, for Vāmanadatta, is the eschatologically expected infinity of the subject "mythically present", in which the subject dissolves in his own emancipation.

Bibliography

Primary Literature

SPr

Saṃvitprakāśa, Vāmanadatta: *Saṃvitprakāśa by Vāmanadatta*. Edited with English introduction by Mark S. G. Dyczkowski. Varanasi 1990.

Secondary Literature

Oberhammer 2005

Gerhard Oberhammer, Überlegungen zur Hermeneutik religiöser Traditionen. In: Torsten Larbig, Siegfried Wiedenhofer (eds.), *Kulturelle und religiöse Traditionen. Beiträge zu einer interdisziplinären Traditionstheorie und Traditionsanalyse.* [Studien zur Traditionstheorie 1]. Münster: LIT Verlag, 2005, 191–211.

Oberhammer 2016

Monistische Gotteslehre und Spiritualität Vāmandattas. Ein religionshermeneutischer Versuch. [Publications of the de Nobili Research Library, Occasional Paper 9]. Wien 2016.

Renou 1957
Louis Renou, *Terminologie grammaticale du sanskrit.* [Bibliothèque de l'Ecole des Hautes Etudes 4, Section Sciences Historique et Philologiques 280/282]. Paris: Librarie ancienne honor Champion 1957.

Schwarz Linder 2014
Silvia Schwarz Linder, *The Philosophical and Theological Teachings of the Pādmasaṃhitā.* [Sitzungsberichte der Österreichischen Akademie der Wissenschaften, Philosophisch-Historische Klasse 853]. Vienna: Austrian Academy of Sciences Press 2014.

(T)
Critical edition of the *Saṃvitprakāśa* (up to IV,55) by Raffaele Torella (T).

Wittgenstein 1960
Ludwig Wittgenstein, *Tractatus Logico-philosophicus. Diaries 1914–1916 Philosophische Untersuchungen.* Frankfurt am Main: Suhrkamp 1960.

Gérard Colas

Evolution of deism and theism up to the 12th century: Some considerations

Problems related to terminology

One of the problems in interpreting pre-13th century Indian metaphysical conceptions concerns the applicability of terms such as theology, theism and atheism. The values attached to these terms also vary according to the scholars' personal views or their professional affiliation to a particular academic discipline. A specialist of Indian logic, for example, describes Udayana's approach as a rational theology.[1] A theologian designates non-dualist Advaita as a theology.[2] An Indian philosopher[3] refuses to call Viśiṣṭādvaita a theology, arguing that it is philosophy. The common designation of Mīmāṃsā as atheist is perhaps motivated by the wish to show that ancient Indian systems could be perfectly "rationalist"; this as a reaction against the prevalent belief that all Indian philosophy is theistic and therefore does not meet the rational prerequisites of Western philosophy. Anthropologists and ethnographers working on India seem to adopt yet another attitude: they often designate as theological any text or human discourse involving metaphysical aspects.

Hasty and indiscriminate labelling of Indian speculative systems as theologies leads one to the misconception that all metaphysical approaches which demonstrate the existence of a supreme creator-God are invariably sectarian or religious. Moreover, it overlooks the difference,

---

1 See the title of G. Chemparathy's work on Udayana's *Nyāyakusumāñjali* (1972): "An Indian Rational Theology".

2 Clooney 1993: 26.

3 R. Balasubramanian, in a conversation in Chennai (January 2013).

not explicit in the texts, between two conceptions: that of a creator-God as a generic or paradigmatic model for the various sectarian creator-gods, and that of a metaphysical creator-God beyond sectarian gods. Although the cryptic refutation of creator-God in the early Buddhist texts does not reveal the exact nature of the object of their criticism, it seems that the Buddhist works up to 6th century targeted the paradigmatic conception of creator-God.

This paper will try to throw light on the subtle distinction between some conceptions of creator-God in India up to the 12th century, and the evolution of the debates on this topic. It does not intend to give an exhaustive account of all available views[4] but aims to offer a hypothetical framework for further research in this field.

Deism

I propose to introduce the notion of "deism" as a working concept to describe the Indian systems of thought which, on the basis of reasoning and not belief, accept the concept of a creator-God that is different from the sectarian notions of creator-gods like Śiva and Viṣṇu. Generally called Īśvara (or Īśa) in the texts, this creator-God is not the object of any specific belief, devotion or ritual.

This deism is to a certain extent comparable to the deism of 18th-century Europe, the historical context being, of course, completely different. Many European thinkers of the 18th century believed that the notion of God was necessary in order to explain the creation and existence of the universe. Adopting a purely rational approach, not subscribing to the tenets or rituals of any revealed religion,[5] they often strongly criticized Christian religion. Another feature of European deism was that it was not unique; there were various deisms whose definition and

4 Mīmāṃsaka and Jaina positions, for instance, are not examined here. Only a few Buddhist views are taken into account (see Jackson 1986: 317–323, 335–338, for some Buddhist and non-Buddhist views).

5 For example, Voltaire's notion of *dieu horloger*, God clockmaker.

content varied according to authors.[6] In contrast with 18th-century European deism, Indian deism did not defy established religion. On the contrary, it appears to have developed as a philosophical compromise to defend religious practices, as seen in the œuvre of Udayana.

Theism

The term theism in this paper will designate any approach that is devotional and associated with a specific divine form. This form can be a god like Viṣṇu, Śiva, Brahmán (nom. Brahmā), or a particular god-form like Kṛṣṇa, a temple deity with a local name and origin. Theism, based on belief, is closely associated with devotional, ritual and social tradition, and is nourished by religious literature like Purāṇic stories and devotional hymns. But the expression "Hindu theism", as one would speak of Christian theism, is not suitable in the Indian context. The vast majority of Hindus worshipped a multitude of gods and did not believe in the existence of a unique God over and above the particular deity or deities which they venerated.

Theisms could also form the basis of speculative systems that were theologies which often used argumentative styles and were in debate with non-theistic speculative systems. It is beyond the scope of this contribution to examine the innumerable definitions of theology. In this contribution, theology signifies a speculative system that legitimates theism in an intellectually organized way. Thus, a system cannot be called theology merely because it defends and legitimates a corpus of scriptures, as Mīmāṃsā defends the Veda.

Brahman

The notion of Brahman, important for our discussion, is difficult to situate between those of deism and theism. It has no single unified meaning in the texts over the immense span of time from the Vedic to

---

6 Hazard 1963: 117–20, 382.

the modern period. In the oldest Vedic text, the *Ṛksamhitā*, it designates predominantly a formula or an enigma.[7] In the ancient Upaniṣads the word Bráhman uniformly denotes a supreme metaphysical principle above gods. Modern scholars often identify it either as a supreme god, or as an abstract metaphysical principle that is not really a god.

The question of a creator of the universe and of gods is present in the ancient Vedic texts. A hymn of the *Ṛksaṃhitā* speculating about the origin of the creation inquires into the principle, referred to as "the One", which preceded all gods. Certain hymns mention the "One" that is above the universe and rules it.[8] But these hymns do not identify the "One" with the Bráhman.

Sectarian theistic corpuses and their concepts of God

The situation in the second half of the first millennium was paradoxical to a certain extent. On the one hand, it saw the development of a deism advocating either the impersonal Bráhman above the gods or the creator-God Īśvara without sectarian affiliation. On the other hand, it was a period when major sectarian theistic corpuses, both devotional and ritual, were composed. For instance, most of the corpus of the *Nālāyira Tivyappirapantam* of the Vaiṣṇava saint-poets, the Āḻvārs, was composed from the 6th to the 9th century;[9] the Śaiva *Periyapurāṇam* was composed between the 6th and the 12th century.[10] Several works of the Purāṇic genre, centered around certain gods, like the *Harivaṃśa* (3rd–4th c.?),[11] were written before the second half of the millenium. As regards ritual texts, not many pre-8th century ritual Tantras and Saṃhitās are ex-

---

7 Renou 1978: 83–89.

8 See hymns 10.129, 8.58.2, 3.54.8. For the Bráhman (neutral), Brahmā (nom. of the masculine Brahmán) and the gods in early Vedism, cf. Steinkellner 2006: 17.

9 Hardy 1983: 269.

10 Zvelebil 1973: 186.

11 Couture 1991: 73.

tant but there are indications that several sectarian theistic scriptures, like some of Pāśupata and Pāñcarātra followers, were composed before the 8th century. Around the end of the first millenium, sectarian traditions had built theologies for their adherents. These consist of, for example, the brief "Knowledge section" (*jñānapāda*) of the Vaikhānasa *Vimānārcanakalpa* or the voluminous *vidyāpāda* sections of certain Śaiva Tantras.

Ritual and other texts of the first millenium testify to the efforts to conceive the pantheon of gods in an organized way. Besides the well-known series of the Vaiṣṇava *avatāra*s and the concept of *trimūrti*, one may mention, for instance, the complex Pāñcarātra theogonic construction that hierarchizes various levels of divine presence and manifestation, *para*, *vyūha*s and *vibhavas*.[12] The pre-6th century *Vaikhānasasmārtasūtra* mentions the four divine aspects of Viṣṇu-Nārāyaṇa, namely Puruṣa, Satya, Acyuta, Aniruddha, which became a characteristic feature of the later theology of medieval Vaikhānasas.[13] These texts sometimes allot specific spiritual functions to distinct divine aspects. For example, the *Vaikhānasasmārtasūtra* seems to associate Viṣṇu more often with ritual action and Nārāyaṇa with meditation.[14]

Buddhism, creator-gods and creator-God up to the 6th century
Early Buddhism

The earliest Buddhism as illustrated in the older part of the Pāli canon was neither deist nor theist, nor could it be called atheist. These texts considered gods as forming a category of living beings like men, ghosts, animals, etc., that belonged to the cosmological organization of the universe. Gods live a long life but are doomed to die and are bound by *karman* like other beings.[15] They live in pure heavens away from the

---

12 *Sātvatasaṃhitā* 1; 9; etc.; Colas 2003: 235.

13 Colas 1996: 25, 110–115.

14 Colas 1996: 27.

15 *Vibhaṅga* 18.6, pp. 422–426; *Mahāvibhāṣā* (1st c. CE?, available in Chinese version), according to *EIP* 7: 526; McDermott 1983: 173.

ordinary world; they converse, see, have sexual activity, etc.[16] The Buddhist attitude vis-à-vis the notion of a god being the creator of the universe may be considered as anti-speculative scepticism rather than atheism. This is illustrated, for example, in a story of the *Tevijjasutta* (*Dīghanikāya* 13). To two young Brahmins who believe that the god Brahmán is the lord (*issara*), maker, designer, chief, creator, master and father of all beings, but disagree about the path to reach him,[17] the Buddha declares such a quest to be futile. The *Devadahasutta* (*Majjhimanikāya* 101) reports a thesis that holds that "God" (*issara*) is one of the five alleged causes of pleasure and pain and concludes that the origin of suffering is only individual craving.[18]

Early stage of Buddhist criticism of the notion of creator-God up to the end of the 3rd century

The beginning of our era saw a split developing between speculative and religious Buddhism. The speculative scepticism towards the existence of a creator-God strengthened over the course of time in Buddhist literature. Concomitantly, the deification of the Buddha developed along with his iconic representation (attested from the 1st century BCE).[19] The tendency to puranicize and iconify the Buddha and his mythology grew with Mahāyāna, following patterns found in non-Buddhist religious movements. Even though the Buddha was never considered as creator-God, non-Buddhists as well as Buddhists came to consider him

---

[16] Vasubhadra's *Caturāgamavibhāga* (350 CE?; available in Chinese version), summarized in *EIP* 8: 353 (for the date, p. 747, fn. 409).

[17] Hayes 1988: 6–7. For a discussion about Bráhman (neutral) and Brahmán (masculine, nominative Brahmā) in early Buddhism, see Maithrimurthi 1999: 14–17.

[18] Hayes 1988: 6–9.

[19] Colas 2012: 94. For the tension between anti-deism and the deification of Buddha, see Steinkellner 2006: 21–22.

as the god of Buddhists.[20] We also see a parallel development of beliefs about *bodhisattvas* and Kṛṣṇa.[21] The progressive deification of the Buddha, on the other hand, was accompanied by the rise of Buddhist criticism of the very notion of creator-God. The criticism of creator-God apparently gained importance in the 2nd century CE. It had two aspects: mere rejection of the existence of any creator-God and rejection of the possibility of a god being the exclusive cause of the world. For example, the *Mahāvibhāṣā* (2nd c. CE?)[22] states that considering creator-God, etc., which are not causes, to in fact be causes is a wrong view.[23] Harivarman's *Satyasiddhiśāstra* (253 CE?)[24] lists the belief that a God is the cause of the world among the beliefs of heretics.[25] Aśvaghoṣa (1st–2nd c.), in his *Buddhacarita*, states that if a God (*īśvara*) were the creator, human effort would be purposeless.[26] Chapter 18 of the text, extant in a Chinese version (4th c.),[27] contains a long list of criticisms. If a creator-God were the cause, the world would be unchanging, no one would doubt his existence, he would not be resented by those

---

[20] See, for example, the installation ritual in the *Bṛhatsaṃhitā* (60.19) that is also meant for the icon of Buddha.

[21] The sports of the *bodhisattvas* in the *Vimalakīrtinirdeśasūtra* (250 CE?), *Saddharmapuṇḍarīkasūtra* (beginning of our era?) and *Sūtrālaṃkāra* (1st c. CE) are comparable to those of Kṛṣṇa in the *Harivaṃśa* (3rd or 4th c. CE?). The apparent moral laxism of *bodhisattvas* and Kṛṣṇa coexists with their detachment; the term *upāya* in both contexts refers to their extraordinary action to save human beings or help humanity to reach higher aims, etc. See Couture 1991: 53–57; Magnin 1998: 39–42; Colas 1998: 161–162.

[22] *EIP* 7: 511. For the dates of authors mentioned in this contribution, see *EIP*, *Bibliography*.

[23] *EIP* 7: 517.

[24] Also known as *Tattvasiddhi*. *EIP* 8: 255.

[25] 3.2, p. 306, in the Sanskrit text reconstructed from the Chinese translation.

[26] *Buddhacarita* 9.63.

[27] See Willemen (2009: xvi–xvii) for the date of the Chinese version and the question of its fidelity to the original. References to chapter 18 in the present contribution are to his translation.

who face suffering; he would not be "Sovereign" if he were to produce ceaselessly with toil or be obliged by an intention; and it would be a childish action if he produced without an intention; creating suffering or happiness under the sway of love and hate, he would not be "Sovereign", etc.[28] The other aspect of Buddhist criticism was that a creator-God could not be the *only* cause of the universe. For example, the *Akṣaraśataka*, attributed to Āryadeva (*fl.* 180 CE?), states that "God", along with mind, space and time are "relative causes" and being "subjected to existence", they are non-eternal.[29]

Buddhist criticism of the notion of creator-God from the 4th to the 6th century

Buddhist criticism of the notion of creator-God grew in the 4th and 5th centuries. However, the attacks of Buddhist scholars were not uniform; some were mild, some more structured and direct. According to Buddhaghosa's *Visuddhimagga* (5th c.), for example, to believe that this world is caused by a creator-God (*issara*), primordial matter (*padhāna*), time (*kāla*), nature (*sabhāva*) and so on, is to consider as a reason that which is not.[30] Buddhaghosa also states that the conditioned production (*paṭiccasamuppāda*) is caused by ignorance, etc., and not by a creator-God. Ignorance again is the source of the belief that the self, atoms, a creator-God, etc. are the cause of a body that arises with a new birth.[31]

---

[28] *Buddhacarita* 18.21-32. Johnston (1936b: 53–54), on the basis of the Chinese and Tibetan translations, translates *īśvara* by "a Creator", which seems to refer to the paradigmatic notion of creator-God (see his fn. 1, p. 53). According to Willemen's translation from Chinese (2009: 131), this passage deals with "the god Īśvara", that is, a specific god.

[29] Translated from a Chinese version by Gokhale 1930: 7. Āryadava is attributed with another text refuting Īśvara, the *Skhalitapramathanayuktihetusiddhi* (Qvarnström 1989: 63, fn. 15).

[30] *Visuddhimagga* 16, p. 511. See *Śvetāśvataropaniṣad* 1.2, which states that neither time, nature, fate, chance, elements, a womb, a person nor a combination of these can be the cause.

[31] *Visuddhimagga* 17, pp. 528 and 544.

The creator-God, etc. does not exist[32] apart from name and form (*nāma-rūpa*). He who searches for spiritual liberation should consider that all formations (*saṅkhara*) are "alien, empty, vain, void, ownerless, with no Overlord (*issara*), with none to wield power over them, and so on."[33] Here Buddhaghosa does not directly criticize the notion of creator-God, be it a non-sectarian God or other.

The criticism of some other authors was more direct, even though the topic was not central to their works. A passage of the *Yogācārabhūmi*[34] attributed to Asaṅga (4th–5th c.)[35] refutes the existence of a God (*īśvara*) as creator of the universe, arguing that such a God cannot be a part of the universe that he himself had created; he would be bound by a purpose or, if the creation were accidental, he would not be the creator of the universe. Again, God and universe would be a tautology if God alone were the creator, and he would cease to be the creator if he depended on something other than himself for creation, etc.[36]

In the *Abhidharmakośa*, Vasubandhu (said to be Asaṅga's younger brother) rejects the thesis that a God (*īśvara*), etc. could be a unique cause of the universe;[37] moreover, it would presuppose the existence of an eternal self.[38] A discussion between the Buddhist and a theistic (or deistic?) opponent in the *Abhidharmakośabhāṣya*[39] (whose attribution to Vasubandhu is debated) is important in the history of Buddhist attacks against the notion of creator-God, for it synthetizes the arguments on this topic: if the cause of the universe were unique, all things would

---

32 Ibid.19, p. 598.

33 Ibid. 21, p. 652 (Bhikkhu Ñāṇamoli's translation, p. 680).

34 *Bahubhūmikavastu*, chapters 3–5 [*Savitarkādibhūmi*], pp. 144–145.

35 For the problems related to this attribution, see Schmithausen 1987: 183–193.

36 Analysis and translation of this passage in Chemparathy 1969: 86–89, 94–96.

37 *Abhidharmakośa* 2.64.

38 Ibid. 5.8.

39 In the commentary on 2.64, pp. 279–281.

emerge simultaneously, but it is seen that things arise in succession; if succession in creation were due to the succession in the wishes of the unique God, then plurality of wishes would presuppose plurality of causes, and if wishes were simultaneous, the cause (God) would be unique (which would bring one back to the starting point of this reasoning). Other arguments are: that if a God created for his own pleasure, he would not be sovereign (*īśvara*) with regard to his pleasure and other entities, for he would depend on means like creation; that this creation for pleasure would imply cruelty because it also includes hells where creatures suffer; that the presence of auxiliary causes, if any, is a mere matter of belief; that their existence would mean that such a God is not the unique cause of the universe; etc. Some of these objections, such as the cruelty of a God who creates suffering and the contradiction between his alleged eternity and the temporariness of his creation, often recurred in the following centuries.[40]

It is difficult to decide whether the term *īśvara* in this context refers to the notion of a supreme creator-God above other gods or to a quintessential concept applicable to all creator-gods. Does Hiun-tsang in the 7th century interpret this passage of the *Bhāṣya* as a rejection of both deistic and theistic creators?[41] In commenting on this passage in the 9th century, Yaśomitra (*fl.* 850) seems to interpret the term *īśvara* as a quintessential concept which could apply to creator-gods such as Mahādeva or Vāsudeva. It is not certain as to whether or not these later interpretations reflect the meaning of *īśvara* as intended by the *Abhidharmakośa* passage and its *Bhāṣya*.

If the hypothetical date (4th c.) of the *Abhidharmakośabhāṣya* is confirmed and if its criticism targeted a metaphysical deistic notion of a creator-God above sectarian gods, it proves that this notion was a known speculative position by that time. But the question would be, who were the followers of this position? Naiyāyikas do not seem to

---

[40] See also Hayes 1988: 10–18.

[41] Unfortunately, La Vallée Poussin's translation does not help to make this point clear: "Que les chose soient produites par une cause unique, par Dieu, Mahādeva ou Vāsudeva, c'est inadmissible pour plusieurs raisons" (translation by La Vallée Poussin, p. 311).

have adopted it before the 6th century although the notion of creator-God is referred to in the *Nyāyasūtras* (1st–3rd c.).[42]

That the Buddhist attack against the creator-God hypothesis gathered importance at the beginning of the 5th century is proved by works like the *Īśvarakartṛtvanirākṛtiḥ viṣṇor ekakartṛtvanirākaraṇa.*[43] In spite of its title,[44] this short tract (tentatively dated around 400)[45] does not refute either Viṣṇu's creatorship or that of any other religious god.[46] The notion of Īśvara as creator-God (*kartṛ*) is disproved pointing out contradictions. For example, such a divine person can create neither an already known entity (like man, for instance) nor an unknown entity (for instance, oil extracted from sand or wool growing on tortoise); both the hypotheses of the creation or non-creation of that creator lead to contradiction.

Similar criticisms continued in the 6th century with Bhavya, who, in his *Madhyamakahṛdaya*, refuted the notion of creator-God (*īśvara*) identified with such gods as Viṣṇu. A passage of chapter 3 (verses 215-224) refutes the notion of creator-God and concludes that time, *puruṣa*, matter (*pradhāna*), atoms or Viṣṇu cannot be the cause of this world. The Vedānta position criticized in chapter 8 (*Vedāntatattvaviniścaya*)

---

42 Colas 2011: 47–48.

43 Edition and translation in Stcherbatsky 1975 (1969): 1–11. Analysis and translation in Chemparathy 1969: 89–94, 97–99. Stcherbatsky translates *īśvara* as "God". Chemparathy's summary tends to render *īśvara* as "the Iśvara" while his translation of the text uses "Īśvara" without article, that is, as a proper name.

44 This is the title as it appears in the colophon (Stcherbatsky 1975: 11). Chemparathy 1969 (see fn. 23, p. 89) retains the title *Viṣṇor ekakartṛtvanirākaraṇa*; La Vallée Poussin and von Glasenapp refer to the same text under the name of *Īśvarakartṛtvanirākṛtiḥ*.

45 Perhaps erroneously attributed to Nāgārjuna, it could have been authored by one of his disciples (*EIP* 9: 100), or by a Nāgārjuna who lived in the 7th century (see the discussion in Chemparathy 1969: 90–92).

46 The term *īśvara* having a generic meaning, the text could lend itself to debates against any sectarian opponent, including Vaiṣṇavas as suggested by the title.

appears to be based on the *Śvetāśvatara-Upaniṣad* and the *Gauḍapādīyakārikā*.[47] According to Bhavya, the Vedāntins call the supreme creator-God by different names: *puruṣa*, *ātman*, Īśvara, Maheśvara.[48] Though he is one, he exists in all embodied beings. All-pervasive and eternal, he is the agent (*kartṛ*) and enjoyer (*bhoktṛ*) of the universe, without being defiled by it. Bhavya naturally refutes the existence of any self, as well as the all-pervasiveness, eternality, agenthood and enjoyerhood attributed to that self.

Chapter 9 criticizes the Hindu mythological gods Brahmán, Śiva and Viṣṇu, pointing out their immoral behaviour and incompetence to create the universe (verse 59). The double form of Viṣṇu, higher and incarnated, is rejected with the argument that incarnations would make him impermanent. Bhavya also criticizes the existence of a creator-God in addition to *karman*; the production of variegated effects by a unique god; the contradiction between the admission of a creator-God as a subtle partless entity and its omnipresence in the gross and manifold world; the notion of creation by God for his own pleasure (because dependence on his own self or on another entity for pleasure would jeopardize his status of being almighty); etc., and he mocks the cruelty of such a God (identified as Rudra) that delights in the creation of hell and the sufferings of human beings.

Sectarian theism is used as an argument to refute the notion of creator-God in a text dated back to the 6th century, the *Abhidharmadīpa*. It is argued, for example, that the universe has no creator because the different sects reject others' Gods as creators of the universe: Bhāgavatas censure Śiva while Śaivas censure Viṣṇu.[49]

The Naiyāyika–Buddhist debate: Vaiśeṣika and Naiyāyika deism

The question of the existence of a creator-God does not appear, or is at best secondary, in the early speculations of the schools of Nyāya and

---

[47] Qvarnström 1989: 22, fn. 7.

[48] Qvarnström 1989: 62, fn. 13; 110.

[49] *EIP* 9: 551–552.

Vaiśeṣika. As regards gods in general, the early authors of these schools accepted them as a category of living beings. The *Vaiśeṣikasūtras* (probably 1st c.), as well as the early Vaiśeṣika author Candramati (probably 5th c.) do not refer to God. The notion of God appears but secondarily and casually in the *Nyāyasūtras* (1st–3rd c.). Three *sūtras* (4.1.19-21) examine the thesis that God (*īśvara*) is the cause of the universe. But it is not presented as being the thesis of the author of the *Nyāyasūtras*. Vātsyāyana's *Bhāṣya* (perhaps 5th c.), the first extant commentary on the *Nyāyasūtras*, seems to accept this as the Nyāya thesis, though not explicitly.[50]

The situation evolved in the 6th century with Praśastapāda and Uddyotakara, who were probably contemporaries of Bhavya. They clearly support the notion of a creator-God in their commentaries on the *Vaiśeṣika-* and *Nyāyasūtras*, without identifying this creator-God with any religious creator-God. According to Praśastapāda, God (Maheśvara) periodically dissolves the universe to give rest to souls, and re-creates it to allow souls to exhaust their *karman* through experience in the created world.[51] However, his function in the creation and destruction of the universe is limited. Firstly, because he operates according to the time cycles of destruction and creation, as well as the *karmans* of the individual souls. Secondly, because he entrusts the task of creating the material universe to a secondary god, Brahmán.[52] Thus his incorporality is not compromised. According to Uddyotakara, the activity of creation is God's very nature, but he cannot incessantly create the universe because he has to take into account aspects like the maturation of *karman*, etc. Uddyotakara rejects the notion of a god who creates out of fantasy or free will.[53]

---

50 Colas 2011: 47–48.

51 Some authors identify Maheśvara in this context as being Śiva: see Steinkellner 2006: 20.

52 Colas 2011: 48.

53 Ibid.

The situation takes a different turn in the 11th century with Udayana's *Nyāyakusumāñjali*. Udayana was a devout worshipper of Śiva,[54] as the introductory and concluding verses of several chapters in his *Nyāyakusumāñjali* and *Lakṣaṇāvali* show. But his personal belief and devotion do not interfere with his philosophical stand. The main aim of the *Nyāyakusumāñjali* is to establish the existence of the creator-God (*īśvara*) and his qualities through reasoning. Since that has already been accomplished by his predecessors, we may suppose that Udayana's redoubled attempt to establish deism was perhaps due to an external factor, ideological or religious.

It seems that the Nyāya-Vaiśeṣika authors from the 6th century to 11th century were keen that their deism should not be confused with ordinary theism or a mere belief in any god. In Praśastapāda's thesis, Brahmán is delegated to create, but the being who is responsible is the non-sectarian Īśvara. A significant aspect in this connection is the refusal of the Naiyāyikas to attribute a body to the creator-God. This refusal is understandable because they defined body as the receptacle of pleasure and pain, caused by the *karman* of the soul. It is unacceptable to the Naiyāyikas that a creator-God experience pain or be subject to the law of *karman*.[55] The absence of a body also distinguishes the creator-God from the Puraṇic or what we may call "religious" type of god, for example, an *avatāra*.[56]

But why did the Nyāya and the Vaiśeṣika schools introduce the notion of creator-God into their systems? Since the admission of a supreme deity sustained only by faith and religion was not acceptable to them, they had to defend the notion of creator-God only through reasoning. In this process they constantly faced criticisms connected with this notion, such as the creation of the universe by a creator-God with-

---

54 Chemparathy 1972: 32.

55 Colas 2011: 50–52. However Udayana admits that the creator-God can take a body of manifestation (*nirmāṇakāya*) in certain occasions, for instance, for teaching or emitting the Veda, an idea that is also found in his predecessor Jayanta Bhaṭṭa (Chemparathy 1972: 153; Colas 2004: 160).

56 Colas 2011: 50.

out his possessing a body.[57] Was the notion of creator-God introduced and demonstrated through reasoning in response to socio-religious compulsion? The importance given to deism in the *Nyāyakusumāñjali* seems to point to this. It answers the criticisms of that epoch that rites are motivated by the quest for social prestige, that they are deceitful and are means to self-interest and influence. The *Nyāyakusumāñjali* supports sacrifices and religious foundations (*iṣṭāpūrta*). It also legitimates icon consecration, but on different lines from those of priestly circles.[58]

Buddhist scholastic anti-deism from the 7th century

The Nyāya-Vaiśeṣika effort to build a deism by presenting a philosophical creator-God different from the common religious gods, in turn influenced the attitude of Buddhist scholastic authors, who strengthened their arguments against the metaphysical creator-God. A milestone in the history of Buddhist anti-deism are several verses of the Dharmakīrti's *Pramāṇavārttika* (600–660).[59] Bhavya's lengthy attacks on the belief in creator-gods were often sarcastic and were not developed on logical grounds. Dharmakīrti's refutation of creator-God in the *Pramāṇasiddhi* chapter is short but well-argumented.[60] The aim of this chapter is to demonstrate that Buddha is the authority (*pramāṇa*) for those who strive for spiritual liberation. In this context, Dharmakīrti rejects the authority of God, Īśvara. His criticism concerns the contradiction between the ephemeral character of the effects and the alleged permanent character of divine cause. These verses also challenge the causality attributed to God's invisible power.[61] However, Dharmakīrti neither explicitly records nor criticizes several features of Praśastapāda's and Uddyotakara's con-

---

57 Chemparathy 1972: 140–148, 152–154.

58 Colas 2004: 160–164.

59 Hayes 1988: 5.

60 See Jackson 1999: 477.

61 For a detailed analysis and study of this passage, see Jackson 1986: 323–335; Jackson 1999; Steinkellner 2006: 27–30.

ceptions which could have been easy targets for Buddhist criticism. For as we saw above, according to Praśastapāda and Uddyotakara, God's sovereignty is constrained by various factors such as compliance with cycles of creation and dissolution, assistance by gods like Brahmán and dependence on *karmic* maturation of human souls.

According to modern research Dharmakīrti inaugurated a Buddhist scholastic tradition of systematically and logically refuting the deistic notion of creator-God.[62] His effective criticism helped to a certain extent to give shape, by reaction, to the definition of and arguments for the creator-God by the Naiyāyikas. Dharmakīrti's anti-deistic arguments were followed and developed in the 8th century by Śāntarakṣita in his *Tattvasaṅgraha* and in the commentary on it by Kamalaśīla.[63] The non-existence of a creator-God, alongside the non-existence of a permanent soul, is one of the corollaries of the Buddhist theory of *pratītyasamutpāda*.[64] In this context, the *Tattvasaṅgraha* refutes others' metaphysical explanations of the universe, deistic as well as theistic. The refutation includes theories of *prakṛti*, creator-God (who is the instrumental but not the material cause of the universe as in Naiyāyika theory), the pair God–Prakṛti (a thesis attributable to the deistic Sāṃkhya) and the *śabdabrahman* (of Bhartṛhari's followers). Śāntarakṣita's refutation of *puruṣa*,[65] who is both instrumental and material cause of the universe, ends with the statement that other creator-gods like Viṣṇu, Brahmán, etc. stand refuted by the same arguments: if this *puruṣa* creates prompted by another being or under the impulse of the invisible factor (*adṛṣṭa*), then he is not independent; if he creates out of compassion, it would mean that suffering beings existed before his creation and it is also not reasonable for them to suffer after his creation; if he creates out of sport (*krīḍā*), he is dependent on pre-existent means of sport; if he creates automatically without any specific intention, he cannot be considered intelligent. It should be noted that Śāntarakṣita distinguishes between the

---

62 See Jackson 1999: 486.

63 *Tattvasaṅgraha* 1–6.

64 For this notion, see, for instance, Stcherbatsky 1923: 28–31; Williams 1974; Shulman 2008: 315–317 (bibliography).

65 *Tattvasaṅgraha* 6, 153–170.

creator-God of the Naiyāyikas and a creator-God called *puruṣa* that could be understood as the paradigm for all other creator-gods. The Buddhist criticism of the notion of Īśvara creator of the universe continued up to the 11th century in the works of authors such as Śaṅkaranandana[66] (10th–11th c.) and Jñānaśrīmitra (11th c.).[67]

Nyāya's reaction to anti-deistic Buddhist attacks around the 11th century

The Naiyāyikas of the 11th century, more concerned with the attacks from Mīmāṃsā,[68] do not seem to have paid much attention to the Buddhist criticisms of deistic conceptions. Udayana and Yāmuna, both of the 11th century, attest to this fact. In his *Ātmatattvaviveka*, which deals with the notion of individual soul, Udayana refutes Buddhist arguments, including those of Jñānaśrīmitra, against the existence of *ātman*. But in his *Nyāyakusumāñjali*, which is intended to prove the existence of creator-God, he rarely mentions the Buddhist point of view. It should also be noted that he does not refer to Jñānaśrīmitra's objection to the uniqueness of Īśvara.[69] Yāmuna, the Vaiṣṇava logician, in his *Īśvarasiddhi* reports the Mīmāṃsaka rejection of the notion of creator-God, but not that of the Buddhists.[70] Thus while Buddhist scholars were eager to demolish the Naiyāyika concept of creator-God in the 11th

---

66 Cf. Krasser 2002.

67 See his *Īśvaravāda*.

68 In Jayanta Bhaṭṭa's defence of deism (9th c.), which answers criticism from Mīmāṃsakas, Buddhist criticism of deism is not the principal target: see *Nyāyamañjarī*, pp. 175–188. For the slow response of Nyāya-Vaiśeṣika to Dharmakīrti's critique, see Jackson 1986: 335, 337.

69 Chemparathy 1972: 179.

70 One may say that their view is discussed in a missing part of this work reputed to be incomplete, but the beginning of the *Īśvarasiddhi* only mentions the Mīmāṃsaka as the opponent to be rejected and not the Buddhist, whereas Yāmuna announces his aim of refuting Buddhism at the very beginning of his *Ātmasiddhi* and deals with it in several parts of that work.

century, it remains to be proved that the Naiyāyikas of the same period cared about the Buddhist opinion on *īśvara*, even though they were engaged in refuting the Buddhist view of individual soul.

Brahman and Īśvara

Brahman (= the neutral Bráhman in the following lines), said to be the ultimate reality and the origin of the universe in the Upaniṣads, is a central concept in all Vedāntic schools. It has been interpreted differently, sometimes unconnected with any deism and theism, sometimes connected with a deistic view and sometimes with a theistic one.

According to Bhartṛhari (5th c.), who is the heir of two traditions, grammar and Upaniṣads, Brahman is the central metaphysical notion. It is eternal, the essential reality Speech, the indestructible Phonem that transforms into the universe of objects. Even though Brahman is the origin of the manifested universe,[71] it is not a personal god or creator-God; the manifestation of the world is nothing but the unfolding of Brahman's own nature.

The perspective of Śaṅkara (8th c.) on the other hand, meets two concerns: to preserve the metaphysical principle Brahman detached from all religion and to justify a deistic principle that legitimates all rites and religious conceptions. As is well known, Śaṅkara distinguishes between three levels of existence. The *pāramārthika* level is that of the "absolutely real", that of Brahman, the supreme and non-dual self. The *vyāvahārika* level is the practical or "practically existent" level, in which Brahmanical values and enjoined socio-religious practices of everyday life have validity. The third level, that of error and dreams (*prātibhāsika*), only has reality as long as it lasts. Śaṅkara considers Brahman as the only metaphysical reality. It is both the material and the efficient cause of all existence.[72] But cause and effect are in reality not

---

[71] *Vākyapadīya* 1.1–4.

[72] *Brahmasūtrabhāṣya*^{S} 1.4.23.

different because, from the transcendental point of view, effect is an illusionary superimposition upon the cause.[73]

Thus, Śaṅkara has no need for a creator-God from the highest metaphysical point of view, but still accepts it at the practical level. He identifies the creator-God Īśvara with Brahman possessing attributes (*saguṇa*), citing the Upaniṣadic passages that speak of Brahman having attributes (*saguṇa-śruti*) in support of his notion of Īśvara. Īśvara is both the material and efficient cause of the universe.[74] He creates the world as a pastime (*līlā*) but can be charged with neither partiality nor cruelty, for he takes into account factors like *karman*. Being their cause,[75] Īśvara is distinct from, and above ordinary gods. He is not considered as quintessential of the sectarian creator-gods, such as Viṣṇu, nor is he identified with Vedic gods. Further, Īśvara cannot have a body, for that would imply his transmigration.[76] The notion of Īśvara, the creator-God, helps Śaṅkara explain the appearance of the world while at the same time preserving the unity and absoluteness of the non-dual Brahman. Since Śaṅkara relied on the authority of the Upaniṣads and because, according to him, a creator-God pertains to the level of relative reality, unlike the Naiyāyikas he has no need for logical proofs to demonstrate the existence and activities of Īśvara.

We may consider the *bheda-abheda* philosophy of Bhāskara (between 8th and 11th c.) as a transitional doctrine between Śaṅkara's monism and Rāmānuja's theism. Here the term *transitional* is not taken in a historical sense, for upholders of *bheda-abheda* preceded Śaṅkara.[77] According to Bhāskara, Brahman is both: the material and efficient cause of the universe which is real, neither a lower reality nor

---

73 Ibid. 2.1.14-15.

74 Ibid. 2.2.37.

75 Ibid. 2.1.34.

76 Ibid. 2.2.40. When Śaṅkara defends the concept that gods possess a body (*vigraha*) (1.3.26–33), he refers not to Īśvara the creator-God, but to the Vedic gods (Colas 2004: 156–157).

77 See, for instance, Ingalls 1954: 294. For an introduction to Bhāskara's philosophy, see Ingalls 1967 and Rüping 1977.

illusory. Bhāskara names Brahman "Īśvara" and "Supreme self" (*paramātman*).[78] It is both cause and effect,[79] because it transforms itself into the universe. It possesses two powers (*śakti*): the power of being enjoyed (*bhogya*), which transforms into insentient entities like space, and the power of being the enjoyer (*bhoktṛ*), which exists as the individual soul (*jīva*). Just as the sun, having sent its rays retracts them, the supreme God (*parameśvara*) deploys his capacity of infinite variety and retracts it.[80] Bhāskara accepts the view of the Pāñcarātra according to which the god Vāsudeva is the material and efficient cause of the universe because it has scriptural sanction, but he rejects its thesis that individual souls originate from the *paramātman*.[81]

At the beginning of the 12th century, Rāmānuja went one step further, from deism to theism. In his *Śrībhāṣya* on *Brahmasūtra*, he identifies Brahman with Īśvara who is Viṣṇu, also named Vāsudeva and Nārāyaṇa.[82] Rāmānuja believes, like Śaṅkara, that Brahman can be proved to exist only through Scriptural authority, not by the other means of knowledge like perception or inference, which are inadequate in this matter.[83]

Brahman-Viṣṇu is the instrumental and material cause of the world; he is both cause and effect; he manifests the world to enable individual souls to experience their merits and demerits.[84] He has conscious beings and non-conscious things as his body[85] but this does not affect his immutability.[86] Rāmānuja's definition of the body as a substance that is

---

78 Bhāskara's *Brahmasūtrabhāṣya*^{B} 1.3.30, p. 65.

79 Ibid. 1.1.4, p. 19.

80 Ibid. 1.4.25, p. 85; 2.1.27.

81 Ibid. 2.2.41.

82 *Śrībhāṣya* 1.1.1, p. 223[a]; 224[a]; p. 49[b]; also p. 43[b].

83 Ibid. 1.1.3, p. 119[b]-120[b]; 123[b], 127[b]. Rāmānuja uses preferably the term *śāstra*, which includes not only Veda, but also other texts like *Mahābhārata* and several Purāṇas.

84 Ibid. 1.1.1, pp. 77[b] and 37[b].

85 Ibid. 1.1.1, p. 76[b]. See also 1.1.1, p. 131[b].

86 Ibid. 1.1.1, p. 77[b].

completely and always capable of being controlled and supported by a sentient soul[87] wards off the objections that could arise with respect to God, namely the dependence of the body on *karman*, the presence in it of pleasure and suffering, etc. It is wide enough to include the possession of bodies by Viṣṇu during his incarnations and to conceive the universe of conscious and unconscious entities as his body. It is applicable to all sentient beings: other gods, human beings, ghosts, animals, etc. Thus the Nyāya-Vaiśeṣika criticism of the possession of a body by the creator-God does not apply to Rāmānuja's conception of the body;[88] Viṣṇu is different from ordinary gods even though they constitute his body along with other individual selves.[89] His nature is pure knowledge and he is not subject to *karman*, unlike the selves of gods, men, etc., whose embodiment is caused by *karman*.[90] Gods other than Viṣṇu are subject to transmigration like all embodied beings, demons, ghosts, men, animals and immovable things.[91]

Unlike Yāmuna, his predecessor, Rāmānuja did not rely merely on logical reasoning but built a new Vedāntic doctrine, centred on Brahman-Viṣṇu. He had to confine his discourse in the *Śrībhāṣya* to the topics and the nature of the text on which he was commenting. But his commentary on sūtras 2.2.39-42, which Śaṅkara and Bhāskara understood to refer to Pāñcarātra, gave him the opportunity to legitimate this Vaiṣṇava sect. He states that Nārāyaṇa, who is Brahman, is the author of the Pāñcarātra scriptures and that this system is incomparable, for it teaches the nature and mode of worshipping Nārāyaṇa.[92]

---

87 Ibid. 2.1.9, p. 222. For a discussion on the bodies and manifestations of Brahman-Viṣṇu according to Rāmānuja, see Colas, 2020.

88 See also *Śrībhāṣya* 1.1.3, pp. 131–132, and 2.2.36–37.

89 Ibid. 1.1.1, p. 69[b]; see also pp. 48[b], 49[b].

90 Ibid. 1.1.1, p. 45[b].

91 Ibid. 1.1.4, p. 163[b].

92 Ibid. 2.2.42, p. 329[b].

Conclusion

From the 5th to the 11th century, Bhartṛhari, various Nyāya-Vaiśeṣika authors, Śaṅkara and Bhāskara all built doctrines that did not have sectarian theistic affiliation. Their concept of a supreme being was established on structured reasoning, not religious faith, although Bhartṛhari, Śaṅkara and Bhāskara valued scriptural authority over logical reasoning. It is probable that the antagonistic forces of Buddhism and of Mīmāṃsā indirectly helped them to strengthen their argumentation to a certain extent, and up to a certain period.

Early Buddhism was not much concerned with theism or deism and refrained from speculating about notions such as creator-God. Buddhist criticisms of theism is seen to have emerged in the beginning of our era and gathered strength from the 4th to the 6th century, paradoxically at the time when Buddha came to be viewed as a god (though not as a creator-God). Buddhism criticized the generic notion of Īśvara creator-God, on the one hand, and creator-gods like Viṣṇu and Śiva, on the other. There is no definite proof that the early upholders of the notion of creator-God, which Buddhism criticized, were Naiyāyikas.

The progressive development of deism in Nyāya and Vaiśeṣika from the 6th century onwards forced Buddhism to concentrate its attacks on the metaphysical notion of Īśvara creator-God. Buddhist criticism continued up to the 11th century, but by then Nyāya-Vaiśeṣika was more preoccupied with the attacks from the Mīmāṃsakas in this regard than it was with those of the Buddhists. Nyāya-Vaiśeṣika speculation about creator-God culminated in Udayana's deism advocated in his *Nyāyakusumāñjali*.

Brahman was the cardinal notion in the works of Bhartṛhari and Śaṅkara. Bhartṛhari did not make room for the notion of Īśvara in his system, while Śaṅkara confined Īśvara to the limited field of empirical reality, clearly distinguishing him from other ordinary gods. He thus preserved a deism that could match that of the Nyāya-Vaiśeṣika, although their definition of Īśvara is not the same. Bhāskara did not make any distinction between the notions of Brahman and Īśvara. His doctrine was historically followed by what may be described as the transformation of deism into theism: Rāmānuja identified both Īśvara and Brahman as Viṣṇu.

While Vedāntic theistic philosophy gained ground after Rāmānuja with Madhva, Vallabha, Śrīkaṇṭha (*fl.* 1400?) and others, a deistic thought without specific religious affiliation persisted in various forms. Udayana had consolidated deism as a distinctive feature of his school; later Naiyāyikas perpetuated deism without developing it further. Buddhist anti-deism disappeared with Buddhism in most parts of India. Post-śaṅkarian non-dualism sometimes was influenced by devotional theism as was the case with Madhusūdana Sarasvatī, but mostly held deism and theism at bay, relegating them to the empirical level only. Mīmāṃsā maintained its rejection of all notion of creator-God. The *Sāṃkhyasūtra*s (perhaps 15th c.) were not just indifferent to the notion of a supreme God, they even rejected it. The ancient non-Vedāntic Vaiṣṇava and Śaiva theologies like Pāñcarātra, Vaikhānasa, Śaivasiddhānta, etc., also developed speculative, sometimes elaborate systems. But they were absent from supra-sectarian debates, the reasons for which can only be conjectural: possibly the vedicity of some of these theologies was an issue, or perhaps the sectarian metaphysical dogmas of some were not acceptable to all, and so on. Perhaps the purpose of these theologies was not to enter the field of formal scholastic debates, but rather to guide their respective religious communities and to assert their place among Hindu theisms.

Bibliography

Primary texts

Abhidharmakośa: *Abhidharmakośa* of Vasubandhu with *Bhāṣya* attributed to him and *Sphuṭārtha Commentary* of Ācārya Yaśomitra, 2 vols., ed. by Dwarikā Dās Śāstrī. [Bauddha Bharati Series 7-8]. Varanasi: Bauddha Bharati, 2008 (2nd ed.).

Brahmasūtrabhāṣya^B: *Brahmasūtrabhāṣya* of Bhāskara, ed. by Vindhyeśvarī Prasāda Dvivedin. [Chowkhamba Sanskrit Series 20]. Varanasi: Chowkhamba Sanskrit Series Office 1991.

Brahmasūtrabhāṣya[S]*: Brahmasūtrabhāṣya* of Śaṅkara, *with the Commentaries Bhāmatī, Kalpataru and Parimala*, ed. by Anantakrishna Shastri and Vasudev Laxman Shastri Pansikar. [Krishnadas Sanskrit Series 25]. Varanasi: Krishnadas Academy. 2000 (reprint).

Bṛhatsaṃhitā: Bṛhatsaṃhitā of Varāhamihira, ed. and transl. by M. R. Bhat, 2 vols, Delhi, 1981–1982.

Buddhacarita: Buddhacarita of Aśvaghoṣa. See E. H. Johnston 1936a, below.

Īśvarasiddhi: Īśvarasiddhi of Yāmuna. In: *Sri Yamunacharya's Siddhitraya with a Sanskrit Commentary by U. T. Viraraghavacharya, with an Introduction in English by R. Ramanujachari, and Translation in English by R. Ramanujachari and K. K. Srinivasacharya.* Madras: Ubhayavedanta Granthamala Book Trust. 1972, 87–98.

Īśvaravāda: Īśvaravāda of Jñānaśrīmitra. In: *Jñānaśrīmitranibandhāvali*, ed. by Anantalal Thakur. Patna: Kashi Prasad Jayaswal Research Institute 1959, 233–316.

Madhyamakahṛdaya: Madhyamakahṛdaya of Bhavya, ed. by C. Lindtner. [The Adyar Library Series 123]. Chennai: The Adyar Library and Research Centre 2001.

Nyāyamañjarī: Nyāyamañjarī of Jayanta Bhaṭṭa, vol. I, ed. by Sūryanārāyaṇa Śukla. [Kashi Sanskrit Series 106]. Benares: The Chowkhambha Sanskrit Series Office, 1936.

Nyāyasūtra: Nyāyasūtras and commentaries = Nyāyadarśana with Vātsyāyana's Bhāṣya, Uddyotakara's Vārttika, Vācaspati Miśra's Tātparyaṭīkā, and Viśvanātha's Vṛtti, ed. by Taranātha and Amarendramohan. Delhi 2003 (reprint of the 1st ed.: Calcutta, 1936–1944).

Sātvatasaṃhitā: Sātvatasaṃhitā with Alaśingha Bhaṭṭa's commentary, ed. by V. V. Dwivedi. [Library Rare Texts Publications Series 6]. Varanasi 1982.

Satyasiddhiśāstra: Satyasiddhiśāstra of Harivarman, Vol. I: Sanskrit Text, reconstructed by N. Aiyaswami Sastri. [Gaekwad's Oriental Series 159]. Baroda 1975.

Śrībhāṣya: Śrībhāṣya of Rāmānuja with Sudarśanasuri's *Śrutaprakāśikā*, ed. by U. T. Vīrarāghavācārya, Madras: Sri Visishtadvaita Pracharini Sabha 1989 (reprint; 1st ed.: 1967). Two volumes, each with separate pagination (I contains *Śrībhāṣya* 1.1 to 1.2; II contains 1.3 to 4.4); vol. I has three successive paginations: one in Arabic figures (editor's Sanskrit introduction, not referred to here), two in Nāgarī figures (here followed respectively by [a] and [b]).

Śvetāśvataropaniṣad: Śvetāśvataropaniṣad ed. and transl. by A. Silburn. Paris: Adrien-Maisonneuve, 1948.

Tattvasaṅgraha: Tattvasaṅgraha of Śāntarakṣita with Kamalaśīla's *Pañjikā* commentary, ed. by E. Krishnamacharya. [Gaekwad's Oriental Series 30-31]. Baroda 1926.

Vaikhānasasmārtasūtra: Vaikhānasasmārtasūtra (containing *Vaikhānasagṛhyasūtra* and *Vaikhānasadharmasūtra*), ed. by W. Caland, Calcutta, 1927.

Vākyapadīya: Vākyapadīya of Bhartṛhari, *Kāṇḍa I*, ed. by K.A. Subramania Iyer [Deccan College Monograph Series]. Poona: 1966.

Vibhaṅga: Vibhaṅga, ed. by C. Rhys Davids. [Pali Text Society, Text Series 144]. London: Pali Text Society 1978 (reprint).

Visuddhimagga: Visuddhimagga of Buddhaghosa, ed. by C.A.F. Rhys Davids, London: Pali Text Society, 2 vols., 1920–1921.

Yogācārabhūmi: Yogācārabhūmi of Asaṅga, ed. by Vidhushekhara Bhattacharya, Calcutta: University of Calcutta 1957.

Studies and translations

Chemparathy 1969
George Chemparathy, Two Early Buddhist Refutations of the Existence of Īśvara as the Creator of the Universe. In: *Wiener Zeitschrift für die Kunde Süd- und Ostasiens* 12-13 (1968-1969) 85–100.

Chemparathy 1972
Id., *An Indian Rational Theology. Introduction to Udayana's Nyāyakusumāñjali.* [Publications of the De Nobili Research Library 1]. Vienna: De Nobili Research Library 1972.

Clooney 1993
Francis X. Clooney, *Theology after Vedānta. An Experiment in Comparative Theology*. [Monumenta Indica Series 2]. Delhi: Sri Satguru Publications 1993.

Colas 1996
Gérard Colas, *Viṣṇu, ses images et ses feux. Les métamorphoses du dieu chez les vaikhānasa*. [Monographies n° 182]. Paris: Presses de l'École française d'Extrême-Orient 1996.

Colas 1998
Id., Jeux humains, jeux divins. Vues indiennes. In: F. Martin, J. Pigeot, K. Chemla (eds.), *Du divertissement dans la Chine et le Japon Anciens*: *"Homo Ludens Extrême-Orientalis"*. [Extrême-Orient/Extrême-Occident 20] Paris: Presses universitaires de Vincennes. 1998, 157–163.

Colas 2003
Id., History of Vaiṣṇava Traditions: An Esquisse. In: Gavin Flood (ed.), *The Blackwell Companion to Hinduism*. Oxford: Blackwell Publishing. 2003, 229–270.

Colas 2004
Id., The Competing Hermeneutics of Image Worship in Hinduism (Fifth to Eleventh Century AD). In: P. Granoff and K. Shinohara (eds.), *Images in Asian Religions: Texts and Contexts*, Vancouver/Toronto: UBC Press. 2004, 149–179.

Colas 2011
Id., God's Body: Epistemic and Ritual Conceptions from Sanskrit Texts of Logic. In: A. Michaels and C. Wulf (eds.), *Images of the Body in India*, London/New York/New Delhi: Routledge. 2011, 45–55.

Colas 2012
Id., *Penser l'icône en Inde ancienne*. [Bibliothèque de l'École des Hautes Études-Sciences religieuses 158]. Turnhout: Brepols 2012.

Colas 2020
Id., Le corps du Dieu créateur selon Rāmānuja: le dépassement d'un obstacle épistémologique dans la scolastique indienne. In: Émilie Aussant and G. Colas (eds.), *Les scolastiques indiennes: naissances, développements, interactions*. Paris: Publications de l'École Française d'Extrême-Orient 2020, 113–126.

Couture 1991
André Couture, *L'enfance de Krishna*, Paris: Les Presses de l'Université Laval/ Les Éditions du Cerf, Patrimoines Hindouisme.

EIP
Bibliography = Potter, Karl H., *Encyclopedia of Indian Philosophies. Bibliography.* Delhi: Motilal Banarsidass 1983 [2nd revised Edition].

EIP 7
EIP 7 = Potter, Karl H., with R.E. Buswell, P.S. Jaini and N. Ross Reat (eds.). 2006. *Encyclopedia of Indian Philosophies, vol. 7. Abhidharma Buddhism to 150 A.D.* Delhi: Motilal Banarsidass [Reprint 1st edition 1996].

EIP 8
EIP 8 = Potter, Karl H. (ed.). 2002. *Encyclopedia of Indian Philosophies, vol. 8. Buddhist Philosophy from 100 to 350 A.D.* Delhi: Motilal Banarsidass [Reprint 1st edition 1999].

EIP 9
EIP 9 = Potter, Karl H. (ed.). 2003. *Encyclopedia of Indian Philosophies, vol. 9. Buddhist Philosophy from 350 to 600 A.D.*, Delhi: Motilal Banarsidass.

Gokhale 1930
Vasudev Gokhale, *Akṣara-çatakam. The Hundred Letters. A Mādhyamaka Text by Āryadeva, after Chinese and Tibetan Materials, translated by Vasudev Gokhale*. Heidelberg: Institut für Buddhismus-Kunde 1930.

Hardy 1983
Friedhelm Hardy, *Viraha-bhakti. The Early History of Kṛṣṇa Devotion in South India*. Delhi: Oxford University Press 1983.

Hayes 1988
Richard P. Hayes, Principled Atheism in the Buddhist Scolastic Tradition. In: *Journal of Indian Philosophy* 16 (1988) 5–28.

Hazard 1963
Paul Hazard, *La pensée européenne au XVIIIe siècle de Montesquieu à Lessing*. Paris: Fayard 1963.

Ingalls 1954
Daniel H. H. Ingalls, Śaṅkara's Arguments against the Buddhists. In: *Philosophy East and West* 3 (1954) 291–306.

Ingalls 1967
Daniel H. H. Ingalls, Bhāskara the Vedāntin. In: *Philosophy East and West* 17 (1967) 61–67.

Jackson 1986
Roger Jackson, Dharmakīrti's Refutation of Theism. In: *Philosophy East and West* 36 (1986) 315–348.

Jackson 1999
Roger Jackson, Atheology and Buddhalogy in Dharmakīrti's Pramāṇavārttika. In: *Faith and Philosophy* 16 (1999) 472–505.

Johnston 1936a
E. H. Johnston, *The Buddhacarita or Acts of the Buddha*. 2 vols., Lahore, 1936.

Johnston 1936b
E. H. Johnston, The Buddha's Mission and Last Journey: Buddhacarita, xv to xxvii (xv–xvii). In: *Acta Orientalia* [The Scandinavian Insitute of Asian Studies, Copenhagen]. 15, Pars I, 26–62.

Krasser 2002
Helmut Krasser, *Śaṅkaranandanas Īśvarāpākaraṇasaṅkṣepa mit einem anonymen Kommentar und weiteren Materialien zur buddhistischen Gottespolemik*. [SbÖAW 689 = Beiträge zur Kultur und Geistesgeschichte Asiens 39]. Vienna: Austrian Academy of Sciences Press 2002.

La Vallée Poussin 1923
Louis de La Vallée Poussin, *L'Abhidharmakośa de Vasubandhu, Traduit et Annoté. Premier et Deuxième Chapitres*. [Société Belge d'Études Orientales]. Paris/Louvain: Paul Geuthner 1923.

Maithrimurthi 1999
Mudagamuwe Maithrimurthi, *Wohlwollen, Mitleid, Freude und Gleichmut, Eine ideengeschichtliche Untersuchung der vier* apramāṇas *in der buddhistischen Ethik und Spiritualität von den Anfängen bis hin zum frühen Yogācāra*. Stuttgart: Franz Steiner Verlag 1999.

McDermott 1983
James P. McDermott, Karma and Rebirth in Early Buddhism. In: W. D. O'Flaherty (ed.), *Karma and Rebirth in Classical Indian Traditions*. Delhi: Motilal Banarsidass 1983 [1st Edition 1980]. 165–192.

Magnin 1998
Paul Magnin, Le divertissement dans le bouddhisme chinois, entre ascèse et 'moyens appropriés'. In: F. Martin, J. Pigeot and K. Chemla (eds.), *Du Divertissement dans la Chine et le Japon Anciens, "Homo Ludens Extrême-Orientalis"*. [Extrême-Orient/Extrême-Occident 20]. Paris: Presses Universitaires de Vincennes. 1968, 31–62.

Ñāṇamoli 2010
Bhikkhu Ñāṇamoli, *The Path of Purification (Visuddhimagga) by Bhadantācarira Buddhaghosa, Translated from the Pali*. Kandy: Buddhist Publication Society (4th ed.) 2010.

Qvarnström 1989
Olle Qvarnström, *Hindu Philosophy in Buddhist Perspective: The Vedāntatattvaviniścaya Chapter of Bhavya's Madhyamakahṛdayakārikā*. [Lund Studies in African and Asian Religions 4]. Lund: Plus Ultra 1989.

Renou 1978
Louis Renou, *L'Inde fondamentale. Études d'indianisme réunies et présentées par C. Malamoud*. Paris: Hermann, Collection Savoir 1978.

Rüping 1977
Klaus Rüping *Studien zur Frühgeschichte der Vedānta-Philosophie. Teil I: Philosophische Untersuchungen zu den Brahmasūtra-Kommentaren des Śaṅkara und des Bhāskara*. Wiesbaden: Franz Steiner Verlag 1977.

Schmithausen 1987
Lambert Schmithausen, *Ālayavijñāna. On the Origin and the Early Development of a Central Concept of Yogācāra Philosophy*. 2 vol. [Studia Philologica Buddhica, Monograph Series IV a and b]. Tokyo: The International Institute for Buddhist Studies 1987.

Shulman 2008
Eviatar Shulman, Early Meanings of Dependent-Origination. In: *Journal of Indian Philosophy* 36 (2008) 297–317.

Stcherbatsky 1923
Theodore Stcherbatsky, *The Central Conception of Buddhism and the Meaning of the Word "Dharma"*. London: Royal Asiatic Society 1923.

Stcherbatsky 1975
Id., *A Buddhist Philosopher on Monotheism. Text with Translation and Critical Introduction of Nāgārjuna's Īśvara-kartṛtva-nirākṛtiḥ-viṣṇoḥ-ekakartṛtva-nirākaraṇa.* In: *Papers of Th. Stcherbatsky, translated for the first time into English by Harish C. Gupta, ed. with an Introduction by Debiprasad Chattopadhyaya.* [Soviet Indology Series 2]. Calcutta: Indian Studies Past and Present, [Reprint; 1st ed.: 1969]. 1–11, 1975.

Steinkellner 2006
Ernst Steinkellner, Hindu Doctrines of Creation and Their Buddhist Critiques. In: P. Schmidt-Leukel, *Buddhism, Christianity and the Question of Creation, Karmic or Divine?* Hants: Ashgate Publishing Limited 2006, 15–31.

Willemen 2009
Charles Willemen 2009. *Buddhacarita. In praise of Buddha's Acts*. Numata Centre for Buddhist Translation and Research, BDK English Tripiṭaka Series. [Taishō volume 4, 192]. 2009.

Williams 1974
David M. Williams, The Translation and Interpretation of the Twelve Terms in the Paṭiccasamuppāda. In: *Numen* 21/1 (1974) 35–63.

Zvelebil 1973
Kamil Zvelebil, *The Smile of Murukaṉ. On Tamil Literature of South India.* Leiden: E.J. Brill 1973.

Erin McCann

Agency, surrender, and community

Piḷḷai Lokācārya's indwelling Lord

The works of Piḷḷai Lokācārya (13th–14th century) are an invaluable resource for understanding the development of the Śrīvaiṣṇava tradition in the post-Rāmānuja period. He was the author of eighteen philosophical treatises (*rahasya*), collectively known as the *Aṣṭadaśarahasyaṅkaḷ*, which, along with Maṇavāḷamāmuni's commentary, are an early formulation of Teṅkalai theology. From about the mid-13th century, two distinct schools of thought are identifiable within the Śrīvaiṣṇava tradition, i.e., the "Kāñci" and "Śrīraṅgam" schools, precursors to the Vaṭakalai and Teṅkalai branches of the tradition, respectively.[1] One of the key differences emerging from these two schools is the status and definition of the correct means (*upāya*) to attaining the Lord.

Though Piḷḷai Lokācārya, the foremost representative of the Śrīraṅgam school, does not understand himself to be the founder of a new branch of the Śrīvaiṣṇava tradition, he does articulate a position on the question of *upāya* that, though not completely absent from the works of Rāmānuja, is an important factor in the bifurcation of the tradition's soteriological paradigm.

Rāmānuja and, to a certain extent, the Kāñci school emphasize the necessity of self-effort through the meditative and ritual practices of *bhaktiyoga*.

Piḷḷai Lokācārya, on the other hand, argues strongly against the ultimate efficacy of self-effort on the part of the devotee. For him, the only *upāya* is God Himself and the only mode appropriate to the devotee is the recognition of his utter dependence on God for all things, including, and most importantly, salvation. Piḷḷai Lokācārya's position

---

1 Mumme 1988: 1–27.

on the question of the correct means for attaining salvation is a clear articulation of the shift in emphasis that we find in the works of the post-Rāmānuja Ācāryas away from the Supreme Lord (*paratva*) favoured by Rāmānuja toward a God who is first and foremost accessible (*saulabhya*) to *all* of His devotees.

For Piḷḷai Lokācārya, the Śrīvaiṣṇava community of believers is itself a manifestation of God's accessibility. Indeed, the primary concern of his theology is more about the creation and maintenance of correct relationships between members of the Śrīvaiṣṇava community, including God, than it is about defining His essential nature. In fact, I think that for Piḷḷai Lokācārya it is in the "between" that we find the true nature of God.

> According to him, the whole essence of Vaiṣṇava philosophy is to conduct oneself as a *bhāgavata* (devotee) and to respect other *bhāgavatas*.[2]

God in His transcendent aspect (*paratva*)

Of the three primary texts I have consulted, *Śrīvacanabhūṣaṇam*, *Mumukṣuppaṭi* and *Tattvatraya*, the only descriptions of the essential nature of God in His transcendent aspect (*paratva*) reminiscent of the tone used by Rāmānuja are found in the *Tattvatraya* in the third chapter dedicated to an exposition on the nature of God, called the *Īśvaratattva.* The opening *sūtra* of this chapter, *Tattvatraya* 74, is a summary of God's auspicious qualities, as follows:

> The essential nature of God is that He is opposed to all kinds of evil. He is infinite and self-luminous. He is full of the auspicious qualities of knowledge, power, etc. He is the cause of creation, maintenance and destruction of the world; according to the *Gītā* He is resorted to by the four kinds of people; those who are miserable, those who are curious to know, those who desire wealth, and those who are wise.[3]

---

2 Venkatachari 1978: 37.

3 Awasthi/Datta 1973: 46.

Though Piḷḷai Lokācārya's references to the *paratva* form of the Lord are sparse, here we find that he is largely in agreement with Rāmānuja. As, for example, in Rāmānuja's definition of "Supreme *brahman*" from the *Gītābhāṣya* 18.73:

> [...] "Supreme *brahman*", who is the great ocean of all auspicious qualities such as knowledge, strength, sovereignty, valour, power and glory, each of limitless excellence and natural (to Him), whose essential nature consists solely of auspiciousness, who is opposed to all that is evil without exception, and to whom the rise, protection and dissolution of the entire universe are sport [...].[4]

There are three important points in common here: that God is opposed to all evil, that He is the cause of the creation, maintenance, and dissolution of the entire world, and that He is endowed with all "the auspicious qualities". The auspicious qualities both authors refer to are what in Pāñcarātric doctrine are called the *ṣaḍguṇa*s, or "six qualities". Traditionally given as knowledge (*jñāna*), power (*śakti*), sovereignty (*aiśvarya*), strength (*bala*), valour (*vīrya*), and glory (*tejas*), they are understood to be, along with Lakṣmī, the first emanation from the eternal and unchangeable Lord. Though Piḷḷai Lokācārya does not emphasize this aspect of the Lord, nor make many references to the *ṣaḍguṇa*s outside of this chapter of the *Tattvatraya*, it is clear that his understanding of the Lord's transcendent form is in line with Rāmānuja and his predecessors.

Paratva in the world

The four *sūtra*s that immediately follow Piḷḷai Lokācārya's opening statement in *Tattvatraya* 74 (above) serve as brief explanations for each of the qualities mentioned. With the exception of *sūtra* 76 each of these are only about two lines long and rather general in nature. There is, however, one additional point made by Piḷḷai Lokācārya here. That is, "He is infinite and self-luminous". *Tattvatraya* 76, which ex-

---

4 Sampatkumaran 1969: 532.

plains the infinite self-illuminating nature of the Lord, gives us a closer look at Piḷḷai Lokācārya's priorities in discussing His essential nature:

> "God is endless (infinite)" means that God is eternal. His immanent presence is in both the conscious and the unconscious (or in the sentient and the non-sentient). A doubt arises from the fact of the immanence of God that if He is immanent in everything, then, He must be equally present in the evil things also and thus may be Himself partly evil. But this doubt is not correct; for as the soul in the body has no relation to childhood, youth and old age (these states belong to the body only.). Therefore, the imperfections of the sentient and the non-sentient things do not affect Him.[5]

Though, to be sure, this may be a point of importance in the works of Rāmānuja as well, the attention Piḷḷai Lokācārya gives to it in this context is telling. Not only does he feel the need to explain with greater detail the quality of *anantatva* (limitlessness or infiniteness), it is also the only point for which he sees the need to define and defend against possible objection. I think that he is attempting here to introduce into this discussion of the qualities of the Lord the connection between the Lord in His transcendent form and the mundane world as its *antaryāmin*, or "Inner Controller". This suggests to me that, for him, God's transcendent quality of limitlessness is directly relevant to His immanent role as the Inner Controller of all sentient and non-sentient matter.

Indeed, much of Piḷḷai Lokācārya's work tends to treat the *paratva* aspects of God's essential nature as if they are in service of, or immanently applicable to His devotees. Even in this chapter dedicated to expressing the essential nature of *Īśvara* his descriptions thereof are quickly followed by explanations of the ways in which such divine qualities are manifested for the aid of sentient beings (*cetana*). For example, *sūtras* 79 and 80 of the *Tattvatraya*:

> Of the numerous above-mentioned qualities, the subjects of His affection are His devotees and the subjects of His might are His opponents. The affection and might, etc. are due to his qualities of knowledge and power, lordship, *tejas*, etc. and all are His subjects. Of the endless qualities of God, knowledge is for the ignorant, power for the weak, forgiveness for those

---

5 Awasthi/Datta 1973: *Tattvatraya*, 47.

> who have sinned, compassion for those who are in misery, affection for those who have shortcomings, superior conduct for the inferior ones, straightforwardness for the crooked ones, friendliness for those who are hard-hearted, softness for those who are afraid of separation (from Him) and easy accessibility for those who yearn to see Him, etc.[6]

Rāmānuja too follows up his statement of God's supremacy at *Gītā-bhāṣya* 18.73, as given above, with a statement on the nature of the relationship between God and His devotee. The imperative for him, however, is not how or why God manifests for us, but rather how we may cultivate devotion for Him.

> [...] and the knowledge that You are Vāsudeva, the Supreme Person, He who is to be known from the *Vedānta*, and who can be attained only by the worship of the Supreme Person which has taken the form of devotion, which can be brought into being by restraint of the senses and control of the mind, the giving up of forbidden actions and the performance of occasional and obligatory rituals having the sole objective of the satisfaction of the Supreme Person, which is to be intensified day by day and which rests on the discriminatory knowledge of the higher and lower principles as being really of this kind and on its practical application—(all this) has been gained.[7]

The difference between these two statements on the relationship of God to His devotees is only more pointed for the near identity of their preceding statements on the essential nature (*svarūpa*) of God. Piḷḷai Lokācārya's interpretation of the Lord's status as *antaryāmin* is what makes this difference possible. In his *Mumukṣuppaṭi*, *sūtra*s 100-101, Piḷḷai Lokācārya concludes that the Lord's supremacy (*paratva*) and accessibility (*saulabhya*), or "status as the Inner Controller (*antarya-min*), means (*upāya*), and goal (*upeya*)"[8] results from His being the

---

6 Ibid., 48–49.

7 Sampatkumaran, *Gītābhāṣya* 532.

8 Mumme 1987: 85–86.

support and/or locus of the entire collection of *naras* (interpreted here as referring only to sentient beings).[9]

Accessibility (*saulabhya*) of the Lord as *arcāvatāra*

Though Rāmānuja, of course, also understands the Lord as the Inner Controller of all sentient beings, he sees that for the purpose of expiating one's sins, a means, an *upāya*, is necessary to find favour with the Lord. For Piḷḷai Lokācārya, on the other hand, there can be no means but the Lord. Because He is the Inner Controller, because all things—sentient and non-sentient—are Him, are His body, the only means to attaining salvation is admitting to one's absolute dependence upon Him. Thus, out of compassion the Lord condescends to make Himself accessible to His devotees—makes it possible for them to realize their love for Him, to find their way to accepting and trusting in Him. The Lord makes himself accessible to His devotees in a number of ways, as *antaryāmin*, as the *avatāras* (Rāma, Kṛṣṇa, etc.), and most importantly in the form of *arcāvatāra*. At the end of a series of passages in the *Tattvatraya* describing the five forms of God as enumerated by Pāñcarātra, he defines *arcāvatāra* as follows:

> The *arcāvatāra* (God in the form of idols, etc.) is the fifth and the last form of God. He accepts this form under the control of His devotees. The devotees uphold that God resides in the material of their choice, like gold, silver, jewels, etc. and in whatever they imagine He resides in. God resides at Ayodhya, Mathura, etc. without reference to time and rules as an object of worship. He overlooks the shortcomings of His devotees, and

9 Maṇavāḷamāmuni comments here that whether we read *Nārāyaṇa* as a *bahuvrīhī* or a *tatpuruṣa* compound determines the meaning respectively as either 1) [His] status as the Inner Controller (*antaryāmī*)—that is, as the Controller situated in the inner soul of all sentient and insentient beings, as stated in the *Antaryāmi Brāhmaṇa*, or 2) [His] status as the means (*upāya*) and goal (*upeya*), which is shown in the instrumental and passive formation of the word *ayana*—whose root is either *i*-, "to go," or *ay*-, "to go". (Mumme 1987: 86)

> He is under the control of His devotees for bathing, eating, sleeping, etc. He abides in the idols, in the temples and in the homes, etc.[10]

There are two important qualities of the *arcāvatāra* that highlight the accessibility of this form. The first, discussed here, is the radical reversal of roles inherent to the *arcāvatāra*. Being present for the devotee in idol form allows one to care for the Lord, to cultivate the feelings of a mother for her child (*vatsālya*), to feel the attachment to a dependent that mirrors the Lord's own feelings for His devotees. The second and related point is discussed in the *Mumukṣuppati*. Emphasizing the importance of being able to *see* the *arcāvatāra*, Piḷḷai Lokācārya writes that it is this form that is "the farthest extent of the [Lord's] accessibility", that

> this, unlike his supreme (*para*) and evolutionary (*vyūha*) forms, or his incarnations (*vibhava*), is visible to the eye.[11]

Indeed,

> His very posture—the divine weapons clutched in his holy hands, his hand held in a gesture saying not to fear, his head crowned, his face, his smile, his holy feet pressed into the lotus seat—is our refuge.[12]

The Lord both accommodates Himself to the desires of His devotees and conceals His supremacy in such image forms, allowing His devotees to approach Him for refuge without fear. In his *Arthapañcaka*, Piḷḷai Lokācārya further marvels at the mystery of the Lord's appearance in the image saying,

> [... He is] all-knowing, but seeming as if not-knowing; all-powerful, but seeming as if powerless; all-sufficient, but seeming as if needy;—thus seeming to exchange places, the worshipped with the worshipper, and choosing to be ocularly manifest to him in temples and homes, in short, at all places and at all times desired.[13]

---

[10] Awashti/Datta, *Tattvatraya* (*sūtra* 112), 68.

[11] Mumme, *Mumukṣuppati* (*sūtras* 139–140), 122.

[12] Ibid. (*sūtra* 140), 123.

[13] Govindacarya/Grierson 1910: 565–607.

The paradox of the Lord's presence as *arcāvatāra* can only be explained, according to Piḷḷai Lokācārya, by the depth and breadth of the Lord's compassion. Because He is perfect, full of all the auspicious qualities (*kalyānaguṇas*), we cannot understand this incarnation (or any incarnation, for that matter) as arising due to *karman.*[14] Thus, it must be His love of and desire for communion with His devotees that provides the impetus for His radical condescension. As such, the devotee can be assured that even in the presence of the Supreme Lord, the Lord of *karman*, he will find refuge:

> The quality of *arcāvatāra īśvara* is that He is the master and His devotees are His dependents and servants. He reverses the relationship or He becomes their innocent and powerless servant. He has unbound compassion and feels overpowered and bestows on His devotees whatever they desire, thus, graciously satisfying all their desires.[15]

In the *Śrīvacanabhūṣaṇam* the only descriptors of the Lord we find are of His image forms. These *sūtra*s, however, are more about identifying the devotee's proper object than they are about expressing the greatness of the Lord. Piḷḷai Lokācārya does insist, though, that the fullness of qualities inherent to the proper object of devotion are indeed present in the *arcāvatāra.*[16] Moreover, he invokes the Āḻvārs as proof, or *pramāṇa*, for this claim by stating in *sūtra* 38,

---

[14] Awasthi/Datta, *Tattvatraya* (*sūtra* 108), 66. "The reason for the previously mentioned different incarnations of God is His will and not the Karma etc. And, the objective of these incarnations is to protect the good (and to destroy the wicked, and the establishment of righteousness)."

[15] Ibid., *Tattvatraya* (*sūtra* 114), 69.

[16] Piḷḷai Lokācārya, *Śrīvacanabhūṣaṇam, sūtra* 37: *viṣayaniyamam āvatu guṇapūrtiyuḷḷaviṭame viṣayam ākai; pūrttiyuḷḷatum arccāvatārattile.* Please note that all translations from the *Śrīvacanabhūṣaṇam* are mine, based on my forthcoming edition and translation of the text.

> The Āḻvārs, in many places, performed *prapatti* to the *arcāvatāra* especially.[17]

The Lord is so powerful as an *arcāvatāra*, in fact, that even for those who cannot be corrected by *śāstra*, those concentrated on other objects, and those who are disinclined toward the Lord, seeing the image of the Lord will convert their aversion to taste (*ruci*).[18] Though Piḷḷai Lokācārya in the *Śrīvacanabhūṣaṇam* is clearly extolling the benefits of seeing the Lord, he equally recognizes that there is an inherent danger in the beauty of the Lord's image form. It is not only possible but entirely likely that a man may become so engrossed in the pleasure of seeing His beauty in this form that he will assume the pleasure to be his own, that he will become attached to the pleasure of seeing rather than to the Lord. Thus, Piḷḷai Lokācārya reminds his readers that,

> It is not from seeing [His] qualities that one engages with the Lord; it is due to the essential nature (of the soul).[19]

Thus, the only thing one can do is surrender to Him—and even this, for Piḷḷai Lokācārya, cannot be called an *upāya*. It is merely a mental acknowledgment of one's essential nature as being utterly dependent upon the Lord. This acknowledgement is called *prapatti*, it is a state of surrender that is reflective of the soul's true nature—merely an acknowledgement of one's pre-existent, if unacknowledged, state of being.

---

[17] Ibid., *sūtra* 38: *āḻvārkaḷ palaviṭaṅkaḷilum prapatti paṇṇiṟṟum arccāvatāratile*. The final *–ē* of *arccāvatāratill-ē*, as an emphatic particle, can be translated here as either "alone", "only", or "especially".

[18] Ibid., *sūtra* 43: *itutāṉ śāstraṅkaḷāl tiruttav oṇṇāte viṣayāntaraṅkaḷile maṇṭi vimukhar-āyp porum cetanaṟku vaimukhyattai māṟṟi ruciyai viḷaikkak kaṭavat-āy ruci piṟantāl upāyam-āy upāyaparigraham paṇṇiṉāl bhogyamum-āy irukkum*. The word *ruci* could also be interpreted here as "hunger", implying a predilection toward the object.

[19] Ibid., *sūtras* 108–109: *bhagavad viṣayattil iḻikiṟatum guṇaṅ kaṇṭu aṉṟu; svarūpaprāptam eṉṟu*.

Salvation through grace or good deeds?

In a long passage that attempts to explain the mind of God in relation to His devotees, Piḷḷai Lokācārya tells us that like the gold-merchant who tests gold against a touchstone accumulating the tiny fragments left over, the Lord takes all the purposeful, incidental and inevitable moments in the series of births of His devotees and multiplies them by ten. Thus, imagining His devotee is worthy of grace thinking,

> [...] you spoke of my town, you said my name, you saw my devotees, you removed their thirst, you gave them shelter [...].[20]

The granting of His grace seems random, as if totally undeserved. And, indeed, because of His perfection, to be touched by His glance is always more than the devotee, who is full to the brim with the faults of humanity, deserves. Moreover, it is only the good works that are done without a claim to agency that are worthy of the Lord's attention.

> Therefore, having clung to the unknown good deeds alone the Lord casts the gracious favour of His glance.[21]

The Lord's grace is not something to be won through adherence to *āśramadharma*, through the performance of daily and occasional ritual action, or even through the meditative techniques of *bhaktiyoga*. In fact, Piḷḷai Lokācārya is absolutely clear that for *prapatti* any intentional action in seeking the Lord's favour is to be considered a fault.

> For other *upāyas*, refraining from action (*nivṛtti*) is a fault; for this one, action (*pravṛtti*) is a fault.[22]

Maṇavāḷamāmuni clarifies the issue even further:

---

20 Ibid., *sūtra* 384: [...] *eṉṉ uraic coṉṉāy eṉ pēraic coṉṉāy eṉṉ aṭiyārai ṉokkiṉāy avarkaḷ viṭāyait tīrattāy avarkaḷuk kotuṅka niḻalaik koṭuttāy* [...].

21 Ibid., *sūtra* 389: *ākaiyāl ajñātam-āna naṉmaikaḷaiyē paṟṟācākak koṇṭu kaṭākṣiy āniṟkum.*

22 Mumme, *Mumukṣuppaṭi* (*sūtra* 232), 170. This comes very close to Rāmānuja's stance on the importance of fulfilling one's obligations according to *aśramadharma* and *bhaktiyoga* without attachment. It is important to note, however, that for Piḷḷai Lokācārya the unconsidered good deeds referred to here are not restricted to those prescribed by *śāstra*.

Upāyas other than this one—the accomplished *upāya* (*siddhopāya*)—are fulfilled by the *cetana*'s activity (*pravṛtti*); thus, it is a fault if the *cetana* refrains from making his own efforts (*svayatnanivṛtti*). This *upāya*, however, is intolerant of association with other aids. Therefore, with it the only fault would be the *cetana*'s activity.[23]

Indeed, *sūtras* 390–391 of the *Śrīvacanabhūṣaṇam* state clearly that there is literally nothing to be done, that all things come from the Lord alone.

Even these [unknown good deeds] were produced for him [i.e., the *cetana*], just as He [the Lord] first produced him [i.e., the *cetana*]. If this is examined, it will become [clear] that it is not necessary for him [i.e., the *cetana*] to do even one thing for himself.[24]

It is only in recognizing one's utter helplessness that one affirms his relationship with God and his total dependence upon Him.

The *cetana*'s essential nature (*svarūpa*)

The essential nature of sentient beings is, perhaps, the topic upon which there is the most agreement between Piḷḷai Lokācārya and Rāmānuja. Like Piḷḷai Lokācārya,

According to Rāmānuja, the human's sole delight is to be found in the Lord, and in his/her own subservience to and dependence on him.[25]

Both agree that devotion to the Lord, dependence upon Him, and delighting in subservience to Him are preliminary to the granting of God's grace and that salvation is a gift that only the Lord may grant. They do not, however, agree on the means to attaining this state of devotion, nor on the nature of salvation. For Rāmānuja, acquiring the

---

23 Ibid. (*sūtra* 232), Maṇavāḷa's commentary, 170–171. *Siddhopāya* here should be understood to be a direct reference to the Lord.

24 Piḷḷai Lokācārya, *Śrīvacanabhūṣaṇam*, *sūtras* 390–391: *ivaiy uṅ kūṭa viḷaiyum paṭiyiṟē ivaṉ taṉṉai mutalile sṛṣṭittatu. atu taṉṉai nirūpittāl ivaṉ taṉakku oṉṟuñ ceyya veṇṭāta paṭiy-āy irukkum.*

25 Nayar 1988: 111–132.

gift of salvation requires effort on the part of the devotee. He makes this clear in the passage from *Gītābhāṣya* 18.73 (quoted above) where he states that devotion must be cultivated through

> restraint of the senses and control of the mind, the giving up of forbidden action and performance of occasional and obligatory rituals ....[26]

Rāmānuja thus affirms the necessity of Vedic study and adherence to the injunctions of *āśramadharma*. For him this is the only sure way to clear the *karman* that prevents one from embarking on the path of *bhaktiyoga*, and the only sure way to develop the love for the Lord that leads to salvation.

Piḷḷai Lokācārya, on the other hand, seeing that the preliminary of love for the Lord is always already fulfilled simply by the fact of existence proclaims that man cannot and in fact should not presume to be capable of contributing anything toward the attainment of his salvation. The initial impulse to reach for the Lord, seemingly based in apprehending His divine qualities, is, in fact, based in an innate overpowering love for Him that occurs because of the soul's original relationship to Him.

> The basis for it (striving after the Lord) is love.
> The basis for that [love] is the relationship [with the Lord].
> That [relationship] indeed is unconditioned;
> It is that which arises from existence.[27]

Śrīvacanabhūṣaṇam 127–129 make the futility of self-effort on the part of the devotee (the *prapanna*) abundantly clear:

> Like a cowry to a jewel, like a lemon to a kingdom, [the means] is not equal to the fruit. Since he [the *prapanna*] is poor, there is not even one thing to give to Him [the Lord]. Giving that which is His, even if giving

---

[26] Sampatkumaran, *Gītābhāṣya* 532.

[27] Piḷḷai Lokācārya, *Śrīvacanabhūṣaṇam*, *sūtras* 115–117: *ataṟku aṭi pirāvaṇyam. ataṟku aṭi campantam. atutāṉ oḷapātikam aṉṟu; cattāpiray uktam.*

> in the proper manner and place, is not the means; and if [one] is to give in the improper manner it will be exposed as theft.[28]

In other words, everything that one could possibly give to the Lord was already His. For one to think that their offering to the Lord is worthy of Him is folly, and, worse, to think that the offering does not already belong to the Lord, to presume ownership over that offering, is a sin. Along these lines and following from Rāmānuja's formulation of the *śarīri-śarīra* (soul-to-body) relationship of the Lord to material existence, Piḷḷai Lokācārya describes the nature of the human soul in the *Tattvatraya* as follows:

> Subservient to God" means that it has nothing of its own; just as sandal (wood), flower, betel, etc. exist for the use of others, similarly, soul is all devotion to God with no interest of its own. The relation is not like ours with house, land, son, wife, etc. that they can exist independently. Just as body cannot exist separately from the soul, similarly, the soul (*cit*) cannot exist separately from God. (Because soul is the body of God).[29]

As is evident here, for Piḷḷai Lokācārya the soul's essential nature is one of absolute dependence upon the Lord. Both independence and dependence upon another God are understood to be external to the true nature of the soul. They are harmful modes of being that are acquired through association with the material world, from the "name that comes with village, family, etc."[30]

> Independence and subservience to another are introduced from the outside. Independence opposes subservience; subservience to another opposes subservience to Him. If the bondage caused by pride (*ahaṃ-*

---

28 Ibid., *sūtras* 127–129: *ratnattukkup palakaṟai pōlēyum rājyattukku elum iccam paḷam pōlēyum phalattukku sadṛśam aṉṟu. tāṉ daridraṉ ākaiyāle taṉakkuk koṭukku alāvatu oṉṟum illai. avaṉ taṉttaik koṭukkum iṭattilē aṭa-ivilē koṭukkil aṉupāyamām; aṭaivu keṭak koṭukkil kaḷavu veḷip paṭum.*

29 Awasthi/Datta, *Tattvatraya* (*sūtra* 23), 20.

30 Piḷḷai Lokācārya, *Śrīvacanabhūṣaṇa*, *sūtra* 79: *grāmakulādikaḷāl varum per anartthahetu.*

kāra) is removed, the unperishing name for the soul is "servant".[31] Carman defines Rāmānuja's understanding of this relation as follows:

> Since this rule is that exercised by the self within its body, God in this aspect of His relation to finite beings may be called the *antaryāmī*, the "Controller within" or the "Inner Ruler".[32]

Fundamentally, Piḷḷai Lokācārya is in agreement with Rāmānuja on the nature of God's relationship to the soul. What is distinct about his understanding is the degree of agency he attributes to the individual soul. Piḷḷai Lokācārya, preserving the singular and absolute autonomy of God, insists that the human soul is wholly incapable of independent action and any claim to it is not only prideful, it is an obstacle to acting in accordance with God's will. Rāmānuja, preserving the sense of God as ultimately judicious, as the Lord of *karman*, on the other hand, insists on the importance of an individual's volitional effort.

Upāya: *bhakti* and *prapatti* as the means of salvation

The distinction between the approaches of Rāmānuja and Piḷḷai Lokācārya to the question of the correct path to salvation and, by extension, their respective understandings of God's role in the process is most clearly seen in their interpretations of *Bhagavadgītā* 18:66 (the *Caramaśloka*). The verse runs as follows:

Abandoning all duties,	*sarvadharmān parityajya*
adopt me as thy sole refuge;	*mām ekaṃ śaraṇam vraja*
from all sins I thee	*ahaṃ tvā sarvapāpebhyo*
shall rescue: be not grieved!	*mokṣayiṣyāmi mā śucaḥ*.[33]

Like Piḷḷai Lokācārya, Rāmānuja takes *sarva dharmān* ("all duties") to mean *karman*, *jñāna*, and *bhakti yoga*. That is, all the paths previ-

---

[31] Ibid., *sūtras* 76–78: *svātantryamum anyaśēṣatvamum vanteṟi. śeṣatvavirodhi svātantryam; taccheṣatvavirodhi taditaraśeṣatvam. ahaṃkāram—ākiṟav ārppaittu uṭaittāl ātmāvukku aḻiyāta peraṭiyāṉ eṉṟiṟe.*

[32] Carman 1974: 136.

[33] Ibid., 215.

ously taught by Kṛṣṇa to Arjuna in the course of the *Bhagavadgītā*. The difference between their interpretations rests primarily on one word, *parityajya*. Literally read, *parityajya* means "having abandoned." As a gerund, it functions as a non-finite verbal form signifying an action done before the action of the finite verb, in this case *vraja*—an imperative second person singular verb from the root *vraj* indicating a command to approach, or proceed toward. Piḷḷai Lokācārya interprets this literally, as in *Mumukṣuppaṭi* 202,

> The gerund form (*lyap*) states that we have to first completely relinquish other means and then surrender, as in the statement, "Having bathed, one should take food."[34]

He goes even further in *Mumukṣuppaṭi* 203 by interpreting this gerund form as imparting an explicitly negative connotation to *sarvadharman*, "It says that these are not only non-*upāya*s, but impediments."[35] Maṇavāḷamāmuni, Piḷḷai Lokācārya's chief commentator, explains this statement as follows:

> ...if there remains even the slightest involvement in these other *upāya*s, they will not only fail to be effective means (*upāya*) to the goal, they will actually turn out to be obstructions to the ultimate attainment.[36]

Rāmānuja, on the other hand, understands that,

> These disciplines are not to be abandoned but to be performed as a worship pleasing to God and entirely in the spirit of love, in a manner accordant with the devotee's own position in society and spiritual qualifications.[37]

For Rāmānuja, the gerund ("having abandoned") refers to one's attachment to the outcome, the fruit (*phala*), of *jñāna*, *karman*, and *bhakti*. Where Rāmānuja takes these *dharma*s, so long as they are done without attachment to their outcomes, as necessary *upāya*s to attaining

---

34 Mumme, *Mumukṣuppaṭi* (*sūtra* 202), 158.

35 Ibid. (*sūtra* 203), 159.

36 Ibid. (*sūtra* 203), Maṇavāḷamāmuni's commentary, 159.

37 Carman 1974: 215.

the Lord, Piḷḷai Lokācārya sees them as further obstructions to the absolute surrender that is the only true path to the Lord.

In an alternative interpretation of the *Caramaśloka*, Rāmānuja understands taking refuge in the Lord as a means of expiating sin so that one may properly perform *bhaktiyoga*:

> Since there is an infinite weight of such sins, since the ceremonies designed to remove them are also countless and difficult to perform, and since life is short, the Lord counsels Arjuna not to practise such expiatory rites but instead to take refuge in Him, and He will remove the sins that prevent Arjuna from undertaking *bhaktiyoga*.[38]

This particular interpretation does seem to provide the scope for understanding *prapatti* as a means to salvation. Indeed, Vedānta Deśika (13th–14th c. CE), the foremost representative of the Kāñci/Vaṭakalai branch of the tradition, comments that Rāmānuja's discussion here is suggestive of a later elaboration of the doctrine of *prapatti*. Namely, that both *prapatti* and *bhaktiyoga* are *upāya—bhaktiyoga* is for those who are qualified (twice-born), while *prapatti* is for everyone else.

There is a hint, Deśika says, contained in the second interpretation, for it shows that just as a man may give up expiatory ceremonies and surrender to the Lord in order to be able to begin *bhaktiyoga*, so one who considers that he cannot perform *bhaktiyoga* at all may give up *bhakti-*, *jñāna-* and *karmayoga* and may surrender to attain Him directly; that is, to secure *mokṣa*.[39] Piḷḷai Lokācārya too allows a place for the practice of *bhaktiyoga* according to one's station in life.

> As previously stated, service of the Lord will be known by the *śāstra*; service of the Ācārya will be known by the *śāstra* and by the word of the Ācārya. Service itself is of two kinds. That is to say, doing what is desired and abstaining from what is not desired. That which is desired and that which is not desired depends upon *varṇāśrama* and the essential nature of the soul. [40]

---

38 Ibid., pp. 215–216.

39 Ibid., p. 216.

40 Piḷḷai Lokācārya, *Śrīvacanabhūṣaṇam*, *sūtra*s 279–282: *kīḻ coṉṉa bhagavat kaiṅkaryam aṟivatu śāstramukhattālē*; *ācārya kaiṅkaryam aṟivatu*

Though he retains a place for service of the Lord according to *śāstra*[41] and *varṇāśramadharma* in his soteriological paradigm, they are subordinate to *prapatti*. He is absolutely clear that the *only* reason for acting in accordance with these principles is that it is pleasing to the Lord—in no circumstance should practising the discipline of *bhaktiyoga* be understood as contributing anything toward one's salvation. Moreover, with the understanding that *prapatti* is the only mode appropriate to the essential nature of the human soul, Piḷḷai Lokācārya states,

> There is no restriction of place, time, manner, worthiness or fruit for *prapatti*. The only restriction is of the object [of surrender].[42]

Because Piḷḷai Lokācārya understands that the proper *upāya* is the Lord Himself, the only obligation for *prapatti* is that one surrenders to the appropriate object—the Lord. The prescriptions of *śāstra* on ritual action, time, manner, etc., ultimately have no power over the Lord, who is the *Siddhopāya* (perfected means). *Bhaktiyoga*, which is subject to the prescriptions of *śāstra* and *varṇāśramadharma*, is dependent on the actions of sentient beings that are afflicted by *karman*. Thus, it is an insufficient means to attaining salvation.

Though God is the perfect and only means to this goal, Piḷḷai Lokācārya sees that man is incapable of realizing his utter dependence upon the Lord without aid. Man's dual nature, his ontological relationship to the Lord alongside his basic inclination toward the world of sense objects, necessitates mediation in order to realize his true identity.

śāstramukattālum ācārya vacanattālum. kaiṅkaryantāṉ iraṇṭu. atāvatu iṣṭam ceykaiyum aniṣṭam tavirukaiyum. iṣṭāniṣṭaṅkaḷ varṇāśramaṅkaḷaiyum ātmasvarūpattaiyum avalambittu irukkum.

41 I think it is safe to assume that *bhaktiyoga* falls into this category.

42 Piḷḷai Lokācārya, *Śrīvacanabhūṣaṇam*, *sūtra*s 24–25: *prapattikku deśaniyamamum kāla niyamamum prakāraniyamamum adhikāriniyamamum phalaniyamum illai. viṣayaniyamamēy uḷḷāvatu.*

> To bring about this awareness and to reconcile the salvific dialectic of grace versus co-operation, the role of the Ācārya or *guru* is brought in and insisted upon.[43]

Even a man absolutely devoted to the image of the Lord requires the intercession of an Ācārya. His reliance on the image, understood by Piḷḷai Lokācārya to be an object of enjoyment, is not itself the problem as it is motivated by attachment to the Lord. However, it is an attachment that nurtures self-interest (for example, gaining the pleasure of seeing the Lord's form) and promotes man's inability to relinquish all selfish motives.[44] But, what is impossible to abandon becomes possible with the aid of an Ācārya. And, in truth, for Piḷḷai Lokācārya, coming to the realization of dependence upon the Lord by way of association with an Ācārya is preferred. Accordingly, Piḷḷai Lokācārya writes,

> That which is common to both bondage and release is the relationship to the Lord; the cause for release is the relationship to the Ācārya.[45]

And, in fact, correcting man's relationship to God by grace is a last resort,

> When the *cetana* is not returned [to its proper state] by instruction, then there is rectification by grace.[46]

However, Piḷḷai Lokācārya, in a number of statements, makes it clear that already before the Ācārya can be engaged there are certain intrinsic qualities of the soul that must be made manifest. *Sūtra*s 96 and 97 of the *Śrīvacanabhūṣaṇam*, for example:

> Tranquillity and self-restraint are the most important among the qualities of the soul. If these two [qualities] exist, the Ācārya enters the hand, the

---

43 Amaladass 1990: xvi.

44 Piḷḷai Lokācārya, *Śrīvacanabhūṣaṇam*, *sūtra* 276: *viṣayadoṣattāle varum avaiy ellām dustyajamāy iṟey iruppatu.*

45 Ibid., *sūtra* 436: *īśvara saṃbandham bandhamokṣaṅkaḷ iraṇṭukkum potuv-āy irukkum*; *ācārya saṃbandhaṃ mokṣattukkē hetuv-āy irukkum.*

46 Ibid., *sūtra* 14: *upadeśattāl mīḷāpotu cetanaṉaiy aruḷāle tiruttum*; *īśvaraṉaiy aḻakāle tiruttum.*

> Ācārya being in hand, the divine *mantra* enters the hand, the divine *mantra* being in hand, God enters the hand, God being in hand, [one] subsequently [attains] the great city of Vaikuṇṭha.[47]

The transformative power of community

What makes the soul ready for the Ācārya? Ready for the essential teachings that will lead him to the Lord? I think that Piḷḷai Lokācārya answers this question via his discussion of devotees of low birth:

> The defect coming from low birth will perish because of the relationship with those who are different (i.e., the *bhāgavata*s).[48]

That is to say, the defect is annulled because of association with other devotees, not the Ācārya, not God—other devotees. And, in a passage explaining why *anyone* may suffer the consequences of disrespecting a devotee of the Lord he states:

> Even though without knowledge and practice for the blessing [of the Lord], the relationship to [the *bhāgavata*s] prepares [one] as if there were knowledge and practice; [thus] disrespectful conduct toward [*bhāgavata*s] is sufficient for destruction.[49]

Just having contact with this community is taken as sufficient preparation for understanding their beliefs and code of conduct. A relationship with the *bhāgavata*s is not only educational, it is transformative. Piḷḷai Lokācārya's emphasis on the role of the Ācārya as intercessor

---

47 Ibid., *sūtra*s 96–97: *ātmaguṇaṅkaḷil pradhānam śamamum damamum. ivaiy iraṇṭum uṇṭāṇāl ācāryaṉ kaipukurum ācāryan kaipukuntavāṟe tirumantraṅ kaipukirum: tirumantram kaipukuruntavāṟe īśvaraṉ kaipukurum; īśvaraṉ kaipukuntavāṟēv "vaikuṇṭamāṉakar maṟṟatu kaiyy atuvēy eṉkiṟa paṭiyē prāpya bhūmi kaipukurum.*

48 Ibid., *sūtra* 221: *nikṛṣṭajanmattāl vanta doṣam camippatu vilakṣaṇa saṃbandhattālē.*

49 Ibid., *sūtra* 207: *jñānānuṣṭhānaṅkaḷaiy oḻintālum peṟṟukku avarkaḷ pakkal saṃbandhamō yamaikirāppōlēy avaiy uṇṭāṉālu miḷavukku avarkaḷ pakkal apacāramē porum.*

and thus the importance of *ācāryābhimāna* in attaining salvation, along with his focus on the importance of having a relationship with this community of believers may seem to contradict his understanding of surrender to the Lord alone as the only means to salvation. I would suggest, however, that for him the Śrīvaiṣṇava community itself is the worldly manifestation of the Lord's grace. And as such, the relationships that Piḷḷai Lokācārya defines and defends (particularly in the *Śrīvacanabhūṣaṇam*) are themselves the means (*upāya*) and goal (*upeya*) of devotion. He sees God not only as the focus of this community, but as its foundation, as the pervading force of its existence.

Conclusion

As much as the point of individual agency is the primary difference between the soteriological paradigms of Piḷḷai Lokācārya and Rāmānuja, I think that the underlying difference on the question of *upāya* is about community. Rāmānuja's focus is on the individual, Piḷḷai Lokācārya's is on the community of Śrīvaiṣṇavas as a whole.

This is as true of their respective audiences as it is of their understanding of God's essential nature and His role in salvation. That is, in Rāmānuja's conception of God as *paratva* and even as *antaryāmin* he sees that God in His infinite and singular perfection maintains a state of separation from the individual. Thus, the aspirant must work to transform himself into one who is worthy of union with the Lord. The weight of *karman* on the individual soul, however, makes this transformation near impossible.

> Nevertheless, the soul is responsible for its good or evil actions, for the Supreme Self, who is the Inner Controller, causes this action (*pravartayati*) by giving His assent or permission (*anumati*) when He has taken note of the soul's volitional effort (*udyogam*).[50]

Thus, it is the individual's effort to make himself worthy rather than one's ability to actually complete such a transformation that, for Rāmānuja, allows the Lord to remove the *karman* obstructing his path.

---

[50] Carman 1974: 138–139.

Though there is some indication that Rāmānuja thought *prapatti* may partly meet the requirement of volitional effort on the part of the soul,

> there is no evidence that Rāmānuja believed that prapatti alone sufficed... Nowhere the word has the later sense of "complete" self-surrender of the devotee to God who, moved by the devotee's utter desolation, lifts him to beatitude by a mere act of grace.[51]

In fact, even when the grace of the Lord is mentioned by Rāmānuja, the self-effort required of the individual in the form of *bhaktiyoga* is also emphasized:

> God's grace may crown the aspirant's efforts, but he first has to deserve it.[52]

Piḷḷai Lokācārya, on the other hand, sees that God as *antaryāmin* and even as *paratva*, though infinite and perfect, chooses to be intimately connected to His devotees. Even the auspicious qualities (*kalyānaguṇas*) manifested in the Lord's *paratva* form are revealed, according to Piḷḷai Lokācārya, for the benefit of His creatures. The Lord as *antaryāmin*, rather than taking account of the soul's volitional or intentional effort and either rewarding or punishing the soul on this account, takes and multiplies only the unintentional actions of the soul. And the *arcāvatāra*, the most accessible form of the Lord, shows the profound nature of the Lord's love and compassion for the individual soul through His condescension to the radical reversal of roles explicit in this form.

The nature of the individual soul is such that its union with the Lord is inherent to its very existence. Knowledge of this fact is obstructed only by the perception of autonomy created by pride and involvement with the world outside the Śrīvaiṣṇava fold. As such, it is clear to Piḷḷai Lokācārya that any intentional effort to remove one's faults (*doṣa*) on the part of the aspirant is an impediment to understanding one's self as being utterly dependent upon the Lord, and thus an impediment to experiencing the Lord's love.

---

51 van Buitenen 1968: 26.

52 van Buitenen 1968: 28.

> Goodness sought for its own sake is prohibited just like evil. Just as the clothes put on for beauty are an obstruction to embracing. Even a necklace.[53]

The work of transforming the self is, I think, transferred by Piḷḷai Lokācārya away from the individual to the community of Śrīvaiṣṇavas. This is possible because of the Lord's very real presence within each and every Śrīvaiṣṇava and, because of their relationships with each other, in the community as a whole. Piḷḷai Lokācārya's aspirant needs first and foremost to be a member of the community in which God has manifested Himself.

Though Piḷḷai Lokācārya proclaims *prapatti* as the means to salvation, he equally reminds the aspirant that approaching God without the support of a community, particularly without the support of an Ācārya whom God Himself has brought to him, is fraught with potential dangers. It is only within a community supported by God that one may find his path to true salvation.

> Just like one field standing full of water oozes out to the neighbouring field, by relation with these people, for those without these [knowledge, devotion and renunciation], distress will be caused to vanish.[54]

Only here can the devotee see his utter dependence upon the Lord. Only here can he find the courage to completely surrender.

---

53 Piḷḷai Lokācārya, *Śrīvacanabhūṣaṇam*, *sūtra*s 164–166: *ta<u>n</u>akkuttā<u>n</u> tēṭum na<u>n</u>mai tīmaiy ōpāti vilakk-āy irukkum. a<u>l</u>akuk kiṭṭa caṭṭaiy aṇaikkaikku virodhiyām āppōle. hāropi.*

54 Piḷḷai Lokācārya, *Śrīvacanabhūṣaṇam*, *sūtra* 264: *oru cey nirampa nīr ni<u>n</u><u>r</u>āl acal ceya pocintu kāṭṭum āppōlēy ivaiy illātā<u>r</u>kkum ivarkaḷ eṭṭai saṃbandhattāle u<u>r</u>āvutal tīrakkaṭavatāy irukkum.*

Bibliography

Primary Literature

Śrīvacanabhūṣaṇammūlam
Piḷḷai Lokācārya, *Śrīvacana Bhūṣaṇam Mūlam*. Tiruvarangam: Śrī Vaiṣṇava Śrī 2001.

Śrīvacanabhūṣaṇam
Piḷḷai Lokācārya, *Śrīvacana Bhūṣaṇam*. EO 0408. Manuscript Collection. École française d'Extrême-Orient, Pondicherry.

Śrīvacanabhūṣaṇam EO 0947
Manuscript Collection. École française d'Extrême-Orient, Pondicherry.

Śrīvacanabhūṣaṇam EO 1008
Manuscript Collection. École française d'Extrême-Orient, Pondicherry.

Secondary Literature

Amaladass 1990
Anand Amaladass, *Deliver Me, My Lord.* A Translation of Maṇavāḷamāmuni's Ārtiprabandham. Delhi: Satguru Publication 1990.

Awasthi/Datta 1973
Awasthi B.M. Awasthi and C.K. Datta. *The Tattvatraya of Lokacarya: A Treatise on Viśiṣṭādvaita Vedānta*. Sanskrit text with English and Hindi translation. Delhi: Indu Prakashan 1973.

van Buitenen 1968
J.A.B. van Buitenen, *Rāmānuja on the Bhagavadgītā. A Condensed Rendering of His Gītābhāṣya with Copious Notes and an Introduction*. Delhi: Motilal Banarsidass 1968.

Carman 1974
John Carman, *The Theology of Rāmānuja. An Essay in Interreligious Understanding*. New Haven: Yale University Press 1974.

Govindacarya/Grierson 1910
Alkondavilli Govindacarya, G.A. Grierson, The Artha Pancaka of Pi̤l̤lai Lokācārya. In: *Journal of the Royal Asiatic Society of Great Britain and Ireland* (July 1910) 565–607.

Mumme 1987
Patricia Mumme, *The Mumukṣuppati of Pi̤l̤lai Lokācārya with Maṇavāḷamāmuni's Commentary*. Text and translation. Bombay: Ananthacharya Indological Research Institute, 1987.

Mumme 1988
Patricia Mumme, *The Śrīvaiṣṇava Theological Dispute: Maṇavāḷamāmuni and Vedānta Deśika*. Madras: New Era Publications, 1988.

Nayar 1988
Nancy Nayar, The Concept of Prapatti in Rāmānuja's "Gītābhāṣya". In: *Journal of South Asian Literature* 23 (1988) 111–132.

Purushothama 1970
Naidu B.R. Purushothama, *Śrī Vacana Bhūṣaṇam Mūlamum*. Maṇipravāḷa text with commentary of Maṇavāḷamāmuni. Cuddaloore, Tamil Nadu: T.K. Narayanasami Naidu 1970.

Rangaswami 2006
J. Rangaswami, Appendix-I: The original sūtras of the text, *Śrīvacana Bhūṣaṇa* in *Maṇipravāḷa* Language. In: *Śrīvacana Bhūṣaṇam of Pi̤l̤lai Lokācārya. Translation and Commentary of Manavalamanuni. Critical Evaluation of the Theo-Philosophy of the Post-Rāmānuja Srivaisnavism*. Delhi: Sharada Publishing House 2006.

Sampatkumaran 1969
M.R. Sampatkumaran, *The Gītābhāṣya of Ramanuja*. Sanskrit text and English translation. Madras: Prof. M. Rangacharya Memorial Trust 1969.

Venkatachari 1978
K.K.A. Venkatachari, *The Maṇipravāḷa Literature of the Śrīvaiṣṇava Ācāryas*. Bombay: Ananthacharya Research Institute 1978.

Marcus Schmücker

Veṅkaṭanātha on the God Viṣṇu-Nārāyaṇa as the ultimate ground

Introductory remarks

The divine concept of Viṣṇu-Nārāyaṇa as put forward by Veṅkaṭanātha (1268–1369) was the result of a complex development shaped by discussions and disputes with several other philosophical and theological schools. In Veṅkaṭanātha's time, the focus of his Vedāntic tradition was the belief in a highest personal Being, referred to as both Viṣṇu and Nārāyaṇa.[1] Conceptually, this belief involved the relationship of this highest Being to a world made up of manifold individual souls and the material world.

The Viśiṣṭādvaita Vedānta theistic tradition was influenced from several directions. Important textual influences include the *Nālāyirat Tivyappirapantam*, the "Four Thousand Divine Compositions" of the Śrīvaiṣṇava canon composed by the twelve Āḻvārs (6th–9th cent.), the *Viṣṇupurāṇa*, Pāñcarātra texts, and above all, the Upaniṣads. The tradition thus had two important strands, one in Sanskrit, the other in Tamil, whereby the Tamil strand later included texts in Maṇipravāḷa, a Tamil-Sanskrit hybrid language. Since both strands were important, Veṅkaṭanātha not only expounded his doctrines in Sanskrit when debating with other traditions, he also composed works in Tamil and Maṇipravāḷa,[2] such as the *Rahasyatrayasāra* (*The Essential Nature of the Three*

---

1 Because the (later) Viśiṣṭādvaita tradition employs the names Viṣṇu and Nārāyaṇa for the same God, the double name Viṣṇu-Nārāyaṇa is used here.

2 For Veṅkaṭanātha's work in Prakrit, the *Acyutaśatakam*, cf. Hopkins 2002: 216–231.

Secrets[3]; henceforth RTS), and the *Paramatabhaṅga* (*The Refutation of Other [Schools'] Doctrines*; henceforth PMBh). Both texts are mostly written in Tamil and Maṇipravāḷa, but they also contain passages (verses) in Sanskrit.

In his works, Veṅkaṭanātha adopts the basic ontological concepts of his most important predecessor, Rāmānuja (c. 1017–1137). However, not only he examines and develops the topics discussed by Rāmānuja and his predecessors, but he also adds many *new* ones.

Veṅkaṭanātha repeatedly refers to Rāmānuja's central teachings. But as will become clear in the course of our contribution, while he accepts Rāmānuja's views, he also takes the teachings of Rāmānuja's successors into account. He elaborates on certain theses and, above all, confronts the doctrines of other schools.[4] As can be seen, he systematically expands on the doctrin of Rāmānuja, but as we also can demonstrate never deviates in Rāmānuja's fundamental views.

The aim of Veṅkaṭanātha was not to unify the various traditions of his time—the Pāñcarātra tradition, the tradition of the *Nālāyirat Tivyappirapantam*, or the Vedāntic tradition. For him it was clear that these traditions were completely different from his own in the topics they discussed,[5] the style of their compositions, and their religious practices.[6] But he does attempt to integrate the

---

[3] The three secrets referring to the three *mantras*, i.e., the *Tirumantra*, the *Dvayamantra*, and the *Caramaśloka* (*Bhagavadgīta* 18.66).

[4] For example, in his *Paramatabhaṅga* (chapter 5–20) Veṅkaṭanātha rejects 15 doctrines of other Schools such as Lokāyata, Mādhyamika, Yogācāra, Sautrāntika, Vaibhāṣika, Advaita, Jaina, Bhāskara, Bhartṛhari, Vaiśeṣika, Naiyāyika, Kumārila, Sāṅkhya, Yoga and Pāśupata.

[5] For remarks on this relationship, see Hardy 1983: 301.

[6] It is clear that the *Tivyappirabandham* as read by the Viśiṣṭādvaita is understood based on their own philosophical and theological terminology. This has been mentioned by Hardy, who has examined the later philosophical tradition of commentaries on the *Tiruvāymoḻi*; see Hardy 1983: 244.

lines of thought of these different traditions into his own and relate them to one another. He examines the different traditions regarding *one* God, a God called Viṣṇu in some sources and Nārāyaṇa in others.[7] In his examinations of earlier traditions and their ideas regarding God's uniqueness, not only is Veṅkaṭanātha's theological basis important, but also its conceptual roots. He tries to unite different directions of religious traditions under the concept of *one* God. In the following an attempt will also be made to demonstrate how Veṅkaṭanātha's concept of God is dependent on his understanding of central Upaniṣadic statements.

Overview

To begin, a short overview of the main characteristics of Veṅkaṭanātha's concept of God will be presented, followed by a discussion of the cosmological context of this concept by looking at how (only) one central sentence from the *Bṛhadāraṇyaka Upaniṣad* (BĀU 1.4.7) is quoted in different contexts and interpreted by both Rāmānuja and Veṅkaṭanātha to substantiate various central ideas in their works. Especially the concept of manifestation—expressed as the transformation of name and form (*nāmarūpe*) from being non-differentiated (*avyākṛta*) to being differentiated (*vyākṛta*)—is fundamental for Veṅkaṭanātha's cosmological and ontological viewpoint. As will be shown, even though he presents an independent line of thought, he remains close to central concepts of Rāmānuja's ontology.

This concept of manifestation is not only helpful for understanding many of the theological and philosophical topics developed by Veṅkaṭanātha in his various works, but also relevant for several of other key concepts he discusses. The concept of manifestation is related to abstract terms such as substance (*dravya*), including its states (*avasthā*), its properties (*dharma*) and its mode

---

7 Also Veṅkaṭanātha uses the terms *brahman*, Viṣṇu, and Nārāyaṇa interchangeably.

(*prakāra*). It also concerns the mode possessor (*prakārin*), as well as the more general qualifier (*viśeṣaṇa*) and qualificand (*viśeṣya*) and the relationship between these two.[8]

The ontology developed by Veṅkaṭanātha is a decisive factor in his view of monotheism. It establishes that God is always connected to all things, regardless of whether they are present or not. In this sense, there is nothing with which God does not stand in relation, or by which He cannot be qualified. As the most qualified entity, everything refers eternally to Him. The condition of an all-encompassing *Being* implies that also non-being (*asattva/abhāva*) is not only defined in its difference to being (*sattva/bhāva*) but is grounded by such a *Being* and can therefore defined as "another kind of being" (cf. Veṅkaṭanātha's expression of *bhāvāntara-abhāva* in SAS 726.8f. *ad* TMK 5.52).[9]

The onto-theological conception of God clearly elaborated by both Rāmānuja and Veṅkaṭanātha is inseparably connected to access to the ultimate ground through language. If conscious and material entities are *a priori* connected with words that signify them—whereby the use of conventional language is excluded—

8 For pointing out a difference in meaning between *viśeṣaṇa/viśeṣya* and *prakāra/prakārin*, cf. Bartley 2002: 82.

9 A point that has already been taken up several times for Veṅkaṭanātha's predecessors in the secondary literature on this subject. See for example Ram-Prasad (2013), who analyzes Rāmānuja's commentary (in the *Gītābhāṣya*) *ad Bhagavadgītā* 2.16. Regarding Rāmānuja's statement: *vināśasvabhāvo hy asattvam*; *avināśasvabhāvaś ca sattvam*, Ram-Prasad explains (ibid. 43): "This does not mean that, just because the body is perishable, it is non-being. Rather, it just means that the perishable, or that which undergoes destruction, is called "non-existent". It is being itself that can be polarized into two orders of being, the indestructible, imperishable selves and destructible, perishable bodies. There are simply two orders of being under being as such." Therefore, in this article I make a distinction here between *Being* that underlies everything and being (*sattva*) as opposed to non-being (*asattva*). It is essential that there is *Being* of being (*sattva*) and *Being* non-being (*asattva*).

then not only can the infinite multiplicity of entities be grounded in God, but also the words that denote every entity. If the foundation of the world is linguistic, then also words with their meanings must refer to God. Insofar as this God is the Being toward whom everything is linguistically aimed, every word thus denotes Him. Discussions emphasizing precisely this aspect revolve around the concept of co-referentiality (*sāmānādhikaraṇya*), a term frequently used by both authors.

Against the background of the concept of co-referentiality, it can be illustrated how both authors attempt to establish their monotheism of the one God Viṣṇu-Nārāyaṇa. According to their understanding of the relationships in the world, whether between material objects or conscious subjects, a single reason for everything is only possible if all distinctions are based on *one* Being. Only by successfully demonstrating this can one justifiably speak of a *unity* (*aikya*) of all differentiations with their underlying ground. Decisively, it is still possible to have differences between conscious subjects, between material objects, and between conscious subjects and material objects.

In the view of Rāmānuja and Veṅkaṭanātha, coordinating objects or words with their meanings is possible because a *third* grounding aspect defined as a substance (*dravya*) is necessarily involved. Even though it is accepted that this *third* grounding aspect ultimately serves to establish a metaphysical reason, which could neither directly perceived nor inferred, its descriptions by our two authors can be interpreted in the way that it has to be presupposed for every kind of knowledge. Both explain this in many examples, but also through their criticism of other schools, of which only a few examples will be given here.

But, before this in addition to the fundamental ontological view of both authors, the eternal (*nitya*) and non-eternal (*anitya*) will of God must also be emphasised, which also comes into play as the ultimate ground in relation to the two different substances such as primordial matter (*prakṛti*) and eternal manifestation (*nityavibhūti*).

Finally, Veṅkaṭanātha's criticism of central doctrines of other schools is addressed, such as the Nyāya-Vaiśeṣika concept of inherence (*samavāya*) and the Sāṅkhya concept of the relation between cause (*kāraṇa*) and effect (*kārya*). The contrasting views of these two schools shed another light on Veṅkaṭanātha's theistic ontology and his concept of God.

Before presenting how Veṅkaṭanātha's central ontological concepts follow those of Rāmānuja, I will discuss the most important features whereby Veṅkaṭanātha characterizes the supremacy of his God as ultimate ground. He leaves nothing out that might serve to presuppose God as the ultimate basis for everything.

Key cosmological and ontological concepts and their relevance for theological issues

How does God remanifest the world? Probably the most important concept that is relevant for the ontology of the Rāmānuja School and its orientation towards God is the Upaniṣadic concept of the "Inner Controller" (*antaryāmin*) and God's act of entering.[10] Rāmānuja[11] used the term *antaryāmin* to explain that when

---

[10] The concept of entering has a central position, because without such an act no remanifestation can take place; cf. Rāmānuja's Śrībh III 131,17 *ad* BS 1.4.15: *kāryānupraveśanāmarūpavyākaraṇaprasiddheś ca.* "And because it is well known that *brahman*, which is creator, omniscient and supreme, unfolds name and form by entering its effects." To describe the process of entering, Rāmānuja refers to *Taittirīya Upaniṣad Āraṇyaka* 6.2.3 and *Taittirīya Upaniṣad* 3.11.3. Another relevant earlier passage similar to the concept of the Inner Controller is Prajāpati's entering the *nāmārūpe*, found in *Taittirīya Brāhmaṇa* 2.2.7.1: *prajāpatiḥ prajā asṛjata. tāḥ sṛṣṭāḥ samaśliṣyan. tā rūpeṇānuprāviśat. tasmā āhuḥ. rūpam vai prajāpatir iti. tā namnā 'nuprāviśat. tasmād āhuḥ. nāma vai prajāpatir iti.* "Prajāpati brought forth creatures. Those brought forth were conjoined. He entered them by means of form. That is why one says: Prajāpati truly *is* form. He entered them by means of name. That is why one says: Prajāpati truly *is* name."

[11] For the reception and development of the concept of *antaryāmin* (Inner Controller) in the Rāmānuja school, see Oberhammer 1998.

God initiates a new creation by virtue of His will (*icchā*), His effort (*prayatna*) and His act of knowledge (*jñāna*), He remains eternally present and effective in every individual soul (*cit*), but also, as we will see, in material mass (*acit*).

It is through His body that He manifests everything and is connected to everything ("conscious and material entities," *cidacid-vastu*).[12] In this sense this God is *one* (*eka*), meaning that no other divine being is equal to Him as this kind of Inner Controller. God is always present inwardly. "Inward" does not mean that the individual soul (*jīvātman*) can recognize God by looking inside, but means that He is present in the heart[13] of each individual soul—a central topos that can also be found in earlier texts such as the Upaniṣads[14] and the poems of the Āḻvārs.[15] It is due to God's act of entering that all terms denoting the soul also denote God. This is for example also the case for the self-referring term "I," by which the individual soul refers to his-/herself, but which denotes at least the all-enabling ground, i.e., God Himself. Conversely, God's outward presence is also connected to everything, meaning that for each constitutive material element of the world, God is the common basis.[16] Nonetheless, when He is present as the Inner Controller, either by the self-reference of the somehow limited

---

[12] For the history of the concept of body (*śarīra*) in the tradition of Viśiṣṭādvaita Vedānta, the polemical discussion with the tradition of Nyāya-Vaiśeṣika, and the difference between the two traditions, cf. Colas 2020: 116ff.; cf. also for the same polemical discussion after Rāmānuja up to Veṅkaṭanātha cf. Oberhammer 1996: 53–98.

[13] Oberhammer (1998: 67f.) has pointed out for Rāmānuja a different usage of language: when Rāmānuja speaks of God's presence in the heart of the soul he changes from the common Inner Ruler (*antaryāmin*) to the One who is internally present (*antarvartin*).

[14] Cf. Olivelle 2006: 54.

[15] Cf. Schmücker 2020b: 367–369.

[16] Common basis refers to the central concept of co-referentiality (*sāmānādhikaraṇya*), which is explained below, starting on below p. 377.

individual soul, or His presence in the time and space limited material mass, He Himself is not limited[17] by a certain time (*kāla*), certain place (*deśa*), or a particular entity (*vastu*).[18]

Other characteristic marks (*lakṣaṇa*) of God enumerated by Veṅkaṭanātha in his *Nyāyasiddhāñjana* (=NSi) at the beginning of the chapter on God (*īśvaraparicheda*, 271,1ff.) are the following: He is the Lord over all (*sarveśvaratvam*); He is conscious while all-pervading (*vyāpakatve*[19] *sati cetanatvam*); He is the Principal of everything (*sarvaśeṣitvam*) and propitiated by all [ritual] actions (*sarvakarmasamārādhyatvam*); He gives the results of every [ritual act] (*sarvaphalapradatvam*); He supports everything (*sarvādhāratvam*); He is the cause of every effect (*sarvakāryotpādakatvam*); He has every other substance except His own knowledge as His body (*svajñānasvetarasamastadravyaśarīratvam*)[20]; and He has [qualities] such as "having the will to be realized by itself" (*svatas satyasaṃkalpatvādikam*).

God's possessing a knowledge that qualifies Him, i.e., His *dharmabhūtajñāna*, raises the question of whether this knowledge belongs to His body. In Veṅkaṭanātha's NSi (cf. NSi 160,1–162,5), he adopts and repeats Rāmānuja's three definitions of God's body but goes beyond Rāmānuja and adds a fourth defini-

---

[17] Cf. Oberhammer 1996 on the development of *triparicchedarāhitya* in the Rāmānuja school.

[18] NSi 271,3–272,1ff.: *sarveśvaratvam, vyāpakatve sati cetanatvam, sarvaśeṣitvam, sarvakarmasamārādhyatvam, sarvaphalapradatvam, sarvādhāratvam, sarvakāryotpādakatvam, svajñānasvetarasamastadravyaśarīrakatvam, svatas satyasaṅkalpatvādikañ ca īśvaralakṣaṇam.*

[19] Cf. van Buitenen (1956: 236) for Rāmānuja's use of *vyāpaka* in a general sense and not in the more technical as "invariably concomitant".

[20] Cf. NSi 166,5 Veṅkaṭanātha's definition of a body: *īśvaratajjñānavyatiriktaṃ dravyaṃ śarīram*. "A body is a substance other than God *and* His knowledge."

tion (*taṭasthalakṣaṇa*).[21] In a fifth definition he explains the above-mentioned word *cetana* to emphasize that God is qualified by consciousness (*caitanya*) that does *not* belong to His body (NSi 166,5): "A body is a substance different from God and His knowledge" (*īśvaratajjñānavyatiriktaṃ dravyaṃ śarīram*). This means that God's knowledge and His will do not belong to His body.[22] Even if God's knowledge is not explicitly a topic in this contribution, it is nevertheless highlighted in some places that it is not only an ontology that is accepted as the ultimate ground, but also the divine will. Needless to say, such a divine will must be distinct from what it brings about. Hence the body is separated from His Gods knowledge, of which the will is a state. What other qualifications does Veṅkaṭanātha ascribe to God, and how close is he to Rāmānuja's views? Rāmānuja identifies God with the Vedic Puruṣa as follows (Śrībh I 17,1 *ad* BS 1.1.1):

> The word *brahman* signifies the supreme Puruṣa, who is free of all defects in His nature, and who is characterized by the multitude of innumerable excellent qualities, and of unsurpassed superiority.[23]

Following this example, Veṅkaṭanātha refers to the Puruṣa-hymn of the *Ṛgveda* (ṚV 10.90),[24] and names his God as the "Lord of

---

[21] NSi 165,1ff.: *yasya cetanasya yadavastham apṛthaksiddhaviśeṣanaṃ dravyaṃ tat tasya śarīram*. "For a conscious being, that substance found in a certain state, which is an inseparable attribute, is its body."

[22] Cf. NSi 160,2–3: *cetanasya caitanyaviśiṣṭasyety arthaḥ*. "The meaning is: for a conscious being is qualified by consciousness."

[23] Śrībh I 17,1: *brahmaśabdena ca svabhāvato nirastanikhiladoṣo 'navadhikātiśayāsaṅkhyeyakalyāṇaguṇagaṇaḥ puruṣottamo 'bhidhīyate.*

[24] Cf. SAS 346.8-9 *ad* TMK 3.7, where Veṅkaṭanātha explicitly refers to the *Puruṣasūkta*: *sarvakartṛtvaṃ puruṣasūktārthapratyabhijñayā siddham. akhilatanutvaṃ ca puruṣa evedaṃ sarvam itivat tenedaṃ pūrṇaṃ puruṣeṇa sarvam ity anena vyañjitam.* "That [God] is the [highest] agent for everything is established by recognizing the meaning of the *Puruṣasūkta*; and that He has everything as His body as [it is said in the words], 'Exclusively the Puruṣa is this every-

the creatures" (*prajāpati*). This expression is related to God's desire to create living beings. However, the will (*icchā*) of the "Lord of the creatures" not only depends on His desire to create, but also on whether what He manifests is already eternally related to Him. Acting out of compassion as well as for His own amusement (cf. *Tattvamuktākalāpa* (=TMK) 3.1b: *krīḍākāruṇyatantraḥ sṛjati*), He initiates a new cycle of world creation for the sake of the final redemption of the unreleased souls, distributing their *karman* individually and impartially[25] (TMK 3.1c: *samatayā jīvakarmānurūpam*). Independent (*nirapekṣa*) and free (*svatantra*), He remanifests everything, i.e., every conscious and material being (*cidacidvastu*).

His presence as the Inner Controller of and in everything (*viśvāntaryāmin*) also has the function of removing the individual soul's fear during the stay in *saṃsāra*.[26] He is characterized by the fact that nothing exists in the past, present or future[27] that has not been eternally supported and directed by Him through His initiating the creation as the remanifestation of His body (*śarīra*).

---

thing,' is revealed [in the words of *Śvetāśvatara Upaniṣad* 3.10]: 'Therefore this [All] is completely filled by Puruṣa.'"

25 For the concept of the Lord's "impartiality" (*sāmya*), see also AS (= *Adhikaraṇasarāvali*) verse 237ff. *ad* BS 2.3.6. Cf. also the explanation in Mumme 1986: 106: "The Lord does not instigate or cause action forcibly, but always through the *guṇa*s, in accordance with the *jīva*'s past *karma*. Vedānta Deśika interprets this as the Lord's *sāmya* or egalitarism, which delivers Him from the possibility of cruelty or partiality."

26 Cf. TMK 2.32b, where it is stated that the knowledge (*vidyā*) of the abode (*ālambana*) i.e., the Inner Controller of everything (*viśvāntaryāmitattva*), destructs the fear of the *saṃsāra* (*bhavabhayaśamanī*) for the one who desires to be free of rebirth (*vītarāgasya*).

27 On Veṅkaṭanātha's view of time (*kāla*), cf. TMK 1.65–70; NSi 130,10–141,8. See also Schmücker forthcoming².

In Veṅkaṭanātha's description, since God is able to manifest everything due to His inconceivable potency[28] (*acintyaśakti*), He is said to have the potency for everything (*sarvaśakti*), i.e., of all actions; further, He is omniscient (*sarvajña*) and omnipresent (*vibhu*), encompasses everything (*sarvavyāpin*),[29] and is completely (*pūrṇa*) present in everything, including other gods.[30] He just goes so far as to say that names of other gods also refer to *one* God, even for example Śiva. Thus, God is said to enter every soul[31] and remains by this act (indirectly) present in material mass (*acit*). What does this mean? We already mentioned that Veṅkaṭanātha describes the process of remanifestation as being initiated by God's wish/will (*saṅkalpa/icchā*); this also implies that God manifests Himself due to His own will as the Inner Controller. He does not distance Himself from what He has manifested. He is considered to *be* the "form of all" (*viśvarūpaḥ*). But how is this kind of omnipresence explained, and does He manifest Himself in everything directly or indirectly?

As I will demonstrate, every entity God enters is also an entity whose denotation refers directly to God Himself. The following passage of the first chapter of his NSi provides a detailed description of the order of God's manifestion of everything and His entering. In this description, Veṅkaṭanātha repeatedly refers to details for which central sentences are in the background. For

---

28 The compound *acintyaśakti*, God's "inconceivable potency" is mentioned in TMK 3.25; cf. also NSi 393,3 (verse 98a).

29 Cf. the quotation of *Mahānārāyaṇa Upaniṣad* XI. 6 in the NSi (482,4–5) and SAS 215.10 *ad* TMK 1.69: *antar bahiś ca tat sarvaṃ vyāpya nārāyaṇaḥ sthitaḥ*. "Nārāyaṇa exists by encompassing all of this inwardly and outwardly."

30 Cf. for example the passage in the third chapter (*īśvarapariccheda*) of Veṅkaṭanātha's NSi (285ff.), where he discusses that God is "perfectly complete in three forms" (*tisṛṣu ca mūrtiṣu paripūrṇa eveśvara*).

31 The god Śiva is declared to be an individual soul into which the Inner Controller enters (cf. NSi 285,4).

example, when he mentions that God desires to create of His own will, he is clearly referring to ChU 6.2.2[32]; or when he speaks of desiring to manifest name and form, he is referring to ChU 6.3.2[33]; this sentence is then mentioned together with BĀU 1.4.7, which refers to the process of manifestati-on and which will be frequently dealt with in the following.

> Each principle is first created *at His wish* by God, who has each previous principle preceding it as His body. Then *He wishes* to manifest individual names and forms; and because these separated principles are not capable of individual creation, *He wishes* to mix them mutually.[34] Thus having made the quintuplication with [a half of] each element and one-eighth of other four elements in the order described in texts such as "a half of ether is fourfold: wind, fire, water and earth",[35] *He makes* a group of individual selfs *entered* by Himself,

---

[32] Cf. ChU 6.2.2: *tad aikṣata bahu syāṃ prajāyeyeti.* "And it thought by itself: 'Let me become many. Let me propagate myself'." (Quoted from Olivelle 1998: 247).

[33] ChUp 6.3.2: *hantāham imās tisro devatā anena jīvenātmanānupraviśya nāmarūpe vyākaravāṇi.* "Come now, why don't I establish the distinctions of name and appearance by entering these three deities here with this living self (*ātman*)". (Quoted from Olivelle 1998: 247).

[34] Compare the following verses of the order of creation with *Viṣṇupurāṇa* (ViP) 1.2.51–52,53cd:
nānāvīryāḥ pṛthagbhūtās tatas te saṃhatiṃ vinā.
nāśaknuvan prajāḥ sraṣṭum asamāgamya kṛtsnaśaḥ. .
sametyānyonyasaṃyogaṃ parasparasamāśrayāḥ
ekasaṃghātalakṣāś ca saṃprāpyaikyam aśeṣataḥ.
mahadādyā viśeṣāntā hy aṇḍam utpādayanti te.
"These [principles], possessing various valours and being separated, are without mixture; accordingly, they, not having combined together, could not create living beings. Having got mutual conjunction, they depend upon one another; and having merged into complete oneness, they have one composite unit as their result. [...] They, from *mahat* to a particular produce the cosmic egg."

[35] Quote not identified.

enters into them, and from these principles *He produces* the cosmic egg (*brahmāṇḍa*) composed of elements attaining to the change called gold, enclosed by the seven covers, [namely, water, fire, air, ether, *ahaṃkara*, *mahat* and *prakṛti*], each following one that is ten times thicker[36] than the previous.[37]

In this cited passage Veṅkaṭanātha describes not only a sequence, but also how each step is the ground for the next step in the course of manifestation.[38] In this course, everything is seen as grounded in the beginning in God's own volition (*svasaṅkalpād*) and continuing in an interplay of his creating, willing acting, and entering, which is described in the quote above in a sequence of

---

36 For *daśaguṇitottara-*, cf. *Viṣṇupurāṇa* 1.2.58:
vārivahnyanilākāśais tato bhūtādinā bahiḥ
vṛtaṃ daśaguṇair aṇḍaṃ bhūtādir mahatā tathā.
"The egg is wrapped in water, fire wind and space and other elements, and by the individuation that is their source. Each layer is ten times greater than the one within, and the whole is covered by Greatness, the origin of the elements." (Translation quoted from Coman 2021: 49).

37 NSi 143,6–146,2: *etāni tattvāni prathamam īśvaraḥ svasaṅkalpād eva tattadavyavahitapūrvapūrvatattvaśarīrakaḥ sṛṣṭvā vyaṣṭināmarūpavyākaraṇaṃ saṅkalpya teṣāṃ tattvānāṃ pṛthagbhūtānāṃ vyaṣṭisṛṣṭyaśakteḥ parasparasaṃmiśraṇañ ca saṅkalpya, 'vyomnordhabhāgaś catvāro vāyutejaḥpayobhuvām' ityādikrameṇa ekaikabhūteṣu bhūtāntarāṇām aṣṭamāṃśacatuṣkaiḥ pañcīkaraṇam kṛtvā teṣu svānupraviṣṭajīvavargam anupraveśya tair eva tattvair daśaguṇitottarasaptāvaraṇaveṣṭitaṃ hemākhyapariṇāmagatabhūtamayaṃ brahmāṇḍam ārabhya* [...]. (Translation adopted from Mikami [pdf]).

38 The same kind of the manifestation is described in TMK 1.16ab: *niḥśeṣaṃ kāryatattvaṃ janayati sa paro hetutattvaiḥ śarīrī tattatkāryāntarātmā bhavati ca, tad asau viśruto viśvarūpaḥ.* "The Highest, having a body, produces restless [each] principle to be effected by principles which are their respective causes, and becomes [after that] the Inner Self of each effect; therefore He [i.e., God] is proclaimed [everywhere as] the One who has the form of everything." For the concept of quintuplication (*pañcīkaraṇa*), cf. also TMK 1.17 and Srinivasa Chari's explanations thereon in id., 2004: 321.

absolutiva (*sṛṣṭvā, saṅkalpya, saṅkalpya, kṛtvā, anupraveśya, ārabhya*). The process of creation, dependent on His will, leads to the manifestation of His body, thus everything proceeds only within Him, i.e., nothing can exist outside of His body. Even the individual souls belong to His body. He creates name and form from a mutually presupposed sequence of principles (*tattva*) and mixes them. He is not described as entering these material principles, but first enters individual souls. After His entering, these souls again enter name and form.[39] After the manifestation of the cosmic egg, gods like Brahman and Rudra receive their special functions, enabled by God as their Inner Controller. The sequence described here is important insofar as Veṅkaṭanātha later discusses whether God's being effective happens directly or indirectly in material mass.

In the next step during creation, God creates out of His grace the four-faceted Brahman, and out of His anger, Rudra. God enters as the Inner Controller into Brahman, whose "form is filled with all conscious beings dwelling inside of this cosmic egg" (NSi 144,4: *sakalatadaṇḍāntarvarticetanabharitavigrahaṃ*), and who is created in any one of seven places,[40] starting with a lotus in His navel. This is caused by the Veda, which is said at this point to be composed by Him to form in the cosmic egg, the fourteen worlds, and to give names and forms.[41]

> And immediately after this, God as the Inner Controller of Brahman created by Himself, causes by Brahman, who is magnified by knowledge and power for the wonderful creation, which [both] are

---

[39] NSi 176, 4–5: *idañ ca vyaṣṭināmarūpāṇāṃ sarveṣāṃ jīvānupraveśa-śrutibalāvalambanenoktam.* "And it is said based on the authority of Scriptures that all individualized names and forms are entered by individual selves."

[40] The seven places are mentioned according to MBh 12.335.36–39 (Nārāyaṇīya-section).

[41] Verses/sentences to which Veṅkaṭanātha implicitly refers in this context are *Viṣṇupurāṇa* 1.5.63, *Manusmṛti* 1.23, *Ṛgveda* 10.90.1, fully quoted in fn. 169 below; and *Brahmasūtra* 1.3.27.

offered by Himself through knowledge acquired by the Vedas composed by Himself, and for whom the various dangers such as Madhu and Kaiṭabha[42] are removed by Him, to create in this cosmic egg various and wonderful names and forms[43], such as gods, animals, human beings, plants which are abiding in the fourteen worlds [of the cosmic egg], and [to create] a particular direction, etc.[44]

There is no independence either for the gods Brahman or Rudra. He creates, i.e., manifests the cosmic egg, as Veṅkaṭanātha repeats, having the god Brahman as His body, and He causes the god Rudra having him as His body to take back the world.

Identification of *brahman* with Viṣṇu-Nārāyaṇa

The uniqueness of God is due to His identification with the *one* secondless *brahman*. Through this identification it is ascertained that He indeed is the *only* basis to which everything refers and on which everything depends.

Both Rāmānuja and Veṅkaṭanātha explicitly state that *brahman* is identical with Viṣṇu-Nārāyaṇa. The Advaitic meaning of *brahman*, "being without a second", relates to the concept that God and His body (*śarīra*) are not to be understood in the sense of a dualism of soul and body, but as a *relational unity*,[45] beyond

---

42 For these two demons, cf. the contribution of Charlotte Schmid in this volume, pp. 115, 117, 121.

43 Note the synonymity of *saṃjñāmūrti-* and *nāmarūpe* mentioned before in the quotation.

44 NSi 145,5–146,1: *sa ca bhagavān anantaraṃ svavihitabrahmāntaryāmirūpeṇāvasthitaḥ svaprahitavedopajñśavijñānena svārpitābhyāṃ vicitrasṛṣṭiviṣayabuddhiśaktibhyām upabṛṃhatena svanirdhūtamadhukaiṭabhādividhāpadā brahmaṇā brahmāṇḍāntaścaturdaśabhuvanasaṃsthānatadadhikaraṇakadevatiryaṅmanuṣyasthāvarādidigviśeṣadivividhavicitravyaṣṭisaṃjñāmūrtisṛṣṭiṃ kārayati.*

45 I have adopted the expression *relational unity* to describe God's relation to conscious and material beings from Gerhard Oberhammer; cf.

which no other divine god can be established through any means of valid knowledge. Veṅkaṭanātha demonstrates the meaning of God as *one* (*eka*) by explaining that *only* such a God can be omnipresent (*vibhu*). Identifying *brahman* with God implies that *brahman* is identical with the *one* God Viṣṇu-Nārāyaṇa, who has no other god beside Him. Gods like Śiva or Brahman are subordinated as we have seen above.[46] In his *Nyāyasiddhāñjana*, at the beginning of the chapter on God (*īśvaraparicchedа*), Veṅkaṭanātha summarizes this fundamental view of his tradition as follows:

> This [God] is *one*, because it is revealed [by authoritative Scriptures] that He has no second [equal being beyond Himself] and [that there is] no [being of] equal value or superior to Him. Exclusively this [God] is [identified as] *brahman*, because only He who is free of threefold limitation is said in Scripture (*śruti*) to be of unsurpassed

---

Oberhammer 1999: 201: "As 'Inner Controller' and God Nārāyaṇa, the Brahma is no longer a transcendent without inner relation to the world, but a Being that relates its inner Being to the being of the world and forms a relational unity with it." On this, see also Oberhammer 1996: 101, where he uses the expression "a common horizon of being" in this context: "The worldly being, that is, the conscious and the material being and the Brahma have a common horizon of being, [...] in which both become comprehensible as a dynamic unity, without, however become identical, nor even the same." [English Translation by M.S.].

46 Cf. NSi 284,5–6: *evaṃ ca nārāyaṇasyaiva paramakāraṇatvamumukṣūpāsyatvasarvāntaryāmitvādisiddheḥ trimūrtisāmyaikyottīrṇavyaktyantaraparatvapakṣāś catvaro 'pi nirastāḥ nirmūlāḥ veditavyāḥ.* "Because exclusively Nārāyaṇa is established as the supreme cause, to be worshiped for one who desires to be released and as the Inner Controller of all, etc., also the four theses are to be known as baseless after it has been refuted that [1] there is equality in the *trimūrti* [i.e., Śiva, Viṣṇu, Brahman are equal]; that [2] there is unity [between these gods]; that [3] there is one god beyond; or [4] another being [is the Supreme]." Cf. also TMK (chapter 3, *nāyakasara*), verse 14; PMBh (chapter 4, *paratattvādhikāra*) 273–275.

greatness or as having the ability to make great,[47] inasmuch as He is the self of all.[48]

In these words, Veṅkaṭanātha establishes and corroborates his schools's monotheism. The monism of the neutral *brahman* is now the monotheism of the *one* and exclusive God. The relationship of the God Viṣṇu-Nārāyaṇa to what He supports, directs and rules is not a relationship that beings can understand through means of valid cognition (*pramāṇa*) such as perception (*pratyakṣa*) or inference (*anumāna*). Only the eternal Veda, i.e., the words of the Vedic language, reveals God's relationship with individual souls (*cit*) and with the material world (*acit*). We will deal with this means of valid knowledge in more detail (cf. p. 422ff.).

The Goddess Śrī

The identification with *brahman* and the reduction of a personal God to one-ness seems contradictory if God and the Goddess are understood as two different personally acting divine beings.

Therefore, in this context the status of the Goddess Śrī/Lakṣmī must be briefly mentioned. Although God is identified as *brahman*, whereby Veṅkaṭanātha and his tradition corroborate the absoluteness and exclusiveness of God, His equal relationship with the Goddess, His female counterpart or complement, is accepted.[49] While Veṅkaṭanātha subordinates all divine beings to the

---

47 Based on the derivation of the word *brahman* from the verbal root *bṛṃh* "to increase, to expand", the word *brahman* is understood as "that which has the potential to expand". Cf. also Śrībh II 110,5–6 *ad* BS 1.1.2: *upalakṣyam hy anavadhikātiśayabṛhad bṛṃhaṇaṃ ca, bṛhater dhātos tadarthatvāt.*

48 NSi 274,1–275,1: *advitīyasamābhyadikadaridratvaśravaṇād asāv ekaḥ. sa eva brahma. tasyaiva trividhaparicchedarahitasya sarvātmakatvena niratiśayabṛhattvabṛṃhaṇatvaśravaṇāt.*

49 However, I have found no passage that explicitly identifies the Goddess with the neuter *brahman*.

one God, the Goddess belonging to God is not considered to be subordinate in the same way as other divine beings are. This results in a contradiction: either the uniqueness of God must be relativized, or the problem of the Goddess not being equal must be resolved. According to Veṅkaṭanātha, insofar as God is eternally related to everything, He must also be connected to the Goddess.[50] Therefore Veṅkaṭanātha sees no contradiction in claiming that God and the Goddess have an eternal conjugal union (NSi 360,5: *dāmpatyaṃ śāśvataṃ*). The context in which he states this view is notable. After discussing in NSi 360,1ff. the body of *brahman* transforming from a subtle state (*sūkṣmacidacidvastuśarīrakaṃ*) into a manifest state (*sthūlacidacidvastuśarīratayā*), and enumerating all the further relationships (*saṃbandhāḥ*) of God, such as the relationship between support (*ādhāra*) and the supported (*ādheya*), ruler (*īśvara*) and ruled (*īśitavya*), principal element (*śeṣin*) and accessory (*śeṣa*), he continues with a verse stating that God has an eternal conjugal union with the Goddess (*śriyā saha*). Due to this, the two are understood as equal (*sāmya*) in their properties, as a unity (*aikya*), and as having the same power (*śaktitva*). Veṅkaṭanātha expresses clearly that the Goddess has exactly the same relations (*saṃbandhāḥ*) as the God has:

> And for this reason, the relations (*sambandhāḥ*), [established by] means of valid knowledge, that [Viṣṇu] has with all [entities] distinct from Him—as Supporter and supported, Controller and controlled, Principal and subordinate, Embodied and body, Cause and effect, etc.—*the same* together with [the Goddess] Śrī.[51]

---

[50] The relation of God and the Goddess is expressed by Veṅkaṭanātha in TMK 3.8 in the following words: "For that *Puruṣasūkta* which is recited in all the Vedas and has stated that exclusively Viṣṇu is the Supreme Being, it is said in a clear manner in the following section that [He] is the consort of the Goddess Śrī; and He is remembered as Nārāyaṇa." *puṃsūktaṃ sarvavedaprapaṭhanam hitaṃ yat paratvaikatānaṃ tasyaiva śrīpatitvaṃ viśadam abhidadhe hy uttaratrānuvāke āmnātaś caiṣa nārāyaṇa iti.*

[51] NSi 360,1–4: *tataḥ siddhaṃ sūkṣmacidacidvastuśarīrakaṃ brahmaiva sthūlacidacidvastuśarīratayā pariṇamatīti vedāntāḥ pratipāda-*

> But *together* with [the Goddess] Śrī, the partnership lasts forever. And for this very reason, the way of both [i.e., God and Goddess] is [according to the authoritative tradition] described with expressions of having [common] qualities such as equality, unity, potency, etc.[52]

All three concepts, i.e., equality (*sāmya*), unity (*aikya*) and potency (*śaktitva*) mentioned in this quote are elaborated by Veṅkaṭanātha. However, all three are to be understood as specifying both, God and Goddess, who cannot be separated in their relation from each other. Their inseparability is proven by their equality, which Veṅkaṭanātha explains as follows:

> Because [their both] knowledge, bliss and etc., are completely equal, and because [they] are equal in [their way of] manifesting the world, being the Principal (*śeṣin*), being fit for surrender, being the goal to be attained, etc., Her equality with Him is clearly justified.[53]

Also the doctrine of unity (*aikya*, *ekatvavāda*) is to be understood in such a way that the inseparably existing Goddess and God are the basis for determining their being one. Their unity can be seen as determining both.

> Even the references to [the Goddess] as one [with Him] by unity with [His] modes are in the same way, insofar as [the Two] are completely equal in the form of a couple and [She] is [also] the substratum of being the Principal to whom only the whole phenomenal world is subordinate.[54]

---

yantīti. tena ca tadvyatiriktasya nikhilasyādhārādheyabhāveśvareśitavyatvaśeṣaśeṣitvaśarīraśarīribhāvakāryakāraṇabhāvādayo yathāgrahaṇaṃ saṃbandhāḥ.

52 NSi 360,5: *śriyā saha tu dāmpatyaṃ śāśvataṃ. tata eva tu tayoḥ sāmyaikyaśaktitvatadvattvādigirāṃ gatiḥ.*

53 NSi 361,1-362,1: *jñānānandādyatyantasāmyāj jagajjanakatvaśeṣitvaśaraṇyatvaprāpyatvādisāmyāc ca sāmyagirāṃ nirvāho vyaktaḥ.*

54 NSi 362,1-363,1: *ekatvavādā apy evaṃ dvandvarūpeṇātyantasamatayā prakāraikyena, samastaprapañcapratiyogikaikaśeṣitvāśrayatvena.*

What is important here is that the Goddess is described as being God's potency (*śaktitva*). Veṅkaṭanātha (NSi 363,1–5) sees this either as a qualifier, whereby he explains the Goddess as God's wife (*patnītvādirūpeṇa*), or as the Goddess having the function relied upon by God for the renewed manifestation of the world.

> Now, the references [to Her] as [His] potency mean that [She] is [His] attribute (*viśeṣaṇatva*) in the form of a wife and the like; or they mean that [She] is helpful in driving [His] operations like the remanifestation, as [She] has the same amusement [as He]. And the reference as "potency" (*śakti*) is always made to the part of the feminine, also in other couples which have the nature of woman and man.[55]

But even as being an attribute (*viśeṣaṇatva*), the Goddess does not have a subordinate status. As this supportive source of God, it is the Goddess who begins a new manifestation of the world.

Finally, Veṅkaṭanātha adds that all the divine embodiments are exclusive to both, God and Goddess. Also forms in which God manifests Himself are defined as being His and Her different states[56] or concrete manifestations.

> The teachings of the different states [of the Lord] such as the *vyūhas* [also] refer to the embodiments, etc., [of Śrī], because these [*avatāras* of Śrī], although they reach the state of an effect on their own will or through the will of the Highest (i.e., the Lord), are different states of the Lord, because everything is of the nature of the Lord.[57]

---

55 NSi 363,1–5: *śaktitvavādās tu patnītvādirūpeṇa viśeṣaṇatvābhiprāyāḥ, sṛṣṭyādivyāpāreṣu samānalīlatayā prerakatvena sahakāritvābhiprāyā vā. prayujyate ca sarvatra strīpuṃsātmakeṣu dvandvāntareṣv api stryaṃśe śaktiśabdaḥ* [instead of *śaktitvavādaḥ*].

56 See Oberhammer 2002: 130–131 for the development of the theological concept of Goddess and her relation to Viṣṇu-Nārāyaṇa. This is also discussed in Oberhammer's as yet unpublished paper on the Goddess Śrī, which he graciously made available to me.

57 NSi 363,3–6: *vyūhavat avasthābhedavādās tv avatārādiviṣayāḥ, sarvasya bhagavadātmakatvena tasya svecchayā parecchayā vā kāryadaśāpannasyāpi bhagavadavasthābhedatvāt.*

It is clear from these words that Veṅkaṭanātha takes the Lord as the ultimate ground; although the will of the Goddess is mentioned, the Lord's will is equal to it. Nevertheless, if something is defined as a specific attribute, mode or state, this does not imply that in their relationship there is a higher and a lower part. The fact that everything has God as His nature describes God as Inner Controller who manifests everything; this means that on the one hand He is inseparable from everything, but at the same time strictly different. His inseparable relations are as manifold as the totality of the world is. His relation to the Goddess is of special intimacy. But despite Veṅkaṭanātha's emphasis on unity (*aikya*) and equality (*sāmya*) or necessary potency (*śakti*), for him every relation remains constituted by a fundamental difference, i.e., a difference either between Him and other divine beings, a difference between Him and the material (*prākṛta*) and immaterial (*aprākṛta*) world, or between Him and every soul that is living in either of these worlds.

Rāmānuja and Veṅkaṭanātha on the (re)manifestation of name and form (*nāmarūpe*)

If everything, i.e., conscious and material entities, refer to *one* God as having Him as their *one* base, it must be pointed out how Rāmānuja and Veṅkaṭanātha reflect their manifoldness, together with their different denotations, in relation to His oneness.

In the following, I first refer to Rāmānuja's views, as these are the basic ideas, and then I demonstrate how Veṅkaṭanātha follows his predecessors' central ideas, adopting them in most cases, but also expanding upon them considerably.

How can the concept of a *Being* characterized in this way be reconciled with the concept of transformation? And what ontological implications does this have? To demonstrate how Rāmānuja and Veṅkaṭanātha understand the transformation of *one* and the *same* base as having different states, I will first focus on their understanding of *Bṛhadāraṇyaka Upaniṣad* (= BĀU) 1.4.7. Using the terms *avyākṛta* (translated here as "non-differentiated" or "non-separated") and *vyākṛta* (rendered as "differentiated" or "separated"), both authors explain that the universe consisting of name and form (*nāmarūpe*) has been transformed from being non-differentiated to being differentiated—in fact, two states referring to a *third* grounding aspect. During this transformation, what existed in the past becomes manifested again in the present in the same way it existed earlier. The central statement in the BĀU referred to by Rāmānuja and Veṅkaṭanātha—referred to quite often—reads as follows:

> All this was non-separated (indistinguishable) [at the beginning of creation]. Then it became separated by name and shape [so it became possible to say]: "This particular one is of the name NN and of such and such a shape." Therefore, even to-day distinction is made by name and shape: "This particular one is of the name NN [and] of such and such a shape."[58]

Prior to Veṅkaṭanātha, these sentences were cited several times by Rāmānuja, such as in his *Vedārthasaṅgraha* (=VAS) and his *Śrībhāṣya* (=Śrībh), especially the first words: "All this was non-separated (indistinguishable) [at the beginning of creation]" (*tad dhedaṃ tarhy avyākṛtam āsīt*). Considering this quotation on its own and not only how it is contextualized in the works of our two authors, we can also understand that the second sentence refers to the existence of name and form and to their transformation from being unrecognizable to being recognizable, this dependent on their differentiation. The final sentence introduces also a temporal

---

[58] I cite here the translation of Thieme 1982/83: 23. *tad dhedaṃ tarhy avyākṛtam āsīt. tan nāmarūpābhyām eva vyākriyatāsau nāmāyam idaṃ rūpa iti. tad idam apy etarhi nāma rūpābhyām eva vyākriyate. asau nāmāyam idaṃrūpa iti.* Cf. also Olivelle's (1998: 47) translation, which renders *rūpa* as "visible appearance": "At that time this world was without distinctions; it was distinguished simply in terms of name and visible appearance—'He is so and so by name and has this sort of an appearance.' So even today this world is distinguished simply in terms of name and visible appearance, as when we say, 'He is so and so by name and has this sort of an appearance'."

factor and refers to this process of manifestation up to the present time (*etarhi*). Thus, this process of differentiation is repeated in the same way from the past until the present.

How was this passage interpreted to explain fundamental theological tenets or issues?[59] Both authors introduce this BĀU passage into their theological concepts according to their theistic background. In their interpretations, they both emphasize God's relation to every conscious and material entity, and that the creation as a kind of (re)manifestation must derive from something already *being* there but cannot arise from nothing. It is therefore important to examine the context where they introduce BĀU 1.4.7 into their works, and how they interpret its meaning regarding their views of their God Viṣṇu-Nārāyaṇa.

Both Rāmānuja and Veṅkaṭanātha refer to BĀU 1.4.7 in the context of describing God's remanifestation as constituting His body—His remanifestation of the world after the period of dissolution (*pralaya*)—and when describing non-differentiated (*avyākṛta*) names and forms (*nāmarūpe*). For both authors, during the period of dissolution everything is in a subtle state (*sūkṣmāvasthā*). When everything manifests, this involves differentiation into the *same* nameable variety of things that already existed in the subtle, non-manifested state. Thus, the fundamental concept of Rāmānuja and Veṅkaṭanātha is that nothing can emerge or be manifested completely anew. Things re-emerge after having been in the state of non-being, i.e., the subtle state. Consequently, if

[59] It should be noted that when examining the concept of correspondence, Johannes Bronkhorst mentions several central Upaniṣad quotations to illustrate his central thesis, among them and in particular BĀU 1.4.7 (cf. Bronkhorst 2011: 10), which he convincingly and insightfully discusses regarding the various philosophical schools of India. It is therefore interesting to see how this quotation is interpreted by Rāmānuja and the thinkers of his tradition. As I will demonstrate, the important nuance here is the eternally given and unchangeable correspondence between *nāman* and *rūpa*. Rāmānuja and Veṅkaṭanātha understand them as modifying states.

something is described as subtle (*sūkṣma*), i.e., as non-differentiated (*avyākṛta*), it still continues to *be*, even if during the period of dissolution (*pralaya*) it is defined as non-being. Moreover, if something becomes recognizable by being differentiated in name and form, it is still in *unity* with God, not only as that which He eternally supports and directs, but also as that which He finally terminates (*paryanta*) in its meaning. From this perspective, not only do all conscious beings, i.e., souls and material objects refer only to Him, but also linguistically, their designations, i.e., their names (*nāman*).

To elaborate on this central view of Rāmānuja and to demonstrate how it is adopted and developed further by Veṅkaṭanātha, I will start with a passage from his *Vedārthasaṃgraha* (VAS), Rāmānuja's earliest work. Here, he discusses whether primordial matter (*prakṛti*) and the individual souls (*puruṣa*) forming the body of *brahman* are non-being (*asat*) during the period of dissolution (*pralaya*). In this period, primordial matter and the individual souls are in an unrecognizable state of subtleness and *brahman* is in the state of cause (*kāraṇāvasthaṃ*), a state in which name and form are non-differentiated. This is clearly expressed in Rāmānuja's words of VAS §74 (113,8–9), when he says: "[*Brahman*,] having as its body primordial matter and souls, which having obtained a subtle state are incapable of the distinction of name and form."[60]

What is important about this statement is that it is not *brahman* itself that is the cause, but only *brahman* whose body consists of souls (*puruṣa*) and matter (*prakṛti*). When in its non-differentiated form, it is defined as non-being and, as such, as having a special state, i.e., the state of the cause (*kāraṇāvasthā*). Determining *brahman* as cause and as being in the subtle state (*sūkṣmāvasthā*) does not affect its essential nature (*svarūpa*), even if it is in another state, i.e., the manifest state (*sthūlāvasthā*), differentiated (*vibhakta*) in name and form. It has merely altered its state, no-

---

60 VAS §74 (113,8–9): *nāmarūpavibhāgānarhasūkṣmadaśāpannaprakṛtipuruṣaśarīraṃ*.

thing else. Having the state of effect it is nevertheless still *one brahman*. What is called the manifestation of the world is not different from *brahman* itself.[61] For Rāmānuja, it is a state of the *one* God/*brahman* that becomes present. This alternation does not occur by itself, but is caused, for example, by God's will or, as already described, by His entering (*anupraveśa*) as Inner Controller. But even the act of entering presupposes a will/a desire (*saṅkalpa/icchā*) to perform such an act. Rāmānuja describes this way of *brahman*'s (i.e., God's) transformation from cause to effect in his VAS §74 (113, 6–7):

> If it is the case that God Himself (*eva*) is one who is in the state of cause, then He Himself is also one who is in the state of effect (*kāryāvasthaḥ*) for the world whose material cause He is. Therefore, between cause and effect there is no difference and there is no contradiction with any authoritative Scripture.[62]

Rāmānuja expresses the same thought in his *Śrībhāṣya* (=Śrībh). Differentiated name and form is connected to *brahman*'s being in the state of effect, while being non-differentiated is always connected to *brahman*'s state as the only and secondless cause (*ekam eva advitīyaṃ kāraṇam*):

> The highest *brahman*, in all cases the self of all, inasmuch as it has every conscious and material being as its body, has at some time differentiated name and form, but at another time non-differentiated

---

[61] Cf. VAS §74 (113,9–10): *brahmaṇas tathāvidhasthūlabhāva eva jagataḥ sṛṣṭir ity ucyate.* See Bartley's (2002: 74) remark on the concept of creation according to Rāmānuja, namely: "Creation is emphatically not *ex nihilo*. Just as there is no substantial change in a piece of clay when it is made into a pot, so there is no substantial change in *Brahman* when its body passes from the causal to the effected condition that is the plural world about us." Cf. also Barua's (2009: 97) helpful distinction between "productive" and "creative" concerning God's activity to remanifest the world.

[62] VAS §74 (113,6–7): *tathā ca sati kāraṇāvastha īśvara eveti tadupādānakajagatkāryāvastho 'pi sa eveti kāryakāraṇayor ananyatvaṃ sarvaśrutyavirodhaś ca bhavati.*

> name and form (*kadācid vibhaktanāmarūpam, kadācic cāvibhaktanāmarūpam*). When it has differentiated name and form it is known as manifold and as effect; when it has non-differentiated name and form it is known as the one cause, without having a second.[63]

The following quotation, again taken from Rāmānuja's Śrībh demonstrates that he relates subtle and manifest conscious and material entities that constitute the body of God with the respective state of God as cause and as effect. His important statement in the following passage—that knowledge of everything can be understood through the realization of the *One* (*ekavijñānena sarvavijñānam*), which is often quoted (cf. VAS §12 (78,1), §36 (92,8), §69 (111,1), §70 (111,5)) refers to ChU 6.1.3 (*yenāśrutaṃ śrutaṃ bhavati*), but alludes also to the fact that knowledge of the cause implies knowledge of its possible effect, since both refer to *one* and the *same* ground. The effect is only another state of God/*brahman* who is in the state of the cause. In this way the effect is "not another" (*ananya*) than the cause. He concludes in his Śrībh:

> Therefore, the Highest Self has a body consisting in subtle or manifested conscious and material entities, depending on the state of the effect and the state of the cause. Thus, the desired knowledge of everything through the knowledge of *one* is very well demonstrated, insofar as the effect is known by the knowledge of the cause, because the effect is nothing other than the cause.[64]

---

63 Śrībh III 163,11–13 *ad* BS 1.4.23: *sarvacidacidvastuśarīratayā sarvadā sarvātmabhūtaṃ paraṃ brahma kadācid vibhaktanāmarūpam, kadācic cāvibhaktanāmarūpam. yadā vibhaktanāmarūpaṃ, tadā tad eva bahutvena kāryatvena cocyate. yadā cāvibhaktanāmarūpaṃ, tadā ekam advitīyaṃ kāraṇam.*

64 Śrībh II 76,15–77,1 *ad* BS 1.1.1: *ataḥ kāryāvasthaḥ kāraṇāvasthaś ca sthūlasūkṣmacidacidvastuśarīraḥ paramapuruṣa eveti kāraṇāt kāryasyānanyatvena kāraṇavijñānena kāryasya jñātatayā ekavijñānena sarvavijñānaṃ* [*ca*] *samīhitam upapannataram.* Cf. also Rāmānuja's statement in VAS §35 (92,5): *kāraṇam evāvasthāntarāpannaṃ kāryam.*

Rāmānuja relates name and form (*nāmarūpe*) to cause and effect: either they are both differentiated (*vyākṛta*) or they are both non-differentiated (*avyākṛta*). In fact, he explains that the cause is not different from the effect, because name and form (*nāmarūpe*) remain the *same* whether manifest, i.e., differentiated, or subtle, i.e., non-differentiated. As we will see below, Veṅkaṭanātha keeps this central view of Rāmānuja, even though he sometimes uses a different terminology. As he points out, it is not contradictory that there are different states (such as the state of cause and the state of effect) for one and the same substance. Neither of these states refers to creation out of nothing or from nothing. When a state ceases to be present, i.e., unable to be known by perception this does not imply its complete destruction. Transformable different states of eternal *Being* imply not a transformation of such a Being, but a *Being* of transformation in a beginningless and endless sequence of states. This concept, called *pariṇāma* by Rāmānuja, does not imply the imperfection of *brahman*, but serves to give it an "exclusive unrestricted supremacy" (*niraṅkuśaiśvaryāvahatvam*, Śrībh I 167 *ad* BS 1.4.27). Numerically, *brahman* therefore remains *one* (*eka*), and the God identified with *brahman* is *only* Viṣṇu-Nārāyaṇa. However, in this context we might point to discussions in which Rāmānuja turns his arguments critically against other positions, such as when he responds to the Sāṅkhya opponent's doctrine of *satkāryavāda*, in which it is assumed that an effect is not non-being, but simply *being* before it becomes present. It is also important for Veṅkaṭanātha to refute this claim of *satkāryavāda* and disengage it from the doctrines of his own school.[68]

---

68 Cf. also below p. 454. For the before mentioned concept of *pariṇāma* also in contrast to the Sāṅkhya tradition see the remark of Carman (1974: 132): "Similarly, in discussing *pariṇāma*, the modification which Brahman undergoes in changing from the state of cause to the state of effect, Rāmānuja explains, 'The *pariṇāma* we teach is not of such a nature as to ascribe the imperfections to the Supreme Brahman. On the contrary, it ascribes to Him unrestricted lordship [niraṅkuśa-aiśvarya]'." Cf. also Bartley 2002: 72; referring to Rāmā-

For Rāmānuja, the state of a substance's non-being can only appear if it is neither currently being (in which case it would already be present as real), nor completely non-being (like emptiness, which is something inacceptable for him). It is precisely the distinction from absolute non-being, i.e., emptiness (*tuccha/śūnya*) that is important: a current *non*-being state can in fact be asserted as one that *is* non-being. This will also be the decisive point for Veṅkaṭanātha. Not only is the ontological status of non-being significant, but also the necessary relation between substance (*dravya*) and state (*avasthā*). The terminology used by Rāmānuja to explain this is clear, for example, in his Śrībh in the discussion on *Brahmasūtra* 2.1.18. In his commentary on this *sūtra* he refers to the central statement in the *Chāndogya Upaniṣad* (ChU 6.2.1) that describes the beginning of the remanifestation also from non-being (*asat*). According to him, manifest (*sthūla*) and subtle (*sūkṣma*) states define his understanding of ontology, since non-being (*asattva/abhāva*) and being (*sattva/bhāva*) are only different states of *one* and the *same* basis, i.e. *Being*. He develops this idea using the terms substance and state/property, whereby being and non-being are assigned to different properties/states of a substance. In the following quotation Rāmānuja positions himself in opposition to the Buddhists, for whom non-being has no basis und thus implies emptiness (*tucchatva*). He clearly explains in the following passage that being and non-being belong to a fundamental substance as its properties.

> The denotation as non-being of this very substance as [being in the state of] an effect is due to the different property at a prior time, i.e., due to a different generic structure (*saṃsthāna-*), not as you [i.e., the

---

nuja's tradition (not the Sāṅkhya), he says: "*Satkārya* theorists understand production as cases of phase-changes (*avasthā-pariṇāma*) where a substancial continuant (*dravya*) undergoes qualitative changes [...]. Phase changes may be contrasted with substantial changes which usually involve either a coming-to-be-*simpliciter* (*utpatti*) or ceasing-to-be (*vināśa*) on the part of an individual substance."

> Buddhist] claim due to emptiness, because being and non-being are taught as two properties of the substance. In this case, non-being is a property that is different from the property of being. For the world that is designated by the word "this," name and form are of the property of being. The property of non-being, on the other hand, is the subtle state [of name and form] contradicting that [i.e., the property of being]. Therefore, non-being of the world which is [still] connected to name and form means the attainment of a subtle state that contradicts the property of being [i.e., the manifest state of name and form].[69]

This passage refers to substance as being in the state of effect and cause. If a substance is in the state of effect, the *nāmarūpe* are manifest; if a substance is in the state of non-being (*asattva/abhāva*), i.e., the state of cause, the *nāmarūpe* are non-differentiated/subtle. Thus, subtle (*sūkṣma*) and manifest (*sthūla*) are equated in this passage with "non-being" (*asattva*) and "being" (*sattva*). Both are defined as different but are based on a substance that is inseparable from its states. The question of how non-being can become being, or how being can become non-being is not relevant, insofar as both states are always based on *Being*, i.e., refered to as substance (*dravya*).[70]

---

69 Śrībh III 259, 13–16 *ad* BS 2.1.18: *sa khalv asadvyapedeśas tasyaiva kāryadravyasya pūrvakāle dharmāntareṇa saṃsthānāntareṇa. na bhavad abhipretena tucchatvena. sattvāsattve hi dravyadharmāv ity uktam. tatra sattvadharmāt dharmāntaram asattvam. idaṃ śabdanirdiṣṭasya jagataḥ sattvadharmo nāmarūpe. asattvadharmas tu tadvirodhinī sūkṣmāvasthā. ato jagato nāmarūpayuktasya tadvirodhisūkṣmadaśāpattir asattvam.*

70 Something else is striking not only in this quotation but also in the passages cited above (such as Śrībh III 163,11-13 *ad* BS 1.4.23), namely the aspect of time (*kāla*), which Rāmānuja does not address explicitly in this context. But indicated by the words *kadācit...kadācit*, the different ontological determinations, or states of *brahman* can only be described under the condition of different times.

Also, in a passage in his earlier VAS, Rāmānuja refers to ChU 6.2.1 when discussing the process of remanifestation. In this famous passage, the father Uddālaka Āruṇi explains to his son Śvetaketu how name and form become manifested, i.e., differentiated (*vyākṛta*). Rāmānuja points out that in this statement, the pronoun "this" (*idam*) refers to the world, which *is* before its remanifestation.

> Here [in the statement of ChU 6.2.1] the word "this" (*idam*) denotes the "world"; "in the beginning" (*agre*) means "the time before manifestation"; and [by words] "only being" (*sad eva*) it is declared that during that time *before* creation, the world was essentially *Being* (*sat*). He means to say that at the very time of its manifestation, the world was still non-differentiated: so, with [with the words:] *ekam eva* he is stating that the world in the state of *being* was at that time not yet differentiated into names and forms.[71]

In his Śrībh, Rāmānuja discusses the controversial matter of whether the term non-differentiated (*avyākṛta*) refers to primordial matter (*prakṛti*) or to the body (*śarīra*) of God/*brahman*, to which, for him, primordial matter (*prakṛti*) belongs (cf. Śrībh II 128,3–130,7 *ad* BS 1.4.14).

According to Rāmānuja's Sāṅkhya opponent, the word *avyākṛta* refers only to primordial matter (*prakṛti*), which is defined as both being (*sat*) and non-being (*asat*). For his opponent, this implies that while primordial matter (*prakṛti*) is eternal in its essential nature, it is also transforming. But since *brahman* cannot be defined as both, i.e., as being (*sat*) *and* as non-being (*asat*), the opponent claims that only primordial matter is the cause of the world. As presented by Rāmānuja, the opponent argues that although primordial matter (*prakṛti*), as the basis of transformation (*pariṇāmāśrayatvena*), does not imply a contradiction between

---

[71] VAS §16 (80,3–6): *atredam iti jagannirdiṣṭam. agra iti ca sṛṣṭeḥ pūrvakālaḥ. tasmin kāle jagataḥ sadātmakatāṃ sadeveti pratipādya, tatsṛṣṭikāle 'py aviśiṣṭam iti kṛtvaikam eveti sadāpannasya jagatas tadānīm avibhaktanām arūpatāṃ pratipādya tatpratipādanenaiva sato jagadupādānatvaṃ pratipāditam.*

being and non-being, in case of the *one brahman*, a contradiction would be unavoidable.

Of course, Rāmānuja disagrees. In his response he clearly states that during the period of dissolution (*pralaya*), *brahman is* non-being (*asat*). Thus, being (*sat*) and non-being (*asat*) must be defined as having *one* and the *same* base. He further explains the relationship between *brahman* and *avyākṛta*. First Rāmānuja demonstrates that it is not primordial matter (*prakṛti*) that should be equated with *avyākṛta*, but the body (*śarīra*) of *brahman*. From this, Rāmānuja derives another argument: being and non-being do not refer to *brahman* itself—as the opponent supposes—but to its body (cf. Śrībh II 128,3ff. *avyākṛtaśabdena avyākṛtaśarīraṃ brahmaiva abhidhīyate*). Only the body is transforming, not *brahman* itself. Nevertheless, we say that *brahman* is alternating between the states of being and non-being, i.e., between the states of being differentiated and being non-differentiated.

Also important in this context is how the cause for the manifestation of the *nāmarūpe* is described. Rāmānuja mentions again the view that *brahman*/God has entered (*praviṣṭa*) its/His body. This is a further contrast to primordial matter (*prakṛti*), which is seen as generally unable to produce such an enlivening act of consciousness. It is another reason why the word *prakṛti* is not applicable for *brahman*.

If the two terms *avyākṛta* and *vyākṛta* denote states of *brahman*/God's body, and conscious and material entities belong to *brahman* in both the subtle state and the manifest state, then Rāmānuja must specify what happens to the *nāmarūpe* and to conscious beings and material objects when they form the imperishable body of *brahman*/God. The following passage of his Śrībh combines the discussion with the metaphor of the body. As Rāmānuja concludes:

> Therefore, insofar as *brahman* has conscious and material entities as its body, they are modes (*tatprakāram*) of *brahman*. At one time, this [i.e., *brahman*] exists by itself as one whose body has conscious and material entities, which being in a subtle state are unable to have differentiated designations; at that time, *brahman* is in the state of the cause. But at another time, *brahman* is one whose body is of

> manifest conscious and material entities, whose name and form are differentiated; and at that time, *brahman* is in the state of effect.[72]

In this passage again, the states of *brahman* are described as cause and effect. In the state of cause, i.e., in the subtle state of the body of *brahman*, everything is still there but nothing is recognizable. In the state of effect, everything is recognizable through its own specific being. Rāmānuja's objection demonstrates that the Sāṅkhya representative is relating cause and effect only to primordial matter (*prakṛti*).

Veṅkaṭanātha also addresses this matter, arguing that God is quite capable of reconciling both in *one* and the *same* basis. In his SAS, his auto-commentary on TMK 3.1, it is obvious that he takes up Rāmānuja's point of discussion with the Sāṅkhya opponent. Here he elaborates not only on a concept of ontology in relation to a God, but he also discusses the need to accept that a divine conscious act initiates the remanifestation, insofar as souls and material mass have a common base with God/*brahman* since God/*brahman* has both as His body. In this, Veṅkaṭanātha follows Rāmānuja's understanding of BĀU 1.4.7 and ChU 6.2.1, namely, that it is not primordial matter (*prakṛti*) but the *one* God who initiates, through His knowledge, the remanifestation of His body, which is constituted by the plurality of souls and the material world.

Thus, Veṅkaṭanātha repeats Rāmānuja's criticism of the concept of primordial matter (*prakṛti*), and points to the concept of co-referentiality (*sāmānādhikaraṇya*). In this context, co-referentiality means that different states belong to *one* and the *same* basis. The Sāṅkhya opponent refers to BĀU 1.4.7, identifying what is mentioned in this passage with the word *avyākṛta* with undeveloped matter (SAS 332.5: *avyaktāparaparyāyasya pradhānas-*

---

[72] Śrībh III 358, 3–5 *ad* BS 2.3.18: *ataḥ sarvadā cidacidvastuśarīratayā tatprakāraṃ brahma. tat kadācit svasmād vibhaktavyapadeśānarhāti-sūkṣmadaśāpannacidacidvastuśarīraṃ tiṣṭhati; tat kāraṇāvasthaṃ brahma. kadācic ca vibhaktanāmarūpasthūlacidacidvastuśarīram; tac ca kāryāvastham.*

yābhidhānād). But Veṅkaṭanātha responds in the same way as his predecessor, and mentions God's conscious and desiring act, without which the remanifestation of everything could not start:

> [That *prakṛti* is the cause] is not the case, because for the undeveloped [i.e., primordial matter (*prakṛti*)], manifestation, etc., preceded by an own desire, expressed in the words: "It thought to itself" [ChU 6.2.3] [...]. "He had this desire" [*Taittirīya Upaniṣad* 2.6.9] would not be possible.
> If one objects that the cause is material because of co-referentiality with something material due to the words, "Being, my dear, was this in the beginning" [ChU 6.2.1], then this is not the case because co-referentiality is also possible due to the intention to speak [of the cause, i.e., God] as qualified by the manifest and subtle conscious and material entities. Thus, the whole world is taught [in the Veda] as the body of the creator [in the words of *Śvetāśvatara Upaniṣad* 4.9:] "From this [body], the possessor of Māyā creates all this", and such a creation is magnified [by the statement from *Manusmṛti* 1.8a], [which reads:] "This one, [as one who wishes to create created manifold beings from his own body] by thinking [of it]."[73]

Both Rāmānuja and Veṅkaṭanātha underline that only *brahman*/God can be present in everything. In contrast, primordial matter cannot. What was previously described as a state of cause and effect is again related to an act of entering. It is *brahman*, with its non-differentiated body (*avyākṛtaśarīra*), that in the manifest state unfolds the differentiation of name and form. For Rāmānuja the transformation from *avyākṛta* to *vyākṛta* describes the relation between cause and effect, and is expressed as the fact that

---

[73] SAS 115.4–10 *ad* TMK 3.1: *tan na; avyaktasya 'tadaikṣata', 'so 'kāmayata' ityādyuktasvasaṅkalpapūrvakasṛṣṭyādyasaṃbhavāt* [...]. '*sad eva somyedam agra āsīd' ityādyacetanasāmānādhikaraṇyāt kāraṇam acetanam iti cen na; sāmānādhikaraṇyasya sthūlasūkṣmacidacidvastuviśiṣṭavivakṣayāpy upapatteḥ. sarvaṃ ca jagat kartuś śarīratayāmnātam 'asmān māyī sṛjeta viśvam etad' iti, īdṛśī ca sṛṣṭiḥ 'so 'bhidhyāya śarīrāt svād' ity upabṛṃhitā.*

one *and* the *same* "substance obtains another state" (*dravyasyāvasthāntarāpatti*).[74]

Already Veṅkaṭanātha's teacher Ātreyarāmānuja (1220–1280) connects this description of the "substance which is entering in another state" (*dravyāntarāvasthāpatti*) with the concept of co-referentiality.[75] This expression is also frequently used by Veṅkaṭanātha to describe causality. Relying upon this expression for causality implies that cause and effect are in unity with each other, in that there is a *third* grounding aspect underlying both.

---

[74] Śrībh III 358,8–9 *ad* BS 2.3.18: *kāraṇāvasthāyā avasthāntarāpattirūpo vikāraḥ prakāradvaye prakāriṇi ca samānaḥ.* "The alternation of the cause state as getting into another state [i.e., the state of effect] is common for the two modes and their mode possessor." Cf. also Śrībh III 258,12–13 *ad* BS 2.1.16, where Rāmānuja provides the analogy to life-stages, and concludes: *ato bālayuvādivat kāraṇabhūtam eva dravyam avasthāntarāpannaṃ kāryam iti gīyate.* "Therefore, it is described, that like [in cases of life stages such as being a] child, youth etc., the substance as [being in the state of] cause is [in the state of] effect, when it has obtained another state." Cf. also Śrībh III 161,14–162,1 *ad* BS 1.4.23: *kāraṇam evāvasthāntaram āpannaṃ kāryaṃ na dravyāntaram iti.* "Only the cause which has obtained another state is the effect, which is not different from substance."

[75] Cf. Ātreyarāmānuja's words in chapter 8 of his *Nyāyakuliśa* (NyKul), which certainly influenced Veṅkaṭanātha. Here, in NyKul 147,7–9, Ātreyarāmānuja defends the concept of *dravyāvasthāntarāpatti* against an opponent (a Naiyāyika?) who holds the view that an effect cannot exist before it is produced, i.e., at an earlier time: "If one objects that the continuity of the material cause is observed, but beingness of an effect is not [observed] even at earlier times, we respond that this is not the case, because one can recognize for such a substance [, i.e., the material cause] of getting another state, because one cannot perceive something different from a substance if it is continuing to exist; therefore the application of co-referentiality is possible." *nanu upādānānuvṛttir eva dṛśyate; na tu kāryasya prāg api satteti cen na, tasyaiva dravyasyāvasthāntaraprāptir iti pratīteḥ. na hi tasminn anuvartamāne dravyāntaraṃ samastīti pratyeti. ata eva samānādhikaraṇapratyayopapattiḥ.*

Since cause-and-effect refer to *one* and the *same* basis, one can speak of their unity (*aikya*).

Both states of God/*brahman* relate to each other, insofar as the state of cause must be presupposed for the state of effect to occur. For Veṅkaṭanātha (and for Rāmānuja as well) there is no completely new production (*utpatti*) and no complete passing away (*vināśa*), but rather the renewed manifestation of what already existed.

The connection between manifestation and ontology is treated in detail because both authors are dealing with the difficulty of how different designations/attributes that exclude each other can be related without any contradiction so that they co-refer due to their grounding in *one* and the *same* basis. The aforementioned concept of co-referentiality has its origin in a grammatical tradition, but for Rāmānuja and Veṅkaṭanātha it is decisive in an ontological context, as introduced here. This will be explained in more detail below. The doctrine that *one* and the *same brahman* can have different states is also seen in context of language in the question: How is it possible for different words with different meanings to be related through co-referentiality? Before we deal with this important term of co-referentiality (*sāmānādhikaraṇya*) we must understand how both authors connect their ontology with language.

Words denoting conscious (*cit*) and material (*acit*) entities also denote the Highest Self (*paramātman*)

The above-quoted passages from Rāmānuja's VAS and Śrībh demonstrate that name and form (*nāmarūpe*) can exist in different states. Nonetheless, it is not necessary to first bring them into a relationship with each other. Since for Rāmānuja and his successors the meanings of words are not determined by human conventions but are given in the unchangeable language of the Veda, name (*nāman*) and form (*rūpa*) correspond eternally. Not only is the ontological aspect of name and form relevant, but also the linguistic aspect. In the following discussion on the linguistic level of words and what they refer to, I start again from Rāmānuja to connect his central ideas to parallel discussions in works of Veṅkaṭanātha. How does Rāmānuja relate not only conscious and material entities to *one* ground, but also their denotations through countless numbers of words?

The following passage we consider (Śrībh II 76–77 *ad* BS 1.1.1) examines how, under the aspect of language, all entities refer to *one* God. From an ontological perspective of remanifestation, cause and effect are states (*avasthā*). But both states are also denoted by words, i.e., linguistic expressions with different meanings. Thus, a plurality of meanings contrasts a unity. Nevertheless, the concept of God's entering is essential in this context to understand that He is the ultimate ground for every denotation. Since God enters the soul, the soul thus denotes *who* entered it and to *whom* it is inseparately related due to this divine act of entering. But what about material mass? According to Rāmānuja, God is not *directly* qualified by material objects, only the soul qualifies Him. But *one* and the *same*, i.e., God/*brahman* can be both: in the state of cause *and* in the state of effect. Referring to this aspect of language, Rāmānuja points out that words like "cause" and "effect" have different meanings but still refer to *one* and the *same brahman*.[76]

> In the sentence [of ChU 6.3.2]: "This deity thought: Let me separate name and form (*nāmarūpe*), entering with this living soul into these three deities," the words "these three deities" denote material mass; and because the sentence expresses that [God] manifests name and

---

[76] For another discussion of this passage, see Bartley 2002: 83–84. His concluding remark on ChU 6.3.2 is as follows: "So the passage teaches that all distinctions of name and form are brought about by God's entering *acit* via the individual self whose inner identity is God himself. As a result all words signify the Supreme Self whose modes are the individual selves with their material bodies." Cf. also Bartley 2002: 107: "Since words denoting modes ultimately refer to the mode possessor, it follows that words denoting bodies ultimately refer to the embodied self."

form entering individual souls that are His selfs, in the same way, *all denoting words are denoting only (eva) the Supreme Self*, which is qualified by the soul, which in turn is qualified by material mass. Hence co-referentiality between a word denoting the state of effect and the word denoting the Highest Self in the state of cause is applied in its primary meaning.[77]

The mention of the primary meaning of co-referentiality is situated directly in the context of how God is expressed in language. Co-referentiality implies that a word denoting an entity also denotes God, since God manifests Himself and everything by His own willing/desiring act of entering as Inner Controller. The meaning of a word for something—either conscious or material—can therefore not be used indirectly but denotes God only directly.

To demonstrate how everything relates to God, God must be the actual and final referent. He is the *one* that is always referred to by words and what they denote. But how Rāmānuja explains God's entering the souls and how far he describes whether God reaches the material body by which the soul is qualified? How are name and form (*nāmarūpe*) related to terms like "mode" (*prakāra*) and "mode possessor" (*prakārin*)?

The different states of name and form (*nāmārūpe*) are modes (*prakāra*) of one mode possessor (*prakārin*), such as the name "lump" and the form, i.e., the object "lump" consisting of clay, refer to just one mode among other modes of the *one* mode possessor clay (*mṛd*). A standard example is the following: inasmuch as clay is modified when a lump (*piṇḍa*) is produced, the word denoting a lump also implies denoting modified clay. And an example for conscious entities would be the following: words de-

---

[77] Śrībh II 77,1–5 *ad* BS 1.1.1: '*aham imās tisro devatā anena jīvenātmanānupraviśya nāmarūpe vyākaravāṇi*' *iti*, '*tisro devatā*' *iti sarvam acidvastu nirdiśya tatra svātmakajīvānupraveśena nāmarūpavyākaraṇavacanāt sarve vācakāḥ śabdāḥ acidviśiṣṭajīvaviśiṣṭaparamātmana eva vācakā iti kāraṇāvasthaparamātmavācinā śabdena kāryavācinaḥ śabdasya sāmānādhikaraṇyaṃ mukhyavṛttam.*

noting souls also denote the soul's possessor, i.e., God Himself.[78] This is because He is embodied (as the entering Inner Controller) in the souls, and their bodies are called a mode (*prakāra*) of the embodied, i.e., the mode-possessor (*prakārin*). In Rāmānuja's words:

> Words denoting conscious beings [i.e., souls] also denote the Highest Self, which is embodied by [these] souls of which He is the self. Just as words denoting a lump, which is the generic structure of material mass, like gods, etc., they denote the individual soul whose body consists in this or that [material object]. [...] This is because the body is a mode of the embodied and because *words which denote modes ultimately refer only to the mode possessor, it follows that words denoting bodies ultimately refer to the embodied self.* When something is conceived in the form: "This is of such and such a kind of thing", the aspect conceived from "is of such and such a kind" is a mode [of the mode possessor].[79]

The passage relates God's embodiment with the linguistic concept of denoting. The reason why material and conscious entities refer to God by their names is that they all form the body of God. Their bodies cannot be thought of as independent from God. But

---

78 Cf. Śrībh III 19,12–15 *ad* BS 1.3.8: *ahamarthasya pratyagātmano 'pi hy ātmā paramātmety antaryāmibrāhmaṇādisūktam. ataḥ pratyagarthasya paramātmaparyavasānād ahaṃśabdo 'pi paramātmaparyavasāyīti.* "In the praising words of the *Antaryāmin-Brāhmaṇa*, etc., it is said that the Highest Self is also the self of the (individual) inward directed self, who is the referent of the word 'I.' Therefore, even the word 'I' results in the Highest Self, because the inward referent [for the word 'I'] is reduced to the Highest Self."

79 Śrībh II 222,1–5 *ad* BS 1.1.13: *ataḥ cetanavācino 'pi śabdāḥ, cetanasyāpi ātmabhūtaṃ cetanaśarīrakaṃ paramātmanam eva abhidadhati. yathā—acetanadevādisaṃsthānapiṇḍavācinaḥ śabdāḥ tattaccharīrakajīvātmana eva vācakāḥ*; [...] *śarīrasya śarīriṇaṃ prati prakāratvāt, prakāravācināṃ ca śabdānāṃ prakāriṇy eva paryavasānāt, śarīravācināṃ śabdānāṃ śarīriparyavasānaṃ nyāyyam. prakāro hi nāma idam ittham iti pratīyamāne vastuni, ittham iti pratīyamānaḥ aṃśaḥ.*

this means that every entity constituting a body must also refer to Him as the basis of that body. In this context, the function of denoting of words can also be explained: A word that denotes a state/property of a substance co-refers to or can be coordinated in a sentence with another word of another attribute or other attributes of *one* and the *same* substance.

> Whenever a thing has actual being (*sadbhāvaḥ*) as its mode […] the words denoting it, as they designate a substance characterized by the attribute denoted by them, appropriately enter into co-referentiality with other words denoting the *same* substance as characterized by other attributes.[80]

Again, we understand from this passage that words do not only belong to what they denote, they also denote that upon which the denoted object is based. Therefore, the base, the mode-possessor (*prakārin*), namely, the embodied God (*śarīrin*), is *also* always denoted by every word denoting modes (*prakāra*) of conscious beings and/or material objects. Our standard example: Without clay, neither lump nor pot could become manifested. Even if a potter, the instrumental cause, turns clay into another state, this state still refers to clay. In other words: If the self-grounding mode-possessor (i.e., clay) would not already *be*, then no other mode (*prakāra*) could be manifested. Thus, although the two different states or modes of lump and pot have their own different denotations, each of these also denotes differently their *one* basis.

In the relation between modes (*prakāra*) and their possessors (*prakārin*), it is not necessary to prove how a certain mode belongs to its possessor and not to another. But it is necessary to understand that a further possessor^2 (*prakārin*^{2}) can also become underlying both, mode^1 (*prakāra*^{1}) and mode possessor^1 (*prakārin*^{1}). To explain: a mode possessor (*prakārin*^{1}) can be understood as a mode of another mode possessor (*prakārin*^{2}), which then is

---

80 Śrībh II 223,8–10 *ad* BS 1.1.13: *yasya padārthasya, kasya cit prakāratayaiva sadbhāvaḥ,* […] *tadvācināṃ śabdānāṃ svābhidheyaviśiṣṭadravyavācitvād dharmāntaraviśiṣṭataddravyavācinā śabdena sāmānādhikaraṇyaṃ yuktam eva.*

the fundament of that mode possessor (*prakārin*^{1}) together with its different modes (*prakāra*^{1}).

This can be illustrated by referring to another standard example: What kind of presupposition are we accepting when we utter the sentence "The lotus is blue"? We are presupposing a *third* grounding aspect upon which the two are based, in this case, a *flower*. Both the lotus and its blue color are understood as what our authors call modes (*prakāra*) and mode possessors (*prakārin*). If we refer to a particular mode possessor (*prakārin*), this does not imply that it is not possible to accept another mode possessor (*prakārin*^{2}). Thus, the lotus as a mode possessor (*prakārin*^{1}) must be understood as a mode, i.e., lotus-ness, of another mode possessor, i.e., the *flower* (*prakārin*^{2}).

What causes difficulties in most cases is that the basis, upon which different qualities/attributes are accepted, in this case *flower*, is not expressed in the sentence.[81] Moreover, it is possible that even *flower* is not the *third* grounding aspect, since one could perhaps also grasp the being of *flower* as a quality, namely, *flower-ness*. And while the neutral concept of substance (*dravya*) could be applied as the *third* grounding aspect to be presupposed, we would rarely admit to a kind of substance referred to as *flower*.

Applying this concept of mode possessor to the relationship between soul and God, this means that if material matter belongs to the soul's body and the soul belongs to God's body, they *both* belong to the body of God. This seems to establish a sequence from material matter *via* the soul to God. Rāmānuja, however, only states that God has everything as His body. Because the soul has material mass as its body, but God has the soul *and* the individual soul's material body as His body, consequently also words denoting material mass refer to God *via* the soul. How one principle is based on the other is taught by Rāmānuja in the following passage.

---

[81] To illustrate: we simply say: "The lotus is blue", instead of: "This is a flower-substance, which is a lotus and which is blue".

> Since the mode depends upon its mode possessor, knowledge of the mode also implies knowledge of the ultimate possessor of all modes. In the same way a word for a mode refers also to the ultimate mode possessor. Words such as 'cow,' 'horse' and 'man,' denoting generic forms (*ākṛti*) that are modes, *also* refer to individualized material forms that are mode possessors. Since material mass is a mode in that it is the body of a conscious being [i.e., a soul] and since the conscious being as embodied is a mode of the Highest Self, these words ultimately refer to the Highest Self, which is the ultimate referent of every naming word; thus, co-referentiality with a word expressing the Highest Self has exclusively a primary meaning.[82]

In this context we must give some more explanations: All considerations relating to the fact that the designations of entities refer to God are also to be understood in the context of the correct exegesis of the most important *Mahāvākya* (ChU 6.8.7) *tat tvam asi*. One could say that coreferentiality ultimately serves for Rāmānuja to establish this *relational unity* between the two denotations *tat* and *tvam*. Based on the concept of Gods/*brahman* being embodied in everything, which means that the name of the soul is also designating God/*brahman*, it follows that both words *tat* and *tvam* when they are in the relation of correferentialiy, even if they are two different words, can only do so, because they are grounded in a *third*, i.e., *one* and the *same* basis. Thus, by the two words exactly two modes of *brahman* are coreferring. By *tat* referring to *brahman* it is expressed as cause (*jagatkāraṇa*), and by *tvam* referring to *brahman* it is designated as Inner Controller

[82] Śrībh II 222,6–223,5 *ad* BS 1.1.13: *ata eva gauḥ, aśvaḥ, manuṣyaḥ ityādiprakārabhūtākṛtivācinaḥ śabdāḥ prakāriṇi piṇḍe paryavasyantaḥ, piṇḍasyāpi cetanaśarīratvena tatprakāratvāt, piṇḍaśarīrakacetanasyāpi paramātmaprakāratvāc ca paramātmany eva paryavasyantīti, sarvaśabdānāṃ paramātmaiva vācya iti paramātmavāciśabdena sāmānādhikaraṇyaṃ mukhyam eva.*

of the individual soul (*jīvāntaryāmirūpeṇa*) as being modified by it.[83]

Let us turn to Veṅkaṭanātha to see how he follows Rāmānuja's view, namely, that words denoting modes also refer always to God, i.e., the ultimate mode possessor. Nevertheless, if material mass at first qualifies the conscious soul and not God directly, the question arises as to how God can be present to be denoted by everything. Veṅkaṭanātha comments on this in both his TMK and his NSi. At first, I give an example of his TMK. He confirms Rāmānuja's view when he explains in TMK 4.82cd that words and what they denote exist always together even during the period of dissolution and appear again when God enters everything as Inner Controller to manifest in what He enters:

> Even during the period of [God's] non-connection [i.e., the period of dissolution (*pralaya*)] with the individual self, the forms of gods, mortals, etc., do not vanish. The omnipresent Lord on His part (*api*) unfolds name and form in the world due to His entering into the individual self.[84]

Veṅkaṭanātha also discusses this in his *Sarvārthasiddhi* (SAS), his auto-commentary on the verse, where he emphasizes—perhaps more emphatically than Rāmānuja—that denotations for souls as well as for material objects also denote God. In this context, he again refers to God entering souls:

> It is well established by the Veda that God, after entering the individual souls, manifested name and form. Therefore, the meaning that the denotation of words for conscious beings [i.e., souls] and

---

[83] Cf. VAS §19–20 (82–83), where Rāmānuja explains this *mahāvākya* against the background of his own ontology by applying the concept of *sāmānādhikaraṇya*.

[84] TMK 4.82cd:
ātmāsaṃbandhakāle sthitir anavagatā devamartyādimūrteḥ
jīvātmānupraveśāj jagati vibhur api vyākaron nāmarūpe.
For *ātmāsaṃbandhakāle* see Veṅkaṭanātha's explanation in his SAS 618.10: *na hi mṛtasya śarīraṃ kṣaṇam api tatsaṃsthānasaṃsthitam avatiṣṭhate.*

material mass extends to the Lord is correct, because the soul has the material world as its body, [but] God has the conscious [soul] *and* material mass as His body.[85]

What this passage does not yet sufficiently clarify is how everything, i.e., also material entities, become the body of God. More explanation was necessary, especially regarding how God is connected to the bodies of the souls, which are themselves directly bodies of God. Could it be possible that words denoting material mass refer to Him only indirectly? Wouldn't this contradict the authoritative passage of God as the Inner Controller entering everything (*viśvāntaryāmin*)? Veṅkaṭanātha refers to this in his NSi. He first discusses the different positions on this matter. One position is that God is *directly* connected to souls and material mass, the view held by Rāmānuja and later also by Parāśarabhaṭṭa in his *Tattvaratnākara*.[86] The other position is presented through a quotation from Rāmamiśra's *Ṣaḍarthasaṃkṣepa*: "Not so, because material being becomes the body of *brahman* [only] through the individual self."[87] Although Veṅkaṭanātha sees no contradiction between these two postions, he ultimately decides that God is directly present in the material world (*acit*). The

---

[85] SAS 619, 1–2 *ad* TMK 4.82d: *jīvātmānam anupraviśya nāmarūpe vyākarod īśvara iti hi vedaprasiddhiḥ. ato 'cciccharīrako jīvaḥ, acijjīvaśarīraka īśvara iti cetanācetanaśabdānāṃ bhagavatparyantābhidhānaṃ yuktam iti bhāvaḥ.* Cf. also SAS 621,7–8 *ad* TMK 4.83: *īśvaraśarīratayā śrutiśataprasiddheṣu pṛthivyādiṣv etal lakṣaṇam asti cet, avivāda eva; prapañcavācināṃ śabdānaṃ parabrahmaparatve 'pi virodhābhāvāt.* The discussion continues TMK 4.85 and 4.86.

[86] *Tattvaratnākara*, Fragment 60, quoted from Oberhammer 1979: 80-81: "Conscious and material beings are equally His body." *cetanācetanayor aviśiṣṭaṃ taṃ prati śarīratvam* [...]. (English trans. M.S.). Cf. also the explanations to this passage in Oberhammer 1979: 217–222.

[87] NSi 178,6: *na, acito jīvadvārā brahmaśarīratvāt.* Rāmamiśra's work *Ṣaḍarthasaṃkṣepa* is lost; the sentence is quoted in Veṅkaṭanātha's NSi (ibid., 178f.).

reason is the following: The soul cannot remain in the saṃsāric world without having a body to which it is intimately related. And God could not be the Inner Controller of everything (*viśvāntaryāmin*) if He were not also effective in what the soul has as its material body, which again is connected to the material world. Veṅkaṭanātha describes God's efficiency and explains why he chooses the first alternative. The decisive argument is that the soul ultimately cannot completely leave its body at any time, also not while that body is asleep or in a state of fainting. God is therefore needed as an Inner Controller to carry on the life of the soul by being present in its body, which is said to consist of material mass.

> Because the Lord is the Inner Controller for separated elements and [sense faculties] such as touch, they are for this reason, mentioned in authoritative Scripture (*śruti*) as God's body. And during [an unconscious] state [of the soul] such as deep sleep and fainting, it is observed that the body and the one who possesses that body are controlled by God only, which is inherent for them. Due to this reason, this direct control would not be possible according to the [second] opinion. And mere existence of the individual self does not bring about control of the body; due to being without knowledge and will in that state, it is the same as for the [material] ether. Therefore, all substances in every state are themselves the bodies of God only; their being the bodies of the individual selves is caused by their *karman*. Thus, this way, [namely, the first opinion], proves to be better.[88]

---

[88] NSi 179,5–9: *vyākṛtabhūtatvagādīn prati ca īśvarasya antaryāmitvāt. tata eva ca teṣāṃ taccharīratvaṃ śrūyate. suṣuptimurcchādyavasthāsu ca svābhāvikam īśvaraniyāmyatvam eva dehadehinor dṛśyate. ata idam advārakaniyamanaṃ tatpakṣe na syāt. jīvasattāmātrañ ca na dehaniyamanaupayikam; tadānīṃ jñānecchārahitatayā tasya gaganādisattātulyatvāt. ataḥ sarvāvasthānāṃ sarvadravyāṇāṃ praty eva svataś śarīratvam. jīvaṃ prati tu tatkarmakṛtam iti samīcīno 'yaṃ panthāḥ.*

Also the question of whether God is directly (*dvāraka*) or indirectly (*advāraka*) connected with everything had to be resolved, insofar as the above-mentioned concept of co-referentiality (*sāmānādhikaraṇya*) would otherwise not be applicable. Some more attention must be given now to this central concept.

Co-referentiality (*sāmānādhikaraṇya*)

Even though the concept of co-referentiality is often referred to in different philosophical traditions, the reception by Rāmānuja and his followers is quite unique. They all rely on only one definition expressed in a single sentence, a definition that is repeated several times in their works.[89] The only sentence in question is of *Kāśikāvṛtti ad* Pāṇiṇi 2.1.49. It is first quoted by Rāmānuja to refer to the topic we have discussed above: While there can be several modes/designations by words that are different from one another, while keeping that difference, they are able to refer to *one* and the *same* basis.

> The functioning of words whose base meanings are distinct in referring to the same object is [the definition of] co-referentiality (*sāmānādhikaraṇya*).[90]

[89] For Rāmānuja, cf. VAS §26 (86,8–9); Śrībh I 191,7 *ad* BS 1.1.1; *Śrībhāṣya* II 208,4 *ad Brahmasūtra* 1.1.13. For Veṅkaṭanātha, cf. fn. 101.

[90] *Kāśikāvṛtti* ad Pāṇiṇi 2.1.49: *bhinnapravṛttinimittānāṃ śabdānām ekasminn arthe vṛttiḥ sāmānādhikaraṇyam*. I quote the translation of Cardona 1970: 234. Other translations of this sentence are as follows: "[...] the application to one thing of several words possessing different reasons of application constitutes co-ordination" (Thibaut). "Co-referentiality is the application to one object of several words in different functions" (van Buitenen). "Co-referentiality is the reference to one entity of words having different grounds for their application" (Bartley).

This sentence is originally found, of course, in a grammatical context, to explain how a compound can be formed from words with different meanings.[91] The unity of different word-meanings is given by the same case ending.[92]

Rāmānuja applies co-referentiality not only in a grammatical sense, but also to all denotable entities.[93] He refers to a unity (*aikya*), which he describes as a "relation" between different attributes resulting from their inseparability (*apṛthaksiddhi*) from a basis, i.e., a substance, i.e., finally God as ultimate ground. To deal with the co-referentiality of the attributes, such a basis must already be accepted. Through co-referentiality, different attributes can be understood as/in a unity (*aikya*) precisely because they refer to a *third* aspect, i.e., they are grounded on/by something else.[94]

It is not the case that sentences can only be formed according to the scheme of co-referentiality. Although related to each other, two entities and the words denoting them can indeed be different, as seen in terms of the relationship between a support and what is being supported (*ādhāra-ādheya*). A famous example of this is

---

91 For the former complex history of this concept and important textual references, cf. Ogawa 2017: 83–151.

92 This is also clear in Liebich's (1892: 33) translation: "Congruenz ist das in ein und demselben Sinne Stehn eines Wortes mit einem andern, während seine Entstehungsursache eine verschiedene ist." [The example in the footnote is: "Vgl. Ostpreussen, Hinterpommern."]

93 Cf. also Lipner 1986: 29: "The point is that the Vedāntin took the grammar of correlativly predicated statements to have certain ontological implications. […] the correlatively predicated expression indicates that a particular thing (i.e., the referent) is the locus of a co-presence of more than one determination such that it gives grounds for the predication of several non-synonymous terms in respect of it."

94 Cf. VAS §26 (86,7–10): *yathā bhūtayor eva hi dvayor aikyaṃ sāmānādhikaraṇyena pratīyate* […] *tathā bhūtayor evaikyam upapāditam asmābhiḥ*. "Just as the identity of two beings is conceived by co-referentiality […] we have declared that the two beings are identical."

"The jar is on the ground" (*bhutale ghaṭo*), a sentence whose words have no common base (*vyadhikaraṇa*). Rāmānuja also mentions another important relationship between two different yet related entities, namely, the relationship marked by a possessive suffix.[95]

While the meaning of co-referentiality is cited in the various traditions in various contexts, in the Rāmānuja tradition it is usually found in polemical contexts involving the Advaitic understanding of the term.

One must point out that Rāmānuja's predecessor Yāmuna already opposed the view that the co-referentiality of two terms cannot be understood in a literal sense, but only with the help of an indirect denotation (*lakṣaṇā-vṛtti*).[96] The dispute with the Advaita position[97] focuses on the divergent Advaitic understanding of unity and its avoidance of any reference[98] to a *third* grounding

---

95 Indeed, Rāmānuja favors co-referentiality since ultimately, theologically speaking, nothing can be independent of God that could not be subsumed under the concept of the divine body. However, he does describe what can occur separately: "And if a substance that may have a separate function is, in some place at some time, wanted as a mode for another substance, then it has a possessive suffix." VAS § 68 (110,7–8): *yasya punar dravyasya pṛthaksiddhasyaiva kadācit kvacid dravyāntaraprakāratvam iṣyate tatra matvarthīyapratyaya iti viśeṣaḥ.* Cf. also NSi (3. chapter) 322,1 (verse 79c): *matvarthīyaḥ pṛthaksiddhe.* "The possessive suffix is used when things are established separately."

96 On Yāmuna, cf. Mesquita 1990: 226ff. For thinkers prior to Yāmuna, cf. Mesquita's discussion of Nāthamuni. Nāthamuni does not use the term co-referentiality (*sāmānādhikaraṇya*) but does refer to the unity of carrier and constitution that can be asserted with co-referentiality. Mesquita (1990: 85ff.) sees in Nāthamuni's definition of the *saṃyoga* (*aikyaṃ sākalyena saṃyogaḥ*) a pre-form of the term. Cf. also Schmücker forthcoming[3].

97 For an overview of these polemical discussions and Rāmānuja's criticism of the Advaitic understanding of scripture, cf. van Buitenen 1956: 59–69.

98 Cf. Marlewicz 2003: 264ff.

aspect as being qualified. The Advaita position favors a *brahman* with no qualities/attributes, which is the basis for the Advaitic understanding of the *Kāśikāvṛtti* statement.

Rāmānuja's follower Varadaguru (1190–1275) uses this *Kāśikāvṛtti* sentence in his *Prameyamālā* to refute the Advaitic teaching of *brahman* as an "indivisible object" (*akhaṇḍārtha*).[99] And also Veṅkaṭanātha's teacher Ātreyarāmānuja opens the seventh chapter of his *Nyāyakuliśa* with this sentence from the *Kāśikāvṛtti*, using it to refute not only the Advaitic understanding of co-referentiality, but also the view put forward by a representative of the "difference *and* identity" (*bheda-abheda*) doctrine.[100] Finally, Veṅkaṭanātha applies the concept of co-referentiality several times in his works when taking up the various discussions of his predecessors.[101] Like his teacher Ātreyarāmānuja, Veṅkaṭanātha not only criticizes the Advaitic concept of co-referentiality, but also argues against views relating attribute and substance with difference *and* identity, like the view of the Jainas, as well as that of Bhāskara and Yādavaprakāśa (cf. below p. 404ff.).

To understand how co-referentiality is applied to establish monotheism, Veṅkaṭanātha's use of the term must be examined in detail. Nevertheless, we must again begin with Rāmānuja's readaption of the definition in the *Kāśikāvṛtti* since it is even influential on how Veṅkaṭanātha subsequently uses the same definition.

Rāmānuja explains unity (*aikya*) with (grammatical) co-referentiality. Unity is established because different words can refer to one and the same basis. When *we* form sentences, *we* unite oppo-

---

[99] For an analysis of this discussion, cf. Marlewicz 2002: 103–129. In addition to Varadaguru, her paper also deals with other authors who criticized the Advaitic understanding of the *akhaṇḍavākyārtha*, i.e., "the indivisible 'object' of a sentence".

[100] Cf. also the sixth chapter of Nārāyanārya's *Nītimālā*, p. 42ff.

[101] Cf. for example: NP, chapter 3.1 (*śabdādhyāya*; *satyaṃjñānavākyārtha*, II., p. 58); SAS *ad* TMK 4.94, 4.98; ŚDū, *akhaṇḍavākyārthakhaṇḍanavāda* (*vāda* 38, p. 161,16–17).

site categories. But this kind of a unifying is only possible by presupposing a *third* grounding aspect, a basis. Without accepting such a *third* grounding aspect, not even a sentence could be formed.[102]

To illustrate: In the following passage, Rāmānuja starts by defining co-referentiality, illustrating this with the sentence "The cloth is red." He explains that two different terms, such as "red" and "cloth," can be related to each other by referring to the concept of substance (*dravya*). Without presupposing a substance, no relationship could be formed between "red" and "cloth." In fact, nothing can be said or known if the grounding aspect of substance is not accepted. Thus, Rāmānuja paraphrases the sentence in question as "The cloth is a substance to which red color belongs."

> The purport of co-referentiality is the unity of the substance which is qualified by attributes. Because the distinctive character of co-referentiality is [expressed in the definition]: "The functioning of words whose base meanings are distinct in referring to the same object is [the definition of] co-referentiality." For the same reason the unity of sentences such as "The cloth is red" follows from all the words re-

---

102 I am using "grounding" in two different ways. First, as already dealt with, grounding explains the case of co-referentiality between two words/entities/attributes, which can only be related by accepting a *third* aspect that grounds them. For Rāmānuja and for Veṅkaṭanātha a substance (*dravya*) has such a grounding function. In this function, substance grounds something other (*paranirvāhaka*) than itself. But in order not to fall into an infinite regress, such a substance must ground itself also, i.e., has to be self-grounding (*svanirvāhaka*). Therefore the relation of co-referentiality can only come about through self-grounding substances. Veṅkaṭanātha defines the substance as *svaparanirvāhaka*. Remarkably, Veṅkaṭanātha also speaks of attributes/qualities of a substance as *svaparanirvāhaka*. See also Srinivasa Chari 2004: 3: "A *dharmin* reveals itself and also the object to which it belongs. This technical term is called *svaparanirvāhaka*. Light reveals objects but it does not require another light to reveal objects. It reveals itself as well as the objects. The same explanation holds good for *dharma* also."

> ferring to one thing. [...] And what is ascertained from co-referentiality is only that the cloth is a substance to which red color belongs.[103]

We read in the last sentence that Rāmānuja introduces the neutral term substance (*dravya*), which belongs neither to the quality of red color nor to the respective possessor of such a color. Nonetheless, it is indispensable and therefore inseparable from red color and the cloth.

Another standard example used by Rāmānuja is: "This [person] is that Devadatta" (*so 'yaṃ devadattaḥ*). In this example, a temporal modification is expressed by attributing different temporal units to *one* and the *same* person.[104] On the Advaitic side, Padmapāda and afterwards Prakāśātman seem to have been the first to have discussed this statement in detail.[105]

Let us follow how Rāmānuja explains this example and then examine how Veṅkaṭanātha takes it up. At first, we must explain what the *third* grounding aspect is in this case: Is it the person Devadatta or is it time (*kāla*) itself? Again, the discussion is about whether different attributes can be unified in *one* basis. Is it pos-

---

[103] Śrībh II 211,1–4 *ad* BS 1.1.13: *viśiṣṭadravyaikyam eva hi sāmānādhikaraṇyasyārthaḥ. 'bhinnapravṛttinimittānāṃ śabdānāṃ ekasminn arthe vṛttiḥ sāmānādhikaraṇyam' iti hi! sāmānādhikaraṇyalakṣaṇam. ata eva hi 'raktaḥ paṭo bhavati' ityādiṣu, aikārthyāt ekavākyatvam.* [...] *'rāgasambandhi dravyaṃ paṭaḥ' ity etāvan mātraṃ sāmānādhikaraṇyāvaseyam.*

[104] Cf. van Buitenen's (1956: 64) paraphrase of this example: "'This is that Devadatta' means nothing but 'Our Devadatta here was, at some previous time, somewhere else, he is the same person who was there at the time.'"

[105] For Prakāśātman's position and his central arguments, see *Pañcapādikāvivaraṇa* (=PañcPV) 714–715. Bartley (2002: 103–105) also discusses this example and presents the position of Padmapāda and Prakaśātman.

sible for *one* and the *same* person to be connected to different places at different times?[106]

As mentioned above, the main opponent in this discussion is the Advaitin, who concludes that any difference between two distinct designations or attributes is incompatible with *one* and the *same* basis. What is significant in this discussion is how that difference is understood. The Advaitin argues that different attributes cannot belong to *one* and the *same* basis, because in further consequence it would have to be assumed that *brahman* possesses innumerable qualities (*saguṇa*). Consequently, the Advaitin argues that there is only a distinctless *brahman*.

In response, the Advaitin is asked if the opposition of past and present can be unified in terms of Devadatta, i.e., a person who is in different places at different times. Time (*kāla*) is now assumed to be the basis of co-reference. For Rāmānuja, in this example, time (*kāla*), with its different temporal limitations, is the *third* grounding aspect and therefore the reason why the same person we saw yesterday at *that* place is now seen here in the present in *this* place.

According to Rāmānuja—and Veṅkaṭanātha follows him on this point, as we shall see below—if one does not accept this grounding aspect, the consequence would be momentariness: By accepting a contradiction between different temporal definitions, it would follow that all things are not permanent, but only momentary. For Rāmānuja it is thus time (*kāla*) that enables us to speak of *one* and the *same* person across different times and places. In his VAS he concludes his discussion with the Advaitic opponent as follows:

---

[106] Cf. also the explanation in Bartley 2002: 107: "Rāmānuja insists that there is not a trace of oblique predication in the statement, 'This is that Devadatta' since there is no contradiction involved in being associated with two sets of spatio-temporal conditions. [...] The contradiction implied by relation to two places is removed by the difference in times. In 'this is that Devadatta,' the terms 'this' and 'that' denote one object with several spatio-temporal properties which are the differerent ground for the application of those terms."

> Therefore, the declaration of the identity [of a person] involved in two actions, past and present, contains no contradiction, for the contradiction of a presence in two different places is solved by the difference in time.[107]

Rāmānuja discusses this example also in his Śrībh, where he repeats this view. In this work he refers to a different argument which adds the perspective of the speaker of the sentence "He is that Devadatta" (*so 'yam devadattaḥ*). The speaker, i.e. the one who recognizes Devadatta, can make this statement due to his/her recollection (*pratyabhijñā*), which enables them to refer to or verify *one* and the *same* person across different times and different places.

From the perspective of the speaker, who is also the one who recollects different times, we can combine places associated with different times (past/present) in *one* and the *same* basis due to our recollection, a recollection that unites a remembering like "I saw this person yesterday" with our present awareness "I see the same person just now." To do this, we must have presupposed continuity in time that *unites* the movement between different places. For Rāmānuja, there is no contradiction between something past connected with that place and something now connected with this place. This is only due to recollection, which brings together "that person" (*sa*) who is remote in time and space with "this person" (*ayam*) who is in the present. Thus, there is *unity* of the person with different temporal attributes. In Rāmānuja's words:

> Therefore, those who maintain the permanency [of things] prove oneness of an object related to two moments in time based on a recollection (*pratyabhijñā*): "He is that [Devadatta]"; otherwise, if there were really a contradiction between these two representations [i.e. this, that], it would follow that all things are [not permanent, but] momentary (*kṣaṇikatvam*) only. The contradiction involved in

---

[107] VAS §25 (86,1–2): *ato bhūtavartamānakriyādvayasaṃbandhitayaikyapratipādanam aviruddham. deśadvayavirodhaś ca kālabhedena parihṛtaḥ.*

one object being connected to two places is removed by the difference of the correlative moments of time.[108]

Rāmānuja's reference to recollection (*pratyabhijñā*) is probably because the Advaitic side, represented by Prakāśātman, polemicizes at length against this means of cognition for the sentence *so 'yam devadattaḥ*. One argument against it is its necessary implication of difference, which for the Advaitin is inacceptable.

Veṅkaṭanātha deals with exactly this Devadatta example in several of his works. While he unfolds his arguments following Rāmānuja closely, he adds far more explanations.[109] I will refer here only to selected passages from his *Nyāyapariśuddhi* (=NP) and his TMK. Not only does he develop in the first work the concept of co-referentiality, providing in a sixfold[110] classification, but he also compares it to the Advaita position, drawing the same conclusion as Rāmānuja and reducing the Advaitin's view to the Buddhist position of momentariness. Veṅkaṭanātha defeats the Advaitin who gets caught in self-contradictions: In order to negate attributes for the pure *brahman*, he must accept such attri-

---

108 Śrībh 211,2–4 *ad* BS 1.1.13: *ata eva hi 'so 'yam' iti pratyabhijñā, kāladvayasambandhino vastunaḥ aikyam upapādyate sthiratvavādibhiḥ. anyathā pratītivirodhe sati, sarveṣāṃ kṣaṇikatvam eva syāt. deśādvyayasambandhavirodhas tu kālabhedena parihriyate.*

109 It is beyond the scope of my paper to deal with Ātreyarāmānuja's detailed chapter on co-referentiality (*sāmānādhikaraṇya*), but he also provides an important argument there to support time as the basis for the statement *so 'yam devadattaḥ*. Cf. NyKul (chapter 7) 141,12–14: *idānīṃ tatkālasambandho viruddha iti cet, kim idānīm asyāpi kālasya saṃyogaḥ? na hi kālasya kālāntarāpekṣā, anavasthānāt.*

110 Cf. NP 3.1 (47,5–6). The six types of co-referentiality are: the description of cause and effect (*kāryakāraṇabhāva*); when something is inseparably related (*apṛthaksiddhabhāva*); when something enters into something (*āveśabhāva*); when something is similar/equals something else (*anukārabhāva*); when something is regarded as something (*dṛṣṭibhāva*); and when something influences/affects something (*uparāgabhāva*). For further explanations, see Vedavalli Narayanan 2008: 117–118.

butes to be existent. Therefore the self-contradiction is: the Advaitin states that the difference between two attributes does not exist but to prove this, he has at the same time presupposed at least two attributes standing in relation to each other.

Veṅkaṭanātha adds precision to Rāmānuja's words by stating that "this-ness" (*tattā*) and "that-ness" (*idantā*) exist independently of each other, because they refer to different times and therefore can never be recognized as simultaneously happening. Nevertheless, both come together in *one* and the *same* person when one speaks about a person who is now the *same* person one has seen on earlier occasions. In the following passage, Veṅkaṭanātha explains once again the difference between cognizing *one* and the *same* person in different times and considering falsely two mutually exclusive times as identical. Neither the person disappears, nor is our recognition of the same person impossible because times like past time, present time, exist independently from each other. The past belongs to the person in the past; the presence belongs to the person in the presence. One and the same person cannot be past and present at the same time, because the past has disappeared when *one* and the *same* person appears in the presence.

> If one were to object that both [references in this sentence, i.e., thisness and that-ness,] are contradictory [when they take place] simultaneously, we say no, because no simultaneity is presented and, because of their independence; on the contrary, recognition [of this-ness and that-ness] at the same time is not a mistake.[111]
> But how are past and present possible for one and the same person? [Both are possible] because at the time of their disappearance, they are gone by themselves, but the person did not disappear because [his/her] being present is recognized [again].[112]

[111] NP 55,2–6: *yugapat tayor vyāghāta iti cen na, yaugapadyasyānabhidhānād anākṣepāc ca. yugapatpratipattis tu na doṣaḥ.*

[112] NP 56,1–3: *tathāpy atītatvavartamānatve katham ekasyeti cet svapradhvaṃsakāle hi svayam atītaḥ syāt na cāsau pradhvastaḥ vartamānatvopalambhāt.*

Important in this quotation is Veṅkaṭanātha's statement that for a person temporal change can be described. Having existed in the past, does not imply that one has passed away. Being present again implies that one has existed in the past. And to be here now, i.e., in a specific place, can be explained as having been related to a particular condition which has past (cf. NP 56,3 *atītopādhiviśeṣasambandhitayā*). Veṅkaṭanātha deals with the same example in the fourth chapter of his TMK. Again, he takes issue with the interpretation of co-referentiality offered by the Advaitin, reducing the Advaitic view to the position of Buddhist doctrine if he does not accept different temporal attributes for *one* and the *same* thing. Here he offers all his arguments together in a nutshell, beginning with the Advaitin's contradictions. In verse 4.97 of the TMK, Veṅkaṭanātha gives three reasons why the Advaitic understanding of co-referentiality is mired in self-contradictions. Each reason points out an inherent flaw based on incoherence between assertion and proof: A statement like "That thou art" (*tat tvam asi*) implies two designations, but then one cannot refer to a distinctless *brahman* and thus this statement must be rejected (*bādha*). A sentence like *so 'yaṃ devadattaḥ* presupposes distinctions, and so claiming a distinctless entity thus implies the flaw of over-extension (*aticāra*). Perhaps the most evident contradiction—asserted many times by Veṅkaṭanātha especially in his ŚDū—is that the Advaitin constantly uses designations when trying to demonstrate, by means of co-referentiality, that *brahman* is without designation. Thus, the Advaitin is destroyed by his own speech (*svavacanahati*), because to be able to thematize the *brahman* without any designation, he is still speaking, i.e., using designations and must therefore already have accepted different designations.[113]

Further since one can conceive *one* and the *same* person in different times, these times must be contradictory. Veṅkaṭanātha responds that different times can be known without contradiction. And further, not the person itself but only time is the reason that

---

[113] For further explanations, see Vedavalli 2008: 119–120.

one can identify *one* and the *same* person in different places at different times. Verse 97 of the fourth chapter (*buddhisara*) of the TMK refers to the above points:

> [Advaitic opponent:] Based on the conclusion: "This [here and now] is [the same as] that [there and in that time]" one would indicate something distinctless about which one disagrees due to employing co-referentiality.
>
> [Our view:] This is not the case, insofar as due to rejection, over-extension and destruction by your own speech, faults exist for the examples [i.e., *tad idam*,] expressed in your own words.
>
> For in [this] sentence there is no contradiction between this-ness and that-ness [of Devadatta] by way of such a recognition.
>
> If you do not accept this, everything would be momentary for you; but here the difference of places does occur due to the succession [of time].[114]

Veṅkaṭanātha bases his claim that the identification *tad idam* (i.e., *so 'yam devadattaḥ*) is true in the same way he used recollection as a reason. Based on this perception, it cannot be refuted that *one* and the *same* person remains *one* and the *same* throughout different times. If this were not accepted, the result would be the position of momentariness, which the Advaitin would be forced to accept, because he has no argument at his disposal to prove *brahman* as an "indivisible object" (*akhaṇḍārtha*). We could also say that the Advaitin has no argument to prove that different designations are connected. To do so, the Advaitic opponent would have to accept a difference (*bheda*), something he vehemently denies.

---

[114] TMK 4.97:
aikādhāryād vigītaṃ tad idam iti nayāl lakṣayen nirviśeṣam; maivaṃ,
bādhāticārasvavacanahatibhiḥ svoktadṛṣṭāntadausthyāt
tattedantāvirodho vacasi na hi bhavet tādṛśādhyakṣanītyā;
no cet, syād vas samastaṃ kṣaṇikam; iha punar deśabhedaḥ kramāt syāt.

The cognition of different times being discussed here would not be valid at all if there were no one to connect the different times indicated in the judgement *so 'yam devadattaḥ*. The basic prerequisite can only be a qualified entity (*viśiṣṭavastu*). Thus, Veṅkaṭanātha rejects the view of the Advaitin:

> And if this is expressed here by you [the Advaitin, in a sentence like], "He is that Devadatta," this is indeed faulty as an example of something having distinctlessness (*nirviśeṣa-*) as its content, because the co-referentiality through "this-ness" and "that-ness" in the sentence "He is that Devadatta" has a specified entity (*viśiṣṭavastu*) as its content.[115]

Veṅkaṭanātha clearly responds to the decisive question—how things that contradict each other can be compatible in *one* and the *same* thing—by referring to the facticity of our perception. To identify someone/something we form such a sentence and we would not be understandable if "thisness" and "thatness" do not refer to *one* and the *same* person/object. Once more adressing his advaitic opponent, who sees different time modes only as contradicting to each other, Veṅkaṭanātha provides an answer:

> [If you ask,] how is it possible to say that one (*ekasya*) [person] can be qualified by this-ness and that-ness since both are contradicting, our response is: This is not the case, because there is no contradiction [between this-ness and that-ness]. If this-ness and that-ness were contradictory in reference to one [person], then there would be a contradiction for the knowledge by perception: "This [person] there is that Devadatta."[116]

---

[115] SAS 638.6–8 *ad* TMK 4.95: *svokte ca so 'yaṃ devadatta ity atra nirviśeṣaparatvadṛṣṭānte 'pi dauḥsthyam eva; so 'yam iti sāmānādhikaraṇyasya tattedantā viśiṣṭavastuparatvāt.*

[116] SAS 638.8–10 *ad* TMK 4.95: *nanu tattedantāvaiśiṣṭyam ekasya katham ucyate? tattedantayoḥ parasparaviruddhatvād iti; tan na, virodhābhāvāt. yadi tattedantayor ekatra virodhaḥ, tarhi so 'yaṃ devadatta iti pratyakṣopalambhavirodhaḥ syāt.*

> If one were not to accept that one is connected to two times, the doctrine of momentariness would result. Therefore, there is no contradiction with time [as a substance]. With the word "here," he [i.e., Rāmānuja already] says that the contradiction of [Devadatta's] presence in two different places is solved by the difference in time.[117] The meaning is: The difference of space in the recollection [of Devadatta] is solved by the difference of time. Here we give the following final decision: Two different times do not contradict one [basis, i.e., time as a substance], because we do not accept the doctrine of momentariness.[118]

How, then, can one represent identity (*abheda*) if one has presupposed a difference (*bheda*) between two attributes which again represent two different designations? If one cannot demonstrate that there is a relation between "this" and "that" remaining exclusively different in the statement "This [person] is that Devadatta," then indeed momentariness would be unavoidable.

At this point, Veṅkaṭanātha analyzes time (*kāla*) referring to co-referentiality to prove that two temporal designations like past (*atīta*) and present (*vartamāna*) belong to *one* and the *same* basis, i.e., time not only as an omnipresent but also as a necessary *third* grounding aspect. But he goes into more detail: For our judgment, we presuppose time (*kāla*) as the necessary common basis (substance) that allows different times. Only the acceptance of time as a *third* grounding aspect enables us to have a knowledge based on temporal change, insofar as temporal designations belong to *one* and the *same* subject. Nevertheless, in a sentence "This [person] is that Devadatta," time as the *third* grounding aspect is not men-

---

[117] Here, with this sentence Veṅkaṭanātha repeats Rāmānuja's words almost literally.

[118] SAS 638.11–13 *ad* TMK 4.95: *ekasya kāladvayasaṃbandhānaṅgīkāre kṣaṇabhaṅgavāda eva prasajyeta. ato na kālavirodhaḥ. deśadvayasaṃbandhavirodhas tu kālabhedena parihṛta ity āha–iheti. pratyabhijñāyāṃ deśabhedaḥ kālabhedād eva parihṛta ity arthaḥ. ayam atra nirṇayaḥ—kāladvayam ekasyāviruddham; akṣaṇikatvāṅgīkārāt.*

tioned at all in this sentence. Nonetheless, co-referentiality can be proven for this statement due to the co-referentiality of time with its different temporal modes. Thus, one could say that co-referentiality of different temporal designations in a *one* (*ekasya*) time is the needed presupposition for building such a sentence.

Moreover, Veṅkaṭanātha describes in more detail the relation of different times with the one substance time. "This time" and "that time", i.e., present time and past time, contradict each other. He explains them as (temporal) parts (*aṃśa*) of time. Both parts (*aṃśau*) are different from each other. Each part of time contradicts (*viruddha*) another part of time. But why for Veṅkaṭanātha such an obvious contradiction does not lead to the acceptance of the doctrine of momentariness? The reason why two contradicting times are in no contradiction with *one* time is given by the concept of self-grounding. Time as an omnipresent substance is for Veṅkaṭanātha self-grounding, but in the following passage he explains that this also implies that time grounds something else, i.e., the two contradicting parts of time (*aṃśau*). In this way Veṅkaṭanātha describes the functioning of the self-grounding time in the following sentence: "In contrast [to the two parts of time] time itself in its totality does not contradict itself, because it is only time by itself [and nothing else]" (SAS 638.14: *svakālas tu sarvo 'pi svakālatvād eva svasyāviruddhaḥ*). Even if each part of time contradicts another part, time itself does not contradict its different parts. In this way, time is not only grounding itself, but necessarily also something else (*paranirvāhaka*). Only by virtue of such a concept, it is for Veṅkaṭanātha reasonable that *one* and the *same* thing/person can be connected with different times.

> And the two parts of time itself, as this time and that time, are not contradicting to time itself. This [part of] time relates to an object in this time, whereas that [part of] time is connected [with the same object] in that time. Inasmuch as time is independent from another time, because it grounds itself *and* something else [i.e. parts of time],

neither an infinite regress occurs, nor does a mutual presupposition of one another.[119]

Any alternative to this fundamental[120] position of self-grounding substances, which Veṅkaṭanātha (and Rāmānuja as well) calls as doctrine of permanence (*sthiravāda*), would imply to accept the doctrine of momentariness (*kṣaṇabhaṅgaprasaṅa*).

Thus, the Devadatta example clearly demonstrates that by accepting time as a substance in which different mutually exclusive units of time can be based, we can speak of the unity (*aikya*) of different temporal designations in *one* time. Independent temporal designations that differ from each other can still be united in *one* and the *same* basis, the *third* grounding aspect, i.e., time as a substance (*dravya*). We can understand this argument as an application of co-referentiality. One might ask why time (*kāla*), as well as the factor of recollection, is introduced here as an important argument. If time is defined as a substance (*dravya*) that can unite mutually exclusive time units, it must ultimately be related to the one God Viṣṇu-Nārāyaṇa, insofar as everything has a single final base, one God, one *Being*, one Inner Controller (*antaryāmin*) of everything. For this, too, Veṅkaṭanātha applies the concept of co-referentiality. We recognize the model: mode and mode possessor (i.e., time with its time units) are based once again on a single mode possessor (i.e., God). Thus, time as the possessor of different time modes (like past, present, future) has a common basis with God, in the sense that time together with all its specific time units ultimately denote God. Veṅkaṭanātha refers to such an ultimate grounding by an ultimate *Being* when he states:

---

[119] Cf. SAS 638.15 *ad* TMK 4.95: *svakālāṃśau ca tadetadkālau svasyāviruddhāv eva. tatkālas tatkāle vastuni saṃbadhyate; etatkālo 'py etatkāle. kālasya svaparanirvāhakatvena kālāntarānapekṣaṇān nānavasthādoṣaḥ, nāpy ātmāśrayadoṣaḥ.*

[120] The concept of *svaparanirvāhaka* is not only applied for substance but also for non-substances (*adravya*). For Veṅkaṭanātha no state of a state is possible; cf. the first sentence of chapter 5 of the NSi, 443,2: *saṃyogarahitam adravyam.*

> Also, in the case of time, as in the case of the respective other [mentioned] categories, co-referentiality grounds [the relationship between God and time]. Therefore, he says: Because He [i.e., God] is the Inner Controller (*kālantaryāmitāder*), etc., of time.[121]

Time therefore always belongs to God's body; and can therefore be thought of as an omnipresent substance together with God's omnipresence. The inseparability as Inner Controller renders any further link to time dispensable and we will see—in the context of the critique of inherence—that this is just another expression for God's eternal conjunction with time.

Different states are based on *one* and the *same* ground insofar as different mutually excluding entities (for Veṅkaṭanātha, including different substances with their different properties/states) are combined in *one* and the *same* principle, namely God/*brahman* Himself/itself. With this, we can return to ontology: different temporal units like past and present are also ontological designations reflecting being, which could be the present time, and non-being, which could be the past or future time. For the discussed example: "being" belongs to the present Devadatta and "non-being" to Devadatta in the past or future. A past being as well as a present being in time can be understood ontologically, if one identifies past being as a "non-being" and the present as "being". This means that *one* and the *same* person can be connected to different ontological categories.

It may seem that we have gotten far off our topic. Indeed, these explanations illustrate how Veṅkaṭanātha develops an idea begun by Rāmānuja and refines it. But if looking at Rāmānuja's, and following him also Veṅkaṭanātha's sentences about *brahman*, has initiated and continued a conflict with some of his most important allies. The correct understanding of *brahman* in the context of statements about it remains, of course, a central concern of

---

121 SAS 208.5–6 *ad* TMK 1.66: *kāle 'pi sāmānādhikaraṇyaṃ tattatpadārthāntareṣv iva nirvahatīty āha—kālāntaryāmitāder iti.*

both Vedānta traditions, i.e., Advaita and Viśiṣṭādvaita. The differences between them regarding this understanding are based on their nearly incompatible premises. But one would completely misunderstand the polemical discussion between the two Vedānta traditions if one takes the Advaitic thesis as the one arguing for the unknowability of *brahman*, and Rāmānuja's view, in contrast, as the one arguing for its knowability. For Rāmānuja as for Veṅkaṭanātha, approaching an entity is in fact only possible through its designations. This always presupposes something that is inseparable from it: its substance. The different understandings of co-referentiality demonstrate that it is exactly these presuppositions that bring about the polemic with the Advaitin, who says that because *brahman* is unknowable and ultimately unnameable, we can only communicate about it indirectly. But Veṅkaṭanātha draws detailed attention to the fact that even indirect communication presupposes exact knowledge of what one wishes to communicate. To say that something is unknowable already presupposes that the speaker *knows* what he or she is talking about. One cannot say to be not knowing without knowing *what* one is not knowing; thus, one must have therefore already presupposed something knowable (*vedya*), which is expressed (*vācya*) in words. This preposition leads the Advaitin into different ways of contradiction: He must confirm exactly what he denies. But also, Veṅkaṭanātha must respond to the question of how the *brahman* is knowable and nameable by words. It is certainly not the essential nature (*svarūpa*) of *brahman* that is denotable or knowable; if this were the case, the Viśiṣṭādvaitin would not contradict the Advaitin's view! What is knowable qualifies the substance. By referring to substance, *brahman* cannot be separated from a concept of substance itself, because it is the ultimate basis for every reference. Countering the Advaitins' apophatism, Veṅkaṭanātha even adds that speaking of the unknowability of *brahman* is already a means to its knowability.[122] By applying co-referentiality,

---

[122] We can also understand against this background that Veṅkaṭnātha defines *brahman* as knowable (*vedya*) and nameable (*vācya*), but at

our two authors also demonstrate a central concept in their proof of God as the *one* in whom all entities, together with their denotations, are based.[123] By co-referentiality it is explained that the different states (either subtle or manifest) of *brahman*/God can have the *same* base. This basis can support entities and their denotations that are mutually exclusive.

---

the same time can also claim that it cannot be grasped by the human mind or language. Cf. for example the first two lines of TMK 3.3ab (339,7-10): *vācyatvaṃ vedyatāṃ ca svayam abhidadhati brahmaṇo 'nuśravāntāḥ. vākcittāgocaratvaśrutir api hi parichittyabhāvaprayuktā.* "The Upaniṣads themselves state that *brahman* is nameable and knowable. For even the authoritative Scripture states [that] *brahman* is beyond speech and mental thought, it is [positively] understood insofar as it is not limited [by them]." The last sentence expresses *brahman* negatively; but exactly in this way it is knowable and expressed in language.

123 TMK 3.5: *niḥsādhāraṇyanārāyaṇapadaviṣaye niścayaṃ yānty abādhe sadbrahmādyās samānaprakaraṇapaṭhitāś śaṅkitānyārthaśabdāḥ antaryantā ca nārāyaṇa iti kathitaḥ; kāraṇaṃ cāntarātmeti* [...]. "The words that are feared to have a different meaning, such as *Being*, *brahman*, etc., and which are recited in the same context, find, if there is no abrogation, their final determination in the word meaning 'Nārāyaṇa,' which is not general; and [this] Nārāyaṇa is called the Inner Controller. The Inner Self is [also] the cause."

For different designations of *brahman* with all the central Upaniṣadic concepts, see Veṅkaṭanātha's description in the *Īśvarapariccheda* of his NSi (NSi 275,3–4): *sa eva sadasadavyākṛtabrahmātmākāśaprāṇaśivanārāyaṇādiśabdaiḥ kāraṇaprakaraṇagataiḥ sāmānyato viśeṣataś ca vyapadiśyate.* "Exclusively this God is generally [i.e., in general terms] and in particular [i.e., with his own name] expressed with the words 'being' (ChU 6.2.1), 'non-being' (ChU 3.19.1/6.2.1), 'non-differentiated' (BĀU 1.4.7), '*brahman*' (BĀU 1.4.10,11),' '*ātman*' (AitU 1.1), 'ether' (ChU 1.9.1), 'breath' (ChU 1.11.5), 'Śiva' (ŚveU 4.18), 'Nārāyaṇa' (MahānārU 1), etc., which can be found [in the Upaniṣads] in the chapters on cause." See also SAS 344.1–4 *ad* TMK 3.5, where Veṅkaṭanātha lists the designations *sat*, *brahman*, *ātman*, *puruṣa*, *prāṇa*, and *akṣara*.

While taken separately, due to their basis, i.e., the *third* grounding aspect, they can be coordinated linguistically and ontologically.

Veṅkaṭanātha on non-differentiated (*avyākṛta*) and differentiated (*vyākṛta*) name and form (*nāmarūpe*)

The following passages quoted from Veṅkaṭanātha's work, take up the ontological basic idea as it was developed by Rāmānuja. The focus, however, is on elaborating the central idea of the unity of different attributes with a single basis. The question is whether this applies to all substances, which are mentioned in Veṅkaṭanātha's works, in the same way. The subsequent explanations refer at first only to the world to be manifested; they do not refer to the world in which the already released (*mukta*) and the eternally released (*nityasūri*) souls "live". Therefore, we will ask afterwards[124] whether the essential distinction between *vyākṛta* and *avyākṛita*, has some relevance for a substance like the eternal realm/manifestation (*nityavibhūti*) of God?

To clarify how Veṅkaṭanātha follows Rāmānuja's ontological understanding of differentiated and non-differentiated entities, we must look at the *Adhikaraṇasarāvali* (=AS), Veṅkaṭanātha's verse-commentary on Rāmānuja's *Śrībhāṣya*. In this work he refers to Rāmānuja's concept of manifestation of name and form. Taking Rāmānuja's view, Veṅkaṭanātha affirms that during the period of dissolution (*pralaya*), the world is not completely dissolved. He clearly explains that such a period is a state that cannot be considered completely as non-being/inexistent.

Concerning another example: It is remarkable that in the first sentence of the AS, Veṅkaṭanātha mentions the "non-being" (*asat*) of the ChU (ChU 6.2.1) quote. According to his understanding, what is called non-being (*asat*) refers to *avyākṛta*. Defining the universe as *asat* implies accepting it as "having no phe-

---

124 Cf. below pp. 433ff.

nomenal existence,"[125] rather than accepting it as being completely inexistent. Veṅkaṭanātha explains this as follows:

> What is expressed only as a state of dissolution in the *Upaniṣad* [ChU 6.2.1] quotation by the words: "In the beginning, however, this [universe] was nothing but non-being (*asat*)" deals with the dissolution expressed also by words [like]: "Something did not even exist," because emptiness, etc., [i.e., a complete non-existence of the world at the time of *pralaya*] is rejected. Due to the absence of distinction [i.e., not being differentiated in name and form], everything is non-differentiated; therefore, the Inner Self, in the totality of substances with their respective states, is to be addressed by words such as "being," "non-being," "non-differentiated."[126]

During the world's dissolution, i.e., while in the subtle state, what remains still *is* and can be manifested again.[127] Since everything

---

125 The interpretation of this passage in Acarya 2016: 845 is very close to Veṅkaṭanātha's understanding: "It appears to me that this discourse, like all other older and contemporary Vedic discourses on cosmogony, characterised the entity at the beginning of time as nothing but *asat* and originally began with *asad evedam agra āsīt*. Moreover, what it meant by the term *asat* was not 'non-existent,' in either a literally descriptive or ontological sense, but 'having no phenomenal existence.'"

126 *Adhikaraṇasarāvali* verse 138 (*kāraṇatvādhikaraṇa* section p. 244,1–4): *āsīd agre tv asad vā idam iti vilayāvasthatāmātram uktaṃ naivāsīt kiñcid ityādy api vilayaparaṃ, śūnyatāder niṣedhāt. sarvasyāvyākṛtatvaṃ vibhajanavirahāt tādṛśāvasthatattaddravyastomāntarātmā tad iha sadasadavyākṛtādyuktivācyaḥ.*

127 This is also demonstrated in Kumāravedānta's commentary on the AS, the *Adhikaraṇacintāmaṇi* (245,5–2): *vilayo hi nāma vedāntasiddhānte avasthāntaraprāptir eva na punar dravyasvarūpanāśaḥ. tat katham ity atrāha śūnyatāder niṣedhād iti. dravyasvarūpavināśo vilaya iti hi vaiśeṣikādīnāṃ pralāpaḥ.* "For in the doctrine of Vedānta, the dissolution [of the world] exclusively signifies the attainment of another state, but not the destruction of the essential nature of the substance (*dravyasvarūpanāśa*). How is that possible? Here he says: Due to the denial of emptiness, etc. For that dissolution (*vilaya*) sig-

remains identical to how it was, non-differentiated (*avyākṛtam*) means that each individual entity, both conscious souls and material mass, continue to *be*, even if this is not recognizable during the period of the world's dissolution (*pralaya*) due to its being non-differentiated. Being non-differentiated (*avyākṛta*) means "being in a subtle state". Thus, each entity remains preserved in its respective state.

The passage illustrates that Veṅkaṭanātha is adopting the main point of Rāmānuja's explanations of BĀU 1.4.7 and ChU 6.2.1–4. Veṅkaṭanātha explains that the term *pralaya* does not mean absolute annihilation, but only a temporary state that will be replaced by another state at the next point in time.

The concept of manifestation as described in BĀU 1.4.7 is thus relevant not only in the context of Veṅkaṭanātha's cosmological thinking, but is also important for his ontology, including his explanations of what conscious and material entities (*cidacidvastu*) in their essential nature (*svarūpa*) are, what kind of states (*avasthā*) they have, how these states alternate, and how, when alternating, they are related to their respective grounding basis, i.e., their substances. Veṅkaṭanātha develops the basic idea of an irreducible *Being* based on the distinction between that *Being* in its essential nature (*svarūpa*) and its transformation into alternating states. He applies it to God in relation to souls and the objective world, to the world itself, and to individual souls in their relation to the world, to other souls, and to God.

Another important and central concept taken up by Veṅkaṭanātha again and again is Rāmānuja's view, mentioned above, that *brahman* enters all things to manifest them. For Veṅkaṭanātha, the Veda expresses that it is God, after having entered the individual souls, who differentiates everything in name and form.

Before demonstrating how Veṅkaṭanātha applies the concept of transformation as expressed in BĀU 1.4.7 in his own theology, I will present passages from several of his works to demonstrate

---

nifies a destruction of the essential nature of the substance (*dravyasvarūpavināśo*), as the Vaiśeṣika, etc., are prattling."

how he begins to integrate this idea into his own views. The first passage is from the 53rd *vāda* of the *Śatadūṣaṇī* (ŚDū 203,23–204,1).[128] Here, Veṅkaṭanātha explains the significance of the term *avyākṛta* by referring to BĀU 1.4.7:

> For it is like this: With the word *avyākṛta* in the statements about the cause, which begin with [the statement of BĀU 1.4.7]: "All this was non-differentiated (indistinguishable) [at the beginning of creation]," the mere essential nature of *brahman* (*brahmasvarūpamātram*) is not to be known, because there is no conventional meaning for the essential nature of *brahman*, as in the case of the word *brahman*, etc., and because the intention of a connection [of *brahman* with name and form] has been made clear exclusively with [the words of BĀU 1.4.7:] "This is non-differentiated in name and form."
> Therefore, the meaning [of the word] "this" (*idam*) [in the statement of BĀU 1.4.7] at the time of the dissolution (*pralaya*) intends only the cessation of being manifest of name and form [but not a complete non-being of name and form].[129]

From Veṅkaṭanātha's words, it is clear that he does not link *avyākṛta* to *brahman* altogether, but—in the same way as Rāmānuja did—only to *brahman* that *has* non-differentiated (*avyākṛta*) name and form (*nāmarūpe*). For him, in the same way as Rāmānuja before him, the subtle form disappears through the perceptible appearance of a manifest form. According to his understanding, both terms, "being" (*sat*) and "non-being" (*asat*), can refer to *brahman*, because whatever is classified by them is not identified by its essential nature (*svarūpa*), but refers only to its different states, which inseparately belong to the *svarūpa*.

---

128 A short summary of the 53rd *vāda* is found in Srinivasa Chari 1976: 111–116.

129 ŚDū, *vāda* 53, 203,23–203,27: *tathā hi taddhedaṃ tarhy avyākṛtam āsīt tannāmarūpābhyāṃ vyākriyatetyādiṣu kāraṇavākyeṣv avyākṛtādiśabdena na brahmasvarūpamātraṃ pratipādyate, brahmādiśabdavat brahmasvarūpe rūḍhābhāvāt, tannāmarūpābhyāṃ vyākriyatety anenaiva yogavivakṣāyāḥ spaṣṭatvāc ca. ataḥ idamarthasyaiva pralayakāle nāmarūpavyākaraṇanivṛttimātraṃ vivakṣitam.*

Another example illustrating this concept is the next passage of the same work. Here, what is defined as "subtle" (*sūkṣma*) is related to darkness (*tamas*). Again, what is denoted by "words like non-differentiated etc." (*avyākṛtādiśabdena*) does not refer to *brahman* itself (*svarūpa*) i.e., its essential nature, but to the conscious (*cit*) and material (*acit*) entities qualifying it. Veṅkaṭanātha again quotes ChU 6.2.1. (*asad vā idam agra āsīd*) to show that the word *asat* (*asacchabdena*), non-being, refers to *brahman*, whose body transforms from a non-differentiated/subtle state (*avyākṛta/sūkṣma*) to a differentiated/manifested state (*vyākṛta/sthūla*).

> If one were to object: How could an undesirable consequence be possible for *brahman* in this [state of darkness], [we answer:] Because even subtle darkness that is presented by words like "Darkness has become one" [SubālaUp 2], is known as the body of *brahman* by words starting with: "Whose body is darkness," [BĀU 3.7.13], and because darkness is in other sentences about the cause kown as a state of *brahman*, it is ascertained that the word "non-differentiated" (*avyākṛta*) means *brahman* as specified by non-differentiated conscious and material entities.
> In the same way, the word *asat*, non-being, here [in the statement of ChU 6.2.1]: "In the beginning this [world] was simply non-being", "Non-being was this world in the beginning", is used to indicate *brahman* as having conscious and material entities as its body, specified by a subtle form, which passes by [the occurrence of] a manifest form; [the word *asat* does] not refer to pure *brahman*, because this contradicts its non-beingness.[130]

---

[130] ŚDū, *vāda* 53, 203,27–204,1: *tarhi brahmaṇas tatra kathaṃ prasaṅga iti cet; tama ekībhavatītyādipratipannasya sūkṣmatamaso 'pi yasya tamaś śarīram ityādibhiḥ brahmaśarīratvapratīteḥ kāraṇavākyāntareṣu brahmāvasthānapratīteś cāvyākṛtaśabda evāvyākṛtacidacidviśiṣṭabrahmapara iti niścīyate. evam asad vā idam agra āsīd, asad evedam agra āsīd, ity atrāpy asacchabdena sthūlākārapradhvaṃsāyamānasūkṣmākāraviśiṣṭacidacriccharīrakaṃ brahmābhidhīyate, na tu kevalaṃ brahma, asattvavirodhāt.*

"Darkness" (*tamas*) in this case does not mean that *brahman* disappears completely. Darkness refers to the body of *brahman* in the subtle state when nothing is perceptible. This needs some explanation: When discussing the view that nothing disappears completely, Veṅkaṭanātha compares his God to other gods. As he explains, the time of dissolution (*pralaya*) is also the time of darkness (*tamas*). Darkness and the above-mentioned subtle state (*sūkṣmāvasthā*) are related to each other: Darkness is a subtle state that cannot be differentiated from *brahman* but is nevertheless *not* identical to *brahman* (cf. Śrībh I 167 *ad* BS 1.4.27). Also in this case, darkness is *based* on God. Veṅkaṭanātha defines it as an eternal substance (following Parāśarabhaṭṭa[131]) belonging to God's body,[132] which during the time of dissolution is not completely inexistent, but only in another state.

We understand this discussion only against the background of Veṅkaṭanāṭha's basic ontological premises. He presupposes darkness to be a kind of *Being*; for him darkness *is*. In this, he sets himself apart from the opposing position, which considers darkness to represent the case of nothing existing, a position that sees beginning as coming from nothing. For Veṅkaṭanātha, the world could not be remanifested under such circumstances. His basic premise is that there is an eternal existence of the one *brahman*, which only changes its states. He also refutes the opponent's argument that the god Śiva is the cause of the universe, because, as he argues, *brahman* alone exists continuously during the period of dissolution, i.e., in the time of darkness[133] (SAS 345.8 *ad* TMK

131 For Parāśarabhaṭṭa's view on darkness (*tamas*) as a substance cf. Oberhammer 1979: 35f.; 95; 235f.

132 Cf. NSi 121,4–6, in accordance with Rāmānuja: *antaryāmibrāhmaṇe ca, yasya tamaḥ śarīram iti tejasā saha tamasaḥ śarīratvenābhidhānāt. tatra ca bhāṣyam evam ambvagnyantarikṣavāyvādityadikcandratārakākāśatamas tejasv ityādi.* For the view that *tamas* does not mean complete non-existence, see also NSi 119,1ff.

133 SAS 345,8 *ad* TMK 3.6: *ataḥ prasiddhaśivaḥ kāraṇam ity atrāha—śiva eveti.*

3.6: *ataḥ prasiddhaśivaḥ kāraṇam ity atrāha—śiva eveti*). Veṅkaṭanātha elaborates on this by describing darkness as a substance that functions as a quality. The God Viṣṇu-Nārāyaṇa is the *basis* for the time-phase of darkness. Since this God supports everything (*viśva*), He is neither identified with darkness itself nor subordinated to it. God, denoted as Śiva (Rudra), is rather described as the support and only cause of darkness.[134] Hence he also explains that the designation "Śiva" actually refers to the Highest God Viṣṇu, concluding in TMK 3.6ab that with the name Śiva, what is meant is Viṣṇu.[135]

Finally, I would like to cite two more important quotations, which not only demonstrate God as being the ground of darkness, but the self-grounding basis of everything through His own will or His inconveivable potency. The world's manifestation based on God and its ontological implications can be found in the third chapter (*nāyakasara*) of the TMK (3.25ab), where he describes the body of God as transforming in various ways:

> [Viṣṇu-Nārāyaṇa], the creator of all, whose power is inconceivable, is Himself the material cause of this world, because He, whose body

---

[134] TMK 3.6cd: *uktaṃ nārāyaṇādhiṣṭhitam iti ca tamo 'nekabādho 'nyathā syāt brahmeśāder mahatyām upaniṣadiṣi vilayādyam; evaṃ tu nātra.* "And darkness is said to be dependent on Nārāyaṇa. In the contrary case, many passages would contradict this. In the *Mahātmya Upaniṣad*, dissolution, etc., is said to be for gods like Brahman, Rudra; but it is not the same here, [i.e., for Viṣṇu]." Cf. also SAS 345.11–19 *ad* TMK 3.6: *ataḥ kāraṇatamodhiṣṭhātṛtvena prasiddho nārāyaṇa evātra śabdāntaraparāmṛṣṭaḥ.*

[135] TMK 3.6ab: *viṣṇor apy asty abhikhyā śiva iti; śubhatārūḍhir atrānupādhis tasmād dhyeyaḥ śruto 'sau śiva iti; śiva eveti vākyaṃ tv anūktiḥ.* "Śiva is also a designation for Viṣṇu. The conventional meaning of the *śubhatā* is without limitation. Hence Nārāyaṇa is described in authoritative Scripture (*śruti*) as Śiva, who is to be meditated upon. But the sentence 'only Śiva' is a re-statement."

> consists in the subtle Undeveloped, etc., transforms manifoldly due to [His] modification into a manifest [state of His body].[136]

Another example is from the third chapter on God (*īśvaraparic-cheda*) in the *Nyāyasiddhāñjana*. Here it is stated that God is not only eternally connected with everything as a material cause, but also acts comprehensively and omnipresent by virtue of His will as an instrumental cause. Again, Veṅkaṭanātha takes up the distinction between separated/differentiated (*vibhakta*) and non-separated/non-differentiated (*avibhakta*) names and forms. For God, Veṅkaṭanātha says, both material cause and instrumental cause must be recognized as His specific characteristics. It is therefore important to refer to Veṅkaṭanātha's statement in the following passage; here it is expressed that it is only God Himself who is the material cause of the transformation from subtle to manifest.

> For it is established that [God], who has as a body whose conscious being and whose material mass have [during the period of dissolution] non-differentiated name and forms, is the material cause in relation to [Himself], who has as a body whose conscious and material entities have differentiated names and forms, and it is also established that [He] is the efficient cause in such a form which is other than "having as a body non-differentiated conscious and material entities"—for instance, in the form of having a particular will, which is common to a potter and the like.[137]

---

136 TMK 3.25ab: *asyaivācintyaśakter akhilajanayitus syād upādānabhā-vas sūkṣmāvyaktādidehaḥ pariṇamati yato 'nekadhā sthūlavṛttyā.* In TMK 3.26, Veṅkaṭanātha also explains how God is connected to everything. He refers to the individual soul, which as an agent causes its own happiness through its own effort. But what the soul is doing individually for itself, God, as cause and agent, is doing for everything, i.e., material and conscious beings. Thus Veṅkaṭanātha concludes: "Therefore, in reference to this agent of everything [i.e., God], it is possible that He is the material cause of everything." *sar-vopādānabhāvas tata iha ghaṭate sarvakartary amuṣmin.*

137 NSi 359,5–7: *avibhaktanāmarūpacidaciccharīrakasya vibhaktanā-marūpacidaciccharīrakatvāpekṣayopādānatvasiddheḥ, avibhaktacid-*

As can be concluded from these passages, whatever belongs to God's body can never pass away completely. Moreover, God Himself is not relativized in his eternal *Being*. An important implication of Veṅkaṭanātha's teaching (as for Rāmānuja, as demonstrated above) is that the difference between being (*sat*) and non-being (*asat*) does not exclude the fact that they can co-exist in *one* and the *same* ground; they merely represent two different states of one and the same basis, which is defined as eternal *Being*. If such a *Being*, identified with a personal God, is accepted, and if what He carries and directs has always existed, absolute non-being (*atyantābhava*) would be incongruous and impossible to prove. If complete non-being were the case, God would have to create out of nothing, with no relationship to anything existing in the past. Thus, Veṅkaṭanātha's central idea (and already Rāmānuja's) is based on the view that due to the undeniable presupposition of *Being*, the concept of emptiness (*śūnyatā*) taught by the Buddhist tradition cannot be proven by any means of valid cognition.

Of course, it could be argued that such a God, endowed with all perfections, should also be able to be related to nothing or be able to create everything again out of nothing. But in the theistic tradition of Vedānta, this possibility is not part of the understanding of *Being* (*sat*). God is identified as *Being*, which is at the root of everything, and when His body modifies, it can be determined as both being (*sattva/bhāva*) and non-being (*asattva/abhāva*).

Refuting the concept of "difference *and* identity" (*bheda-abheda*)

In the following the difference between attributes that specify a substance, can be pointed out by another important philosophical

---

aciccharīrakatvātiriktena kulālādisādhāraṇasaṅkalpaviśeṣavattvādy-ākāreṇa nimittatvasiddheś ca.

and theological position mostly identified by Veṅkaṭanātha with the view of the Jainas, but also Bhāskaras (9th c.) and Yādavaprakāśas (10th c.), whose doctrin is called by him as "the thesis of the half Jainas" (*ardhajainapakṣaṅkaḷ*, cf. PMBh p. 283,4 (chapter 24)). They do not take into account that there is also a difference between grounding substance and its respective different attributes additionally to the difference (*bheda*) between specifying attributes.

At this point, it is important to reiterate how the above-mentioned term of unity (*aikya*) differs from the rather simple notion of identity (*abheda*). This is illustrated in Veṅkaṭanātha's critique of the notion of defining co-referentiality as difference *and* identity, a view that contradicts his own understanding of this concept. We already developed the central view that for differently classified entities/attributes to be brought into unity, they must relate to a *third* grounding aspect. This *third* aspect is implicitly presupposed in the references of two attributes, which are classified differently. This is the only reason why there is no contradiction in the common appearance of different things, even if there is still a distinction. If we perceive something that we say is both a lotus *and* blue, then we clarify that the underlying substance (e.g., a flower) to which being blue and being a lotus, both belong is the reason why both attributes can appear together as a unity.

In contrast, the presupposed substance (*dravya*), in this example the flower, remains distinct, even though it cannot be separated from its attributes. There is no such a thing like a pure flower. As we have pointed out above, our tradition defines attributes and the third grounding aspect as different.

Now, the Jaina, who also refers to the concept of co-referentiality, is the position to be refuted. He accepts a difference between attributes like blueness and lotusness but denies a difference between these and an underlying *third*. He argues for a concept of "difference *and* identity," (*bheda-abhedavādin*) and explains co-referentiality on the background of this doctrine. While there are different attributes/qualities, they are merged with the substance into a unity.[138] Veṅkaṭanātha represents the Jaina position in the first half of TMK 4.94ab against the background of coreferentiality (*sāmānādhikaraṇya*):

> Since it is established that unity (*aikya*) is intended in a sentence [which expresses] coreference for words, which are used differently, it is a futile wish for doctrinal representatives like those of the Jainas etc., (*ārhatāder*) that this (*idam*) [i.e., coreferentiality] is also true for the one who represents [the doctrine of] difference *and* identity.[139]

And in his commentary (SAS) Veṅkaṭanātha describes his opponent as arguing a simplified form of co-referentiality as follows:

> Wherever there is difference *and* identity, there is co-referentiality, [as in the sentence:] "The lotus is blue".[140]

Again, on the background of his own definition of coreferentiality, such a sentence cannot be analyzed. In the second half of the verse, Veṅkaṭanātha refutes this view: Even if one says that the substance is inseparable from that which the substance is grounding, co-referentiality is only possible if the ultimate basis is *different* from what it is grounding. But this is not the case for the opponent. For him, there is on the one side unity (*aikya*), i.e., identity (*abheda*) with the substance, on the other side there is difference (*bheda*), because by the word *paryāya* i.e., "modification" different properties are expressed (cf. SAS 637.1–2 *paryāyaśabdena dharmā ucyante*). Following such a view of the opponent, the consequence would be that one and the same entity is stated twice: based on being blue, the substance would be blue,

---

138 For an explanation of difference and non-difference (identity) between between substance (*dravya*) and "state of appearance" (*paryāya*) according to the Jaina view, cf. Trikha 2012: 59–62.

139 TMK 4.94ab:
dvāre bhinne samānādhikaraṇavacasām aikyatātparyasiddheḥ
bhedābhedasthitānām idam anuguṇam ity ārhatāder durāśā.

140 SAS 636.10–637.2 *ad* TMK 4.94: *yatra bhedābhedau tatraiva sāmānādhikaraṇyam, nīlam utpalam iti.*

and based on being a lotus, it would be a lotus. Such an absurd consequence results from accepting a difference between the properties *and* at the same time an identity with the underlying substance; therefore, against the background of the teaching of *bheda-abheda*, a sentence/cognition like "The lotus is blue" would be impossible. Thus, Veṅkaṭanātha expresses in the second half of the verse TMK 4.94cd that only difference must be accepted:

> A sentence which indicates in another way something regarding uniformity with [the essential] nature of things, is unlikely to be a means of valid cognition.
> Based on such a cognition, a single entity would exist twice, and this is not right because [co-referentiality] is possible if there is only difference.[141]

In his commentary (SAS) to the second half of the verse, Veṅkaṭanātha draws attention to the fact that the unity of words used in different contexts does not mean that they must be identical with what they refer to. Attributes such as blue-ness and lotus-ness remain differentiated from one another but appear in a unity only when they are related to a *third* grounding aspect.

> Because in the quote [of *Kāśikāvṛtti ad* Pāṇini 2.1.49] "The functionning of words whose base meanings are distinct in referring to the same object is [the definition of] co-referentiality," the characteristic of co-referentiality is that [words] are dependent on a single object due to their different application. For this reason, saying that difference *and* identity are established by co-referentiality has a basis in poor expectations due to contradictory speech. If co-referentiality establishes difference *and* identity, then there would be no means of cognition for it, because co-referentiality establishes an object that contradicts the means of valid cognition.[142]

---

141 TMK 4.94cd:
vastusthityaikarūpye vacanam itarathā bodhayat syān na mānaṃ
tanmānatvād dvidhaikaṃ sthitam iti ca na sat, bheda evopapatteḥ.

142 SAS 637.3–6 *ad* TMK 4.94: *bhinnapravṛttinimittānāṃ śabdānām eka[tra]sminn arthe vṛttis sāmānādhikaraṇyam iti pravṛttinimittabhe-*

Now it remains to be shown to what extent difference *and* identity as a basic thesis also led to absurd consequences for other doctrinal proponents of the *bheda-abheda* doctrine in a theistic Vedānta tradition such as that of Bhāskara or Yādavaprakāśa. The view of difference *and* identity as followed by both is analogous to the concept of substance mentioned above. Bhāskara asserts the same of *brahman*, saying that it is imposed properties (*upādhi*) with which it is equated. In this case, the absurd consequence of identity (*abheda*) leads these thinkers to conflate God/*brahman* directly with suffering. For Veṅkaṭanātha, asserting that *brahman* is simultaneously identical *and* different leads him therefore to the following words of critique:

> But the followers of Bhāskara [hold the view that] the substance *brahman*, which is differentiated into partial manifestations of conscious and material entities, transforms itself into material partial manifestation and wanders about in *saṃsāra* as the conscious partial manifestation endowed with the transformation of the material partial manifestation.[143]

When there is no longer any distinction between the partial manifestations, and their change, then it is *brahman* itself, in its essence, that changes; identical with the soul endowed with a body, it wanders as such in the *saṃsāra* and becomes bound and released. Veṅkaṭanātha also highlights how identity is misinterpreted in the teaching of Yādavaprakāśa; he takes the difference

---

denaikārthaniṣṭhatvalakṣaṇatvāt sāmānādhikaraṇyasya, tenaiva sāmānādhikaraṇyena bhedābhedasiddhir iti vacanaṃ viruddhabhāṣaṇatvād durāśāmūlam eva. yadi bhedābhedaṃ bodhayet sāmānādhikaraṇyam, pramāṇaviruddhārthapratipādakatvāt pramāṇam eva na syād.

143 SAS 381.3–6 *ad* TMK 3.27: *bhāskarīyās tu—cidacidaṃśavibhaktaṃ brahmadravyam acidaṃśena vikriyate, tadvikāropahitena cidaṃśena saṃsaratīti.* Cf. also NSi 217,2–218,3: "As for Bhāskara's opinion, it is ridiculous that eternal and omniscient [*brahman*] is associated with an imposed property (*upādhi*)."

between released and bound souls as an opportunity to demonstrate the absurd consequences of the doctrine:

> Similarly, the doctrine of [Yādavaprakāśa's] being and conscious *brahman*, which is at once identical *and* different from all word-objects, should also be refuted, because [Yādavaprakāśa] holds [the view] that even the soul which is still bound in *saṃsāra* at the time of the world's dissolution becomes identical with the released one and that even the released soul, who is omniscient would be bound at the beginning of creation with infinite [souls] in *saṃsāra* through the realization of identity with all things to be abandoned. Therefore, there is no difference between attachment and release.[144]

So far we can summarize: When the doctrine of difference *and* identity (*bheda-abheda*) is applied to the relationship between *brahman* and conscious and material entities, as in the case of these two authors, Veṅkaṭanātha points out that neither the binding of the soul nor release can be assumed; but this is precisely what Veṅkaṭanātha has in mind with the criticism of co-referentiality interpreted against the background of *bheda-abheda*; in order to be able to assert co-referentiality, the *third* grounding aspect, even if it is not named in the sentence, a substance must be distinct from its attributes. Within such a distinction, the *inseparability* of the basis but not its identity (*abheda*) must be accepted. If no *third* grounding aspect were presupposed, which is *distinct* but inseparable from its attributes, which are also designations, co-referentiality would not be acceptable.

What functions as a substance (*dravya*)?

Let us now look briefly at how Veṅkaṭanātha finally coordinates all substances with God Himself, the one basis for everything,

---

144 NSi 217,3–218,1: *evaṃ sakalapadārthabhinnābhinnasaccidbrahmavādo 'pi dūṣyaḥ, baddhasyāpi pralaye muktāviśeṣasadāpattyabhidhānāt. muktasyāpi sarvajñasya sṛṣṭau sarvaheyatādātmyānusandhānena anantasaṃsārayogāt. ato bandhamokṣāviśeṣa eva.*

and how he tries to reconcile the multiplicity of designations that are the basis of the substances that form God's body.

Although Veṅkaṭanātha considers substances, which are the indispensable basis of their states, to exist in and of themselves, he does not see them as isolated from each other. Moreover, each must be able to exist together with God.

How are substances related to God? A description of the relation between God and substances is found in the first verse of the fifth chapter (*adravyasara*) of the TMK, where Veṅkaṭanātha explicitly refers to the analogy of how a substance is related to its state. It is like the relation of God to all substances together with their states:

> The totality of non-substances (*adravyajātaṃ*) is established as unseparated (*apṛthaksiddham*) and restricted (*niyatimad*) to their respective substances. It is similar with everything for the Supreme (*parasya*) [i.e., the Supreme Self, God].[145]

In his auto-commentary on the TMK, Veṅkaṭanātha explains his sentence of the verse in more detail:

> The meaning is: For that substance which is said [to be characterized by a quality, i.e., a non-substance], it is exclusively limited to it. And the totality of [the qualities which are] non-substances is inseparately established in/for each of these substances. In the same way, the totality [of substances together with their non-substances] is also inseparately established from the Highest.[146]

Regarding to God and His *relational unity* these sentences of Veṅkaṭanātha demonstrate once more that the feature of different states, non-substances (*adravya*), consists in the transformation of *one* and the *same* substance, at least God Himself. And while *one* and the *same* substance can have states, which are independent

---

[145] TMK 5.1ab: *tattaddravyeṣu dṛṣṭaṃ niyatimad apṛthaksiddham adravyajātaṃ tadvat viśvaṃ parasya.*

[146] SAS 680.7–8 *ad* TMK 5.1: *yasya dravyasya yad ucitaṃ tat tatraiva niyatam ity arthaḥ. tac ca tatra tatrāpṛthaksiddham adravyajātam. tadvad eva viśvam api parasyāpṛthaksiddham.*

from each other, they do not appear simultaneously. Nevertheless they are intimately connected to their basis. If we refer to a state, then we have inevitably presupposed a substance, which is determined by that state in a specific way. For this reason, too, a state and its basis cannot be presented as separate.

The temporal implication of different states has already been pointed out. As Veṅkaṭanātha explains, on one hand, the states of a substance cannot exist as separated from it, but, on the other hand, they exist temporarily and do not remain permanently present. If infinite states did not qualify substances at certain times, this would lead to the erroneous assumption that only a single state determines a substance, or that all states determining a substance must occur simultaneously. Neither is possible for Veṅkaṭanātha.

If a state cannot be separated from its substance, how can a sequence of states be conceptualized? The fact that something is always perceptible is because a state can be either non-differentiated (*avyākṛta*), that is, in a subtle state (*sūkṣmāvasthā*), or differentiated (*vyākṛta*), that is, in a manifest state (*sthūlāvasthā*). And because everything can be defined as already *Being*, there is no need for further mediation possible between a substance and how it is specified. For Veṅkaṭanātha, this is not the only reason not to accept the concept of inherence (*samavāya*), by which relata like substance and its attributes are connected. Another reason would be that one cannot say what exists earlier or later: substance or non-substance (*adravya*). Rather, it is only possible to grasp a substance simultaneously (*yugapat*) with its respective determining state/property.

In reply to an objection that since a substance is given before its non-substance, if non-substance does not exist, both are not given due to their interdependence, Veṅkaṭanātha says that substance and non-substance rely mutually on each other. Therefore, in only a single moment (*ekasminn eva kṣaṇe*), i.e., in a *single* knowledge, is a substance and its state, i.e., designation and what is to be designated, able to be grasped. This only could happen based on the thesis of inseparability of substance and state,[147] but also of the intimate relation of its states and its designation by different words. Thus, to whatever one refers in the world we have access to it only by language *and* knowledge. As we have pointed out above, already Rāmānuja connected the modes of a mode possessor with designations. Therefore knowing the world implies always knowing the world by language. Veṅkaṭanātha mentions the relation between a cognitive act and its linguistic character. The act of knowing always takes place simultaneously with the use of words, even if the words for both (*tacchabdau*) are given by the speaker of a sentence in succession (*anukramād*). This is Veṅkaṭanātha's *linguistic paradigm*. He concludes that words are performed simultaneously whereby there is no contradiction between what happens first and what happens later.[148] To demonstrate this he refers to the fact that children learn the original meaning of the words of Vedic language by recognizing objects in their own world. After all, when they learn language, they also grasp properties and their basis at the same time, learning what has been handed down to denote objects in the world before they were born. As described by Veṅkaṭanātha,[149] children do not create their own way of speaking.

[147] Another example is SAS 682.11ff. *ad* TMK 5.3, where Veṅkaṭanātha states that substance and state/non-substance (*avasthā/adravya*) cannot be considered two separate entities: *avasthāvaddravyam iti hi dravyaṃ lakṣyate. avasthā cādravyam eva. tathā cānyonyasāpekṣatvād dravyam adravyaṃ ca dvayam api na sidhyatīti.* "The substance is defined as a substance that is characterized by a state. And the state is a non-substance. And in the same way, because of their interdependence, both substance and non-substance are not established as a pair." Cf. also the important discussion in TMK 1.10 and the important consequence in his commentary thereon, that both, qualifier and qualified, can be said as qualified (cf., SAS 31.4: *ataḥ saṃbandhyubhayaṃ viśiṣṭaśabdārtha iti syat.*).

[148] SAS 682.20 *ad* TMK 5.3: *ato dravyādravyaśabdayor vyutpattau vyavahāre tatpratipattau ca parasparapaurvāparyābhāvān na virodhaḥ.*

[149] For Rāmānuja's view on this topic, see Lipner 1986: 13.

> Children indeed know simultaneously (*yugapad*) the essential nature of an entity due to the relation of specifier and specified. And in the beginningless *saṃsāra* they learn only simultaneously through the [Vedic] use of the words in earlier times. [...] Therefore, determining the difference between substance and non-substance as conforming to the difference between specifier and specified, etc., as [they are] known in the world, is correct.[150]

Even if we express objects designated by words in our language in a sequence, we immediately perceive not only differentiated objects, i.e., specific states/properties denoted by words, we also reconstruct by our linguistic knowledge always the *same* world in the *same* eternal vedic language. But before we continue to illustrate how Veṅkaṭanātha deals with vedic language, a few more examples and explanations.

More examples of substances and their states/properties

Like Rāmānuja, when Veṅkaṭanātha describes "transformation" (*pariṇāma*) in terms of substance (*dravya*) and state (*avasthā*), it is against the background of his understanding of God's being in (relational) *unity* with every conscious and material entity (*cid-acidvastu*). Even if a state (*avasthā*) is defined as "non-being," it nevertheless *is* because it can become present again. This is what presupposes *being*: effects have a supporting basis, even at the time of their non-being (*abhāva*). Otherwise they could not be determined as *being* non-being for any period. The difference between being and non-being is the difference between two states of a substance; while both *are*, at the same time both are not. Each state appears in its own part of time of being present. Also non-

---

150 SAS 682.22–683.16 *ad* TMK 5.3: *bālāḥ khalu viśeṣaṇaviśeṣyabhāvena vastusvarūpaṃ yugapad upalabhante. anādau ca saṃsāre pūrvapūrvavyavahārair yugapad eva śikṣyante* [...]. *ato lokadṛṣṭaviśeṣaṇaviśeṣyādivibhāgānusāreṇa dravyādravyādivibhāgaparikalpanaṃ nyāyyam.*

being (*abhāva*) is therefore something concrete, something that can be fixed to a condition, place and time in its specific nature (*svabhāva*). Non-being (*abhāva*) is recognizable as a state of something that *is* not present.[151]

Accepting an eternally existing substance means there is no first state from which transformation begins. Insofar as a substance is never without a state, nor determined by only one state, it is impossible to define a substance's first or last state. This can be explained by the basic ontological idea presented above: It is contradictory to say that *Being* (*sat*) starts at a certain point in time, since if this were the case, one would have to accept a first beginning. But to assert that there was a first beginning, one must already have presupposed *Being* to know what the first beginning *is*.

Without accepting that what is called substance (*dravya*) is eternal, it would be impossible to speak of a beginningless (*anādi*) and endless (*ananta*) ever-continuing sequence of states (*avasthāsantāna*). And without the beginninglessness of different states, the eternity of their base could not be assumed either. If different states are recognized, then also the substance, which is always in a special state, is recognized. If, for example, an effect of primordial matter (*prakṛti*) is recognized, then this is also grasped in its respective state; if a temporal designation is recognized, then also the substance "time" is grasped as being temporally specified. It is not the substance "time" (*kāla*) itself that is recognized, but time in its respective temporal state.

As stated above, substance is seen as the *third* aspect. If substance is equated with *Being*. *Being* is thus also always inevitably presupposed and ultimately the condition of every judgement. Substance (*dravya*), i.e., *Being*, is never conceivable in and of it-

---

[151] Cf. the statement in SAS 726.8 *ad* TMK 5.52: *niṣedhakapramāṇagocaro hy abhāvaḥ*. See also TMK 5.129: *so 'bhāvo yaḥ svabhāvaṃ niyamayati daśādeśakālādibhedaḥ*. "That is [defined as] non-being, whose different states, places, times, etc., restrains the characteristic nature [of such a non-being]."

self. It is only perceived in its specific designation, i.e., the state that is manifest at a certain time (*kāla*) and in a certain place (*deśa*). There is never a cognition that separates the two factors *that* something is and *what* it is.

One of the many examples of the alternation of states in Veṅkaṭanātha's works is the following passage from the *Nyāyasiddhāñjana*. In this passage, Veṅkaṭanātha illustrates the change from *ekatva* to *bahutva*, i.e., from oneness to manifoldness, using as his example the relationship between earth and grass. In response to an opponent's idea that the manifoldness (*bahutva*) of the world disappears completely in the state of its dissolution, Veṅkaṭanātha explains that this is not the case insofar as there is no state of complete dissolution. The fact that the period of dissolution (*pralaya*) is only a temporary state is demonstrated by the example of grass (*tṛṇa*). Here, too, a transformation occurs through a sequence of different states. Indeed, when in the state of grass, the earth ceases to be. However, the existence of grass indicates that the earth is now in the state of grass. It is not the grass itself that changes when it withers at certain times of the year, but it is the earth ceasing to be in the grass state. Veṅkaṭanātha does not see grass as a part (*avayava*) of the earth, but as its temporary state. If the grass vanishes and the earth appears, then the earth has returned to the state that follows the state of grass. Instead of talking about the grass state or the earth state, Veṅkaṭanātha says that the earth changes from the state of manifoldness back to that of unity. The substance "earth" is the material cause for its state of being grass.

> For instance, when [earth] is transformed into modifications such as grass and stone, people begin to use the expression: "[They are] different from earth"; when the same are transformed into another modification, people again begin to use the expression: "[It is now] earth." But this does not mean the mutual oneness of each part, such as grass or stone, nor [does it mean their oneness] with great earth.

> What then [does it mean]? [It means] the mere attaining of the state of the same kind by abandoning the state of a different kind.[152]

Veṅkaṭanātha follows Rāmānuja's viewpoint closely, as a passage from Rāmānuja's commentary (Śrībh III 253.11–12) on the *Brahmasūtra* demonstrates. Rāmānuja states that if something changes, it does not become another different substance but has only reached a different state.

> As the state of the pot [arises] after states as a bowl, dust [or] lumps have been given up, in the same way a state of manifoldness [occurs] by giving up the former state of oneness (*ekatvāvasthāprahāṇena*), or the state of oneness (*ekatvāvasthā*) [occurs] by giving up the state of manifoldness (*bahutvāvasthā*).[153]

Veṅkaṭanātha refers to this remark in his NSi. Again, for him the transformation from unity to manifoldness does not occur through an attribute connected to many properties (*anekadharmayogopādhikaṃ*), but rather through the alternation from the state of unity to that of manifoldness:

> [Objection:] Unity as a state (*avasthārūpasyaikatvasya*) may not be contradicted by manifoldness (*bahutvena*) that exists in the future or in the past; but there may be a contradiction due to the unity of the [eternal] essential nature of substances.
> [Our view:] This may not be the case, for there would be a contradiction if one substance becomes another [substance]. But there is no [contradiction] in the case of an existent (*sat*) [substance] attaining plurality by a limiting condition, namely, the connection with many attributes (*dharma*). And in a *smṛti*, the Venerable Parāśara

---

[152] NSi 514,2–515,2: *yathā tṛṇopalādipariṇāmakalāyāṃ pṛthivītaḥ pṛthagvyavahāro jāyate, teṣām eva pariṇāmāntaram āpannānāṃ punaḥ pṛthivītvavyavahāraḥ. na ca tāvatā tṛṇopalādyaṃśānāṃ parasparaṃ tāvad aikyam, atha mahāpṛthivyā vā. kiṃ tarhi vijātīyāvasthāprahāṇena sajātīyāvasthāpattimātram.*

[153] Śrībh III 253,11–12 *ad* BS 2.1.15: *kapālatvacūrṇatvapiṇḍatvāvasthāprahāṇena ghaṭatvāvasthāvat, ekatvāvasthāprahāṇena bahutvāvasthā, tatprahāṇenaikatvāvasthā ceti.*

says: "Identity of [an individual] self with the Highest Self is admitted as the highest goal, but this is false, since one substance cannot become another (substance)" (ViP 2.14.26).[154]

The last sentence indicates yet another consequence in Veṅkaṭanātha's doctrine of each other differing substances. Substances with their attributes never become identical in a way that they become a distinctless union. They are inseparable but remain different. Again, the quoted verse from the *Viṣṇupurāṇa* suggests identity between the Highest Self and the individual soul, but in fact explains that they remain always independent.[155]

The quoted passage also demonstrates that Veṅkaṭanātha sees several different states as grounding in *one* and the *same* basis. Veṅkaṭanātha's idea (as well as Rāmānuja's) that *one* and the *same* ground, i.e. *brahman* is in different states does not mean that these states occur simultaneously. They are in a "sequence" (*santāna*)[156] that proceeds without beginning, with one state presupposing the next. The next state always follows a previous one.

---

154 NSi 47,3–6: *bhavatu avasthārūpasyaikatvasya pūrvāparabhāvinā bahutvenāvirodhaḥ, taddravyasvarūpaikyena tu virodha syāt. na syāt, taddravyasya hy ataddravyatvam viruddham. na tu tasyaiva sato 'nekadharmayogopādhikaṃ bahutvam. smarati ca bhagavān parāśaraḥ, paramātmātmanor yogaḥ paramārtha itīṣyate mithyaitad anyadravyaṃ hi naiti taddravyatāṃ yataḥ iti.*

155 Cf. also the discussion in *vāda* 37 (*jīveśvaraikyabhaṅgavāda*) of Veṅkaṭanātha's *Śatadūṣaṇī*.

156 For Veṅkaṭanātha, this "sequence of states" (*avasthāsantāna*) means that each state in the sequence (*santāna*) is individually recognizable, even if there is always a flow (*pravāha*) from one state to the following state. The concept of *santāna* is interpreted in a completely different way in the Buddhist doctrine of momentariness, in which the uninterrupted flow of causal moments does not allow an individual moment to be recognized as such. In contrast, according to the Viśiṣṭādvaita Vedānta, a moment is a substance's temporal qualifier and is a state of that substance. (For Veṅkaṭanātha's discussion of this concept and his refutation of *kṣaṇikatva* cf. TMK 1.27, and Schmücker forthcoming[2]).

There is no "first" or "last" state of a substance, but only an earlier (*pūrva*) or a later (*uttara*) one; the later one, in turn, becomes the earlier one for the next. This alternation of states takes place infinitely.

As in the passage from Rāmānuja's VAS (§74,113,8f.) cited above (p. 356), Veṅkaṭanātha explains that it is at least only *brahman* which has states. When he speaks of substances, this is based on the idea that a substance cannot be the basis for something else (i.e., another substance) except in the case of the *dharmabhūtajñāna*, the "knowledge that functions as a property," which is always in a specific state.[157] In the same way, God/*brahman* cannot be based on something else. As we have seen before, Veṅkaṭanātha expresses this with the already above mentioned compound *svaparanirvāhaka*: A substance is self-grounded (*svanirvāhaka*), but at the same time gives *Being* to its respective states/characteristics, i.e., to something different (*para*).[158]

In explaining the co-referentiality of different times, I have already demonstrated that time as a substance is self-grounding. But it accomplishes also something else, namely, the temporal measuring of things. Thus, it is not time itself that alternates in its essential nature (*svarūpa*), but its temporality, i.e., its different respective temporal states. The self-grounded substance time as the *third* aspect is the basis of all temporal classifications. When Veṅkaṭanātha defines time as the present (*vartamāna*), he clarifies what is recognizable *in* time: It is not the temporality of the present that is perceptible, but the temporal classification of time.

Veṅkaṭanātha applies the concept of *svaparanirvāhaka* also to the concept of "difference" (*bheda*) itself. Difference is self-grounding (*svanirvāhaka*), i.e., one difference cannot be recognized from another difference.[159] A difference of difference can-

---

[157] Cf. Schmücker 2020a: 78; 85.

[158] Cf. fn. 120 above.

[159] For the opposite position, which holds the "difference" of difference in Navya-Nyāya, cf. Matilal 1986: 155–163.

not be proven by any means of knowledge without falling into an infinite regress. Rather, difference being given by itself (*svataḥ*) is the reason that various objects can be recognized as different; it is the reason that there is a difference between things. Thus, self-grounding difference is the ground for other (uncountable) differences between various things (*paranirvāhaka*).[160]

Properties defining the essential nature of a substance (*svarūpanirūpakadharma*)

If everything is only recognizable through states that are temporal properties, how can the eternity of a substance be explained? According to Veṅkaṭanātha, substance is imperishable and inseparably connected to its states. "Being eternal" is defined by the essential nature (*svarūpa*) of the substance itself. And yet a substance itself can never become a state (*avasthā*). If the imperishable *Being* itself were only a state, it would be contradictory to assume the *relational unity* of God. This is why Veṅkaṭanātha accepts that the definition of the eternity of a substance is not linked to the alternation of its states; a substance is known or can be determined as eternal only through the state by which it is defined.

It is due to the properties, which define the essential nature (*svarūpanirūpakadharma*) that one can speak of a substance existing eternally even though it continuously has different states. Essential properties disprove the argument that a substance only exists when its respective states are recognized. If the sequence of states (*avasthāsantāna*) is considered to be without beginning, it is not possible to claim that a substance is without being in a specific state. Saying that a substance is eternal can only be expressed—according to our context outlined so far—that the substance is qualified by the qualifier "eternity". But this is in fact a paradox and provokes the question if "eternity" can really be

---

160 See Schmücker 2022: 147ff. on how Veṅkaṭanātha develops the concept of difference (*bheda*) regarding God's divine knowledge.

expressed through a qualifying propertiy? For this, Veṅkaṭanātha distinguishes between the above-mentioned alternating states and essential properties. He defines such properties as *nirūpitasvarūpadharma*, i.e., "properties of the essential nature [of a substance] that has already been determined [by properties]". Thus, there are always two "types"[161] of properties, or two ways of qualifying a substance: the mentioned *svarūpanirūpakadharmas*, "properties that determine/define the essential nature," *and* secondary properties that further specify the essential nature/substance (*svarūpa/dravya*).[162]

In chapter five (*tattvatrayacintanādhikāra*) of his *Rahasyatrayasāra* (RTS), in the last sentence of the passage cited below, Veṅkaṭanātha clearly explains that defining an essential nature (*svarūpa*) is only possible by defining the properties qualifying that essential nature. In the context of the cognitive process, he describes the use of the means of valid cognition in the following terms:

> The means of valid cognition, when they reveal entities, also reveal the essential nature of the respective entities, its properties that define the essential nature, and the (further) specifications of the es-

---

161 For a further discussion on properties as seen by thinkers after Veṅkaṭanātha, see Kassan-Hann 1992: 126. Citing *Yatīndramatadīpikā* (IX: 15), in addition to the two properties discussed here, also named are: *sṛṣṭa-upayuktāḥ dharmāḥ*, "attributes useful for creation"; *āśrayaṇa-upayuktāḥ dharmāḥ*, "attributes useful for providing refuge"; and *rakṣaṇa upayuktadharmāḥ* "attributes for protection."

162 Also Rāmānuja distinguishes between the two properties of *svarūpanirūpakadharma* and *nirūpitasvarūpadharma*; see Carman 1974: 72: "Statements that He is sheer knowledge and bliss are maintained because they express the defining property of the essential nature [*svarūpanirūpaka-dharma*] of the Supreme Brahman, who is different from all, the support of all, the cause of the origination, subsistence, and dissolution of all, faultless, immutable, the Self of all." See also VAS §24 (84,14–15): *nanu ca jñānamātraṃ brahmeti pratipādite nirviśeṣajñānamātraṃ brahmeti niścīyate. naivam, svarūpanirūpaṇadharmaśabdā hi dharmamukhena svarūpam api pratipādayanti.*

sential nature that has been determined [by primary properties] and their usages. Among these, [the means of valid cognition] reveal the essential nature [of the respective entity] as specified by properties that define it. An explanation of that essential nature (*svarūpa*) without an explanation of its properties is not possible.[163]

In Veṅkaṭanātha, the elaboration of these two qualities is found only in conscious entities, i.e., for God and for the souls.[164] For God, he distinguishes between the following qualities:

> In this way, God's essential nature, which is characterized by the fact that every being (*sarvasattā-*) depends on Him, has the form of *Being*, recognition, unlimitedness, joy [and] purity, because they are His qualities that determine His essential nature. [...] Other qualities and the divine and auspicious embodiments specify God's essential form, which has already been determined [by the qualities mentioned before]. Among these qualities, the six *guṇa*s—cognition, ability, power, guideship, power and splendour—serve His greatness. Gracious condescension, parental love, etc., serve His attainability. All these qualities belong every time to His essential nature.[165]

---

[163] RTS (chapter 5) 141,2–7: *pramāṇaṅkaḷ vastukkaḷaik kāṭṭum potu avvō vastukkaḷin svarūpattaiyum svarūpanirūpakadharmaṅkaḷaiyum nirūpitasvarūpaviśeṣaṇaṅkaḷaiyum vyāpāraṅkaḷaiyum kāṭṭum. atil svarūpattai svarūpanirūpakadharmaṅkaḷālē viciṣṭam ākavē kāṭṭum. anta svarūpattaic collum potu avvō tarmaṅkaḷaiy iṭṭallatu collav oṇṇātu.*

[164] The difference for the soul between these two kinds of properties is also explained in chapter 5 of the RTS, as well as in the PMBh (cf. 2. chapter, *jīvatattvādhikāra*).

[165] RTS (chapter 5) 111,24–112,10: *ippaṭi svādhīnasarvasattādikaḷaiyuṭaiyavaṉ-āy irukkiṟa īśvaraṉuṭaiya svarūpam satyādikaḷākiṟa svarūpanirūpakadharmaṅkaḷālē satyam-āy jñānam-āy anantam-āy ānandam-āy amalam-āy irukkum.* [...] *maṟṟuḷḷa guṇaṅkaḷum divyamaṅgaḷavigrahādikaḷum ellām īśvaraṉukku nirūpitasvarūpaviśeṣaṇaṅkaḷ-āy irukkum. ik guṇaṅkaḷil jñānabalaiśvaryaśaktitejassukkaḷ eṉṟu aṟu guṇaṅkaḷ paratvopayuktaṅkaḷ-āy irukkum. sauśilyavātsalyādikaḷ saulabhyopayuktaṅkaḷ-āy irukkum. ik guṇaṅkaḷ ellām sarvakālattilum svarūpāśritaṅkaḷ-āy irukkum.*

Because all properties are dependent on a single base, for Veṅkaṭanātha there is no case in which the real world, the plurality of individual souls, or the transcendent reality, i.e., God and His divine manifestation (*nityavibhūti*), cannot be considered as permanent on one hand, and connected to alternating properties on the other, even if Veṅkaṭanātha's description of alternating states/properties varies—as I will describe later in more detail (see p. 434)—for example for the divine manifestation in contrast to material matter (*prakṛti*).

As Veṅkaṭanātha clarifies, a sequence of states in which different states arise and pass away again is possible with the substance itself remaining. After listing various substances and their respective states, Veṅkaṭanātha describes this as the "flowing along" (*pravāha*) of states, which he understands in the sense of an uninterrupted sequence of states. He describes this in a passage also in chapter 5 of the RTS:

> All these substances are eternal in their essential nature. After they have been declared as being qualified by their particular states, which may be divided into different names, some of their states are non-eternal. Because of the uninterrupted flow of other states of the same kind that pass away, one speaks of their eternal flows.[166]

These "eternal flows" are just as central a concept for Veṅkaṭanātha as the "sequence of states" (*avasthāsantāna*) described above. For him, flowing along means that although something alternates eternally, it nonetheless remains the same in its essential nature (*svarūpa*). There is nothing excluded from this flow. According to Veṅkaṭanātha, it even includes the desire/will (*icchā*) of God and the states of His divine knowledge (*dharmabhūtajñāna*).[167]

---

[166] RTS (chapter 5) 110,24–111,2: *it travyaṅkaḷ ellām svarūpēṇa nityaṅkaḷ-āy irukkum. nāmāntarabhajanārhāvasthāviśeṣaviśiṣṭataiyaiy iṭṭuc cila vaṟṟai anityaṅkaḷ muḻukka eṉkiṟatu. aḻintatōṭu sajātīyaṅkaḷ-āṉa avasthāntaraṅkaḷ mēlum muḻukka varukaiyālē pravāhanityaṅkaḷ eṉṟu collukiṟatu.*

[167] Cf. Schmücker 2022: 140ff.

For Veṅkaṭanātha, this divine knowledge is eternal and non-eternal. As a substance it is eternal, but concerning its alternating states it is also non-eternal due to its moving through an obligatory sequence in which each preceding state enables the following one.

The (re)manifestation of the eternal Veda

For Veṅkaṭanātha the Veda is identical with differentiated and non-differentiated name and form (*nāmarūpe*). He follows the view of Rāmānuja, who explicitly identified names (*nāman*) with the words of the Veda. As Rāmānuja says, it is through the Highest Self, i.e., God, that the words of the Veda are applied to objects. These are identical with what was defined in the Upaniṣadic quote as form (*rūpa*).[168] In this context, Rāmānuja cites *Ma-*

[168] As already Rāmānuja writes in his VAS §83,12–14: *vaidikā eva sarve śabdā vedādāv uddhṛtyoddhṛtya pareṇaiva brahmaṇā sarvapadārthān pūrvavat sṛṣṭvā teṣu paramātmaparyanteṣu pūrvavan nāmatayā prayuktāḥ.* "All words are Vedic: the Supreme Brahman extracted them from the Veda and, after having created all the corresponding objects as He did earlier, applied these words as names to those objects, which terminate in the Supreme Spirit." See also Rāmānuja's commentary on BS 1.3.29, as well as Lipner's summary (1986: 9) thereof, where it is pointed out that Rāmānuja does not advocate the doctrine of the authorlessness of the Veda but sees the Veda merely as a "carrier" that preserves its words. Referring to Rāmānuja's commentary on BS 1.3.29, Lipner states (ibid, p. 9): "But in what sense, we may ask, do the Vedas pre-exist (and indeed post-exist) eternally, and 'where' do they do this? Rāmānuja would answer that the Vedas in some way exist continuously, eternally, in the mind of Brahman—their source and goal—who is eternal. Just as during a great dissolution the aggregate of conscious and non-conscious beings remains deindividualised and collapsed in Brahman, in potency proximate as it were to individualisation, so too the Vedas repose deep within the consciousness of Brahman in potency proximate to their pre-established empirical form. When the time for re-emitting the world arrives, they are evoked or manifested (Rāmā-

nusmṛti 1.21, *Viṣṇupurāṇa* 1.5.64 and *Ṛgveda* 10.90.1.[169] For him these passages confirm that from the words of the Veda, the Supreme Being remanifests names, functions, special generic forms and gods in the same way they existed in other, earlier eons (*kalpa*).

For Veṅkaṭanātha, too, the Veda is the totality of all the words (*vedākhyaḥ śabdarāśiḥ*) denoting conscious (*cit*) beings and material (*acit*) entities. Thus, for him only that which is expressed in the language of the Veda, and nothing else, exists as the world of material beings (*acit*) and as individual conscious souls (*cit*). At the beginning of a new eon (*kalpāntara*), God does not remember a Veda that was completely dissolved during the period of dissolution (*pralaya*), but rather the same Veda of past eons.

For Veṅkaṭanātha, this implies that the Veda, when promulgated by God at the beginning of His remanifestation, reappears as a totality in exactly the same way that it was found in the be-

---

nuja uses the Sanskrit term *āviṣkṛ* in this context) rather than composed by the supreme Person who transmits them via Brahmā and the ancients to mankind. [...] Their [i.e., the Vedas] periodic empirical manifestation (as of the world) may depend on the divine will, but their content—their structure and form—by revealing the divine essence (so far as this is possible) is directly rooted in it and cannot change since the divine essence at heart is unchanging. In short, if the supreme being is to be revealed through language, it must be in the form of the Vedas as we have them."

169 *Manusmṛti* 1.21:
sarveṣaṃ tu sa nāmāni karmāṇi ca pṛthakpṛthak
vedaśabdebhya evādau pṛthaksaṃsthāś ca nirmame.
"In the beginning He created the various names and activities and distinct forms of all things out of the words of the Veda."
Viṣṇupurāṇa 1.5.64:
nāma rūpaṃ ca bhūtānāṃ kṛtyānāṃ ca prapañcanam
vedaśabdebhya evādau devādīnāṃ cakāra saḥ.
"In the beginning He made the name-and-form of beings—gods, etc.—and the variety of duties out of the words of the Veda."
Ṛgveda 10.90.1: *sūryācandramasau dhātā yathāpūrvam akalpayat.*
"Having created sun and moon, He gave them names as before."

ginningless flowing along (*anādipravāha*) of the previous eon (*kalpa*). Even if it is pointed out that something disappeared and has now reappeared, God does not manifest it in a different way than it existed before, i.e., in another eon (*kalpa*), because as perfect as God is, so too does He perfectly preserve the Veda. The way Veṅkaṭanātha relates God to the Veda—in fact identifies with the Veda—not only characterizes his concept of God but plays a significant role in how something can be understood as being referred to through the words of the Veda, i.e., how words and objects are related, or more generally expressed, how worldly entities are related to language. Since it is unchangeable, i.e., eternally fixed which word denotes which object, the question of conventional usage of language is irrelevant, as is the question of the indirect denotation (*lakṣaṇā*) of a word.

This can be explained more precisely in the context of the central question of how the eternal Veda is related to God's remanifestation. As may be clear by now, Rāmānuja and Veṅkaṭanātha both consider the remanifestation to be the transformation from non-differentiated (*avyākṛta*) name and form into differentiated (*vyākṛta*) name and form (*nāmarūpe*). *Before* a new manifestation, everything that obtains concrete form due to God's will already *is*. With a renewed manifestation, forms (*rūpa*) have the same name they had before the period of dissolution (*pralaya*) and thus, they must be denoted with the same words. Veṅkaṭanātha explains that the name (*nāman*) of an object or a person does not dissolve into nothing, even if what that name denotes is no longer perceptible. They still have an ontological status in the period of dissolution due to being in the subtle state (*sūkṣmāvasthā*). Neither the denotations for objects nor the names of persons disappear completely, despite one speaking of their non-being (*abhāva*). Non-being refers only to the temporary task of the signifier. It does not mean definitive disappearance. This also applies to the sounds (*varṇa*) of the words (*pada*) for Vedic sentences.

In his *Seśvaramīmāṃsā* (= SeMī)[170] Veṅkaṭanātha provides more evidence for the eternal existence of the Veda during the period of dissolution and why everything becomes manifested again completely. According to Veṅkaṭanātha, the reason the Veda does not dissolve completely is the relationship between *vācya*, i.e., the denoted object (i.e., the form, *rūpa*), and *vācaka*, i.e., the denoting word (i.e., the name, *nāman*). Even if the first is dissolved, they still belong together always and are inseparable. Also in this context, Veṅkaṭanātha argues that non-being, in this case the non-being of the denoted object, does not imply complete destruction at all. For example, a person who has died has vanished, but the denotation of such a person remains. As he continues:

> [...] and speaking of the dissolution of the designator due to the dissolution of what is to be designated (*vācyapralayād vācakapralayoktiḥ*) is not the case here, because with regard to [an object] like a pot, etc., the complete disappearance of their designation (*nāman*) is not observed, inasmuch as it is generally well known that names of people who have died remain.[171]

When referring to BĀU 1.4.7 in another passage of the SeMī, Veṅkaṭanātha provides an example of the same concept. Here the designation of an object, in this case a ring (*kuṇḍalanāma*), is shown to be independent of the fact that the object was lost and newly produced. Veṅkaṭanātha concludes that the name continues to be, even if the form (*rūpa*) is absent:

> Just as when a ring disappears, the ring's designation (*kuṇḍalanāma*) is no longer seen [but] when a ring is produced again, its name is such a ring, so it is [also] here. [...] For the separation of names in the case of separation from form is not contradictory if the form does

---

170 Especially in his commentary on *Mīmāṃsā Sūtra* 1.1.7; 1.1.13; 1.1.23, Veṅkaṭanātha refers to the idea that nothing disappears completely during the period of dissolution.

171 SeMī 37,7–8: [...] *na cātra vācyapralayād vācakapralayoktiḥ, ghaṭādiṣu tannāmapradhvaṃsādarśanāt, vinaṣṭeṣu nareṣu nāmaśeṣatvaprasiddheḥ.*

not exist, insofar [as in BĀU 1.4.7, the statement] is handed down: "For this [universe] was non-differentiated at that time; [then] it was differentiated in name and form."[172]

Due to the ontological status of Vedic reality, Veṅkaṭanātha holds the view that no word of the Veda is derived from the conventional (*sāṅketika*) language of human beings. If there were such a word, not only would the Vedic language be of human origin, but it also would not be the eternal Vedic language. Moreover, since it is eternal, he criticizes the view of the Veda's "acceptance by a majority of people" (*mahājanaparigraha*).[173]

To claim that the meaning of a Vedic word is based on human conventions, one would have to prove a creator who gives words their meaning.[174] Such an agent, however, cannot be justified for the beginning of the remanifestation of the world.[175] Also in this context, Veṅkaṭanātha repeats his teaching that it is God who manifests name and form, when he for example TMK 4.71d: says

---

172 SeMĪ 41,6–12: *yathā kuṇḍale vilīne kuṇḍalanāma na dṛśyate, punaḥ kuṇḍale kṛte tad eva nāma gacchati, evam ihāpi.* [...] *rūpavibhāge hi nāmavibhāgas tadabhāve tatra tan na prayujyata ity abhipretya taddhedaṃ tarhy avyākṛtam āsīt tan nāmarūpābhyāṃ vyākriyata ity āmnātam.*

173 For Veṅkaṭanātha's discussion on the concept of consensus-based acceptance of a majority of people (*bahujanaparigṛhītatva*), cf. TMK 4.114.

174 See TMK 4.71ab, where Veṅkaṭanātha explains that God does not remanifest words based on usage according to human convention: *śabdaḥ saṃketito 'rthaṃ gamayati vimato 'pīti śāstrapratīpaṃ; tatkartā 'dya hy asiddhaḥ* [...]. "It is contrary to the *śāstra* to say that the Vedic word expounds its meaning by being based on human language conventions. Because an agent [i.e., a creator] for this [i.e., the Veda or human language] cannot be proven here [even now]."

175 TMK 4.71c: *sa ca duradhigamas sṛṣṭikāle 'numānaiḥ. śrutyā cet pratyutaitad.* "And at the time of creation such an agent is difficult to be obtained by means of inferences. If one argues that by authoritative Scripture [such an agent can be established as being based on human convention], the opposite is the case."

(quoted above fn. 84): "The omnipresent [Lord] on His part (*api*) unfolds name and form based on the Veda."[176] The remanifestation does not contradict everything remaining as it has always been. After all, the thesis that meanings must be assigned anew by a divine agent (i.e., God) would only be valid if there were a final destruction and all things, with their denotations, etc., had to be created anew. We can therefore also understand the difference to the view of that kind of creator-God, who must set up anew everything after the period of complete dissolution (*pralaya*), but cannot be proved by inference.[177] In contrast, for Veṅkaṭanātha, every sentence of the Veda has intrinsic validity (*svataḥprāmāṇya*), which implies eternal evidence. Intrinsic validity remains independent from the person who is articulating such a sentence.[178] Therefore Veṅkaṭanātha speaks of the "beginninglessness flowing along of [vedic] sentences [only] of one form" (*ekarūpavākyapravāhānādi*).[179] No word of the Veda completely

---

[176] TMK 4.71d: *vibhur api tanute vedato nāmarūpe.*

[177] Cf. TMK 4.71c quoted in fn. 175 above.

[178] Even from the perspective of the validity of a means of knowledge, which implies a contradiction between the authorlessness of the Veda and a personal God, Veṅkaṭanātha agrees with both, saying in SAS 647.16–648.1 *ad* TMK 4.103: *yathā nityam īśvarajñānaṃ kāraṇadoṣābhāvāt pramāṇam, evaṃ vedavākyam api kāraṇadoṣābhāvāt pramāṇam; tadvākyajanitaṃ jñānam api nirdoṣavākyajanitatvāt pramaiveti. itthaṃ ca svataḥprāmāṇyaṃ nirvahati.* "Just as the eternal knowledge of God is a means of valid cognition, because there is no flaw [of God being] the cause, in the same manner also a Vedic sentence is a means of valid knowledge because [here] there is not the fault of being caused [either]. Also, knowledge that is produced from a Vedic sentence is a valid cognition, because it is produced from a flawless sentence. And in this way, the intrinsic validity of knowledge is accomplished."

[179] Also in his PMBh (chapter 5) 355,2–359,2, Veṅkaṭanātha takes up his designation of the Veda as having one form (*ekarūpa*): *varṇapadavākyaṅkaḷukku pratyakṣādikaḷālē anityatvam tōṉṟāniṟka vedam nityam ām paṭi eṉ eṉṉil, padattukum vedattukkum nityatvam āvatu, sarvakālattilum ekarūpakramaviśeṣaviśiṣṭam-āy koṇṭu prayogikkap*

disappears, nor is any other new word added. Thus, the entirety of the sentences of the Veda (*vedavākyarāśi*) is eternal, even if they are promulgated by a personal God at a certain point in time, i.e., the time of creation (*sṛṣṭikāle*). Thus, Veṅkaṭanātha sums up his view by describing the words and sounds of sentences as non-eternal (*sarvam etad anityam eva*). In contrast, "the sentences [of the Veda] have [eternally] the same form; and only this [i.e., having the same form] is [their] being eternal."[180] But even if the Veda remains always the same without any modification, it neither can be promulgate itself, nor could it remanifest by itself. For this a personal God is necessary. And God's articulation of the Veda presupposes His particular intention (*īśvarābhisandhiviśeṣa*). This particular intention is to make the Veda remanifest. Such an intension presupposes knowledge of a divine and conscious Being. According to Veṅkaṭanātha, unity of God's knowledge (*aikyarūpya*) corresponds to the one form or unity of His intention (*ekarūpābhisandhi*), this in turn corresponds to the Veda having eternally one form (*nityaikarūpa*), which preserves its unity (*vedaikya*) of the totality of different words (*śabdarāśi*). Therefore the intension to promulgate the Veda has the same form in each eon (*pratikalpam*), as does God's sentence of command (*ājñāvākya*). God's recollection of the Veda in *one* and the

---

paṭukaiy ākaiyālē. kramavṛttikaḷukku pōlē varṇattukkum vedoktamāṉa utpattināśaṅkaḷai koṇṭālum, īśvaraṉum maṟṟuḷḷa pravartakarum ellām ekarūpam āka pravarttippikkaiyālē padataiyum vedattaiyum nityam eṉṉalām. "If one objects that the Veda, which is eternal, does not appear as eternal, because the sound, word and sentences [of the Veda] are perceptible, [our answer is that] it is [nevertheless the case that] word and Veda are eternal, because they are *always* applied as specified by a particular succession, which has a single form (*ekarūpa-*). And because there is no need to fear that the sounds come into being and pass away, as it were, by their succession, when the Veda is proclaimed, the word and Veda are eternal because God, the Creator, creates everything as having one form."

180 SAS 706.8–9 *ad* TMK 5.26: *sarvam etad anityam eva*; *vākyānāṃ sajātīyatvamātraṃ tv avaśiṣyate, tad eva nityatvam iti.*

same form and His promulgating through His command (*ājñā*) preserves its eternity. As Veṅkaṭanātha explains in the TMK 4.113c:

> And for these [authoritative Scriptures] the form of His command is no deminish, because for an omnipresent [Highest Self] the intention has one form.[181]

And in his commentary on this line, Veṅkaṭanātha gives his version of the eternity of the Veda. For him there is no contradiction, because God's intention, even if it is a particular one in each eon, His command, and what is promulgated in each eon, i.e., the Veda, correspond to each other, in so far as they have only one form (*ekarūpa*/*aikarūpya*):

> God, whose intention has one form (*ekarūpābhisandhi-*), utters a command in every eon (*pratikalpam*). Only this is the eternity of the Veda, what is promulgated [by God] in each eon in one form.[182]

Thus, for Veṅkaṭanātha there is no contradiction between God's particular intention and the eternity of the Veda because the Veda and His command have one and the same form. When a sentence consisting of a sequence (*krama*) of sounds, words, etc., is uttered, this does not then imply that it is non-eternal (*anitya*) since God manifests everything in just the same way as it was. What has passed has not passed in such a way that it cannot re-appear again. One could also say in this case that the Veda is neither absolutely non-existent nor transient, nor is it absolutely (eternally) existent, for in both cases it would then be a contradiction that

---

181 TMK 4.113: *ājñārūpatvam āsāṃ na ca galati vibhor *ekarūpābhisandher* [*instead of: *aikyarūpya-*].

182 SAS 658.2–4 *ad* TMK 4.113: *pratikalpam ekarūpābhisandhir īśvara ekarūpam evājñāvākyaṃ vadati. etad eva vedasya nityatvam, yad aikarūpyeṇa sarveṣv api kalpeṣūccāryamāṇatvam.*

Cf. also NP 258,9–17, where Veṅkaṭanātha defines the totality of the Veda as *tādṛkkramayogitāmātram*.

sounds disappear.[183] Further, for him the Veda is not something that exists apart from the world, it *is* the world. It describes the world through language, whereby each word denoting an object eternally forms an indiscernible unity with it. There is nothing in the world that is not described in the language of Veda. *The complete world is given as the Veda.* This has epistemological consequences. In our knowledge of the world, we do not perceive name and form—i.e., word and object—as separate from each other, even if the object of a word is absent. If this is applied to the relationship between God and the Veda, nothing exists in the world to which God is not related. When the world as God's body becomes manifest again after the period of dissolution, *He Himself is manifested as the Veda*. Indeed, in a sense, He *is* the Veda in a personalized form. If name and form (*nāmarūpe*) always correspond, worldly knowledge can also be explained. As soon as any piece of knowledge is directed toward the world, it is directed toward recognizable objects, namely, forms with their names, i.e., with their denotations. This is linked to the discussion above explaining that all names ultimately refer to God. Here, too, the concept of *ekarūpa* indicates that it is not contradictory if different words connect to form sentences.

God's will (*icchā*) against the background of substance (*dravya*) and state (*avasthā*)

Veṅkaṭanātha understands the process of transformation as being guided by the will (*icchā*) of *one* God. The will of God is itself an alternating sequence of states that determines everything and touches all substances to cause their transformation. God's independent will is further proof that God is directly present in every-

[183] Veṅkaṭanātha propitiates the very frightened (*aticakita*) representatives of the Mīmāṃsā; they should not care about the non-eternity of the Veda even if its sounds are declared as non-eternal, cf. TMK 5.26.

thing and not through the individual soul. It can also be clearly shown that Veṅkaṭanātha does not distinguish God's will from material things, but that here, too, he sees His will as the ultimate basis. Even if the *relational unity* with God is demonstrated by examples that do not involve God's will, the transformation of the flowing along (*pravāha*) does not have an independent dynamic. After determining that everything is based on different substances, Veṅkaṭanātha examines how these are always and thus already related to God. Substances are based on God; even if they are self-grounded, they are not independent from God, since He is the ultimate base of each substance, and also indirectly supports every state of each substance. We might take a glance at a passage of the third chapter of the RTS:

> Just as the Lord Himself is the support for the properties qualifying His essential nature and the properties that define the essential nature already defined, in the same way He is, in His [own] essential nature, the unseparated support of all substances different from Him. He is the abode *via* substances for the states that belong to [these] substances. [...] In this way, because everything is inseparable (*apṛthak*), in reference to the essential nature of the Lord, their *being* depends on the *Being* of their support [i.e., the Lord].[184]

For Veṅkaṭanātha, not only is every substance together with its states grounded in God's *Being*, but every substance is also directed by His will, which is eternal *and* non-eternal.

> Therefore, it is said that because also the preservation, having the form of continuity of being, depends on the will of God, *everything relies on the will of God* [...]. The being caused by the non-eternal will for non-eternal entities and the being established by the eternal

184 RTS (chapter 3) 50,15–51,6: [...] *īcvaraṉ taṉ svarūpanirūpakadharmaṅkaḷukkum nirūpitasvarūpaviśeṣaṇaṅkaḷ-āṉa guṇaṅkaḷukkum pōlē svavyatiriktasamastadravyaṅkaḷukkum avyavahitam āka svarūpeṇa ādhāram-āy irukkum. avvō dravyaṅkaḷai āśrayittirukkum guṇādikaḷukku avvō dravyadvārā ādhāram-āy irukkum.* [...] *ippaṭi sarvamum īcvarasvarūpattaip paṟṟa apṛthaksiddhaviśeṣaṇam ākaiyālē ivaṟṟiṉ sattādikaḷ āśrayasattādhīnaṅkaḷ.*

> will for eternal entities is defined as the dependency on *Being* of all entities [i.e., conscious and material]. The will of the Highest Self classifies the entities that rely on the essential nature of the Highest Self. In this manner, all entities are grounded in the essential nature of God and depend on the will of God Himself.[185]

Every substance remains due to God's *Being*, and with it, the inseparable states of every substance remain as well. For Veṅkaṭanātha, substances that are analyzed with regard to their aspects of essential nature (*svarūpa*), their permanence (*sthiti*), and their activity (*pravṛtti*), and which are provided with the quality/state of being (*sattātikaḷ*) as well as other properties, do not exist without being grounded in God's *Being* and by His will.[186]

God's divine manifestation (*nityavibhūti*) of pure being (*śuddhasattva*)

As seen by the many references to BĀU 1.4.7 discussed above, a central concept for Rāmānuja and Veṅkaṭanātha is the remanifestation of the world, which is developed into the concept of grounding substances (*dravya*) which are characterized by different states/properties. Based on this concept we have been able also to demonstrate that for both authors, God/*brahman* is thought

---

[185] RTS (chapter 3) 51,10–52,3: *ittālē sarvattiṉuṭaiyavum sattānuvṛttirūpaiy-āṉa sthitiyum īśvareccādhīnaiy-āṉa paṭiyālē sarvamum īśvarasaṅkalpāśritam eṉṟu collukiṟatu.* [...] *sarvavastukkaḷuṭaiyavum sattai saṅkalpādhinaiy ākaiy āvatu anityaṅkaḷ anityecchaiyālē utpannaṅkaḷāyum, nityaṅkaḷ nityecchāsiddhaṅkaḷ-āyum irukkai. paramātmāviṉuṭaiya iccai iv vastukkaḷai paramātmāviṉ svarūpāśritaṅkaḷ āka vakuttu vaikkum. ippaṭi sarva vastuvum īśvarasvarūpāśritamum-āy īśvarecchādhīnamum-āy irukkum.*

[186] Cf. RTS (chapter 5) 111,6: *īśvarasattaiyayum oḻiya īśvarecchaiyayum oḻiya ivaṟṟukku sattātikaḷ kūṭātu oḻikai.* "The *Being* of these substances would not be possible without the *Being* of God and without the will of God."

of as the ultimate ground that can be related to everything based on His body, which itself consists of different substances with different states/properties. We also pointed out that there is nothing which can be thought of as beyond God's will (*icchā*), which is considered *the* ultimate ground. Whatever is non-eternal depends on His non-eternal (*anitya*) will; whatever is eternal depends on His eternal (*nitya*) will. God's divine manifestation is described in some places as His dominion (*sthāna*). Thus, we can also demonstrate that Veṅkaṭanātha takes this will as the ultimate ground to avoid contradictions resulting in a difference between material (*prākṛta*) manifestation (*prakṛti, līlavibhūti*) and immaterial (*aprākṛta*) divine manifestation (*nityavibhūti*).

Veṅkaṭanātha's distinction between eternal and non-eternal has consequences for his interpretation of God's body. Establishing that substances are eternal in their essential nature (*svarūpa*) implies that the body of God must also be eternal. Eternal substances belong to the eternal body of God. But how can something non-eternal (*anitya*) like appearing and disappearing states/properties belong to something eternal like the body of God? Still more problematic is the question of whether the eternity and non-eternity of the two substances, i.e., material matter (*prakṛti*) and divine eternal manifestion (*nityavibhūti*), are the same?[187]

As has already been mentioned, nothing occurs separately from substances. Every alternation of states belongs to the non-eternal part of God's body. In this context, Veṅkaṭanātha distinguishes between modifications caused by *karman* and modifications not caused by *karman*. This means that there are two kinds

---

[187] Although Veṅkaṭanātha discusses the *nityavibhūti* as a separate substance in his works, he does not devote an individual chapter to the topic as he does for other substances in both the TMK and the NSi. He rather examines the topic of the *nityavibhūti* in sub-chapters in the chapters on God: one in the *nāyakasara* of the TMK (verse 61–80), another in the *īśvarapariccheda* of the NSi (384–398). He also devotes a small section in his PMBh to the topic of *śuddhasattva* (cf. *acidadhikāra* pp. 198–206).

of non-eternal modifications. One is caused by *karman* and belongs to the material (*prākṛta*) realm of *prakṛti*. The other, the uncaused modification, belongs to the immaterial realm of the eternal manifestation (*nityavibhūti*). The following passage deals with this classification; it concludes a lengthy discussion regarding the definitions of God's body (cf. also above, p. 340). It also examines whether God's body can include opposites, such as eternalness and non-eternalness. We can relate the following passage to the above-mentioned passage (RTS chapter 3 [pp. 51,10–52,3]; cf. fn. 185 above) that everything is based on God's will. Analogous to His eternal and non-eternal body, this division corresponds to His eternal and non-eternal will. The substances listed first in the passage correspond to God's eternal will. The division into *karman* conditioned and non-*karman* conditioned corresponds to God's non-eternal will.

> That very body [of God] is of two kinds: an eternal one and a non-eternal one. Of these, the eternal one is the body of God composed of substance made up of the three *guṇa*s [i.e., primordial matter, *prakṛti*], time, the individual self, the auspicious place [His form as Vāsudeva], and so on. And the eternal [sages] have the natural forms of Garuḍa, Śeṣa, and so on. The non-eternal [body] is of two kinds: that which is not made by *karman* and that which is made by *karman*. The former [i.e., that not made by *karman*] is God in form of *mahat* and so on. So are the forms of Ananta, Garuḍa, the auspicious place, etc., and those who are liberated, which are made at will. That which is made by *karman* is also of two kinds: that made by *karman* with the help of one's own will and that made purely by *karman*. The former is of great [sages] such as Saubhari, [who controlled many bodies at once]; the latter is of other insignificant beings.[188]

---

[188] NSi 174,6–175,1: *tad etat śarīraṃ dvividham—nityam anityañ ceti. tatra nityaṃ triguṇadravyakālajīvaśubhāśrayādyātmakam īśvaraśarīram nityānāñ ca svābhāvikagaruḍabhujagādirūpam. anityañ ca dvividham akarmakṛtaṃ karmakṛtañ ceti. prathamam īśvarasya mahadādirūpam. tathā anantagaruḍādīnāṃ muktānāṃ cecchākṛtatattadrūpam. karmakṛtam api dvividham. svasaṅkalpasahakṛtakarmakṛtaṃ*

Important for Veṅkaṭanātha's understanding of "eternal" manifestation (*nityavibhūti*) in contrast to the other substances is his remark that there are modifications not subject to *karman*. This must also include, for example, souls who have not been released eternally, because at a certain point in time they are released from *karman*. But how does Veṅkaṭanātha define this kind of modification which is non-eternal but independent of *karman?* A few more remarks are necessary to explain the difference from material matter (*prakṛti*). One important point by which Veṅkaṭanātha differentiates the two *vibhūti*s is their synonymity of qualities (*guṇa*). In verse TMK 5.19bc, Veṅkaṭanātha clearly states that, even if the qualities of both manifestations have the same designations, their meaning is different.

> In both manifestations' qualities like sound, etc., depend on the three *guṇas* [i.e., material matter, *prakṛti*] *and* on the substance [i.e., the *nityavibhūti*], which surpasses material matter. [But] if one arrives at a decision based on the knowledge of *śāstra*s, a mutual mixture [of the qualities of the two manifestations] is in no way to be supposed.[189]

---

kevalakarmakṛtañ ceti. pūrvaṃ mahatāṃ saubhariprabhṛtīnām. uttarañ ca anyeṣāṃ kṣudrāṇām. (Translation adopted from Mikami [pdf]).

189 TMK 5.19bc:
[…] *śabdādayo 'mī triguṇatadadhikadravyaniṣṭhā guṇāḥ syuḥ.*
niṣkṛṣṭe śāstradṛṣṭyā na katham api mithas saṃkaraḥ śaṅkanīyaḥ.

Emphazising such a difference between material (*prākṛta*) and immaterial (*aprākṛta*), Veṅkaṭanātha comments in his SAS 699.7–8: *aprākṛte punar vibhūtyantare śrutismṛtītihāsapurāṇaprasiddhāḥ prakāraviśeṣāḥ tattadanubhavādhīnānandaviśeṣāś cāpalapituṃ na śaknuyanta iti bhāvaḥ.* "The intension is: One cannot doubt that, in contrast, regarding the other [divine] manifestation, which is immaterial, specific modes and specific bliss which depend on the experiences of these modes, are well established in authoritative Scripture (*śruti*), Smṛti, Itihāsa and Purāṇa."

Another difference between the two kinds of manifestation is the spatial limitation between both realms, described by Veṅkaṭanātha in NSi 40,3–41,2. In the lower direction, primordial matter (*prakṛti*) is infinite, but in the upper directions, it is limited by the manifestation of enjoyment. Veṅkaṭanātha refers to two authoritative sources, when he says:

> Because authoritative Scriptures (*śruti*) mention that eternal manifestation (*nityavibhūti*) is beyond darkness (*tamas*) and material matter (*triguṇa*); because it is mentioned [in ViP 2.7.25] like: "It is infinite and its extent cannot be enumerated."[190]

There is another central point of difference between the two manifestations. As we have seen, the distinction between non-differentiated (*avyākṛta*) and differentiated (*vyākṛta*) is fundamental for explaining the remanifestation of the world. But does this distinction also play a role when Veṅkaṭanātha describes divine manifestation (*nityavibhūti*)? When he again cites BĀU 1.4.7 in the following verse, how does he understand the *nityavibhūti* in this context? If Veṅkaṭanātha does not understand God's divine manifestation (*nityavibhūti*) as consisting of pure being (*śuddhasattva*) under the same conditions as other substances, the period of dissolution (*pralaya*) consisting of *tamas* concerns only primordial matter (*prakṛti*), whose beginningless and endless flowing along (*anādipravāha*) characterizes its eternal nature. This difference

---

190 NSi 40,3–41,2: *nityavibhūtes tamaḥparatvaśruteḥ triguṇasya ca, tad-anantam asaṅkhyātapramāṇañ ceti vacanāt.* Also in the next sentences Veṅkaṭanātha distinguishes material matter: *tac ca vicitrasṛṣṭyupakaraṇatvān māyā, vikārān prakarotīti prakṛtiḥ, vidyāvirodhādibhir avidyādiś cocyate. samaviṣamavikārasantānāṃś ca kālabhāgabhedābhyām ārabhate.* "And it is also called '*māyā*' (mysterious power) because it is the instrument of the wonderful (*vicitra*) creation, '*prakṛti*' because it generates (*prakaroti*) modifications, and '*avidyā*' (ignorance) and so on because it is opposite from knowledge and other things. And [it] begins a series of modifications (*vikāra*) characterized by similarity or dissimilarity in accordance with the difference in time and place (*bhāga*)." (Translation adopted from Mikami [pdf]).

becomes clearer when Veṅkaṭanātha elaborates on the relationship between the two types of substances in TMK 3.61, the opening verse of the *nāyakasara*'s sub-chapter on the eternal manifestation (*nityavibhūti*). This verse contains a statement concerning the difference between the eternal manifestation (*nityavibhūti*) consisting of pure *sattva*, and primordial matter. The eternal manifestation (i.e., *nityavibhūti* consisting in pure being, (*śuddhasattva*)) is described as an eternal place, based on references in authoritative sources.

> It is told [according to authoritative Scripture] that there is an order of the impure [i.e., primordial matter, *prakṛti*] creation [and an order] of the pure creation; with regard to the reality of pure being (*śuddhasattva*), an eternal dominion is mentioned in authoritative Scripture (*śruti*); the same [reality of pure being] is said according to Smṛti. There, [i.e., in the eternal manifestation,] the states of the bodies, etc., exist due to a particular concretization. Even the Vedic statement that there is only one [*brahman* without a second] before creation depends on what will be created.[191]

To conclude, Veṅkaṭanātha differentiates his view from those of the three Vedāntins Śaṅkara, Bhāskara and Yādavaprakāśa, who do not accept this process of remanifestation. What is more important in our context is how he distinguishes between *two* types of manifestations that are both eternal. Veṅkaṭanātha points out that such a dominion is attested in *śruti-* and *smṛti*-literature. Remanifestation and demanifestation do not apply to the divine manifestation of God in the same way as they characterize the eternity, i.e., the constant transformation (*santatiparināṃa*) of primordial matter.

Nevertheless, both manifestations are characterized by non-eternal things, but also by eternal ones. In his commentary on the

---

[191] TMK 3.61abc:
śuddhasyāśuddhasṛṣṭikrama iti kathitaḥ; śuddhasattve tu tattve
sthānaṃ nityaṃ śrutaṃ tat smṛtam api kalayā tatra dehādyavasthāḥ.
sṛṣṭeḥ prāg ekam evety api nigamavacas srakṣyamāṇavyapekṣaṃ
[…].

verse, Veṅkaṭanātha therefore states that there are non-eternals in the *nityavibhūti*, just as there are eternals for everything consisting of the matter of *prakṛti*. As we have mentioned several times above, there is no complete dissolution, something both manifestations (*vibhūti*) have in common. The difference is in the manner of manifestation. But a manifestation is also true of the *nityavibhūti* in the form of partial manifestations. Veṅkaṭanātha tries to clarify the puzzling multitude of eternal and non-eternal things as follows:

> If one were to object that the distinction between eternal and non-eternal manifestation is impossible because here [i.e., in the worldly *vibhūti*] also the essential nature of the individual soul is eternal, but there [i.e., in the *nityavibhūti*] the desired body, etc., is not eternal, he answers in the verse [TMK 3.61 with] the expression "due to a partial manifestation" (*kalayā*). The meaning is: Because an eternal and a non-eternal multitude (of things) is intended, the distinction [between the two *vibhūti*s] is in such a way, for there is no manifestation and dissolution of the earth, etc., located here [in the worldly realm] and of the divine bodies located there [in the *nityavibhūti*]. Indeed, according to the *Mahābhārata* [MBh 12.326.31] it is said: "For there is no being (*bhūtam*) in the world, immovable or movable, that is permanent, except this one conscious being, the eternal Vāsudeva."[192]

The point is that even a partial manifestation in the *nityavibhūti* must have a "reason," because God's eternal and non-eternal will is also effective in this eternal realm. A kind of dissolution may take place. But complete dissolution after which everything is manifested again does not apply. This is also true for Vāsudeva,

---

[192] SAS 447.4–6 *ad* TMK 3.61: *nanv evam api nityānityavibhūtivibhāgo 'nupapannaḥ, atrāpy ātmasvarūpāder nityatvāt, tatrāpy aicchadehāder anityatvāt, tatrāha—kalayeti. nityānityaprācuryavivakṣayā tathā vibhāga iti bhāvaḥ. na hi tatratyānāṃ pṛthivyādīnām īśvaradehādīnāṃ cātratyavat sṛṣṭipralayau. uktaṃ hi mahābhārate nityaṃ hi nāsti jagati bhūtaṃ sthāvarajaṅgamam. ṛte tam ekaṃ puruṣaṃ vāsudevaṃ sanātanam iti.*

who is qualified by everything and who is the highest divine manifestation of God in His eternal manifestation. Thus, Veṅkaṭanātha explains the verse from the *Mahābhārata*:

> The word *bhūta-* has here [in the verse of MBh 12.326.31] the meaning of a partial manifestation to be caused. Therefore, speaking of the dissolution of the soul is to be understood in a figurative sense.[193]

To distinguish between eternity in worldly and divine manifestation in terms of *pralaya*, Veṅkaṭanātha claims that for the latter, any implication of dissolution can only have a secondary meaning. He further explains: "Because it is established for Vāsudeva, even if he is qualified by everything, a particular dissolution takes place" (SAS 447.9: *viśiṣṭalayasya vāsudeve viśvaviśiṣṭe 'pi siddhatvāt*). The kind of dissolution (*laya*) mentioned in this sentence is therefore also different from what is mentioned in the third line of verse 61, which refers to the secondlessness of *brahman*/God, and which, as we have demonstrated, in combination with BĀU 1.4.7, refers to the subtle state of the material world at the time of dissolution (*pralaya*). Veṅkaṭanātha explains his statement of verse 61 in his commentary in more detail:

> The intention is: The One-ness is understood as non-differentiated name and form during the dissolution of the world, which is created as dependent on the specific time of creation, [and according to BĀU 1.4.7] is denoted by [the word] "this" (*idaṃ*) depending on the time of instruction. For this very reason indeed, the authoritative tradition reveals only this [Being] as having the modes of one-ness and manifoldness in the words [of BĀU 1.4.7]: "All this was non-separated (indistinguishable) [at the beginning of creation]. Then it became separated by name and form."[194]

---

[193] SAS 447.6–9 *ad* TMK 3.61: *bhūtaśabdo 'tra kāryāṃśaparaḥ. ata eva jīvalayoktir aupacārikī.*

[194] SAS 447.11–14 *ad* TMK 3.61: *ayaṃ bhāvaḥ—sṛṣṭikālāpekṣayā srakṣyamāṇasya jagata upadeśakālāpekṣayā idaṅkāragocarasya pralayadaśāyām avibhaktanāmarūpatayā ekatvam avadhāryate. ata eva hi,*

The important thesis that *brahman*/God remains secondless as this quoted passage establishes seems inapplicable for the *nityavibhūti*, because what dissolves into a subtle state during the state of dissolution (*pralaya*) relates here only to the material matter that is connected to the individual *karman* of the souls. Important in this context is also the mention of the future participle in the verse (*srakṣyamāṇa*), which implies that there is no "future" time and thus no past and present concept for the eternal manifestation Such is only the case for material (*prākṛta*) matter.

However, I understand Veṅkaṭanātha's citing of BĀU to mean that a change from subtle to manifest occurs only for *one* realm; this does not mean that God/*brahman* is no longer without a second. What keeps God one without a second is the dependence of everything on His non-eternal as well as on His eternal will. As Veṅkaṭanātha states, the remanifestation of the *karma*-conditioned world as dependent on God's non-eternal will or the promulgation of the eternal Veda happens at a certain time of the beginning manifestation of the *līlāvibhūti*, i.e. material matter. This does not apply to the *nityavibhūti*, in which eternally released (*nityamukta*) souls or souls that are released (*mukta*) at a certain time do not need to be taught.[195]

As far as the two types of manifestation are concerned, it can be said that in the state of *pralaya*, primordial matter "dissolves", hence its name *avyakta* (non-manifest). Constant transformation

---

tad dhedaṃ tarhy avyākṛtam āsīt tannāmarūpābhyāṃ vyākriyateti śrutir ekatvabahutvaprakāram etam eva vyanakti.

195 In this context the quote of *Ṛgveda* 1.22.20: *tad viṣṇoḥ paramaṁ padaṃ sadā paśyanti sūrayaḥ* is relevant. "That is the highest footstep of Viṣṇu; the patrons always see it". On the status of these patrons/seers during *pralaya* cf. Veṅkaṭanāth's remark NSi 224,2–3: *evaṃ sadādarśanādibalād eva nityamukteśvarāṇāṃ pratisargāvasthāyāṃ suṣuptakalpatayā 'vasthānaṃ vadantaḥ pratyuktāḥ.* "In this way, those who hold that the state of the eternal [seers] and God is like that of deep sleep during the time of dissolution are rejected on account of [their] eternal vision and so on."

(*satatapariṇāma*) applies only here. The statement of the BĀU can only be applied to this manifestation.

But let us refer to another passage that clearly expresses God's will as the sole and final cause, and thus as the common or final reason. It is found in the NSi chapter on God's eternal manifestation (*nityavibhūti*).[196] In this relevant passage, Veṅkaṭanātha describes the realm of the *nityavibhūti*, whereby he confirms that there is a difference between what is eternal and what is non-eternal. He also gives more reasons for how "pure being" (*śuddhasattva*) is distinct from primordial matter, insofar as during the process of remainfestation for the *nityavibhūti*, a preceding element is not the material cause of the following one, as it is in case of the remanifestation of the *karman*-dependent world.[197] He rejects a manifestation being explained according to the evolution of

---

[196] For more references concerning the difference of the *nityavibhūti* to *prakṛti,* as well as other important points like the issue of being self-illuminating while being material, which Veṅkaṭanātha discusses extensively, as does the tradition after him, such as Raṅgarāmānuja (16th c.) in his commentary on the NSi, cf. Oberhammer 2000: 72ff. Oberhammer deals here with the *nityavibhūti* part in the NSi, translates (ibid. pp. 58–71), interpretes it. He also mentiones Veṅkaṭanātha's comprehensive references on Pāñcarātra literature such as the *Paramasaṃhitā*, the *Padmasaṃhitā*, the *Sātvatasaṃhita*, the *Pauṣkarasaṃhitā* or the *Viṣvaksenasaṃhitā* (ibid. pp. 89f., pp. 94–98).

[197] Cf. Veṅkaṭanātha's important definition of *śuddhasattva* in difference to the *sattva* of the *prakṛti*: NSi 444,2–4: *prakāśasukhalāghavādinidānamatīndriyaṃ śaktyatiriktam adravyaṃ sattvam. tat dvidhāśuddham aśuddhañ ceti. rajastamaḥśūnyadravyavṛtti sattvaṃ śuddhasattvam, tat nityavibhūtau. rajastamassahavṛtti sattvam aśuddhasattvam, tat triguṇe.* "*Sattva* is that non-substance beyond sense faculties and different from potency which causes illumination, happiness, lightness etc. It is of two sorts: pure one and impure one. Pure *sattva* is that *sattva* which exists in substance devoid of *rajas* and *tamas*. It belongs to [His] eternal manifestation (*nityavibhūti*). Impure *sattva* is that *sattva* which coexists with *rajas* and *tamas*. It belongs to the *triguṇa*."

prakṛti and distinguishes between various types of entities, which can also be understood as a demarcation from *prakṛti*. He thus differentiates the concept of non-eternity in the *nityavibhūti* from that concept of non-eternity of material matter (*prakṛti*).

In the following quote, Veṅkaṭanātha refers to two different views describing the *nityavibhūti*. One follows the tradition of the Pāñcarātra, but also includes principles of material matter; the other (*ke cit*, according to some) accepts only the principles of material matter, but emphasizes that they are not modified in the same way as the eternal transformation of *prakṛti*.

> And this [transcendent dominion] is, as it is taught in the *Pañcopaniṣad* (i.e., the Pāñcarātra), composed of the five gross elements and the [eleven] sense faculties (*indriya*); it forms the bodies, the sense faculties and the vital breaths, as well as the objects of the eternal (*nitya*) souls, the liberated souls and God in accordance with their own will.
>
> According to some, it is also composed of the twenty-four principles (*tattva*), as in the case of [the material universe] made up of the three *guṇas*. Yet, these principles are *not* modified by *prakṛti*, because the authoritative Scripture (*śruti*) describes the bodies and so forth in the divine universe as constant. As well as [the gross elements] like ether [and the corporal faculties], there exist [the intermediate principles], namely, *mahat*, [*ahaṃkara* and the five *tanmātras*], though they are not derived from material matter.
>
> In fact, there [in the divine realm], [each preceding entity], say, ether, is not the material cause of [each following entity], say, air […].
>
> Further, there are objects that are ornaments, arms, arrows, attendants, mansions, gardens, wells, artificial mountains for playing, and so forth—they are excessively wonderful and eternal. Some [objects], however, are products and non-eternal.[198]

---

[198] NSi 389,2–17: *iyañ ca pañcopaniṣatpratipādyapañcabhūtendriyamayī nityamukteśvarāṇām icchānurūpaśarīrendriya[?]prāṇaviṣayarūpeṇāvatiṣṭhate. triguṇavad iyam api caturviṃśatitattvātmiketi ke cit. tathāpi na tattvānāṃ prakṛtivikṛtibhāvaḥ. divyamaṅgaḷavigrahāder nit-*

Also in another passage, Veṅkaṭanātha distinguishes between changes in the *nityavibhūti* and those that are *karman*-related. Here, too, he emphasizes the will of God, to which everything is ultimately subject. As a special difference from primordial matter, Veṅkaṭanātha also mentions in this context time (*kāla*), by which God only brings about changes in the material (*prākṛta*) manifestation of material matter (*prakṛti*).

> For even there [in the eternal dominion], trees have transformations (*pariṇāmāḥ*) such as buds, flowers and fruits; rivers [have modifications] such as foam, waves and bubbles; and [His] body has [modifications] such as [His] divine manifestations (*vyūha*) and [His] incarnations *(vibhava). Only those modifications that are caused by time and dependent upon karman are negated there, but not those caused merely by the will of God.* The bodies are this way, too: the bodies of some eternal seers and of God are eternal because of being held with their eternal will; some are non-eternal because of being held with their non-eternal will. [The bodies] of those who are liberated, however, are caused and are non-eternal also.[199]

This passage, also from Veṅkaṭanātha's NSi, indicates that alternations take place due to the will of God. In this sense, a kind of transformation can also be accepted for the pure manifestation (*śuddhasṛṣṭi*). In this context, too, the basic idea can be recognised that two different types of substances can be based on *one*

---

yatvaśravaṇāt. aprākṛtānām api mahadādīnāṃ sadbhāva ākāśādivat. na hi ākāśādyupāttās tatra vāyvādayaḥ. [...] *viṣayāś cātra bhūṣaṇāyudhāsanaparivārāyatanodyānavāpikākrīḍāparvatādayo 'tivicitrā nityāḥ. ke cit tu kṛtakā anityāś ca.*

199 NSi 389,17–390,2: *santi hi tatrāpi taruṣu pallavakusumaphalādayaḥ pariṇāmāḥ, nadīṣu phetataraṅgabudbudādayaḥ, vigrahe ca vyūhavibhavādayaḥ. kālakṛtakarmādhīnapariṇāmamātraṃ hi teṣu niṣedhyam, na tu bhagavatsaṅkalpamātrakṛtam api. tad evaṃ śarīrāṇy api kāni cit nityānām īśvarasya ca nityecchāparigrahāt nityāni. kāni cid anityecchāparigrahād anityāni. muktānāṃ tu kṛtakāny evānityāny api.* (translations adopted from Mikami [pdf]).

and the *same* basis, in this case God's will, which is eternal and non-eternal.

No missing link

Finally, we turn to the polemical discussions involved and consider once again how Veṅkaṭanātha determines God's relation to everything in his criticism of the concept of inherence (*samavāya*) as taught by the Vaiśeṣika.

It is interesting to compare this very concept with Veṅkaṭanātha's understanding of the relation of substance and attribute (state/properties). We had repeatedly demonstrated that Rāmānuja and Veṅkaṭanātha give (the same) reasons under which conditions substance and attribute can be related, under which conditions we recognise, or form sentences. We elaborated on their views and tried to demonstrate that their fundamental understanding consisted in presupposing a *third* grounding aspect that must necessarily be distinct from the respective attributes/states/words, which had to correlate to each other. But for such a correlation we did not speak of a copula,[200] because such a copula, as an intermediate third, would have to be connected with those determinations that are related to each other, which is precisely different from the Viśiṣṭādvaita view of inseparability of substance and state/property, for which there is no need of any copula, becauseboth are always inseparately connected. Thus, Veṅkaṭanātha does not consider inherence (*samavāya*) to link two relatas.

---

[200] Cf. for example Phillips (1997: 48) explanation: "Thus when we say "This pot is blue," the pot is a substance and blue is a quality, and the "is" means inherence, *samavāya*. From an ontological perspective, in response to the question, "What relates the blue to the pot?" the answer is inherence. Inherence is a special glue that binds qualities to substances ...". Cf. also Halbfass (1992: 72; 149) remarks describing the *samavāya* as "the cosmological and ontological foundation of the possibility and legitimacy of predication. It is, in a sense, the hypostatized, reified copula, or the cosmic prototype of the copula."

What has become clear thus far is that Veṅkaṭanātha's view of substance and property/state implies that neither needs any further link to be inseparately related to each other.[201]

At first, we explain, which reasons are given to reject the concept of inherence: Against the background of Rāmānuja's and Veṅkaṭanātha's concept of unity needing a basis, we can understand that the relation of mutually different designations is a relation in which such a basis and its various attributes, inseparably grounded in that basis, are relevant.

Veṅkaṭanātha critizises the Vaiśeṣika concept of *samavāya*, and accepts conjunction (*saṃyoga*). His own view can be summarized as follows: Since substance and state are defined as inseparately established and are therefore linked, an "unborn" (*aja*) conjunction (*saṃyoga*) must be accepted especially for the relationship of eternal and omnipresent (*vibhu*) substances like God and time (*kāla*). I will briefly present also a few other arguments related to this. We will see that Veṅkaṭanātha interprets conjunction (*saṃyoga*) as a state (*avasthā*), i.e., a substance being in the state of conjunction (*saṃyuktāvasthā*).[202] For this he follows

---

[201] The Vaiśeṣika concept of inherence is also criticized in the Jaina tradition, which as we have seen above (p. 401) argues for "identity" (*abheda*) between substance and property. Even if the meaning of such an "identity" stands in contrast to the Viśiṣṭadvaitic concept of being inseparately established (*apṛthaksiddha*) we can observe some similarity between the Jaina refutation and Rāmānuja's—in fact already of Nāthamuni's critique of *samavāya* (cf. fn. 96 above).

[202] Veṅkaṭanātha enumerates the following *adravya*s at the beginning of chapter 6 (*adravyapariccheda*) of the NSi 443,8–10: *sattva*, *rajas*, *tamas*, and five [qualities] beginning with sound (*śabda*), conjunction (*saṃyoga*) and potency (*śakti*). For him they cover the following states/properties, under which also the concept of inherence is mentioned: *gurutva-dravatva-sneha-saṃskāra-saṅkhyā-parimāṇa--pṛthaktva-vibhāga-paratva-aparatva-karmasāmānya-sādṛśya-viśeṣa-samavāya-abhāva-vaiśiṣṭyādīnāṃ.* "Weight (*gurutva*), fluidity (*dravatva*), viscidity (*snehatva*), latent impression (*saṅskar*a), number (*saṅkhya*), size (*parimāṇa*), separateness (*pṛthaktva*), disjunction (*vibhāga*), remoteness, (*paratva*), nearness (*aparatva*), action

Yāmunas statement in his *Ātmasiddhi* (see below). To give an example, I refer at first to passages from chapter 5 (*adravyasara*) of the TMK and from the NSi.[203] I will then shortly introduce Veṅkaṭanātha's own definition of conjunction.

The central argument taken up by Veṅkaṭanātha was already developed by Rāmānuja,[204] namely, the argument that accepting inherence leads to an infinite regress. If one assumes a relation between two relata, a regress arises when one asks what connects both. This reasoning is also adopted by Veṅkaṭanātha. For him, too, there is no way to prove that the relation (*saṃbandha*) between a substance and its states or properties is constituted by inherence as a *third*. Nevertheless Veṅkaṭanātha does not reject that we can speak of a relation; one has only to take into account that substance and different properties/states are self-grounding and therefore mediated by themselves individually. It is in vain to consider how a property/state is related to what must be specified (*viśeṣya*) or regarding its inseparable occurrence. If inseparability defines how properties can ground without mediation in a sub-

---

(*karman*), generality (*sāmānya*), similarity (*sādṛśya*), particularity (*viśeṣa*), inherence (*samavāya*), non-being (*abhāva*), qualifiedness (*vaiśiṣṭya*) etc."

203 The 15th chapter (*vaiśeṣikabhaṅgādhikāra,* pp. 167–221) of the PMBh provides many more points of Veṅkaṭanātha's criticism; see especially pp. 176–187 of this chapter, which refutes the relation of time (*kāla*) and inherence (*samavāya*); cf. also Schmücker forthcoming².

204 Cf. Śrībh III 292,2–3 *ad* BS 2.2.12–13. Rāmānuja refers here to Praśastapādas's definition of *samavāya* (*Pādārthadharmasaṃgraha* (PDhS) 773): *ayutasiddhānām ādhārādheyabhūtānām iha pratyayahetur yaḥ saṃbandhaḥ, sa samavāya iti samavāyo 'bhyupagamyate.* "Inherence is the relation that causes here the cognition of an inseparably related carrier [i.e., the substance] and that which is to be carried [i.e., the property]." For more information about Rāmānuja's critical treatment of the Nyāya-Vaiśeṣika, cf. Lott 1976: 126–145.

stance, inherence no longer fulfils any function.[205] He therefore explains transformation of a substance due to the respective connected state (*saṃyuktāvasthā*). Such a conjunction (*saṃyoga*) can not be *caused* by a third, i.e., inherence (*samavāya*). The relationship is given by itself.[206]

It is not possible here to go into the way in which these objections influenced the later representatives of the Nyāya, or were already reflected[207] earlier in the Vaiśeṣika, and led to new considerations as to how the concept of inherence can be maintained. The central claim was that the reaction of the Nyāya-Vaiśeṣika to the accusation of infinite regress was to explain that inherence is a relation in and of itself, i.e., self-linking.[208] However, Veṅkaṭanātha's reaction should also be mentioned in this context.

Against such an argument two examples can illustrate why, also in this case, for Veṅkaṭanātha nothing is needed to link by a third instance substance and its states. If the concept of relation is used, it must be justified that relata can still be spoken of when speaking of a substance and its states. From the inseparable link between substance and property, it follows, however, that not only is a mediating third aspect not necessary, but such a third aspect cannot be proved by any means valid cognition. Does it therefore make any sense to speak of a relation? If it is spoken of at all, then it is seen as a designation of substance, since substances

---

[205] Cf. already Rāmānuja's remark in Śrībh III 292,4–5 *ad* BS 2.2.12–13: *samavāyasya tadapṛthaksiddhatvaṃ svabhāva iti parikalpyate cet—jātiguṇānām evaiṣa svabhāvaḥ parikalpanīyaḥ.* "If one objects that being inseparately established is the characteristic nature of inherence, then this nature would also have to be assumed for genus, property, etc. [and therefore inherence is unnecessary]."

[206] The Naiyāyikas argue for a self-linking relation and accordingly declare inherence as such: "A self-linking relation is non-different from one or both of its loci: it is not a third reality connecting them." (Bartley 2002: 85).

[207] Cf. for such a position Trikha 2012: 233ff.

[208] Cf. for more explanation cf. Bartley 2002: 84–85.

are defined as being connected to something else. Only in this way it can be maintained that no third aspect mediates between a property and its basis. Whatever is considered a relation is therefore reduced to the assertion of inseparable togetherness of the substance and its attribute. Ultimately, it is this togetherness which—as already explained—constitutes a specified thing (*viśiṣṭavastu*), which in turn is the reason why it can be an object of perception. With this we arrive at the concept of experience, which is for Veṅkaṭanātha another argument against the acceptance of inherence.

In his commentary on TMK 5.2, Veṅkaṭanātha explains why no additional member binds the properties/states of a substance listed under "non-substance" (*adravya*). A substance is qualified differently only due to its alternating characteristic nature (*svabhāva*). As Veṅkaṭanātha states:

> And this [non-substance], which is without any further designation, may only qualify this, i.e., a substance, by virtue of its own characteristic nature (*svabhāvād eva*), insofar as relations such as inherence, etc., do not exist.[209]

The transformation of a substance would also not be possible if one accepts the concept of an additional link between substance and property/state. To know *what* something *is* is only possible through a knowledge that reveals its property or state of a grounding substance, that is, its characteristic nature (*svabhāva*). Nothing can be known if there is no base/substance presupposed, which is self-grounding (*svaparanirvāhaka*) together with its self-grounding property/state as well—without any mediating part.

> Because the characteristic nature of things is not to be blamed, the form/shape accessible to means of valid knowledge is called characteristic nature (*svabhāvo nāma prāmāṇikaṃ rūpam*) in contrast to the essential nature [of substances]. Non-substances are recognized inas-

---

[209] SAS 681.9–10 *ad* TMK 5.2: *idaṃ cānupadhikaṃ samavāyādisaṃbandhābhāvena svabhāvād eva tat—dravyaṃ viśiṃṣyāt.*

> much as they are distinguishing qualifiers proven as unseparated with regard to their [grounding] substances.[211]

In response to his opponent who accepts inherence (*samavāya*), Veṅkaṭanātha repeats his argument that inherence is nothing other than inseparability between non-substance (*adravya*) and substance (*dravya*).

> For you, the relation is established only as inseparable between which [relata] the inherence is accepted due to their being inseparably established; but inherence is not assumed to be this relation, because that is the more difficult assumption, insofar as inherence cannot be known as being different from establishing inseparability that is naturally given. Therefore, the contact (*upaśleṣaḥ*) between substance and non-substance is only due to their own characteristic natures.[212]

Although Veṅkaṭanātha draws an analogy between self-linking inherence and self-linking non-substance, another important argument is that if one accepts inherence (*samavāya*), there would be no sequence of different states and thus no explanation for any (temporal) modification. For Veṅkaṭanātha, what is accessible as a means of cognition is the way of appearance. There is no characteristic nature (*svabhāva*) without an essential nature (*svarūpa*), which in turn is inseparable from what appears as characteristic nature (*sva hava*); but only what appears, i.e., the characteristic nature, is recognizable through a means of valid knowledge.

Thus, the point of critique is the following: the relation establishhed by inherence is not self-linking; what is self-linking is the

---

[211] SAS 681.12–12 *ad* TMK 5.2: *aparyanuyojyatvād vastusvabhāvānām, svabhāvo nāma prāmāṇikaṃ rūpam. apṛthaksiddhaviśeṣaṇatvenopalabhyante dravyaṃ praty adravyāṇi.*

[212] SAS 681.14–16 *ad* TMK 5.2: *bhavatā yayor ayutasiddhyā samavāyaḥ kalpyate tayor ayutasiddhir eva saṃbandhaḥ, na punas tatkalpanīyaḥ samavāyaḥ, kalpanāgauravāt, svābhāvikāpṛthaksiddhivyatirekeṇa samavāyasyānupalambhāt. ataḥ svabhāvād eva dravyādravyayor upaśleṣaḥ.*

substance and its properties/states, which are proven as inseparable of each other. If we recognize something when dealing with an object, then we do not reflect on how its states are connected to their basis but we recognize immediately the thing itself. When we speak about something or when we recognize something, we presuppose that its substance and its state are one. We therefore accept that dealing with objects would not be possible if they were not recognized as qualified (*viśiṣṭa*).[213] In the same chapter (chapter 5, *adravyasara*) of the TMK, in the context of the refutation of inherence (*samavāya*), Veṅkaṭanātha exemplifies that we cannot recognize anything beyond substances and their constituent properties. He thus refutes that inherence is perceptible, because there is *nothing* to be recognized *between* a substance and its state due to their inseparability:

> We are not aware of a relation (*bandhaṃ*) between two inseparately established [entities] as being different from their essential nature.[214]

---

[213] See also SAS 793.9–14 *ad* TMK 5.127, where Veṅkaṭanātha argues that assuming inherence between two relata (*saṃbandhin*) is useless (*nirarthikā*). As he concludes: "Therefore even for the one who accepts inherence, the specific characteristic nature of two relata must be accepted. And in this way, accepting inherence between two relata is in vain." *tasmāt samavāyāṅgīkāravādināpi saṃbandhinoḥ svabhāvaviśeṣaḥ svīkāryaḥ. tathā ca madhye samavāyakḷptir nirarthikā.*

[214] TMK 5.126: *bandhaṃ nādhyakṣayāmaḥ samadhikam apṛthaksiddhyos tatsvarūpāt.* In the commentary on this verse (SAS 792.9–11), Veṅkaṭanātha again explains that inherence cannot be known by perception: "We cannot perceive the relation accepted as different from the essential nature of the two [i.e., substance and state], which are inseparately established. Therefore establishing inherence on the basis of perception is difficult to obtain." *apṛthaksiddhayos samavāyākhyaṃ svarūpād adhikaṃ kalpyamānaṃ saṃbandhaṃ na pratyakṣayāmaḥ. ataḥ pratyakṣāt samavāyasiddhir iti dūrāpāstam.*

Cf. also the next sentence of his commentary: SAS 792.12–13: *ayam arthaḥ guṇaguṇinau, avayavāvayavinau, jātivyaktī, parasparaṃ, svabhāvād eva saṃbadhyete iti.* Cf. also the explanations in Shastri 1993: 241 referring to this passage, ibid., 243: "If, however, inherence is assumed to be related to its relata by dint of its own merit, the

Assuming a link between qualifier and what is qualified would also imply a decision regarding eternalness. The link is either eternal (*nitya*) like the substance, or non-eternal (*anitya*) like its states. Again, for Veṅkaṭanātha it is not a contradiction for the states of a substance to be determined as non-eternal (*anitya*) and the substance as being eternal. Why should a pot, which is made of clay, contradict clay? The link between the eternal and the non-eternal is not a contradiction; they are compatible in the beginningless sequence of states of one and the same substance.

It can be asked in which context the expression "a state which is in conjunction" (*saṃyuktāvāsthā*) is used, after having demonstrated that it is possible for the substance to have a state without linking it through inherence to the substance. In the following section, it is demonstrated that conjunction is not a mediating designation between property possessor and the property itself. To describe this, Veṅkaṭanātha adopts Yāmuna's explanation that there is "no interspace" (*nairantarya*), i.e., "no gap". He also draws attention to the fact that a quality/property cannot have conjunction because otherwise it would have to be a substance. It might be clear that Yāmuna is reading this description of extreme proximity as another expression of the central concept of being inseparately established (*apṛthaksiddhi*). It is the equation of *samavāya* with *saṃyoga*, but it is also what is expressed by the concept of inseparability, the abiding difference in the description of extreme proximity.

> By how it is stated in the *Ātmasiddhi* [ĀS 82,9f.] that: "Conjunction (*saṃyoga*) is synonymous with *nairantarya* (being without any gap) and is but extreme proximity." This very [conjunction] is, in the Vaiśeṣikas, categorized as inherence (*samavāya*) when it takes resort in a dependent [entity]. Accordingly, an alternative based on the assumption that [inherence] is different [from conjunction] is impossible. This also signifies that there is no other relation than [conjunc-

---

two relata may also do so, and substance and attribute, whole and part, etc. are mutually related to each other due to their own characteristic nature."

tion] because, in our opinion, the inherence accepted by other [schools] is not accepted and *[inherence is] nothing but a variety of [conjunction] itself*; but not that the relation between quality and what has quality (*guṇin*) is [also] characterized with conjunction. Should one say "quality and what has quality are in conjunction," this usage would be metaphorical—in order to teach this, the author says: "synonymous with *nairantarya*." The usage "being in conjunction" is merely because there is no gap/interruption [between the two].[215]

The basic thesis that God enters everything, in the sense that He manifests everything anew, is now valid for all substances, also for those that are—as He Himself is—omnipresent (*vibhu*) like time (*kāla*). However, Veṅkaṭanātha (NSi 480,4–481,5) distinguishes between two forms, namely, a conjunction between a limited entity and an omnipresent entity. Such a conjunction can be caused by action of both entities or by an action of one or the other. For instance, a conjunction between two lambs, or a conjunction between a pillar and a hawk. In contrast, an unaffected conjunction is between two substances that have no gap (*nairantarya*) and are unmovable. They are related by an eternal conjunction as a state of an omnipresent substance.

What are the theological implications of all this? What consequences does Veṅkaṭanātha draw? To give an example for two omnipresent substances: The opponent argues that no conjunction can arise between omnipresent substances, insofar as there is no one to cause it. Again, Veṅkaṭanātha responds that such sub-

---

215 NSi 422,3–11: *yat tu—nairantaryāparaparyāyamatyantasāmīpyamātrañ ca saṃyogaḥ. sa eva paratantrāśritaḥ samavāyapadaparibhāṣābhūmir vaiśeṣikāṇām apīti nārthāntaratvamurarīkṛtya vikalpaḥ saṃbhavatīty ātmasiddhā vaktum—tad api parābhyupagatasamavāyān abhyupagamāt svamate svarūpaviśeṣānatirekāt, na tu guṇaguṇino saṃyogalakṣaṇasaṃbandhaparam. guṇaguṇinau saṃyuktāv iti yadi kecit prayuñjīran, tadānīm aupacāriko 'yaṃ vyavahāra iti jñāpayitum, nairantaryāparaparyāyam ity uktam; nirantaratvamātrāt saṃyuktatvavyavahāraḥ.* (Translation adopted from Mikami [pdf]).

stances depend on God's entering (*anupraveśa*) for being in the state of conjunction, in his words:

> Even for omnipresent [entities like time (*kāla*)], their production of effects and so on are dependent upon God's entering [i.e., conjunction].[217]

We can note that the term *saṃyoga* is another description of how ultimately everything exists inseparably from Him due to His entering as Inner Ruler. It is the conjunction of an all pervasive entity that enables any modification; similarly, such a conjunction enables also modifications in omnipresent substances like time (*kāla*), because God Himself is connected to everything through an eternal conjunction (*ajasaṃyoga*).

> As the conjunction of an omnipresent [entity] is said [to be inevitable] to enable a particular modification of a shaped [entity], in the same way the conjunction [of an omnipresent entity like time] with God must be inevitably accepted to enable modifications of time and other [omnipresent entities]. Otherwise, it would be impossible for [such an entity] like time even to be the body of God.[218]

We have already pointed out in the context of the explanation of co-referentiality that time has a common basis with God; time cannot be thought of independently of God. The concept of inseparability is a consequence of the doctrine of the Inner Controller. This assumption of divine immediacy not only underlies Veṅkaṭanātha's rejection of the concept of inherence relationship, it also justifies—as the last quotation demonstrates—the assumption that there is no contradiction between two omnipresent (*vibhu*) eternal substances if they are connected by an eternal conjunction

---

[217] NSi 483,3: *vibhūnām api svakāryajananāder īśvarānupraveśanibandhanatvāt.*

[218] NSi 483,8–484,2: *yathā mūrtagatavikāraviśeṣasiddhyarthaṃ vibhusaṃyoga uktaḥ, tathaiva kālādigatavikārasiddhyartham api īśvarasaṃyogo 'viśyābhyupetyaḥ. anyathā īśvaraśarīratvam api kālāder na syād iti.*

(*ajasaṃyoga*), whereby this is nothing other than a description of God's inseparability from everything as Inner Controller.

Refutation of other views of cause and effect: The Sāṅkhya

As has been shown, Rāmānuja's and Veṅkaṭanātha's understanding of the ontological implications of BĀU 1.4.7 developed into a concept of substance and properties/states. However, the above outline would remain incomplete if no ontological view of other schools were examined. We already referred to Rāmānuja's critique and could also illustrate how Veṅkaṭanātha followed closely Rāmānuja's arguments against Sāṅkhya ontology. But Veṅkaṭanātha again took much effort to reclaim for his own tradition the so called *satkāryavāda*. Thus, in the following, Veṅkaṭanātha's criticism of the ontology of the atheistic Sāṅkhya will be discussed briefly, although length constraints prevent a presentation of all arguments Veṅkaṭanātha develops. Here the emphasis will be on the contrast between the atheistic Sāṅkhya arguments and the theistically inspired dynamics of Veṅkaṭanātha's ontology. We mentioned already, he and his predecessors[219] also call their ontology *satkārya*, i.e., the fact that an effect always *is*.

As we have seen, for Veṅkaṭanātha, *satkārya* implies that a substance (*dravya*), i.e., *Being* must be accepted as the basis for every alternating state. Against his Sāṅkhya opponent, he claims the *satkāryavāda* as his own doctrine, and refers to his central view that an effect is only a state of a substance, which exists before in another state, i.e. the state of the cause: "The substance which exists even earlier [in the state of the cause], is [in the state of an effect], insofar as it appears as qualified by another state".[220] Again we see how Veṅkaṭanātha's view of creation, i.e., remani-

---

219 Cf. for example, chapter 8 of Ātreyarāmānuja's *Nyayakuliśa* (pp. 143–152, esp. p. 147).

220 SAS 93.7–8 *ad* TMK 1.20.

festation, based on an Upaniṣadic background, is distinct from the teaching of *satkāryavāda* as developed by Sāṅkhya authors.

Veṅkaṭanātha does not advocate the doctrine that an effect (*kārya*) *is* already completely (manifest) in the cause, but rather teaches that an effect can only be manifested when the needed circumstances are given. As has been demonstrated, for him the effect *is* insofar as it *is* the subtle state (*sūkṣmāvasthā*), also if it is not yet in a present and perceptible state. As he criticizes, the Sāṅkhya does not accept this concept of ontology, since being can neither become non-being, nor can non-being become being: what is, is being only. The consequence of this view: Nothing can cause non-being to become being. From this, the conclusion is reached that there is only being. Therefore also an effect must already be being before it is produced.[221]

Veṅkaṭanātha's criticism of the Sāṅkhya not only concerns disagreements regarding ontology. Concerning the view on the remanifestation of the world, it is for him exactly the question of how previous non-being comes into being again, and how this kind of transformation can be brought together with a highest, eternal God who is identified with *Being*. Indeed, at first glance

[221] The ontologies of the two schools have neither have been compared nor distinguished from each other very often. However, the fact that the same sources can be seen as a starting point in the development of both schools has been noted by Wezler (1988). On Sāṅkhya and Viśiṣṭādvaita Vedānta, he remarks (ibid., p. 180): "Both schools could have had this concept of being in common but should have greatly differed from each other as regards their respective 'Weltanschauung', a dualistic and non-theistic one in the case of (Proto-sāṅkhya) and a theistic and perhaps monistic one in the case of the others. That is to say, we should assume that the tradition going back to this teaching of Uddālaka Āruṇi's evolved into two views when some thinkers interpreted the concept of *sat* in Chānd Up. 6.2.1f. as unintelligent material prima and basis (*prakṛti*) of the phenomenal world, and others took it to mean a personal god out of whom this world emanates." For the development of atheistic Sāṅkhya and theistic ontology of the Viśiṣṭādvaita Vedānta based on the *sarvasarvātmakavāda*, cf. also Wezler 1992: 290ff.

Veṅkaṭanātha's view seems to have much in common with that of the Sāṅkhya, namely, that properties continue to *be* when they vanish, and therefore they also already *are* when they are produced again. But—as we have mentioned many times—an important Viśiṣṭādvaita development consists in not explaining an effect as based on a cause, but in basing both on *Being*, i.e., *brahman*, which is identified with the God Viṣṇu-Nārāyaṇa.

To understand how Veṅkaṭanātha sets his own ontology against that of the Sāṅkhya, a few remarks on the ontology of the Sāṅkhya are necessary so that the differences in the polemical debate become clearer.

In disputes regarding the ontological status of effect, one relevant question among others was to understand an effect if it is defined as being. In the context of the early history of Sāṅkhya ontology, the answer given by the early Sāṅkhya teacher Vārṣagaṇya, namely, that *no* non-being can be caused remained influential. This thesis is clearly mentioned as the first reason in verse nine of Īśvarakṛṣṇa's *Sāṅkhyakārikā* (= SK) and is also discussed in that work's commentaries. The most famous commentary thereon, the *Yuktidīpikā* (=YD), as well as the later *Tattvakaumudī* by Vācaspati, were based in part on the teaching of Vārṣagaṇya.

Briefly their ontological argument can be reconstructed as follows: According to the YD, an effect is the result of a process of transformation (*pariṇāma*), which is explained in terms of appearance (*āvirbhava*) and disappearance (*tirobhava*). Speaking of disappearance (*tirobhāva*) does not mean dissolving into nothingness. The YD augments this concept by stating that the manifestation of one effect disappears due to the manifestation of another potentiality (*śakti*) contradicting the first. Referring to the followers of Vārṣagaṇya, it is stated in this text (YD p. 128)[222] that although the three-world de-manifests, it does not withdraw from *being*: "And even though it withdraws (*apetam api*) [from mani-

---

222 YD 128–129: *tad etat trailokyaṃ vyakter apaiti na sattvāt. apetam api asti vināśapratiṣedhāt.* For the many references of the discussion to this passage see Ratié 2013: 136, fn. 38.

festation], it *is*, because [we] deny destruction."[223] The YD thus explains every change as disappearance and reappearance of qualities, while the qualified base continues to *be*.[224] The question remains as to how completely the manifestation (*abhivyakti*) can be dissolved in disappearance and subtlety (*saukṣmya*) if it is not to become non-being. According to the Sāṅkhya teaching, it must still *be*, despite not being perceptible due to the subtlety of primordial matter. All this sounds quite like Veṅkaṭanātha's view. So, what is the decisive difference and what is his point of critique?

From the fact that it would be contradictory to claim that non-being can be produced, the Sāṅkhya followers concluded that the effect is already there: it was real in advance. However, this led them to the difficult position of no longer being able to claim non-being. The explanation that although the manifestation disappears, it continues despite not being perceptible because of subtlety (*saukṣmya*) is also found in Vācaspatimiśra's commentary on SK 9. Just as the limbs of a tortoise disappear when they are withdrawn and reappear when they are stretched out, so it is the same case with a pot that comes into appearance from a lump of clay and then disappears within it. In both cases, neither is anything that *is* finally destroyed, nor does anything arise from non-being.[225] Veṅkaṭanātha criticizes the example of the tortoise

---

[223] And the passage continues in YD 129f.: *saṃsargāc cāsya saukṣmyaṃ saukṣmyāc cānupalabdhi. tasmād vyaktyapagamo vināśaḥ.* "And because of its merging [into primordial nature, the world] is subtle; and due to its subtlety, it is not perceived. Therefore, destruction is the disappearance of manifestation."

[224] YD 163f.: *yadā śaktyantarānugrahāt pūrvadharmaṃ tirobhāvya svarūpād apracyuto dharmī dharmāntareṇāvirbhavati tad avasthānam asmākam pariṇāma ucyate.* "We call 'transformation' the state [that occurs] when, after making a previous property disappear by assuming another power, the property possessor (*dharmī*), which does not abandon its essential nature, appears with another property."

[225] Cf. for this example Vācaspati's TK (ed. Srinivasan pp. 100ff.) on SK 9. The limbs of the tortoise, when they appear and when they disappear neither arise nor are destroyed, because there is no arising of

several times, as will be discussed in the following. He not only refutes the Sāṅkhya's concept of manifestation (*vyakti*) in his TMK, similar criticism can be found in the eighteenth chapter of his *Paramatabhaṅga* (*nirīśvarasāṅkhyādhikaraṇa*) where he refutes the Sāṅkhya position, as well as in passages of his *Śatadūṣaṇī*. He demonstrates that the Sāṅkhya opponent can never speak of *Being* of non-being without contradicting his own ontological presuppositions. But according to Veṅkaṭanātha's own view, non-being *is*, just as being *is*. They do not have to appear simultaneously; rather, for an effect to occur, non-being and being can alternate. For the Sāṅkhya, such alternation is impossible: non-being (*asat*) can never become being (*sat*).

The following example is to illustrate the different views on their ontology: In verse 24 of the first chapter (*jaḍadravyasara*) of his TMK, Veṅkaṭanātha has his Sāṅkhya opponent argue that before states are present, it must be assumed that they are already being (*santi prāg*). According to Veṅkaṭanātha, such an understanding of the ontological status is wrong, insofar as the Sāṅkhya opponent, if he accepts already being, cannot claim non-being. The verse refers to an opponent who defends the Sāṅkhya ontology by relying on SK 9.[226] This provides Veṅkaṭanātha a platform for responding to central Sāṅkhya doctrines.

> If [the Sāṅkhya opponent asserts that] states are [already] being given before [they become manifest], (1) because one does not observe

---

non-being, nor destruction of being. To establish his view Vācaspati quotes in this context *Bhagavadgīta* 2.16: "There is no thing such as being of non-being or non-being of being."

[226] It is clear that it is SK 9 being referred to: "Because non-being is not produced, because a material cause is known, because a particular object cannot arise from everything, because a cause capable of producing a particular object produces what it is capable of producing, and because [the product] has as its nature the cause, the effect *is* [before the operation of its cause]." *asadakaraṇād upādānagrahaṇāt sarvasaṃbhavābhāvāt. śaktasya śakyakaraṇāt kāraṇabhāvāc ca satkāryam.*

> that something different from being is brought forth, and (2) because one does not observe that something which has not yet already appeared comes into being, [and] also (3) because of the distinction between capable and incapable, [then] we deny [these reasons] because one observes the arising of the effect from something [i.e., the cause] that is suitable to produce it. If it is so, then its production from the cause is also established, insofar as it presupposes an instrumental cause, etc.
>
> [For you, the Sāṅkhya, the view is that] the manifestation (*vyaktiḥ*) that is [already] manifested, enters into an infinite regress. But you do not claim that the manifestation is already realized; in such a way, it is not the case for us in reference to the manifestation.[227]

The Sāṅkhya opponent argues that one cannot *observe* something different from being (*sat*) as being caused. Could this be true for Veṅkaṭanātha as well? In fact, Veṅkaṭanātha lists several conditions that must be fulfilled before an effect is perceptible and explains an effect as something that can only be produced under *specific* conditions. Only when an effect is actually perceived by *someone* it is really there, i.e., in a certain place and at a specific time. It cannot be said to be present at an earlier time because there is no means of valid knowledge. Nevertheless, one must take into concern the following case: before that, i.e., being present, one has to accept that the effect was also not non-being, as otherwise it could not be produced. But as long as an effect is not perceptible, one must say that it is not yet present.

How does Veṅkaṭanātha unfold the arguments in his autocommentary on this verse? On one hand, he refutes the view that an effect already *is*: If earlier non-being is not present, one cannot say that it is completely not. Definable as non-being, it is merely not perceivable in its unmanifested state. He elaborates that the

---

[227] TMK 1.24:
santi prāg apy avasthāḥ saditarakaraṇāprāptaniṣpattyadṛṣṭeḥ
śaktāśaktaprabhedādibhir api yadi, na; svocitāt kāryadṛṣṭeḥ
tasmin saty eva tasmāj janir api niyatā tannimittādinīter
vyaktir vyaktānavasthāṃ bhajati na ca kṛtām āttha naivaṃ kṛtau naḥ.

explanation of the Sāṅkhya opponent is incorrect, namely, that something can be in the state of non-being but nevertheless must be accepted as being. We have explained that this is for Veṅkaṭanātha the "subtle state" (*sūkṣmāvasthā*). As presumed by the Sāṅkhya opponent, if cause and effect are not different, then if a cause *is*, the effect must also *be*. Therefore, according to him, an effect cannot be defined as non-being if the cause already *is*. Non-being is not an option, because based on his own doctrin, he cannot claim that something arises from non-being. But exactly this is possible for Veṅkaṭanātha, due to his premise that there *is* non-being, i.e., *Being* of non-being. He does not have to follow the thesis that being cannot originate from non-being. Therefore, he can crititisize the Saṅkhya opponent pointing out that according to his premises, he can never explain how non-being becomes being if he has not himself already presupposed a *third* basis, i.e., *Being*. Based on such view of the Sāṅkhya, a Supreme Being would be unable to manifest previous non-being as present being or transform again something being present into later non-being. But for Veṅkaṭanātha this is precisely the task of his God. He objects that being and non-being can be states of an object. The Sāṅkhya counters with the beginninglessness existence of an object that cannot be perceived earlier as non-being. Veṅkaṭanātha responds that the effect is a state which is not present before it is not really there. And what we do not perceive we cannot speak of as being, although this does not imply to accept complete non-being but *Being* of non-being.

> However, for us, non-cognition [of an effect] is declared to be due to [being in] an unmanifested state. Someone saying: "[Things like a] non-being pot, etc., are not non-pots" is childish[229] prattle.[230]

---

229 This sentence is repeated in the PMBh's Mādhyamika chapter (*mādhyamikabhaṅgādhikāra*, pp. 98–100). Here he again explains: If something has no existence at all we cannot raise any question about its characteristic nature; we can only address a question toward a person or an object which is. Finally, he concludes ibid.: *ittālē*, *na hy asan ghaṭādir na ghaṭādiḥ e̲ṉ̲ra khaṇḍanajalpam nirastam.* "There-

Veṅkaṭanātha tells the Sāṅkhya opponent that to claim that an effect can be being (present), he must have presupposed the non-being he himself so vehemently denies. Thus, the decisive argument he elaborates here consists in showing the opponent that he cannot but accept non-being becoming actual being. Otherwise, the Sāṅkhya opponent would represent the absurd opinion that an effect is already real *in* its cause, which can be thoroughly proven to be false due to the lack of any means of valid knowledge. Again, Veṅkaṭanātha develops his argument against the background of his own doctrine, which claims that an effect is merely a state made possible by the preceding one. Therefore, he rejects the Sāṅkhya opponent's thesis that it cannot be assumed that an effect which is different from its cause is manifest *before* it is present. He justifies his own answer in another passage of his SAS on TMK 1.24:

> In the first place, something like an effect is *not* not observed, because [otherwise] it would contradict the complete [reality of the] world and the [authority of] the Veda, and because also bringing about a manifestation would be without a basis. [...] And one does not recognize even being as not different from the cause, because the answer is already given, and because otherwise the difference between primordial matter, its transformation, etc., would be refuted.
> Therefore, you also involuntarily adopt the opinion that the effect observed as different from the cause (*kāraṇād bhinnatvena*) did not previously exist in this form. Because for something that has arisen in the form of a pot, there is not again the necessity that an activity arises by means of a stick, etc.[231]

---

fore, also the *khaṇḍana*'s prattle that 'non-existent pots, etc. are not non-pots, etc.' is refuted."

[230] SAS 95.6–7 *ad* TMK 1.24: *asmākaṃ tu avyaktāvasthayā 'nupalabdhir apy uktā. 'na hy asan ghaṭādir na ghaṭādiḥ' iti tu kasyacid vacanaṃ bālapratāraṇam.*

[231] SAS 95.1–4 *ad* TMK 1.24: *na tāvat kāryam iti kim api na dṛṣṭam, sarvalokavedavirodhāt; vyaktisādhanasyāpi nirāśrayatvaprasaṅgāc ca.*[...]. *na ca satyam api na kāraṇād vyatirekeṇa gṛhyate; uktottara-*

The essential point here may be the following: We wouldn't strive for something or have the wish to produce something if it were already present before our eyes. We have something in mind of what we can bring forth and what we want to bring forth. In this, we presuppose that the effect can be brought forth. But we also presuppose that what we want to bring forth is not *already* present befor us. Otherwise, any intention to produce it would be in vain. In fact, we can say that *Being* of the non-being of what we want to produce is the necessary condition for any production of an effect to become real. By accepting *Being* as a third grounding aspect helps Veṅkaṭanātha not to fall into the same dilemma as the Sāṅkhya opponent, i.e., to accept cause and effect at the same time as being. Veṅkaṭanātha has the possibility to speak of being.

Our standard example of a material cause is the lump of clay. It is true that a lump already *is* before a pot becomes manifested, yet for the opponent, as a prerequisite for a pot to be made, it is not necessary for the pot to be already *real* in the lump of clay. The pot is only real *after* it has been made, i.e., after it has become a real product (made by a potter), but not before. Also, in the case of an instrumental cause, a real pot does not already spatially exist *in* the potter's wheel.

As Veṅkaṭanātha argues, the change of the state of a substance—in this case, the change from a lump of clay to a pot of clay—is not the manifestation of something pre-existent and latently hidden that is then made visible again. It is rather something that actually appears from one moment to the next under the condition of given circumstances, i.e., through appropriate causes such as the material (*upādānakāraṇa*) and an agent (*nimittakāraṇa*) conditioned by space and time.

---

tvāt, prakṛtivikṛtītyādivibhāgabhaṅgaprasaṅgāc ca. ataḥ kāraṇād bhinnatvena dṛṣṭaṃ kāryaṃ tenākāreṇa pūrvaṃ nāsīd iti tvayaivākāmenāpi svīkartavyam. na hi ghaṭākāreṇa niṣpannasya punar api daṇḍādivyāpāraniṣpādyatvam asti.

We know already Veṅkaṭanātha's main thesis that although the states of a substance alternate, the substance itself does not. Clay remains clay, even if it is transformed into a pot. In terms of material, the pot as a state of clay is never separate from the clay itself (*apṛthaksiddha*). At the same time, the pot as a state of clay is not identical with clay itself, but different (*bhinna*). All states are real existing states, as are all supporting causes that bring about change. The following passages of Veṅkaṭanātha's *Paramatabhaṅga* and his *Śatadūṣaṇī* illustrate again the week point of the Sāṅkhya's view on ontology.

In chapter 18 of the *Paramatabhaṅga* (PMBh), which deals with refutations of the atheistic Sāṅkhya school (*nirīśvarasāṅkhyanirākaraṇādhikāra*), Veṅkaṭanātha points out that if one assumes everything to be eternal, no manifestation depending on a certain time can be identified.

> For the one who says that everything is eternal because he is attached to the doctrine that the effect is being, it is not possible to say that there is a manifestation at a certain time, because he must also accept that the manifestation is eternal. If you [i.e., the Sāṅkhya opponent] then accept the manifestation of a manifestation you arrive at an infinite regress.[232]

Again, the main point of criticism is that even if the Sāṅkhya opponent explains change, he cannot explain why something which is not here now can later become a real object. How does a Banyan tree become a Banyan tree out of a seed? The seed is of course the potential state of the tree, but again what does "*is*" mean here? We cannot find a tree already fully present *in* the seed. Again, we can understand Veṅkaṭanātha's argument against his background of the grounding third as his main argument. He can argue, based on his ontological background, that seed and tree are different states of one and the same substance. The poten-

---

232 PMBh (chapter 18) 11,1–12,3: *satkāryavādaśraddaiyālē sarvanityatvam collukiṟa ivaṉukku abhivyakti nityatvamum koḻḻa vēṇṭukaiyālē kālaviśeṣattil abhivyakti colla virak' illai. abhivyaktikku abhivyaktikoṇṭāl anavasthaiyām.*

tial state is the subtle state, and a subtle state already *is*. But "*is*" does not have the meaning of being present now, which would also imply being eternally present. Also the two following passages from the *nirīśvarasāṅkhyanirākaraṇādhikāra* (chapter 18) of the PMBh refer to the absurd consequence of things being considered manifest before they are really manifest.

> Leaving aside the statement that a substance which is in another state shares the designation of developed (*vyakta*) and undeveloped (*avyakta*), etc., demonstrated also by means of valid cognition, like perception, etc., the statement that *mahad*, etc., remains manifest also within the main cause, like the designs in rolled up clothes and like the legs and arms inside the shell of a tortoise, is contradicted by hundreds of means of valid cognition, as in [ViP 6.4.18c]: "If water in the state of fire"; and [in ViP 6.4.22d]: "If fire in the state of wind".[233]

The same criticism is expressend in the following passage of the same chapter:

> A subtle substance that is capable of being transformed into a tree is the basis of this saying that the tree exists inside the seed, because there is no tree inside the seed, as in the example like a Banyan tree exists inside a Banyan seed. For one, who says that everything is eternal because he believes in the *satkāryavāda*, it is impossible to say [that there is] a manifestation at a certain time, because he has also to accept that the manifestation is eternal. If you accept the manifestation of a manifestation, you arrive at an infinite regress.[234]

---

[233] PMBh (chapter 18) 8,4–10,1: *pratyakṣādisarvapramāṇaṅkaḷum kāṭṭukiṟapaṭiyē dravyam avasthāntarāpannam-āy avyaktavyaktādisaṃjñaikaḷai bhajikkiṟatu eṉṉum atu oḻiya, cruṭṭiṉ cavaḷiyil toḻilkaḷ pōlavum, kūrmakarparattukku uḷḷē kālum talaiyum pōlavum mūlakāraṇattukku uḷḷē mahadādikaḷum abhivyaktam-āy kiṭak kiṉṟaṉa eṉṉum atuvum agnyavasthe ca salile* [ViP 6.4.18c], *vāyvavasthe ca tejasi* [ViP 6.4.22d] *ityādipramāṇaśataviruddham.*

[234] PMBh (chapter 18) 10,3–5: *ālam vitaiyiṉ uḷḷē ālirukkumāy pōlē eṉṉum dṛṣṭāntamum vitaiyiṉuḷḷē vṛkṣam illāmaiyālē, vṛkṣamāy pariṇamikka valla sūkṣmadravyam vitaiḷiṟat eṉkaikkuṭalām. satkāryavā-*

I will conclude with a passage from Veṅkaṭanātha's *Śatadūṣaṇī*. Here he again establishes his ontology by means of a rich debate with a Sāṅkhya opponent. While he repeats the arguments regarding infinite regress found in the TMK and the PMBh, his arguments here are more nuanced. Despite being situated in a polemical discussion in the *Śatadūṣaṇī* dealing with refutations of Advaitic theses, this discussion must again be understood against the background of Veṅkaṭanātha's thesis of the world being God's body. Since the Sāṅkhya ontology cannot substantiate alternating states of entities, the becoming and non-being of effects must be examined also here. Once again, the passage in question demonstrates Veṅkaṭanātha's view of the ontological status of an effect. His view that different states are subtle or manifest only at specific times and in specific places is his basis for discussing the being and non-being of an effect that manifests differently. As has been repeatedly dealt with in this chapter, he refutes two arguments. The first argument is, that effects are already manifest and therefore present in the cause; the second is, that effects do not exist at all, with the consequence that nothing arises. The aim of his discussion is precisely the ontological status of being, namely, the *being* of non-being. In this context, however, quite different criteria are used, including empirical verification: *Something can only be known as being when it can be verified by means of valid cognition as being present in a certain time, in a certain place.* Veṅkaṭanātha repeats the dilemma of the Sāṅkhya opponent, namely, that negation implies the assumption of prior being and thus the futility of bringing about an effect that is not different from the being-ness of the cause. He first formulates a series of counter-arguments, all of which are already well known: If an effect is non-being, its cause cannot be being. And if an effect is already being, then it does not need to be produced since we would not need anyone to produce the effect. Regarding the manifesta-

---

daśraddhaiyālē sarvanityatvam collukiṟa ivaṉukku abhivyakti nityatvamum koḻḻa vēṇṭukaiyālē kālaviśeṣattil abhivyakti colla virakillai. abhivyaktikku abhivyaktikoṇṭāl anavasthaiyām.

tion of an effect, Veṅkaṭanātha repeats the argument of an infinite regress, as well as the other another undesirable consequence mentioned above, i.e., eternal manifestation.

> Furthermore, if an effect is at an earlier time non-being in its cause, how is it possible for it to be caused by this? If one assumes that it is beforehand, then it should not be possible to bring it into being, insofar as it is already established. Therefore, the activity of an agent would also be in vain. If one were to say that it must be manifested, then this is not the case, because a being and a non-being of the manifestation are not assumed, insofar as an infinite regress occurs if the manifestation is also to be manifested [again], and because in the case of an eternal manifestation, the undesirable consequence would also be for things like a pot, etc., to be an eternal manifestation.[235]

The Sāṅkhya opponent just denies again non-being. Veṅkaṭanātha's response is that then nothing could come into being, because by denying non-being, one has accepted affirmation. One way out is the *abhivyakti* theory: Something is already there and thus only needs to be manifested. While Veṅkaṭanātha can claim that the effect is being, he can also say that it is non-being at a different time. This would defeat the objection that a non-being effect can become being. First, he shows that it is not a contradiction to assert that a substance is being, since otherwise a change of state would not be possible; the substance could not change from the state of cause to that of effect if the respective following state were not already (potentially) present.[236]

---

235 ŚDū, *vāda* 55, 208, 15–34: *kiṃ ca yadi kāraṇe pūrvaṃ kāryam asat, kathaṃ tena janayituṃ śakyam?* […] *atha pūrvam eva tatra sat, siddhatvād eva na sādhyaṃ syāt. tata eva kārakavyāpāranairarthyaṃ ca. vyaṅgyatvam astv iti cen na; vyaktisadasadbhāvayor apy anuyogāvatārāt. vyakter api vyaṅgyatve 'navasthānāt, nityavyaktatve ghaṭāder api nityavyaktiprasaṅgāt.*

236 Also in the nondualist Śaiva tradition, the topic of manifestation in discussion with the Sāṅkhya plays a major role. In some cases, arguments like those of Veṅkaṭanātha are developed. Cf. the analysis in Ratié (2014: 160–164): "The Śaivas claim to solve this problem by saying that the effect is always manifest in some way, even when it is

It is therefore also not a contradiction to say that something is *Being* non-being before it is real being. For Veṅkaṭanātha, this is "his" *satkāryavāda*. As non-being, it is potential being but not yet present. He makes this possible change of perspective clear in the following words:

> [Sāṅkhya opponent:] But when one asks if the effect in the cause is either being or non-being beforehand, what is its purpose?
> [Our response:] Does one ask whether the substance [in the state of] an effect is known as [the same] substance in the state of the cause, or is it not known? Then we accept the effect as being (*sat*). Nevertheless, there is no contradiction with what can be brought into being because it [i.e., substance] is possible as obtaining [another] state [i.e., the state of effect]. And for this very reason the activity of an agent has a result; and only what is in such a manner is for us the *satkāryavāda*.

---

not perceptible to the individual consciousness as a sensory object, because the all-powerful universal consciousness must ever be conscious that it manifests the whole universe by taking its shape—just as when we imagine an apple, we remain aware that our consciousness creates the apple by merely taking its shape or its aspect (*ākāra*)." Cf. also p. 166ff.: "[…] if the advocate of the *satkāryavāda* chooses to say that this manifestation already exists before the operation of the cause so as to save the *satkāryavāda*, he must either contradict his own principle that the effect only exists in some *unmanifest* state before the operation of the cause, or admit that the *manifestation* of the pot is already present in the clay and nonetheless *is manifest for nobody*. The problem vanishes in the idealistic system of the Pratyabhijñā, because the pot can be ever manifest as an internal form grasped by the absolute consciousness and yet remain unperceived as an external form for the various limited individuals, and because even when the pot becomes perceptible as an external form for the limited individuals, this manifestation is nothing new, but only amounts to the individuals' limited awareness of the ever manifest internal form of the pot."

> Do you then ask whether the state of the effect [already] is in the state of the cause, or not? Then [we say] that [such a state] is certainly not [already present in its cause].[237]

In retrospect, these examples of the Sāṅkhya position as found in three different works of Veṅkaṭanātha show that according to him, the Sāṅkhya position is not an ontology that can manifest the world anew, because it cannot establish a connection between past being and present being.

Summary

To the reader, the many topics unfolded here may seem to range quite widely. However, the aim has been to elaborate on the central figure of Veṅkaṭanātha, a figure fundamental for the theology of the god Viṣṇu-Nārāyaṇa as it developed in the tradition of Rāmānuja. The development of this monotheistic tradition was dependant on relating the world, i.e., conscious beings and material mass, as well as uncountable differing and denotating words, to a single ground. What our authors call unity (*aikya*) of two different entities with their different designations is only achieved by referring to a *third* aspect. This *third* aspect is inseparably related to these two entities, which have a fixed correspondence in linguistic expression. However, statements of these designations do not express explicitly this *third* aspect. God/*brahman* is indispensable as this *third* aspect, but the concept laid down here is repeated in detail for every individual substance (*dravya*), all defined as grounding in themselves. They can thus form the basis of

---

[237] ŚDū, *vāda* 55, 210,27–210,30: *yat punaḥ kāraṇe kāryaṃ pūrvaṃ sad asad veti, tasya ko 'rthaḥ? kiṃ kāryadravyaṃ kāraṇāvasthāyāṃ dravyarūpeṇa vidyate na veti? tadā sad ity aṅgīkurmaḥ. tathāpi na sādhyatvavirodhaḥ, avasthāpattirūpeṇa tadupapatteḥ. tata eva kārakavyāpārasāphalyaṃ ca. etāvān eva ca nas satkāryavādaḥ. atha kāryāvasthā kāraṇadaśāyām asti na veti pṛcchasi, tadā nāsty eva sā.*

different designations, thus avoiding the problem of an infinite regress.

In the tradition up to Veṅkaṭanātha, there are many approaches to different designations that are states or properties of *one* and the *same* substance. Given the indissoluble correspondence of name and form (*nāmarūpe*), one important approach concerns the inseparability between ontology on one hand and language on the other. Name and form correspond eternally; they merely exist in different states. In their different states, they are inseparable from the one *brahman*/God. This ontological aspect is highlighted by Rāmānuja and Veṅkaṭanātha in their frequent references to the sentence of BĀU 1.4.7. Both authors illustrate the linguistic aspect through the concept of co-referentiality (*sāmānādhikaraṇya*). Even though other descriptions exist of how objects relate to each other, such as being denoted by a possessive suffix, co-referentiality can be underscored as one of the most central and frequently used terms of Veṅkaṭanātha to describe ontological and linguistic dependence on the irreducible, self-grounding basis called substance (*dravya*). Indeed, it might be possible to say that in every discussion of Veṅkaṭanātha regarding the self-grounding substance, the basic idea of co-referentiality is at work.

When referring to the world, we deal with words and objects for which we must have already presupposed a basis (*dravya*) making them possible. This applies to the self-reference of the individual soul in exactly the same way. But theologically speaking, there is nothing that is not grounded in the ultimate substance of all substances, that is, God Himself, a God in whom everything must have its basis and who is inseparably connected—desbribed as eternal conjunction (*ajasaṃyoga*)—with other substances, of which time is like God defined as omnipresent (*vibhu*). Without this inseparability, it would not be possible to speak meaningfully of unity (*aikya*). This is what is many times being referred to with the metaphor of the body and its Inner Controller (*antaryāmin*).

The Vedāntic doctrine of God's (relational) *unity* with all eternally changing things forming his body, i.e., all substances and their states (*śarīra*), makes it understandable why this tradition not only defines God's body as all-encompassing, but also as manifold as is possible. A detailed analysis of the categories in which worldly phenomena are grasped does not contradict the idea of an omnipresent and all-encompassing God. Rather, it supports God's *relational unity* with everything. The more specifically the world can be classified the more detailed God is related to everything. Moreover, before the world is recognized, it is determined (*niyata*) as being specific (*viśiṣṭa*) and as always remaining so.

Veṅkaṭanātha takes recourse in basic ontological assumptions to explain how having a multitude of states is not contradictory. The states of a substance do not exist simultaneously, nor is there a single state that excludes all others. There are rather some states that are present, and others (like the past or the future) that are not. It is never the case that something passes away completely or arises anew from nothing, from emptiness. Nor is there, as made clear by Veṅkaṭanātha's criticism of the Sāṅkhya opponent, something that *is* real before it becomes real. Also here, co-referentiality is applied, insofar as cause and effect can be related to one and the same substance, i.e., *Being*.

The sequence of states (*avasthāsantāna*) also disproves the idea that substance and state are connected through external linking principle. Substances together with their states are self-grounding—*Being* is not based on *Being*, time is not based on time, qualifying knowledge is not based on qualifying knowledge, etc. Moreover, they are not only the basis for themselves (*sva*-), but they are also the basis for others (*para*). No further link is necessary, even if, as here the case, one substance specifies another. Concerning the sequence of states, despite states being different, they form a unity due to referring inseparably to their respective substance. This unity ultimately reflects God's *relational unity* with everything, which remains even if there are other substances in addition to God with alternating states.

However, it is not only the ontology that provides the ground for everything, but it is also—and this is a clear step beyond Rāmānuja—the foundation in a divine will for eternal and non-eternal entities, in which they ultimately finds their reason.

What do we get out of it theologically if we refer everything back to the fundamental act, an act decisive for our authors, namely, the act of transformation? God's work as the Inner Controller never ends. If His never-ending omnipresence is taken seriously, then God works continuously in every transformation. He remains effective, no matterwhat substance and conditions are involved. For God to be the Inner Controller directly connected to everything, it is inconceivable for any entity to be independent from Him.

Bibliography

Primary Literature

AS

Adhikaraṇasarāvalī, Veṅkaṭanātha: *Adhikaraṇasarāvaliḥ Kumāravedāntācāryānugṛhītena cintāmaṇinā* [...] *sametā*. Madras: Kapeer Printing Works 1940.

ĀS

Ātmasiddhi, Yāmunācārya: In: Sri Yamunacharya's Siddhi Traya with a Sanskrit Commentary by Sri U. Ve. Abhinava Desika Uttamur T. Viraraghvacharya with an Introduction in English by R. Ramanujachari and an English Translation by R. Ramanujachari & K. Srinivasacharya, ed. T. Viraraghvacharya, Ubhayavedāntagranthamālā, Madras 1972.

NSi

Nyāyasiddhāñjana, Veṅkaṭanātha: *Veṅkaṭanāthaviracitaṃ Nyāyasiddhāñjanam. Raṅgarāmānujasvāmiviracitasaralaviśadavyākhyayā Kṛṣṇatātayāryaviracitayā Ratnapeṭikākhyayā vyākhyayā ca sametam*. Madras: Ubhayavedāntagranthamālā 1976.

NP

Nyāyapariśuddhi, Veṅkaṭanātha: Nyāyapariśuddhiḥ by Sri Venkatanatha Sri Vedāntāchārya with a Commentary called Nyayasar by Srinivāsāchārya, ed. with Notes by Vidyābhusan Laksmanāchārya of Brindāban. [Chowkhamba Sanskrit Series 251]. Benares 1918–1923.

PañcP/PañcPV
Paṇcapādikā/Pañcapādikāvivaraṇa, Padmapāda/Prakāśātman: Pāñcapādikā of Śrī Padmapādācarya [with commentaries] and Pañcapādikāvivaraṇam of Śrī Prakāśātman [with commentaries]. [Madras Government Oriental Series 155]. Madras: Government Oriental Manuscript Library 1958.

PDS
Padārthadharmasaṅgraha, Praśastapāda: Praśastapādabhāṣyaṃ of Praśastapādācārya with the Commentary Nyāyakandalī by Śrīdhara Bhaṭṭa along with Hindi Transl. by Paṇḍita Śrī Durgādhara Jhā. Varanasi: Sampurnand Sanskrit Vishvavidalaya 1997.

PM
Prameyamālā, Vātsya Varadaguru: Prameyamālā by Vātsya Varadaguru, ed. by R. Rāmānujachari and K. Srinivasacharya. *Journal of the Annamalai University* 10:3 (1941) 1–28.

PMBh
Paramatabhaṅga, Veṅkaṭanātha: *Śrīkavitarkikasiṃha-sarvatantra-svatantra-śrīmadveṅkaṭanātha śrīmadvedāntadeśikaviracitaḥ paramatabhaṅgaḥ dvitīyo bhāgaḥ* [...] *vatsya śrīnārāyaṇācāryeṇa viracitayā deśikāśayaprakāśābhimukhyayā vyākhyayā sahitaḥ*. Madras: Elango Achukoodam: 1940.

RTS
Rahasyatrayasāra, Veṅkaṭanātha: *Śrīmadrahasyatrayasāra*. Ramadesikacaryar Swami [ed.]. Srirangam: Sri Marutthy Laser Printers 2000.

SAS
Sarvārthasiddhi, Veṅkaṭanātha; see TMK.

ŚDū
Śatadūṣaṇī, Veṅkaṭanātha: *Veṅkaṭanātha, Śatadūṣaṇī*, ed. by Aṇṇaṅgarāchārya [*Śrīmadvedāntadeśikagranthamālā*]. Conjeevaram: Śrīmadvedāntadeśikagranthamālā 1940.

SeMī
Seśvaramīmāṃsā, Veṅkaṭanātha: *Seśvara Mīmāṃsā of Vedānta Deśika*. Edited by Vachaspati Upadhyaya. Delhi: S. N. Publications 1981.

Śrībh

Śrībhāṣya, Rāmānuja: *Śrībhāṣya* of Rāmānuja with Sudarśanasuri's *Śrutaprakāśikā*, ed. by U. T. Vīrarāghavācārya, Madras: Sri Visishtadvaita Pracharini Sabha 1989 (reprint; 1st ed.: 1967). Two volumes, each with separate pagination (I contains *Śrībhāṣya* 1.1 to 1.2; II contains 1.3 to 4.4).

TK

Tattvakaumudī, Vacaspatimiśra: *Vācaspatimiśras Tattvakaumudī, ein Beitrag zur Textkritik bei kontaminiertert Überlieferung*, vom S.A. Srinivasan. [Alt und Neu-Indische Studien 12]. Hamburg: De Gruyter and Co. 1997.

TMK

Tattvamuktākalāpa, Veṅkaṭanātha. *Śrīmadveṅkaṭanāthārya Vedāntadeśika viracitaṃ Tattvamuktākalāpaḥ. tadvyākhyā ca tadviracitā sarvārthasiddhir nāma vṛttiḥ.* Madras: Ubhayavedāntagranthamālā 1973.

VAS

Vedārthasaṃgraha, Rāmānuja: *Rāmānuja's Vedārthasaṅgraha. Introduction,* Crit. Ed. and Annotated Transl. by J.A.B. van Buitenen. Poona 1956.

ViP

Viṣṇupurāṇa. The Critical Edition of the Viṣṇupurāṇam, ed. by M.M. Pathak, 2 Vols., Vadodara: Oriental Institute 1997–1999.

YD

Yuktidīpikā. The most Sigificant Commentary on the Sāṃkhyakārikā, critically edited by Albrecht Wezler and S. Motegi. Vol I [Alt und Neu-Indische Studien 44]. Stuttgart: Franz Steiner Verlag 1998.

YMD

Yatīndramatadīpikā, Śrīnivāsadāsa: Yatīndramatadīpikā by Śrīnivāsadāsa. [Text] English Translation and Notes by Swāmī Adidevānanda. Mylapore Madras: Ramakrishna Math Printing Press 1949.

Secondary Literature

Acarya 2016
Diwakar Acarya, 'This World, in the Beginning, was Phenomenally Non-Existent': Āruṇi's Discourse on Cosmogony in Chāndogya Upaniṣad VI.1–VI.7. In: *Journal of Indian Philosophy* 44 (2016) 833–864.

Bartley 2002
Bartley, Christopher, *The Theology of Rāmānuja*. London: Routledge 2002.

Barua 2009
Ankur Barua, *The Divine Body in History: A comparative study of the symbolism of time and embodiment in St. Augustine and Rāmānuja* [Religions and Discourse 45]. Bern: Peter Lang, Internationaler Verlag der Wissenschaften 2009.

Bronkhorst 2011
Johannes Bronkhorst, *Language and Reality: On an Episode in Indian Thought* [Brill's Indological Library 36]. Leiden: Brill 2011.

Carman 1974
John Carman, *The Theology of Rāmānuja: An Essay in Interreligious Understanding*. New Haven: Yale University Press. [Indian reprint: Bombay: Anantha Indological Research Institute 1981.]

Hardy 1983
Friedhelm Hardy, *The Early History of Kṛṣṇa Devotion in South India*. Oxford: Oxford University Press 1983.

Halbfass 1992
Wilhelm Halbfass, *On Being and What There Is: Classical Vaiśeṣika and the History of Indian Ontology*. Albany: State University of New York Press 1992

Hopkins 2002
Steven Paul Hopkins, *Singing the Body of God: The Hymns of Vedāntade-śika in their South Indian Tradition*. Oxford: Oxford University Press 2002.

Colas 2020
Gérard Colas, Le corps du Dieu créateur selon Rāmānuja: le dépassement d'un obstacle épistémologique dans la scolastique indienne. In: Émilie Aussant and Gérard Colas (eds.), *Les scolastiques indiennes: Genèses, développements, interactions*. Paris: Publications de l'École Française d'Extrême-Orient 2020, pp. 113–126.

Kassam-Hann 1992
Zayn Kassam-Hann, The Viśiṣṭādvaita Idea of Pervasion (*vibhu*) according to the *Yatīndramatadīpikā*. In: Katherine K. Young (ed.), *Hermeneutical Paths to the Sacred Worlds of India: Essays in Honour of Robert W. Stevenson*. Atlanta, GA: Scholars Press 1992, pp. 123–136.

Liebich 1892
Bruno Liebich, *Zwei Kapitel der Kāçikā: Übersetzt und mit einer Einleitung versehen.* Breslau: Preuss & Jünger 1892.

Lipner 1986
Julius Lipner, *The Face of Truth: A study in Meaning and Metaphysics in the Vedāntic Theology of Rāmānuja.* Albany: State University of New York Press 1986.

Lipner 2013
Julius Lipner, Rāmānuja. In: Knut A. Jacobsen, Helene Basu, Angelika Malinar, Vasudha Narayanan (eds.), *Brill's Encyclopedia of Hinduism.* Brill Online 2014.

Lott 1976
Eric J. Lott, *God and the Universe in the Vedāntic Theology of Rāmānuja.* Madras: Rāmānuja Research Society 1976.

Marlewicz 2002
Halina Marlewicz, *Vātsya Varadaguru on the Akhaṇḍavākyārtha Theory of Advaita Vedānta*. In: Gerhard Oberhammer, Marion Rastelli (eds.), *Studies in Hinduism III. Pāñcarātra and Viśiṣṭādvaita Vedānta* [Beiträge zur Kultur- und Geistesgeschichte Asiens 40]. Vienna: Verlag der Österreichischen Wissenschaften 2002, 103–129.

Marlewicz 2003
Halina Marlewicz, *Advaita Vedānta Hermeneutics of Revelation Key-Statements*. In: Gerhard Oberhammer, Marcus Schmücker (eds.), *Mythi-*

sierung der Transzendenz als Entwurf ihrer Erfahrung [Beiträge zur Kultur- und Geistesgeschichte Asiens 41]. Vienna: Verlag der Österreichischen Akademie der Wissenschaften 2003, pp. 249–280.

Matilal 1986
B.K. Matilal, *Perception: An Essay on Classical Indian Theories of Knowledge*. Oxford: Oxford University Press 1986.

Mikami [pdf]
Mikami, Toshihiro (unpublished manuscript), Nyāyasiddhāñjana of Vedāntadeśika: An Annotated Translation. University of Tokyo.

Mesquita 1990
Roques Mesquita, *Yāmunācāryas Philosophie der Erkenntnis: Eine Studie zu seiner Saṃvitsiddhi* [Veröffentlichungen der Kommission für Sprachen und Kulturen Südasiens 24]. Vienna: Verlag der Österreichischen Akademie der Wissenschaften 1990.

Mumme 1985
Patricia Mumme, Jīvakartṛtva in Viśiṣṭādvaita and the Dispute over Prapatti in Vedānta Deśika and the Teṅkalai Authors. In: S. Kuppuswami Sastri and S.S. Janaki (eds.), *Professor Kuppuswami Sastri Birth-Centenary: Selected Research Papers Presented at the Birth-Centenary Seminars*. Chennai: Kuppuswami Sastri Research Institute 1985, pp. 99–118.

Vedavalli Narayanan 2008
Vedavalli Narayanan, *The Epistemology of Viśiṣṭādvaita. A Study Based on the Nyāyapariśuddhi of Vedānta Deśika*. Delhi: Mushiram Manoharlal 2008.

Oberhammer 1979
Gerhard Oberhammer, *Materialien zur Geschichte der Rāmānuja-Schule I: Parāśarabhaṭṭas Tattvaratnākara.* [Veröffentlichungen der Kommission für Sprachen und Kulturen Südasiens 14]. Wien: Verlag der Österreichischen Akademie der Wissenschaften 1979.

Oberhammer 1996
Id., *Materialien zur Geschichte der Rāmānuja-Schule II: Vātsya Varadagurus Traktat von der Transzendenz des Brahma in der kontroverstheologischen Tradition der Schule.* [Veröffentlichungen zu den Sprachen

und Kulturen Asiens 28]. Wien: Verlag der Österreichischen Akademie der Wissenschaften 1996.

Oberhammer 1998
Id., *Materialien zur Geschichte der Rāmānuja-Schule IV: Der "Innere Lenker" (antaryāmī). Geschichte eines Theologems.* [Veröffentlichungen zu den Sprachen und Kulturen Asiens 31]. Wien: Verlag der Österreichischen Akademie der Wissenschaften 1998.

Oberhammer 2000
Id., *Materialien zur Geschichte der Rāmānuja-Schule V: Zur Lehre von der ewigen vibhūti Gottes.* [Veröffentlichungen zu den Sprachen und Kulturen 34]. Wien: Verlag der Österreichischen Akademie der Wissenschaften 2000.

Oberhammer 2002
Id., *Materialien zur Geschichte der Rāmānuja-Schule VI:* Die Lehre von der Göttin vor Veṅkaṭanātha. [Veröffentlichungen zu den Sprachen und Kulturen Asiens 35]. Wien: Verlag der Österreichischen Akademie der Wissenschaften 2002.

Oberhammer (unpublished)
Id., Zur Diskussion der Natur der Göttin in der Rāmānuja Schule.

Ogawa 2017
Hideyo Ogawa, The Qualifier-Qualificand Relation and Coreferentiality. In: Patrick McAllister (ed.), *Reading Bhaṭṭa Jayanta on Buddhist Nominalism*, Patrick McAllister (ed.). Vienna: Austrian Academy of Sciences Press 2017, pp. 83–151.

Olivelle 1998
Patrick Olivelle, The Early Upaniṣads. Annotated Text and Translation. New York: Oxford University Press 1998.

Olivelle 2006
Patrik Olivelle, Heart in the Upaniṣads. In: *Rivista di Studi Sudasiatici* I (2006) 51–67.

Phillips 1995
Stephen H. Phillips, *Classical Indian Metaphysics. Refutation of Realism and the Emergence of New Logic.* Chicago/La Salle, Illinois: Open Court 1995.

Ram-Prasad 2013
Chakravarthi Ram-Prasad, *Divine Self, Human Self. The Philosophy of Being in Two Gītā Commentaries*. London: Bloomsbury 2013.

Ratié 2014
Isabelle Ratié, A Śaiva Interpretation of the *Satkaryavāda.* The Sāṃkhya Notion of *Abhivyakti* and Its Transformation in the Pratyabhijñā Treatise. In: *Journal of Indian Philosophy* 42/1 (2014) 127–172.

Schmücker 2007
Marcus Schmücker, The *vyūha* as the "State of the Lord" (*bhagavadavasthā*): Vedāntic Interpretation of the Pāñcarātra Doctrines According to Veṅkaṭanātha. In: Marion Rastelli, Gerhard Oberhammer (eds.), *Studies in Hinduism IV. On the Mutual Influences and Relationship of Viśiṣṭādvaita Vedānta and Pāñcarātra* [Beiträge zur Kultur- und Geistesgeschichte Asiens 54]. Vienna: Verlag der Österreichischen Wissenschaften 2007, pp. 89–106.

Schmücker 2011
Id., Zur Bedeutung des Wortes 'Ich' (*aham*) bei Veṅkaṭanātha. In: Gerhard Oberhammer, Marcus Schmücker (eds.), *Die Relationalität des Subjektes im Kontext der Religionshermeneutik* [Beiträge zur Kultur- und Geistesgeschichte Asiens 70]. Vienna: Verlag der Österreichischen Akademie der Wissenschaften 2011, pp. 309–40.

Schmücker 2020a
Id., Soul and Qualifying Knowledge (*Dharmabhūtajñāna*) in Later Viśiṣṭādvaita Vedānta of Veṅkaṭanātha. In: Ayon Maharaj (ed.), *The Bloomsburry Research Handbook of Vedānta*. London: Bloomsbury 2020, pp. 75–104.

Schmücker 2020b
Id., Theological concepts according to the three early *Antāti*-s of Poykaiyāḻvār, Pūtattāḻvār and Pēyāḻvār. In: Eva Wilden (ed.) in collaboration with Marcus Schmücker, *The Three Early Tiruvantātis of*

the Tivyappirapantam [Collection Indologie 143; NETamil Series 7]. Pondicherry: École Française d'Extrême-Orient 2020, pp. 359–380.

Schmücker 2022
Id., On the relation between God and time in the later theistic Vedānta of Madhva, Jayatīrtha and Veṅkaṭanātha. In: Marcus Schmücker, Michael Williams, Florian Fischer (eds.), *Temporality and Eternity: Nine Perspectives on God and Time.* Berlin: De Gruyter 2022, pp. 123–160.

Schmücker forthcoming[1]
Id., Veṅkaṭanātha's critique of Bhāskara's and Yādavaprakāśa's doctrine of *bheda-abheda* according to the *Paramatabhaṅga* (chapter 13).

Schmücker forthcoming[2]
Id., Veṅkaṭanātha's concept of time (*kāla*).

Schmücker/Oberhammer forthcoming[3]
Id./Oberhammer, Fragments of Nāthamuni. Towards a Reconstruction of Early Viśiṣṭādvaita Vedānta.

Shastri 1993
Biswanarayan Shastri, *Samavāya Foundation of Nyāya-Vaiśeṣika Philosophy.* Delhi: Sharada Publishing House 1993.

Srinivasa Chari 1976
S.M. Srinivasa Chari, *Advaita and Viśiṣṭādvaita: A Study based on Vedānta Deśika's Śatadūṣaṇī.* Delhi: Motilal Banarsidass [2]1976.

Taylor 2021
McComas Taylor, The Viṣṇu Purāṇa – Ancient Annals of the God with Lotus Eyes. Translated from the Sanskrit by MacComas Taylor. Australian National University Press 2021.

Thibaut 1904
George Thibaut (trans.), *The Vedānta-Sūtras with Commentary by Rāmānuja* [Sacred Books of the East, Vol. 48]. Oxford: Clarendon Press 1904.

Thieme 1982/83
Paul Thieme, Meaning and form of 'grammar' of Pāṇini. In: *Studien für Indologie und Iranistik* 8/9 (1982/83) 3–34.

Trikha 2012
Himal Trikha, *Perspektivismus und KritikPerspektivismus und Kritik. Das pluralistische Erkenntnismodell der Jainas angesichts der Polemik gegen das Vaiśeṣika in Vidyānandins Satyaśāsanaparīkṣā*. [Publications of the De Nobili Research Library, Volume 36]. Wien 2012.

Varenne 1960
Jean Varenne, *La Mahānārāyaṇa Upaniṣad*. Paris: Éditions E. de Boccard 1960.

Wezler 1987
Albrecht Wezler, Remarks on the *sarvasarvātmakavāda*. In: R.R. Mukhopadhyaya et al. (eds.), *Philosophical Essays: Professor Anantalal Thakur Felicitation Volume*. Calcutta: Sanskrit Pustak Bhandar 1987, pp. 166–181.

Wezler 1992
Id., Paralipomena zum *Sarvasarvātmakavāda* II: On the *Sarvasarvātmakavāda* and its relation to the *Vṛkṣāyurveda*. In: *Studien zur Indologie und Iranistik* 16/17 (1992) 287–315.

Wilden 2020
Eva Wilden (ed.) with the collaboration of Marcus Schmücker, *The Three Early Tiruvantātis of the Tivyappirapantam* [Collection Indologie 143; NETamil Series 7]. Pondicherry: École française d'Extrème-Orient 2020.

General index

About the contributors

Gérard Colas is Emeritus Senior Research Fellow at the Centre national de la recherche scientifique. Before1985, he was in charge of the Indian manuscripts at the Bibliothèque nationale de France. His PhD thesis was devoted to the study of the architectural guidelines laid out in the *Vimānārcanakalpa*, as compared to temples in South India (published, 1982). The medieval Sanskrit corpus of Vaikhānasa literature was the topic of his Habilitation thesis (published, 1994). His research concerns Indian epistemologies in relation to religious problematics, especially the icon (*Penser l'icône en Inde ancienne*, 2012), rites, Vaiṣṇavism, theism and deism. Transmission of Sanskrit texts (*Écrire et transmettre en Inde classique*, ed. with Gerdi Gerschheimer, 2009), palaeography and 18th century missionary literature in Sanskrit and Telugu (by French Jesuits and Halle-Tranquebar Pietists; *Catalogue of the Telugu Manuscripts of the Franckesche Stiftungen*, with U. Colas-Chauhan) are his other fields of research. Most recently he edited together with Emilie Aussant the volume: *Les scolastiques indiennes: genèses, developpements, interactions*, Paris 2020.

Erin McCann finished her PhD in the Faculty of Religious Studies at McGill University in Montreal, Canada. She is a postdoctoral researcher at the Centre for the Study of Manuscript Cultures of the University of Hamburg. Her recent research project, titled "The Linguistic and Material Aspects of Mixed-Language Manuscripts in the Śrīvaiṣṇava Tradition", focused on the convergence of multilingualism with the production and use of multiple-text manuscripts in the Śrīvaiṣṇava tradition of South India. Her main research interests include Śrīvaiṣṇava theology, Maṇipravāḷa literature, manuscript studies, and the socio-cultural manifestations of multilingualism. Most recently she co-edited together with Giovanni Ciotti the volume *Linguistics and Textual Aspects of Multilingualism in South India*, Pondichérry 2020.

Gerhard Oberhammer is Professor Emeritus of Indology of the University of Vienna. His research interests focus on schools of Indian philosophy such as Nyāya, Yoga and the Vedānta traditions as well as hermeneutics of religion. His most important publications with regard to the topic of this volume are the *Materialien zur Geschichte der Rāmānuja-*Schule (Vienna 1979-2008) of which ten volumes have appeared to date. Recently he has published an Occasional Paper in the de Nobili Research Library: *Meghanādārisūris Lehre vom Jivaḥ als Subjekt des Erkennens. Eine begrifflich kritische Rezeption der überlieferten Lehre*, Wien 2023.

Marion Rastelli is a senior scientist at the Institute for the Cultural and Intellectual History of Asia of the Austrian Academy of Sciences, Vienna. Her research focuses on the teachings and ritual of Pāñcarātra. She has authored numerous articles and the two monographs *Philosophisch-theologische Grundanschauungen der Jayākhyasaṃhitā. Mit einer Darstellung des täglichen Rituals*, Vienna 1999, and *Die Tradition des Pāñcarātra im Spiegel der Pārameśvarasaṃhitā*, Vienna 2006. Since 2006 she is co-editor of *Tāntrikābhidhānakośa: A Dictionary of Technical Terms from Hindu Tantric Literature.* Together with Nina Mirnig and Vincent Eltschinger she co-edited the volume*: Tantric Communities in Context*, Vienna 2019.

Charlotte Schmid is director of studies of the École française d'Extrême-Orient. She divides her research between two areas of fieldwork, the north and the south of the Indian subcontinent. After studying the earliest known representations of a major Hindu deity of Bhakti, those of Kṛṣṇa in Mathurā, she had spent several years in the Tamil-speaking South. Poring over inscriptions and sculptures produced during the Pallava and the Cōḻa period (6th-12th century) and reading texts with the help of the Pandits at the centre of the École française d'Extrême-Orient in Pondichérry enabled her to produce her books: *Sur le chemin de Kṛṣṇa : la flûte et ses* voies, Paris 2014, and *La Bhakti d'une reine*, Pondichérry 2014, as author, and in association with Emmanuel Francis (CNRS) *The Archaeology of Bhakti* (2 volumes, Pondichérry 2014/2016) as editor.

Marcus Schmücker is a senior scientist at the Institute for the Cultural and Intellectual History of Asia of the Austrian Academy of Sciences, Vienna. His research interests focus on the traditions of Advaita Vedānta and of Viśiṣṭādvaita Vedānta. In collaboration with Eva Wilden he published the volume *The Three Early Tiruvantātis of the Tivyappirapantam*, Pondichérry 2020. Working also at the intersection between theology and philosophy he co-edited together with Mike Williams and Florian Fischer a volume on *Temporality and Eternity. Nine Perspectives on God and Time*, Berlin/Boston 2022. Together with Bernhard Nitsche he co-edited the volume *God or the Divine? Religious Transcendence beyond Monism and Theism, Between Personality and Impersonality*, Berlin/Boston 2023.

Peter Schreiner studied Indology, History of Religions and Philosophy at the universities of Mainz, Munich and, after obtaining a MA in Religion from Temple University in Philadelphia, of Münster and Tübingen. He wrote his dissertation on Premcand (Münster 1972), his habilitation on the *stotra*s in the *Viṣṇupurāṇa* (Tübingen 1981), he worked for the Tübingen Purāṇa Project (1982-86) and was lecturer of Sanskrit at the SOAS in London (1988-89) before becoming professor of Indology at the University of Zürich (retired since 2008). His publications include, apart from numerous articles and reviews, a German translation of the *Bhagavadgīta*, the volumes on the *Brahmapurāṇa* in the series *Purana Research Publications Tübingen* (in collaboration with Renate Söhnen) and a German translation of the *Viṣṇupurāṇa*: *Viṣṇupurāṇa. Althergebrachte Kunde über Viṣṇu*, Berlin 2013.

Eva Wilden studied Indology and Philosophy at the University of Hamburg, where she took a doctorate on Vedic ritual and afterwards specialized in Classical Tamil under the guidance of S.A. Srinivasan. Her habilitation *Literary Techniques in Old Tamil Caṅkam Poetry: The Kuṟuntokai* was published in 2006. After being employed (since 2003) as a researcher at the École Française d'Extrême-Orient in Pondicherry she is since 2017 professor of Classical Tamil and Manuscript Studies at Universität Hamburg and a member of the Cluster of Excellence Understanding Written Artefacts the Hamburg Centre for the Study of Manuscript Cultures. Her recent book publications are: *A Gram-*

mar of Old Tamil for Students, Pondichérry 2018; *A Critical Edition and an Annotated Translation with Glossary of the Akanāṉūṟu* (three Volumes), Pondichérry 2018; *The Three Early Tiruvantātis of the Tivyappirapantam*, Pondichérry 2020. Since August 2023 she heads at the Academy of Sciences and Humanities in Hamburg the long termed project: *Tamilex*. Compiling an electronic corpus of classical Tamil literature and a historical dictionary, taking into account indigenous exegetical and lexicographical sources.

Katherine K. Young is Professor Emeritus in the Faculty of Religious Studies at McGill University (Montreal Canada) and an Associate Fellow at the Centre for the Study of Religion and Society at the University of Victoria (Victoria Canada). She published in the fields of Hinduism, especially Tamil Vaiṣṇavam, Gender and Religion including women in Hinduism, and Hindu Ethics. Some publications on South Indian Hinduism include topoi of Śrīvaiṣṇavism: Constructing a South Indian Sect through Place" in *Mapping the Chronology of Bhakti: Milestones, Stepping Stones, and Stumbling Stones.* Valérie Gillet (ed.), Pondichérry 2014; "The Hermeneutics of Bhagavadgītā 9:32" in the *Journal of Hinduism*, Oxford 2009; "Brāhmaṇas, Pañcarātrins, and the Formation of Śrīvaiṣṇavism" in *On the Mutual Influences and Relationship of Viśiṣṭādvaita Vedānta and Pāñcarātra*, Gerhard Oberhammer, Marion Rastelli (eds.), Vienna 2006; "Śaṅkara on the Liberation of Women and Śūdras" in *Goddesses and Women in the Indic Religious Tradition*, Arvind Sharma (ed.), Leiden 2005; and "Oṃ, the Vedas, and the Status of Women with Special Reference to Śrīvaiṣṇavism" in *Jewels of Authority: Women and Textual Tradition in Hindu India*, Laurie L. Patton (ed.), Oxford 2002. Her most recent publications are *Turbulent Transformations: Non-Brahmin Śrīvaiṣṇavas on Religion, Caste and Politics in Tamil Nadu* (Orient Blackswan 2020), and *Nāthamuni's Divyaprabandham and Tangled Tales: A New Approach to Śrīvaiṣṇava History.*